Managing Diversity in the Military

Managing Diversity in the Military

Research Perspectives from
the Defense Equal Opportunity
Management Institute

Mickey R. Dansby
James B. Stewart
Schuyler C. Webb
editors

Transaction Publishers
New Brunswick (U.S.A.) and London (U.K.)

Library of Congress Catalog Number: 2001027545
ISBN: 0-7658-0046-2
Printed in the United States of America

Library of Congress Cataloging-in-Publication Data

Managing diversity in the military : research perspectives from the Defense Equal Opportunity Management Institute / Mickey R. Dansby, James B. Stewart, and Schuyler C. Webb, editors.
    p. cm.
    Includes bibliographical references and index.
    ISBN 0-7658-0046-2 (alk. paper)
    1. United States—Armed Forces—Personnel management. 2. United States—Armed Forces—Minorities. 3. Diversity in the Workplace—United States. I. Dansby, Mickey R. II. Stewart, James B. III. Webb, Schuyler C.

UB417 .M35 2001
335.6'1' 0973—dc21
                      2001027545

Contents

Part 4: Military Discipline and Race

Part 5: Where Do We Go From Here?

Acknowledgements

We are indebted to a number of individuals for their timely contributions and assistance. First and foremost are the authors, all of whom have participated in one of Defense Equal Opportunity Managemnet Institute's (DEOMI) research programs or research symposiums. They responded to target dates and revisions with patience and uncommon enthusiasm. Authors, we sincerely thank you. Without your perseverance and creative scholarship, this text would not be possible. We are also grateful to the DEOMI staff, particularly, Mrs. Kiyoko Dornan for assistance in preparing the manuscript. We thank Mr. Jerry Scarpate, Mr. William Herrmann, (USA RET.), Dr. Judith Johnson, Dr. Stephen Knouse, Dr. Leonard Missavage, Dr. Rupert Nacoste, Dr. Gary Whaley, Captain April Dillard, USAF, Dr. Paul Rosenfeld, and members of the Research and Evaluation Committee for their critical and constructive review. We also thank Mr. Rufus Tolbert (USN-ret) for sharing his encouragement and professional experiences of over thirty years of military experience. To all these and many others not named, but not forgotten, our thanks. All the errors contained herein are ours alone.

Mickey R. Dansby
James B. Stewart
Schuyler C. Webb

Preface

The Department of Defense (DoD) has a rich history of diversity management going back to when it became the first American institution to be racially integrated by Executive Order 9981 signed by President Truman on July 26, 1948. During the last half of the twentieth century, the DoD has faced racial unrest and sex discrimination and has gone on to pioneer equal opportunity initiatives that make it one of the most forward looking institutions in the United States. Currently, the Office of the Secretary of Defense, Deputy Assistant Secretary of Defense for Equal Opportunity has the responsibility to lead and direct equal opportunity programs and initiatives throughout DoD. As part of that mandate, it recommends and monitors research efforts of the DEOMI Directorate of Research. The Directorate has been prolific in producing a variety of applied research reports used in the management of diversity and equal opportunity in DoD.

This book provides an introduction to diversity management and equal opportunity research in the U.S. military. The twenty-four papers included in the volume explore a variety of topics that are salient for the effective management of diversity in the Armed Services. The organization and, to a significant degree, the content of this work is designed to offer a balance of theoretical and applied presentations relevant to military equal opportunity and diversity management. To that end, it is not intended to be an "elite discourse" designed strictly for an academically inclined readership. On the contrary, this work is expected to be a resource for equal opportunity researchers, Equal Opportunity Advisors, EO Program Managers, commanders, and students, in addition to others having their first introduction to military equal opportunity and diversity research. With that in mind, the editors have opted for inclusiveness in subject matter coverage. Authors were encouraged to report their ideas, studies, and research findings in detail rather than cursorily or illustratively. The level of detail provided in each section allows portions of the text to be used selectively as a resource for in-depth exploration of specific topics.

Coverage of topics is not intended to indicate that a section is more important or relevant than the others. Consideration regarding the inclusion of papers in the book involved both pedagogical and practical decisions. Pedagogically, the book strives to inform the reader by exploring topics, which will hold the most relevance for the majority of the readership. Practically, it was necessary to limit the length of the book. Even though the coverage is intended to be comprehensive, one underlying goal is to scrutinize the usefulness of traditionally held views about equal opportunity in a military setting, and to offer alternative perspectives where appropriate. Although this is not a value-free text, it is not directed against any particular view. At the same time, it is demonstratively and unapologetically supportive of diversity management and equal opportunity policies instituted by the U.S. military. The views expressed are, however, those of the editors and authors alone, and do not necessarily represent those of the DoD.

Commandant's Statement

Diversity is a twentieth-century term for a concept that has been studied since ancient times. The human tendency to identify the manners and morals of people different from or similar to our own is not a new issue. Today, the global debate over status and rights continues among different races, genders, and cultures. And, as the United States enters the twenty-first century, the issue of diversity in society and in organizations is becoming more complex than ever before. The demographic changes of the 1980s and 1990s in the United States are creating a society where racial lines, culture uniqueness and equity are increasingly blurred. These changes engendered efforts to forge a new sense of collective identity than can be embraced by all Americans.

Historically, the majority of Americans have, at best, tolerated the differences in culture and tradition. The unprecedented diversity of our present society and its expected increase in the near future will, most likely, create new problems unless our nation's citizens prepare to cope with it now. Indeed, the time is ripe to move beyond "tolerance" of diversity to the "celebration" of diversity as an asset that enriches the lives of all citizens. To accomplish this new celebration, or appreciation, of diversity, whether it be cultural or gender based, an effort must be made to alter the values of society in general and in organizations like the military in particular.

Along with the ongoing demographic and political shifts that will impact society and the military, the "new" playing field will feature less stability and predictability and more change and uncertainty. It is a time and environment I refer to as *"VUCA,"* which is an acronym meaning volatile, uncertain, complex, and ambiguous. All four attributes characterize our dynamic military environment. Technological advancements, budget constraints, mission creep, and competition for, and retention of, talented personnel will force the military to improve continually its organizational structures to achieve optimum use of resources, especially its human resources.

Managing the diversity of the force in the twenty-first century is now one of our greatest leadership challenges. Unfortunately, this is not due to the nature of America becoming "kinder and gentler" towards diverse groups, but because military leaders must attain specific outcomes such as mission success and, ultimately, organizational survival. The effectiveness of diversity programs is contingent on leadership commitment that embodies the value of diversity. The evolution and development of this type of organizational commitment needs to be better understood in order for organizations to determine the best approaches to support their own particular style of diversity management.

One primary factor in the effective management of a diverse organization is the leader's understanding of the cultural beliefs and values of the organization. Research is one key to creating the necessary knowledge base. While this collection of articles offers no panacea for the issues of diversity management in the military, it does offer empirical support that is a necessary precursor to sound decision making. That is, the reports provide the verifiable and sound data that military personnel planners and policy makers undoubtedly require. DEOMI research is an outstanding example of how applied research can aid policy formulation. Based on DEOMI research, military planners, trainers, and policy makers are better able to deal with issues of race and gender. To be sure, these articles help separate fact from journalistic sensationalism and exaggeration leading to misinformation, misinterpretation, and faulty decision-making.

In summary, this book presents a collection of research studies conducted at DEOMI, addressing some of the equal opportunity and diversity issues in the military and exploring how the military is attempting to resolve them. Anyone interested in the dynamics of military equal opportunity and diversity management should find this book interesting. It should be of assistance to those facing challenges related to diversity management, race/gender relations, and equal opportunity. These challenges will continue to impact mission accomplishment, operational readiness, and ultimately the stability and health of our nation in the future. In addition, I believe it offers insights, practical methodologies, and effective management guidelines for commanders, civilian sector executives, and human resource practitioners responsible for equal opportunity programs and outcomes. The research presented in this text will assist professionals in utilizing the best of what diversity has to offer as they lead the way in fostering an all-inclusive military and workforce.

Jose Bolton, Sr., Ph.D.
Colonel, USAF
Commandant, DEOMI

Overview

"We pass through this world but once. Few tragedies can be more extensive than the stunting of life, few injustices are deeper than the denial of an opportunity to strive or even to hope, by a limit imposed from without, but falsely identified as lying within."

— Stephen Jay Gould, *The Mismeasure of Man* (1996)

Introduction

The price of freedom is not free. Indeed, protecting the security of our nation, at all costs, is the primary mission and constitutional duty of every service member. As our military enters the twenty-first century, it has an unprecedented opportunity to make our nation safer and more prosperous. Our military might is unparalleled and the community of democratic nations is growing, enhancing the prospects for political stability, peaceful conflict resolution, and greater hope for the people of the world.

At the same time, the dangers that our military faces are unprecedented in their complexity. Newspaper headlines list a variety of external threats—acts of terrorism, proliferation of weapons of destruction, etc.—that potentially could compromise our political and economic stability. The necessity for ready Armed Services to meet these dangers is of paramount importance. In the midst of technological and materiel advancements we must not forget that the most important element of our Armed Services is our people. Throughout history our armed forces included a mixture of different racial, ethnic, and gender groups working in coordination to meet and overcome those threats. Today's multicultural and multiethnic force is a continuation of that legacy and a testament to American interracial and inter-gender cooperation, achievement, and success.

In many ways the military has always been a mirror of American society, reflecting back the scars and blemishes as well as the character that defines the face of the nation. For women and minorities, it has meant gender and race policies that too often prevented them from openly serving in the front lines. And yet they did serve as best they could, and in doing so brought out the best in themselves, if not the best in America. Minorities have taken part in all of this country's wars. Although white America usually restricted the participation of women and minorities in military affairs until a crisis unfolded, minority Americans have viewed their military record as proof of loyalty and as a claim to the benefits of full citizenship.

Since United States law and tradition require male citizens to participate in the Armed Services, restriction of a group from fulfilling this obligation could provide a dubious rationale for denying that group its full rights to citizenship. Aware of this reasoning, women and minorities sought to participate in America's wars in the hope that sacrifices on the battlefield would bring the reward of increased rights for all women and minorities in civilian life.

Women

Although women have always played an integral role in the military, the roles assigned to them have shifted and changed throughout their years in the armed services. In fact, women have increasingly been integrated into the armed services and they have continuously faced gender discrimination at every stage in their military career. During the Revolutionary, Civil, and Spanish American Wars, women were officially prohibited from joining the military. Because of their exclusion, women were rendered powerless in the Armed Services. During these wars, the military hired civilian nurses as its first female employees, marking the entrance of women in the military. During both World War I and World War II, women in the Armed Services were restricted to noncombatant auxiliaries or separate units such as medical and administration. Although the situation facing women during World War II was upgraded over their circumstances during World War I, women faced wholesale demobilization after both conflicts. This all too familiar pattern was common for racial minorities as well.

Minorities

The life of Africans in America, in particular, has been a strange paradox since their precarious arrival to these shores. Kidnapped from Africa and enslaved in the United States, Africans were afforded the minimum of rights as human beings. For almost two hundred years most African people were frozen in a dehumanized legal position. No matter what happened in the larger society, they remained enslaved, largely unaffected by the political changes around them. Even after the abolition of slavery, African Americans were in a peculiar situation as citizens without full rights. Their unequal status naturally followed them into the Armed Services.

The history of minorities in the military is replete with examples of honorable and heroic service during periods of war, despite pervasive discrimination and racism. Let us consider a brief historical account. Crispus Attucks, an African American who was first to fall in the struggle for freedom and others were there on the first morning of the American Revolution, fighting for freedom for a nation that would deny their freedom. They volunteered during the War of 1812. They were there on the battlefields of the Civil War, in that fatal assault on Fort Wagner, South Carolina, answering President Lincoln's appeal to "the better angels of our nature." In 1917, they were in Europe, in the Great War, fighting to make the world safe for democracy, only to return to a country where they could be lynched for demanding the basic democratic principle of equal opportunity.

The number of Hispanic Americans serving in the military before the Vietnam War can only be estimated. Records are sketchy because, like the Census Bureau, the military did not closely track Hispanic members. For example, Puerto Ricans were not counted as Hispanic, but as Puerto Ricans. Depending on their skin color, Hispanics were assigned either to segregated Colored/Negro or White units. However, we now know that Hispanic soldiers participated in major battles from the War of 1812 to the present.

The history of Native Americans within the United States is fraught with conflict and ongoing friction. Despite the so-called Indian Wars (considered by some historians as the first Civil War—i.e., American against American), broken treaties, and the re-settlement of Indians in reservations, Native Americans have fought in every American war in which American soldiers participated. From the Revolutionary War when several Indian nations sided with American revolutionaries to fighting on both sides of the Civil War to World War II, they have served under military and societal misperceptions and stereotypes as well as disparate treatment.

Asian Americans (i.e., Japanese, Korean, Filipino, Chinese, Pacific Islanders, and others) have encountered the indignities of racism and bigotry since their arrival to these shores. Until World War II, Asian Americans were subject to discrimination under American law. Their patriotic loyalties were questioned during times of war and, for the most part, were not permitted to serve this country in combat until 1943 when it became a military necessity. For example, an estimated 200,000 Filipino troops fought under General Douglas MacArthur in the Pacific Theater.

African-American as well as Hispanic, Native, and Asian-American veterans of World War II learned painfully that victory over the Axis powers was not synonymous with victory over either *"Jim Crow"* segregation or white supremacy. The coined expression *"Double V"* —victory against Axis powers and racism in America—was a dream deferred for most minority veterans. Like others before them, they returned not to parades or cheering crowds, but to a barrage of continuous bigotry, enforced segregation, and systemic, institutionalized racism. Hispanics returned to their segregated barrios, many Asian Americans returned to their scattered and stigmatized communities, and Native Americans returned to the blight of Indian reservations. Some minority veterans were insulted, humiliated, and/or beaten; others were killed. In 1945, at the close of World War II, the U.S. military establishment was a racially segregated institution whose personnel policies were dominated by prejudices inherent from earlier wars. Some minority veterans must have wondered, as did the poet laureate Langston Hughes, *"I swear to the Lord, I still can't see, why democracy means everybody but me."*

Military Desegregation

At the end of the war came the largest demobilization in the nation's history and while many white service members wanted to be discharged, many African Americans and other minority members wanted to remain on active-duty despite disparate treatment. Because proportionately fewer African Americans discharged than whites, Africa Americans constituted a growing share of the Armed Services. During the aftermath of World War II, there were two significant events contributing to the integration of the Armed Services. African-American leaders began to apply political pressure on the Truman administration and at the same time threaten widespread civil disobedience, if the Armed Services were not opened to African Americans and other minorities. In addition, the Army's *Gillem Report* was issued in 1945. The results led to the conclusion that small African-American units together with larger white units were superior to large African-American units in all measured domains including combat readiness, morale, and discipline. The report also suggested that the Army should limit African-American recruitment to 10 percent of the total Army and continue policies of segregation. As a result of those two significant events, a few months before the 1948 election the President's Commission on Equality of Treatment and Opportunity in the Armed Services was established by President Truman through Executive Order 9981. This historic order instituted a racial desegregation policy of the U.S. Armed Services and set in motion a sense of purpose for military integration by stating:

> ...It is hereby declared to be the policy of the President that there shall be equality of treatment and opportunity for all persons in the Armed Forces without regard to race, color, religion, or national origin. This policy shall be put into effect as rapidly as possible, having due regard to the time required to effectuate any necessary changes without impairing efficiency or morale....

The executive order heralded the beginning of the end of the policy of segregation that had stifled the Armed Services since the Revolutionary War. Even so, desegregation alone did not award minorities the full equality many hoped it would as social forces both inside and outside the Armed Services were gathering to create widespread civil disorders. The order did, however, do more toward eliminating segregation than any other prior institutional effort in the history of the United States. Nonetheless, the effort was not fully implemented until several years later due to the Army arguments that racial integration would erode unit cohesion during a time of preparation for war. President Truman called a special congressional committee chaired by former U.S. Solicitor General, Charles H. Fahy, to study how the Armed Services would implement the order.

Testifying before this committee, Colonel Harold Riegelman succinctly summed up the problem of racial prejudice. He remarked:

> The pressure for immediate action against segregation in the armed forces is made even greater by the unparalleled position of leadership the United States holds today in international affairs. The United States is looked upon as the greatest champion of freedom and democracy in the world, where the dark people outnumber the white, where the concept of racial superiority and white supremacy is an insult to more than half of the earth's population (Greenberg & Morris, 1997).

By the time the Korean War ignited in 1950, military integration was universal in policy although limited in practice. As the first war the United States fought after desegregation and under the influence of the Civil Rights movement, the Korean War was an experiment in race relations. The performance of integrated units during the war was unequivocal according to an important research study. Social scientists of the Operations Research Office of Johns Hopkins University studied the performance of segregated and integrated units both in Korea and the United States under the research project code named *Project Clear*, formally entitled *The Utilization of Negro Manpower in the Army*. In 1954, the researchers concluded that African, Hispanic, and Asian Americans as well as other minorities performed better when not restricted to segregated units and that unit readiness and performance of Army units were considerably enhanced by integration. Further, the study noted that integration throughout the Armed Services was feasible and that a quota on minority participation was unnecessary (Ansell, 1990). Although a seminal study, it did not address how fairly African-American soldiers in integrated units were treated. In the same year the Department of Defense announced that the Army had disbanded all segregated (i.e., all-Negro) units.

Racial Conflict in the Armed Forces

Toward the end of the Vietnam War in the early 1970s, the gathering maelstrom of racial instability in the Armed Services erupted in a surge of racial violence at many military installations both stateside and aboard. General Creighton Abrahams, who commanded the troops in Vietnam, reported that poor race relations were a major problem plaguing combat effectiveness. It was at that time that the Pentagon began to consider race relations a serious problem. The Army experienced a stunning number of race riots. Ugly disturbances pitted soldiers against one another at Fort Bragg, Fort Dix, and at a number of camps in Germany, Korea, and Vietnam. The situation in Germany was particularly grim because of the hostility of German communities toward African-American servicemen and the reportedly flagrant discrimination in off-post housing that exacerbated existing racial tensions.

Historically, the Navy has had the smallest percentage of African Americans in the Armed Services, but it was in the Navy that some of the most dramatic race riots occurred. In October 1972, race riots on two aircraft carriers, USS *Kitty Hawk* and USS *Constellation*, were of such magnitude that they became national issues, commanding the attention of top-level personnel. Four days later, racial turmoil resulted in the cancellation of a training exercise on the *Constella-*

tion and forced the ship to return to port. Within a month of these incidents, race riots were reported aboard the USS *Sumpter* and USS *Hassayampa*. Shore commands, including Midway Island and Norfolk, also experienced race riots.

The Air Force was relatively unscathed until May 1971. One of the key events that brought attention to the state of racial affairs was the four-day riot at Travis AFB, California. African-American airmen sought redress for a number of grievances involving poor housing, the biased operation of the non-commissioned officers (NCO) club, substandard recreational activities, and a perception of severe disciplinary actions awarded to men of color. Further, they questioned an order by the base commander that banned the clenched-fist salute reminiscent of an episode during the 1968 Olympic Games, which had disturbed most of white America. That riot was the catalyst that prompted Air Force leadership to reassess and reappraise its equal opportunity policy and practices. Initially, the Air Force leadership believed that the Travis riot was a mere spillover from the "stream of racial prejudice" that had infected society at large. However, the Air Force soon discovered that the riot had been caused by a failure in leadership, which had led to a critical breakdown in organizational and intercultural communication.[1]

In general, African-American service members, undoubtedly significantly influenced by the social transformation in American society at the time, were protesting demonstratively against discrimination in both on- and off-post housing, promotions, job assignments, and career development; against bias in the administration of military justice; and against the reality and perception of unequal treatment in the Army in general. The level of dysfunction was unprecedented in the Armed Services, and most commanders were untrained, unskilled, insensitive, and unprepared to deal with the conflict. Indeed, there was a wide range of suggestions proposed, from "shooting the rioters" to "permissive understanding" of the problems faced by minorities in the military.

One recommendation, eventually adopted, was a mandatory race relations training program, and it became the single most ambitious training program of its type in terms of training and hours ever implemented by any institution in the United States (Hope, 1979). The onus for its development fell on the Defense Race Relations Institute (DRRI) later to be renamed the Defense Equal Opportunity Management Institute.

Defense Equal Opportunity Management Institute (DEOMI)

Racial turbulence spreading throughout the Armed Services during the 1970s persuaded Pentagon officials to take a more aggressive stance on race relations and equal opportunity matters. In January 1970, the Inter-service Task Force on Education in Race Relations, known as the *Theus Committee* (named for Air Force Brigadier General Lucius Theus), was created to examine the causes of and possible remedies for corrosive race relations in the military. The committee's recommendations initiated a Department of Defense (DoD) directive, and in 1971, the Defense Race Relations Institute (DRRI) was established at Patrick Air Force Base, Florida. Under the DoD Directive 1322.11, DRRI was established to prepare instructors to teach race relations at the base level to all Armed Services personnel, collect research data on programs, and conduct classes throughout the Armed Services. Officials realized that some of the earlier "instructional efforts" actually triggered hostile confrontations when led by inadequately trained, overzealous leaders, and the DRRI program was viewed as a way to develop skilled and perceptive race relations facilitators. Brigadier General Lucius Theus (who later became Major General and chief advisor to the Deputy Chief of Staff/Personnel on racial matters) maintained that an attitudinal change was desired, but it was almost too much to expect from a short seven-week course. Consequently, the initial program was established to modify negative behaviors that exacerbated racial tensions.

To reflect its growing and demanding mission, the Institute's name was changed to the *Defense Equal Opportunity Management Institute* (DEOMI) on July 27, 1979, and eventually expanded its core curriculum to sixteen weeks. Since the first seven-week course, the Institute has continued to evolve to meet requirements of commanders in managing diversity, equal opportunity, and related issues. DRRI originally focused exclusively on race relations, but its scope was widened to include various ethnic groups as well as certain categories of whites as well as sexual harassment and discrimination. The DEOMI curriculum includes a number of equal opportunity courses designed for military and civilian advisors, managers, reservists, and senior executive leaders (i.e., flag officers and senior executive staff). The current mission of DEOMI is to increase combat and essential readiness by enhancing unit organizational leadership and cohesion.

This is accomplished by developing and conducting education and training in the administration of military equal opportunity (EO), equal employment opportunity (EEO), and human relations.

The directive that established DRRI was replaced by DoD Directive 1350.2 and specifies as one of its primary functions that it will "conduct research, [and] perform evaluation of program effectiveness." In 1987, in conjunction with conducting its rigorous training courses, DEOMI began conducting EO, EEO, and human relations research as well as monitoring and disseminating equal opportunity research findings. Since then the program has expanded through specialized programs—i.e., the Topical Research Internship Program (TRIP), Summer Research Faculty Program, and the Shirley J. Bach Visiting Research Chair for an eminent social science and EO scholar.

DEOMI's research program focuses generally on assessing the attitudes, perceptions, and behavior of military personnel of different races, ethnic origins, and gender; developing and analyzing race relations/equal opportunity training techniques and programs. The program also includes developing tools, techniques, and products for use by military commanders and equal opportunity personnel in the management of equal opportunity (and organizational effectiveness) programs and issues. Policy decisions should be based on empirical research or evidence as opposed to popular opinion, intuition, or tradition. By providing timely, relevant research, DEOMI is strategically involved in the formulation and implementation of personnel policies and practices across DoD and the Armed Services. The articles in this book are an extension of that crucial mission.

Organization of the Book

The basic theme underscoring the papers in this collection is a concern with implementing equal opportunity and effective diversity management. The subheadings are "Overview," "Contemporary Approaches to Managing Diversity," "Diversifying Leadership: Equity in Evaluation and Promotions," "Gender Integration and Sexual Harassment," "Military Discipline and Race, Where do We Go from Here?" (i.e., future research perspectives). The papers in each section encompass a broad spectrum of research in the field of military equal opportunity and diversity management. All of the areas explored have counterparts in the civilian sector. The research presented reflects the diverse interests of scholars from various backgrounds who use different models, approaches, and methodologies, many of which are adapted from the study of civilian institutions. It is the unique application of these models, approaches and methodologies to the military context that defines the distinct area of military equal opportunity and diversity management.

Summary of Contents

"Cultural diversity" has became one of the most popular phrases of the 1990s and will probably continue its popularity into the current century. We hear less about equal employment opportunity and affirmative action efforts and programs and more about managing cultural diversity and diversity training. The importance of the cultural diversity movement stems in large part from the predicted demographic shifts that are already underway in America's workforce. These shifts will produce military, public, and private sector workforces that are much more demographically diverse than in the past. Many organizations have begun to respond to these demographic projections. However, because neither law nor federal guidelines mandate it, diversity management is not as prevalent today as are the equal employment opportunity and affirmative action programs that preceded it. For example, a recent report showed that federal agencies have developed few new diversity programs to address demographic changes, but rather have continued their old affirmative action programs. The report further stated that the programs are only aimed at the recruitment of people of color and not their promotion into higher ranks in the bureaucracy (Cameron, Jorgenson, & Kawecki, 1993).

Managing diverse workgroups has become a strategic imperative for many organizations, as well as a crucial element in organizational survival. Different types of organizations are developing programs and opportunities to increase the participation of their employees, especially those who have not been included previously in important positions within their organizations. The discussion of diversity in the workplace has expanded to include a wide variety of differences among individuals and groups. In addition to differences related to age, race, gender, ethnicity, and physical ability, diversity has also come to include individuals or groups who differ according to sexual preferences, marital status, educational background, parental status, work experience, and income. One analyst remarked that diversity management is managing human resource needs that cut across all demographic categories (Jenner, 1994). Most organizational leaders and human resource managers would agree that managing diversity should include many characteristics common to a culture, race, gender, age, or sexual preference.

Many researchers argue that, effectively managed, workplace diversity can create a competitive advantage in areas of cost, resource acquisition, marketing, creativity, problem solving, organizational flexibility, and customer service. In terms of individuals, some of the diversity literature reveals that effectively managed diversity programs can lead to increases in job satisfaction and retention for women and minorities. In addition, there is empirical evidence that an organization that adopts a diversity management policy will provide the necessary professional environment for women and racial minorities to succeed (Gilbert & Stead, 1999).

Organizations that effectively manage their diversity are referred to as "multicultural." These organizations represent the ideal, a place in which differences are appreciated and used to gain competitive advantage. In multicultural organizations, organizational culture promotes both attitudinal and structural integration of majority and minority members through diversity education and training as well as through equitably rewarding employees for wide-ranging contributions. The U.S. Armed Services, although not a utopia by any means, has made substantial strides in improving its equal opportunity climate by top-level support, policy implementation, mandatory and specialized training evolutions, and applied research. The initial section, "Contemporary Approaches to Managing Diversity," examines a variety of diversity research, elements, and perspectives — training, conceptual definitions, diversity, mentoring, senior leader perceptions, and religious accommodations — in the military context. The lead article by Mickey Dansby and Dan Landis provides the history and philosophy of the equal opportunity training conducted at DEOMI and serves to orient the reader to subsequent articles as well as other sections in the book.

Part 2, "Diversifying Leadership: Equity in Evaluation and Promotions," addresses accession and retention issues that are particularly important in the context of the current environment of military drawdown, base closures, and budget reductions. The number of eligible recruits has declined significantly, forcing the military to compete actively against the civilian sector to recruit and retain personnel. For that reason, the issue of retention will continue to be a critical area of inquiry in the future. Moreover, in the military, as in the civilian sector, performance evaluations influence critical personnel decisions concerning promotion, assignment to career enhancing positions, and retention. Performance evaluation systems are undergoing continuous transformation in corporate America. Organizations today are modifying the methods by which their leaders are evaluated, counseled, and promoted. Likewise, every branch of the Armed Services has substantially modified its performance evaluations in ways that parallel corporate practices. The Air Force officer performance report, Officer Evaluation Report (OER), underwent a full-scale review in 1995. The Navy changed its Report on the Fitness of Officers (a.k.a. fitness report or FITREP) from an alphanumerical rating scale to a behaviorally anchored rating scale format in 1996; the Army revised its OER in 1997; and the Marine Corps began its new Performance Evaluation System (PES) in 1998. These efforts are an attempt to make the performance evaluations systems more accurate and timely, as well as fair. The U.S. military, along with its personnel, has much to gain from an evaluation system that accurately reflects the work behavior and potential of its personnel. Although the results of the studies do not generate clear evidence of racial bias, they do indicate that the performance of minority officers is viewed differently compared to white officers. Two of the articles challenge the readership to determine ways to eliminate the potential bias illustrated by the research. No doubt that there are biological differences between males and females, but the number of differences, their specific nature, and the reasons for their existence are all topics of controversy and require ongoing study on the part of researchers in many disciplines. There are also political overtones in gender studies, which have been particularly salient since the beginning of the feminist movement in the 1960s and 1970s. Some writers and researchers on gender issues minimize differences and offer a definitive review of research on gender differences. Others with a feminist orientation emphasize the differences by calling attention to redressing inequities in the status of women in our society.

In general, gender and sex role research deepens our understanding of how institutions respond to the challenge of social change, how they adapt to new realities while striving to protect their essential traditions. It can provide insights into how we as a culture view the human being, assigning talents and limitations to other human beings based on their gender alone and help explain the dynamics for change in previously single-gender environments. Part 3 entitled, "Gender Integration and Sexual Harassment," takes a two-pronged approach to these complex issues.

Specific to the military context, the issue of women in the military has a unique history, but was not seriously debated until the mandatory draft ended in 1973. To place women's role in the modern military in perspective, it is important to note that the concept of American women serving in war is not new. Women have fought and died in every war in American history. It is the extent of their participation and the degree to which they have been integrated into the military forces that sets the present so dramatically apart from the past. For example, the number of women in the military is increasing and they are indispensable as far as operational readiness is concerned. Indeed, in a competitive labor market the military must use women to fill its diverse jobs—there are not enough qualified male volunteers to fill all positions. Women played key combat support roles in the bombing of Libya, the invasions of Grenada and Panama, and during Operations Desert Shield and Desert Storm in the Middle East, the air assault on the former Yugoslavia, and in other military wartime and peacetime operations. This brings us to the question of combat exclusion. This issue is of particular significance because its implementation disqualifies women from specific jobs and experiences that are critical to career advancement, leads to decreased levels of job satisfaction and retention, and generates a host of problems that have implications for combat readiness.

Also considered is the topic of sexual harassment, which has become a highly controversial issue in the workplace. The U.S. Supreme Court's review of four sexual harassment cases in 1998 is a marked increase from prior dockets; since 1986, the court has only reviewed two sexual harassment cases. The proliferation of sexual harassment cases reviewed by the Supreme Court, especially since the court's docket has been reduced in recent years, sends a message to organizations as to the severity of sexual harassment and the possible repercussions. Moreover, the High Court extended the definition of sexual harassment and recently ruled that Title VII of the 1964 *Civil Rights Act* prohibits harassment between members of the same sex. It also mandated that the legal standards governing same-sex claims are the equivalent to those applied to claims of sexual harassment by a member of the opposite sex.

Likewise, sexual harassment has become a primary area of focus in the armed services, particularly since the widely publicized incidents in the military and civilian sectors. Unfortunately, totally eliminating sexual harassment from the workplace is quite difficult due to ambiguities in the legal definition of the construct as well as vast differences in the perceptions of men and women. Throughout the literature it has been reported that sexual harassment of women in the workplace is a pervasive problem that causes physical, psychological, and economic harm to its victims. Moreover, incidents of sexual harassment (and assault) in the military context jeopardize unit cohesion and mission readiness, as well as *esprit de corps*. The articles in this section detail the issues of integration and sexual harassment as well as equal opportunity perceptions.

When the Kerner Commission issued its report in the wake of urban riots that scarred the 1960s, it warned that America was moving perilously toward becoming two societies, "one black, one white, segregated and unequal." A recent report, *The Millennium Breach*, released on the thirtieth anniversary of the Kerner report, seems to confirm the Kerner Commission's prophecy by reporting that the economic and racial divide in the United States not only has materialized, but also is getting wider. Debates about the progress America has made toward eliminating racial discrimination are ongoing. As a case in point, many scholarly and legal debates over the past thirty years in the field of race relations in the United States have linked the issues of race, economic status, and crime. Considering the disproportionate number of African Americans under control of the civilian and military criminal justice systems in the United States, further study is warranted. Reflecting the concerns of the military system as well as the American society, the next section entitled, "Military Discipline and Race," includes detailed studies that provide several perspectives within the military context. Understanding these findings may help us better comprehend how racial and ethnic tensions inform current debates about relationships among crime, law, and society in general and the military in particular.

This volume is only a beginning effort to highlight research examining diversity management in the military. Ideally, it will encourage future compilations of EO and diversity research. DEOMI will continue to play a vanguard role in producing groundbreaking applied research addressing continuing and emerging issues. The last section, "Where Do We Go from Here?" proposes future research directions for military equal opportunity and diversity management. As we know, the military is affected by a number of social forces—demographic shifts, political changes, technological and scientific advancements, economic fluctuations, health trends—that, in turn, influence equal opportunity and diversity research methodology and findings. Significant changes in the nation's demographic composition will strongly affect the military. Ultimately, those changes will influence the way analysts pose research questions as well as frame proposed problem solutions. Thus, this section will give the reader a sense of those future questions and anticipated research efforts.

If sustained research attention is accorded to the many recommendations made by our contributors in the coming years, we will make major strides toward meeting the challenges of diversity management, and begin to realize the full potential of human diversity as one of our most powerful national resources.

Note

1.   Alan Gropman's book, *The Air Force Integrates: 1945-1964*, provides an outstanding documentary account of the turbulent period in race relations and constitutes a seminal contribution to the evolving history from the racially segregated U.S. Army Air Force (USAAF) to its successor United States Air Force (USAF).

References

Ansell, R. (1990). *From segregation to desegregation: Blacks in the U.S. Army 1703-1954*. Carlisle Barracks, PA: U.S. Army War College.

Astor, G. (1998). *The right to fight: A history of African Americans in the military*. Novato, CA: Presidio Press.

Cameron, K., Jorgenson, J., & Kawecki, C. (1993, winter). Civil service 2000 revisited. *Public Personnel Management, 22*, 669-674.

Cox, T. (1991). The multicultural organization. *Academy of Management Executive, 5*, 34-47.

Cox, T., & Blake, S. (1991). Managing cultural diversity: Implications for organizational competitiveness. *Academy of Management Executive, 5*, 45-56.

Cronin, C. (1998). *Military psychology: An introduction*. Needham Heights, MA: Simon & Shuster.

Fuentes, G. (1999, Jan 18). A whole new way to judge Marines. *The Marine Corps Times*, p. 8.

Gilbert, J., & Stead, B. (1999). Stigmatization revisited: Does diversity management make a difference in applicant success? *Group & Organization Management, 24*(2), 239-251.

Glazer, N. (1997). *We are all multiculturalists now*. Cambridge: Harvard University Press.

Gould, S. (1996). *The mismeasure of man*. New York: W.W. Norton & Co.

Greenberg, M., & Morris, W. (1997). *Black Americans in the military*. URL Http://www.dtic.mil/armylink/news/Arp1997/s19970401black.html.

Gropman, A. (1978). *The Air Force integrates: 1945-1964*. Washington, DC: Office of Air Force History.

Hacker, A. (1995). *Two nations: Black and white, separate, hostile, unequal*. New York: Ballantine Books.

Harrison, D., Price, K., & Bell, M. (1998). Beyond relational demography: Time and the effects of surface- and deep-level diversity in work group cohesion. *Academy of Management Journal, 41*(1), 96-107.

Hoberman, J. (1997). *Darwin's athletes: How sport has damaged black America and preserved the myth of race*. New York: Houghton Mifflin.

Hope, R. (1979). *Racial strife in the U.S. military: Toward the elimination of discrimination*. New York: Praeger.

Jenner, L. (1994, Jan). Diversity management: What is does it mean? *HR Focus, 71*(1), 11-13.

Jet (1998, Mar 23). Kerner commission's 'separate and unequal' societies exist today, pp. 4-6.

Larkey, L. (1996). Toward a theory of communicative interactions in culturally diverse workgroups. *Academy of Management Review, 21*, 463-491.

Marine Corps Gazette (1999, Feb). New performance evaluation system goes into effect, *83*(2), pp. 4-5.

Milliken, F., & Martins, L. (1996). Searching for common threads: Understanding the multiple effects of diversity in organizational groups. *Academy of Management Review 21*(2), 402-433.

Moskos, C. (1991, Aug 5). How do they do it? The Army's racial success story. *The New Republic*, pp. 16-20.

Mullin, R. (1973). *Blacks in America's wars*. New York: Monad Press.

Scott, L., & Womack, W. (1988). *Double V: The Civil Rights Struggle of The Tuskegee Airmen*. East Lancing, MI: Michigan State University Press.

Supreme Court to decide four sex harassment cases this term. (1998, spring). *BNAC Communicator, 16*(2), pp. 1, 12, 16.

Tolbert, R. (1999, Jun 20). Personal interview.

West, C. (1994). *Race Matters*. New York: Vintage Books.

Part 1

Contemporary Approaches to Managing Diversity

Introduction to Part 1

Importance of Teamwork and Readiness

Recent trends in organizational practice, such as the increasing use of quality teams, autonomous work groups, project teams, and management task forces, suggest that groupwork is becoming more pervasive in organizations and is recognized as a vital means of maintaining organizational effectiveness and productivity. Reduced bureaucracy, increased employee/member involvement, and high quality products are all potential benefits gained from the use of teams in organizations. In today's business world the use of teams to increase product development, productivity, and profitability is rapidly expanding. Cross-cultural and cross-functional teams that can work effectively to tap the deep reservoir of knowledge possessed by all members have a distinct strategic advantage in the global marketplace. The U.S. Armed Services are effective team-based organizations with strong leadership. To be sure, the history of the U.S. military would strongly suggest that teams, system of teams, and team management—from the Joint Chiefs of Staff to basic training squads—are vitally inherent to the success of mission accomplishment and organizational effectiveness. Fundamentally, the core of military execution relies on preparedness, team cohesion, and responsiveness.

Readiness of the U.S. military has never been more important. Ready forces provide the flexibility needed to shape the global environment, deter potential enemies, and if required, to rapidly respond to a broad spectrum of threats. In addition, readiness, or more specifically personnel readiness, instills the confidence our people need to succeed in a variety of challenging situations. In recent years, DoD policy and budget guidance has made readiness a top priority. Today's challenge is to sustain a high level of readiness. Each service has a different approach to maintain readiness and includes a mixture of elements (i.e., unique force characteristics, deployment levels, and specific materiel). Less tangible, although equally important, factors that influence readiness are quality of life, leadership, and composition of teams and intra-team dynamics.

Command readiness is contingent on the readiness of its collective teams. Without cooperation among teams the execution of operations will be compromised. Intolerance of people of different racial backgrounds, genders, values, and religions may be obstacles to team, unit or command cohesion, effectiveness, and accomplishment. With women and minorities entering the military at unprecedented rates, the challenge of diversity management remains a significant factor in command readiness and ultimately the security of our nation.

Military Diversity

Analyses examining diversity management in the military have been influenced heavily by research examining private sector organizations. This cross-fertilization is to be expected, in part, because the military exhibits many organizational characteristics similar to private sector institutions. As noted by Moskos and Wood (1991), in the wake of the transition to an all-volunteer force, researchers began in the late 1970s to examine the thesis that the U.S. military was evolving from an institutional format to one resembling an occupation. To the extent that this thesis has validity, there is every reason to expect that diversity management techniques developed in the private sector have some applicability in a military environment.

Much of the current research examining the management of diversity in the Armed Services has focused on two issues: (1) the effects of changes in demographic diversity on perceptions of the climate for equal opportunity (EO), and (2) the effects of changes in demographic diversity on organizational effectiveness (OE) or mission readiness. Data from the Military Equal Opportunity Climate Survey (MEOCS) have been used to examine the effect of increases in the proportion of women on perceptions of the quality of the EO climate. Dansby and Landis (1995) found that minority women have the least favorable perceptions of the EO climate, but these perceptions improved as the proportion of minority women in the workgroup increased. Tallarigo (1994) reported that as the ratio of women to men in military organizations increased, women were less likely to see themselves as victims of discrimination, although their overall assessment of the EO climate did not improve.

Research examining the relationship between EO and OE in the private sector has attempted to resolve contradictory predictions regarding the effect of increased demographic diversity on organizational effectiveness (OE). Proponents of the "value in diversity" hypothesis hold that properly managed diversity can be beneficial for organizations and lead to improved performance. Advocates of what might be described as the "deleterious diversity" hypothesis insist that increased diversity invariably has a negative impact on the functioning of groups. The studies conducted to date have failed to generate consistent findings that favor one hypothesis over the other.

Studies focusing on military organizations have also produced inconclusive findings. Siebold and Lindsay (1994) found that the percentage of non-white soldiers in a platoon was not related to group cohesiveness. Rosen et al. (1996) determined that increases in the representation of women had a negative effect on men's rating of group cohesion and effectiveness. Niebuhr, Knouse, and Dansby (1994) concluded that perceptions of racism and sexism within a work group correlated negatively with group cohesiveness and performance. Respondents' race had a significant effect on perceptions of group cohesion and performance, but a similar pattern did not occur for gender. These studies suggest that the effects of increases in racial/ethnic and gender diversity on perceptions of OE may be asymmetrical in military organizations.

Further, EO may affect quality efforts of organization. Knouse (1994) found a systematic relationship among perceptions of quality of work group output, work group effectiveness, commitment, satisfaction, and positive EO behaviors. The degree of demographic diversity was correlated with the total quality (TQ) scale. In a subsequent study, a TQ scale was found to be correlated with work group effectiveness, leader cohesion, job satisfaction, group cohesion, organizational trust, and overall EEO climate (Knouse, 1996).

Research Overview

The findings cited above provide a context for the studies of how the military approaches the management of diversity that are presented in this section. They also support the expectation that when diversity is understood and managed effectively, a military organization can experience higher levels of productivity, more effective communication, greater teamwork, and enhanced morale. "Intercultural Training in the United States Military" by Mickey Dansby and Dan Landis discusses the history and philosophy of intercultural relations in the Armed Services as well as the diversity policies, training, and other methods used to implement equal opportunity and diversity programs.

A clear understanding of the various dimensions of diversity and their potential impact on organizations are prerequisites for the design of effective management strategies. This understanding is continuously evolving as both theoretical and empirical knowledge advances. Several of the articles in this section provide theoretical perspectives on the management of diversity. "Contemporary Models of Racism: Theoretical Perspectives, Institutional Assessment, and Organizational Implications for an Equal Opportunity Climate" by Olenda Johnson examines the relevance of three contemporary models of racism to the United States military. "Three Levels of Diversity: An Examination of the Complex Relationship Between Diversity, Group Cohesiveness, Sexual Harassment, Group Performance, and Time" by Gary Whaley introduces a tripartite typology for classifying different types of diversity. The nature of the relationship among three types of diversity is discussed and a general model of organizational behavior including diversity, group cohesiveness, group performance, sexual harassment, and time is presented. The next paper, "Religious Accommodation in the Military," by Carlos Huerta and Schuyler Webb provides a brief history and overview of religious accommodation guidelines and cases in the military context. "Personality and Leadership in Diverse DoD Workgroups and Teams" by Robert McIntyre and Judith Johnson argues that for teams to be more effective in the military greater attention must be paid to individual psychological diversity in addition to demographic diversity.

Successful management of diversity requires recognition of the importance of developing strategies that promote constructive interpersonal dynamics. This can involve a variety of strategies including enhancement of leadership skills, greater use of team approaches to task performance and decision-making, and focusing special attention on the professional development of new members of the organization. "See No Evil, Hear No Evil: Senior Leaders' Social Comparisons, and the Low Salience of Racial Issues" by Rupert Nacoste examines how the demographic and hierarchical isolation of senior military leaders can lead to inadequate attention to potential racial conflicts. "Mentors, Mentor Substitutes, or Virtual Mentors: Alternative Mentoring Approaches for the Military" by Stephen Knouse and Schuyler Webb asserts that although the traditional mentoring relationship is difficult to establish and maintain in a military environment, a number of adaptations to the traditional relationship can be implemented.

The evaluation of diversity programs is a critical but often overlooked dimension of the diversity management process. "Opportunities for Assessing Military EO: A Researcher's Perspective on Identifying an Integrative Program-Evaluation Strategy" by Jack Edwards addresses the issue of designing effective evaluation techniques. The study examines global efforts by the DoD to assess equal opportunity programs including surveys and formal reporting procedures. Edwards notes that the only large-scale DoD evaluation of EO issues focused on the investigation of the efficacy of the discrimination complaint process which led to the publication of a two-volume document entitled "Report of the Task Force on Discrimination and Sexual Harassment" (Defense Equal Opportunity Council Task Force, 1995).

"Local Effects and Global Impact of DEOMI Training" by Judith Johnson and "Perceptions of Small Group Diversity Training at the Defense Equal Opportunity Management Institute" by Ruth Greene present alternative approaches to the evaluation of the effectiveness of training provided through the Defense Equal Opportunity Management Institute.

Taken together these research studies provide a solid foundation for additional research that can lead to improvements in the management of diversity and equal opportunity in military organizations. These studies further emphasize that diversity management and equal opportunity are military necessities.

References

Dansby, M., & Landis, D. (1995). *Race, gender, and representation index as predictors of equal opportunity climate in military organizations.* DEOMI Research Series Pamphlet 95-12.

Knouse, S. (1994). *Equal opportunity climate and total quality management: A preliminary study.* DEOMI Research Series Pamphlet 94-3.

Knouse, S. (1996). *Diversity, organizational factors, group effectiveness, and total quality: An analysis of relationships in the MEOCS-EEO Test Version 3.1.* DEOMI Research Series Pamphlet 96-6.

Moskos, C., & Wood, F. (1991). Introduction. In C. Moskos and F. Wood (Eds.) *The military, more than a job?* Maclean, VA: Pergamon-Brassey's International Defense Publishers, 3-14.

Niebuhr, R., Knouse, S., & Dansby, M. (1994). *Workgroup climates for acceptance of diversity: Relationship to group cohesiveness and performance.* DEOMI Research Series Pamphlet 94-4.

Rosen, L., et al. (1996). Cohesion and readiness in gender-integrated combat service support units: The impact of acceptance of women and the gender ratio. *Armed Forces and Society, 22*(4), 537-553.

Siebold, G., & Lindsay, T. (1994). *The relation between soldier racial/ethnic group and perceived cohesion and motivation.* Paper presented at the annual meeting of the American Sociological Association (Los Angeles, CA).

Sundstrom, E., DeMeuse, K., & Futrell, D. (1990) Work teams. *American Psychologist, 45*(2), 120-133.

1

Intercultural Training in the United States Military[1]

Mickey R. Dansby and Dan Landis

Introduction

"Our nation was founded on the principle that the individual has infinite dignity and worth. The DoD, which exists to keep the Nation secure and at peace, must always be guided by this principle." Thus begins the Department of Defense Human Goals, a brief charter outlining the broad philosophy for equal opportunity and diversity within the DoD. This document, signed by the Secretary of Defense, Deputy Secretary of Defense, service secretaries, and military chiefs of the Services, lists a number of objectives, including: "To make military and civilian service in the Department of Defense a model of equal opportunity for all..." and "To create an environment that values diversity and fosters mutual respect and cooperation among all persons..." DoD strives to implement these lofty goals through two primary means: policy directives and training.

Military training in matters of intercultural diversity and equal opportunity is multi-tiered, starting with basic instruction at the various service entry points (e.g., basic recruit training, Service Academies, ROTC) and continuing through the senior career levels. Although each service develops its own directives and program of training, the core for this training comes from one source: the Defense Equal Opportunity Management Institute (DEOMI) at Patrick Air Force Base, Florida (formerly known as the Defense Race Relations Institute or DRRI). Since 1971, this institution has been responsible for training the equal opportunity advisors who manage and conduct training programs for the Services. In essence, DEOMI "trains the trainers" for DoD (and the U.S. Coast Guard, which falls under the Department of Transportation) in matters of intercultural relations, equal opportunity, and diversity. Because of its central role, discussion of DEOMI's work plays a crucial role in developing the theme of this chapter.

Our goal in this chapter is to give the reader a perspective on the background, philosophy, and status of intercultural training in the military. We begin with the historical background, to set the context for the rest of the chapter.

Historical Background

Day (1983) has provided an in-depth review of the development of DEOMI and the Services' race relations training programs. Rather than repeat that material, we shall summarize key elements and update Day's work to give the reader an appreciation of current practice in the DoD. We begin with a thumbnail history of intercultural training in the military.

Integration of the Armed Forces

The foundation of intercultural relations in the military is largely based on the integration of blacks into the Services following World War II. Though minority contributions to America's defense prior to World War II are well documented (see, for example, Binkin, Eitelberg, Schexnider, & Smith, 1982; MacGregor, 1981; Nalty, 1986; and Young, 1982), their participation in World War II and decisions in the post-war period are watershed events in understanding intercultural relations in the military.

Substantial numbers of black servicemembers served during World War II. Over 900,000 served in the Army (almost 9 percent of the Army during their peak period), about 167,000 in the Navy (around 4 percent) and over 17,000 in the Marine Corps (2.5 percent) (Binkin et al., 1982). With limited exceptions, these individuals served in segregated units (Lovejoy, 1977; MacGregor, 1981). Their notable contributions to the war effort, though sometimes clouded by controversy (Hope, 1979; Nalty, 1986; MacGregor, 1981), could not be overlooked. As many black servicemembers returning to their homes suffered discrimination at the hands of a society they had fought to defend, President Truman was moved to action (Nalty, 1986;

MacGregor, 1981). Eventually, Truman's concerns resulted in the landmark Executive Order 9981.

Issued July 26, 1948, Executive Order 9981 called for "equality of treatment for all persons in the armed services without regard to race, color, religion or national origin." It also established the President's Committee on Equality of Treatment and Opportunity in the Armed Services (often known as the Fahy Committee) to serve as a vehicle for implementing the policy by advising the President and the service secretaries on how to "effectuate the policy..." (MacGregor, 1981). Despite its broad powers, the committee faced an arduous task in carrying out its charter due to the opposition of many high-ranking military and civilian officials in the military establishment.[2]

It took the impetus of another war (in Korea) and research supporting integration based on the effectiveness of integrated units during this war to move the desegregation effort from policy to reality. (Both the Army's internal study and a contract study called *Project CLEAR* supported integration; furthermore, with larger numbers of black soldiers involved in the Korean conflict, efficiency demanded integration as a pragmatic necessity; MacGregor, 1981.) Finally, by October 1954, the Secretary of Defense was able to announce the abolishment of the last racially segregated (active-duty) unit in the armed forces (MacGregor, 1981).

President Truman's July 1948 executive order racially integrating the forces had a profound effect on the American military services. Another event leading to a permanent change in the face of America's armed forces occurred in the same year. In June, Congress passed the Women's Armed Services Act of 1948 (P.L. 625; Holm, 1992). When President Truman signed this law, he assured a permanent place for women in the armed forces. Though P.L. 625 placed severe limits on women's service (e.g., their strength could never exceed 2 percent of the force and women were restricted from serving as general officers; interestingly, during the life of the law, the 2 percent ceiling was never reached), it made it possible for women, many of whom had served during World War II, to continue in the services during peacetime. In 1967, P.L. 90-130 removed the limits on women's representation and rank in the services.

The integration efforts, for both race and gender, have resulted in an American armed force whose ethnic/racial/gender diversity is quite different today from the force of World War II. For example, at the end of the war, women comprised 2.3 percent of the total active military strength (280 thousand out of 12 million; Holm, 1992); by 1971, they were only 1 percent (about 40 thousand; Holm, 1992); but by March of 1994, they were over 12 percent (over 198 thousand; DEOMI, 1994). Black members' representation has grown from 5.9 percent in 1949 (Young, 1982) to 19.3 percent (over 325 thousand; DEOMI, 1994) in March of 1994. Total minority representation in the active services in March of 1994 was over 28 percent (471 thousand; DEOMI, 1994).

Although the desegregation of the services after World War II set the services on course for these dramatic changes, the pathway to the future would prove to be full of potholes.

The Civil Rights Era

The desegregation of the Services did not lead to an end of racial discrimination and strife, nor did it result in full integration (from an attitudinal perspective) of minority members (Lovejoy, 1977). By the early 1960s, with the civil rights movement in full swing, pressure to improve conditions for minority servicemembers continued to swell. Proponents of civil rights in the public sector and the Kennedy administration urged DoD to take action to end segregation in reserve units and in the housing, schools, etc., serving military members in communities near military bases (MacGregor, 1981).

Secretary of Defense Robert McNamara formed a committee (designated a Presidential committee since DoD requested Presidential appointment of its members) to address the issue (MacGregor, 1981). President Kennedy announced the establishment of the President's Committee on Equality of Opportunity in the Armed Forces on June 24, 1962 (MacGregor, 1981). It is often known as the Gesell Committee, after its chairman, Gerhard Gesell.[3] The work of this committee had greater support within DoD than did the Fahy Committee, perhaps because it had its roots within the DoD rather than directly from the executive branch (MacGregor, 1981). The work of this committee established equal opportunity for minority soldiers, both on and off the installation, as a direct command responsibility and linked equal opportunity to military efficiency (MacGregor, 1981). It resulted in DoD Directive 5120.36 (July 1963), supporting equal opportunity for all servicemembers and giving commanders authority to declare "off-limits" those establishments in the civilian community that discriminated on the basis of race, creed, or national origin (Hope, 1979; MacGregor, 1981). The directive also established a focal point for equal opportunity management within DoD and required the Services to develop their own manuals and regulations to implement the policy. Between 1964 and 1966, such regulations were published (Hope, 1979).

The Vietnam Era

Shortly after the implementation of these policies, the Vietnam War began. With it came increased numbers of black and other minority servicemembers. But many of these servicemembers, inspired by the civil rights era and with enhanced awareness of inequities, were more vocal concerning equal opportunity issues. As they became more militant, racial unrest in the form of riots and incidents occurred across the Services (Binkin et al., 1982; Hope, 1979). Official investigations into the causes of these disturbances resulted in a document (called The Rearden Report after the chairman of the investigating team, Frank Rearden III) supporting charges of discrimination. In response, among other things, the Services were required to establish equal opportunity/human relations officers and human relations councils in all major units, to improve utilization of minority members across the occupational spectrum, and to remove leaders who failed to take action against discrimination (Hope, 1979). Subsequently, other investigations and incidents led to Congressional involvement, culminating in a 1969 directive from the House Armed Services Committee for the DoD to establish mandatory race relations seminars for all servicemembers (Hope, 1979).

In January 1970, Defense Secretary Melvin Laird created the Interservice Task Force on Education in Race Relations to develop a plan to implement the program. Colonel Lucius Theus (a black Air Force officer eventually promoted to major general) chaired the committee, which later came to bear his name. The Theus Committee delivered its report to the Secretary of Defense on July 31, 1970 (Lovejoy, 1977). In September, an implementation committee (the Krise Committee) was directed to test the educational approach outlined in the Theus report. Late that year, Colonel Edward Krise (who became DRRI's first Director), chairman of the committee, delivered a report on the pilot program to DoD. The report gave specific suggestions on how to carry out the Theus Committee's recommendation to establish DRRI (Lovejoy, 1977). A draft DoD directive was developed and the process of "coordination" began within DoD. Finally, spurred by one more racial incident (a particularly destructive riot at Travis Air Force Base in May 1971), the Theus Committee's plan for race relations education was codified into DoD Directive 1322.11 in June 1971 (Hope, 1979; Nalty, 1986). In the words of one observer, "this directive outlined the most comprehensive race relations education program ever attempted by any major institution in this country" (Hope, 1979, p. 41).

Founding of DEOMI

DoD Directive 1322.11 chartered the Defense Race Relations Institute (DRRI; later renamed DEOMI) and the Race Relations Education Board (RREB), a high level committee that was to oversee DRRI and provide policy guidance for race relations education (Day, 1983). Others (Day, 1983; Hope, 1979; Lovejoy, 1977) have chronicled the early history of the RREB and DRRI; we shall not repeat it here. Suffice it to say that the establishment of DRRI (DEOMI) marks the beginning of the modern approach to intercultural training in the military. The following discussion updates the descriptions of DEOMI provided by Day (1983) and others (e.g., Hope, 1979; Lovejoy, 1977).

Current Policy, Training Philosophy, and Programs

Day (1983), Lovejoy (1977), and Hope (1979) chronicle the evolution from DEOMI's initial course (lasting six weeks and primarily focusing on black/white issues and individual racism) to the present 16-week course (with broad inclusion of material relating to other racial-ethnic groups, gender issues, institutional discrimination, and organizational development). Between 1971 and the present, DEOMI has gone through a number of organizational changes, but the basic approach to intercultural training in the military has remained the same. DEOMI still "trains the trainers," using small group interaction, lectures, and exercises as the primary training methods. DEOMI graduates still serve as advisors and trainers in their respective Services. Over the years, however, the size of DEOMI and the scope of its mission have expanded to meet the changing needs of the military. In the next section, we describe current (1995) policy and training practices at DEOMI.

Current Policy

As mentioned previously, the DoD Human Goals outline the broad philosophy for intercultural relations within the military. A number of DoD and service directives provide the regulatory framework for this broad philosophy. The two key documents at the DoD level are DoD Directive 1350.2 (The Department of Defense Equal Opportunity Program, December 1988) and DoD Instruction 1350.3 (Affirmative Action Planning and Assessment Process, February 1988).

DoD Directive 1350.2 amends, cancels, or consolidates a number of previous directives (e.g., DoD Directive 1100.15, The Department of Defense Equal Opportunity Program, and DoD Directive 1322.11, Education and Training in Human/Race Relations for Military Personnel) into a unified policy statement. DoD Directive 1350.2 calls for compliance with standards of fair treatment ("Discrimination...shall not be condoned or tolerated"), establishment of affirmative action programs (with an annual reporting requirement), and "education and training in EO and human relations at installation and fleet unit commands, Military Service accession points, and throughout the professional military education (PME) system...."

Training Philosophy

From its early days, DEOMI's training philosophy has mirrored the military's approach to equal opportunity and cultural diversity. Five main principles provide the foundation: (1) a focus on *behavioral change* and *compliance* with stated policy; (2) emphasis on equal opportunity and intercultural understanding as *military readiness issues*; (3) an understanding that *equal opportunity is a commander's responsibility*, and that the *DEOMI graduate's function is to advise and assist the commander* in carrying out this responsibility; (4) a belief that *education and training* can bring about the desired behavioral changes; and (5) reliance on *affirmative action plans* as a method for ensuring equity and diversity.

Especially important in the military's approach to intercultural training is the emphasis on education as a means to achieve *behavioral change* and *compliance* with directives (Hope, 1979; Lovejoy, 1977; Thomas, 1988). Though the Race [later *Human*] Relations Education Board has been abolished, DoD Directive 1350.2 reemphasizes DEOMI's educational function and charters the Defense Equal Opportunity Council (DEOC) to provide policy advice and guidance on EO matters. The DEOC, in its present form, includes the Deputy Secretary of Defense as its chair and the service secretaries, under secretaries, selected assistant secretaries, Chair of the Joint Chiefs of Staff, and Director of Administration and Management as members. Among DEOC's four objectives is the charge to "assist in developing policy guidance for education and training in EO and human relations for DoD personnel" (DoD Directive 1350.2, December 23, 1988, p. 4-1).

The belief that EO and cultural understanding are *military readiness issues* is clearly iterated in DEOMI's current mission briefing (given to distinguished visitors to the Institute); but this idea was evident in the 1971 issue of DoD Directive 1322.11 (which established DEOMI). That directive says the education program is designed to prevent racial problems from impairing "combat readiness and efficiency" (Hope, 1979). A negative EO climate is thought to detract from readiness by leading to racial incidents or other disruptive events, while a positive EO climate may be an enhancer of readiness by improving cohesion and other organizational factors (Knouse, 1994).[4]

DoD Directive 1350.2 also reinforces the concept that *equal opportunity is a commander's responsibility.* The directive identifies the chain of command as the "primary and preferred channel for correcting discriminatory practices and for ensuring that human relations and EO matters are enacted" (p. 2). Commanders are also given broad powers in dealing with discrimination (affecting military members, their families, and DoD employees) arising from non-military sources (such as housing or service providers, various organizations associated with the military, etc.). The desire to help commanders with this responsibility led the first DEOMI staff to develop a handbook for commanders, designed to be "supportive of the commander's responsibility to develop a program in race relations" (Lovejoy, 1977, p. 106). This Commander's Notebook contained a statement that the EO program "must be...consistent with the philosophy and behavior of the local commander..." (Day, 1983, p. 246). The DRRI Program of Instruction identified one of the major objectives as giving the students the "capability and judgment to work with commanding officers in determining the specific needs of a race relations...program" (Hope, 1979, p. 42).

As we have discussed previously, the belief that *education and training* can bring about behavioral changes leading to enhanced intercultural relations permeates DEOMI's history. The primary purpose of the Theus Committee was to develop a plan for an education program to improve race relations (Lovejoy, 1977), and DRRI and HREB were subsequently founded to implement this plan. The Krise Committee, charged with planning the implementation, "was responsible for a significant innovation...that of concentrating on behavioral rather than attitude change" (Lovejoy, 1977, p. 24). According to Judge L. Howard Bennett, Deputy Assistant Secretary of Defense for Civil Rights at the founding of DRRI and perhaps the driving force behind the philosophy of behavioral change through education, the educational program could work by providing greater understanding, appreciation, and respect among the groups that make up the military (Hope, 1979).

Use of *affirmative action plans* to manage EO and diversity has also been a standard practice in the military Services. DoD Directive 1350.2 establishes ten reporting categories for which the Services must provide plans and assessments on an annual basis. The categories include: (1) Recruiting/Accessions, (2) Composition, (3) Promotions, (4) Professional Military Education (PME), (5) Separations, (6) Augmentation/Retention, (7) Assignments, (8) Discrimination/ Sexual Harassment Complaints, (9) Utilization of Skills, and (10) Discipline. Details of the reporting process are spelled out in the supplement to the directive, DoD Instruction 1350.3. DEOMI's curriculum includes training for EO advisors on these requirements and how to implement affirmative action programs.

Staffing

Current DEOMI staff includes seventy military and thirty-five civilians, divided into seven primary directorates (Training, Curriculum, Support, Research, External Training, International Affairs, and Civilian EEO). In addition, at any given time, there may be as many as 300 students enrolled in the courses described below.

Training Programs

Over the years, DEOMI has adapted to the times, providing expanded or specialized training programs and adding research and consulting capabilities to meet the needs of the Services. The present course offerings include the following:

The Equal Opportunity Staff Advisor Course. This is the linchpin of DEOMI's training programs. A resident course of 16 weeks' duration, it is designed to train equal opportunity staff advisors for commanders throughout all Services. It evolved from DEOMI's original course (discussed previously) and is thought to epitomize the "DEOMI experience." While a variety of training techniques are used, the focus is on small group exercises, practicums, and lecture presentations. Students are led through a carefully designed curriculum, designed to develop intrapersonal awareness, interpersonal understanding, and organizational skills. It covers cultural factors and unit cohesion (139 hours), communication skills (62 hours), staff advisor skills (50 hours), leadership (31 hours), and service-specific skills (20 hours). In addition, there is an extensive guest lecture series (94 hours) covering diverse topics related to EO in the military.

In DEOMI's early years, students were generally volunteers. Currently, students may volunteer, but many, especially from the Army, are simply assigned EO duties as part of their normal career rotation. Assignment to EO duties varies by service (for example, Army graduates serve for only two or three years as EO advisors, then return to their original military specialty; Air Force graduates serve for a career). Most of the students are mid- to senior-grade noncommissioned officers, with the largest numbers coming from the Army. As with all DEOMI courses, civilians employed by the Services may also attend. Few officers (other than DEOMI staff and some reserve components officers) have attended the course during recent years. However, the Army sent sixteen officers to the course in 1994, reversing a trend away from officer involvement in EO programs. These officers are to serve at the major command level throughout the Army. Another watershed event in 1994 was the training of Marine Corps EO advisors in this course for the first time (though Marines had participated in other DEOMI courses and a few Marine officers had graduated from the 16-week course because they were to join the DEOMI staff). The American Council on Education recommends 23 semester hours of undergraduate credit for graduates of this course. Although the 16-week resident course is the crown jewel in DEOMI's course offerings, several other courses supplement it.

The Reserve Components Course. This course is designed to parallel the Equal Opportunity Staff Advisors Course, yet be offered on a schedule that is compatible with reserve component training. It consists of two resident phases at DEOMI, each two weeks long, plus a nonresident correspondence phase. The graduates are qualified to serve as EO advisors in the various reserve components (e.g., National Guard, Reserves). Its curriculum and training methods are similar to those for the 16-week course. Students may be officers or mid- to senior-grade noncommissioned officers.

The Equal Opportunity Program Orientation for Managers. This is a two-week course designed to acquaint program managers at the higher levels of command with EO issues. It includes an orientation to such topics as prejudice and discrimination, program management, and service policies. Students are typically senior noncommissioned officers or officers in the grades of O-3 (lieutenants from the Navy and Coast Guard; captains from the other Services) to O-6 (captains in the Navy or Coast Guard; colonels in the other Services).

Equal Employment Opportunity Courses. Beginning in 1994, DEOMI assumed responsibility for training civilian employees of the Services who are responsible for equal employment opportunity (EEO) programs. There are three courses, designed to serve the needs of EEO advisors at different strata (from counselor to managerial levels) in the EEO system. The courses are each two weeks long and cover cultural awareness, EEO complaint processing, EEO law, communications skills, counseling skills, and dispute resolution techniques.

Senior Noncommissioned Officer Equal Opportunity Workshop. This is a one-week course that orients senior noncommissioned officers toward EO issues. The students are typically first sergeants, master chiefs, sergeant majors, or chief master sergeants. They have considerable influence over the day-to-day management of personnel within their commands and can contribute much toward the human relations climate. The course uses many guided discussions, exercises, and case studies to involve the students in their own learning process.

Senior Executive Leaders Equal Opportunity Training. In March 1994, the Secretary of Defense (Mr. Perry) issued a memorandum calling for DEOMI to train newly selected admirals and general officers, as well as Senior Executive Service personnel, in EO topics. The two-day workshops are designed to give these senior leaders personal insight into broad EO and diversity issues and to help them become more effective as senior managers within the Services.

Mobile Training Teams. Since 1990, DEOMI has conducted a number of mobile training seminars at the request of military and civilian agencies. The mobile training interventions are focused on the specific needs of the organization. For example, perhaps a unit has a need for sexual harassment and sex discrimination training. A team from DEOMI will develop an appropriate program and deliver it on site. The requesting unit pays the travel costs for the team, but there is no charge for the training. Members of DEOMI's staff are also available for consultation to help identify training needs and other EO/diversity concerns within the units.

Other Services

Besides its extensive training programs, DEOMI offers a number of other services to help military commanders improve the EO and diversity climate within their commands. These services include the following:

Research. When DEOMI was founded, research (in the sense of student and program evaluation) was an integral part of the institution. It was used to validate and develop curriculum, to assess the impact of training on students and those in the field, and to supplement curriculum materials. After the institute programs were well established, the interest in research waned, however. In 1986, the research program was reinstituted, and a research directorate was established. The research services include conducting original research on areas of interest in military EO, monitoring and disseminating findings, and providing resource materials to policy makers, commanders, EO advisors, and other interested individuals. Adjunct researchers from the Services and civilian institutions of higher learning augment the DEOMI research staff through internships, summer faculty research programs, and the DEOMI visiting professor (sabbatical) program.

The summer research program, currently administered through the Office of Naval Research, has been the vehicle through which the Research Directorate is able to magnify its efforts to provide a research input to the military's equal opportunity programs. Since the initiation of the summer program in 1987, close to thirty university faculty members have participated, several of them more than once. Approximately 20 percent were from Historically Black Colleges/Universities (HBCUs) and a number of the remainder were members of minority groups on the faculties of predominately white institutions. The research topics have been quite broad, reflecting the interests of both DEOMI and the individual faculty member. At least one effort, the measurement of equal opportunity climate (discussed below and in a separate chapter) has had significant impact on the various services. Thirteen of the summer projects have dealt with aspects of equal opportunity climate; thirteen have also focused on women's issues, including sexual harassment; five researched accessions policy; and the same number dealt with racial disparities in the system of military justice. The remainder looked as such diverse topics as evaluating the DEOMI curriculum (two projects), Hispanic issues (two projects) and equal opportunity policy (three efforts).

Climate Analysis. The Directorate of Research also conducts the Military Equal Opportunity Climate Analysis Survey (MEOCS) program (Landis, 1990; Dansby & Landis, 1991; Landis, Dansby, & Faley, 1993). MEOCS is an organizational development survey covering equal opportunity and organizational effectiveness issues. It is offered free to commanders of military organizations. DEOMI provides a confidential feedback report to the commanders and maintains a database of survey results by service. The feedback report provides comparisons between unit and database results, as well as internal comparisons (e.g., minority-majority, men-women) to help commanders better plan actions to improve the climate. This voluntary program has been quite popular with commanders (over 2000 requested the survey between June 1990 and January 1995), resulting in a database of nearly 300,000 records. MEOCS is discussed further in another chapter of this book.

Electronic Bulletin Board. The electronic bulletin board allows EO advisors, service leadership, researchers, and interested others to access and share information. Many of the research publications, statistics, case studies, and other resources are available for download. Also, the system serves as a vehicle for networking and E-mail among EO advisors and DEOMI staff.

EO Conference and Research Symposium. The Worldwide Equal Opportunity Conference (hosted by DEOMI December 5-9, 1994) was meant to be the first of many such conferences. In addition to training programs, seminars, and workshops, a research symposium was also conducted. Paper presentations and panel discussions contributed toward increased awareness of EO/EEO research and sharing of ideas for future projects and practical application.

Library. Over the years, the DEOMI library has developed an extensive collection of materials relating to EO and diversity issues.

It contains over 12,000 books and 250 periodicals, as well as CD-ROMs for 1500 periodicals and 100 ethnic newspapers. Its selected journals, books, reports, and CD-ROM resources are perhaps the best source for military EO information in the world. The library is a resource for staff, students, and adjunct researchers.

National/International Initiatives. Since 1993, DEOMI has also provided consultation and assistance for national and international efforts to improve intercultural training and understanding. In 1994 a separate directorate was established to further the national/international goals of the Institute. DEOMI teams have worked with universities, police departments, fire departments, the Department of Justice, Chambers of Commerce, schools, youth groups, and other agencies to help improve the diversity climate. In the international arena, DEOMI has consulted with agencies from Russia and other former Eastern Bloc nations, South Africa, Canada, Great Britain, and Germany. These efforts support national democratization initiatives.

Summary and Discussion

In this chapter, we have described the history and philosophy of intercultural relations in the armed forces, the current policies, and the training programs and methods used to implement the programs. Central to the military training effort is the DEOMI, a unique institution dedicated to training and research in equal opportunity and diversity issues within the military. Since 1971, DEOMI has served as a focal point for intercultural training.

In keeping with the military culture, intercultural training in the services, as we have indicated, is a pragmatic business. Using a system of centralized training (based at DEOMI) for the trainers and decentralized delivery at various levels throughout the Services, military leaders hope to influence the *behavior* of servicemembers to maintain *compliance with stated policy*. And that policy endorses principles of equity, opportunity, and fair treatment, not limited by a person's color, race, ethnicity, or gender.

Many would argue that this approach has made the military the most successful major institution in America in implementing the goal of equal opportunity for people of all racial/ethnic backgrounds. Indeed, in March 1994, there were fifty-four minority generals and admirals serving on active duty (DEOMI, 1994; there were also eleven women in the general/flag officer ranks). This representation at the most senior levels of the services is even more impressive given that the military must "grow its own" generals and admirals. There is no opportunity for lateral recruitment from other societal institutions; all general/flag officers must come through the ranks, a process that takes about twenty-six years. Therefore, the current generals and admirals started in the system about 1968. Based on the numbers of minority officers within the personnel "pipeline," we predict the number of minority general/flag officers will double by 2005 (if force levels are maintained at predicted levels). General Colin Powell, an African-American who rose to the highest military position in the nation, serves as an important and symbolic reminder that minority members with the right abilities have the opportunity to reach the top in today's military services.

Clearly, the integration of women and minorities into the military has been a success. In examining the reasons for this situation, one of us has pointed out five possibilities that, taken together suggest patterns to be followed by other organizations:

1. Speedy change is better than slow incremental policies. The integration of blacks was achieved in a fairly fast fashion due to wartime needs. Women, on the other hand, have had to endure a much slower process to no clear benefit.

2. Providing opportunities for contact (Allport, 1954; Amir, 1976) acts to weaken prejudice and lay the foundation for later integration policies. Hence, the experience of whites who served with blacks in the Second World War made acceptance of integration possible in 1948.

3. Making salient the contrast between segregationist policies and the fundamental precepts of the society can act to increase dissonance around the past practices. Having fought a world war to eliminate racism , the country was less willing to accept segregation at home. Gunnar Myrdal (1944) called this an "American Dilemma."

4. The role of top leadership cannot be overemphasized. President Truman provided strong leadership which when combined with the tradition of military compliance with civilian authority led to efforts to produce change.

5. Efforts to institutionalize nondiscriminatory behavior (the subject of this chapter) are important. In the military, this was accomplished by:

    a. Development of a cadre of people whose *raison d'etre* was to eliminate discrimination. While this approach eventually caused problems with the chain of command, the foundation was established for equal opportunity to be an important aim of the service. Paradoxically, because this cadre was composed of a disproportionate number of minorities and women, they were sometimes not taken seriously by commanders.

b.   Development of a body of knowledge about minority groups and women which could be used to counter stereotypes when they arose in the field.

c.   Development of a technology directed toward changing behavior and attitudes. This technology consists of curricula, lesson plans, group exercises, films, and videotapes (modified from Kauth & Landis, 1994).

Despite these successes, the senior leadership in the military understands the need to press its efforts in this area. In a pivotal memorandum to all the services, Secretary of Defense Perry stated it this way: "Equal opportunity is not just the right thing to do, it is also a military and economic necessity... The Military Services have led our nation in expanding opportunities for minority groups... However, I believe we can and should do better..." (March 3, 1994 memorandum from Secretary of Defense William J. Perry to all service chiefs and department heads). In the memorandum, one of five initiatives designed to accomplish this objective states the Secretary's desire that all personnel receive equal opportunity training, and specifically mentions training for senior leaders (generals, admirals, and Senior Executive Service civilians). DEOMI's programs serve as the fulcrum for leveraging the training across the services.

The military approach to intercultural training, while recognizing the importance of affective predispositions and responses, is clearly focused on behavioral modification. Through education designed to enhance intercultural sensitivity and awareness, and through sanctions designed to ensure compliance, military leaders hope to intervene in the intercultural behavior process to support principles of equity and diversity. This approach is based on the hypothesis that such behaviors, with reinforcement from the recipient, or host, will strengthen, especially if the social system supports such interactions.

Balance theories of attitude change (e.g., Heider, 1958; Osgood & Tannenbaum, 1955; Festinger, 1957; Brehm & Cohen, 1962), especially cognitive dissonance theory (Festinger, 1957; Brehm & Cohen, 1962), predict some positive attitude change as a result of behavioral compliance if the compliance is not perceived to be the result of extreme coercion or large incentives and if the new behavior is seen as central to the individual's self-perception. The perceptions of coercion and incentive are individual matters; some military members who come into the services with negative attitudes toward EO policies may justify their counterattitudinal intercultural behaviors based on the level of coercion or incentives, while others may change their attitudes if coercion and incentives are perceived as weak. In any case, from the military perspective, if behavioral interventions lead to increased positive affect toward others from diverse backgrounds, it would be a bonus. But attitude change, per se, is not the stated goal.

No program, particularly one as complex and far reaching as the military's human relations efforts, is free of problems which may limit overall effectiveness. We will mention just two. First, the theoretical orientation of the DEOMI curriculum was fundamentally set in the 1970s. Hence, the discussion of the conceptual underpinnings of intercultural or equal opportunity training include a focus on dissonance and institutional discrimination. The group exercises tend to reinforce a view of racism that is "traditional" to use McConohay's (1986) term. Contact theory is briefly, if at all, mentioned and there is virtually no recognition of the newer conceptualizations derived from Tajfel, Brewer, Gaertner, Larwood, and others (Tajfel & Turner, 1979; Brewer & Miller, 1984; Gaertner & Dovidio, 1986; Larwood & Gattiker, 1985; Larwood, Gutek, & Galliker, 1984). These approaches have been shown (e.g., Shachar & Amin, 1996) to be quite useful in changing both attitudes and behaviors.

A second issue revolves around the organization and utilization of research on equal opportunity issues. The permanent research staff across DoD focused exclusively on equal opportunity issues is quite modest, given the size and importance of the issue. At DEOMI, the current staff consists of two Ph.D. level research psychologists (one of whom is the Director and the other a military officer scheduled to retire shortly), three M.A. level researcher/administrators (one of whom is a military officer), and several noncommissioned officers and secretaries who perform the various administrative duties necessary to keep the operation on track. Several of the staff spend most of their time ministering to the MEOCS database and in preparation of survey feedback reports for commanders (see Landis, Dansby, & Tallarigo, 1996). Until recently (1993), the Director was an Air Force lieutenant colonel and thus subject to rotation every three or four years. These staff are supplemented by summer researchers (see above) who are in residence for ten weeks and a recently added full-time sabbatical leave faculty member (who spends an academic year in the Directorate). Under these circumstances it is very difficult to maintain a coherent and consistent research program. As compensation, the directorate has placed most of its effort into the development and enhancing of the MEOCS, leaving other issues to be handled on an "as time is available basis." What the group does, it does extremely well with limited resources; but it has hardly reached its potential as the military's center for equal opportunity research, a role that was envisioned for it by the DEOC in 1987, a role that was assigned without the necessary funding.

If equal opportunity research is underfunded at DEOMI,[5] the situation elsewhere in DoD is hardly better. The Army Research Institute (mentioned earlier) has conducted little significant research in the equal opportunity arena since the later 1970s (Thomas, 1988). To our knowledge, the only Navy program is centered at the Navy Personnel Research and Development Center (NPRDC) in San Diego (Rosenfeld, Thomas, Edwards, Thomas, & Thomas, 1991), an excellent effort which is being scaled back at this time. Except for an occasional graduate thesis, the situation is even grimmer in the Air Force. All of these considerations must make us cautious in anticipating high impacts from the EO research programs described in this chapter.

The long-term result of the military's program remains to be seen. What will happen to intercultural relations as the force reductions continue? How will societal demographic and attitudinal changes impact the military of the future? Will there even be a need for such training as the twenty-first century unfolds? How will increases in the numbers of women in the military affect intercultural relations in the military? Will backlash from majority men (the "reverse discrimination" concerns) have a significant impact on the services? Will policies regarding homosexual participation be revised, and how might this affect the services? (Kauth & Landis, 1994) All these and other questions remain to be answered. Truly, at least for intercultural relations and training in the military, these are interesting times.

Notes

1. The opinions expressed in this paper are those of the authors and do not necessarily reflect positions of the Department of Defense or any of its agencies. Reprint requests and/or comments should be addressed to the first author at: Directorate of Research, Defense Equal Opportunity Management Institute, 740 O'Malley Road, Patrick AFB, FL USA 32925.
2. For example, Senator Richard Russell (D-GA) had this to say: "[T]he mandatory intermingling of the races throughout the services will be a terrific blow to the efficiency and fighting power of the armed services.... It is sure to increase the number of men who will be disabled through communicable diseases. It will increase the rate of crime committed by servicemen" (Power of the Pentagon, 1972). Also typical of the early attitude toward women in the military is a 1945 statement by

Brigadier General C. Thomas, Director of the Division of the Plans and Policies at Marine Corps Headquarters, who commented, "The opinion generally held by the Marine Corps is that women have no proper place or function in the regular service in peacetime....The American tradition is that a woman's place is in the home" (Stremlow, 1979, p. 1).

3.   Gesell at the time of his appointment was a Washington lawyer and acquaintance of Secretary McNamara's special assistant, Adam Yarmolinsky, and a close friend of Burke Marshall, then head of the Department of Justice's Civil Rights Division.

4.   Although this is a quite reasonable rationale, it is important to note that it has never been subjected to an empirical test, even though cohesion does seem to be related to unit effectiveness (Siebold & Lindsay, 1991). One of the problems has been the lack of agreement on what constitutes cohesion. In addition, it has been difficult to carry out a field test under realistic conditions.

5.   The total DEOMI (operating) budget (FY 94) is about $2.5 million. Even with the addition of the salaries and benefits for the assigned military personnel on staff, the total is considerably less than $7.0 million. Considering the size of the active duty and reserve force, this amounts to less than $3 annually per servicemember. At the same time, one must be mindful of the fact that this amount is greater than is being spent by any other governmental agency, at any level!

References

Allport, G. W. (1954). *The nature of prejudice*. Reading, MA: Addison-Wesley.

Amir, Y. (1976). The role of intergroup contact in change of prejudice and ethnic relations. In P. A. Katz (Ed.), *Towards the elimination of racism*. Elmsford, NY: Pergamon.

Binkin, M., Eitelberg, M. J., Schexnider, A. J., & Smith, M. M. (1982). *Blacks and the military*. Washington, DC: The Brookings Institution.

Brehm, J. W., & Cohen, A. R. (1962). *Explorations in cognitive dissonance*. New York: Wiley.

Brewer, M., and Miller, N. (1984). Beyond the contact hypothesis: Theoretical perspectives on desegregation. In N. Miller & M. Brewer, *Groups in contact: The psychology of desegregation*. Orlando, FL: Academic Press.

Day, H. R. (1983). Race relations training in the U.S. military. In Landis, D., & Brislin, R. W. (Eds.), *Handbook of intercultural training (volume II): Issues in training methodology*. New York: Pergamon Press.

Dansby, M. R., & Landis, D. (1991). Measuring equal opportunity in the military environment. *International Journal of Intercultural Relations, 15*, 389-405.

DEOMI (1994). *Semi-annual race/ethnic/gender profile of the Department of Defense active forces, reserve forces, and the United States Coast Guard* (Statistical series pamphlet no. 94-4). Patrick Air Force Base, FL: Defense Equal Opportunity Management Institute.

Festinger, L. (1957). *A theory of cognitive dissonance*. Stanford, CA: Stanford University Press.

Gaertner, S. L., & Dovidio, J. (1986). The aversive form of racism. In. J. Dovidio & S. Gaertner (Eds.), *Prejudice, discrimination and racism*. Orlando, FL: Academic Press.

Heider, F. (1958). *The psychology of interpersonal relations*. New York: Wiley.

Holm, J. (1992). *Women in the military: An unfinished revolution*. Novato, CA: Presidio.

Hope, R. O. (1979). *Racial strife in the U.S. military: Toward the elimination of discrimination*. New York: Praeger.

Kauth, M., & Landis, D. (1994, August). *Applying lessons learned from ethnic and gender integration to the United States Military*. Paper presented in a workshop "Gays and lesbians in the military: Psychological perspectives on implementing the new policy" given at the 1994 American Psychological Association Convention, Los Angeles.

Knouse, S. B. (1994). *Equal opportunity climate and total quality management: A pre-liminary study* (DEOMI Research Pamphlet 94-3). Patrick Air Force Base, FL: Defense Equal Opportunity Management Institute.

Landis, D. (1990, January). *Military equal opportunity climate survey: Reliability, construct validity, and preliminary field test*. Oxford: University of Mississippi, Center for Applied Research and Evaluation.

Landis, D., Dansby, M. R., & Faley, R. H. (1993). The Military Equal Opportunity Climate Survey: An example of surveying in organizations. In P. Rosenfeld, J. E. Edwards & M. D. Thomas (Eds.), *Improving organizational surveys: New directions, methods, and applications*. Newbury Park, CA: Sage Publications.

Landis, D., Dansby, M.R., & Tallarigo, R. (1996). The use of equal opportunity climate in intercultural training. In D. Landis & R.S. Bhagat (Eds.). *Handbook of intercultural training, 2nd edition*. Thousand Oaks, CA: Sage.

Larwood, L. & Gattiker, U. E. (1985). Rational bias and interorganizational power in the employment of management consultants. *Group and Organization Studies. 10*, 3-17.

Larwood, L., Gutek, B. & Gattiker, U. E. (1984). Perspectives on institutional discrimination and resistance to change. *Group and Organization Studies, 9*, 333-352.

Lovejoy, J. E. (1977). *A history of the Defense Race Relations Institute (DRRI)*. Patrick AFB, FL: Defense Equal Opportunity Management Institute.

MacGregor, M. J. (1981). *Integration of the Armed Forces, 1940-1965*. Washington, DC: Center of Military History, United States Army.

McConohay, J. (1986). Modern racism, ambivalence, and the modern racism scale. In J. Dovidio & S. Gaertner (Eds.), *Prejudice, discrimination, and racism*. Orlando, FL: Academic Press.

Myrdal, G. (1944). *An American dilemma*. New York: Harper & Row.

Nalty, B. C. (1986). *Strength for the fight: A history of black Americans in the military*. New York: The Free Press.

Osgood, C. E., & Tannenbaum, P. H. (1955). The principle of congruity in the prediction of attitude change. *Psychological Review, 62*, 42-55.

The power of the Pentagon (1972). *Congressional Quarterly Weekly Report*, 34-35.

Rosenfeld. P., Thomas, M. D., Edwards, J. E., Thomas, P. J., & Thomas, E. D. (1991). Navy research into race, ethnicity, and gender issues: A historical review. *International Journal of Intercultural Relations, 15*, 407-426.

Shachar, H. & Amir, Y. (1996). Training teachers and students for intercultural cooperation in Israel: Two models. In D. Landis & R.S. Bhagat (Eds.). *Handbook of intercultural training, 2nd edition*. Thousand Oaks, CA: Sage.

Siebold, G. L. & Lindsay, T. J. (1991). Correlations among ratings of platoon performance. *Proceedings of the 33rd Annual Conference of the Military Testing Association*, (pp. 67-72). San Antonio, TX: U.S. Air Force Armstrong Laboratory Human Resources Directorate and the U.S. Air Force Occupational Measurement Squadron. October 28-31.

Stremlow, M. V. (1979, March). *A history of women marines 1946-1977*. Washington, DC: History and Museums Division, Headquarters U.S. Marine Corps, p. 1.

Tajfel, H. & Turner, J. (1979). An integrative theory of intergroup conflict. In W. Austin & S. Worshel (Eds.). *The social psychology of intergroup relations*. Monterey, CA: Brooks/Cole.

Thomas, J. A. (1988). *Race relations research in the U.S. Army in the 1970s: A collection of selected readings*. Alexandria, VA: U.S. Army Research Institute for the Behavioral and Social Sciences.

Young, W. L. (1982). *Minorities and the military: A cross-national study in world perspective*. Westport, CN: Greenwood Press.

2

Contemporary Models of Racism: Theoretical Perspectives, Institutional Assessment, and Organizational Implications for an Equal Opportunity Climate

Olenda E. Johnson

Introduction

In recent years, the social psychology literature exploring racism and racial prejudice has focused primarily on "contemporary" models of racism—more subtle forms of racial prejudice. In contrast to "traditional" or "old-fashioned" racism, in which belief about the innate inferiority of specific races (blacks in particular) is displayed through open bigotry, subtle racism appears to be nonracial on the surface.[1] Yet, beneath the surface are negative attitudes and stereotyped beliefs that ultimately affect personal interactions. It is these more subtle forms of racism that are thought to be most prevalent in today's society, and perhaps the most pernicious (Dovidio & Gaertner, 1991; Kinder & Sanders, 1996; Wolfe & Spencer, 1996).

Scholars have offered several conceptualizations of subtle or covert racism. Among them are aversive racism (Gaertner & Dovidio, 1986), symbolic racism (Kinder & Sears, 1981), and modern racism (McConahay, 1986). Each model asserts that, with the exception of the separatist minority (e.g., KKK, skinheads), most whites reject blatant displays of racial prejudice, yet often expose their own anti-black sentiment through their seemingly nonprejudiced behaviors and the ideologies they espouse.[2] When brought to the surface in an organizational context, this subtle racism will negatively impact interpersonal relations, often breeding institutional racism in which informal barriers to advancement create disadvantages for racial minorities (Dovidio, 1993; Howitt & Owusu-Bempah, 1990; Sears, 1988).

For organizations aiming to establish an equal opportunity climate for all its members, an understanding of racism in its various forms is essential. Particularly important is an assessment of its pervasiveness in an existing environment. Given this, the purpose of this paper is threefold: (1) to distinguish between aversive, symbolic, modern, and traditional racism; (2) to describe the relationship between the subtle forms of racism and institutional racism; and (3) to empirically assess the impact of subtle racism in the current military environment.

Contemporary Theories of Racism

Aversive Racism

The theory of aversive racism (Gaertner & Dovidio, 1986) is based on the assumption that many whites genuinely have strong egalitarian attitudes and consider themselves to be nonracist. However, by the mere nature of their existence in a historically racist society, theory argues that these whites also harbor negative feelings toward other races. Gaertner and Dovidio (1986) characterize aversive racists as persons who: (1) sympathize with victims of past injustices; (2) support public policies that, in principle, promote racial equality; (3) identify more generally with a liberal political agenda; (4) regard themselves as nonprejudiced and nondiscriminatory; and (5) unavoidably possess negative feelings and beliefs about blacks. Theory posits that the antipathy is developed from the legacy of racism in the United States that has produced enduring stereotypes, creating unavoidable racial prejudices. As a consequence, even without conscious knowledge or intention, evaluations and treatment of blacks and other racial minorities by many whites may be unfairly biased (Wolfe & Spencer, 1996).

The subtlety of aversive racism is unveiled by the discomfort, uneasiness, and apprehension exhibited by many whites in interracial contexts. Because of this interracial anxiety, aversive racists are motivated to avoid interaction with blacks and other racial minorities. When avoidance is not available, they will be guided by the norms of socially appropriate behavior and try, in earnest, to demonstrate that they are not racist. However, oftentimes seemingly nonracial behavior and statements actually relay underlying fears and prejudiced beliefs. In a situation that threatens to make their negative feelings salient, aversive racists may overreact and try to emphasize their egalitarian beliefs by expressing, for instance, that they "don't see color" and they "just see [you] as a regular person" (cf., Dovidio, 1993; Dovidio & Gaertner, 1991). At the very least such statements imply that to be thought of as 'black' is somehow to be considered *irregular*.

In an experiment examining prosocial behavior, Gaertner (1973) (reported in Gaertner & Dovidio, 1986) tested the propositions that aversive racists prefer to avoid interaction with other races and that their behavior often contradicts their expressed egalitarian views. In the study, the likelihood of black and white persons receiving assistance from members of the liberal and conservative party was examined. Liberals and conservatives residing in Brooklyn received supposed wrong-number phone calls in which the callers, distinguished as black or white based on identifiable dialects, indicated that their car was disabled and that they were trying to reach a service garage from a public phone on the expressway. The callers further indicated that they were out of change and requested the person contact the garage. It was predicted that black callers would be helped less frequently by members of the conservative party than by members of the liberal party.

The results showed that conservatives were indeed less helpful toward blacks than whites, whereas liberals helped both relatively equally. However, liberals hung up more prematurely (i.e., prior to hearing the request for help) on blacks than on whites; whereas, there was no difference in premature hang ups between blacks and whites for conservatives. Therefore, persons professing to treat everyone equally responded differently to blacks and whites, prior to the request for assistance, based on the racial dialect of the individual callers. So in one regard, their egalitarian ideals were upheld, in the other the subtlety of their racial beliefs was revealed.

In another study, Dovidio and Gaertner (1981) examined whether the relative status and ability of an individual had any bearing on the extent to which assistance would be offered. White students were paired with a black or white confederate who was identified as their supervisor or subordinate and described as high- or low-ability relative to the task that was to be completed. Prior to the experiment, the subjects completed a prejudice assessment and were classified as either high- or low-prejudice. Before the task began, the confederate accidentally knocked a container of pencils on the floor. The researchers then examined whether the subject offered assistance in picking up the pencils.

The results showed that black supervisors were helped less than black subordinates, but white supervisors received slightly more assistance. There was no difference in prosocial behavior towards blacks based on ability; however, high-ability whites were helped more often than low-ability whites. There was no significant difference in overall helping behavior for high- and low-prejudiced subjects. Thus, irrespective of ability, even low-prejudiced subjects responded the least favorably toward black supervisors. Post-experiment interviews revealed that both high- and low-prejudiced subjects felt that even high-ability blacks were still less intelligent than themselves and consequently resisted being subordinated to black supervisors. The rejection of the traditional role reversal (i.e., blacks as supervisors, whites as subordinates) manifested itself in the subjects' decision not to offer assistance. In a similar study, Dovidio and Gaertner (1983) found that regardless of the high or low prejudice score, whites were also less likely to *seek* (emphasis added) assistance from blacks, even though they reported blacks to be equally capable and willing to assist as whites.

The seemingly nonracist chain of events and the subtlety of the racism revealed make these studies intriguing. More importantly, with the exception of those classified as high-prejudice, subjects in these studies appeared cognitively unaware of the racial undertone of their actions. The implications for organizations are manifold. First, interracial anxiety that spurs avoidance can lead to the exclusion of racial minorities from informal networks. Research indicates that such networks are critical for organizational advancement and a key factor in the lack of advancement for racial minorities (Thomas & Alderfer, 1989; Ibarra, 1995). Secondly, the reluctance to offer assistance can negatively impact the ability of racial minorities to attract a mentor. Again, research indicates that the absence of a mentoring relationship is a hindrance to career success, particularly for blacks (Dreher & Cox, 1996; Thomas & Alderfer, 1989). Moreover, when mentoring is available, interracial discomfort combined with the failure to assist can impede the effectiveness of cross-race mentoring relationships (Thomas, 1993). Third, to the extent that whites are inhibited from seeking assistance from blacks and instead seek assistance from a white peer, the authority of the black supervisor or manager can be undermined. Ultimately, this could hinder the black supervisor's ability to manage and impede organizational effectiveness (e.g., Lovelace & Rosen, 1996).

In sum, aversive racism speaks to the conflict between egalitarian values and negative racial affect. Said differently, this form of subtle racism represents the incongruity between the belief in racial equality and discriminatory behavior toward racial minorities. Because of the stereotypes entrenched in our culture, the aversive racist's disdain of racial prejudice is belied by unintentionally negative behavior. Though not consciously motivated by racial hatred as would be the case for traditional racism, the harmful consequences of this form of racial prejudice remain.

Symbolic Racism

Whereas aversive racism reflects the blending of egalitarian values and embedded, culturally-defined stereotypes, symbolic racism speaks to the amalgam of anti-black feelings and traditional American values that embody the Protestant work ethic (Kinder & Sears, 1981; Sears, 1988). The foundation of symbolic racism lies within the ideology of individualism, which argues that all people regardless of race have equal opportunity and it is up to the *individual* to work hard enough to succeed (Sears, 1988). At the same time, symbolic racists also believe that blacks do not adhere to the value of a strong work ethic and could get ahead if they just worked harder. The belief that blacks simply do not work hard enough is concordant with the stereotype that blacks are lazy. Therefore, the symbolic racism perspective suggests that racial prejudice is subtlety veiled by the espousal of traditional American values.

The mixture of valued work ethic and anti-black affect translates into opposition to programs and policies designed to redress past discrimination and promote racial equality (e.g., affirmative action, school busing, bilingual education) (Huddy & Sears, 1995; Kinder & Sanders, 1996). For symbolic racists, programs such as affirmative action challenge their individualistic value system and threaten the American culture—and, hence, their way of life. In this respect, racial prejudice surfaces as resistance to change in the racial status quo. Furthermore, because of the persistent belief that blacks are unwilling to work (see Kinder & Sanders, 1996; Kluegel, 1990), expressed resentment toward any organized efforts that offer assistance to blacks frequently results in allegations of reverse discrimination (Sniderman & Piazza, 1993).

Research on symbolic racism has focused primarily on its consequences, rather than directly measuring the construct (Sears, 1988; Sniderman & Tetlock, 1986). Mostly, the research has examined the effect of whites' racial attitudes on their political opinions and voting behavior (see Sears, 1988 for a review). Typically, researchers assess whether certain beliefs predict opposition to racially-themed political policies or support for black political candidates. Table 2.1, for example, shows items used by Kinder and Sears (1981) in their study examining the impact of symbolic racism on the racially charged Los Angeles mayoral campaigns of 1969 and 1973. The measures were, for the most part, an assessment of political beliefs that suggested racial antipathy (i.e., that symbolized racial prejudice). Kinder and Sears found that the antagonism and resentment reflected in the items predicted opposition to the black political candidates and racial policy that was believed to benefit blacks.

Such anti-black sentiments have important implications for racial minorities in organizations. The underlying belief that racial minorities could succeed if they only worked harder, combined with the symbolic racists' belief that they also receive preferential treatment, may make it difficult for racial minorities to attain equal opportunity (Sears, 1988). Because symbolic racists endorse an individualistic ideology, they tend to ignore systemic barriers that impede progress for racial minorities (e.g., Baron & Pfeffer, 1994; Braddock &

Table 2.1
Items Used to Measure Symbolic Racism
(Kinder & Sears, 1981)

Do you think blacks who receive money from welfare programs could get along without it if they tried, or do you think they really need the help?

Blacks shouldn't push themselves where they're not wanted.

Because of past discrimination, it is sometimes necessary to set up quotas for admission to college for minority group students.

Do you think Los Angeles officials pay more, less, or the same attention to a request or complaint from a black person as from a white person?

McPartland, 1987). As a result, they are likely to resist supporting equal opportunity efforts because they presume that these programs are simply a way for racial minorities to obtain unfair advantage.

Attached to the belief of unfair advantage is the presumption that racial minorities are also less competent than their white counterparts (Heilman, Block, & Lucas, 1992). In this regard, individual ability is smothered by the stigmatizing assumption of inability (Pettigrew & Martin, 1987). Heilman et al. (1992), for example, conducted a field investigation in which 184 employed white men completed a questionnaire regarding their impression of the changing composition of the American work force. Subjects were asked to identify a co-worker and indicate whether affirmative action played a role in the hiring decision as well as the extent to which they thought the co-worker was competent. Heilman et al. (1992) found a strong and inverse relationship between presumed affirmative action status and perceived competence, particularly for black co-workers. The greater the role affirmative action policies were presumed to play in the hiring decision, the lower the co-worker's competence was perceived to be. Furthermore, when black co-workers were presumed to be affirmative action hires, they were also projected to have the least career potential.

A consequence of these attribution processes is that the performance evaluations of racial minorities may be negatively biased. Given that assessments of others are shaped by individual beliefs (Brewer & Kramer, 1985; Ryan, Judd, & Park, 1996), it could be expected that the stereotypes and assumptions embraced by symbolic racists would be reflected in their evaluation of racial minorities (cf., Jackson, Sullivan, & Hodge, 1993; Kraiger & Ford, 1985). To the extent that the performance evaluations are colored by these presumptions, racial minorities are likely to have lower evaluations because actual performance is minimized or disregarded (Greenhaus, Parasuraman, & Wormley, 1990; Ilgen & Youtz, 1986). Moreover, even when performance is acknowledged as good, it is likely to be attributed to situational factors (e.g., assistance from others) or luck rather than individual capability (Greenhaus & Parasuraman, 1993; Pettigrew & Martin, 1987). Thus, the inability of racial minorities to obtain a fair and accurate performance appraisal hinders their promotion and reward opportunities, resulting in a pattern of institutional discrimination. In other words, career progress is stymied by inaccurate evaluations that prevent racial minorities from advancing in the organization (Greenhaus, et al, 1990; Thomas & Alderfer, 1989).

Taken together, the argument for traditional Protestant work values, coupled with its underlying assumptions, amounts to an ostensibly nonracial justification for opposition to the advancement of racial minorities. Where traditional racists engage in flagrant discrimination, symbolic racists display their racial prejudice through less public means (e.g., voting behavior, performance evaluations). In either regard, both approaches have the same consequence of disadvantaging racial minorities.

Modern Racism

Modern racism is a close relative of symbolic racism. Like symbolic racism, modern racism is based on a value system that conflicts with negative feelings toward racial minorities. In this instance, it is the "belief in a just world" that collides with the view that blacks are undeserving of special efforts to redress past inequities (McConahay, 1986). According to theory, modern racists believe that discrimination is a thing of the past and that blacks have unbound opportunities for advancement (Kinder, 1986; McConahay, 1986). Modern racists also subscribe to an abstract principle of justice, which argues that the universe is ordered in such a way that people are fairly rewarded based on their own actions and moral character (Lerner, 1980). Therefore, the outcomes people receive are assumed to be the outcomes they deserve. From this viewpoint, society is believed to provide equal opportunity for all people.

Since modern racists reject the notion of abject inequality, any attempts to advance the status of racial minorities (e.g., affirmative action) are considered unfair. Thus, similar to symbolic racism, efforts to attain racial equality are perceived by modern racists as "[racial minorities] pushing too hard and too fast into places where they are not wanted" (McConahay, 1986; Sears, 1988). The caveat is that modern racists see themselves as nonracist and are attentive to preserving this image. In racial contexts, modern racists are careful to exhibit socially appropriate beliefs and behaviors, invoking principles of fairness to justify their racial convictions (Peterson, 1994).

The belief that racial minorities violate norms of fairness precludes modern racists from recognizing the racial advantages accorded whites. In other words, they do not see themselves as benefiting from their racial group membership (see Kluegel & Smith, 1986).

Yet, research shows that white-dominated power structures and the legitimacy of white social status provide advantaged outcomes for some, while creating disadvantage for others (cf., Baron & Pfeffer, 1994; Berger, Fisek, Norman, & Zelditch, 1977; Major, 1994). Dreher and Cox (1996), for example, examined the influence of the mentoring experiences of MBA graduates on compensation outcomes. They found that MBAs (of any race or gender) who had mentoring relationships with white men received greater overall compensation (i.e., salary, commission, and bonuses) than those who had mentors of other races and gender. The researchers reasoned that the advantaged status of white men, in both formal and informal power structures, accorded mentees greater access to information and increased visibility—factors important to career success (see Kanter, 1989)—thereby generating enhanced career outcomes for the protégés. In addition, the researchers found that mentoring relationships with white men were more common among white MBAs than black and Hispanic MBAs. Hence, there were clear advantages associated with racial group membership for whites.

Nonetheless, modern racists believe the playing field is level for all races. In this regard, they believe in the equality of opportunity, but not necessarily in the equality of outcome (Kinder & Sanders, 1996; McConahay, 1986). As with symbolic racism, this form of subtle racism can have a significant impact in organizations. In particular, to disavow the existence of white advantage is to perpetuate racial disadvantage. This denial, in turn, propagates institutional racism. Uneven access to information, professional visibility, and career-enhancing support minimizes career opportunities and career outcomes for racial minorities, while advancing the career progress of racial majorities (Greenhaus et al., 1990; Thomas & Alderfer, 1989). Thus, the serendipitous equality advocated by modern racists creates continual inequities for racial minorities. Though the discriminatory behaviors may not be as overt as traditional racism, modern racists sanction racial discrimination by assuming that a general principle of fairness is equally applicable to all races, irrespective of racial history and the current racial climate.

Summary

Table 2.2 summarizes the distinctions between the subtle forms of racism and traditional racism. As noted in the table, the fundamental ideology of each model forms the basis for differentiation. The racial schema highlights the central tenet of each theory, which, for the subtle forms of racism, reflects the mixture of individual ideals with underlying racial beliefs. In total, the table shows that the value systems associated with each model ultimately shape racial attitudes and behavior.

The overarching implication for military organizations is clear—subtle racist attitudes (overt prejudice notwithstanding) can hinder the military's ability to establish an equal opportunity climate. To begin with, the inherent conflict between individual value systems and negative racial affect is likely to inhibit acceptance of any efforts to promote racial equality (cf., Kossek & Zonia, 1993; Kravitz & Platania, 1993; Witt, 1990). Next, to the extent that subtle racism evokes interracial anxiety, the effectiveness of diverse workgroups is likely to be impacted (cf., Konrad, Winter, & Gutek, 1992; Watson, Kumar, & Michaelsen, 1993). Finally, job satisfaction for both racial minorities and majorities may be negatively affected because of the differential attention perceived to be granted to the other group (i.e., advantaged opportunities for majorities versus unfair advantage for minorities; Perry, 1993; Witt, 1990). In total, the indication is that subtle racism is a phenomenon with significant organizational consequences.

Institutional Assessment

Much has been written about the disparate experiences of black and white military personnel, particularly as related to tenure and promotion. Research shows that black officers (but not necessarily enlisted members) have traditionally had lower retention and promotion rates than their white counterparts (Baldwin, 1996; Stewart, 1992). Typically researchers point to socioeconomic and educational explanations for the incongruous career experiences. However, few have examined the social psychological factors that contribute to the differences. In an effort to address the latter, the present study investigates the influence of subtle racial prejudice on institutional barriers to advancement in the military. Specifically, this study examines the relationship between white racial attitudes and individual behaviors that create obstacles to career progress for blacks and other racial minorities.

The theoretical arguments for aversive, symbolic, and modern racism suggest a relationship between subtle racism and institutional

Table 2.2
Models of Racism

	Aversive	Symbolic	Modern	Traditional
Ideology	Egalitarianism *"I believe in racial equality."*	Individualism, Protestant Work Ethic *"I believe individual effort is the key to success."*	Belief in a Just World *"People get what they deserve."*	Biological Superiority *"I believe whites were created as the superior race."*
Beliefs about blacks[3]	Victims of past injustices	Could succeed if worked harder	Undeserving of special efforts to redress past inequities	Innately inferior
Racial schema	Incongruity between egalitarian values and unavoidable negative feelings toward blacks	Conflict between work values and anti-black sentiment	Conflict between values of fairness and anti-black sentiment	Racial hatred Complete separation of the races
Attitude toward discrimination	Nondiscriminatory practices favored	Systemic barriers to advancement ignored	A thing of the past	Deemed justifiable and desirable
Attitude toward policies that address racial equality	Publicly supported	Threat to the cultural ideals that symbolize American ethos	Violation of norms of fairness	Affront to superior status of white race
Behavioral consequences	Avoidance Interracial anxiety Unintentional discrimination	Opposition to policies designed to promote racial equality (e.g., school busing, affirmative action)	Opposition to policies designed to promote racial equality (e.g., school busing, affirmative action)	Bigoted language Overt discrimination Violence

racism. The argument presented here is that the presence of subtle racism in a military environment, in conjunction with the existence of overt (traditional) racism, elicits the behaviors that create barriers to advancement for racial minorities. The nuances in interracial interactions often cause racial majorities to react in ways that yield discriminatory outcomes for racial minorities (e.g., Cose, 1993). Underlying racial beliefs can stifle valued input (Sessa & Jackson, 1995), impede decision making ability (Lovelace & Rosen, 1996), and restrict the position power of racial minorities (see Thomas & Alderfer, 1989). The suggestion is that subtle racial undertones can result in negative consequences for racial minorities in organizations.

From the perspective of racial majorities, subtle racism is likely to influence job satisfaction and organizational commitment. Racial majorities who ascribe to the ideologies embodied in subtle forms of racism may experience some level of dissatisfaction because attention to the predicament of racial minorities is interpreted as inattention to the situation of racial majorities (e.g., Lynch, 1991; 1997). Furthermore, the discomfort with the organization's approach to racial matters may cause racial majorities to reevaluate their loyalties to an organization that they perceive as not being committed to all of its members (e.g., Tsui et al., 1992). Taken together, the potential impact of subtle racism for both racial majorities and minorities necessitates an assessment of its prevalence and consequences in the existing military environment.

Methodology

The existence of subtle racism in organizational contexts is usually demonstrated through laboratory experiments (e.g., Pettigrew & Martin, 1987) or anecdotal evidence (e.g., Cose, 1993). The absence of field studies suggests there is a need for empirical research in organizational settings (Bielby, 1987). For the present study, the opportunity for an empirical field investigation was provided by the ongoing climate assessment conducted by the United States military. For the last seven years, the military has been analyzing its equal opportunity climate through the distribution of surveys to its military and civilian personnel (Military Equal Opportunity Climate Survey; Dansby & Landis, 1991). Included in the measurement instrument are items that assess racial attitudes and perception as well as the racial climate of individual units. The questionnaire also contains measures of job satisfaction, organizational commitment, and unit effectiveness. As such, an examination of institutional and other forms of racism and their relation to specific organizational variables was possible. For the present analysis, items from the survey were used to create measurement scales for the various types of racism and other organizational variables. Data collected through the climate assessment process were used to assess the impact of subtle racism on the career experiences of certain military personnel.

Sample

Data gathered in 1996 were used for this empirical investigation. Respondents were active duty personnel from each of the five service branches (Air Force, Army, Marine Corps, Navy, Coast Guard). The members were stationed in the United States, in units of fewer than 2,000 persons. Consistent with previous research on subtle racial attitudes (e.g., Gaertner & Dovidio, 1986; McConahay, 1986; Sears, 1988), only white service personnel were selected for this study (n=22,495).

Fifty-four percent (12,052) of the sample were in the Army. The Navy, Marines, Air Force, and Coast Guard represented 16 percent, 14 percent, 10 percent, and 6 percent of the sample, respectively. Seventy-one percent (15,986) indicated that they were enlisted members; twenty-two percent (4,871) indicated that they were officers.[4] Eighty-five percent of the sample were male (19,083); fourteen percent were female (3,028).

Factor Analysis

A principal components factor analysis was conducted to determine if distinct forms of racism could be captured from the climate assessment instrument. Twenty-five items were selected from the instrument based on their representativeness of the racism constructs and their similarity to existing measurement scales. All of the items were measured on a 5-point scale with "1" generally representing high likelihood of a behavior or agreement with a statement and "5" generally indicating low likelihood or strong disagreement (see Appendix A for specific wording). Relative to institutional racism, items that corresponded with Barbarin and Gilbert's (1981) climate for racism scale and Feagin and Feagin's (1986) description of discriminatory organizational norms were selected. Items reflecting blatant bigotry (i.e., racial superiority and racial separation) were included as possible designates of overt racism. Subtle racism was represented by items associated with modern and symbolic racism. No items related to aversive racism were identified. Dovidio and Gaertner (1991) argue that survey methodologies are not suitable for measuring aversive racism because of their susceptibility to socially desirable responses. Previous attempts to create aversive racism scales have yielded only moderate reliabilities (e.g., Kleinpenning & Hagendoorn, 1993). Therefore, items reflecting the ideals and beliefs of modern and symbolic racists and those which paralleled measures from previous studies (e.g., Sears, 1988) were added to the list of items for the factor analysis.

An oblique rotation was used for the factor analysis because of the related racial content of each item, which suggested inter-item correlation (Kim & Mueller, 1977). The factor analysis resulted in four factors with eigenvalues greater than 1.00. Table 2.3 shows the factor loadings for each of the items, sorted by factor in descending order. For clarity, only factor loadings greater than or equal to .4 are shown. With the exception of three items, all of the items had substantial factor loadings (>.5). Thus, the analysis yielded four different factors representing distinct underlying components.

Factor 1, for the most part, reflects differential treatment for racial majorities and minorities. The unfavorable experiences depicted for racial minorities are indicative of institutional racism (cf., Greenhaus et al., 1990; Ilgen & Youtz, 1986). Items regarding the denial of promotion and career-enhancing educational opportunities indicate racial disadvantage relative to career progress. The item regarding the different forms of motivational speeches, in which the focus for majorities was promotion opportunities and for minorities the lack of opportunities, indicates the absence of comparable career support, which prevents minorities from advancing in organizations. Finally, items regarding interracial dating, racially-toned reprimands, less desirable office space, and changing duty assignments based on race reflect a climate for institutional racism such that disparate treatment results in less favorable experiences for racial minorities. In total, Factor 1 is interpreted as representing institutional racism.

Factor 2 reflects the racial attitudes consistent with the anti-black sentiments embodied in modern and symbolic racism theories. The items regarding minorities crying "prejudice" rather than acknowledging personal faults and not taking advantage of educational op-

Table 2.3
Factor Loadings for Institutional, Subtle, and Overt Racism

	Factor 1	Factor 2	Factor 3	Factor 4
Institutional racism items (I)				
A supervisor discouraged cross-racial dating among personnel who would otherwise be free to date within the organization.	.74			
A majority member complained that there was too much interracial dating among other people in the organization.	.73			
A minority member was assigned less desirable office space than a majority member.	.72			
The Commander/CO changed the duty assignments when it was discovered that two persons of the same minority were assigned to the same sensitive area on the same shift.	.72			
A Commander/CO giving a lecture took more time to answer questions from majority members than from minority members.	.72			
A majority supervisor did not select a qualified minority subordinate for promotion.	.70			
A motivational speech to a minority subordinate focused on the lack of opportunity elsewhere; to a majority subordinate, it focused on promotion.	.66			
When reprimanding a minority man, the majority supervisor used terms such as "boy."	.63			
A qualified minority first-level supervisor was denied the opportunity for professional education by his/her supervisor. A majority first-level supervisor with the same qualifications was given the opportunity.	.61			
Subtle racism items				
Minorities and women frequently cry "prejudice" rather than accept responsibility for personal faults.		.83		
Some minorities get promoted just because they are minorities.		.76		
Many minorities act as if they are superior to majority members.		.70		
Minorities don't take advantage of the educational opportunities that are available to them.		.53		
In this organization, I have personally felt discriminated against because of my race.		.43		
Institutional racism items (II)				
More severe punishments are given out to minority as compared to majority offenders for the same types of offenses.			-.83	
Minorities get more extra work details than majority members.			-.83	
Majority supervisors in charge of minority supervisors doubt the minorities' abilities.			-.77	
Majority members get away with breaking rules that result in . punishment for minorities.			-.68	
Majority members assume that minorities commit every crime that occurs, such as thefts in living quarters.			-.48	
Overt racism items				
Minorities and majority members would be better off if they lived and worked only with people of their own races.				-.81
After duty hours, people should stick together in groups made up of their race only (e.g., minorities only with minorities and majority members only with majority members).				-.80
I dislike the idea of having a supervisor of a race different from mine.				-.78
Trying to bring about the integration of women and minorities is more trouble than it's worth.				-.62
Power in the hands of minorities is a dangerous thing.				-.60
Minorities were better off before this equal opportunity business got started.				-.40

portunities corresponds with the belief that racial minorities could succeed if they worked harder.[5] The item regarding minorities getting promoted because of their race relates to the belief that minorities receive preferential treatment. The item concerning minorities acting superior to majorities hints at the notion that the actions of minorities threaten the racial status quo. Finally, the item related to feeling discriminated against due to race reflects the idea of reverse discrimination. Thus, Factor 2 is characterized as subtle racism.

Factor 3 depicts other elements that constitute institutional racism. These items relate to differential treatment for racial minorities due to embedded organizational systems. In particular, the items regarding different levels of punishment and types of work assignments reflect unfavorable treatment that disadvantage minorities. The other items regarding skepticism of minorities' abilities and assumptions about their responsibility for organizational thefts suggest further disadvantage since such actions are likely to lead to lesser work responsibilities and more intensive monitoring of their conduct. Hence, Factor 3 is also representative of institutional racism.

Lastly, Factor 4 reflects the ideals of overt racism. Items regarding living and working with people of one's own race, disliking the idea of a supervisor of another race, along with the view that racial integration is futile, all conform to the belief in racial separation. In addition, the item stating that "power in the hands of minorities is a dangerous thing" insinuates racial hatred and can be associated with the belief that minorities are innately inferior. Finally, the item concerning the situation of minorities being better prior to the institution of equal opportunity suggests a preference for the racial status quo where racial majorities maintain superior status to racial minorities. Therefore, Factor 4 is identified as representing overt racism.

In sum, the results of the factor analysis confirm that distinct forms of racism could be captured from the climate assessment instrument. The strength of the factor analysis is demonstrated by the size of the factor loadings, which were generally greater than .6. The potency of the conclusions is further evidenced by the lack of overlap in the factor loadings. The individual items loaded highly only on their respective factors. Given this, scales for the three types of racism were formed from the results of the factor analysis. These scales were used for the remaining data analyses.

Measures

Forms of racism. Factors 1 through 4 were converted to scales that measured institutional, subtle, and overt racism. The measure of institutional racism was a 14-item scale constructed from Factors 1 and 3. The individual items were coded on a 5-point scale and were then averaged to produce a mean score (1 = a high level of institutional racism; and 5 = no indication of institutional racism) (a = .90). The 5-item subtle racism scale was derived from Factor 2 and also had sufficient reliability (a = .74). Again, the items were averaged on a 5-point scale to produce a degree of subtle racism (1 = high degree of subtle racism; 5 = no subtle racism). Similarly, the overt racism scale was comprised of the six items that loaded on Factor 4 (1 = high degree of overt racism; 5 = no overt racism) (a = .81). Overall, the reliabilities for each of the racism measures were fairly strong.

Job satisfaction. Three items from the climate assessment instrument were used to measure job satisfaction. Two items measured the level of satisfaction with certain aspects of the job, while the other measured overall job satisfaction (see Appendix B). These items were averaged together as a global measure of job satisfaction (1 = very satisfied; 5 = very dissatisfied) (a = .75).

Organizational commitment. Four items from the climate assessment instrument were used to measure organizational commitment. The items assessed loyalty and intent to stay with the organization (see Appendix B). These items were also averaged (1 = highly committed; 5 = not committed) (a = .76).

Control variables. Age, branch, education level, gender, military category, and unit size were included as control variables. Gender and military category were coded as dichotomous variables (1 = female, 2 = male; 1 = officer, 2 = enlisted). The other control variables had multiple categories and are listed in Appendix C.

Data Analysis

Regression analysis was the primary method used in this examination. To examine the impact of subtle racism on institutional racism beyond the influence of overt racism, a hierarchical multiple regression was performed. Military category, age, and education level were entered as the first set of controls in step one, followed by branch and unit size as the next set of control variables in step two.

Overt racism was entered in step three, with subtle racism entered in step four. Military category, age, and education level were entered as control variables in order to minimize method bias generated from the use of self-report questionnaires to measure institutional racism. Previous research on racial discrimination indicates that demographic variables such as age and occupation influence perceptions of institutional bias (Kinder & Sanders, 1996; Kluegel, 1990). Since the primary focus of this study is the impact of subtle racism on institutional discrimination, it was important to assess the characteristics of the organization—i.e., the organizational processes that produce disadvantages for racial minorities—absent individual perceptual biases. On the other hand, categorical differences were important to the assessment of individual racial attitudes and to engender further understanding of the individuals that comprise the organization (Feagin & Feagin, 1986; Pettigrew & Martin, 1987). The second set of control variables (branch and unit size) were included to account for organization-level determinants of institutional racism.

Simple linear regression was used to test the predicted relationship between subtle racism and job satisfaction and organizational commitment. The proposition is that inverse relationships between subtle racism and the two other variables would exist for racial majorities. Results of the analyses are discussed below.

Results

Table 2.4 provides the summary statistics and correlations of the variables included in the analysis. The correlations reveal that enlisted personnel were more likely to sanction overtly racist beliefs than were officers. Enlisted personnel were also more likely to endorse subtle racist beliefs. Officers were more satisfied with their jobs and more organizationally committed than were enlisted members. Accordingly, the older the member of the service, the greater the level of job satisfaction and organizational commitment. Relative to education level, the higher the level of educational attainment, the lower the degree of overt and subtle racism.

Table 2.5 shows the results of the regression analysis used to test the relationship between subtle racism and institutional racism. Again, control variables were entered in steps 1 and 2 followed by overt and subtle racism in steps 3 and 4. As expected, the control variables explained some of the variance in institutional racism (R^2=.07; p<.01). The findings revealed significant main effects for each of the control variables except branch of service. Therefore, a relationship between institutional racism and specific branches of the military was not indicated. Overt racism accounted for the greatest amount of variability in the regression model (b=.52), indicating a strong direct relationship with institutional racism. Subtle racism likewise was a significant predictor of institutional racism (b=.14), explaining additional variance above that explained by overt racism.

Table 2.6 shows the results of the simple linear regression analyses used to examine the relationship between subtle racism and job satisfaction and organizational commitment. Supporting the predictions, the findings show a significant inverse relationship between subtle racism and the dependent variables ($t = -41.54$; $p<.01$ and $t = -45.70$; $p<.01$ for job satisfaction and organizational commitment, respectively). As the degree of subtle racism increased, the levels of job satisfaction and organizational commitment decreased. The same analysis was also conducted relative to overt racism. As with subtle racism, Table 2.7 shows that job satisfaction and organizational commitment were likewise inversely related to overt racism. The greater the degree of overt racism, the lower the levels of job satisfaction and organizational commitment.

Discussion

The findings from this research point to individual-level contributors of institutional discrimination, namely overt and subtle racism. The more organization members endorsed beliefs representative of overt and subtle racism, the greater the likelihood of behaviors indicating institutional racism. Furthermore, organization members who sanctioned overt and subtle racist beliefs were more dissatisfied with their jobs and less committed to the organization than were members who opposed such racial beliefs. Importantly, the findings did not reveal a relationship between branch of service and levels of institutional, subtle, and overt racism. Hence, there was no indication that one particular branch experienced greater degrees of racism, in its various forms, than another branch.

The results of this study illustrate the negative consequences of subtle racism for both racial minorities and majority group members. On the one hand, subtle racism creates obstacles to advancement for one set of organization members; on the other hand, it contributes to discontentment among another set of members. Both outcomes are detrimental to efforts to create an equal opportunity cli-

Table 2.4
Means, Standard Deviations, and Correlations

Variables	Means	s.d.	1	2	3	4	5	6	7	8	9	10	11
1. Institutional racism	4.38	.63	1.00										
2. Overt racism	4.25	.75	.54**	1.00									
3. Subtle racism	3.43	.92	.39**	.53**	1.00								
4. Job satisfaction	2.40	1.03	-.26**	-.26**	-.27**	1.00							
5. Organizational commitment	2.74	1.10	-.26**	-.25**	-.29**	.54**	1.00						
6. Officer vs enlisted	1.77	.42	-.19**	-.19**	-.15**	.19**	.22**	1.00					
7. Education level	3.22	1.01	.20**	.21**	.10**	-.16**	-.17*	-.67**	1.00				
8. Age	3.10	1.17	.20**	.20**	.12**	-.18**	-.17**	-.32**	.42**	1.00			
9. Gender	1.86	.34	.06**	-.08**	-.05**	.01	-.02*	.01	-.04**	-.05**	1.00		
10. Branch of service	2.52	1.04	.02**	.00	-.00	-.07**	-.11**	-.04**	-.07**	.01	.03**	1.00	
11. Unit size	3.25	1.29	-.11**	-.09**	-.09**	.07**	.08**	.13**	-.12**	-.10**	-.00	-.16**	1.00

* $p < .05$
** $p < .01$

Table 2.5
Results of Hierarchical Regression Analysis Predicting Institutional Racism

Variables	β	t	R^2	R^2D
Step 1			.06	
Gender	.07	9.08**		
Officer vs enlisted	-.08	-8.62**		
Age	.14	18.39**		
Education level	.09	9.71**		
Step 2			.07	.01**
Branch of service	.01	1.84ns		
Unit size	-.08	-11.13**		
Step 3			.32	.25**
Overt racism	.52	86.15**		
Step 4			.33	.01**
Subtle racism	.14	20.13**		

* $p < .05$
** $p < .01$
ns - not significant

Table 2.6
Results of Regression Analysis for Subtle Racism as a Predictor of
Job Satisfaction and Organizational Commitment

Dependent Variables	β	t	F
Job satisfaction	-.27	-41.54**	1725.53**
Organizational Commitment	-.29	-45.70**	2088.25**

* $p<.05$
** $p<.01$

Table 2.7
Results of Regression Analysis for Overt Racism as a Predictor of
Job Satisfaction and Organizational Commitment

Dependent Variables	β	t	F
Job satisfaction	-.26	-40.52**	1641.47**
Organizational Commitment	-.25	-38.35**	1470.42**

* $p<.05$
** $p<.01$

mate. In essence, individual attitudes translate into behaviors that yield disparate career experiences for racial minorities and majorities. Ultimately, this creates racial advantage and disadvantage within the organization. The implication for the military is that stated policies alone may not be sufficient for establishing and maintaining an organization that provides equal opportunity for all of its members. In other words, attention must be given to the attitudes of the individuals that comprise the organization in addition to aspects of the organization itself.

Dovidio (1993) suggests that one way of addressing subtle racism is to enhance whites' understanding of their own subtle biases. According to Dovidio, training people to recognize subtle bias may promote greater equality and attenuate the likelihood of discriminatory behaviors. At the same time, racial minorities may bear the onus of helping to reduce interracial anxiety by offering to educate and enlighten others about their culture, organizational experiences, and the subtle discrimination they encounter. Indeed, a central theme of subtle racism theories is that racial majority group members are often unaware of the racial undertones and the sense of discomfort displayed by their actions. Enhancing their understanding may decrease anxiety and bias. Ultimately, the goal is to maximize the benefits of racial diversity for the total organization.

In total, this research supports the anecdotal literature that describes incidents of subtle racial discrimination in the workplace (e.g., Cose, 1993). Too often such incidents are interpreted as racial minorities being "too sensitive" (Dovidio, 1993). The present study offers some validation that these experiences might occur. The findings also support the proposition that subtle racism can be as consequential as overt racism. This suggests that there is a need for a continuous (and perhaps closer) examination of racial attitudes, particularly when investigating the incongruous career experiences of some military personnel. Equally important is future empirical research that explores the perception of subtle racism by racial minorities and the perceived consequences of those actions. This additional research will further the understanding of the impact of race and race relations in organizations.

Notes

1. The theories discussed in this paper were developed in the 1970s and 1980s. As such, the use of the terms "black" and "white" to describe racial group members (as opposed to African-American and white American) is consistent with their original conceptualizations. For continuity, "black" and "white" are used throughout the paper, even for present-day analyses.
2. Most theoretical perspectives on racism, including Allport's (1954) seminal work, discuss racial prejudice in terms of whites' attitudes toward blacks.
3. These theories of racism were developed based on whites' attitudes toward blacks.
4. Missing demographic data accounted for seven percent (1638) of the sample. Previous research involving gender/race issues conducted in a military context revealed a reluctance on the part of some members to provide complete demographic information for fear of compromising their anonymity (see Johnson, 1996).
5. Two of the items included in the factor analysis read "minorities and women." Because both items loaded highly on their respective factors with other items specifically related to racial minorities they were retained in the analysis.

References

Allport, G. W. (1954). *The nature of prejudice*. Reading, MA: Addison-Wesley.

Baldwin, J. N. (1996). The promotion record of the United States Army: Glass ceilings in the officer corps. *Public Administration Review, 56*, 191-198.

Barbarin, O. A., & Gilbert, R. (1981). Institutional racism scale: Assessing self and organizational attributes. In O. A. Barbarin, P. R. Good, O. M. Pharr, & J. A. Siskind (Eds.), *Institutional racism and community competence* (pp. 147-171). Department of Health and Human Services. No. (ADM) 81-907.

Baron, J. N., & Pfeffer, J. (1994). The social psychology of organizations and inequality. *Social Psychology Quarterly, 57*, 190-209.

Berger, J., Fisek, M. H., Norman, R. Z., & Zelditch, M. (1977). *Status characteristics and social interaction: An expectation-states approach*. New York: Elsevier.

Bielby, W. T. (1987). Modern prejudice and institutional barriers to equal employment opportunity for minorities. *Journal of Social Issues, 43*, 79-84.

Braddock, J. H., II, & McPartland, J. M. (1987). How minorities continue to be excluded from equal employment opportunities: Research on labor market and institutional barriers. *Journal of Social Issues, 43*, 5-39.

Brewer, M. B., & Kramer, R. M. (1985). The psychology of intergroup attitudes and behavior. *Annual Review of Psychology, 36*, 219-243.

Cose, E. (1993). *The rage of a privileged class*. New York: HarperCollins.

Dansby, M. R., & Landis, D. (1991). Measuring equal opportunity climate in the military environment. *International Journal of Intercultural Relations, 15*(4), 389-405.

Dovidio, J. F. (1993, April). The subtlety of racism. *Training & Development*, pp. 51-57.

Dovidio, J. F., & Gaertner, S. L. (1981). The effects of race, status, and ability on helping behavior. *Social Psychology Quarterly, 44*, 192-203.

—— (1983). Race, normative structure, and help-seeking. In B. M. DePaulo, A. Nadler, & J. D. Fisher (Eds.), *New directions in helping* (Vol. 2), pp. 285-302. New York: Academic Press.

—— (1991). Changes in the expression and assessment of racial prejudice. In H. J. Knopke, R. J. Norrell, & R. W. Rogers (Eds.), *Opening doors: Perspectives on race relations in contemporary America* (pp. 61-89). Orlando, FL: Academic Press.

Dreher, G. F., & Cox, T., (1996). Race, gender, and opportunity: A study of compensation attainment and the establishment of mentoring relationships. *Journal of Applied Psychology, 81*, 297-308.

Feagin, J. R., & Feagin, C. B. (1986). *Discrimination American style: Institutional racism and sexism*. Malabar, FL: Krieger.

Gaertner, S. L., & Dovidio, J. F. (1986). The aversive form of racism. In J. F. Dovidio & S. L. Gaertner (Eds.), *Prejudice, discrimination, and racism* (pp. 61-89). San Diego: Academic Press.

Greenhaus, J. H., & Parasuraman, S. (1993). Job performance attributions and career advancement prospects: An examination of gender and race effects. *Organizational Behavior and Human Decision Processes, 55*, 273-297.

Greenhaus, J. H., Parasuraman, S., & Wormley, W. M. (1990). Effects of race on organizational experiences, job performance, and career outcomes. *Academy of Management Journal, 33*, 64-86.

Heilman, M. E., Block, C. J., & Lucas, J. A. (1992). Presumed incompetent? Stigmatization and affirmative action efforts. *Journal of Applied Psychology, 77*, 536-544.

Howitt, D., & Owusu-Bempah, J. (1990). The pragmatics of institutional racism: Beyond words. *Human Relations, 9*, 885-899.

Huddy, L., & Sears, D. O. (1995). Opposition to bilingual education: Prejudice or the defense of realistic interests? *Social Psychological Quarterly, 58*, 133-143.

Ibarra, H. (1995). Race, opportunity, and diversity of social circles in managerial networks. *Academy of Management Journal, 38*, 673-703.

Ilgen, D. R., & Youtz, M. A. (1986). Factors affecting the evaluation and development of minorities in organizations. In K. M. Rowland & G. R. Ferris (Eds.), *Research in personnel and human resources management: A research annual.* (Vol. 4, pp. 307-337). Greenwich, CT: JAI Press.

Jackson, L. A., Sullivan, L. A., & Hodge, C. N. (1993). Stereotype effects on attributions, predications, and evaluations: No two social judgments are quite alike. *Journal of Personality and Social Psychology, 65*, 69-84.

Johnson, O. E. (1996). *Justice in the eye of the beholder: The effect of category salience on fairness judgments in organizations*. Unpublished doctoral dissertation.

Kanter, R. M. (1989). *When giants learn to dance: Mastering the challenge of strategy, management and careers in the 1980s*. New York: Simon & Schuster.

Kim, J., & Mueller, C. W. (1978). *Factor analysis statistical methods and practical issues*. Beverly Hills, CA: Sage Publications.

Kinder, D. R. (1986). The continuing American dilemma: White resistance to racial change 40 years after Mydral. *Journal of Social Issues, 42*, 151-171.

Kinder, D. R., & Sanders, L. M. (1996). *Divided by color.* Chicago, IL: University of Chicago Press.

Kinder, D. R., & Sears, D. O. (1981). Prejudice and politics: Symbolic racism versus racial threats to the good life. *Journal of Personality and Social Psychology, 40*, 414-431.

Kleinpenning, G., & Hagendoorn, L. (1993). Forms of racism and the cumulative dimension of ethnic attitudes. *Social Psychology Quarterly, 56*, 21-36.

Kluegel, J. R. (1990). Trends in whites' explanations of the black-white gap in socioeconomic status, 1977-1989. *American Sociological Review, 55*, 512-525.

Konrad, A. M., Winter, S., & Gutek, B. A. (1992). Diversity in work group sex composition: Implications for majority and minority members. In P. Tolbert & S. B. Bacharach (Eds.), *Research in the sociology of organizations* (Vol. 10, pp. 115-140). Greenwich, CT: JAI Press.

Kossek, E. E., & Zonia, S. C. (1993). Assessing diversity climate: A field study of reactions to employer efforts to promote diversity. *Journal of Organizational Behavior, 14*, 61-81.

Kraiger, K., & Ford, J. K. (1985). A meta-analysis of ratee race effects in performance ratings. *Journal of Applied Psychology, 70*, 56-65.

Kravitz, D. A., & Platania, J. (1993). Attitudes and beliefs about affirmative action: Effects of target and respondent sex and ethnicity. *Journal of Applied Psychology, 78*, 928-938.

Lerner, M. J. (1980). *The belief in a just world: A fundamental delusion.* New York: Plenum.

Lovelace, K., & Rosen, B. (1996). Differences in achieving person-organization fit among diverse groups of mangers, *Journal of Management, 22*, 703-722.

Lynch, F. R. (1991). *Invisible victims: White males and the crisis of affirmative action.* New York: Praeger.

Lynch, F. R. (1997). *The diversity machine: The drive to change the "white male workplace."* New York: Free Press.

Major, B. (1994). From social inequality to personal entitlement: The role of social comparison, legitimacy appraisals, and group membership. In M. P. Zanna (Ed.), *Advances in experimental social psychology* (Vol. 26, pp. 293-355). San Diego, CA: Academic Press.

McConahay, J. B. (1986). Modern racism, ambivalence, and the modern racism scale. In J. F. Dovidio & S. L. Gaertner (Eds.), *Prejudice, discrimination, and racism* (pp. 91-125). San Diego: Academic Press.

Perry, L. S. (1993). Effects of inequity on job satisfaction and self-evaluation in a national sample of African American workers. *Journal of Social Psychology, 133*, 565-573.

Peterson, R. S. (1994). The role of values in predicting fairness judgments and support for affirmative action. *Journal of Social Issues, 50*, 95-115.

Pettigrew, T. F., & Martin, J. (1987). Shaping the organizational context for black American inclusion. *Journal of Social Issues, 43*, 41-78.

Ryan, C. S., Judd, C. M., & Park, B. (1996). Effects of racial stereotypes on judgments of individuals: The moderating role of perceived group variability. *Journal of Experimental Social Psychology, 32*, 71-103.

Sears, D. O. (1988). Symbolic racism. In P. A. Katz & D. A. Taylor (Eds.), *Eliminating racism: Profiles in controversy* (pp. 53-84). New York: Plenum Press.

Sessa, V. I., & Jackson, S. E. (1995). Diversity in decision-making teams: All differences are not created equal. In M. M. Chemers, M. A. Costanzo, & S. Oskamp (Eds.), *Diversity in organizations: New perspectives for a changing workplace* (pp. 133-156). Newbury Park, CA: Sage.

Sniderman, P. M., & Piazza, T. (1993). *The scar of race.* Cambridge, MA: Harvard University Press.

Sniderman, P. M., & Tetlock, P. E. (1986). Symbolic racism. Problems of motive attribution in political analysis. *Journal of Social Issues, 42*, 129-150.

Stewart, J. B. (1992). Looking for a few good men: Predicting patterns of retention, promotion, and accession of minority and women officers. *American Journal of Economics & Sociology, 51*, 435-458.

Thomas, D. (1993). Racial dynamics in cross-race development relationships. *Administrative Science Quarterly, 38*, 169-194.

Thomas, D. A., & Alderfer, C. P. (1989). The influence of race on career dynamics: Theory and research on minority career experiences. In M. B. Arthur, D. T. Hall, & B. S. Lawrence (Eds.), *Handbook of career theory* (pp. 133-158). Cambridge, MA: Cambridge University Press.

Tsui, A. S., Egan, T. D., & O'Reilly, C. A. (1992). Being different: Relational demography and organizational attachment. *Administrative Science Quarterly, 37*, 402-423.

Watson, W. E., Kumar, K., & Michaelsen, L. K. (1993). Cultural diversity's impact on interaction processes and performance: Comparing homogeneous and diverse task groups. *Academy of Management Journal, 36*, 590-602.

Witt, S. L. (1990). Affirmative action and job satisfaction: Self-interested v. public spirited perspectives on social equity—some sobering findings from the academic workplace. *Review of Public Personnel Administration, 10*, 73-93.

Wolfe, C. T., & Spencer, S. T. (1996). Stereotypes and prejudice. *American Behavioral Scientist, 40*, 176-185.

Appendix A
Factor Analysis Items Selected from the MEOCS*

Use the following scale to estimate the *chances* that the actions listed below COULD have happened (in your unit during the last 30 days):

> 1 = There is a *very high chance* that the action occurred.
>
> 2 = There is a *reasonably high chance* that the action occurred.
>
> 3 = There is a *moderate chance* that the action occurred.
>
> 4 = There is a *small chance* that the action occurred.
>
> 5 = There is *almost no chance* that the action occurred.

ITEM
A supervisor discouraged cross-racial dating among personnel who would otherwise be free to date within the organization.
A majority supervisor did not select a qualified minority subordinate for promotion.
A majority member complained that there was too much interracial dating among other people in the organization.
A minority member was assigned less desirable office space than a majority member.
The Commander/CO changed the duty assignments when it was discovered that two persons of the same minority were assigned to the same sensitive area on the same shift.
A Commander/CO giving a lecture took more time to answer questions from majority members than from minority members.
When reprimanding a minority man, the majority supervisor used terms such as "boy."
A motivational speech to a minority subordinate focused on the lack of opportunity elsewhere; to a majority subordinate, it focused on promotion.

(cont.)

* MEOCS = Military Equal Oppurtunity Climate Survey

In this section, we are asking for your opinions about certain issues. On your answer sheet, mark your response to each of the items as follows:

> 1 = *totally agree* with the statement
> 2 = *moderately agree* with the statement
> 3 = *neither agree nor disagree* with the statement
> 4 = *moderately disagree* with the statement
> 5 = *totally disagree* with the statement

ITEM
Minorities were better off before this equal opportunity business got started.
More severe punishments are given out to minority as compared to majority offenders for the same types of offenses.
Majority supervisors in charge of minority supervisors doubt the minorities' abilities.
Minorities get more extra work details than majority members.
After duty hours, people should stick together in groups made up of their race only (e.g., minorities only with minorities and majority members only with majority members).
Trying to bring about the integration of women and minorities is more trouble than it's worth.
Majority members assume that minorities commit every crime that occurs, such as thefts in living quarters.
Minorities and majority members would be better off if they lived and worked only with people of their own races.
I dislike the idea of having a supervisor of a race different from mine.
Majority members get away with breaking rules that result in punishment for minorities.
Some minorities get promoted just because they are minorities.
Power in the hands of minorities is a dangerous thing.
Minorities and women frequently cry "prejudice" rather than accept responsibility for personal faults.
In this organization, I have personally felt discriminated against because of my race.
Minorities don't take advantage of the educational opportunities that are available to them.
Many minorities act as if they are superior to majority members.

Appendix B
Job Satisfaction and Organizational Commitment
Measures Selected from the MEOCS

The questions in Part IV are used to determine *how satisfied you are with some specific job-related issues*. Indicate your degree of satisfaction or dissatisfaction by choosing the most appropriate response:

> 1 = *very* satisfied
> 2 = *moderately* satisfied
> 3 = *neither* satisfied or dissatisfied
> 4 = *somewhat* dissatisfied
> 5 = *very* dissatisfied

ITEM
The chance to help people and improve their welfare through the performance of my job.
The chance to acquire valuable skills in my job that prepare me for future opportunities.
My job as a whole.

In this part of the survey, answer the following questions regarding *how you feel about your organization.*

> 1 = *totally agree* with the statement
> 2 = *moderately agree* with the statement
> 3 = *neither agree nor disagree* with the statement
> 4 = *moderately disagree* with the statement
> 5 = *totally disagree* with the statement

ITEM
I would accept almost any type of assignment in order to stay in this organization.
I am proud to tell others that I am part of this organization
I feel very little loyalty to this organization.*
It would take very little change in my present circumstances to cause me to leave this organization.*

* Item reverse coded.

Appendix C
Measurement Codes for Control Variables

Code	Age	Branch	Education Level	Unit Size
1	20 or under	Air Force	Less than high school	100 or less
2	21 - 25	Army	High school grad or GED	100 - 299
3	26 - 30	Navy	Some college	300 - 599
4	31 - 40	Marines	College degree	600 - 999
5	41 - 49	Coast Guard	Advanced college work	1000 - 1999
6	50 or over			

3

Three Levels of Diversity: An Examination of the Complex Relationship Between Diversity, Group Cohesiveness, Sexual Harassment, Group Performance, and Time

Gary L. Whaley

Introduction

Workforce 2000 (Johnston & Packer, 1987) put the spotlight on the changing demographic character of the American workforce. This report popularized the slowly emerging idea that the basic character of the labor pool in the United States is changing from the white male dominated resource that it had always been, to a more feminine and more variegated well spring. It was predicted that by the year 2000 the workforce would be 47 percent women (Johnston & Packer, 1987). Further, it was stated that between 1985 and 2000 non-whites would comprise 29 percent of the net additions to the workforce (Johnston & Packer, 1987).

Workforce 2020 (Richard & D'Amico, 1997), the sequel to *Workforce 2000*, projects the continued diversification of America. The authors report that, according to Census Bureau projections, for year 2020: white non-Hispanics will comprise only 68 percent of the American labor force; Hispanics will increase their representation in the workforce from 9 percent in 1995 to 14 percent in 2020; and, Asians will be the most rapidly growing minority group increasing their representation in the labor force to 6.5 percent in 2020 from 1.6 percent in the 1980s (Richard & D'Amico, 1997).

The active-duty military, of course, can expect to experience the same evolution of its demographic makeup as that experienced in the nation that it defends. An examination of the demographic profile of the active duty military for the years 1987 to 1997 affirms this (see Tables 3.1a, 3.1b, and 3.1c). For all active-duty military personnel across all services the proportion of all race/ethnic minority groups has increased from 27.3 percent in 1987 to 32.3 percent in 1997, a net increase of 18.3 percent over the ten-year period. For women in the active-duty forces the increase was from 10.2 percent to 13.7 percent, a net increase of 34.3 percent for the same ten years. As in the general population, the fastest growing race/ethnic groups in the active-duty forces are Hispanics and Asian Americans. Hispanics have realized a net change in their proportional representation of 74.4 percent, from 3.9 percent of the total in 1987 to 6.8 percent in 1997. Asian-American representation changed from 2.2 percent in 1987 to 3.2 percent in 1997, a 45.5 percent increase. However, within the officer ranks, Asian-American representation increased from 1.3 percent to 2.5 percent, a 92.5 percent increase in ten years! While the numbers are still small, the rates of change are significant. Indeed, the military does contain an increasingly culturally diverse membership.

Today, most would agree that diversity can no longer be thought of as simply a defensive action against potential charges of discrimination towards a minority group. This change is explained by the realization by interested parties of three facts:

1.   The labor pool today is becoming more and more diverse.

2.   Business is becoming globalized necessitating the diversification of global organizations.

3.   Diversity is an important organizational dynamic which needs to be understood.

The purpose of this paper is to examine the diversity concept and to develop a comprehensive and practical operationalization of the concept. Further, this paper will examine the relationship of diversity to important organizational outcomes such as work group performance and sexual harassment.

Diversity Defined in the Literature

While interest in workforce diversity has spanned some 30 years in the literature, an employer's interest in the topic was largely dic-

Table 3.1a
Demographic Distribution of Active Duty Forces- All Ranks (% of Total)

YEAR	TOTAL (1000's)	WOMEN	BLACK	HISPANIC	NATIVE AMERICAN	ASIAN AMERICAN	OTHER
1987	2139.5	10.2	19.3	3.9	0.6	2.2	1.3
1988	2123.7	10.4	19.8	4.1	0.6	2.3	1.3
1989	2138.5	10.7	19.9	4.3	0.6	2.3	1.3
1990	2065.6	10.9	20.5	4.6	0.6	2.4	1.2
1991	2008.4	10.9	20.3	4.8	0.6	2.4	1.3
1992	1831.6	11.4	19.8	5.0	0.6	2.6	1.3
1993	1730.5	11.7	19.4	5.3	0.6	2.7	1.4
1994	1633.0	12.1	19.2	5.4	0.6	2.8	1.5
1995	1540.8	12.6	19.3	5.8	0.6	2.9	1.6
1996	1457.6	13.2	19.6	6.3	0.6	3.0	1.7
1997	1425.5	13.7	19.8	6.8	0.7	3.2	1.8

Table 3.1b
Demographic Distribution of Active Duty Forces- Enlisted (% of Total)

YEAR	TOTAL (1000's)	WOMEN	BLACK	HISPANIC	NATIVE AMERICAN	ASIAN AMERICAN	OTHER
1987	1826.3	10.2	21.4	4.2	0.6	2.3	1.3
1988	1818.7	10.4	22.0	4.5	0.6	2.4	1.3
1989	1825.2	10.7	22.1	4.7	0.7	2.4	1.3
1990	1761.9	10.9	22.9	5.0	0.7	2.5	1.3
1991	1710.5	10.8	22.6	5.2	0.7	2.6	1.3
1992	1550.7	11.3	22.0	5.5	0.7	2.7	1.4
1993	1466.1	11.5	21.6	5.8	0.7	2.8	1.4
1994	1379.8	12.0	21.4	6.0	0.6	2.9	1.5
1995	1295.5	12.5	21.5	6.4	0.7	3.0	1.6
1996	1224.9	13.2	21.8	6.9	0.7	3.2	1.7
1997	1197.9	13.7	22.1	7.5	0.7	3.3	1.8

Table 3.1c
Demographic Distribution of Active Duty Forces- Officers (% of Total)

YEAR	TOTAL (1000's)	WOMEN	BLACK	HISPANIC	NATIVE AMERICAN	ASIAN AMERICAN	OTHER
1987	313.3	10.3	6.5	1.7	0.4	1.3	1.3
1988	304.9	10.7	6.7	1.8	0.4	1.4	1.2
1989	313.3	10.8	6.7	1.9	0.4	1.5	1.2
1990	303.7	11.4	6.9	2.1	0.4	1.7	1.1
1991	297.9	11.7	7.1	2.2	0.4	1.8	1.2
1992	280.9	12.0	7.2	2.3	0.4	1.9	1.3
1993	264.4	12.4	7.1	1.7	0.4	2.0	1.4
1994	253.3	12.8	7.3	2.6	0.4	2.1	1.5
1995	245.4	13.0	7.5	2.8	0.4	2.3	1.6
1996	232.7	13.4	7.8	3.0	0.5	2.4	1.7
1997	227.6	13.6	8.0	3.2	0.5	2.5	1.7

Note: These data were gathered from the *Semi-Annual Race/Ethnic/Gender Profiles of the Department of Defense Forces, (Active and Reserve), the United States Coast Guard, and Department of Defense Civilians* 1987-1997 prepared by the Research Directorate, Defense Equal Opportunity Management Institute, 740 O'Malley Road, Patrick AFB, Florida 32925-3399.

tated by the federal government. Only with the passage of the 1964 Civil Rights Act was there a general awakening of interest in the demographic composition of an organization's membership. Specifically, Title VII prohibited employers from intentionally using race, skin color, age, gender, religious beliefs, or national origin as the basis for making decisions regarding employment, promotions, dismissals, and other job related issues (Hunt, 1984). Additional federal equal employment opportunity laws such as the 1967 *Age Discrimination in Employment Act*; the *1973 Vocational Rehabilitation Act*; and, the 1972 *Vietnam Era Veterans Readjustment Assistance Act* have all served to further sensitize employers to the issue of workforce composition so as to protect themselves against charges of discrimination. In most cases the measurement of the race/ethnicity and gender mix of the organizational membership was necessitated by the Equal Employment Opportunity Commission and the need for affirmative action plans and goals.

It has been a more recent occurrence, since the 1980s, that an interest in diversity has gone beyond the effort to demonstrate compliance to state and federal laws regarding discrimination. Interest in the concept began to shift from being a measure of integration in the workforce to an interest in diversity as an important organizational characteristic linked to such organizational issues as member satisfaction (e.g., Verkuyten et al., 1994; Meglino et al., 1989), turnover (e.g., Jackson et al., 1991; Tsui et al., 1992), creativity (e.g., Watson et al., 1993; Bantel & Jackson, 1989), and productivity (e.g., Judge & Ferris, 1993; Ancona & Caldwell, 1992). As the researchers' interests in diversity heightened during this period, they began to utilize a much wider, more general, perspective of diversity consistent with the dictionary definition of diversity which is "the condition of being different...(or) an instance or a point of difference" (Mish, 1984).

The review of the management literature by Milliken and Martins (1996) demonstrates this expanded operationalization of the diversity concept. They identified twelve different dimensions of diversity. Included in their review were studies which focused on the traditional demographic measures of diversity: race/ethnic background, nationality, gender, and age. Also reviewed were studies examining diversity in: personality and values, educational background, functional background, occupational background, industry experience, organizational membership, organizational tenure, and group tenure.

To organize their thinking about the different types of diversity, Milliken and Martins (1996) suggested a typology of diversity dimensions: "observable" and "less observable." Observable attributes of diversity include such characteristics as race, ethnic background, age, or gender. Less observable attributes include such attributes as education, technical abilities, functional background, tenure in the system, social economic background, and personality characteristics or values.

Milliken and Martins (1996) argued the distinction between "observable" and "less observable" diversity characteristics is useful because of the different group dynamics they evoke in an organizational setting. Observable, or visible, characteristics of diversity are particularly likely to stimulate responses that are the direct result of personal biases, prejudices, or stereotypes. These, of course, are important elements in the study of group dynamics. The less observable characteristics of diversity tend to influence a different set of group dynamics. Milliken and Martins argued that diversity in educational backgrounds, job experiences, and skills, for example, create different underlying schema, or conscious and unconscious preconceptions and beliefs, that organize one's thinking about a problem.

Harrison, Price, and Bell (1998), in reviewing the diversity literature, have suggested a similar typology for different measures of diversity. They posited a distinction between "surface-level diversity" and "deep-level diversity." The surface level was defined as "differences among group members in overt, biological characteristics that are typically reflected in physical features" (Harrison et al., 1998). This category includes much the same demographic variables that Milliken and Martins had categorized as observable (i.e., race/ethnicity, gender, and age). The deep-level characteristics of diversity, which they did not define, included such factors as attitudes, beliefs, and values (Harrison et al., 1998), somewhat different from Milliken and Martins "less observable" category.

Harrison et al. (1998) argued that past researchers' interest in the "surface-level" diversity characteristics was due to the widespread belief that these characteristics are reasonable, easily assessed proxies for underlying psychological characteristics, which are considerably more difficult to assess. Perhaps, a rethinking of Harrison et al.'s classification scheme may help reconcile the difference between their typology and that of Milliken and Martins, as well as provide some consensus between the two models of classification of diversity dimensions.

A General Typology for Diversity

This author suggests that the theme not fully expressed in the Harrison et al. method of classification of diversity is the ease of measurement of the variable itself. What Harrison et al. referred to as "surface-level" characteristics are those they describe as most easily measured and validated (i.e., race, gender, and age). Variables they classified as "deep-level" are those less easily measured and validated (i.e., attitudes, beliefs, and values). Thus, their categorization scheme may be redefined as a single dimension (measurability) with two categories (easily measured and less easily measured).

If the Harrison et al. classification method can withstand the slight augmentation suggested here, then their measurability dimension can be integrated with the observability dimension of Milliken and Martins. In Figure 3.1 below on the horizontal axis Milliken and

Martins' "observability" dimension is divided into two categories: easily observable and less observable. The vertical axis represents Harrison et al.'s, "measurability" classification dimension, also divided into two categories: easily measurable and less easily measurable. The result is a four-cell classification scheme for diversity variables summarized in Figure 3.1.

Cell 1 contains variables which are easily observable and easily measurable. The traditional measures of diversity such as race, gender, age, and physical disabilities, for example, lie within this cell. These factors are generally apparent from simple observation. They can also be readily measured in highly reliable and valid ways, typically with a simple survey form.

Cell 2 identifies variables which are less observable but easily measurable. Within this cell lie the variables religion, national origin, education, job-related experience, marital status, organizational membership, political affiliation, socio-economic status, and the like. These are aspects of diversity which are not readily apparent when first meeting an individual or a group. But they are easily measured with a job application, a survey, or a poll, for example. Milliken and Martins, using their single dimension of observability, had also included personality characteristics and values within this set. The classification method suggested here places these very different variables into a separate category.

Figure 3.1
A Typology for Diversity Measures

		Observability	
		readily obser.	less observable
Measurabilty	easily measured	Cell 1 Race/Ethnicity Gender, Age	Cell 2 Nat'l Origin Education Org. Membership
	less easily measured	Cell 3 Task Behavior Enacted Roles Skills	Cell 4 Values Attitudes Personality

Cell 3 contains variables which are classified as easily observable and less easily measured. Included within this cell are the behavioral variables such as task-related behaviors, enacted roles within a group, and individual skills, for example. Whereas one can readily observe on-the-job behavior of others, it is not easy to obtain valid assessments of the quantity and quality of their work, the reliability of their work, or the variability of their level of effort, nor is it easy to assess quantitatively the different roles one fulfills within a task group or what behaviors are specifically serving what role. Valid and reliable measures of these variables, as anyone involved in job performance evaluation knows, are difficult and time consuming to devise and administer.

Cell 3 represents a class of diversity variables which have not heretofore been considered in the diversity literature. However, the literature on "teams" contains a great deal of information on the concept of roles within a work group. An obvious analogy is that of a basketball team. A coach must assess each player's special strengths and make them responsible for specific roles within the team. For example, there must be individuals assigned to the role as ball handler, the 3-point specialist, the power scorer, and the rebounder for a team to be successful. Everyone cannot perform all tasks; rather, individuals must perform certain tasks which are, ideally, consistent with their unique experiences and skills. Successful work groups must have persons to fulfill specialized roles based on their skills and preferences.

Cell 4 delineates variables which are less observable and less easily measured. Within this cell lie the diversity variables Harrison et al. have labeled "deep-level" diversity (i.e., attitudes, beliefs and values, as well as the personality characteristics and values which Milliken and Martins had simply labeled as "less observable"). These characteristics are not directly observable, although persons observe the behavior of others and, via an attribution process, make an inference as to what attitudes, values, and personality characteristics an individual may possess. But, reliable and valid measures of these characteristics are difficult to create.

Three Levels of Diversity

The value of the classification scheme discussed above and summarized in Figure 3.1 may be as a heuristic device to assist researchers and practitioners in their thinking about the impact diversity has upon the dynamics of a work group. For example, Cell 1 defines a set of diversity variables which are referred to here as Level I diversity variables. Level I variables are *"surface-level"* variables which pertain most directly to questions of equal opportunity, affirmative action, and equity within a system across various demographic or minority groups. Surface-level variables have not, however, been found to be useful in the study of predictors of work group outcomes. When this level of diversity variables is examined for relationships with such outcome variables as performance ratings, organizational commitment, or turnover, for example, the findings are inconsistent within and across those studies (Harrison et al., 1998; Pulakos et al., 1989).

Cells 2 and 3 contain many of the skill-based and role-set diversity variables which have been shown to be most closely related to such group processes and outcomes as group performance, turnover, and creativity (Milliken & Martins, 1996). These two cells comprise the variables which will be referred to here as Level II, *"working-level"* diversity variables, because they focus on the different types of skills, experiences, knowledge, and roles sets individuals bring to a work group.

Cell 4 contains those diversity variables that are characterized here as *"deep-level."* Level III includes differences among members' attitudes, beliefs, and values. Harrison et al. (1998) report finding few studies that have examined these diversity variables. Those which were reviewed demonstrated Level III diversity variables to be associated with group cohesiveness, performance, group processes, and turnover.

Comprehending the systemic nature of these three levels of diversity and their relationships to one another is essential to understanding the important dynamics of the impact of diversity on work group performance. Elsass and Graves (1997) have posited a general model of cognitive and behavioral processes which will help us to understand these dynamics. Drawing from social identity theory (Ashforth & Meal, 1989), Elsass and Graves explained how members of a newly formed group will categorize one another based on each individual's salient features such as race, ethnicity, and/or gender (Level I diversity variables). The category to which one is assigned is based upon members' prototypes of various racial, ethnic, and/or gender groups (Lord & Foti, 1986) and is influenced by a number of different contextual factors. These contextual factors can include particular racial, ethnic, or gender groups which are associated with certain tasks within an organization (Deaux & Major, 1987), job functions or levels linked to specific groups within an organization (Brewer & Miller, 1987; Wharton, 1992), or the relative smallness of the representation of a particular demographic group within an organization (Kanter, 1977; Taylor & Fiske, 1978; Wharton, 1992). The categorization process utilizing Level I diversity variables results in members of a group developing a set of role expectations for themselves and the other members of the group, status judgments (Level II diversity variables), and a set of judgments and attitudes towards an identifiable demographic group (Level III diversity variables). Thus, Elsass and Graves (1997) demonstrated how Level I variables influences a work group's perceptions of the membership's Level II and Level III diversity characteristics.

The interdependent nature of these diversity variables is also suggested in other social-psychological theories. Social role theory recognizes that different persons within a group may be expected to perform different roles based on their gender, for example (Eagly, 1987; Eagly, Makhijani, & Klonsky, 1992), thus linking Level I and Level II diversity variables. Additionally, as explained in Heider's (1958) attribution theory, individuals construct either internal or external attributions from the observed behaviors of others. Heider points out that there is a natural tendency to make an internal attribution pertaining to the other's attitudes, character, or personality based on observed behaviors (Heider, 1958; Jones, 1990). Thus, behavior patterns—those enacted, expected, and perceived (Level II)—are linked to group members' perceptions of others' personal goals, personality, and attitudes (Level III).

A Model of Diversity, Sexual Harassment, and Group Performance

In the paragraphs below, the author will propose a simple model depicting the relationships among diversity, sexual harassment, and group performance. The model suggested in Figure 3.2 below may be helpful in demonstrating and summarizing the central role that diversity plays in a number of important organizational issues such as individual satisfaction and commitment, work group performance, work group cohesiveness, and sexual harassment.

Figure 3.2
Behavioral Model of Diversity, Sexual Harassment, and Performance

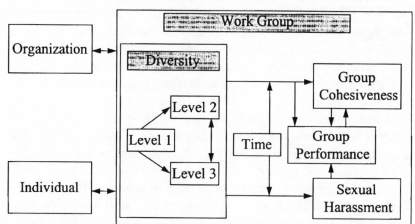

The focal point of the model presented in Figure 3.2 is work group diversity. As explained earlier, diversity is conceived in three levels. The manner in which Level 1, surface-level diversity, can influence the working-level and deep diversity variables, was also explained above as was the cross-level influence between working-level diversity and deep-level. The model also suggests that diversity has an influence on work group cohesiveness, sexual harassment, the individual, and the organization. These relationships will be discussed in the paragraphs below.

Diversity, Group Cohesiveness, and Time

The literature is consistent in demonstrating that diversity has a negative impact upon work group cohesiveness. Cohesiveness is defined as the degree to which group members are attached to each other and are motivated to stay in the group (Robbins, 1996). Milliken and Martins (1996) summarized their review of the literature by stating that the research suggests the more diverse a group is with respect to gender, race, or age (Level 1 diversity), the higher its turnover and the more likely it is that dissimilar individuals will be absent and leave the group (i.e., lower its cohesiveness). Byrne's (1971) similarity-attraction paradigm supports the proposition that Level 2 and 3 diversity variables also influence group cohesiveness. Specifically, Byrne posits that similarity with respect to opinions, personality traits, and social background characteristics tend to increase the degree of attraction between individuals. Terborg et al. (1976) found that attitudinal similarity (Level 3 diversity) was associated with higher group cohesiveness. Finally, Harrison et al. (1998) found variables representing surface-working and deep-level diversity to be significantly and negatively correlated with group cohesiveness.

Harrison et al. (1998) suggested that the negative impact that diversity has upon group cohesiveness is softened with the passage of time. Their argument is that when new members are introduced to a group it is the readily apparent differences (i.e., age, race, and gender) that are used as the basis for inferring similarity in attitudes, beliefs, or personality. This position is supported by Tsui et al. (1992). Over time, as people acquire additional information through their interactions and observations, the initial assumptions which were based upon stereotypes are replaced by more accurate information pertaining to one another's beliefs and values. This results in a reduction of prejudice and conflict and greater cohesiveness (Harrison et al., 1998). Thus, Figure 3.2 suggests that time moderates the relationship between diversity and cohesiveness.

Diversity and Group Performance

Many studies demonstrate that Level 1 diversity has a negative impact upon factors generally associated with productivity such as member satisfaction, absenteeism, and turnover. Other diversity studies have shown benefits. For example, it has been demonstrated that the number of alternatives considered in decision-making tasks and the degree of cooperation within the group increases with diversity (Cox et al., 1991; McLeod & Lobel, 1992; Watson et al., 1993). Watson et al. (1993) demonstrated that these positive effects occurred only after the diverse group had been together for a period of time.

Some Level 2 diversity variables have also been linked in a positive fashion with some cognitive benefits in the decision-making process of groups. For example, Bantel and Jackson (1989) have linked diversity in educational background to increased innovativeness of a work group. Ancona and Caldwell (1992) have linked functional background to enhanced team performance. Whereas Level 3 diversity variables have been linked to issues pertaining to group cohesiveness (discussed below), which is linked to group performance, no studies were found demonstrating a direct relationship between values, attitudes, or personality diversity and group performance.

Diversity, Sexual Harassment, and Time

While not examined in the diversity literature, the relationship between diversity and sexual harassment has been the subject of investigation in the sexual harassment literature for a long time. The socio-cultural models predict patterns of sexual harassment based on diversity of gender (Level 1) and power/status diversity (Level 2) between men and women (e.g., Farley, 1978). Or, the harassment is the result of a socialization process which creates sets of gender based role expectations (Level 2 diversity) that men are to act aggressively and women are to act submissively (e.g., Terpstra & Baker, 1986). Or, the harassment is the result of men and women perceiving harassing behaviors differently as the result of possessing different gender-based attitudes (Level 3) towards women (e.g., Fitzgerald & Ormerod, 1991). In summary, the literature suggests that as diversity increases, the likelihood of sexual harassment tends to increase.

For the relationships among diversity, sexual harassment and time, the same logic could be applied as Harrison et al. applied to the relationships among diversity, cohesiveness, and time. The argument could apply here that as men and women look beyond the most readily observable differences and acquire more accurate information about one another's roles, status, beliefs, and values, the result could be a weakening of the positive relationship between diversity and sexual harassment. Thus, Figure 3.2 suggests that time moderates the relationship between diversity and sexual harassment as well as cohesiveness. Of course, this is an area in which specific empirical research could enlighten us greatly.

Group Cohesiveness, Sexual Harassment, and Group Performance

The research on group cohesiveness and group performance has generally shown that highly cohesive groups are more effective than less cohesive groups (e.g., Greene, 1989). However, the relationship is somewhat more complex than it might seem. Cohesiveness is both a cause and a result of group success. The closeness of a highly cohesive group reduces internal tensions and provides a supportive environment for the attainment of the group's goals. The achievement of the group's goals in turn reinforces the closeness of the group. Problems pertaining to performance can, however, arise if the group's norms are not consistent with high performance (see Robbins, 1996) or if the group suffers from "groupthink" (Janis, 1973) brought on by a misdirected desire for maintaining high cohesiveness.

Sexual harassment has been demonstrated to have a significant impact on the level of performance of those individuals experiencing the harassment. Victims often experience both psychological and physical maladies from harassment, resulting in sick leave, absenteeism, and turnover (e.g., Dansky & Kilpatrick, 1997). The financial impact of sexual harassment on an organization can also be significant. It has been reported that sexual harassment costs the typical firm $6.7 million per year in reduced productivity, increase absenteeism, and employee turnover (Wagner, 1992).

Work Group Diversity, the Organization, and the Individual

From a systems perspective one understands that the performance of the whole system depends, in part, on the performance of each of its subsystems. The degree of the impact that a particular work group has upon the whole organization depends upon the work group's centrality in the organization's workflow and the role the group plays in that workflow. The research of Ely (1994) suggests that the level of diversity of the senior level management team may be an important determinant of the acceptance of diversity throughout the lower levels of the organization. Milliken and Martins argued that when there is a lack of diversity at the top of an organization "not only does the organization lose possible cognitive benefits of having diversity in the membership of its management teams, but the organization may be systematically affecting the behavior of all members who observe the homogeneity at the top and react to it in ways that are detrimental to the achievement of organizational goals" (Milliken & Martins, 1996). Blau (1977) suggests that the perception of diversity may be a relative phenomenon. The sensitivity of an individual to diversity may be a function of the level of diversity for the organization as a whole. In other words, the more heterogeneous or diverse an organization, the less likely diversity will be associated with problems within a work group of that organization.

With respect to the individual, the literature is consistent in suggesting that Level 1 diversity has a negative impact on such individual outcomes as job satisfaction, absenteeism, and turnover (e.g., Jackson et al., 1991; Tsui et al., 1992; Wagner et al., 1984). The same has been demonstrated to be true for Levels 2 and 3 diversity variables (e.g., Meglino et al., 1989; Cummings et al., 1993). Tsui et al. (1992) found that diversity has a greater negative impact on whites than it does on non-whites and a greater negative impact on men than it does on women.

Conclusion

This paper has examined some important issues pertaining to the concept of diversity and understanding the impact of diversity on some important work-group, individual, and organizational outcomes. The most significant contribution this paper makes lies in the development of the typology for diversity variables and in the identification of the three levels of diversity: surface, working, and deep levels of diversity. Understanding the cross-level influence which these groups of diversity variables can have upon one another and the impact they have upon a number of other performance-related factors is crucial to the effective management of diversity within a system. Without proper management of diversity, its potentially negative consequences can and will outweigh the positive.

Future research might focus on testing various relationships posited in the behavioral model developed in this paper. While there is empirical support in the literature for the relationships delineated by the model, it has not been consistent. As these relationships become more clearly and accurately understood, more effective organizational strategies for leadership, total quality, human resource training, and communication within diverse groups may be developed. For effective management to take place, a precise understanding of organizational diversity is essential.

References

Ancona, D. G., & Caldwell, D. F. (1992). Demography and design: Predictors of new product team performance. *Organization Science, 13*, 468-494.

Ashforth, B. E., & Meal, F. (1989). Social identity theory and the organization. *Academy of Management Review, 14*, 20-39.

Bantel, K. A., & Jackson, S. E. (1989). Top management and innovations in banking: Does the composition of the tip team make a difference? *Strategic Management Journal, 10*, 107-124.

Blau, P. M. (1977). *Inequality and heterogeneity*. New York: Free Press.

Brewer, M. B., & Miller, N. (1984). Beyond the contact hypothesis: Theoretical perspectives on desegregation. In N. Miller & M. B. Brewer (Eds.), *Groups in contact: The psychology of desegregation*, pp. 281-302. Orlando, FL: Academic Press.

Byrne, D. (1971). *The attraction paradigm*. New York: Academic Press.

Cummings, A., Zhou, J., & Oldham, G. R. (1993). *Demographic differences and employee outcomes: Effects on multiple comparison groups*. Paper presented at the Annual Meeting of the Academy of Management, Atlanta, GA.

Cox, T. H., Lobel, A. A., & McLeod, P. L. (1991). Effects of ethnic group cultural differences on cooperative and competitive behavior on a group task. *Academy of Management Journal, 34*, 827-847.

Dansky, B. S., & Kilpatrick, D. G. (1997). Effects of sexual harassment. In W. O'Donohue, (Ed.) *Sexual Harassment: Theory, Research and treatment*, Needham Hights, MA: Allyn Bacon, pp. 152-174.

Deaux, K., & Major, B. (1987). Putting gender into context: An interactive model of gender-related behavior. *Psychological Review, 94*, 369-389.

DEOMI. (1987-1997). *Semi-annual race/ethnic/gender profile of the Department of Defense Forces, (active and reserve), the United States Coast Guard, and Department of Defense Civilians*. Statistical Series Pamphlets 1987-1997 prepared by the Research Directorate, Defense Equal Opportunity Management Institute, 740 O'Malley Road, Patrick AFB, Florida, 32925-3399.

Eagly, A. H. (1987). *Sex differences in social behavior: A social-role interpretation*. Hillsdale, NJ: Erlbaum.

Eagly, A. H., Makhijani, M. G., & Klonsky, B. G. (1992). Gender and the evaluation of leaders: A meta-analysis. *Psychological Bulletin, 111*, 3-22.

Elsass, P. M., & Graves, L. M. (1997). Demographic diversity in decision-making groups: The experiences of women and people of color. *Academy of Management Review, 22* (4), 946-973.

Ely, R. J. (1994). The effects of organizational demographics and social identity on relationships among professional women. *Administrative Science Quarterly, 39*, 203-238.

Farley, L. (1978). *Sexual shakedown: The sexual harassment of women on the job*. San Francisco: McGraw Hill.

Fitzgerald, L. F., & Ormerod, A. J. (1991). Perceptions of sexual harassment. *Psychology of Women Quarterly, 15*, 281-294.

Greene, C. N. (1989). Cohesion and productivity in work groups. *Small Group Behavior*, February, 70-86.

Harrison, D. A., Price, K.H. & Bell, M. P. (1998). Beyond rational demography: Time, and the effects of surface- and deep-level diversity on work group cohesion. *Academy of Management Journal, 41*, 96-107.

Heider, F. (1958). *The psychology of interpersonal relations*. New York: Wiley.

Hunt, James W. (1984). *The law of the workplace: Rights of employers and employees*. Washington, DC: The Bureau of National Affairs, Inc.

Jackson, S. E., Brett, J. F., Sessa, V. I., Cooper, D. M., Julin, J. A., & Peyronnin, K. (1991). Some differences make a difference: Individual dissimilarity and group heterogeneity as correlates of recruitment, promotions, and turnover. *Journal of Applied Psychology, 76*, 675-689.

Janis, I., (1973). *Victims of group think: A psychological study of foreign policy decisions and fiascoes*. Boston: Houghton Mifflin.

Jones, E. E. (1990). *Interpersonal perception*. New York: Freeman.

Johnston, William B., & Packer, Arnold E. (1987). *Workforce 2000: Work and workers in the 21st century*. Indianapolis, IN: Hudson Institute.

Judge, T. A., & Ferris, G. R. (1993). Social context of performance evaluation decisions. *Academy of Management Journal, 36*, 80-105.

Kantor, R. M. (1977). *Men and women of the corporation*. New York: Basic Books.
Lord, R. G., & Foti, R. J. (1986). Schema theories, information processing and organizational behavior. In H. P. Sims & D. A. Gioia (Eds.), *The Thinking Organization: Dynamics of Organizational Social Cognition*. San Francisco: Jossey-Bass.
McLeod, P. L., & Lobel, S. A. (1992). The effects of ethnic diversity on idea generation in small groups. *Academy of Management Best Paper Proceedings*, 227-231.
Meglino, B. M., Ravlin, E. C., & Adkins, C. L. (1989). A work values approach to corporate culture: A field test of the value congruence process and its relationship to individual outcomes. *Journal of Applied Psychology*, 74, 424-432.
Mish, F. C., Editor (1984). *Webster's Ninth New Collegiate Dictionary*. Springfield, MA: Merriam-Webster Inc.
Milliken, F. J., & Martins, L. L., (1996). Searching for common threads: Understanding the multiple effects of diversity in organizational groups. *Academy of Management Review*, 21, 402-433.
Richard, W., & D'Amico, C. D. (1997). *Workforce 2020: Work and workers in the 21st century*. Indianapolis, IN: Hudson Institute.
Robbins, S. P. (1996). *Organizational behavior: Concepts, controversies, applications*, 7th Edition. Englewood Cliffs, NJ: Prentice Hall.
Taylor, S. E., & Fiske, S. T., (1978). Salience, attention, and attribution: Top of the head phenomena. In L. Berkowitz (Ed.), *Advances in Experimental Social Psychology*, 11, pp. 249-288. New York: Academic Press.
Terborg, J. R., Castore, C., & DeNinno, J. A. (1976). A longitudinal field investigation of the impact of group composition on group performance and cohesion. *Journal of Personality and Social Psychology*, 34, 782-790.
Terpstra, D. E., & Baker, D. D. (1986). Psychological and demographic correlates of perception of sexual harassment. *Genetic, social and general psychology monographs*, 112, 459-478.
Tusi, A. S., Egan, T. D., & O'Reilly, C. A. (1992). Being different: Relational demography and organizational attachment. *Administrative Science Quarterly*, 37, 549-579.
Verkuyten, M. de Jong, W., & Masson, C. N. (1994). Job satisfaction among ethnic minorities in the Netherlands. *Applied Psychology: An International Review*, 42, 171-189.
Wagner, E. J. (1992). *Sexual harassment in the workplace: How to prevent, investigate, and resolve problems in your organization*. New York: AMACOM.
Wagner, G. W., Pfeffer, J., & O'Reilly, C. A. (1984). Organizational demography and turnover in top-management groups. *Administrative Science Quarterly*, 29, 171-189.
Watson, W. E., Kumar, K., & Michaelsen, L. K. (1993). Cultural diversity's impact on interaction process and performance: Comparing homogeneous and diverse task groups. *Academy of Management Journal*, 36, 590-602.
Wharton, A. S. (1992). The social construction of gender and race in organizations: A social identity and group mobilization perspective. In P. T. Tolbert & S. B. Bacharach (Eds.), *Research in the sociology of organizations*, 10, pp. 55-84. Greenwich, CT: JAI Press.

4

Religious Accommodation in the Military

Carlos C. Huerta and Schuyler C. Webb

Introduction

Religious liberty was one of the principles on which America was founded. This was partly due to the European immigrants' experience of religious persecution in Europe. There was such a wide diversity of religious groups in Colonial America that the Founding Fathers resisted favoring any particular religion. This resistance was partly due to the fact that no one religious group had enough political power to dominate permanently. It should be noted that the dominant faith was Protestant Christianity. To insure "domestic tranquility" the Founding Fathers wrote into the First Amendment to the U.S. Constitution *"Congress shall make no law respecting an establishment of religion, or prohibiting the free exercise thereof."*

Implementing the First Amendment has never been an easy task. The quest to understand the intent and meaning of these words has been prominent in many cases in state and Federal courts. The conflict between individual rights to religious freedom and the claims of the state has been part of American history and continues to be with us to the present.

Even though the military has attempted to integrate the individual's right of religious freedom into its mission-oriented environment since its inception before the American Revolution, the struggle between individual rights of religious expression and the concerns of the organization is perhaps more intense in the military than anywhere else in the society. What happens to *esprit de corps*, combat readiness, unit cohesiveness, and mission accomplishment when individual service members are permitted free exercise of their religion? Or what happens to the above if service members are not allowed the free exercise of religion?

The Department of Defense (DoD), the U.S. Congress, and the Courts, including the Supreme Court of the United States, have considered these questions. What has become clear in this litigation is that there are no hard and fast answers, as this paper will discuss. Specifically, this paper explores the social function of religion, religious diversity, America and religious liberty, religion in the military, including the tradition of religious support in the Armed Services, Federal Courts, religion and the military, and the DoD and religious accommodation.

Background

The Social Function of Religion

Religion is a universal experience and force of human life. It has been known to promote both good and evil. There have been many theories about the origin of religion. Yet, it seems that creating religion is something that human beings have always done. Some of the earliest archaeological digs reveal human artifacts used as religious symbols or in rituals. Some of the art works found in prehistoric caves in Europe, Asia, and Australia include wall paintings that were clearly intended to convey religious symbols and imagery.

Religion can be the major factor that gives a people, a culture, a nation, or a social movement, its distinct character and motivation to exist. Pakistan, for example, was founded independently from India so that the rights and interests of the Islamic minority in India could be protected from those of Hindus. Fifty years after its formation, national identity remains a problematic issue for Israel. Conceived as a Jewish homeland, religion plays a paramount role in individual as well as collective life. At the same time, because of prolonged security threats to the state, it has been a nation at arms and is being defended by mandatory conscription (Cohen, 1999).

Religious Diversity

In contemporary religious discussions there is a high level of interest in the implication of the diversity of religious beliefs on social stability. One can see the importance that religious issues have in current affairs and their impact on military strategy by just observing the turmoil in the former Yugoslavia. Here one sees that much of the fighting is divided on religious lines. Similar disputes are evident in Northern Ireland, the Middle East, Tibet, Nigeria, and other countries.

The five major faith groups commonly recognized by scholars and historians are Hindu, Buddhism, Judaism, Islam, and Christianity. These groups are the largest populated and most geographically diverse among currently practiced religions compared to many other smaller faith groups. Even within them, there is enormous diversity. The Buddhists have three major subdivisions: Mahayana, Iberavada, and Mantrayana (Wangu, 1993). The Jewish tradition in America has three major subgroups with a fourth one growing. They are the Orthodox, Conservative, and reform movements with the Reconstructionist quickly growing in significance (Morrison & Brown, 1991). Islam contains two major subdivisions, Shiite and Su'uni with others organized in America (Bulliet, 1994; Murphy, 1999). Within Christianity, there are three major subgroups: Roman Catholic, Eastern Orthodox, and Protestant. As for Protestantism, there are at least 65 different church bodies in America with membership of at least 60,000 people (U.S. Commission, 1986).

There are hundreds, if not thousands, of other religions that have been and are a part of the history of humankind. Though they do not have a large number of adherents, they are important to their followers. Some of these religions are limited to specific geographic areas or nations. Examples of this are Confucianism and Taoism in China, Shintoism in Japan, and Native-American religions in the United States.

Statistics enumerating adherents of the world's religious groups are only rough approximations (*Information*, 1986). Although Christianity keeps some detailed statistical records, the method of counting membership varies widely. Some religious organizations count only adults while others include infants and children. To further confuse matters, individuals may practice more than one religion, as in China (e.g., Confucianism, Taoism, and Buddhism) or in Japan where most are Buddhist and Shinto. In America, there is the Messianic Jewish faith where elements of Judaism and Christianity are practiced together. Therefore, demographic religious data must be reviewed carefully and only the broadest of conclusions should be made.

America and Religious Liberty

The military is but a microcosm within the macrocosm of American society. The military, therefore, reflects the attitudes and expectations of that society. Its service members come from a society with a rich heritage of religious faith and practice. The need for religious accommodation in the military comes from the society that the military defends. The conflicts between the military organization and the individual's need for religious accommodation can only come from a society that permits such conflicts to happen, that is, gives them the freedom to happen.

From the founding of the first colonies to the writing of the Constitution, religion played an important part in American life. Religious liberty, freedom of conscience, toleration (in the negative sense of just allowing to exist but not necessarily respecting) of dissenting faith and practice, and the reluctance to endorse any one single church organization because it would threaten the survival of others, characterized the unique direction American politics was taking on religious matters. The Founding Fathers decided that religion was important enough to be protected from the "wiles" of government. The motivation for writing the First Amendment is often misunderstood. Stephen L. Carter (1993) reminds us that:

> One must be careful not to misunderstand what the doctrine and the First Amendment that is said to embody it were designed to do. Simply put, the metaphorical separation of church and state originated in an effort to Protect religion from the state, not the state from religion. The religion clauses of the First Amendment were crafted to permit maximum freedom to the religious. (p. 105).

There were many factors that influenced this outcome in the writing of the Constitution and the civil practice, which provided for religious liberty. One factor was the need of some immigrants who came to America to escape religious persecution in Europe. Another factor was that there was a variety of church bodies so that no one body could muster enough permanent political power to be singled out as the one denomination to be solely sponsored and supported by the state. It is for this reason that, although the Church of England was established as the "official" church in nine of the colonies during the infancy of this nation, it did not take long for it to be quickly disestablished in the first states (Barret, 1982). Its disestablishment was accelerated because many of the colonists had experienced some of the abuse and conflicts arising from state-sponsored religion in Europe. It was also made easier after the Revolutionary War due to the perceived tie between Anglicanism and Great Britain.

Another important factor was "Enlightenment Thought" that held reason, education, tolerance, and compromise in high regard. This new perspective influenced such leaders as Thomas Jefferson, Thomas Paine, James Madison, and Benjamin Franklin. Dissenting opinions and freedom of conscience were generally widely respected. Along with "Enlightenment Thought" came the principle of religious tolerance and moderation of religious practice and conviction. Some of the early political leaders were Deists, who believed in a Supreme Being, but were not bound by church teachings or dogma. Some writers who influenced Jefferson, like Thomas Paine and John Milton, were also critical of the church and clergy.

It should not be assumed that toleration meant respect and equality. Many Protestant dissenters, i.e., Methodists, Presbyterians, and Baptists suffered various penalties and persecutions. The Jewish and Catholic faiths were not recognized as legitimate faiths in many of the colonies (Peterson, 1994). There was strong anti-Catholic bias in all of the colonies except Rhode Island and Pennsylvania (Barret, 1982). Even Jefferson was alleged to be an infidel by some of his detractors and was claimed to have a hostile agenda against Christianity. Despite this, many colonies made attempts at protecting the religious liberties of their various Protestant constituents.

Several colonies, for example Pennsylvania, Rhode Island, and Maryland, included in their charters general provisions for religious tolerance and privileges. Although some articles of confederation, such as those of the Massachusetts Bay Colony, were somewhat restrictive due to their Puritan influence, they too addressed religious issues of faith and practice. The Constitution of North Carolina maintained that "all persons shall be at liberty to exercise their own mode of worship" (Boorstin, 1966). William Penn widely advertised the attractiveness of his colony of Pennsylvania, which was founded on religious tolerance. His "Frame of Government," written in 1682, guaranteed religious freedom to all "who confess and acknowledge the one almighty and Eternal God" (Boorstin, 1958).

In spite of these general provisions, there were serious incidents of religious persecution in colonial America. There was considerable conflict between the Quakers of Pennsylvania and the Puritans of other colonies. Quakers were beaten, imprisoned, and expelled.

As immigration increased, other European religious traditions were introduced. Many dissenting religious groups who had objected to established, state-sponsored, churches came to America.

Connecticut in 1818 and Massachusetts in 1833 repealed compulsory tax support of churches. For the Founding Fathers, separation of church and state did not imply indifference toward religion but reflected a determination to protect any individual faith group from being dominated by any other within the colonies. "Perhaps the overriding factor in deciding the general issue in the United States, however, was the practical consideration that the extreme multiplicity of sects in the country meant that in the long run the embodiment of any one of them, or even a combination, was not politically feasible" (Magill, 1975). Pluralism was already an operating factor, which was to influence political compromise. It was a political attempt to protect the wide variety of religious practices in colonial America. The effort tried to avoid placing any one religious organization in a favored position over another. As a result this helped to diminish the abuse, taxation, discrimination, corruption, and persecution often associated with state religion.

Contemporary Religious Diversity

The history of religious plurality in the twentieth century has prepared America for the future of religious accommodation and policy. Should recent sociological trends hold, and if predictions are to be believed, there will be a continuing increase in religious diversity in America. The recent influx of Asians from Vietnam, Cambodia, and Korea, as well as Cuban and Haitian exiles and others from the Caribbean Islands has increased religious diversity. Asian immigrants have strengthened Buddhist, Taoist, and Confucianist practice, as well as introduced folk religions to America. Due to the immigration of Cuban exiles into Florida in the last two decades, unfamiliar religious practices, such as Santeria, have come into the national consciousness. From the followers of Reverend Sun Myung Moon (i.e., Moonies) to the Rajneeshi and Bah'is, from the Church of Scientology to Wicca to Rastafarians, there have been newly formed religions of great diversity (Stuttaford, 1999). Between 1965 and 1970, over 120 newly formed religious groups were founded in America alone (Melton, 1977). In 1990, membership in "miscellaneous" religious groups in America (i.e., not Christian, Jewish, or Buddhist) was at over 157,000 (U.S. Bureau, 1994).

Moreover, in the past five decades, the diversity of religions in western societies has significantly increased. There has been a dramatic increase in the number of new religions; some of them newly imported to the West, principally from Asia. The earlier religious pluralism, which was almost entirely confined to variations within Christianity, has been extended to embrace new conceptions of spirituality and new movements from other religious traditions. The orientations, teachings, practices and patterns of these various religions —whether indigenous or imported—are widely diverse, and often entirely different from the corresponding characteristics of traditional churches or sects. Toleration for which they are certainly eligible has not been easily extended to them. Thus, tolerance is the continuing challenge and responsibility of a democratic society.

Religion in the Military

The Tradition of Support of Religion in the Armed Forces

Famous military leaders, including Napoleon and military tactician Carl von Clausewitz, have spoken of the importance of troop morale in winning battles and eventually the war. Religion may indeed be one critical factor that determines the outcome of combat. Troops that are convinced of the ultimate justice of their cause may be more likely to fight with commitment and determination.

The American military has always been supportive of religion. For example, General George Washington provided for his troops to be served by clergy during the Revolutionary War. The Army Chaplain Corps predates the Declaration of Independence. As early as 1775 the Second Article of Navy Regulations stated that "Commanders of ships in the thirteen United Colonies are to take care that Divine services be performed." Not only did the Army of the Revolution allow the free exercise of religion; it actually encouraged religious worship. Many of the leaders of the Revolutionary War were devout men who were convinced that faith in God would vindicate their cause.

The all-volunteer force is another factor driving religious accommodation. In order to make military life attractive to recruits some of their civilian activities, such as church attendance, are encouraged to continue in the military environment. Military service may appear more acceptable to parents and families if opportunities for worship, religious education, and pastoral counseling are available to their children, should they need or want them.

The religious composition of the U.S. Armed Services, depicted in the Joint Survey Study of Religious Matters, is very diverse. Table 4.1 provides statistical information, and as with all such tables one must be careful in drawing all but the most general conclusions. For example, it would be wrong to assume that those service members who marked "no religious preference" are not religious. In fact, many of those service members are very religious and attend a variety of services but just chose not to be identified with any one group. On the other hand, there are service members that pick the religious preference of a parent or other loved one, but in fact, they have no personal religious preference.

Table 4.1
Armed Forces Religious Demographics-June 1995

Faith Group	Number	Percent
PROTESTANT		
Specified Protestant		
Episcopal	15,494	0.97%
Baptist	337,097	21.19%
Lutheran	52,698	3.31%
Methodist	59,939	3.77%
Presbyterian	20,175	1.27%
Other	87,604	5.51%
Christian Scientist	1,808	0.11%
Jehovah's Witness	501	0.03%
Latter-day Saints	16,093	1.01%
Reorganized	423	0.03%
Seventh-day Adventists	4,317	0.27%
Friends (Quaker)	422	0.03%
Salvation Army	270	0.02%
Protestant (No Preference)	77,113	4.85%
Christian (No Preference)	77,412	4.87%
ROMAN CATHOLIC	366,252	23.02%
EASTERN ORTHODOX	1,249	0.08%
JEWISH		
Orthodox	26	0.00%
Conservative	11	0.00%
Reform	25	0.00%
Non-Specified	4,404	0.28%
OTHER RELIGIONS		
Buddhist	2,010	0.13%
Hindu	336	0.02%
Muslim	3,112	0.20%
Other (Bhai, Druid, Wicca, etc.)	7,526	0.47%
NO PREFERENCE	290,417	18.25%
ATHEIST	1,230	0.08%
UNKNOWN	163,079	10.25%

A review of the table shows the percentage of "other" religious groups, not Christian, is just 1.1 percent of the force. As a result, one might think that the question of religious accommodation is blown out of proportion. It was the intention of the Founding Fathers that the rights of the few should be protected and it is that vision that makes this country so unique.

Chaplaincies of all the Services take their duty of providing religious support to all service members very seriously (Fuentes, 1998; Jordan, 1997). They do not adopt the attitude, and neither do aware commanders, that one's religious accommodation is only as important as the numbers of one's faith group in the service. Such an attitude will only lead to more adjudication and a breakdown in service member welfare and morale.

Federal Courts, Religion, and the Military

The Federal courts have maintained that commanders and military regulations can have greater authority than individual rights and conscience when the military mission is involved. In *Parker v. Levy* [*417 U.S. 733* (1974)] the court ruled that although "members of the military are not exempted from the protection granted by the First Amendment, the different character of the military community and of the military mission requires different application of these protections." Even where civil rights or constitutional factors are considered, the courts have accepted the right of the Armed Services to reasonably limit religious practice due to reasons of military necessity, mission requirements, command authority, discipline, obedience, etc. The Court, in *Schlesinger v. Councilman* [*420 U.S.* 738 (1975)], decided that in order to perform its vital role "the military must insist upon respect for duty and discipline without counterpart in civilian life."

Although there is no Constitutional right to religious exemption from military service, Congress has allowed for conscientious objection. In *United States v. Seeger* [380 U.S. 163 (1965)], the U.S. Supreme Court allowed for the validity of a claim of conscientious objection by a person not a member of a traditional pacifist groups, such as Quakers or Mennonites. On the issue of selective conscientious objection i.e., opposition to a particular war, the Supreme Court held that the First Amendment provided no such protection.

In an important case for civil rights and constitutional appeal for military members, *Chapel v. Wallace* [103 S. Ct. 2362 (1983)], the

U.S. Supreme Court held that "enlisted military personnel may not maintain a suit to recover damages from a superior officer for alleged constitutional violations." Due to the unique structure of the military and its special status, the U.S. Supreme Court "has long realized two systems of justice, to some extent parallel: one for civilians and one for military personnel." Even where alleged Constitutional violations are involved; the courts will not consider efforts on the part of military personnel to recover damages from superiors.

In summary, the Supreme Court has rendered several conclusions on both sides of the argument/discussion. On one hand, it clearly states that the service member is not exempt from the First Amendment right of free exercise of religion. It also states that this right at times can be reasonably limited due to military necessity. On the other hand, the Court is not saying what military necessity is and under what conditions military commanders can evoke military necessity to limit the free exercise of religion. Currently, that interpretation and decision is determined by the commander.

Goldman v. Weinberger Case

One of the most outstanding examples of how religious practice and a commander's discretion can come into conflict is the *Goldman v. Weinberger case [106 S. Ct 1310* (1986)]. This case involved an Air Force officer, Captain S. Simcha Goldman, who was an ordained orthodox rabbi that observed the Jewish tradition of keeping his head covered at all times. His challenge to Air Force regulations was based on First Amendment principles.

Captain Goldman was working as a psychologist at March Air Force Base Mental Health Clinic in California. He had earned a doctoral degree sponsored by an Air Force scholarship program. For several years he wore the Jewish skullcap, the yarmulke, when in military uniform and on duty at the hospital. During these years, his commanders, using their discretion, believed that military necessity did not require them to limit his free exercise of religion. While testifying for a court martial, his religious practice was brought to the attention of a new commander, and he was ordered to remove it while in military uniform and on duty in the clinic. The practice of wearing the yarmulke while in uniform was determined by his commander to be a violation of Air Force Regulation 35-10, which states, in part, that "headgear will not be worn while indoors except by armed security police in the performance of their duties" (Department of the Air Force, 1987). The commander interpreted Captain Goldman's yarmulke, worn for religious purposes, to be the equivalent of military headgear and ordered Goldman to comply with the regulation. Goldman filed suit in Federal court claiming his constitutional rights under the First Amendment had been violated.

The Air Force argued that "the traditional outfitting of personnel in standardized uniforms encourages the subordination of personal preferences and identities in favor of the overall mission." Goldman argued that his religion required him to wear the yarmulke, it was widely practiced in society at large, no one had objected to the practice, and the Constitution guaranteed individual rights freely to pursue religious acts.

The Court record was quite divided on the issue. The Federal District Court in Washington, DC, ruled in Goldman's favor and enjoined the Air Force from enforcing its regulation. Later, the U.S. Court of Appeals reversed the decision "on the grounds that the Air Force's strong interest in discipline justified the strict enforcement of its uniform dress requirement." The U.S. Supreme Court, in a 5-4 decision, affirmed the Court of Appeals decision supporting Air Force policy and the commander's order.

The Court pointed to important differences between military life and civilian status. "To accomplish its mission the military must foster instinctive obedience, unity, commitment and *esprit de corps*." Citing earlier court opinion, it is noted that the essence of military service "is the subordination of the desires and interests of the individual to the needs of the Service."

In a dissenting opinion, it was argued that the Court had "abdicated its role as principle expositor of the Constitution and protector of individual liberties in favor of credulous deference to unsupported assertions of military necessity." Justice Sandra Day O'Connor along with Justice Thurgood Marshall argued that the principles of a free exercise claim should also apply to the military context. The military, they said, should be required to demonstrate that it would be substantially harmed by granting the exception." In their opinion, "no test for Free Exercise claims in the military context is even articulated, much less applied."

The Goldman case raises many unanswered questions. From an equal opportunity perspective, the question looms whether or not institutional discrimination was involved. Was it covert bias toward Jews that affected the outcome of the case? Are our institutions, mili-

tary courts so predisposed to favoring a Christian orientation or secular position that such a visible sign of Jewish reverence is depreci-
ated and denied expression? Did Goldman display of a Jewish religious symbol touch deep emotional resistance? Was it viewed as a
flagrant display, or as the Supreme Court notes, "an eloquent rebuke
to the ugliness of anti-Semitism," rather than seen as a deeply held
practice of reverence?

The Court had noted that Goldman's "devotion to his faith is readily
apparent." Consequently, are the issues of 'uniformity' and *esprit de
corps* pretext for attitudes and prejudice not favorably disposed to
Jewish tradition? The perceived need for conformity may detract
from the more serious issue of bias against religious minorities. Justice Stevens, who was in the majority, noted that there was reason to
believe that the actions against Captain Goldman had retaliatory
motives (Drinan, 1986). Many legal observers were perplexed at the
motives for bringing such a case to the Supreme Court:

> It was hoped in 1981 that the Pentagon would accept the resolution of the issue by the
> trial court. But, for reasons that are not entirely clear, the Defense Department decided
> to spend an immense amount of energy, time and money in vindicating its decision to
> prevent an Orthodox Jew in the military from wearing a yarmulke while in uniform.
> (Drinan, 1986).

Arguing against the uniformity claim is the fact that military uniform guidelines do not strictly forbid any and all individual variation. There are special provisions for watches, rings, bracelets, non-
issue shoes, sunglasses, and women's earrings. The size, number,
composition, and appearance of these items are restricted, although
religious symbols on any of then are allowed. However, this practice simple begs the question: Is the special provision for personal
jewelry more important than the wearing of religious apparel or the
religion rights of the First Amendment?

The issues argued in the Goldman case did not end with the Supreme Court. In 1984, Congress introduced legislation that would
have allowed military members to wear "unobtrusive religious headgear" on a test period basis. This action was withdrawn when the
Department of Defense Authorization Act of 1985 directed:

> In order to promote the free expression of religion by members of the Armed Forces to
> the greatest extent possible consistent with the requirements of military discipline, the
> group to examine ways to minimize the potential conflict between the interests of
> members of the Armed Forces in abiding by their religion tenets and the military interest
> in maintaining discipline.

The study group's efforts culminated with the issuance of the Joint Service Study on Religious Matters in March 1985. Congress again considered the issue in 1986. A bill was introduced which would allow wearing religious apparel for members of the Armed Forces in uniform if "the item is neat and conservative" and if it "is part of the religious faith practiced by the member." The bill was adopted by the House of Representatives and was narrowly defeated in the Senate by a 51-49 vote. Identical legislation was considered in 1987 by the 100th Congress and passed. According to the sponsor, Senator Frank Lautenberg of New Jersey, "Our citizens in uniform should not be deprived of their basic constitutional rights, such as the free exercise of religion, the minute they enter the military."

The current uniform policy of the Services allows for the wearing of the yarmulke and other religious apparel. The current regulation allows the service members to wear religious apparel during and outside of worship while in uniform. There are specific restrictions as each service has its own regulations, conditions and details (Department of the Air Force, 1987). The Army, for example, allows soldiers to wear religious apparel in uniform as long as it does not endanger health, safety, or mission requirements and is not visible or apparent. If it must be visible, then, among other requirements, the rule of neat and conservative applies and it must not interfere with the proper wearing of the uniform or is temporarily or permanently attached to it (Department of the Army, 1992).

Chaplains may wear any required religious apparel in the performance of religious support to service members. Obviously these are general guidelines that cannot apply to all possible military situations. The commanders must use their discretion and current military policy in interpreting them.

The ramifications of the Goldman case have extended to other religious minorities. Muslim service members who wish to observe their religious tradition of keeping their head covered have that opportunity. In the past the Department of the Army had permitted Sikhs to wear turbans while in military uniform but this practice had been reversed. Starting in 1958, Sikhs drafted into the Army had been allowed to wear beards and turbans. In 1974, on a case-by-case basis, they were granted an exception to wear beards and turbans even if they enlist or reenlist. This policy was terminated in 1981

(Hirst, 1981). Those who were in under the old policy were allowed to continue wearing beards and turbans, but since 1981 no practicing Sikhs have entered the military. In 1994, the Senate Armed Services Committee ordered the Pentagon to review its policy on beards and turbans as it relates to the Sikhs. There are observers that believe that the intent of having Pentagon officials' review its policy is to have them change it (Hudson, 1994).

What is obvious is that the conflict between religious liberty and military necessity has had an active past and promises to have a more interesting future. Because these issues are not clear cut the courts and Congress are extremely divided. There are no good or bad people here, rather only people deeply concerned about faithfully carrying out their public duty. When the Pentagon resisted Congress in changing the law, it was not doing so to deny its members their rights under the First Amendment. It did it because it feared that allowing service members to religious articles while in uniform could lessen the effectiveness of the fighting force. Congress thought otherwise and the present law reflects that.

The Department of Defense and Religious Accommodation

Policy

On February 3, 1988, DoD Directive 1300.17, *Accommodation of Religious Practice within the Armed Services*, was issued. This recognized that "a basic principle of our nation is free exercise of religion" and that "the Department of Defense places a high value on the rights of service members of the Armed Forces to observe the tenets of their respective religions," Requests for accommodation of religious practices should be approved by commanders when accommodation will not have an adverse impact on military readiness, unit cohesion, or discipline" (Carter, 1993).

Through the directive, goals were established in the following eight areas for accommodation: (1) worship services, holy days, and Sabbaths; (2) separate rations, diets and food supplements at sea or in the field; (3) waivers for immunization; (4) inclusion of information on various religious traditions in Chaplains', Judge Advocate Generals', and Commanders' courses; (5) statements advising potential enlistees, or reenlistees on religious accommodations; (6) conditions when religious items that are not visible may be worn with the uniform; (7) conditions when religious items may be visibly worn with the uniform; and (8) religious apparel Chaplains may wear while performing religious support for the service member and his or her family.

Because of the diversity in commands in military, the directive recognizes the need for individualized consideration and rests the decisions on religious accommodations on the shoulders of the commander. The directive identifies five factors that commanders should consider when dealing with requests for religious accommodation. There are the following: (1) What is the importance of the military requirements? (2) What is the importance of the request to the individual? (3) What is the cumulative effect of repeated, similar accommodations? (4) What alternatives are available to meet the request? and (5) What have past practices been for similar requests, whether of a religious nature or not?

An important feature of the directive is the stipulation that matters of religious accommodation, which cannot be resolved, should be handled administratively. Judicial procedure should only be considered when there are violations of articles of the *Uniform Code of Military Justice*. According to the directive reassignment, reclassification or separation may still be necessary to resolve the conflict between the individual's religious belief and military necessity (Department of Defense, 1988).[1]

Most requests for accommodation fall into four major categories: worship and Sabbath observance, diet, medical, and religious apparel. Worship, Sabbath observance, and religious days are recognized as being essential to practicing believers. Most religious organizations have some kind of worship or ritual requirement. The Army, Navy, and Air Force have made provisions for Sunday worship services. Currently, the military chaplancy, dedicated to the principle of performing or providing religious support to all service members, is making provisions to meet worship requirements of other faith groups that do not worship on Sunday. Among these are Muslim, Jewish, and Seventh-Day Adventists. The command should recognize this diversity of worship days and do what it can, within the bounds of mission, to accommodate their service members who want to fulfill tenets of their faith on these days. Duty rosters may schedule members of these religions on their Sabbath. However, in many instances, with command approval, these individuals may swap duty with others in order to observe their religious days.

Several religious groups prohibit eating certain foods or require that they are prepared in a specific manner. For example, Muslims, Jews, and Seventh-Day Adventists follow prohibitions against eating pork. The DoD Joint Study Group found that "the overwhelming majority of these needs can be met in garrison with the Services current food preparation and serving procedures" (Department of Defense, 1985). For practicing Muslims and Jews, for example, whose needs cannot be met by current food preparation procedures, separate rations can be a solution. Dietary accommodation must be intentionally planned for these members assigned to the field, at isolated posts, or on sea duty. In the past, service members on extended field or sea duty who wanted to practice the dietary laws of their faith had to bring their own food. In another example, during Ramandan, when Muslims refrain from food and drink for a month during daylight hours, military commanders are urged to accommodate their fasting service members—excusing them in some cases, from rigorous physical exercise. The commanders also allow flexible work hours so Muslims can participate in *iftar*, the traditional fast-ending meal, and attend the social gatherings and community prayers that usually follow (Murphy, 1999).

Presently, due to the requirements of the DoD Chaplain's Board, multi-faith MRE (meals ready to eat) are being planned for distribution to military depots in 1996. These rations are not expected to be distributed to field units until 1999. However, since 1995, some units have ordered Multi-Faith Meals (MFM) through appropriate supply channels to meet the dietary needs of their soldiers and sailors (see Drinan, 1986).

Medical issues may present a greater concern to commanders due to their possible effect on their unit's readiness status and overseas deployment. Christian Scientists, among several religions, have prohibitions against immunization, blood transfusions, and surgery. In peacetime, garrison, or home port situations, this may not present a problem because all military Services presently accept some waivers from immunizations. In a combat scenario, however, denial of blood transfusions and surgery could seriously deteriorate unit strength. There may be a problem with withholding immunizations for personnel deployed overseas. Many countries allow admission only to inoculated individuals.

Since DoD Directive 1300.17, wearing religious apparel has been less of a concern. Some groups require the wearing of religious articles or clothing. Some groups require they be worn under the outer garments and not visible. Those that are visibly worn must conform to the current service regulations and guidelines.

In 1993, new legislation was passed by Congress that might have an impact on religious accommodations in the military in the future, Public Law 103-141, *Religious Freedom Restoration Act of 1993*. The law states that its purpose is "Creating a statutory prohibition against government action substantially burdening the exercise of religion." An important addition to the law is the concept of compelling governmental interest. What this means and how it will impact the DoD and the military is unclear.

Practical Considerations for Implementation

The unique task for a commander is to balance the needs of the military with the needs of the individual. A reasonable, common sense approach is required, which supports both the conscientious expression of religion, and the requirements of military discipline and order. The intent of the DoD directive and military regulations is to minimize potential conflict.

When commanders receive a request for religious accommodation they should determine exactly what is being requested. It should be established that the request is based on religious conviction or belief and not personal whim or individual preference. Part of the inquiry should be to determine to which faith group the individual belongs. It would then be helpful to establish the main tenets of that particular religious body. It should be noted that the individual's own convictions are the primary standard or basis of deciding the case, not just the teachings and guidelines of the religious organization.

Further, the commander should not judge or evaluate the religious belief even though the conviction held may be very different from anything he or she has been exposed to or believes. It is very important that there be no differentiation between those members of a large or generally accepted faith or tradition and those of a small or little known faith or tradition such as Wicca (Stuttaford, 1999). The principles established in the DoD Directive point to the abiding respect that is to be held for persons of religious convictions. Their lifestyles and beliefs are to be taken seriously and their requests are to be handled as directed by DoD within appropriate service regulations.

Obviously, commanders are not in a position to grant every request for religious accommodation. The requirements of the unit mission, the environment of operations, and popuar opinions determine the amount of flexibility that can reasonably be allowed. The chaplain, as the commander's staff officer on religious and ethical matters, should be used as a resource in the commander's information gathering and decision-making process.

One might think that on the battlefield, where the commander is most restricted to support the service member's religious needs, religious accommodation would fall by the wayside. The fact of the matter is that battlefield commanders have understood the importance of religiously accommodating the fighting service member. As a consequence, they have worked very hard and have overcome tremendous obstacles to ensure that the religious needs of all their service members are met. Any improvement that needs to be made is usually at a base, post, or station.

All services have established procedures for commanders to follow in handling requests for religious accommodations for their members. In the Army, for example, commanders can refer to the Committee for the Review of Accommodation of Religious Practices for advice in difficult cases. When soldiers receive unfavorable decisions they may request an appeal by this review committee (Department of the Army, 1993). In any Service, individuals who believe they have been religiously discriminated against may submit a formal equal opportunity complaint (Department of the Air Force, 1994; Department of the Army, 1988; Department of the Navy, 1989).

Common sense is to be used in any decision. In addition, compromise, moderation, and reasonable tolerance on the part of all parties concerned is desirable. What is just, fair, and practical are to be the standards for decision within the context of the mission. Understandably, the needs of individuals are subordinated to the needs of the military organization as a whole. But as most successful commanders know, service members' equal opportunity, welfare and morale are critical to mission readiness and accomplishment.

Note

1.   The Air Force and the Army have issued guidelines for implementing the DoD Directive, AFI 52-101, (Chaplain Service Responsibilities and Procedures, November 1994) and DA. "Pamphlet 60175, (Accommodating Religious Practices,

September 22, 1993. The Department of the Navy has guidance in OPNAVINST 173 0. 1B (Religious Ministries in the Navy, November 23, 1987) and SECNAVINST 17318 (Accommodations of Religious Practice, May 23, 1988).

References

Barrett, D. (1982). *World christian encyclopedia*. New York: Oxford.

Boorstin, D. J. (Ed.). (1966). *An American primer*. Chicago: University of Chicago Press.

Boorstin, D. J. (1958). *The Americans: The colonial experience*. New York: Random House.

Bulliet, F. (1994). *Islam: The view from the edge*. New York: Columbia University Press.

Carter, S. L. (1993). *The culture of disbelief*. New York: Basic Books.

Cohen, S. (1999). *The scroll or the sword? Dilemmas of religion and military service in Israel*. Newark, NJ: Harwood Academic.

Department of Defense. (1988, February 3). *Accommodation of religious practices within the military services*. DoD Directive 000.17.

Department of Defense. (1985, March). *Joint service study of religious matters*. Washington, DC.

Department of the Air Force. (1994, November). *Chaplain service responsibilities and procedures*. AFI 52-101.

Department of the Air Force. (1987. February 1). *Dress and personal appearance of Air Force personnel*. AFR 35-10 (CI). (Note: This regulation has been superseded by AFI 36-2903, July 20, 1994 of the same name.)

Department of the Air Force. (1994, August 15). *Social actions program*. AFI 36-2701.

Department of the Army. (1993, September 22). *Accommodating religious practices*. Pamphlet No. (500-75).

Department of the Army. (1988, March 31). *Army command policy*. AR 600-20.

Department of the Army. (1989, August 31). *Chaplain activities in the United States Army*. AR 165-1.

Department of the Army. (1988, October 7). *Immunization and chemoprophylaxis*. AR 40-562. (Note that this is also Department of the Air Force 48-110 and Department of the Navy, NAVMEDCOMINST 6230.3).

Department of the Army. (1992, September 1). *Wear and appearance of Army uniforms and insignia*. AR 670-1.

Department of the Navy. (1988, May 23). *Accommodations of religious practices*, SECNAVINST 1730.8.

Department of the Navy. (1989, April 13). *Navy equal opportunity*. OPNAVINST 5354.1C.

Department of the Navy. (1987, November 23). *Religious ministries in the Navy*. OPNAVINST 1730.1B.

Department of the Navy. (1991, April 19). *United States Navy uniform regulations*. NAVPERS 155665H.

Drinan, R. F. (1986, July 5). The Supreme court, religious freedom and the yarmulke. *America*, p. 9.

Fuentes, G. (1998, December 7). Chaplains increase leadership role. *Navy Times*, p. 18.

Folk, T. R. (1986, summer). Religion and the military. *Military Law Review*, Vol. 113.

GI chow revamped religiously: New MREs developed for Jews, Muslims, Hindus and vegetarians. (1992, March 23). *The Washington Post*.

Hirst, D. (1981, September 7). Sikhs now in keep beards; others won't. *Army Times*.

Hudson, N. (1994, July 4). Senate supports Sikhs seeking service in Army. *Navy Times*.

Information please almanac, atlas and yearbook 1986. (1986). Boston: Houghton Mifflin Co.

James, W. (1936). *Varieties of religious experience*. New York: Modem Library, Inc.

Jordan, B. (1997, April 28). Air Force orders religious tolerance. *Air Force Times*, p. 4.

Kotkin, J. (1994). *Tribes: How race, religion, and identity determine success in the new global economy*. New York: Random House.

Magill F. N. (Ed.). (1975). *Great events from history, American series, Vol 1*. Englewood Cliffs, NJ: Salem Press.

Melton, G. J. (1977). *A directory of religious bodies in the United States*. New York: Garland Publishing, Inc.

Message, CDR (1995). USAQMC&S, ATSM-CES-OK 101955Z MAR 95, Subject: Multi-Faith menus/meals.

Morrison, M. & Brown, S. F. (1991). *Judaism: World religions*. New York: Facts on File, Inc.

Moseley, J. G. (1981). *A cultural history of religion in America*. Westport, CT: Greenwood Press.

Murphy, C. (1999, Dec 21). Military, muslim life meld on U.S. bases. *The Washington Post*, pp. B1, B6.

Peterson, M. D. (1994, December). Jefferson and religious freedom. *The Atlantic Monthly*, pp. 112-121.

Religious articles of wear again before Congress. (1987, February 2). *Air Force Times*.

Schwarzkopf, H. N. (1992). *It doesn't take a hero*. New York: Bantam Books.

Social Aspects of Religion. (1986). *The New Encyclopedia Britannica, Vol 26*. Chicago: Encyclopedia Britannica, pp. 538-547.

Stuttaford, A. (1999, Jul 12). Strange brew. *National Review*, pp. 32-34.

The study and classifications of religions. (1986). *The New Encyclopedia Britannica, Vol 26*. Chicago: Encyclopedia Britannica, pp. 548-567.

U.S. Bureau of the Census. (1994). *Statistical abstract of the United States 1994* (114th ed.). Washington, DC: Government Printing Office.

U.S. Commission on Civil Rights. (1986, January). *Bigotry and violence in Idaho*. Washington, DC: Government Printing Office.

U.S. Congress. (1987, January 6). *Congressional record*, Senate BM 248.

Wangu, M. B. (1993). *Buddhism: World religions*. New York: Facts on File, Inc.

5

Personality and Leadership in Diverse DoD Workgroups and Teams

Robert M. McIntyre and Judith L. Johnson

Introduction

This chapter examines diverse teams within the Department of Defense (DoD). It is intended to encourage the reader to explore the denotations and connotations of the term, diversity, as it applies to leading DoD teams. We propose that personality adds an important dimension to the diversity construct and report a study that exemplifies several ways in which personality can be examined within diverse teams.

Diversity Defined

One of the most common themes in the diversity literature involves its definition. Originally, the word served as a way to communicate information on the variation of race, sex, religion, and national origin (RSRNO) characteristics among workers within an organization. As researchers explored the deeper meanings of the term, it became clear that diversity might refer to qualities associated with or attributed to RSRNO characteristics. The "valuing diversity" movement led to further implicit (unstated) refinements of the term and possibly to greater confusion as to its definition.

Progress has been made of late on the definition. Larkey (1996) presents a cogent basis for understanding diversity which implicitly acknowledges the role of individual differences. She begins with the assumption that the "core" idea of the diversity construct is culture. From this premise, she posits that diversity refers to perceptible characteristics associated with sets of values, beliefs, and attitudes reflecting a worker's cultural status. In other words, certain cultures share values, beliefs, and attitudes; RSRNO characteristics are the outward signs of an individual's culture. Larkey goes on to present a two-faceted definition of diversity:

> For purposes of understanding current theory, diversity is defined as (a) differences in worldviews or subjective culture, resulting in potential behaviors that may have oral differences among cultural groups, ...and (b) differences in identity among group members in relation to other groups. (p. 465).

This definition implies several things. First, certain cultures and world views lead to behaviors that may differ from behaviors associated with other world views and cultures. Second, individual workers identify with these world views and cultures such that their behaviors (particularly those unique to the world views and culture) are emotionally charged as their own. The emotional element of these behaviors implies that focusing on, referencing, criticizing, or commenting on them by other work group members could be inferred as a denigration of the culture that drives them. This can be illustrated by considering teenagers as having their own culture or world view. The adult who criticizes or even comments on some of their choices in apparel (i.e., dyed hair, baggy trousers, body piercing, tattoos, etc.) creates a chasm between them and the culture that is difficult to cross once created.

In their elaboration of work groups, McGrath, Berdahl, & Arrow (1995) lay the foundation for the effect of diversity on work groups. These authors take a similar but slightly broader view of diversity than is common among "valuing diversity advocates" and other authorities on the topic. They point out that a work group's composition can be relatively homogeneous or heterogeneous on more than just demographic characteristics. They go on to describe the following classes of characteristics where group members may show heterogeneity:

1.   Demographic attributes (DEM) that are socially meaningful in the society in which the organization is embedded (e.g., age, race, ethnicity, gender, sexual orientation, physical status, religion, and education).

2.   Task-related knowledge, skills, and abilities (KSA).

3.   Values, beliefs, and attitudes (VBA).

4.   Personality, cognitive and behavioral styles (PCB).

5.   Status in the work group's embedding organization (ORG; e.g., organizational rank, occupational specialty, departmental affiliation, and tenure. (p.23)

A comparison of the Larkey definition of diversity and the implicit definition by McGrath and his colleagues points to one fundamental difference. In the Larkey perspective—which characterizes the approach by most serious researchers in the field—culture is at the heart of diversity issue. Differences in RSRNO characteristics are essentially reflective of cultural differences that lead to different behaviors. The McGrath et al. perspective indicates that culture is only one of the individual difference characteristics that an individual worker brings to the work group. Ultimately, however, McGrath et al. embrace an "integrative multicultural approach" to explain how demographic diversity in work groups leads to differences in member behavior, group interaction, and task performance. This approach hearkens back to Larkey's underlying assumptions in the sense that it discusses demographic attributes as implying diverse cultural identities. These cultural identities reflect "differential sociohistorical experiences and hence are likely to be associated with actual differences in expertise (KSA), in values (VBA), and in habits (PCB)" (p. 30). In addition, cultural identities are associated with certain behavioral tendencies and correspond to differences in social power.

Personality characteristics such as those represented in the Five Factor Model (FFM) of personality add a fruitful dimension to determinants of workgroup and team processes and are explicitly included in the McGrath et al. (1995) definition of diversity. For example, the factor of Agreeableness dictates the levels of competition versus cooperation experienced and exhibited by an individual, and this certainly influences teamwork. Along similar lines, the factor of Conscientiousness influences individual team member behavior which, in turn, may affect team productivity and output. For reasons such as this, personality may provide an important addition to the description of the critical, elemental, individual differences affecting successful interactional work group processes.

Personality and Its Use as One Basis for Understanding Diversity

We posit that workgroups or team diversity should be examined not only from a demographic perspective but from a more comprehensive personality and individual difference perspective. The basis of this position is that diversity of team members can influence the performance and effective functioning of teams. Note that "effective functioning" is broadly defined and includes members' psychological health and well-being in addition to task completion and team cohesion.

Personality theory has been developed and empirically examined for over one hundred years. The field has received a significant boost in the past fifteen years with the development of comprehensive factor-based theories and enhanced methods of assessment. Organizations in general have recognized the value of personality in human resource management functions. This is true of the DoD as well. The following section reviews literature on the application of the Five Factor Model (FFM) of personality within the DoD. This review was focused on the DoD in particular but also included selected research on teams.

The Five-factor Model of Personality (FFM) and DoD

Although certainly not the first factor-based theory of personality (cf., Eysenck & Eysenck, 1963), the FFM has grown in popularity and is readily measurable through the NEO-PI-R (Costa & McCrae, 1990). Further, consensus has been reached in the literature that the FFM is the current best approach for modeling personality (Wiggins & Trapnell, 1997), although it is not immune from valid and potentially serious criticisms (Hough & Schneider, 1996) . The literature on the FFM has steadily grown although it is far from complete due to the relative recency of the publication of the NEO-PI-R. Despite this, the FFM has been applied within the DoD.

The FFM includes Extraversion (versus introversion), Neuroticism (versus emotional stability), Openness to Experience (versus closed), Agreeableness (versus not agreeable); and Conscientiousness (versus not conscientiousness). These five personality factors are continuous and normally distributed. That is, individuals can be described as having "more or less" of each factor, with 68% of individuals falling somewhere in the middle of the continuum. Thus, the majority of individuals are neither "Extraverted" nor "Introverted". Perhaps, of interest for teams and team leadership are those people who place in the tails of the distribution; yet there is little research on those who scores fall on the extremes of the five factors.

Each of the five factors include six facets or subscales. Extraversion is composed of the facets of warmth, gregariousness, assertiveness, activity, excitement-seeking, and positive emotions. Neuroticism includes the facets of anxiety, angry hostility, depression, self-consciousness, impulsivity, and vulnerability. Openness to experience includes fantasy, aesthetics, feelings, actions, ideas and values. Agreeableness contains trust, straightforwardness, altruism, compliance, modesty, and tender-mindedness. Finally, Conscientiousness is composed of competence, order, dutifulness, achievement-striving, self-discipline, and deliberation.

FFM and Diverse Teams

Relatively little published research is available on the FFM and teams, and diverse teams have not been systematically examined within the FFM framework. However, one researcher (Howard, 1996) has developed a training program that includes a team variable of "comfort and appreciation for diversity" (p. 15). Comfort with and appreciation for diversity is contrasted with a tendency towards prejudice. According to Howard, individuals who are comfortable with diversity have a personality constellation that includes low anger (low N), high openness to experience, and high compliance, modesty, and tender-mindedness (high Agreeableness). This is consistent with Johnson (1997) who hypothesized prejudice and authoritarianism to be moderated by high Neuroticism, low Openness, and low Agreeableness.

Although little empirical research exists on the FFM and diverse teams, the model has been researched in the work setting and information is known regarding factors relating to productivity and other outcome measures. Additionally, leadership and training profiles of respective groups of individuals have been examined. This section will review selected literature with emphasis on DoD research and military samples.

FFM and Teams

Selected group processes can impact team performance. With respect to Army teams, Beck and Pierce (1996) identified several processes impacting team performance that are likely related to the FFM. Out of these processes, environmental stressors, group cohesion, groupthink, and leadership variables are of primary importance for the present chapter.

Environmental Stress

The effect of environmental stressors on team performance has received attention in the literature. One interesting study examined the effects of status and stress on decision making in dyads of U.S. Navy personnel (Driskell & Salas, 1991). Results provide support for the increased receptivity hypothesis (Driskell & Salas, 1991) which holds that stressful situations make both leaders and subordinates very responsive to input from other group members. In short, subordinates are more willing to follow leader guidance, but leaders are also more likely to seek advice from their subordinates. Thus, stressful situations contribute to greater receptivity for all individual team members.

The factor of Neuroticism (N) includes stress-related facets of anxiety, impulsivity, and angry hostility. As an individual difference variable, it is likely that team members with higher levels of N are more vulnerable to stressful situations. Neuroticism may be likened to arousability, or emotional reactivity. Team members who are high on this factor may be exceptionally reactive to stress and less resistant to emotional upheaval typically associated with intense situations or crises. Although the clinical and counseling literature is replete with examples of the effects of High N on adaptive functioning (for a recent study see Bagby, Joffe, Parker, Kalemba, et. al, 1995), no research can be found that addresses this issue with respect to team functioning. For example, it is well documented that High N predisposes an individual to clinical levels of depression and anxiety (Eysenck, 1947) largely related to relative inability to manage stress in a non-emotionally reactive manner. It is of critical empirical and practical importance to ascertain the effects of individuals with High N on team performance, particularly under stressful conditions.

Directly related to N is the notion of negative affectivity (NA: Tellegen, 1982; 1985), which has been examined in the workplace. NA refers to an individual's prevailing emotional experience. Those high in NA tend to experience negative emotions and moods. They frequently experience negative feelings and are distressed both by their own thoughts and experiences as well as those of others (Tellegen, 1982, 1985; Watson & Pennebaker, 1989). Often, this translates into thoughts and actions that result in negative affective experiences. NA is contrasted with Positive Affectivity (PA), which refers to tendencies to experience positive emotions and feelings. Those high in PA experience little distress, with consequent positive mood. NA and PA are related to job performance, particularly work-related strain. In general, those high in NA report their work to be more stressful than those low in NA (Burke, Brief, & George, 1993). To date, NA has not been examined with respect to teams and working groups; although there is recognition of the need for empirical research (George, 1996). Similar to N, NA undoubtedly affects team functioning and performance, and empirical information is notably lacking.

Teamwork Stress: Team Composition and Team Cohesion

Another phenomenon in the literature is that of "teamwork stress" (Morgan & Bowers, 1995 p. 266), which includes many environmental stressors but refers largely to a change in team interaction processes and performance. Often, this involves an alteration in the team's capacity to obtain desired goals and objectives. Although there exist many types of teamwork stressors, team composition and team cohesion constitute two of them. Team composition is defined as the degree to which team members are similar to one another. This has been examined from many perspectives, including gender and ethnicity. In general, it is been found that homogeneous teams may exhibit increased cooperation (Lodahl & Porter, 1961), and experience less conflict than heterogeneous teams (Bass, 1965). However, these findings depend upon the criterion or team outcome variable. When the criterion involves creativity and enhanced problem-solving, heterogeneous teams are more effective (Goldman, Dietz, & McGlynn 1968). Note that heterogeneity has been defined in various ways including such sociodemographic variables as race and gender. Although little is known regarding heterogeneity in terms of individual team member personality, Hoffman and Maier (1961) demonstrated that personologically hetereogeneous teams produced better responses on a team problem-solving task.

Team composition in the military has been examined with respect to gender. In general, however, findings have been mixed (Jackson, May, & Whitney, 1995; Wood, 1987) and Wood's (1987) meta-analytic study suggested the need for examining gender-affected interaction patterns. Elliott, Hollenbeck, and Tower (1996) performed a well-designed laboratory study on high stress tactical decision-making teams. Importantly, this study was embedded in a theoretical model of team performance (Multi-level theory: Hollenbeck, et al., 1995) where team members possessed the type of differential expertise and hierarchical structure common to military teams. Results indicated significant gender-related differences in performance, with all men teams performing most accurately, and teams with a leader who was a man and two woman subordinates performing least accurately. These differences were attributed to gender-based differences in communication style as well as efficiency of information exchange. Team members of low-performing teams did not gain the information necessary for accurate decision-making.

In addition to examining gender-based communication patterns among teams, it is important to note there are some gender-based differences in the five factors of personality. For example, it is known that women tend to score higher on Agreeableness than men (Costa & McRae, 1990; 1992) . This tendency could be manifest in a team through an unwillingness to disagree and a bias towards acquiescence in decision-making. Along similar lines, women tend to score higher on Neuroticism than do men (Costa & McRae, 1990; 1992). In a gender diverse team, this may be manifest in greater levels of reactivity relative to men. The interaction between personality and gender on team performance variables has not been established and constitutes a fruitful area for research.

Team Cohesion

Team cohesion is another form of potential teamwork stress and refers to the mutual attraction among members of a group and the resulting desire to remain in the group (Eddy, 1985) and is an important factor in team performance. Griffith (1988) reported that cohesive Army units are more willing to reenlist in their unit, view their units as more combat ready, are more satisfied with the Army, and report higher personal morale. In general, cohesion has a positive effect on group performance in that cohesive groups are more productive (Driskell & Salas, 1992), more interactive (Fisher & Ellis, 1990), disagree less (Morgan & Lassiter, 1992) and make better decisions (Valacich, Dennis, & Nunamaker, 1992). Recall that team composition is one aspect of team orientation, which is a necessary condition for efficient team performance (Dickinson & McIntyre, 1997).

Cohesion is a multidimensional construct and includes at least two dimensions, task cohesion and interpersonal cohesion (Beck & Pierce, 1996). Task cohesion refers to task performance/commitment, and is more important than interpersonal cohesion (referring to interpersonal support and attraction) for facilitating performance (Zacccaro, 1991). Further, Mullen, Anthony, Salas, and Driskell

(1994) conclude that positive group decision quality is attributable to the influence of task cohesion. When decision quality decreases, this is related to the influence of interpersonal cohesion. Importantly, Mullen et al. (1994) believe that interpersonal cohesion may contribute to groupthink and that cohesion may eliminate or minimize groupthink.

The role that personality plays in group cohesion is unknown but it is highly probable that personality mediates group cohesion. Mutual attraction among members and the desire to remain in the group are likely moderated by the factors of Extraversion, Agreeableness, and Neuroticism. Extraverts are known for their propensity to seek affiliation and gregariousness; hence predisposing them to increased social interaction conducive to group cohesion. On the other hand, introverts often prefer solitary activity and may not be particularly affected by a desire to remain in the group. Introverts may be slower to value group cohesion or less willing to engage in social interaction that foments group cohesion. Agreeableness is another factor that would relate to group cohesion. Individuals low in Agreeableness may be competitive (as opposed to cooperative), lacking in trust, suspicious and skeptical of the motives of others, and tough-minded. These characteristics may impede development of group cohesion, in that individuals who are suspicious of others likely have little inclination to be attracted to and remain in their group. Finally, Neuroticism may affect group cohesion through individual proneness to self-consciousness, anxiety, and anger. These individuals may be high in subjective distress levels sufficient to disrupt other-directedness necessary for group cohesion. All of these potential interactions between personality and group cohesion are in need of empirical examination.

Groupthink

Groupthink describes a problematic phenomenon resulting when stress, high group cohesion, and leadership style combine to reduce disagreement among subordinates (Janis, 1972; 1983). During groupthink, teammates convince one another of the correctness of the leader's decision, and these tendencies are heightened during greater situational stress. Groupthink involves members rallying around the leader and the major danger is that the number of options considered by the team are limited. This occurs because the group leader may believe the team sees the merit of his or her views, when in actuality members are not actively thinking and are instead simply being supportive of the leader's views. Although the prevalence of groupthink in DoD teams is unknown, some authors (Peck & Pierce, 1996) say the phenomenon undoubtedly exists, needs to be acknowledged, and preventative strategies implemented when possible.

Application of the FFM to groupthink may be useful. The factor of Agreeableness may be particularly important in that teams composed of highly agreeable individuals may be prone to unquestioned acceptance of a leader's position. The Agreeableness facet of compliance may be particularly useful in that individuals high in compliance may be predisposed to groupthink. In efforts to be cooperative, individual members may actually impede team processes and decision-making. On the other hand, consider a team composed of individuals high in Extraversion. Extraversion, with its facet of assertiveness, may buffer a team from the potential of groupthink. Extraverts are generally more outspoken and assertive than those lower in this factor, and may serve as individual safeguards of groupthink.

The factors of Openness to Experience and Neuroticism may also be important in groupthink. High openness can lead an individual to value almost any idea and decrease the focus on task accomplishment. Under stress, such individuals may be overly receptive to the input from both leader and team members to the exclusion of pre-held ideas. Hence, their value as a team member would be reduced. Finally, high Neuroticism predisposes an individual to be emotionally reactive to stress and experience frequent anxiety. They may be prone to readily agree with the leader and other team members in an effort to quell internal distress and inadvertently contribute to groupthink. As in the case of high openness, this ultimately reduces their effectiveness as a team member/contributor. When a team is likely to be subjected to stressful situations, it may perform better when composed of members partly selected on the basis of the FFM.

FFM and Leadership

The relation between personality characteristics and leadership is characterized by research that is fragmented and narrow in focus (Nysted, 1997). Leadership has been broken down into areas such as behavioral styles, traits, and environmental constraints and authors such as Nysted (1997) have called for a more holistic approach to integrate complex trait patterns with leadership variables. The FFM is presently being assessed and its relation to leadership is presently being examined (Aditya, 1998), but data collection efforts are presently ongoing and final results are not presently available.

Despite this lack of research, it is known that a flight crew captain's personality affects the performance of his crew. Crews with captains characterized as warm, friendly, self-confident, and stable made fewer errors than crews with egotistical, hostile, and passive-aggressive captains (Foushee & Helmreich, 1988). Notably this study did not use the FFM but did use adjectives and descriptive personality terms consistent with other factor-based models of personality. Specifically, the warmth, friendliness, and self-confidence found in this study of leadership is typical of Extraversion. Similarly, the feature of stability is associated with Neuroticism, or low reactivity.

FFM Group Profiles, Selection, and Training

Although it has recently been acknowledged that personality measurement can be useful in such employment decisions as selection, training, and performance, it is critical to bear in mind that its utility is constrained by the nature of the job. For example, Barrick and Mount (1993) note that some positions are highly scripted and detailed procedures necessary for efficient performance allow little room for personality to affect performance. The work of Hogan and Hogan (1993) addresses this issue. These authors developed the 5 X 6 Model which classifies a job into one of the six Holland occupational categories and then examines the validity coefficients of the five factors of personality (FFM). Use of this model results in higher correlations between personality and job performance, insofar as it takes into account both the five factors of personality and the six occupational types.

Hogan, Hogan and Roberts (1996) illustrate this principle in the example of a truck driver. In Holland's codes, a truck driver is classified as a realistic-conventional occupational type. Well performing people in the realistic-conventional occupation are hard working and likely fit well into an organization. However, they may not perform as well in administrative, leadership, or team member roles which require extensive communication skills. From the FFM perspective, personality characteristics associated with the realistic-conventional occupational type include high Conscientiousness and low Neuroticism and these two factors are associated with the classification of truck driver (Hogan & Hogan, 1995).

Of critical importance is the fact that Agreeableness, Extroversion, and Openness to Experience may be relatively unimportant for the occupation of truck driver with its realistic-conventional job classification. Hence, use of the FFM in employment decisions is maximized when the performance demands of the job are known and used in tandem with the FFM. Use of the FFM may be inappropriate in those instances where a job analysis is lacking or when the job role is so routinized there is little room for personality to serve as a mediator of performance. In this latter instance, the situation must not be so demanding as to overwhelm sources of individual variation in job behavior (Monson, Hesley, & Chernick, 1982). Even in this latter instance, however, the empirical question remains of whether someone extremely low in extraversion can perform effectively as a college professor or platform speaker.

In addition to the above cautions, it is important to note that FFM profiling of the "ideal" candidate for training programs and occupations is in its infancy, likely due to the relatively recent publication of the NEO-PI-R. However, some empirical information is available.

With respect to military samples, Braun, Prusaczyk, Goforth, and Pratt (1994) reported on the personality profiles of U.S. Navy Sea-Air-Land commando (SEAL) trainees. This interesting study addressed the issue of high rates of attrition among SEAL trainees, and incorporated the FFM in an attempt to improve selection and training. Braun et al. noted that selection efforts have been historically directed to intelligence, maturity, physical performance, and combat skills. Hence, introduction of the FFM represented a new and additional variable to assist in selection. Results from this study indicated personality differences between more-experienced and less-experienced SEALs but these were attributed to the effects of age. There were also differences between Commissioned officers and Enlisted SEALs in that Commissioned officers were significantly higher on Extraversion and Consciousness. When compared to published norms for adult men, SEALs were lower in Neuroticism and Agreeableness, average to lower in Openness, and higher in Conscientiousness and Extraversion. Hence, relative to the normative (and civilian) group, the authors provide a description of an "average" U.S. Navy SEAL:

This subset of SEALS appear to be calm, hardy, secure, and not prone to excessive psychological stress or anxiety. They are level-headed, practical and collected even under very stressful or dangerous situations. They are rarely impulsive and have strong control over cravings or urges. Active and assertive, they prefer being in large groups and are usually energetic and optimistic. They seek excitement and stimulation and prefer complex and dangerous environments. They are very competitive, skeptical of others' intentions, and are likely to aggressively defend their own interests, but are not hostile. Finally, they are purposeful, well organized, persistent, and very reliable (p. 16).

Note the lower Neuroticism and Agreeableness and higher Extraversion and Conscientiousness scores manifest in this description.

This study directly pertains to DoD teams, insofar as SEALs often work in tactical teams. Paradoxically, one challenge may lie in the low Agreeableness and Neuroticism scores. For example, teams may be impeded by competitiveness (low scores on Agreeableness) on the part of individual members. Similarly, lack of anxiety (low Neuroticism), could potentially lead to groupthink (Janus, 1972; 1983) and not provide sufficient safeguards against dangerous situations. Although it is likely that low Neuroticism would be essentially valuable in tactical teams, future research needs to be directed to levels of N that are ideal to balance relative lack of anxiety and such factors as appraisal of dangerous situations.

The FFM has also been used to profile the personalities of U.S. Air Force Pilots. With a relatively large sample of both men and women pilots (N = 1301), Callister, King, Retzlaff, and Marsh, 1997 administered the NEO-PI-R and examined pilot scores on the five factors versus standardized norms on the general population. These authors found that both men and women student pilots were higher in Extraversion and lower in Agreeableness than adult norms drawn from the general population. Women student pilots were also higher in Openness than women from the general population. The authors then proceed to discuss the usefulness of the FFM in assessment and possible intervention with student pilots.

This article is noteworthy in documenting personality differences between a military occupational category (such as student pilots) and non-military samples. However, it does not appear that these differences are statistically significant and the results must be interpreted cautiously. Visual inspection and comparison of the Extraversion facets indicate elevated scores emanated from certain facets. Specifically, both men and women student pilots were higher on the facets of assertiveness, activity, and excitement-seeking. They were lower on the Agreeableness facets of compliance and tendermindedness. Women student pilots were also lower on the Straightforwardness facet. Interestingly, both men and women student pilots demonstrated similar personality profiles relative to the general population.

With respect to the FFM and its utility in selection and classification, Pederson, Allan, Laue, Johnson, and Siem (1992) examined its utility relative to alternative personality theories. Comparisons were made between models of personality theory and the authors concluded the FFM was the most appropriate for aircrew selection and classification. Of course, personality is viewed as one more attribute to include in selection and training, in addition to the physical, academic, and aptitude requirements already in place.

Related work is that of Street, Helton, and Nontasak (1994), who examined the FFM in the selection of landing craft air cushion (LCAC) vehicle crew members. Specifically, these authors first used principal component analysis to extract factors from the Adult Personality Inventory (API) and then principal factor analysis to remove unique and error variance and obtain a solution. The factors were then labeled and compared to the FFM and both exploratory principal components analysis and the confirmatory principal factor analysis produced five factor solutions that corresponded to the FFM. Hence, the five factors were derived from the API. The authors conclude the "derived API openness variable includes traits of practicality and conventionality. The significance of the practicality trait is such that individuals who are more conventional and practical tend to do better in the overall LCAC training program". Included in this are indices of psychomotor coordination and decision-making skill drawn from the Landing Craft Air Cushion Vehicle Crew Selection System (LCSS), which is a computerized test battery (see Helton, Nontasak, & Dolgin, 1992 for further information). The major significance of this study is that high Conscientiousness and lower Openness appeared to predict success in the LCAC training program.

Cortina, Doherty, Schmitt, Kaufman, and Smith (1992) examined the FFM, MMPI, and Inwald Personality Inventory and prediction of training success for state police recruits. Hierarchical regression revealed Neuroticism and Agreeableness to add to the predictability of training criteria. In this study, Conscientiousness did not add to the prediction. However, when incremental validity of personality tests over the Civil Service exam were examined, they were small. Thus, incremental yield of information by using the FFM was questionable in this study.

FFM and Work-Related Variables

The FFM has been examined in terms of work-related variables such as job performance, and there is related literature on important correlates such as procrastination and task avoidance. For example, a meta-analytic study found Conscientiousness to be predictive of job performance across five categories of employees (Barrick & Mount, 1991). Job performance was measured through job and training proficiency and personnel data. This study was important in that it included various groups of workers ranging from professionals to skilled/semiskilled workers. Further, Conscientiousness is highly related (inversely) to procrastination and task avoidance (Johnson & Bloom, 1994), which holds implications for efficient job performance and achievement within deadlines. Although Conscientiousness has received empirical attention, relatively little is known regarding the other four factors (Extraversion, Neuroticism, Openness to Experience, and Agreeableness) and job performance criteria.

Examination of the Use of the Five Factor Model in the Training of DEOMI's Study Groups

As a part of the effort to examine the application of the FFM within DoD work groups and teams, data were collected on personality factors and teamwork processes within a class of DEOMI students. DEOMI's primary mission is the training of Equal Opportunity Advisor's (EOAs) from the various defense-related organizations. The job of the EOA after graduating from DEOMI is to serve as a resource person and resident expert in a variety of roles within his or her unit. The position is somewhat fluid and depends on the service within which the EOA works and on the role assigned by the commanding officer.

EOA training covers fifteen consecutive weeks. Intensive in nature, it is designed both to inform as well as change attitudes within the student on the general topics of prejudice, equal opportunity, and diversity. An important aspect of the training is the implementation of C-Groups, which refers to a small group process focusing on the exploration of group identifications, (e.g. racial, religious, ethnic, etc.). C-Groups are implemented in EOA training during the entire 15-week training period. Groups are formed prior to the students' arrival at DEOMI and are composed to equally represent race, gender, ethnicity, and cultural heritage. Therefore, each group reflects a socioculturally diverse group, which provides students with a learning environment that is diverse and interpersonally intense. Clearly, it is anticipated that students will take the experience of working in such diverse groups and apply them to their upcoming EOA positions.

The existence of such groups within DEOMI provided the opportunity to examine the effect of personality diversity within socioculturally diverse groups through a pilot study. Although these work groups were not tactical teams in the classic sense of the term, they did indeed comprise real organization members in a real task—a learning task—for a reasonably long duration. They had a mutual goal to acquire competency in the skills and knowledge required in the EOA position. Students work interdependently both in the C-Groups as well as on occasional joint projects. Based on this line of reasoning, the C-Groups comprising the EOA training represent a type of team. The importance of this training leads to the conclusion that the examination of the FFM within EOA training may provide fruitful insights for future investigations.

We entered this phase of the research with the following questions:

1.   What is the effect of different personality mixes on the C-Group processes?

2.   What is the effect of different personality profiles on the emerging leadership of the small training groups?

3.   Is there any evidence of an interaction effect of the personality of the emergent group leaders of the small groups and the personality profiles of the other group members?

4.   What might be the advantage of educating group instructors in the nuances of the FFM on the effectiveness of instruction?

These questions could not be thoroughly studied with only one EOA 15-week class. However, we did identify research that might be continued in the future.

Method

Participants

The class of 98-2 consists of 98 individuals (65 men and 33 women) who were being trained to work in the equal opportunity field. Each DEOMI small group is composed of 16 or 17 trainees and two DEOMI team leaders. There were six small groups in the present study, and groups are composed to be diverse with respect to gender, rank, service, ethnicity, and education. The following Table 5.1 summarizes the six groups with respect to these variables.

Procedure

Each student completed the NEO-PI-R according to standard instructions. This instrument is known to be reliable and valid (Costa & McRae, 1990; 1992) in measurement of the five factors and their facets. Instructors assigned to each group (two per group) completed a teamwork measurement instrument based on the work of Dickinson and McIntyre (1997). (See Appendix 1.) Rosenstein and Dickinson (1996) evaluated the reliability and construct validity of the measurement instrument and found adequate empirical support for both. This questionnaire assessed team performance on seven components including team orientation (attitudes members have towards each other and the team); team leadership (providing direction, structure and support for other team members); communication (exchange of information); monitoring (observing activities and performance of other team members); feedback (giving, seeking, and receiving of information among team members), back-up behavior (assisting performance of other team members); coordination (execution of activities in a timely and integrated manner); and performance (accomplishment of activities and tasks required of the team). Responses remained anonymous and were numerically coded.

Results

General Characteristics: Class 98-2

Several descriptive analyses were undertaken in this project. First, the class of 98-2 (N = 98) was compared to published norms for the general population across the five factors. The class did not differ substantially from the general population. Across the sample of 98 students, the mean T scores for the factors were as follows: Neuroticism: 50.03 (SD = 8.64); Extraversion: 53.00 (SD = 9.76); Openness to Experience: 51.91 (SD = 10.96); Agreeableness: 47.00 (SD = 11.29); and Conscientiousness = 55.67 (SD = 11.01).

Secondly, between-group analyses were conducted to establish the presence of any gender or racial group differences with respect

Table 5.1
Summary of Ruggeberg's Team Leadership Classification System
(Ruggeberg, 1996)[1]

Type	Team Leadership Descriptor	Summary of Team Leadership
I	Self-management	Very little process management or guidance toward goal attainment; low structure and leader responsibilities; low importance of process management knowledge, skills, abilities, and other characteristics; limited member responsibilities
II	Advisory	Very low involvement in team activities; high guidance toward goal attainment; open communications
III	Transformational	High transformational leadership, integration, initiating structure, involvement with team and shared leadership
IV	By-the-Book	Very low consideration, tolerance of freedom, openness to ideas or concerns, importance of interpersonal KSAOs, representation of team, transformational leadership; high importance of process management KSAOs.
V	Boundary Management	High boundary management behaviors and tolerance of freedom; very low leader role assumption & initiating structure; low integration, team building, & leader responsibility; low importance of process management KSAOs

1 Table 5.1 is based on Table 20, Ruggeberg (1996, p. 205)

to the FFM. There were no significant differences between racial groups on the five factors. However, significant gender differences were present with women displaying greater tendencies towards Agreeableness, F (1, 96) = 4.18, p <.03, and Openness to Experience, F (1, 96) = 6.53, p < .01), than men. Women had a mean score of 50.44 (SD = 9.22) and men a mean of 45.25 (SD = 11.89) on Agreeableness. Means on Openness to Experience were 55.77 (SD = 10.00) and 49.95 (SD = 11.89) for women and men, respectively.

Further analyses indicate certain facet scales contributed to the gender differences in Agreeableness and Openness in this sample. For Agreeableness, the facet of Compliance was significant in that women obtained a mean score of 49.41 (SD = 11.53) and men a mean score of 43.86 (SD = 10.98). Openness to Experience had facets that were significantly different between men and women including Aesthetics and Actions. Women obtained a mean score of 54.81 (SD = 9.88) and men 49.01 (SD = 11.10) on Aesthetics. On Actions women obtained a mean score of 56.78 (SD = 10.58) and men 49.62 (SD = 11.64).

Rank had an effect on one of the five factors. Since the majority of the sample was enlisted, the enlisted individuals were bifurcated into lower (N = 22: E-5 and E-6) versus higher (N = 68: E-7, E-8, E-9) paygrades. These two groups were significantly different on the factor of Neuroticism, F = 13.05 (1, 88), p < .001. The lower rank individuals obtained a mean score of 55.45 and higher ranks obtained a mean score of 48.12 indicating lower levels of Neuroticism among higher ranks. Examination of the facet scales associated with Neuroticism indicates lower ranks experience higher levels of anxiety, F (1, 88) = 5.66, p < .02, angry hostility, F (1,88) = 10.53, p < .002, depression F (1, 88) = 4.06, p < .04, and vulnerability F (1, 88) = 14.53, p < .0001 than higher ranks. Taking these facet scales in this order, lower ranks had means of 54.06, 56.83, 52.30, and 49.06 and higher ranks had means of 49.18, 48.27, 47.59, and 40.64, respectively.

Small Groups: 98-2

The six small groups were also subjected to various analyses. There were significant differences between Extraversion, F (5, 92) = 2.62, p < .02), and Agreeableness, F (5, 92) = 2.35, p < .04). For Extraversion, significant differences were found on the facet scales of Warmth, Activity, and Positive Emotions. Warmth differed between Group

One and Groups Three, Four and Five, F (5,92) = 2.79, p < .02. Group One had a significantly larger value (M = 55.39) than the other three groups where Group Three had a mean score of 47.59, Group Four had a mean of 45.56, and Group Five a mean of 46.13. The facet of Activity was also significantly different, F (5, 92) = 3.64, p < .005, between certain groups. Specifically, Group Five was lower (M = 46.76) than Groups One (M = 53.31), Two (M = 54.46), and Three (M = 53.32). Group Six (M = 60.42) was higher than Groups Three (M = 53.32) , Four (M = 52.47) , and Five (M = 46.76) on Activity. The Positive Emotions factor was significantly different, F (5, 92) = 2.93, p < .01 between Group Four (M = 45.94) and Groups One (M = 56.61), Two (M = 56.50), Three (M = 53.86), and Six (M = 54.69), with Group Four scoring lower than these latter groups. Finally, Group Five (M = 49.03) was significantly lower on Positive Emotions than Groups One (M = 56.61) and Two (M = 56.50).

Agreeableness was also significantly different between some of the small groups, F (5, 92) = 2.35, p < .04. Group Five (M = 43.29) was significantly lower than Groups One (M = 53.69), Two (M = 49.69), and Six (M = 46.23). Examination of the facets indicate Altruism to be significantly lower in Group Five (M = 47.61) than in Group One (M = 57.02), Group Two (M = 56.67), and Group Six (M = 56.14).

Small Groups: 98-2 and Outcome Measures

The six DEOMI small groups (learning teams) were analyzed with respect to outcome measures of group processes. Table 5.2 indicates significant differences across the six learning teams on all seven teamwork components. Post hoc analyses, also summarized in Table 5.2 indicate that the Team 3 is the most effective and Team 5 is least effective. Table 5.3 provide a summary of similar analyses for nine single-item performance measures, an overall composite of the nine items, the stage of development of the team (where 1 is the beginning stage and 4 is the highest stage), and six single items measures of interaction processes. Due to the fact these measures were not as reliable as the multi-item measures corresponding to the seven teamwork components, there were fewer significant differences associated with them across the six learning teams. However, Team 4 did show its superiority on accomplishing its goals, meeting performance goals in a timely manner, and overall performance.

Table 5.2
Summary of Analyses of Variances (ANOVAs)
On Teamwork Process Measures Across 6 Learning Teams

Teamwork Component	F-Statistic and p values	Team Post-Hoc Differences
Team Orientation	11.037, p < .006	1 vs. 5, 4 vs. 5, 4 vs. 6
Team Leadership	9.932, p < .007	1 vs. 5, 1 vs. 6, 4 vs. 5, 4 vs. 6
Monitoring	8.908, p < .010	4 vs. 5
Feedback	6.285, p < .022	4 vs. 5
Communication	13.387 p < .003	1 vs. 5, 2 vs. 5, 4 vs. 5, 4 vs. 6
Backup	7.442 p < .015	4 vs. 5, 4 vs. 6
Coordination	21.793, p < .001	1 vs. 2, 1 vs. 3, 1 vs. 5, 1 vs. 6, 2 vs. 4, 3 vs. 4, 4 vs. 5, 4 vs. 6

Table 5.3
Results of ANOVAs on Team Outcome Measures

Team Outcome Measure	F-Statistics and p Values	Team Post Hoc Differences
Team goals accomplished	10.600, p < .006	3 vs. 5, 4 vs. 5
Meet expectations of the team	Nonsignificant effect	
Meet performance goals in timely manner	10.400, p < .006	2 vs. 5, 2 vs. 6, 4 vs. 5
Team regards output as adequate	Nonsignificant effect	
Team achieved goals with few errors	5.971, p < .025	Only marginal differences
Team produces output suitable to organization	5.200, p < .034	Only marginal differences
Team members regard team accomplishments above average	Nonsignificant effect	
Team feels team performed acceptably	Nonsignficant effect	
Team members said that objectives were met efficiently	5.960, p < .025	Only marginal differences
Overall Team Performance (Composite of previous nine measures)	6.885, p < .018	4 vs.6
Stage of Team Development	6.600, p < .020	Only marginal differences
Mutual Trust shown	6.800, p < .019	Only marginal differences
Mutual Concern shown	6.800, p < .019	Only marginal differences
Mutual Support shown	4.400, p < .050	Only marginal differences
Positive Emotional status of members shown	4.400, p < .050	Only marginal differences
Mutual Respect shown	4.400, p < .050	Only marginal differences
Mutual celebration shown	5.800, p < .027	Only marginal differences

* Based on Table 20, Ruggeberg (1996, p. 205)

Emergent Leaders: 98-2

Each of the learning team facilitators independently selected emergent leaders from their small groups. These emergent leader's ($\underline{N}$=19) personality profiles were averaged and resulted in a summary profile of indigeneous leaders in diverse groups. When a criterion of one-half standard deviation ($\underline{T}$= + - 5) from published norms was used, it was found that these leaders were higher than the general population in Openness to Experience ($\underline{M}$ = 58; $\underline{SD}$ = 11), and Conscientiousness ($\underline{M}$ = 55, $\underline{SD}$ = 12), and lower on Agreeableness ($\underline{M}$ = 45, $\underline{SD}$=9). This sample was average on Negative Emotions ($\underline{M}$ = 51, $\underline{SD}$ = 11) and Extraversion ($\underline{M}$ = 51, $\underline{SD}$ = 9).

These higher scores on Openness to Experience derive from higher than average scores on the facets of Fantasy ($\underline{M}$ = 57, $\underline{SD}$ = 11), Aesthetics ($\underline{M}$ = 55, $\underline{SD}$ = 12), Feelings ($\underline{M}$=55, $\underline{SD}$ = 12), Actions ($\underline{M}$ = 55, $\underline{SD}$ = 11), and Ideas ($\underline{M}$ = 55, $\underline{SD}$ = 10). Higher scores on Conscientiousness derive largely from the facet of Achievement striving ($\underline{M}$ = 57, $\underline{SD}$ = 10). Lower Agreeableness scores derived from the lower scores on Trust ($\underline{M}$ = 44, $\underline{SD}$ = 12) and Altruism ($\underline{M}$ = 44, $\underline{SD}$ = 9).

Discussion

Similar to Braun, Prusaczyk, Goforth, and Pratt (1994), who profiled Navy SEALs, and Callister, King, Retzlaff, and Marsh, (1997) who profiled Air Force student pilots, a general mean personality profile of DEOMI trainees emerges from the FFM. Generally, the group of DEOMI 98-2 average trainees can be described in the following manner:

> Emotional expressiveness and reactivity is within normal ranges. Although they tend to be calm and free from tension under most circumstances, situational stress may precipitate negative affect and occasional anger. However, they are essentially stable and not prone to internal distress or outward hostility. Their orientation to others is affable but they are also capable of working alone, and they move easily between group and solitary activities. When working with others, they are able to be cooperative or competitive as the situation demands, and they are neither excessively dependent upon or independent from surrounding individuals. They are not easily distracted by others nor are they overly stimulated by their environment. That is, they do not exhibit a strong preference for exciting activities or novel experiences. Their range of interests is moderate and they appreciate new ideas; however, they tend to be fairly practical and down to earth in their interests. When there is a task to be accomplished, they tend to be achievement-oriented, disciplined, and responsible. Their strong needs for order and structure serve them well in task completion.

It is important to bear in mind that this is a general group description and may not apply to any single individual within the group. However, similar individualized descriptions can be composed based upon a person's responses on the NEO-PI-R.

The finding of greater Openness to Experience and Agreeableness for women relative to men is consistent with the literature and holds implications for practical use of the FFM. Along similar lines, the finding that lower ranks demonstrate higher levels of Neuroticism (N) than higher ranks is also important when using the FFM in military samples. Essentially, localized norms may need to be developed for DEOMI that take into account these differences. As the NEO-PI-R continues to be administered to DEOMI trainees, scrutiny of potential gender differences should continue. Additionally, although the present sample did not exhibit racial differences in personality, future classes may exhibit differences, and statistical analyses should be performed prior to any practical use of the NEO-PI-R for purposes such as selection or training.

The statistically greater levels of Openness to Experience and Agreeableness for women found in 98-2 is attributable to the fact they were compared to the men in this sample. Hence, these findings must be interpreted with care. Both women and men scored within the average range; however, they were significantly different from each other with the men scoring slightly lower and women slightly higher on these two factors. Thus, this finding may have implications for small group processes but little application to performances in the external environment.

Within the small groups, the higher levels of Openness to Experience and Agreeableness in women may be manifest in greater appreciation for novel ideas and experiences and receptivity to acting on this appreciation. For them, "tested and true" ideas may be questioned and they may be more willing to act on new ideas. However, the women are also more cooperative and open to the opinions of others than the men in this sample, who may be more competitive with and skeptical of others. These differences can create desired diversity, but can also contribute to tension within the group.

With respect to rank, it is important to note that some occupational characteristics are "stronger" than others. When an occupation has a strong demand for prescribed job-relevant behaviors the effects of personality are often not as pronounced as when an occupation leaves more room for personality to affect performance (Hogan

& Hogan, 1995). One such example of this may lie in the variable of rank. Higher ranks may involve occupations with implicit and explicit expectations for non-reactivity and emotional stability (low N) that serve to moderate any existing levels of N. An alternative explanation may be that high ranks demonstrate lower scores on N simply because they are experiencing less anxiety, hostility, depression, and vulnerability when compared to those of a lower, and perhaps more insecure, rank. When used with military samples, interpretation of FFM scores must be made within contextual variables such as type of sample and variables such as rank.

The finding of lower levels of N with higher rank may also indicate the effects of lower rank. Within this data set, average scores for both low and high rank are very close to the standardized mean of 50. However, between group comparisons of relative standing indicate statistical differences between low and high ranks. Indeed, on the N facets of angry hostility and vulnerability, lower ranked individuals are close to one standard deviation above their higher ranked counterparts. Hence, although levels of N are within normal limits for both groups and are likely not of clinical significance, they are suggesting that individuals at the lower end of the rank spectrum are experiencing greater internal dissatisfaction than those at the higher end of the spectrum. Of course, further research would be necessary to clarify the reasons for these differences between low and high ranks.

Some interesting findings were also discovered with regard to teamwork processes and the six small groups (learning teams). In fact, this is the first study that considers small training groups of this sort as learning teams. It appears that this is a worthy addition to the training of these military teams. It presents the trainees with the challenge to perform as team members with shared goals, and commitment to learning as a team. Team processes were different across the different teams which may add insight to the ways that learning teams might be treated in the context of equal opportunity training. We believe that future work by the training development directorate within DEOMI as well as in other training environments employing similar models of training would do well to examine the value of teamwork processes.

The results on emergent leaders suggest these individuals are accepting of new ideas and novel experiences. They also readily act on new suggestions and are probably creative problem-solvers. They tend to have a strong appreciation for art and beauty, and are sensitive to the feelings of others. At the same time, they may be discreet and cautious in their approach to others, and circumspect in their interpersonal interactions. This may generate, in part, from a focus on tasks and the need to achieve. It is important to note this description emanates from team leader ratings; however, there was extensive agreement among individual raters regarding emergent leaders. Further research is needed to describe emergent leaders as well as the interaction between team leaders', emergent leaders, and team/group process measures.

General Discussion

The Role of Team Leadership and Shifting Paradigms

Even if the organization clearly defines its objectives, how does it meet them? In particular, how might the DoD evolve to new and improved "paradigms" or "management models" for diversity? Since teams are so important within the DoD (and this may apply to organizations outside the DoD for teams are becoming increasingly important there as well), team leadership may be the important tool for implementing change. Leadership of teams has critical and essential impact on team outcomes. Therefore, team leaders are involved in the fabric of the performance of an organization. How better to disseminate an evolving model of managing diversity than through the team leadership "network"? Through a commonly designed team leader training program, covering the fundamental aspects and components of team processes, diversity initiatives can be implemented at a deep rather than simplistic level. In particular, the personality perspective on diversity can be disseminated through a training program where team leaders master the basics of the FFM and its importance in group and team processes. This approach holds potential for better management of team performance and for establishing a foundation for valuing diversity in the most profound sense of the term.

Equal Opportunity Advisor Training and the FFM

The FFM was examined in the context of DEOMI EOA training and can be used in a variety of ways. For example, the FFM can become the basis for an expanded definition (or paradigm as the case may be) of diversity. The curriculum within DEOMI can be modified to provide EOA students with a mastery of the basics of the FFM and appreciation for the role of personality in human interactions. The years of research supporting the FFM and a psychometrically valid measurement instrument can serve as a solid foundation for training future EOAs. It should be noted that DEOMI has already begun to train the DEOMI students in the FFM particularly as the factors pertain to them individually. This kind of training might be further developed to provide graduates of DEOMI with sufficient competence to apply the model in the work activities and training.

There is also an opportunity to use the FFM to assist current DEOMI trainers in their small group work. DEOMI training philosophy explicitly values the self-knowledge and awareness promoted by an individual's understanding of their own personality and how it influences individual behavior and emotions. This process of self-awareness is facilitated by information gained from the measurement and description of FFM personality factors. Further, trainers can benefit from knowledge regarding the role of personality in leadership and small group behaviors. For example, rather than confronting a group member on their consistent silence within the group, a trainer could use the knowledge of introversion and its influence on interactional processes to facilitate greater participation of such group members. Conversely, group members (trainees) can view their silence as a product of personality, which is a value-free construal that may enable them to focus on strategies for behavioral change if so desired. Operating within a FFM framework can thus provide a common communication system and opportunity for self-awareness within a value-free (and less stigmatized) individual difference model.

Warning: Life Beyond the FFM

Although the FFM may supplement the concept of diversity, a cautionary note must be added. Consideration of personality and individual differences is important; however, values and attitudes may not be fully captured by the FFM. Yet, values and attitudes are very much a part of an individual team member's makeup and team behavior. Furthermore, although the NEO-PI-R is a well designed and validated instrument, it is not free from random measurement error. Finally, as the analyses of the DEOMI class of 98-2 indicate, local norms are likely more important than standard published norms and there may be within-group differences between categorical variables such as gender or rank. For all of these reasons, the FFM should be applied within an appropriate context and by individuals with appropriate training.

Recommendations for Research

There are many practical questions that require research-based answers including the following:

1. Is there a personality profile of an ideal team leader? Might this profile change as a function of the type of team, and the mix of personalities comprising the team?

2. Alternatively, are we facing a situation of equifinality when it comes to the personality of a team or a team leader? That is to say, individuals with many different profiles may perform the team leadership task equally well?

3. Might it be fruitful to examine the personality "types" who cannot perform effectively in a DoD team or as a team leader? The team process model by Dickinson and McIntyre (1997) may serve as a basis for hypothesizing both those who can and who cannot perform effectively within a team.

4. What are the repercussions of examining the values, attitudes, and personality attributes of individuals in place of or in addition to their sociodemographic characteristics?

5. Is there an ideal profile suited to the job of EOA and EOA instructor? Are there certain profiles that should be avoided?

6. Are the facets comprising the five factors a more fruitful source of information for answering the profile-related questions above? If so, should the reliability of these facets be a matter of psychometric attention?

Conclusion

At the outset, it was argued that leading diverse teams within the DoD is an issue worthy of exploration. A discussion followed that defined diversity, teams, and team leadership. The use of personality theory as an important job-relevant individual difference variable within the DoD was examined. Finally, the manner in which the FFM might serve as a way of understanding and managing diversity within a rather unique group within the DoD—the DEOMI training program—was explored. Suggestions for new ways of thinking about diversity and important questions for future research are offered.

References

Barrick, M.R., & Mount, M.K. (1991). The big five personality dimensions and job performance: A meta-analysis. *Personnel Psychology, 44*, 1-26.

Beck, H.P., & Pierce, L.G. (1996). The impact of selected group processes on the coordination and motivation of army teams. Army Research Laboratory, ARL-CR-292.

Burke, M.J., Brief, A.P., & George, J.M. (1993). The role of negative affectivity in understanding relations between self-reports of stressors and strains: A comment on the applied psychology literature. *Journal of Applied Psychology, 78*, 402-412.

Burgess, K.A., Riddle, D.L., Hall, J.K., & Salas, E. (March, 1992). Principles of team leadership under stress. Paper presented at the 38th annual meeting of the Southeastern Psychological Association, Knoxville, TN.

Cortina, J.M., Doherty, M.L., Schmitt, N., Kaufman, G., & Smith, R.G. (1992). The "big five" personality factors in the IPI and MMPI: Predictors of police performance. *Personnel Psychology, 45*, 119-140.

Costa, P.T., Jr., & McCrae, R.R. (1990). *The NEO Personaltiy-Revised Manual*. Odessa, FL: Psychological Assessment Resources.

Costa, P.T., Jr., & McCrae, R.R. (1992). *Professional manual revised NEO personality inventory (NEO-PI-R) and NEO Five-Factor Inventory (NEO-FFI)*. Odessa, Fl: Psychological Assessment Resources, Inc.

Driskell, J.E., & Salas, E. (1992). Can you study real teams in contrived settings? The value of small group research to understanding Teams. In R.W. Swezey & E. Salas (Eds.), *Teams: Their training and performance*. Norwood, NJ: Ablex Publishing Company.

Driskell, J.E., & Salas, E. (1991). Group decision making under stress. *Journal of Applied Psychology, 76*, 473-478.

Eysenck, S.B.G., & Eysenck, H.J. (1963). On the dual nature of extraversion. *British Journal of Social and Clinical Psychology, 2*, 46-55.

Eysenck, H.J. (1947). *Dimensions of personality*. London: Routledge & Kegan Paul.

Fisher, A.B., & Ellis, D.G. (1990). *Small group decision making: Communication and the group process*. New York: McGraw Hill.

George, J.M. (1996). Trait and state affect. In K.R. Murphy (Ed.), *Individual differences and behavior in organizations*. San Francisco: Jossey-Bass.

Hackman, J. R. (1990). Creating more effective work groups in organizations. In J. R. Hackman (Ed.), *Groups that work and those that don't* (pp. 479-504). San Francisco, CA: Jossey-Bass.

Helton, K.T., Nontasak, T., & Dolgin, D.L. (1992). Landing Craft Air Cushion (LCAC) crew selection system manual (NAMRL-Special Report 92-4). Pensacola, FL: Naval Aerospace Medical Research Laboratory.

Hoffman, L.R., & Maier, N.R.F. (1961). Quality and acceptance of problem solutions by members of homogeneous and heterogeneous groups. *Journal of Abnormal and Social Psychology, 62*, 401-407.

Hogan, R., & Hogan, J. (1995). *Hogan Personality Inventory manual (2nd ed.)*. Tulsa, OK: Hogan Assessment Systems.

Hogan, J., & Hogan, R. (1993, April). The ambiguities of conscientiousness. Paper presented at the 8th Annual Conference of the Society for Industrial and Organizational Psychologists, Inc., San Francisco.

Hogan, R., Hogan, J., & Roberts, B.W. (1996). Personality measurement and employment decisions. *American Psychologist, 51*, 469-477.

Hough, L.E., & Schneider, R.J. (1996). Personality traits, taxonomies, and applications in organizations. In KR. Murphy (Ed.), *Individual differences and behavior in organizations*. San Francisco: Jossey–Bass.

Jackson, S.E., May, K.E., & Whitney, K. (1995). Understanding the dynamics of configuration in decision making teams. In R. Guzzo & E. Salas (Eds.), Team effectiveness and decision making in organizations. San Francisco: Jossey-Bass.

Janus, I.L. (1972). *Victims of groupthink*. Boston: Houghton Mifflin.

Janus, I.L. (1983) Groupthink. In H.H. Blumberg, A.P. Hare, V. Kent, & M.F. Davis (Eds.), *Small groups and social interaction*. (Vol. 2, pp. 39-46). New York: Wiley.

Johnson, J.L. (1997). *Personality and prejudice*. DEOMI Research Series 97-5.

Johnson, J.L. & Bloom, A.M. (1995). An analysis of the contribution of the five factors of personality to variance in academic procrastination. *Personality and individual differences, 18* (1), 127-133.

Larkey, K.L. (1996). Toward a theory of communicative interactions in culturally diverse work groups. *Academy of Management Review, 21*, 462-291.

Larson, C.E., & LaFasto, F.M. J. (1989). *Teamwork: What must go right/what can go wrong*. Newbury Park, CA: Sage.

McGrath, J.E., Berdahl, J.L., & Arrow, H. (1995). Traits, expectations, culture, and clout: The dynamics of diversity in work groups. In S.E. Jackson and M.N. Ruderman (Eds.), *Diversity in teams* (pp. 17-45). Washington, D.C.: American Psychological Association.

Morgan, B.B.Jr., & Lassiter, D.L. (1992). Team composition and staffing. In R.W. Swezey & E. Salas (Eds.), *Teams: Their training and performance*. Norwood, NJ: Ablex Publishing Company.

Mullen, B., Anthony, T., Salas, E., & Driskell, J.E. (1994). Group cohesiveness and quality of decision making: An integration of tests of the groupthink hypothesis. *Small Group Research, 25*, 189-204.

Pedersen, L.A., Allan, K.E., Laue, F.J., & Siem, R. (1992). Personality theory and construction in selection and classification (Tech. Report AL-TR-1992-0021). Brooks Air Force Base, San Antonio, TX: Armstrong Laboratory.

Pratt, J. & Jiambalvo, J. (1981). Relationships between leader behaviors and audit team performance. *Accounting, Organizations, and Society, 6*, 133-142.

Rosenstein, R., & Dickinson, T.L. (1996, August). The teamwork components model: An analysis using structural equation modeling. In R.M. McIntyre (Chair), Advances in definitional team research. Symposium conducted at the annual meeting of the American Psychological Association, Toronto.

Ruggeberg, B. J. (1996). Toward understanding team leadership: The empirical development of a team leadership classification system. Unpublished doctoral dissertation, Department of Psychology, Old Dominion University.

Salas, E., Dickinson, T.L., Converse, S.A., & Tannebaum, S.I. (1992). Toward an understanding of team performance and training. In R.W. Swezey & E. Salas (Eds.), *Teams: Their training and performance*, (pp. 3-29). Norwood, NJ: ABLEX.

Stewart, G.L., & Manz, C. C. (1994, April). Leadership for self-managing teams: A theoretical integration. Paper presented at the Ninth Annual Conference of the Society for Industrial and Organizational Psychology, Nashville, TN.

Street, D.R., Helton, K.T., & Dolgin D.L. (1992). The unique contribution of selected personality tests to the prediction of success in naval pilot training (NAMRL-1374). Pensacola, FL: Naval Aerospace Medical Research Laboratory.

Tellegen, A. (1982). *Brief manual for the differential personality questionnaire*. Unpublished manuscript, University of Minnesota.

Tellegen, A., (1985). Structures of mood and personality and their relevance to assessing anxiety, with an emphasis on self-report. In A.H. Tuma & J.D. Maser (Eds.), *Anxiety and the anxiety disorders* (pp. 681-706). Hlllsdale, NJ: Erlbaum.

Thomas, D.A. & Ely, R.J. (1996, Sep/Oct). Making differences matter: A new paradigm for managing diversity. *Harvard Business Review, 74 (5), 79-91.*

Watson, D., & Pennebaker, J.W. (1989). Health complaints, stress, and distress: Exploring the central role of negative affectivity. *Psychological Review, 96*, 234-254.

Wiggins, J.S., & Trapnell, P.D. (1997). Personality structure: The return of the big five. In R. Hogan, J.A. Johnson, et al. (Eds.). *Handbook of personality psychology*. San Diego, CA: Academic Press, Inc.

Wood, W. (1987). Meta-analytic review of sex differences in group performance. Psychological Bulletin, *102*, 53-71.

Zaccaro, S.J. (1991). Nonequivalent associations between forms of cohesion and group-related outcomes. *Journal of Social Psychology*, 131, 387-399.

Appendix

Teamwork Process Measures

TEAMWORK   Group Number _____

Please use the scale below to rate your team. Consider carefully the aspects of teamwork (e.g., **TEAM ORIENTATION**) and their behaviors (e.g., cooperate fully with one another). Rate how frequently your team members engage in each of the behaviors.

> 5 = Always
> 4 = Most of the time
> 3 = Often
> 2 = Sometimes
> 1 = Never

TEAM ORIENTATION refers to the attitudes that team members have toward one another and the team task. It reflects acceptance of team norms, level of group cohesiveness, and importance of team membership.

Team members:

_____ 1. Willingly participate in all relevant aspects of the team.

_____ 2. Cooperate fully with one another.

_____ 3. Pull together and place team goals ahead of their personal goals and interests.

_____ 4. Display a high degree of pride in their duties and the team.

_____ 5. Display an awareness that they are part of a team and that teamwork is important.

_____ 6. Assign high priority to team goals.

_____ 7. Feel that team experience is personally satisfying.

_____ 8. Feel proud of personal contributions to team output.

_____ 9. Regard other team members in a positive way.

_____10. Feel close to other team members.

_____11. Do helpful things for other members of the team.

_____12. Unify with other members in pursuit of team goals.

_____13. Feel that accomplishment of team goals is important.

TEAM LEADERSHIP involves providing direction, structure, and support for other team members. It does not necessarily refer to a single individual with formal authority over others. Team leadership can be shown by several team members.

Team members:

_____ 1. Encourage other team members to make decisions on their own.

_____ 2. Work with other members to develop communication methods and areas of responsibility.

_____ 3. Explain to other team members exactly what is needed from them for a project.

_____ 4. Review the situation quickly when the team becomes overwhelmed and take action.

_____ 5. Ensure that other members are working up to capacity.

_____ 6. Ask other members to follow standard procedures.

_____ 7. Stress the importance of meeting deadlines.

_____ 8. Strive to maintain definite performance standards.

_____ 9. Give consideration to the needs of other members, especially subordinates.

_____10. Provide encouragement when other members attempt to meet new challenges.

_____11. Are willing to listen to problems/complaints of other members.

_____12. Show concern for the welfare of other team members, especially subordinates.

_____13. Strive to create a friendly team environment.

_____14. Provide needed support for new members.

_____15. Listen to the concerns of other team members.

_____16. Assign experienced members to perform critical tasks.

_____17. Assign extra work only to the more capable members.

_____18. Find someone to fill in for them when leaving work.

COMMUNICATION involves the exchange of information between two or more team members in the prescribed manner and by using proper terminology. Often the purpose of communication is to clarify or acknowledge the receipt of information.

Team members:

_____ 1. Clarify intentions to other team members.
_____ 2. Clarify procedures in advance of assignments.
_____ 3. Pass on complete information to other members.
_____ 4. Acknowledge and repeat messages to ensure understanding.
_____ 5. Communicate with proper terminology and procedures.
_____ 6. Verify information prior to reporting to others.
_____ 7. Ask for clarification of performance status when necessary.
_____ 8. Follow proper communication procedures in passing and receiving information.
_____ 9. Ensure that other team members understand information as it was intended to be understood.
_____10. Communicate information related to the team task.
_____11. Discuss task-related problems with others.

MONITORING refers to observing the activities and performance of other team members. It implies that team members are individually competent and that they may subsequently provide feedback and backup behavior.

Team members:

_____ 1. Are aware of other team members' performance.
_____ 2. Are concerned with the performance of team members with whom they interact closely.
_____ 3. Make sure other team members are performing appropriately.
_____ 4. Recognize when a team member makes a mistake.
_____ 5. Recognize when a team member performs correctly.
_____ 6. Notice the behavior of others.
_____ 7. Discover errors in the performance of another team member.
_____ 8. Watch other team members to ensure that they are performing according to guidelines.
_____ 9. Notice which members are performing their tasks especially well.

FEEDBACK involves the giving, seeking, and receiving of information among team members. Giving feedback refers to providing information regarding other members' performance. Seeking feedback refers to requesting input or guidance regarding performance. Receiving feedback refers to accepting positive and negative information regarding performance.

Team members:

_____ 1. Respond to other members' requests for performance information.

_____ 2. Accept time-saving suggestions offered by other team members.

_____ 3. Explain terminology to a member who does not understand its meaning.

_____ 4. Ask the supervisor for input regarding their performance and what needs to be worked on.

_____ 5. Are corrected on a few mistakes, and incorporate the suggestions into their procedures.

_____ 6. Use information provided by other members to improve behavior.

_____ 7. Ask for advice on proper procedures.

_____ 8. Provide helpful suggestions to other members.

_____ 9. Provide insightful comments when an assignment does not go as planned.

BACKUP BEHAVIOR involves assisting the performance of other team members. This implies that members have an understanding of other members' tasks. It also implies that team members are willing and able to provide and seek assistance when needed.

Team members:

_____ 1. Fill in for another member who is unable to perform a task.

_____ 2. Seek opportunities to aid other team members.

_____ 3. Help another member correct a mistake.

_____ 4. Provide assistance to those who need it when specifically asked.

_____ 5. Step in for another team member who is overburdened.

_____ 6. Take control of a situation when other team members do not know how to perform.

_____ 7. Solve a problem posed by another team member.

_____ 8. Ask for help when needed.

_____ 9. Maintain their own duties in the process of helping others.

COORDINATION refers to team members executing their activities in a timely and integrated manner. It implies that the performance of some team members influences the performance of other team members. This may involve an exchange of information that subsequently influences another member's performance.

Team members:

_____ 1. Complete individual tasks without error, in a timely manner.

_____ 2. Pass performance-relevant data from one to another in a timely and efficient manner.

_____ 3. Are familiar with the relevant parts of other members' jobs.

_____ 4. Facilitate the performance of each other.

_____ 5. Carry out individual tasks in synchrony.

_____ 6. Cause other members to work effectively.

_____ 7. Avoid distractions during critical assignments.

_____ 8. Carry out individual tasks effectively thereby leading to coordinated team performance.

_____ 9. Work together with other members to accomplish team goals.

PERFORMANCE concerns the accomplishment of the activities and tasks required of the team. This team performance occurs with a consideration of the goals and expectations of team members, the supervisor, and the larger organization.

Team members:

_____ 1. Accomplish team goals.

_____ 2. Meet or exceed expectations of the team.

_____ 3. Meet performance goals in a timely manner.

_____ 4. Regard team output as adequate or acceptable.

_____ 5. Achieve team goals with few or no errors.

_____ 6. Produce team output that meets standards of the organization.

_____ 7. Regard accomplishments of the team to be above average.

_____ 8. Feel that the team as a whole performed at an acceptable level.

_____ 9. Met team objectives in an efficient manner.

6

See No Evil, Hear No Evil: Senior Leaders' Social Comparisons and the Low Salience of Racial Issues

Rupert W. Nacoste

Introduction

One of the major responsibilities of a chief executive officer (CEO) is to manage the morale of the company's work force. That responsibility is important because morale has an influence on productivity and turnover rates. Unfortunately for the CEO, management of morale is often done from a distance, through others who channel information to the CEO. That sometimes happens because of the size of organizations, and very often happens because of the extraordinary demands on the CEO's time. Time is often taken up with responsibilities that make it difficult for the CEO to be in direct contact with "line workers." All this is also true for the CEOs, who in the military are senior leaders—Navy and Coast Guard captains and admirals, and Air Force, Army, and Marine Corps colonels and generals.

Like other CEOs, as part of managing morale, senior military leaders must manage the complex issues of race and gender relations. Management of race and gender relations has the major goal of ensuring equal opportunity between race and gender groups. Whether they are aware of it or not, senior military CEOs are trying to manage, then, a system of procedural interdependence.

Personnel systems of all types are systems of procedural interdependence. Procedural interdependence refers to a social system in which groups are linked to each other by decision-making proce-

133

dures. In such a system, the decision-making procedures influence the outcomes available to the groups. Those procedures then influence in what way groups' outcomes are dependent on each other, or interdependent.

Procedural interdependence exists, however, at both a material (or objective) and psychological (or subjective) level (Nacoste, 1996; Nacoste & Hummels, 1994). All CEOs, including senior military leaders, are attempting to manage both these dimensions of their personnel systems. Management of the material level involves setting up policies that ensure equal opportunity for all groups, as well as meeting requirements imposed by outside agencies. Management of the psychological dimension requires establishing policies that meet the subjective standards of the groups affected by the policy, so "as to encourage the continuation of productive exchange" between groups (Thibaut & Walker, 1975). Both these management goals are greatly affected by procedures.

To "line workers," CEOs and senior leaders are often perceived as being out of the loop, and so their ability and even motivation to meet these management goals may often be doubted. Senior leaders, it seems, although fair-minded, may not fully understand whether any action needs to be taken, or if there is a need, what action should be taken to meet the material and psychological management goals. The work reported in this paper was undertaken to develop some formal hypotheses about why senior military leaders may not fully understand how to manage the system of procedural interdependence, as it bears on race and gender relations within their units or agencies.

Two Social Psychological Hypotheses

When it comes to getting authentic information, senior military leaders are faced with certain situational impediments. As with social systems, informational systems are systems of interdependence. That means that the flow of information in these systems is not linear, but dependent on how a person is structurally linked to others. For example, senior leaders are linked to others in the information system in hierarchical fashion. Whereas line workers have co-workers who are on the same hierarchical level, and with whom they have mutual dependence, by contrast senior leaders are less likely to have someone with whom they are mutually dependent. That structure of relationships for the senior leader in the information system of interdependence suggests two possible structural sources that might be influencing the information that senior leaders receive on racial and gender tensions: a demographic isolation source, and a social comparison source.

Demographic and Hierarchical Isolation

Demographic isolation refers to a set of background factors that combined with a leadership position, keeps a person out of the direct flow of information. Where the information in question regards issues of race and gender, certain demographic characteristics of senior leaders may isolate those leaders from the relevant information flow. Those demographic characteristics would include the race of the leader. Being white might make a person less likely to perceive racial concerns, whereas those who are nonwhite might find them to be obvious. When race comes together with education level and rank, an individual might be very unlikely to ever receive authentic reports about racial matters in the unit. For example, highly educated, high-ranking whites would be in a structural niche in the information system that would be isolated from that kind of information. Nonetheless, given the institutional pressure to have a unit where racial and gender tensions are low, these individuals would have to have some way of satisfying their need for information on these matters.

Hypothesis I: Senior leaders fit a demographic profile that isolates them from information about racial issues in their units.

Social Comparison

When an individual has no objective way of gauging reality, they turn to subjective social comparisons to reduce their uncertainty. This concept comes directly from Festinger's (1954) theory of social comparison. If senior leaders fit a demographic profile that isolates them from the information they need, they will turn to some other source for that information.

For senior leaders, the problem is that they are required to monitor and improve race relations in their units, in order to maintain a high level of mission readiness. Under those circumstances, senior leaders need objective information about those matters. Unfortunately, given their demographic and hierarchical isolation, senior leaders are less likely to get this information. Given those circumstances, it follows from Festinger's (1954) social comparison theory that senior leaders will rely on social comparison to reduce the anxiety they experience about monitoring and managing racial issues in their units.

Hypothesis II: Demographic isolation causes senior leaders to rely on social comparison as a source of information about racial issues in their units.

Types of Social Comparison

What possible social comparisons might senior leaders use in response to their demographic and hierarchical isolation? Although a variety of social comparisons are possible, upward and downward for example, it is most likely that social comparisons with similar others will occur. That would mean that senior leaders would cognitively conceptualize how others like them would evaluate and respond to the situation. Given, however, that the point of reference here is senior leaders, there is another, non-contradictory, possibility.

Senior leaders are attempting to manage a policy mandate. As such, the theory of procedural interdependence is particularly applicable. That theory implies, among other things, that there is a social psychological link between the nature of the problem and the procedures that exist in the organization's system of policies and procedures. Attempts to comply with a policy statement will motivate a search for information. Those cut off from relevant information by demographic and hierarchical isolation will then likely use what they think about related policies and procedures as a social source of information. In the case of senior military leaders, that would mean that these leaders would use their own evaluation of the fairness of general personnel systems to evaluate the legitimacy of claims of racial concerns.

Hypothesis III: For senior leaders, two forms of social comparison will be found to be related to the salience of racial issues: general social comparison and system fairness.

Social Comparison Consequences

Generally, although it can reduce anxiety, social comparison does so without reliance on objective information. What consequence will the identified social comparisons have on the salience of racial issues among senior leaders? General social comparison, because it uses similar others as a source, should reduce the salience of racial issues among senior leaders. Why? Similar others will, in this case, be similarly situated, that is demographically and hierarchically isolated. That being the case, the social comparisons are being made with individuals who themselves have little experience with racial issues, and thus little sensitivity to what they involve and how they influence people psychologically. For similar reasons, use of evaluations of general systems will also lead senior leaders to assume that when it comes to race, things are basically going well. Again, if senior leaders fit a particular demographic profile, and given that they have traversed the system so successfully, they will have very little reason to question the operation of the system. As a consequence, they will tend to judge the general personnel systems to be fair, and for them that will reduce the possibility that there are racial problems being created by the system.

Hypothesis IV: The general and systems social comparisons used by senior leaders will reduce the salience of racial issues.

Preliminary test of hypotheses I-IV will be conducted with responses from the Senior Leader Equal Opportunity Climate Survey (SLEOCS).

Method

Senior military leaders' views of equal opportunity in the armed forces may be unique. With that in mind, the Senior Leader Equal Opportunity Climate Survey (SLEOCS) was constructed by the staff of the Defense Equal Opportunity Management Institute (DEOMI) (see Dansby, 1998). From the survey, items for the test of hypotheses to be conducted were drawn from the 18 demographic items, the 25 items to measure Equal Opportunity perceptions in general, the 16 items to measure perceived seriousness of equal opportunity issues, and from 24 items taken from the Military Equal Opportunity Climate Survey (MEOCS) scales. Except for the demographic items, a 5-point Likert item format was employed.

For these preliminary tests of the newly specified hypotheses (I-IV), the decision was made to focus only on active-duty personnel. That being the case, all others were eliminated from the analyses reported, leaving N=671. These participants were mostly white (93 percent), male (88 percent), between 46 and 55 years of age (92 percent), and held a graduate degree (91 percent).

Factor Analysis

Although all of the responses to the SLEOCS had previously been factor analyzed, that factor analysis was not directed by specific psychological hypotheses. That factor analysis was conducted with all of the items included in one factor analysis to capture clustered variance across all surveyed responses. The analysis yields a number of general factors.

In the present case, the hypotheses are much more directed. Consequently, a specific "psychological" factor analysis was conducted using small sets of items, making the statistical assumption that within each survey item set, there will be unique clustering that is based on psychological dimensions of the responses.

Factor Analysis Predictions

Items 19-43 of the SLEOCS were designed to assess a variety of perceptions of equal opportunity issues in the military. Following from the procedural-interdependence perspective developed above, it is expected that, at minimum, items 41-43 would cluster. Theoretically those items reflect "general system procedural fairness." If those items were to cluster, as expected, then there would be support for the approach and an empirical starting point for further analyses.

Items 44-59 were designed to assess the psychological salience of racial and gender problems in the military. Here, it is expected that a factor analysis would show clusters such that racial and gender problem saliences are relatively independent.

Correlation Analysis

On the face of it there were two items that seemed good candidates for use as indicators of general social comparison. Item 60 had to do with the respondent's (i.e., the senior leader's) judgment of how "most people" would rate equal opportunity in the respondent's Service or agency. Item 61 was the respondent's personal rating of the same. A high correlation between these two items would suggest, theoretically, that senior leaders were using some "generalized other" as a source through which to judge how their units were doing when it comes to equal opportunity.

Preliminary Statistical Analysis

Identification of Theoretical Dimensions

General Systems Fairness: Items 19-43 were subjected to principle components factor analysis with variamax rotation. Using 1.0 as the mininum acceptable eigenvalue, six clusters were extracted from the responses, accounting for 55.2 percent of the variance in responses to these items. Results of this factor analysis were consistent with expectations. Most importantly for the theory guiding this research, items 40-43 clustered together; eigenvalue= 3.7, accounting for 14.8 percent of the variance. Together these items seem to reflect the hypothesized "general systems procedural fairness," with items such as "The discipline system in my Service or agency is fair to all groups," and "The promotion system in my Service or agency is fair to all groups." Also included in this cluster was item 40, which reads "EO issues are generally handled equitably in my Service or agency." Inclusion of that item in the "general systems fairness" cluster provides preliminary support for the major hypothesis that evaluations of general systems procedural fairness is the inferential lens through which command level personnel evaluate equal opportunity programs.

Salience of Racial Problems: Separately, items 44-59 were subjected to a principal components factor analysis with varimax rotation. With eigenvalue acceptability set at 1.0, four factor clusters were identified, explaining 75.8 percent of the variance. Given the conceptual direction of the work of most interest was item cluster one which clearly was salience of racial, majority-minority problems. That cluster included items where the respondent is to evaluate the seriousness of a problem in the relationships between "Black (African-American) and white members," "Hispanic and white members," etc. It is certain that this cluster is only racial, since separate item clusters captured both general gender issues (i.e., various combinations of men and women) and gender discrimination (i.e., "Sexual harassment," and "Sexism" or gender discrimination).

General Social Comparison: Senior leaders' personal ratings of the equal opportunity climate, and their judgment of how "most other people" would rate the climate were correlated. That analysis showed the two items to be highly correlated ($r = .78$, $p < .01$). The items were then combined to create an index for "general social comparison."

Major Results

Hypothesis I was that senior leaders are demographically isolated, or insulated from information that should make racial concerns and incidents salient. With that in mind, the demographic backgrounds of respondents were analyzed. Consistent with the hypothesis, those analyses show that senior leaders fit in a certain socio-demographic profile.

Senior leaders were found to be mostly male (92.3 percent), mostly white (93.4 percent), 46 to 55 years of age (88.5 percent), and with college degrees (99.6 percent). Individuals in this profile are much less likely than others to have seen or experienced racial discrimination. And indeed, other data from the SLEOCS show this precisely. Among active-duty senior leaders, 88.7 percent have not experienced discrimination by military personnel, and 84.2 percent have not experienced discrimination by civilian personnel.

Hypothesis II states that the identified demographic isolation will cause senior leaders to use more social psychological sources of information to gauge racial concerns. There are two problems with this hypothesis. First, it is a motivational hypothesis, and the dynamics of motivation are not subject to precise identification with the present data. Second, it is a causal hypothesis, again not testable with the present data, which were collected through a cross-sectional methodology that does not allow for a direct test of causal relationships.

With those problems noted, it was still worthwhile to check for a relationship between the demographic characteristics of the respondents and the two types of social comparison identified. Should a relationship be found, that would be taken as an indication of the influence of demographic features on motivation to use social comparison. Results of separate hierarchical regression analyses for general social comparison and general systems fairness provided evidence that demographic isolation did influence senior leaders to use social comparison. General social comparison was predicted by pay grade ($B = .15$, $p < .001$) and by age of the senior leader ($B = .10$, $p < .009$). Likewise, general systems fairness was predicted by pay grade ($B = -.09$, $p < .02$) and age of the senior leader ($B = .11$, $p < .005$). Thus, hypothesis II was indirectly confirmed, with the evidence indicating that demographic factors were linked to the two types of social comparison. This indirect confirmation was useful as part of the network of logical relations that led to hypothesis III.

Hypothesis III stated that two forms of social comparison would be empirically identified: general social comparison and (evaluations of) general system fairness. Correlational and factor analytic work reported above did identify these forms of social comparison in the responses of senior leaders.

In addition, further analyses showed that the two forms of social comparison were significantly correlated with each other ($r = .41$, $p < .01$). Given their placement in the survey, and their lack of common-sense connection, that these two sets of responses correlate at all suggest that they share a conceptual link. Since, however, the level of correlation was modest, the two were treated independently.

Hypothesis IV indicated that general social comparison and general systems fairness would predict salience of racial issues, such that the more positive these responses, the lower the salience of racial issues. This hypothesis was investigated through the use of hierarchical multiple regression analysis.

As shown above, salience of racial issues exists in a separate, independent cluster. That cluster was subjected to hierarchical multiple regression analysis. Demographic variables, and the two types of social comparison were used as independent variables to test the hypothesis that social comparison influences the salience of racial issues for senior leaders. That regression confirmed the hypothesis. A significant regression model was obtained using these variables as predictors ($\underline{F}$ $(5,661) = 14.5$, $p < .001$, $R^2 = .09$). Only the two types of social comparison were significant predictors of the salience of racial issues: general social comparison ($B = .26$, $p < .001$) and general systems fairness ($B = .11$, $p < .008$).

Having established that social comparison is a significant predictor of the extent to which, for senior leaders, racial issues are salient, it is important to make note of the direction of this influence. Hypothesis IV indicates that social comparison should reduce salience. And indeed, that is what the analysis shows. In all cases, the beta-weight is positive. Given the coding of the social comparison indicators and the coding of the indicators of racial issues salience, the positive beta-weight means that as social comparison information indicates more positive evaluation, salience of racial issues is lowered. For instance, as general social comparison indicates that when a senior leader says that "like others, I" evaluate the equal opportunity climate in my service as "very good," that senior leader is more likely to report that racial relationships in their Service are "no problem at all." The same holds for general systems fairness social comparison. When systems are evaluated as fair by a senior leader, that senior leader perceives that racial relationships are "no problem at all." In both instances, social comparison reduces the salience of racial issues. That can be said with some confidence because, to begin with, responses are skewed towards low salience.

Discussion

What factors might make it less likely that racial issues will be salient to senior leaders? One obvious hypothesis is racial prejudice. Here the claim would be that senior leaders, who are mostly white, carry overt or covert racial prejudice that blinds them to racial inequities.

Another possibility, however, is that there are background factors that do not cause racial prejudice, per se, but that make discrimination less cognitively available as an explanation for racial inequities. It could be, for example, that some senior leaders have no personal experience as victims of discrimination. Being without such a personal experience should reduce the salience of discrimination as a social force, and thus reduce the availability of discrimination in the individual's cognitive system. Analyses conducted for this report showed that most senior leaders surveyed indicated they had no experience with discrimination.

If the experience of discrimination increases the cognitive availability of discrimination as an explanation for events, then command level personnel are much less likely to explain (even) clear racial disparities in terms that rely on the concept of discrimination. Senior leaders would, according to hypotheses II and II, imagine how some similar, generalized other would evaluate the situation and search for an explanation in the procedural systems linked to the racial disparities. Both cognitive strategies, however, would be unlikely to include, or include only at a very low level, the concept of discrimination as an available explanation. Having searched for a reference point in general social comparison and through the general procedural systems, senior leaders would judge the alleged racial event through the lens of their evaluation of the general procedural systems. If those systems are judged to be working fairly, then the alleged racial incident will be discounted in racial terms.

It was with this set of logically connected propositions that the work reported in the current study was undertaken. Four interrelated hypotheses were subjected to preliminary tests. Those preliminary tests confirmed the hypotheses and the underlying set of connected propositions. The evidence suggests, then, that the salience of racial issues among senior level personnel is largely influenced by their demographic isolation and the consequent social comparisons they use to gauge the racial climate in their units.

Demographic isolation and the reliance on social comparison that this isolation seems to motivate in senior leaders are a problem because together they cause senior leaders to ignore, or discount, the voices of those who are closest to the problems—rank and file personnel. Dansby (1998) has shown that there is a discrepancy between senior leaders' and rank and file personnel's evaluation of the equal opportunity climate in their units. While the rank and file are generally positive, senior leaders are much more optimistic than the rank and file. Now there is evidence that this optimism may not be rooted in any hard data, but is primarily based on the two types of social comparison that senior leaders' use to reduce their anxiety about race relations. As a consequence, senior leaders are at risk of being taken by surprise and caught off guard by some racial dynamics that finally come to the fore through some extreme event. And it would take an extreme event even to get their attention since, because of their own social comparisons, senior leaders are desensitized to seeing racial events as racial events.

What can be done to cause senior leaders to pay more attention to the concerns expressed by the personnel in their units? Breaking the "mesmerizing power" of social comparison as it operates in emergency situations is most readily accomplished through training. Once people are aware to how social comparison inhibits actions that they would normally take to help others, social comparison has less power. Senior leaders then should be trained. Given the root cause of their reliance on social comparison, demographic and hierarchical isolation, senior leaders should be trained to use sources of information that are not so isolated. Unlike senior leaders, Equal Opportunity Advisors are not isolated from information about racial climate issues in their units. Quite the contrary, Equal Opportunity Advisors receive a great deal of information about the command's racial climate. Given where Equal Opportunity Advisors sit in the structural flow of information, senior leaders should be trained to use their Equal Opportunity Advisors as a "divining rod" to ascertain the true racial climate of their units.

References

Dansby, M.R. (1998). The Senior Leader Equal Opportunity Climate Survey: An update on what the bosses believe. In M.R. Dansby (Ed.) *Proceedings of the 2ⁿᵈ Biennial EO/ EEO Research Symposium* (pp. 49-53). Defense Equal Opportunity Management Institute, Patrick AFB, FL.

Festinger, L. (1954). A theory of social comparison processes. *Human Relations, 7*, 117-140.

Nacoste, R.W. (1996). Social psychology and the affirmative action debate. *Journal of Social and Clinical Psychology, 15*, 261-282.

Nacoste, R.W., & Hummels, B. (1994). Affirmative action and the behavior of decisionmakers. *Journal of Applied Social Psychology, 24*, 595-613.

Thibaut, J.W., & Walker, L. (1975). *Procedural justice: A psychological analysis.* Hillsdale, NJ: Earlbaum.

7

Mentors, Mentor Substitutes, or Virtual Mentors: Alternative Mentoring Approaches for the Military

Stephen B. Knouse and Schuyler C. Webb

"Mentor was an old friend of Odysseus, to whom the king had entrusted his own household when he sailed, with orders...to keep everything safe and sound.

Athena...assuming the form and voice of Mentor, addressed him with winged words. 'Telemachus, you will be neither a coward nor fool in the future...you can hope to succeed in this undertaking...for am I not your father's friend, and ready to find you a fast ship and sail with you myself? I myself will pick out the best for you.'"

— Homer, The Odyssey, Book 2, Lines 226-296

Introduction

In Homer's *Odyssey*, when Odysseus left his kingdom of Ithaca for the legendary war with Troy, he consigned his son and heir, Telemachus, to the wise and experienced care of his friend and colleague, Mentor. In the ensuing twenty years of Odysseus' absence, Mentor oversaw Telemachus' training in the arts of war and kingship and supported him against opposing countrymen in the governing assembly.

In addition, the warrior goddess, Athena (also the goddess of wisdom and the arts), appeared to Telemachus many times in the form of Mentor to offer guidance, encouragement, and resources. When Odysseus returned at the end of twenty years to find his loyal wife, Penelope, surrounded by hostile suitors who were consuming his wealth, he was able to defeat these interlopers and regain his kingdom with the capable assistance of Telemachus, who had been well tutored by Mentor and his substitute persona, Athena.

From this Greek epic, several parallels for today's mentor can be borrowed—the more senior "father" figure developing a younger colleague (e.g., protégé or mentee) in career and life skills within an atmosphere of friendship and trust. Moreover, there is a substitute mentor stepping in to help on occasion. Indeed, the most unique guidance and strongest encouragement came from this substitute. Interestingly, there is also a powerful mentoring role for a female figure. Eventually, the protégé is expected to go to great lengths in order to honor the work and friendship of the mentor. The authors revisit these metaphors several times again.

In this report the authors will first address the concept of mentoring —definitions; functions; advantages for the protégé, mentor, and organization; stages of the mentoring relationship; research on mentoring; and the unique situation of military mentoring. We argue for several reasons that mentoring is difficult in the military. Therefore, several alternatives to traditional mentoring are examined. Finally, recommendations are discussed for implementing these mentoring alternatives in the military environment.

The Concept of Mentoring

Today, the mentor is seen in relation to the protégé from several perspectives. One type of definition focuses upon traits and behaviors of the mentor: "an individual with advanced experience and knowledge committed to providing upward mobility, and support to protégés" (Ragins, 1997, p. 484). Another type of definition emphasizes the mentor-protégé relationship: "developmental relationship between an individual and a more senior, influential professional or manager" (Dreher & Cox, 1996, p. 298). A third looks at the benefits: "provides protégés with the opportunity to develop skills, gain access to developmental opportunities, build the confidence necessary to tackle challenging tasks, and obtain guidance and counseling" (Eby, 1997, p. 126).

In essence, the mentor provides two basic functions for the protégé: instrumental and psychosocial (Kram & Isabella, 1985). In the instrumental or career enhancing function, the modern mentor, like Telemachus' Mentor, provides sponsorship of the protégé in the organization, thus legitimizing him or her to the established powers in the organization. The mentor also provides coaching on job-related skills and feedback on job performance. The mentor makes the protégé visible to important personnel and protects him or her from powerful individuals in the organization. The mentor recommends challenging work assignments and unique training and development that broaden and deepen job skills. Moreover, the mentor assists the protégé linking into career networks.

In the psychosocial function, the mentor provides the protégé counseling to improve interpersonal skills and to enhance their perceptions of their colleague's thoughts and feelings. Mentors serve as a role model for the correct behavior to exhibit in the organization. In addition, like the original Mentor, the modern mentor is a friend to the protégé. All of these activities require a cost in the form of substantial time and effort spent by both the mentor and protégé in maintaining the relationship. These costs are balanced by numerous benefits to the protégé, to the mentor, and to the organization.

Various Advantages

Protégé. The protégé or mentee experiences better job satisfaction, encounters better opportunities for advancement, enjoys a higher income than nonmentored individuals (Dreher & Ash, 1990), and reports more career satisfaction (Turban & Dougherty, 1994). For example, mentored persons possessing a Masters of Business Administration (MBA) Degree averaged over $22,000 more in annual salary than nonmentored MBAs (Dreher & Cox, 1996). In addition, mentoring empowers the protégé to use his or her skills and knowledge more effectively and efficiently (Gunn, 1995).

Mentor. The mentor takes a risk in terms of time diverted away from his or her own career and even the possibility of a political flare-up from rivals when entering a mentoring relationship. However, this risk is balanced by a number of advantages to the mentor. He or she receives personal satisfaction from helping junior people advance. They may feel that they have repaid a personal debt to their own mentor by continuing the tradition. Moreover, they may feel that they have provided continuity in the organizational hierarchy by sponsoring their own successor (Ragins & Cotton, 1993; Ragins & Scandura, 1993).

The Organization. There are a number of advantages to the organization. A mentored workforce is more skilled, more connected with one another, and more savvy about organizational politics. There is less turnover of valuable junior people. In downsizing, the remaining mentored employees have skill depth and flexibility (Gunn, 1995).

Mentoring grooms future organizational leaders (Jossi, 1997). There is a smooth transition from senior to junior people of corporate memory, unwritten policies, psychological contracts, organizational myths and stories, and connectivity to resources and the outside environment. Finally, from a cost viewpoint, formal or informal mentoring results in highly individualized training and is a relatively inexpensive means of employee development compared to formal workshops and seminars (Jossi, 1997).

Stages of the Mentoring Relationship

Mentoring is a long-term relationship that evolves through several stages (Kram, 1983). This can be a shortcoming with respect to the system of frequent job rotations in a military career.

Initiating. In embarking on the mentoring path, there must be a friendship, like the one between Mentor and Odysseus' family, or some other close "chemistry" between the mentor and protégé. From social psychological research, it is known that friendships typically arise between individuals who share many common characteristics (e.g., same gender and race) and similar psychological traits (e.g., attitudes and values) (Aronson, 1995). Thus, white males may find it easier to find potential mentors among senior managers and professionals, who are predominantly white males, than do women and minorities, who are at a disadvantage (Ragins, 1997). In short, the mentoring needs of women and minorities are less likely to be met.

The organizational leadership can encourage opportunities for such "chemistry" to develop. It can help the mentoring process either through establishing formal programs that structure the process or informal programs that provide opportunities for the chemistry to develop. Such opportunities can arise through informal discussions among junior and senior people, junior and senior people working together on teams, working on special projects, and junior presentations to seniors. In these situations, senior people can see how potential protégés present themselves, deal with interpersonal relations, and solve problems.

Mentoring. An effective mentoring relationship develops over two to five years. Because it focuses on career cultivation, the instrumental or career enhancing function usually develops first. As the mentor-protégé friendship deepens, the psychosocial function then develops.

Disengagement and Separation. The protégé cannot stay in this position throughout his or her career. At some stage protégés must disengage from the mentoring relationship and strike out on their own. This is much like emancipation of a teenager from the parental nest, when he or she goes to college or enlists in the military or takes a first real job. There can be much emotional turmoil at letting go. Indeed, the protégé may return to the mentor during times of stress and crisis.

At times the mentor does not want to let go. Mentors may have defined their careers and even self-identities in the mentoring relationship. Terminating that relationship may be very difficult (Ragins & Scandura, 1997).

Redefinition of Roles. Finally, the protégé is on his or her own. Eventually the old mentor withdraws from power or retires, and the former protégé now becomes a mentor to a new generation of potential rising stars.

Research on Mentoring in the Civilian Sector

Because of its importance to the organization, mentoring has generated a fair amount of research. Our purpose is not to present an exhaustive review of the literature, but rather show a sampling of mentor programs and approaches in several important areas.

Formal Mentoring Programs

Given the many benefits compared to low costs of mentoring, it is logical that many organizations would try to mandate mentoring through formal programs. Indeed, some recommend that formal mentoring programs are a requirement for equal opportunity for all employees (Reid, 1994). There are many suggestions for an effective formal program: link mentoring with the performance evaluation and compensation systems, build mentoring into position succession planning, and be inclusive instead of exclusive in identifying protégés (Kram & Hall, 1996).

Two of the most visible formal programs are at DuPont and General Electric (GE). At DuPont, the mentoring program emphasizes sharing intellectual capital. There are about 7,000 employees in the program, served by a group of voluntary mentors. The major goal was carefully defined as improving business results rather than developing individuals. Mentors, who are managers outside of the individuals' departments, meet with their protégés once a month to discuss work issues (Jossi, 1997). DuPont's success appears to emphasize mentoring as one of many tools to improve its business.

GE also has a formal program. There is a buddy system for new employees paired with more senior employees. Originally the program focused on women and minorities, but a backlash convinced GE to make the program inclusive of everyone. Its unique feature is that focus groups are conducted to evaluate and continually improve the mentoring program (Gunn, 1995). One problem with mentoring that is evident in the 1990s is downsizing. For example, the Internal Revenue Service (IRS) had a fairly successful mentoring program until downsizing forced out many of the mentors (Gunn, 1995).

Mentoring for Women and Minorities

It has been noted above that women and minorities may be at a disadvantage since there are relatively few women and minorities at the top in organizations who can serve as mentors, and many of those there are involved with their own career development. Further, these groups may have difficulty building the crucial "chemistry" with older experienced white males at the top required for effective mentoring to develop (Ragins, 1997).

In addition, women and minorities as potential protégés may have special issues to overcome that require additional mentoring effort, such as stereotyping of performance potential, perceived incompetence (e.g., the belief that they were hired only for Affirmative Action reasons), glaring visibility as a numerical minority in the organization (with concomitant performance pressure), and identity problems (woman or minority versus employee) (Ragins, 1989; 1997).

The research, unfortunately, is not favorable for strong mentoring relationships for women and minorities. Indeed, white men and socioeconomically advantaged people are more apt to be mentored than other groups. Further, more senior white males may be assigned women and minorities as protégés as much to help the white males learn how to coach differing types of people as to help their protégés (Kram & Hall, 1996).

Because there are more men at high levels of organizations and therefore more potential male mentors than female, often a woman who desires a mentoring relationship must acquire a mentor of the opposite sex. Researchers have, however, suggested that women encounter many barriers to establishing cross-gender relationships. Women may be less likely than men to initiate mentoring relationships and others in an organization may perceive such relationships as sexual rather than professional in nature. In addition, men considering such relationships may have a fear of being accused of sexual harassment or improper conduct. Women on the other hand, who are offered mentoring may wonder what male mentors expect in return (Collins, 1983).

Interpersonal power is an important variable in the effectiveness of the cross-gender mentoring relationship. The most effective mentors are experienced, capable, and powerful; usually older white males (Ragins, 1997). In successful cross-gender mentoring relationships, the emphasis is on career enhancement rather than the psychosocial function. Women protégés and male mentors are less likely to interact with each other outside of the work setting (Ragins & McFarlin, 1990).

The research literature shows a similar situation for women and minority networks. A network works like an extended mentoring relationship—identifying resources for career enhancement, friendship, and social support. Networks for women and minorities tend to be smaller, with fewer strong ties, and less stable than networks for white males (Ibarra, 1993).

Qualitative Research

Unfortunately, much of the mentoring research consists of recording anecdotes and experiences gained from mentoring relationships. One interesting and more rigorous study found that informal mentoring relationships generated more personal interaction outside the organization and at social gatherings than did formal mentoring relationships (Tepper, 1997). Thus, the informal mentoring situation again seems to be stronger and more encompassing than the formal relationship.

In general, qualitative research reveals several important factors in successful mentoring. As in the story of Mentor in *The Odyssey*, trust between protégé and mentor is crucial (Reid, 1994). Regular contact between both parties is also important (Coley, 1996). In addition, there must be realistic expectations of what the relationship will produce (Gunn, 1995; Jossi, 1997). For example, mentoring cannot guarantee advancement or high wages.

Military Mentoring

Unique Needs

The military provides a unique situation for mentoring. First, there is a dual rank structure: enlisted and officer personnel. Junior non-commissioned officers (NCOs) or petty officers and junior officers could benefit from mentoring. Second, there are special groups that possess special mentoring needs. The numbers and percentage of women in the military are increasing. They face daunting circumstances, such as the degree to which women will be allowed in combat roles. The numbers of minorities are also increasing. Each minority group has unique needs. For example, Hispanics prefer to have mentors who can understand their culture and extended family orientation (Knouse, 1991; 1992). In addition, those at high risk for encountering the military justice system (both minorities and majorities) may benefit from mentoring on acceptable behaviors when they initially enter the military (Knouse, 1993).

Research on Mentoring in the Military

Perspectives on Mentoring. Several Air Force studies addressed the perspective of the mentor and protégé on mentoring effectiveness. Lewandowski (1985) surveyed colonels and lieutenant colonels destined for Air War College (to parallel upper level business executives) and found most of them previously had mentors and were in continuing mentoring relationships. He concluded that mentoring was a major factor in their success. Gouge (1986) surveyed junior officers attending a technical school and found that these potential protégés perceived a need for mentors to act as role models, advisors, and motivators. However, they did not expect the mentor to protect or sponsor them. Lassiter and Rehm (1990) found the majority of their Air Force sample believed that an informal mentoring program was acceptable and should continue. Over half of the junior officers indicated that there should be some type of education and training about mentoring.

Formal Programs. Some military organizations have attempted formal mentoring programs but with very limited success. Relatively few individuals participate in these programs (Sullivan, 1993; Webb, Knouse, Schwerin, & Bourne, 1998).

Mentoring for Women. The availability of mentors for military women appears to vary across Service and specialty. A survey of female Army officers showed that they received less mentoring than male officers and were less positive about their career development (Ratchford, 1985). On the other hand, a survey of Navy Nurse Corps officers (mostly female) revealed that 67 percent had received mentoring in terms of role modeling, career development, and providing information (Matthews, 1988). A survey of Equal Opportunity Advisor (EOA) students at the Defense Equal Opportunity Management Institute (DEOMI) showed that a majority of all students had been mentored, although a larger percentage of males reported more mentoring relationships than females. In addition, both genders perceived male mentors as more effective than female mentors in the military (Sullivan, 1993).

Mentoring for Minorities. Similar to military women, minorities in the military report a shortage of potential mentors. In a survey of majority and minority members across the Services, minorities reported that mentoring was crucial to career progression, but they had difficulty finding mentors in senior leadership positions and mentoring was even actively discouraged in some cases (Dellums, 1994). A survey of Hispanic officers and NCOs at DEOMI revealed that none had experienced a mentoring relationship in his or her military career (Knouse, 1991). In a survey of African-American Army officers, respondents recognized a need for mentoring, but many failed to attach to a mentor early in their military careers. Moreover, many tended to seek assistance from mentor figures only during crisis situations. Those African-American officers who were able to establish successful mentoring relationships with senior white officers had either been commissioned through a predominately white university or through West Point (U.S. Military Academy). African-American officers commissioned through historically black colleges and universities had more difficulty establishing mentoring relationships with white senior officers (Butler, 1996). In other words, similar educational experience seemed to be a factor in developing successful mentoring relationships across races.

Unique Issues with Military Mentoring

There are several problems unique to the military situation that make mentoring particularly difficult. First, it is difficult for the chemistry to develop that begins an effective mentoring relationship. The military is perhaps the most diverse organization in the United States. Thus, perceived similarities that instigate friendships may not be readily apparent among people with diverse backgrounds. In addition, the military rank structure separates enlisted from officers and even junior enlisted from senior enlisted and junior officers from senior officers. Moreover, there are relatively few situations for seniors to see how juniors comport themselves and thus take an initial interest in embarking on a mentoring relationship (such as the special projects that are more available in the civilian sector).

Second, there are not enough senior women and minorities in either the senior enlisted or officer ranks who could serve as mentors for the relatively large number of women and minorities in the junior enlisted and officer ranks. Third, individuals tend to change assignments and locations frequently in the military, usually every two to four years. It has been noted above that an effective and productive mentoring relationship usually takes a longer time to develop. Thus, transfers may abruptly sever many potentially effective mentoring relationships.

Alternatives to Mentoring for the Military

Similar to the civilian sector, individuals in the military need help and guidance on career enhancement and personal development. Indeed, it can be argued that equal opportunity for all in career development requires equity in mentoring (i.e., everyone has the opportunity to benefit from some type of mentoring experience; Reid, 1994). Moreover, in the present turbulent career environment, one needs mentoring help from multiple sources (Loeb, 1995) in both the civilian and military sectors.

Traditional mentoring as we have seen, however, is particularly difficult in the military. Therefore, we examine now several alternatives to mentoring. After all, Athena, the warrior goddess, was an alternative mentor for Telemachus, and she was highly effective.

Peer Mentors

Instead of trying to find one senior person to serve all mentoring functions, individuals can identify several colleagues who can serve specific mentoring functions. There can be several types of these peer mentors (Kram & Isabella, 1985) or lateral mentors (Eby, 1997). The information peer can share career-enhancing information. The collegial peer can offer career strategizing and feedback on job performance. In addition, he or she can serve as a friend. The special peer can provide the psychosocial functions of emotional support and feedback on personal traits.

A variation on the peer or lateral mentor is the coaching buddy (Gunn, 1995). He or she serves as a short-term mentor for new people entering the organization. Coaching buddies can help the new person get started, introduce them around, indicate where resources reside, and begin their socialization into the organization. The military already encourages sponsors for new people in many units.

Team Mentoring

An increasing amount of work in the military is being accomplished in teams: combat teams, support teams, health care teams, quality teams, and training teams. This provides a unique opportunity for team members to provide guidance and feedback to other team members. Teams can provide technical knowledge to individuals, a sense of identity upon which to build self esteem, training in team skills (such as interpersonal interaction and problem solving), personal feedback, and a buffer from outside pressures (Eby, 1997).

Mentor Circles

Several civilian organizations, like NYNEX, the telecommunications company, are experimenting with mentor circles. Instead of trying to pair protégés and mentors one-on-one, they link protégés to groups of mentors. Individuals may meet with a group of senior people, say once a month, to discuss job performance, career goals, and future endeavors (Kram & Hall, 1996).

Networks

A network is a set of interlocking relationships both inside and outside an organization that can serve many of the mentoring functions (Ibarra, 1993). Military members can maintain networks with former peers in training and education environments and with colleagues from former assignments. The problem is that such networking requires time and effort. One means of minimizing the time and effort is to use computers, particularly e-mail, to communicate with a wide range of colleagues and acquaintances.

Specialty Leaders

The Navy has a unique role in some of its corps, the specialty leader (formerly called specialty advisor). This is a senior person in a community of specialists, such as the medical corps (e.g., physicians), who is either selected by the community or appointed by senior officers for a term of three years. These specialty leaders maintain a relationship with individuals in their community to assess professional needs and skill mixes. They also may lobby unit commanders for individuals who fit particularly well into job or training openings. They keep individuals and unit commanders apprised of career needs and developments. They provide a liaison between the individual and their detailer (e.g., job placement officer) on fitting skill mixes and personal desires.

Retirees

Military retirees constitute a largely untapped group of potential mentors. They retain a closer tie to the military through their benefits and formal associations than do many civilian retirees. They may live physically close to military posts and bases in order to maintain these benefit and association ties. NCOs and chief petty officers may retire as early as age 37 and officers at 41. Thus, they may be young enough to relate to junior NCOs, petty officers, and officers and still maintain fairly close ties to active duty colleagues. Similar civilian programs, such as the Senior Corps of Retired Executives (SCORE), a program that matches retired managers with young entrepreneurs, have a proven record of success.

Virtual Mentors

One of the many benefits of computers is the almost unlimited access to information and personnel resources. Through web pages on the Internet and through e-mail (e-mentoring), individuals can access information and contact colleagues instantaneously around the world. The constraints of time and synchronous communication required of face-to-face mentoring are absent. In short, it is very convenient. Further, it is highly cost effective (Muller, 1998). Moreover, the Internet can be used as a vehicle for supplying tutorials about how to mentor via computers (Bennett, 1997).

Several civilian mentoring groups are setting up Internet and e-mail access. One example is SCORE, whose web page offers conference information, business resources, and counseling by e-mail (SCORE, 1998). Another example is a national program termed "MentorNet," supported by a web page that uses e-mail to connect over 200 women students majoring in science, engineering, and math with mentors in industry and trade organizations (Haworth, 1998). Still another example is "Preparing Future Faculty," a web page where graduate students can link to over 100 university programs to see what roles and responsibilities faculty perform. In addition, students can attempt to recruit mentors through the web page, and mentors can learn how to mentor over the Internet (Guernsey, 1998). There is the Mentor Program for Women at the School of Business, Susquehanna University, linking women students with volunteer mentors from the business community (Cianni, 1998). In medicine, there is the Anesthesiology Mentor Program,whict allows residents to locate anesthetists who can provide guidance and assistance (Anesthesiology, 1998).

There are also virtual mentor groups. In Canada, there is the Mentor Circle, where young business people can contact conference rooms, similar to Internet chat rooms, where they leave a message and one or more mentors can leave a response (Youth in Business, 1998). The Texas Library Association has a Round Table Mentor Program, where new librarians can develop individual mentor relationships or networks over the Internet (Texas Library Association, 1998).

There are numerous opportunities, then, for individuals to develop virtual mentors through computers. These virtual mentors can handle a potentially large number of protégés. Messages can be left and answered day or night. In addition, the relationship is basically informational and not face-to-face, thus interpersonal attraction does not have to develop for traditional mentoring. Further, status differences are not apparent. This means that women and minorities can have easier access to all senior officers as virtual mentors.

Recommendations

From these mentoring alternatives, several recommendations are made for the military.

1. Strengthen sponsorship programs for new assignments. The military currently practices sponsorship of new people in many units. Sponsoring can include help with relocation, family settling in, job tasks, and socialization into that particular unit. To borrow from the Total Quality Management (TQM) literature (Knouse, 1996), this is a "best practice" that should be copied by other units. In addition, sufficient time and resources for effective sponsoring should be allocated. Perhaps sponsoring could even be considered in performance evaluation.

2. *Encourage team mentoring.* In training and team development exercises, the team mentoring function (Eby, 1997) can be stressed. Team members can give each other feedback on contribution to the team and interpersonal skills. Individual training needs in these areas can also be identified.

3. *Experiment with open-group discussions with senior NCOs, Chief Petty Officers (CPOs), and officers.* This is a variation of the mentoring circle in the civilian sector (Kram & Hall, 1996). The emphasis here is upon experimentation to find what works with an individual unit. Some units are more hierarchical and tradition bound than others, and such open discussion may not work well. For others, junior enlisted and officers can learn from their seniors' positive experiences as well as mistakes.

4. *Expand the Navy specialty leader concept to other services.* The Navy specialty leader program serves naval communities well, such as the various medical corps (Webb et al., 1998). There appears to be no reason why it could not be expanded to other corps as well as other services. This liaison role can simultaneously serve the individual, the receiving commander, and the military.

5. *Encourage retired NCO, CPO, and officer groups to set up volunteer mentor lists.* The emphasis would be upon recently retired NCOs, CPOs, and officers, who still have extensive ties to active duty colleagues and to the state-of-the-art technology in their fields. Mentor lists could either focus on specialists for specific career information or generalists for overall career and personal development. Some examples of groups are The Retired Officer Association (TROA) and Noncommissioned Officer Association (NCOA). There are service specific groups, such as the National Naval Officers Association (NNOA), Association of Naval Service Officers (ANSO), Chief Petty Officers Association (CPOA), Air Force Association (AFA), Air Force Cadet Officer Mentoring Program (AFCOMAP), the Army's ROCKS program for minorities (an association named after Brigadier General Roscoe "Rock" Cartwright who was an esteemed role model and mentor to many black officers; Powell, 1996),

Army Warrant Officers Association, and branch regimental associations in the Army. In addition, there are specialty groups, such as the Association of Military Surgeons of the United States (AMSUS).

6. *Publish web pages focusing on NCO and officer career issues and e-mentoring.* These career-oriented web pages could serve the mentoring career enhancing function of informational sources. Moreover, direct mentoring pages could be set up. An unlimited number of individuals could benefit from these pages and access them at any time. Messages could be left via e-mail at any time in e-mentoring (Muller, 1998).

Four examples of interest, from which the military might borrow, are SCORE, MentorNet, Preparing Future Faculty, and the Anesthesiology Mentor/Protégé Program. The SCORE home page displays information on conferences, e-mail counseling, business resources, and frequently asked questions (FAQ) (http://www.score.org). MentorNet for women science students displays general mentoring information, a student area with FAQ, a mentor area with FAQ, and links (http://www.mentornet.net). Preparing Future Faculty has links to campus programs, sample activities, FAQ, and resources (http://www.preparing-faculty.org). The Anesthesiology Mentor/Protégé Program gives program objectives, selection criteria, the rules of the mentor and protégé interaction, and even how to break off the relationship (*http://www.metrohealth.org/clinical/anes/mentor.asp*).

In addition, the mentor circle idea could be converted to a virtual mentor circle through conference rooms, where individuals leave questions for specific mentors or any mentor logging on. In Canada, the Mentor Circle has mentor profiles so individuals can know something about a given mentor and a slot in a conference room where questions can be left (*http://sae.ca/youth/mentors/guidelines/htm*).

7. *Disseminate lists of NCOs and officers who will serve as virtual mentors.* Enlisted and officer personnel who are experienced with computers and the Internet can serve as virtual mentors or e-mentors. They can present themselves through e-mail as specialty resources, information liaisons, and sounding boards for ideas or even complaints. A relatively large number of individuals could benefit from their expertise. Indeed, even the identity of these virtual mentors could be eliminated from e-mail. Thus, women and minorities could link into e-mentors as information sources with minimal problems of mentoring across gender and race.

Conclusions

Although mentoring can serve important career enhancing and personal development functions, the military environment makes traditional mentoring relationships difficult to maintain and even to establish. However, substitute and alternative mentoring options are available. With some creative thinking, innovation, and resource allocation, many junior enlisted and officer personnel could have the opportunity to access some variation of mentoring through peers, teams, retirees, or even their personal computer.

References

Anesthesiology. (1998). Mentor/protégé program. URL http://www.metrohealth.org/clinical/anes/mentor.asp.

Aronson, E. (1995). *The social animal* (7th ed.). New York: W. H. Freeman.

Bennett, D. T. (1997). Providing role models online. *Electronic Learning, 16*(5), 50-52.

Butler, R. (1996). *Why black officers fail in the U. S. Army.* Carlisle Barracks, PA: U. S. Army War College.

Cianni, M. (1998). *Sigmund Weis School mentor program for women.* URL http://susqu.edu/orgs/w_ment/default.htm.

Coley, D. B. (1996). Mentoring two-by-two. *Training and Development, 50*(7), 46-48.

Collins, N.W. (1083). *Professional Women and their mentors: A practical guide to mentoring for the women who wants to get ahead.* Englewood Cliffs, NJ: Prentice-Hall, Inc.

Dellums, R. V. (December 30, 1994). *An assessment of racial discrimination in the military.* Washington, DC: House Armed Services Committee Staff Task Force on Equality of Treatment and Opportunity in the Armed Services.

Dreher, G. F., & Ash, R. A. (1990). A comparative study of mentoring among men and women in managerial, professional, and technical positions. *Journal of Applied Psychology, 75,* 539-546.

Dreher, G. F., & Cox, T. H. (1996). Race, gender, and opportunity: A study of compensation attainment and the establishment of mentoring relationships. *Journal of Applied Psychology, 81,* 297-308.

Eby, L. T. (1997). Alternative forms of mentoring in changing organization environments: A conceptual extension of the mentoring literature. *Journal of Vocational Behavior, 51,* 125-144.

Gouge, J. A. (1986). *Air Force mentoring: The potential protégé's perspective.* Unpublished master's thesis, Air Force Institute of Technology, Wright-Patterson AFB, OH.

Guernsey, L. (January 30, 1998). Site helps Ph.D. students prepare for faculty life. *The Chronicle of Higher Education, 44*(21), A23.

Gunn, E. (1995). Mentoring: The democratic version. *Training, 32*(8), 64-67.

Haworth, K. (April 17, 1998). Mentor programs provide support via e-mail to women studying science. *The Chronicle of Higher Education, 44*(32), A29-A30.

Ibarra, H. (1993). Personal networks of women and minorities in management: A conceptual framework. *Academy of Management Review, 18,* 56-87.

Jossi, F. (1997, August). Mentoring in changing times. *Training,* 50-54.

Knouse, S. B. (1991). Social support for Hispanics in the military. *International Journal of Intercultural Relations, 15,* 427-444.

Knouse, S. B. (1992). The mentoring process for Hispanics. In S. B. Knouse, P. Rosenfeld, & A. Culbertson (Eds.), *Hispanics in the workplace* (pp. 137-150). Newbury Park, CA: Sage.

Knouse, S. B. (1993). *Differences between black and white military offenders: A study of socioeconomic, familial, personality, and military characteristics of inmates at the U.S. Disciplinary Barracks at Fort Leavenworth.* DEOMI RSP 93-2. Patrick AFB, FL: Defense Equal Opportunity Management Institute.

Knouse, S. B. (1996). *Human resource perspectives on TQM: Concepts and practices.* Milwaukee, WI: American Society for Quality Control Press.

Kram, K. E. (1983). Phases of the mentor relationship. *Academy of Management Journal, 26*, 608-625.

Kram, K. E., & Hall, D. T. (1996). Mentoring in a context of diversity and turbulence. In E. K. Kossek & S. A. Lobel (Eds.), *Managing diversity* (pp. 108-136). Cambridge, MA: Blackwell.

Kram, K. E., & Isabella, L. A. (1985). Mentoring alternatives: The role of peer relationships in career development. *Academy of Management Journal, 28*, 110-132.

Lassiter, A., & Rehm, D. (1990). *Should the Air Force establish a formalized mentoring program?* Maxwell AFB, AL: Air War College.

Lewandowski, F. (1985). *Air Force mentoring: The mentor's perspective.* Unpublished master's thesis, Air Force Institute of Technology, Wright-Patterson AFB, OH.

Loeb, M. (November 27, 1995). The new mentoring. *Fortune, 132*(11), 213.

Matthews, K. R. (1988). *Mentoring: Its effect on black officers' career progress within the United States Army.* Unpublished manuscript from *Dialog.*

Muller, C. B. (1998). *MentorNet: The national electronic industrial mentoring network for women in engineering and science.* URL http://www.mentornet.net.

Powell, C. (1996). *My American journey.* New York: Ballantine.

Ragins, B.R., & Scandura, T.A. (1997). The way we were: Gender and the termination of mentoring relationships. *Journal of Applied Psychology, 82*(6), 945-953.

Ragins, B. R. (1989). Barriers to mentoring: The female manager's dilemma. *Human Relations, 42*, 1-22.

Ragins, B. R. (1997). Diversified mentoring relationships in organizations: A power perspective. *Academy of Management Review, 22*, 482-521.

Ragins, B. R., & Cotton, J. L. (1993). Gender and willingness to mentor in organizations. *Journal of Management, 19*, 97-111.

Ragins, B. R., & McFarlin, D. B. (1990). Perceptions of mentor roles in cross-gender mentoring relationships. *Journal of Vocational Behavior, 37*, 321-339.

Ragins, B. R., & Scandura, T. A. (1993, May). *Costs and benefits of being a mentor.* Paper presented at the annual meeting of the Society for Industrial and Organizational Psychology, San Francisco.

Ratchford, D.C. (1985). *Gender analysis of the Professional Develoipment of Officers Study (PDS) Survey.* Unpublished manuscript.

Reid, B. A. (1994). Mentorships ensure equal opportunity. *Personnel Journal, 73*(11), 122-123.

SCORE (1998). *Service Corps of Retired Executives.* URL http://www.score.org.

Sullivan, M. M. (1993). *Mentoring in the military: A preliminary study of gender differences.* DEOMI RSP 93-3. Patrick AFB, FL: Defense Equal Opportunity Management Institute.

Tepper, B. J. (1995). Upward maintenance tactics in supervisory mentoring and nonmentoring relationships. *Academy of Management Journal, 38*, 1191-1205.

Texas Library Association (1998). *New members round table mentor program.* URL http://www.txla.org/groups/nmrt/mentor.html.

Turban, D.B. & Dougherty, T.W. (1994). Role of protégé personality in receipt of mentoring and career success. *Academy of Management Journal, 37*, 688-702.

Webb, S. C., Knouse, S. B., Schwerin, M. J., & Bourne, M. J. (1998, Aug). Perceptions of mentoring among gender and racial groups in the U.S. Navy Medical Service Corps. *MSC Professional Bulletin*, *98*(3), 9-14.

Youth in Business (1998). Mentor circle. URL http://sae.ca/youth/mentors/guidelines.htm.

8

Opportunities for Assessing Military EO: A Researcher's Perspective on Identifying an Integrative Program-Evaluation Strategy*

Jack E. Edwards

Introduction

This paper identifies a rationale for why Department of Defense (DoD) equal opportunity (EO) practices should be evaluated. Then, it provides an overview of major EO-evaluation efforts currently underway in DoD. Third, considerations are identified for designing supplemental program-evaluation plans. Inventories of both what is available today and what awaits tomorrow provide a firm foundation for beginning to identify an integrative strategy for evaluating EO practices.

Rationale for Evaluating EO Practices

With a smaller military force and a decreasing DoD budget, it is imperative that human and fiscal resources be used judiciously. EO is a human resources program intimately tied to readiness. With racial/ethnic minorities and women accounting for larger and larger portions of the military, the military must be seen as an organization that actively seeks to provide EO to all members. Anything less could affect the ability to attract high quality recruits and retain previously trained members. These issues illustrate that EO is more than just "the right thing to do"; it is also something that affects the bottom line—mission readiness.

The military's emphasis on EO comes at a price. Currently, the military spends millions of dollars per year on EO practices such as

---

* The views expressed are those of the author and do not necessarily represent the official positions of the DoD.

complaints investigations and training to combat sexual harassment. These costs are both direct (e.g., producing and mailing surveys) and indirect (e.g., time away from the workplace to attend training). Little is known, however, about the effectiveness of individual EO practices. It might be questioned whether or not the same effect could be obtained for a decreased cost using different methods of information dissemination, complaint resolution, etc.

Like everything else, military EO practices should be evaluated to identify areas of excellence and opportunities for improvement. Initiatives such as Vice President Gore's reinventing government combined with budgetary and force-size considerations suggest now is the time to search for increased efficiencies. For example, one method of obtaining increased efficiencies is to emphasize "jointness." Rather than each Service undertaking independent programmatic and evaluation efforts, cross-Service programs and assessment tools could have multiple benefits. Sharing the cost of, say, developing a DoD-wide complaints-monitoring system could result in a system with (a) a lowered per-Service cost and (b) enhanced capabilities beyond those which could be afforded by any single Service.

For fiscal and practical reasons, our quest now turns to the second objective of this paper: an inventory of current EO assessment efforts. Taking stock of the available information will lead logically to the third objective of this paper—identifying methodological and practical challenges to supplementing current EO-assessment efforts. By building on strengths and identifying challenges, DoD will be provided a firm base for designing an improved and integrative system of EO practices and program evaluation.

EO Assessment: The Current State of Affairs

Many military EO programs and policies have been implemented in response to high-level (e.g., Presidential, Congressional, or Secretary of Defense) initiatives or as a result of crises (e.g., riots on aircraft carriers in the 1970s, Tailhook, or Aberdeen). In the past, the haste to implement a new EO requirement rarely allowed sufficient time to plan a systematic program to evaluate and refine the existing and supplement EO practices. When EO evaluation is done, it is frequently a one-time effort (e.g., see U.S. General Accounting Office, 1995, for an annotated review of military EO studies).

DoD and the Services have taken some steps to monitor EO programs. These efforts have primarily emphasized administering surveys and examining databases for race/ethnicity- and gender-related differences. Less systematic evaluations include the cursory evaluations of EO training. Figure 8.1 shows examples of databases that can be used to evaluate the EO programs. For each source of data, "X" indicates those content areas that could be investigated. The remainder of this section provides an overview of these various monitoring and evaluation efforts.

Surveys

DoD and some of the Services have strong EO-survey programs. These surveys currently provide most of the data used to evaluate military EO programs and EO climate. Descriptions of those programs follow. Although some of the Service efforts were begun before the DoD-wide surveys, the DoD-wide surveys are reviewed first because they span all Services and are required by law.

DoD-Wide Sexual Harassment Survey

Defense Manpower Data Center (DMDC) conducted the first joint-Service, active-duty sexual harassment survey in 1988. In 1994, DMDC was tasked to update that survey and re-administer it. Updating the survey accomplished two important objectives: addressing current policy concerns and incorporating recent advances in the understanding and measurement of sexual harassment. In order to provide an updated survey while maintaining comparability with the 1988 results, DMDC developed three sexual harassment instruments.

- Form A was a re-administration of the 1988 survey for fairly unambiguous comparisons of 1988 and 1995 incident rates.

- Form B was a new questionnaire that built on the content of the 1988 survey, included current policy issues, and incorporated the previously cited methodological advances.

- Form C was a research form that linked the list of sexual harassment behaviors in the 1988 survey (Form A) to the behavior list in the new survey (Form B).

Service EO and survey offices contributed to the development of the new instrument. The surveys were also field tested with multiple groups from each Service.

Figure 8.1
Source of Data to Measure Selected EO Concerns

EO Concern	Current Sources of Information						
	Personnel Surveys		Aggregate from Services		Paper Copy	Electronic Files	
	Sexual Harassment Survey	Equal Opportunity Survey	Military Equal Opportunity Assessment (MEOA)	Archival Records of Complaints	Personnel Folders (at units or from Nat'l Archives)	Officer and Enlisted Master Files	Pay Files
Selection into Military			X			X	
Placement/MOS			X		X	X	
Performance Evaluation	X	X			X		
Assignments	X	X			X	X	
Promotions	X	X	X		X	X	X
Discipline		X	X	X	X	X	X
EO Climate	X	X					
EO Training	X	X					
EO Complaints	X	X		X			

The *1995 Sexual Harassment Survey* was mailed to a worldwide, representative sample of active-duty personnel from the four DoD Services and the Coast Guard. Sample sizes were 30,239 members receiving Form A; 49,752 members receiving Form B; and 9,695 members receiving Form C. The sample was stratified by Service, gender, racial/ethnic group membership, pay grade, occupation, and location inside or outside the U.S. Oversampling of women was used to ensure adequate cell sizes for the analyses. Unweighted response rates were 46 percent for Form A, 58 percent for Form B, and 56 percent for Form C.

Among other things, the results from Form A showed that the percentage of women experiencing at least one incident of sexual harassment decreased from 64 percent in 1988 to 55 percent in 1995 (see Bastian, Lancaster, & Reyst, 1996, for findings from Forms A and B). Form B, which contained the longer behavior list, showed that 78 percent of the women reported experiencing at least one incident of offensive behavior during the prior year. Form B also contained an item that asked respondents if they considered any of the behaviors they checked to be sexual harassment. About one third of the 78 percent indicated "none" of what they checked was sexual harassment. Thus, 52 percent of active-duty women reported experiencing at least one behavior that they considered sexually harassing. For active-duty men, that rate was 9 percent.

Data files were provided to all Services in July 1996. A report of the findings and a technical report were published in December 1996. DMDC provides researchers with a CD-ROM containing public-use data files and final technical documentation.

DoD-Wide Racial/Ethnic Harassment and Discrimination Survey

Congressional staff inserted language in the *National Defense Authorization Act for Fiscal Year 1995* (House of Representatives Conference Report, page 114) requiring this survey. Two years later, legislation (Title 10, USC—Armed Forces, Chapter 23, Section 481) stated that the Secretary of Defense "Shall carry out an annual survey to measure the state of racial, ethnic and gender issues and discrimination...and...hate group activity."

In response to the Congressional mandates, DMDC administered the 16-page *1996 Equal Opportunity Survey* (*EOS*; Edwards, Elig, & Riemer, in process). The survey's EO items can be grouped broadly into five categories: types, frequency, and effects of racial/ethnic incidents; characteristics of the complaints process; opinions about personnel policies and programs; interpersonal relations of service members from different racial/ethnic groups; and comparisons of EO in the military now to EO in the military 5 years ago and to the civilian sector. In addition to addressing EO-related issues, the survey included questions about identification with and commitment to the organization, career issues, characteristics of the workplace, job satisfaction, and demographics.

The *EOS* was sent to 73,496 active-duty DoD and Coast Guard members from late 1996 through Spring 1997. The sampling design considered requirements for analyses by Service, sex, racial/ethnic group membership (Hispanic, non-Hispanic black, non-Hispanic White, Asian/Pacific Islander, and Native American/Alaskan Native), paygrade, location (U.S., Europe, Asia/Pacific Islands) and density in duty occupations of blacks, Hispanics, and total minorities. The design oversampled minority group members to ensure adequate sample sizes for comparisons among racial/ethnic subgroups.

EOS findings will be briefed to the Services in early 1998. Also, the Services will be provided databases for their own data analyses. After the Services have had time to perform their own analyses, databases will be provided to academic, private-sector, and public-sector researchers.

Other EO Surveys

Some Services have also administered their own surveys to obtain EO information. The Navy has administered its biennial *Navy Equal Employment and Sexual Harassment (NEOSH) Survey* to active-duty personnel since 1989 and to Reservists since 1993. Similarly, the Marine Corps has fielded its biennial *Marine Corps Equal Opportunity Survey (MCEOS)* to active-duty personnel since 1994 and to Reservists since 1996. All four of these survey efforts utilize samples representative of the entire Service or Reserve component.

Although the Army and Air Force do not have surveys addressing only EO concerns, they have obtained survey information on these topics. The Army has included items intermittently on its omnibus *Sample Survey of Military Personnel*, with sexual harassment items appearing about every two years. The Air Force does not routinely administer its own survey to assess EO; it has adopted the DoD-wide surveys.

Although the DoD-wide and Service-wide surveys provide extremely valuable information to policy officials for DoD-wide and Service-wide issues, those surveys are not designed to provide information to the local command. To address this problem, some Services have developed command-level assessment programs. The Navy and the Marine Corps have computer-assisted assessments. Both use items from their Service-specific surveys. The assessment aids provide items, norms from the most recent Service-specific survey, and software for analyzing and graphing results (e.g., see Rosenfeld & Edwards, 1994).

Last, but certainly not least, is the *Military Equal Opportunity Climate Survey (MEOCS)*. The Defense Equal Opportunity Management Institute (DEOMI), which is hosting this conference, has had an active *MEOCS* program for the past decade (see Landis, Dansby, & Faley, 1993, for an overview). Portions of all the Services have used the *MEOCS* to assess command-level EO. In fact, several hundred thousand service members have completed the *MEOCS*. DEOMI provides the instruments, and personnel at the local command administer them. DEOMI computerizes the data from the completed surveys and provides a report of findings to the command. When commanding officers obtain results, they can compare the findings from their units to those obtained from prior *MEOCS* respondents. The *MEOCS* has different items than the Services' items or the items found in the DoD-wide surveys.

Complaints Processing

Other than surveys, the only large-scale evaluation of an EO issue has been the investigation of complaints. The largest of these efforts was the Defense Equal Opportunity Council (DEOC) Task Force's investigation of the discrimination-complaints process. The Task Force was co-chaired by the Secretary of the Air Force and the Under Secretary of Defense for Personnel and Readiness. Following extensive data gathering and analysis, the DEOC Task Force issued its two-volume *Report of the Task Force on Discrimination and Sexual Harassment* (Defense Equal Opportunity Council Task Force, 1995). In its report, the Task Force outlined goals and principles for an effective complaints processing system. In addition, the report listed forty-eight recommendations for improving the Services' discrimination-complaints processing as well as EO programs in general.

At this time, DoD-wide information on complaints processing is very limited. The information consists of only the number of complaints handled per year. While this type of data can be used to monitor an overall trend, important evaluative information is being lost by the inability to capture more complaint data.

Although some Services have begun computerizing information pertaining to each complaint, development of these Service-specific tracking systems has proceeded independently. Recently, the Services began discussing the development of a system for consolidating complaints information. DMDC has met with the Services and the Reserve components to identify commonalties among the systems. Developing a single system would provide less ambiguous answers about complaint rates and the nature of the complaints. Still, attention must be given to the special requirements of each Service to ensure that such a joint system could be optimally useful for all parties.

Other Types of Data Useful in EO-Program Evaluation

Other EO evaluations use data from a variety of sources. Two common methods for obtaining such data are by mining electronic or paper personnel files and aggregating data that is supplied to successively higher level commands. Examples are provided to illustrate these other methods of obtaining EO-evaluation data.

Military Equal Opportunity Assessment (MEOA)

DoD annually publishes the *MEOA*. The *MEOAs* are compendia of statistics on topics such as promotion rates, discipline rates, and discrimination and harassment complaints. These findings are compiled by examining electronic databases (e.g., to determine promotion rates) and "rolling" up statistics to successively higher level commands (e.g., to determine discipline rates). Each type of statistic is examined for differences that are related to members' race/ethnicity and gender.

Since each Service supplies DoD with the data from the *MEOAs*, it is possible to examine rates at both the DoD-wide and Service-specific levels. The high level of aggregation contained in the *MEOAs* makes the statistics useful for little more than trend analysis at the DoD-wide or Service-wide level.

Miscellaneous Other Issues

In addition to using electronic files to derive rates such as those appearing in the *MEOA*, the electronic files can be used for other purposes. For example, pay files can be examined for decreases in pay from one month to another. This information has been used at times for the study of military discipline/punishment (e.g., see Edwards, 1997, for a review of sources for Navy discipline data). Since the pay files were not designed for this specific purpose, the types of conclusions which can be drawn are limited and tentative.

Paper personnel records are another source of data for racial/ethnic data. While some of this information is available on personnel while they are still in the military, other types of data (e.g., reason for court martial) cannot be examined for EO-related concerns until after the personnel folders have been retired at the national archives.

Training Evaluations

EO training is probably the EO practice requiring the most time and fiscal resources. In a given year, almost every military member will attend at least 1-hour of EO training (e.g., on cross-cultural awareness or the avoidance of sexual harassment). In addition to regularly mandated training, crises can result in additional training. Such training is often the preferred method for correcting EO problems detected by a survey, a special study group, or another means of evaluation.

Despite being the EO practice requiring the largest amount of human and fiscal resources, EO training is rarely evaluated. When training is "evaluated," the evaluation typically looks much like a short "customer satisfaction" survey and is completed at the end of the training session. A Navy example illustrates the quality of the training evaluations. As a result of sexual harassment at the Tailhook convention, the Secretary of the Navy ordered eight hours of mandatory training for all military and civilian personnel in the Department of the Navy. Following the training, all attendees had to complete a short survey that asked if they had attended the training and if they now knew what sexual harassment was.

Because of limited resources, little effort is usually made to determine if behavior or attitudes are actually changed following the training. More must be done to look at the short-, intermediate-, and long-term effects of EO training.

Identifying Challenges to Supplementing Current EO Evaluation Efforts

Evaluating EO—or any other human resource program—presents methodological and practical challenges. This fact is particularly pertinent to military EO evaluations. Such challenges need to be identified now so that supplemental evaluation tools can be designed to overcome those hurdles. Although no single method will be able to overcome all of these challenges, early identification of hurdles along with rigorous planning can result in a variety of tools that complement one another and decrease the problems caused by any single constraint.

The prior section showed that military EO-evaluation efforts have used a piecemeal approach which has resulted in uneven coverage of the wide range of concerns related to military EO. While some concerns (e.g., military members' perceptions of EO climate) are covered in much depth and evaluated with multiple assessment methods, other issues (e.g., training effectiveness) have little data against which quality can be judged.

Much of the remainder of this paper is devoted to identifying major challenges to designing a comprehensive EO program-evaluation system. Major issues to be included in this section are the lack of norms for judging effectiveness, measuring the race/ethnicity of members, operationally defining harassment and discrimination, and practical concerns to designing an EO evaluation program.

Lack of Norms for Judging Effectiveness

A major impediment to evaluating military EO programs is the lack of a standard against which to compare Service findings. When DoD and the Services gather EO data, there is no non-military group against which military findings can be validly compared. Because of legal considerations, private-sector organizations seldom gather EO data on surveys, much less release that information outside their organizations. Even if survey or complaint information were gathered and released by non-military organizations, it would have little relevance to the military because the "opportunities" for harassment and discrimination are greatly expanded in the military.

Private- and public-sector findings (e.g., U.S. Merit Systems Protection Board, 1995) are computed for civilians who typically spend an 8-hour day in the *workplace*. Since military people often work *and live* on a military installation and use non-work facilities on the installations, harassment or discrimination in the workplace could potentially occur 24 (versus 8) hours per day. Similarly, findings for the active-duty Services may not be a good comparison for Reserve findings. Reservists have a decreased chance to be harassed or discriminated against (relative to that for active duty). Reservists' survey answers would pertain primarily to what occurred one weekend per month and during the two weeks of annual training per year.

Measuring Race/Ethnicity

Two race/ethnicity-related issues must be addressed before designing supplemental EO-assessment tools. The issues pertain to (a) how to handle a member who has a mixed racial/ethnic background and (b) a potential artifact in determining the racial/ethnic composition of the military's total force.

Multi-Race Military Members

Prerequisite to evaluating an EO program is knowing the racial/ethnic background of members. Until recently, most organizations gathered racial/ethnic information by asking respondents to self-report their ethnicity and race using *separate questions*. The ethnicity question asked if a person was (or was not) Hispanic. The race question typically asked the person to select from one of four categories: American Indian/Alaska Native, Asian/Pacific Islander, black/African American, and white.

A month ago, the Office of Management and Budget (1997) issued *Revisions to the Standards for the Classification of Federal Data on Race and Ethnicity*. The question assessing ethnicity now asks respondents if they are "Hispanic or Latino," and the race question has five categories: American Indian/Alaska Native, Asian, black/African American, Native Hawaiian/Other Pacific Islander, and white. Thus, "Latino" has been added to the ethnicity question. For the race question, two changes were made in categories: Native Hawaiians are explicitly mentioned, and they and other Pacific Islanders have been provided a separate category from Asians. While neither of these category modifications should make much of a difference when monitoring race/ethnicity, another change will make a significant difference. Respondents are now permitted to "Mark one or more..." or "Select one or more..." races.

If this new method of measuring race/ethnicity is applied to DoD, it leads to numerous concerns, some of which are faced by other organizations. One particularly thorny question is how to treat the data from an individual who indicates numerous races. Should the person be classified as multi-racial, randomly assigned to one of the selected categories, or have a proportional part of the person assigned to each category? Any one of those alternatives would be a change from the prior racial/ethnic classification scheme. Therefore, norms and trend data (e.g., from surveys or *MEOAs*) could become of limited use.

Under Representation Versus Under-Counting

The military strives to obtain a force that mirrors the composition of the U.S. population. To judge its progress toward this goal, DoD and the Services compare their racial/ethnic compositions to those for similarly aged members of the U.S. population. To be an appropriate comparison, DoD should be using the same methods to gather racial/ethnic data as the methods employed by the Census Bureau (i.e., the questions and self-identification established by the Office of Management and Budget).

DoD race/ethnicity data in administrative records are primarily based on others' (usually recruiters') observations and are not collected using questions that map directly to those used to generate census statistics. Self-reports from DoD surveys and others' observations obtained from DoD databases are fairly consistent for some subgroups (most notably Blacks); however, agreement is less consistent for other subgroups (most notably Hispanics). For example, according to administrative records, Hispanics are less than 4 percent of DoD service members. Findings based on survey self-reports are at least twice that amount and closely parallel U.S. population estimates obtained using questions that are almost identical to those used on the 1990 U.S. Census.

Although it would be expensive to obtain new racial/ethnic data on millions of DoD personnel (active-duty members, Reservists, and DoD civilian employees), DoD cannot judge how well it maps to the U.S. population without such an effort. Until then, it is impossible to determine how much differences are due to under counting versus under representation of some subgroups.

Operationally Defining Harassment and Discrimination

A first step to identifying the degree to which a problem exists is to agree how the problem is to be defined operationally. The DoD-wide and Service-specific surveys operationally define sexual harassment differently. For example, the *1995 Armed Forces Sexual Harassment Survey* (e.g., see J. E. Edwards, Elig, D. L. Edwards, & Riemer, 1997) used 24 behaviors and considered incidents committed on or off duty by military personnel or civilian employees. In contrast, the Navy and Marine Corps surveys use 10 categories of behaviors and consider a more limited context. These variations in item wording, content, and context have at times resulted in confusion about which numbers most accurately reflect sexual harassment in the military.

This same problem does not exist with regard to the operational definition of racial/ethnic harassment and discrimination. The *EOS* is the first military survey to define racial/ethnic harassment and discrimination.

Practical Concerns When Designing an Evaluation Program

While the prior sections have identified methodological challenges, practical concerns must also be considered before the design of an evaluation program begins. The design team must be especially cognizant of five practical concerns that will challenge researchers when they to design EO-evaluation strategies.

- *Type of information needed.* The desired information should direct the choice of the data-gathering method, and not vice versa. No single method (e.g., surveys) can effectively provide a full picture of how well DoD and the Services are doing with regard to all EO issues.

- *Interrelatedness of EO content areas.* Assessments done for one content area will almost surely have implications for other core content areas. For example, information obtained in a content analysis of the sexual harassment complaints could provide valuable lessons learned. That information could be used to amend policy, examined for ways to improve communication, incorporated into training programs, or written into items for a survey.

- *Time between assessments.* Assessment is not a one-time process; instead, it is a continuing effort. The frequency of the assessment is determined by the content and the strategy. If the time between assessments is too short, there will not be sufficient opportunity to complete the process of refining programs, communicating the changes to members, and providing ample time for members to consolidate the changes into their behaviors and attitudes.

- *Balancing costs versus value of the evaluation.* The financial and human re-source costs of some assessment strategies is high relative to such costs for other strategies. Time and fiscal constraints might make it impossible to implement some methods that show particular promise in such program evaluations.

- *Sensitivity to organizational and personal concerns.* Some of the assessments are more disruptive or invasive than others. For example, interviewing com-plainants is more invasive than reviewing court cases. Also, conducting in-depth analysis in a single unit is very disruptive to the mission of the unit.

- *Characteristics of evaluators.* Some assessment strategies should be used by only selected groups of evaluators. For example, the review of court decisions may be most meaningful when done by lawyers. Similarly, an audit of training materials by non-DoD personnel would probably provide a more objective review than would an audit by the people who are involved in the training.

Summary and Conclusions

This paper started with the basic assumption—EO is a human-resource program that affects readiness. From this point, the basis for three objectives were developed.

1.   Limits to fiscal and human resources suggest a need to fine tune all programs so that they work at optimal efficiency and effectiveness.

2.   Currently, the piecemeal development of EO program-evaluation tools has re-sulted in very uneven coverage of EO topics (e.g., attitudes, training effective-ness).

3.   Numerous methodological and practical considerations should be addressed before planning is needed to design supplemental assessment tools that over-come the obstacles to obtaining a clear evaluation of military EO programs.

References

Bastian, L. D., Lancaster, A. R., & Reyst, H. E. (1996, December). *Department of Defense 1995 sexual harassment survey* (DMDC Report No. 96-014). Arlington, VA: Defense Manpower Data Center.

Defense Equal Opportunity Council Task Force. (1995). *Report of the Task Force on Discrimination and Sexual Harassment.* Washington, DC: Department of Defense.

Edwards, J. E. (1997, August). Equity of the Navy discipline system: A review of race-based findings. In P. J. Thomas (Chair), *Understanding disparities in the perception of minority and majority personnel.* Symposium presented at the 105th annual convention of the American Psychological Association, Chicago, IL.

Edwards, J. E., Elig, T. W., Edwards, D. L., & Riemer, R. A. (1997). *The 1995 armed forces sexual harassment survey: Administration, datasets, and codebook for form B* (DMDC Report No. 95-015). Arlington, VA: Defense Manpower Data Center.

Edwards, J. E., Elig, T. W., & Riemer, R. A. (in process). *The 1996 armed forces equal opportunity survey: Administration, datasets, and codebook* (Report No. 97-026). Arlington, VA: Defense Manpower Data Center.

Landis, D., Dansby, M. R., Faley, R. H. (1993). The military equal opportunity climate survey: An example of surveying in organizations. In P. Rosenfeld, J. E. Edwards, & M. D. Thomas (Eds.), *Improving organizational surveys: New Directions, methods, and applications* (pp. 212-239). Newbury Park, CA: Sage.

Office of Management and Budget. (1997). *Revisions of the standards for the classification of federal data on race and ethnicity*. Washington, DC: Author. (available at http://www.whitehouse.gov/WH/EOP/OMB/html/fedreg/Ombdir15.html).

Rosenfeld, P., & Edwards, J. E. (1994). Automated system assesses equal opportunity. *Personnel Journal, 73*(9), 98-103.

U.S. General Accounting Office. (1995, April). *Equal opportunity: DOD studies on discrimination in the military* (GAO/NSIAD-95-103). Washington DC: GAO.

U.S. Merit Systems Protection Board. (1995). *Sexual harassment in the federal workplace: Trends, progress, continuing challenges*. Washington, DC: Author.

9

Local Effects and Global Impact of Defense Equal Opportunity Management Institute Training

Judith L. Johnson

Introduction

This report represents continued effort to evaluate training effectiveness of the Defense Equal Opportunity Management Institute (DEOMI). For a review of the history of program evaluation efforts at DEOMI, the reader is referred to DEOMI Research Series Publication 95-8 entitled "A Preliminary Investigation into DEOMI Training Effectiveness" (Johnson, 1995).

Briefly, evaluation of training effectiveness entails investigation into both local effects and global impact. Local effects of training include variables such as mastery of course content, student attitude change, and acquisition of skills such as problem-solving or mediation. Global impact includes the effect of training when the graduates return in their EO capacity to their home installations. Ultimately, issues addressed by global impact include fostering a productive and efficient work climate and military readiness. It is important to note that selection of both local effect and global impact variables should be based upon the unique needs of the organization (Blake & Heslin, 1993).

Although local effects are useful in documenting training effectiveness on an individual level, global impact addresses the broader question of whether DEOMI has an effect on the military in general. Ideally, assessment of global impact would include longitudinal analyses of EO climate with appropriate comparison groups (such as police units). However, limited personnel and financial resources often preclude such comprehensive and systematic efforts.

Consequently, the present study indirectly assessed global impact through survey of commander and senior leadership satisfaction with DEOMI graduates across certain domains. Two separate surveys were conducted and participants completed the Commander's/Supervisor's Evaluation of DEOMI Graduates (CSEG) and Critical Review. Study One consisted of a resurvey of the commanders and supervisors surveyed in the summer of 1995 regarding DEOMI graduate performance. These individuals received the same survey as before (the CSEG). They were also asked to assume the role of DEOMI's worst critic and generate three criticisms of DEOMI (the Critical Review). This latter request was designed to elicit criticism in that past surveys suggested the presence of positive response bias. Results were then compared with those from the summer of 1995 in order to establish whether satisfaction with DEOMI training was maintained over time.

Study Two consisted of a survey of the commanders and supervisors of three classes of recent DEOMI graduates, 95-2, 95-3, and 96-1. Respondents completed the CSEG regarding level of satisfaction with the DEOMI graduates' performance of EO tasks at their home installations. Respondents also completed the Critical Review.

Study Three consisted of measurement of local effects manifested through two domains: mastery of EO content and degree of attitude change with respect to authoritarianism. The class of 96-2 was surveyed with respect to authoritarianism to assess extent of change ostensibly related to training. A pretest posttest design was used. Mastery of EO content was assessed for the classes of 95-2, 95-3, and 96-1.

Mastery of EO content is a measure of achievement. Students' knowledge of EO issues and policy is assessed, and they are instructed in broad areas such as communication, interface with commanders, and processing of discrimination complaints. Specifically, EO content also includes instruction in identification of sexual harassment and racism and provision of guidance to personnel who perceive discrimination. Since students typically would not possess extensive experience in or knowledge of EO issues, it was expected there would be significant changes in mastery of EO content as a function of DEOMI training.

Local effects were also assessed through measurement of attitudinal change for the class of 96-2. Authoritarianism was selected as an attitudinal measure potentially sensitive to DEOMI training due to its established and well replicated relation with prejudice (Duckitt, 1994; Stephan, Ageyev, Coates-Shrider, Stephan, et al., 1994). Further, this general relationship extends to both traditional prejudice and symbolic racism (Raden, 1994). Therefore, consistent with Hope's (1979) findings on decrements of prejudice as a function of DEOMI training, it was predicted that authoritarian attitudes would show a similar decrease.

Study One

Method

Participants. Commanders and supervisors of graduates from DEOMI classes of 94-3 and 95-1 (N = 147) were resurveyed regarding satisfaction with the graduates' performance. Respondents included 88% male (N = 56) and 12% female (N = 7). Racial/ethnic distribution included 74% Caucasian (N = 47) and 19% African-American (N = 12). There was one Hispanic, two Asians, one Native American, and one "Other." With respect to rank, 52% were officers (N = 33) and 42% were enlisted members (N = 27). Respondents included 63% Army (N = 40), 20% Navy (N = 13), 9% Air Force (N = 6), and 8% Marines (N = 4).

Procedure. Participants were mailed the CSEG to complete anonymously. They also received a "Critical Review," which asked them to pretend to be DEOMI's "worst critic" and generate three major issues with DEOMI. Follow-up procedures resulted in a return rate of 57% (N = 63) for the CSEG as of the writing of this report.

Results

Two important findings emerged from this study. First, commander/supervisor satisfaction for DEOMI combined classes of 94-3 and 95-1 between the summer of 1995 and the summer of 1996 was not significantly different. Specifically, the categories of EO Issues (t = .28, 156 degrees of freedom, p < .77), Command & Leadership (t = .83, 135 degrees of freedom, p < .40), Administrative, Meetings & Training (t = 1.05, 125 degrees of freedom p < .29), Guidance, Advisement, & Processing (t = .38,

150 degrees of freedom, $p < .70$) and General Satisfaction ($t = .78$, 121 degrees of freedom, $p < .43$) were not significantly different between the two survey administrations. This indicates relatively stable levels of satisfaction with DEOMI graduate performance across a one-year interval.

Secondly, summarized ratings indicated high levels of satisfaction across categories of performance for the DEOMI graduate. Specifically, mean ratings of 4.74 (SD = .55) for EO Issues, 4.60 (SD = .58) for Guidance, Advisement, & Processing, 4.56 (SD = .68) for Command & Leadership, 4.58 (SD = .62) for Administrative, Meetings, & Training, and 4.38 (SD = .75) for General Satisfaction were obtained. Note these ratings ranged from a one (1) "Totally dissatisfied," to a five (5) "Totally satisfied." Results are summarized in Figure 9.1.

Preliminary analyses were performed on the Critical Review. Although not subjected to a formal content analysis, it can be reported that approximately 46 percent ($\underline{N} = 29$) of the respondents provided

Figure 9.1
Comparison of Commander/Supervisor Satisfaction
Ratings Between 1995 and 1996

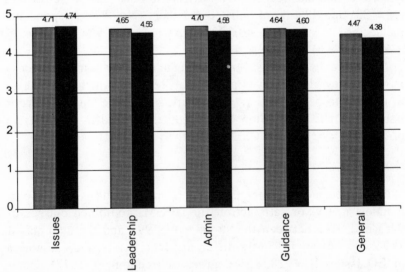

☐ Summer, 1995 (Combined Classes of 94.3 & 95.1)

■ Summer, 1996 (Combined Classes of 94.3 & 95.1)

critical review commentary. Preliminary content analysis indicates three major content areas. The first area concerned leadership support of DEOMI. Eleven comments focused on the need for more leadership representation among DEOMI trainees and greater leadership support of DEOMI's mission. Secondly, six comments focused on the need for more service-specific training. Finally, six comments focused on a perception that DEOMI graduate performance can be viewed by some individuals as counterproductive. That is, a focus on diversity and differences is occasionally viewed as potentially less valuable than a focus on positive EO changes made within the past decade. It must be emphasized these elicited comments have not yet been subjected to formal content analysis and should be viewed as heuristic in nature. It is also important to note that many respondents were unable or unwilling to generate critical commentary.

Study Two

Method

Participants. Commanders and supervisors for the combined classes of 95-2, 95-3, and 96-1 (N = 59) completed the CSEG and Critical Review. Respondents included 86% male (N = 51) and 13% female (N = 8). Racial/ethnic distribution included 67% Caucasian (N = 40) and 18% African-American (N = 11). There were four Hispanics, two Asians, one Native American, and one "Other." With respect to rank, 61% were officers (N = 36) and 33% were enlisted members (N = 20). Respondents included 35% Army (N = 21), 25% Navy (N = 15), 38% Air Force (N = 23), and no Marines. The procedure was the same as in Study One. Although this study is presently ongoing, a return rate of 34% (N = 59) was obtained at the time of this report.

Results

High levels of satisfaction were obtained for summarized ratings of EO Issues (Mean = 4.75), Guidance, Advisement, & Processing (Mean = 4.62), Command & Leadership (Mean = 4.54), Administrative, Meetings, & Training (Mean = 4.46), and General Satisfaction (4.25). Results are summarized in Figure 9.2.

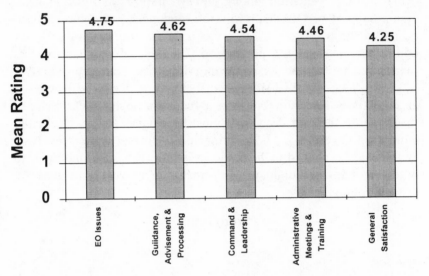

Figure 9.2
Commander's/Supervisor's Evaluation of DEOMI
Graduates' Knowledge and Performance
(N = 59; Combined Classes of 95-2, 95-3, 96-1)

Consistent with Study One, a preliminary content analysis was performed on the 47 percent ($\underline{N}$ = 28) individuals who responded to this request. The first of the three most endorsed categories involved the need for more service specific training. Eight individuals indicated this to be a need. Five individuals reported the length of the training to be excessive. Finally, eight individuals remarked that DEOMI graduates may benefit from more training on assessment of a situation in its entirety and within a contextual framework. Some of these respondents indicated their belief that DEOMI graduates need to be more flexible and holistic in their approach to a potentially problematic situation. As in Study One, it is emphasized these findings are preliminary.

Study Three

Method

Participants. Students from the DEOMI class of 96-2 ($\underline{N}$ = 108) were surveyed with respect to attitude change. Mastery of EO Content was assessed for classes 95-2, 95-3, and 96-1.

Procedure. Students completed the Authoritarianism Scale (AS; Heaven, 1985) upon entry to the training program. This inventory has well established reliability and validity (Heaven, 1985). Students were retested with this instrument upon completion of the fourteenth week of the residential program. Since students are routinely given pretests and posttests regarding EO achievement, information on content mastery was readily available through archival sources.

Results

No significant differences were found on authoritarian attitudes between the pretest and posttest ($\underline{t}$ = .22, degrees of freedom = 207, $\underline{p}$ < .82). The pretest mean on the AS was 102.83 (SD = 7.89) and posttest mean was 103.10 (SD = 9.60).

Mastery of EO content showed significant achievement for all classes. Results are summarized in Figure 9.3. Paired sample t-tests for the classes of 95-2 and 95-3 indicated significant improvement (95-2: $\underline{t}$ = -27.84, 74 degrees of freedom, $\underline{p}$ < .000; and 95-3: $\underline{t}$ = 26.94, 91 degrees of freedom, $\underline{p}$ < .000). The 95-2 pretest mean was 56.21 (SD = 8.83) and the posttest mean was 76.05 (SD 7.5). For 95-3 the pretest mean was 59.23 (SD = 8.31) and the posttest mean

Figure 9.3
EO Achievement Means

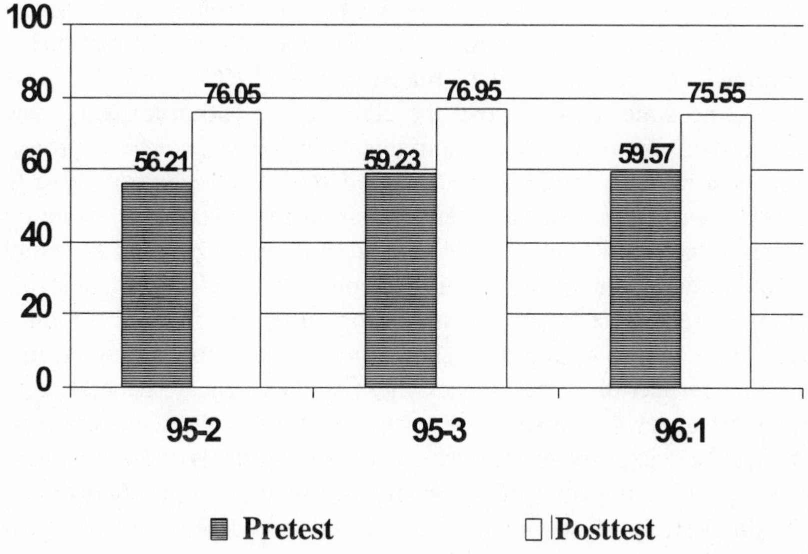

■ **Pretest**   □ **Posttest**

was 76.95 (SD = 6.21). Paired sample t-tests also indicated significant improvement in EO achievement for the class of 96-1 (t = -
22.67, 99 degrees of freedom, p < .000). The class of 96-1 had a
pretest mean of 59.57 (SD = 8.46) and a posttest mean of 75.55 (SD
= 5.10).

General Discussion

Collectively, these three studies generally demonstrate positive
local effects and global impact of DEOMI training. DEOMI is effective in training as demonstrated through the increase in EO achievement posttest scores. This indicates an increase in student proficiency
in areas ranging from equal opportunity policy through interviewing techniques and administrative management. However, as noted
in Johnson (1995), an area of potential improvement may lie in a
focus on mastery of EO achievement. For example, a reasonable
goal for mean posttest scores might be set at a criterion of 85 percent, which would represent a higher standard of achievement than
is currently attained. Along similar lines, it is also useful to consider
an evaluation of curriculum content and its representation in test-
taking materials. Students would benefit from more frequent and
varied evaluation attempts and these, in turn, may more accurately
represent actual course content.

It is uncertain why authoritarian attitudes remained unchanged.
However, there are several possible reasons. First, measurement of
authoritarianism is an indirect assessment of prejudicial attitudes.
Future research efforts should use instruments directly measuring
prejudice such as the Modern Racism Scale (McConohay, 1986). A
second possible reason is that the construct of authoritarianism and
consequent use of the Authoritarianism Scale may not be appropriate for a military sample. The obtained scores were high relative to
established norms for samples similar in organizational structure
(such as police officers). Given the unique organizational structure
of the military, authoritarianism may constitute a selection factor that
tends to remain constant and is reinforced by service and the military hierarchy, as opposed to a construct sensitive to training efforts.

With respect to global impact, these studies indicate general com-
mander/supervisor satisfaction with the DEOMI graduate's performance. Hence, DEOMI training can be appropriately viewed as having a positive impact within military installations. Importantly, longitudinal study of commander/supervisor satisfaction indicates that

levels remained consistently high between June of 1995 and June of 1996. This suggests that the DEOMI classes of 94-3 and 95-1 maintained high levels of performance of their EO duties, as evaluated by their supervisors. Hence, performance decrements possibly related to "burn-out" or decreasing motivation were not present. Instead, a high level of satisfaction with performance of EO duties was maintained over time.

Graduates received mean ratings indicating high levels of satisfaction with management of intercultural/ethnic issues. They are also viewed as competent in managing issues related to racism, sexism, and sexual harassment. There was strong satisfaction expressed regarding the graduate's ability to assess EO climate trends within the command or unit, and provision of guidance to individuals who perceive themselves to be targets of discrimination. Moderate satisfaction was expressed in performance of tasks such as advisement of commanders and staff agencies on EO matters that impact upon EO climate. Finally, moderate to total satisfaction was expressed on conduct of EO training and on conduct of meetings, conferences, and briefings related to EO matters.

As noted earlier, commander/supervisor ratings for the classes of 95-2, 95-3 and 96-1 were also uniformly high. Although caution must be exercised due to the preliminary nature of this survey, obtained ratings indicate moderate to high levels of satisfaction across the domains of EO Issues, Guidance, Advisement & Processing, Command & Leadership, Administrative, Meetings & Training, and General Satisfaction.

As reviewed in Johnson (1995), greater effort could usefully be directed to longitudinal trend analysis of EO climate within the military. That is, EO climate improvement should be manifest in both prospective and retrospective trend analysis of MEOCS data. Although this may be less than ideal, as addressed earlier, presently limited financial and personnel resources preclude more comprehensive efforts.

Conclusions

Although findings from this study are generally positive with respect to local effects and global impact of DEOMI training, there are several areas for improving program evaluation efforts.

First, as noted in Johnson (1995), a comprehensive theory and model of training would promote evaluation efforts. For example, if the training model and curriculum dictates problem-solving skill acquisition as a logical goal, then assessment efforts should be directed towards this discrete area. Comprehensive evaluation efforts would thus entail periodic and systematic assessment of multiple domains on multiple occasions. In order to achieve this, program evaluation should be an ongoing component of the DEOMI mission and integrated throughout the organizational structure.

Secondly, multiple measures and methods of evaluation would enhance interpretation of program evaluation data. For example, conclusions from the present study are constrained by the use of a single method for assessment of global impact. In addition to survey data on commander/supervisor satisfaction, focus groups and gathering of factual information related to complaint management and outcome would generate much needed information on behavioral and "real life" aspects of DEOMI graduate performance. Focus groups and other methods should be directed both to the DEOMI graduate and their supervisor. Ongoing feedback loops could be established between research and evaluation efforts within DEOMI and field installations. This could ensure training consistent with evolving field needs. It would also enable DEOMI training efforts to be continually responsive to dynamic societal and cultural factors encountered in the EO Advisor's responsibilities, and ultimately enhance DEOMI's capacity to meet military readiness needs.

References

Blake, B. F. & Heslin, R. (1983). Evaluating cross-cultural training. In D. Landis & R. W. Brislin, (Eds.). *Handbook of Intercultural Training*. New York: Pergamon.

Duckitt, J. (1994). Conformity to social pressure and racial prejudice among White South Africans. *Genetic, Social, and General Psychology Monographs, 120*(2), 121-143.

Heaven, P. C. L. (1985). Construction and validation of a measure of authoritarian personality. *Journal of Personality Assessment, 49*, 545-551.

Hope, R. O. (1979). *Racial Strife in the U.S. Military*. New York: Praeger.

Johnson, J. L. (1995). A preliminary investigation of DEOMI training effectiveness.

McConohay, J. (1986). Modern racism, ambivalence, and the Modern Racism Scale. In J. F. Dovidio & S. L. Gaertner (Eds.), *Prejudice, discrimination, and racism*. San Diego: Academic Press.

Raden, D. L. (1994). Are symbolic racism and traditional prejudice part of a contemporary authoritarian attitude syndrome? *Political Behavior, 16*(3), 365-384.

Stephan, W. G., Ageyev, V., Coates-Shrider, L., Stephan, C. W., et al. (1994). On the relationship between stereotypes and prejudice: An international study. *Personality and Social Psychology Bulletin, 20*(3), 277-284.

10

Perceptions of Small Group Diversity Training at the Defense Equal Opportunity Management Institute*

Ruth L. Greene

Introduction

For the last twenty-seven years the education and training component at the Defense Equal Opportunity Management Institute (DEOMI) has successfully integrated a variety of training components that include didactic, experiential, behavioral, and group education and training. Historically, the training content at DEOMI focused on three general areas. First, students were made more aware and knowledgeable about intercultural issues on race relations, and equal opportunity. Second, students were to develop skills and knowledge to be effective small group leaders and facilitators on issues related to racial harmony and equal opportunity. Finally, students would be trained in knowledge regarding equal opportunity policies in the military to equip them to serve as resources (i.e., advisors) to commanders.

This chapter begins with a detailed description of the current curriculum, methodology, and philosophy of the DEOMI. Next, student perceptions of the small group experiential learning laboratory activities in the Equal Opportunity Advisor Course are reviewed. Following this is an exploration of trainers' perceptions of DEOMI training needs and trainer styles.

---

* Opinions expressed in this report are those of the author and should not be construed to represent the official position of DEOMI, the military Services, or the Department of Defense.

189

Current data from the Military Equal Opportunity Climate Survey (MEOCS), which measures equal opportunity and organizational effectiveness, have indicated that gender and race affect individual perceptions of the diversity climate. Therefore, descriptive data are used to evaluate differences between gender and racial groups during the training phase. In the second phase, mean scores from low need to high need are used to rank training needs. Recommendations are made to increase training effectiveness.

Research on DEOMI Training Program

Several researchers have written about the historical development of diversity training at DEOMI (Day, 1983; Landis, Hope & Day, 1984; Smith, 1994; Dansby & Landis, 1996). A few studies have focused on the DEOMI training "content" and "processes" (Day, 1983; Adelman & Larkin, 1980; Johnson, 1995). The content and process of the training include the class presentations, effectiveness and relevancy of activities in the lectures and small groups, as well as an evaluation of the degree to which curriculum content is related to EO duties or tasks. In one of the more recent studies, Johnson (1995) reported a preliminary study of the local effects of DEOMI training through pretest and post-test measures of achievement and attitudinal change. However, she was principally concerned with outcome measures of commander/supervisor satisfaction of EO performance after training.

Generally, these studies report that the training at DEOMI has been viewed positively by students. However, there is a dearth of information since the 1980s on the current training processes, specifically those processes in the small group-training component of the curriculum. Because a number of changes have been made since the 1980s to the structure, content, approach, and mission at DEOMI, more research is needed on the current training program. Although the small group experiential methodology has remained a major focus of the training, it is currently less confrontational than it was in the 1970s, with more focus on intergroup processes, awareness, knowledge, and skills that focus on both personal and institutional effectiveness. Moreover, the current curriculum content has addressed many of the recommendations proposed in earlier studies concerning the need for more focus on service-specific information relevant to the duties that students will encounter in the field (Day, 1983).

The DEOMI training program provides a unique opportunity to study training design and effectiveness, as well as trainer effectiveness, in a unique experiential laboratory group that is specifically designed to have a diverse demographic composition. All DEOMI small group-training classes have a diverse membership with respect to race, ethnicity, gender, rank, and organization (i.e., branch of service). Finally, the DEOMI training is a unique combination of awareness, knowledge, and skill training that allows individuals to become effective managers of equal opportunity and human relations training.

Elements of DEOMI Training

The military equal opportunity program has changed continuously over the last twenty-five years to reflect changing missions. Below is a brief description of the current (1) philosophy of DEOMI training; (2) the design of the training; and (3) external organizational assessment of training.

1. *Philosophy of DEOMI Training*: The training program focuses on both education and training and uses a laboratory method of learning that stresses experiential learning and didactic learning approaches. The small group training setting allows faculty and students to participate in understanding, diagnosing, and providing solutions to issues of diversity, organizational change, and intergroup relations. The DEOMI philosophy is based on the adult learning model which focuses on the way adults learn and theories of how different cultural groups work together. Additionally, because diversity training is viewed as a military readiness issue, Equal Opportunity Advisors (EOAs) are trained to advise commanders in implementing EO programs by providing training and education in their units, and serving as group facilitators on issues of diversity.

2. *Design of the Training Program*: DEOMI uses the laboratory experiential approach to education and training. Further, the program requires clearly stated objectives and defined content, and student evaluation is based on the program objectives and content.

The current DEOMI curriculum uses a systems approach to curriculum development that follows an Instructional System Development (ISD) process to develop, implement and evaluate instruction. The goal of ISD is to develop instruction based on job performance requirements and to ensure that graduates have the skills, knowledge, and attitudes to become effective EO Advisors. The curriculum is designed to develop a base of knowledge and skill that will allow graduates to assess human relations climates in the organizations they serve, to provide assistance to commanders, and to reduce discriminatory practices in their organizations.

3. *External Organizational Assessment of Training*: DEOMI views external assessment and recognition as central to the success of its training mission. As a consequence, it participates in appropriate accreditation processes. The Council on Occupational Education (COE) currently accredits DEOMI.

DEOMI Training Methodology

DEOMI currently uses several training activities, techniques, and strategies, which include lectures, small group discussions, guest lectures, simulation techniques, videotapes, case studies, role playing, symposia, student presentations, and practical experiences.

The primary formats include: (1) platform instruction; (2) clarification group, small group instructor led and student led experiential learning; and (3) guest lecture series. Guest lecturers include recognized military and civilian authorities that focus on contemporary equal opportunity issues faced by EOAs. Although this is less of a focus as compared with the 1970s curriculum, students also participate in field activities that take place in surrounding communities.

The Clarification Group Process (C-Group)

The Clarification Group Process (C-Group) is a laboratory-training model that allows participants to gain self-understanding, skills in inter-group relations and leadership, and skills in understanding the kinds of dynamics that underlie conflicts between groups (Bahad, Birnbaum, & Benne, 1978; Birnbaum, 1975). It is a methodology to promote diversity awareness. It is not a therapy group, but rather uses a group format to help each person explore their attitudes and feelings that they have toward other racial, religious, cultural and ethnic groups.

DEOMI's laboratory method includes theory lectures, role-plays, and skill practice exercises that allows students to clarify feelings about their own group identification, attitudes toward other groups, and how other groups view them. This C-Group method of education is an outgrowth of the National Training Laboratory in Group Development, and theory and practice based on the early model by

Kurt Lewin, Kenneth Benne, Leland Bradford, and Ronald Lippit (Benne, Bradford, Gibb, & Lippit, 1975), who pioneered work on inter-group relations training.

The model begins with a structured group interview that helps students understand their group identification that includes age, sex, religion, race, social class, ethnicity, and how the group identification influences attitudes, feeling and actions as an equal opportunity officer. The C-Group focuses on interpersonal, inter-group processes (see Bahad, Birnbaum, & Benne, 1983; Benne et al., 1975). Skills include organizational development skills and effective consulting skills.

Training Evaluation

The DEOMI training course uses a building block approach in which a student progressively makes progress in mastering required behavioral skills in interpersonal relations, group development, and cross-cultural and gender issues. EOAs must be able to (1) demonstrate the ability to understand concepts and knowledge, (2) meet selected behavior, oral and written standards, and (3) apply theoretical principles during the small group exercises. Internal evaluation includes three areas:

1. *Content Knowledge*: Knowledge and concepts are measured by written examinations.

2. *Behavioral Performance*: The Interpersonal Skills Development Evaluation (ISDE) form measures behavioral performance skills. The ISDE reporting system measures students' required behavioral skills throughout the course. Evaluation includes at least four trainer observations and evaluations of students in and out of the classroom. Behavioral areas that are evaluated include: (1) group development skills, cross-cultural and gender awareness, and adaptability skills; (2) communication process skills; (3) effective feedback skills; (4) self-centered functions; (5) self awareness;and (6) standards of conduct. Additionally, trainers provide counseling and feedback to students during the feedback sessions.

3. *Oral and Written Skills*: Finally, students are required to have a basic knowledge of oral and written communication strategies that will enhance the effectiveness of staff communication in their organization. Five oral and four written assignments are measured through performance checklists.

Training Quality Assurance

DEOMI trainers use both platform lecture training and small group facilitation skills. They are required to participate in internal and external training sessions to master the requisite skills. To insure greater familiarity with the training curricula, all DEOMI trainers are required to complete the resident Equal Opportunity Advisor's Course (EOAC) and pass a performance board review before presenting their lessons. In a quality system of evaluation there are two groups of measures that are needed. These include (1) internal measures that measure student reactions and satisfaction and whether they have mastered the course content, and (2) external measures that provide information about on the job behavior and the impact of the training on the business or unit. Both types of evaluation are used at DEOMI.

In addition to student performance in mastering objectives, surveys and individual feedback forms are used to assess the internal process or local effects of training. Periodic graduate surveys and commander or supervisor surveys gauge the external impact of the program. Likewise the Directorate of Research, the research arm of DEOMI, administers the MEOCS, a diagnostic tool which measures equal opportunity and organizational effectiveness in the field and fleet.

DEOMI views self-assessment and evaluation for improvement as an essential part of the mission of the Institute. The Council on Occupational Education (COE) currently accredits DEOMI. Until 1995, COE was under the umbrella of the Southern Association of Colleges and Schools (SACS), which is a regional accrediting association that serves institutions in an eleven-state region. In 1994, COE became an independent accreditation agency and now serves as the national institutional accrediting agency for non-degree granting and applied associate-degree granting, post-secondary occupational education institutions.

DEOMI is unique in focusing on both education and training in the diversity training curriculum. In recent years, particular attention has been given to the area of organizational development and assessment. Students are instructed on the MEOCS administration and use to evaluate and improve the human relations' climate in their organizations. The MEOCS includes items and questions focusing on demographic information, unit EO climate, organizational commitment, work group effectiveness, job satisfaction, and racial attitudes and perceptions. MEOCS results can be used to examine differences by subgroups. More importantly, MEOCS data can be used by EOAs to assist Commanders in developing and implementing a plan for organizational improvement and in organizing action teams to address certain issues revealed by the data.

Equal Opportunity Advisor Training Course Curriculum

The Equal Opportunity Advisor Course (EOAC) is a 68-day (approximately 15 weeks) resident training course for active-duty officers, noncommissioned officers (i.e., enlisted), and civilians, conducted three times a year. It is DEOMI's flagship course. The purpose of the course is to prepare Department of Defense (DoD) personnel to become specialists on equal opportunity issues, program managers, and advisors to commanders. Specifically, it provides a base of knowledge and skill mix that allows graduates to assess the human relations climate within the organizations they serve, and to provide advice and assistance to commanders to prevent, reduce or eliminate discriminatory practices.

The EOAC covers three levels of learning: cognitive, affective, and performance. The cognitive level of learning includes theories and information relevant to the DoD EO program; the affective level covers values, attitudes, and sensitivities related to EO issues; and the performance level covers the actual tasks that EO advisors will perform at their respective commands or units.

The EOAC uses the building block concept in which studies progress through several blocks of study. These blocks or instructional series include course administration, interpersonal skills, communication skills, power and discrimination, cultural awareness, assessments, staff advisor skills and service-specific skills (see Table 10.1). Throughout each instruction block students are given oral and written assignments that require them to research, support and organize their ideas in a position paper and an oral briefing. The curriculum blocks are listed below:

- The *Course Administrative* series provides the curriculum overview and evaluation procedures.

- The *Interpersonal Skills* series provides basic knowledge of oral and written communications theory and includes topics on the communications process, effective and active listening, effective feedback and guided discussion techniques.

- The *Communications Skills* block includes lessons on the communication process and effective feedback.

- The *Power and Discrimination* block provides information to explore and discuss the relationship between power, prejudice and discrimination.

- The *Cultural Awareness* series provides basic information on various cultural relationships that exist within society and the U.S. military. This block contains several lectures and exercises that include various topics, such as the historical, culture and contemporary issues associated with the major ethnic and cultural groups in the United States, various issues associated with women in the military, discrimination, power, sexual harassment, religious accommodation, and affirmative action.

- The *Unit and Organizational Factors* block provides information and techniques to analyze and understand organizational equal opportunity issues.

- The *Advisor Skills Service Specific* block provides basic knowledge and skills required to perform duties as the EO staff advisor to commanders in the field and fleet. These classes include lectures on motivation theory, conflict management, mediation techniques, organizations as systems, services regulations, and managing EO programs, advising the commander and marketing EO programs, interviewing skills, and organizational assessment.

- The *Assessment Skills* Block prepares EOAs to conduct unit EO climate assessments using various survey tools and analysis techniques.

- The *Service Specific* block provides specific information on service regulations, and individual philosophies, procedures and programs within the Army, Navy, Air Force, Marine Corps, Coast Guard and foreign military services (i.e., South Africa, Soviet Union, Korea, Trinidad and Tobago, and others).

Student Perceptions of Small Group Laboratory

The small group laboratory, or C-Group, includes fifteen to twenty-one people who communicate in the group to facilitate common individual and group goals. Experiential learning takes place when group members systematically and critically examine their shared experience, analyze the situation, and generalize and apply the information to performance tasks and simulations in the field and fleet.

The curriculum at DEOMI is designed such that the block lectures are accompanied by structured group experiences that reinforce the theory, skills, and knowledge taught in the large group lectures. More than 60 percent of the training is accomplished using the small group structured experience method. As a result of this methodology, the EOAs have a framework to utilize the knowledge that they are learning and to evaluate their behaviors and the behaviors of others. The curriculum also provides a framework they can use in their work outside of the training session.

Table 10.1
DEOMI Educational Curriculum 1997 EO Advisor Course

DEOMI Course Administration
    Library Orientation   Evaluation Procedures
    Curriculum Overview   Pre & Post Assessment
    Writing Program

Interpersonal Skills
    Group Development, Norms and   Conflict Management
       Expectations   Guided Discussion Techniques
    Socialization Process   Ethics
    Motivation Theory   Role of EO Advisor
    Group Development Theory

Communication Skills
    Effective and Active Listening   Myers Briggs Personality Type
    Effective Feedback Skills   Communication Process
    Perceptions   Presentation Skills
    Student Interviews

Cultural Awareness
    Introduction to the American Experience   Affirmative Actions
    Power and Discrimination   Managing Diversity
    Racism   Communication Across Differences
    Sexism   Personal Dissonance
    Extremism   Concept of Culture
    The White Male Club   Black American Experience
    Racism in the Military   Hispanic American Experience
    Sexual Harassment   Asian American Experience
    Religious Accommodation   Native American Experience
    Anti-Semitism   Arab American Experience
    System/Victim Focus   Jewish American Experience
                                     White American Experience

Unit and Organizational Factors

Advisor Skills
    Managing Dynamic EO Programs   Organizational Assessment
    Organizational Process Theory   Intervention and Action Techniques
    Processing Assessment Data   Observation Techniques

Assessment Skills
    Survey Considerations   Interviewing Techniques

Service Specific Skills
    Service Specific
    Marketing Briefs

The elements of training most commonly evaluated are course design and delivery (Kirkpatrick, 1975). In this preliminary study the focus is on students' perceptions of course design and trainer effectiveness, with special emphasis on comparing these across gender and race/ethnicity. In this study students reported their reactions during four consecutive lessons covering the *Cultural Factors and Unit Cohesion* lessons that spanned a five-week period. Questionnaires were customized to evaluate training design and delivery, and participant learning.

Methodology

Subjects

Participants included 85 students who were enrolled in the 15-week Equal Opportunity Advisor Course. At the beginning of the course students are assigned to a small group which serves as the experiential, laboratory group throughout twelve weeks of the course. Each of the six small groups had two or more trainers and no more than fifteen students. Each group had a mixture of members from each service and included males and females, as well as enlisted and officer personnel. When possible, experienced trainers were paired with inexperienced trainers. Sixty-three percent of the sample was male and 37 percent was female.

Measurement

Data were collected during the ninth week of the 15-week course. Prior to data collection, students had completed instructional blocks on course administration, dynamics of effective leadership, and communication skills. The five lessons that were evaluated were part of the *Cultural Factors and Unit Cohesion* Block and included the small group exercises and discussion on (1) *system victim focus,* (2) *women in the military,* (3) *sexual harassment,* (4) *religious accommodation,* and (5) *affirmative action.* The typical format involved a formal lecture followed by a small group experience. Students from the seven small groups were asked to complete a 22-item survey for five consecutive days after completing the lecture and small group exercises. The survey used a five-point rating scale with 5 representing strong agreement and 1 representing strong disagreement. Each day the survey focused on the class objective for the day and students were asked to evaluate the small group session and the trainers along specific dimensions, and to indicate barriers that they thought may have impeded the accomplishment of the course objectives. The survey measured student reactions and satisfaction on (1) a global rating of the small group activity, (2) nine specific questions about the small group activity, (3) five questions concerning barriers to training, (4) a global rating of the trainer, and (5) four specific questions about trainer effectiveness. The researcher collected the surveys immediately after the students completed them at the end of each day.

Results

The data presented below are disaggregated by race and gender. Each dimension is rated using a Likert-type scale with scores ranging from 5 (high) to 1 (low).

A. Comparisons by Gender

Table 10.2 presents global group means for group reactions to the small group activity. T-tests were used to compare male and female reactions to the small group activity and their perceptions of potential barriers to the success of the training lesson. In general, both men and women held positive perceptions of the activities.

Mean scores for males and females indicated that all participants viewed training favorably. There were no significant differences across gender in perceptions of trainer effectiveness. Mean ratings for all trainer effectiveness indicators ranged from 4.06 to 4.26. There was one significant gender difference in perceptions of barriers to the lessons. Findings show that females compared to males believed that the trainers ability to facilitate could be a barrier to the success of the lesson (t = -2.01; p<.05).

B. Comparisons by Race

Comparisons by race were limited to examination of differences in perception between the two largest groups, African Americans and whites. In the sample of eighty-five students, only eight belonged to another racial/ethnic group and this number was to small to conduct a separate analysis. The composite means scores indicate high levels of satisfaction with the small group experience, 3.63 for whites and 3.92 for African Americans. Global means ratings of the

Table 10.2
Group Statistics by Gender

	Gender	N	Mean	Standard Deviation	T	df	Sig.
Global Ratings Ratings of the small group	Female Male	109 264	3.80 3.84	.887 1.07	-.32	371	.747
Ratings of the trainee	Female Male	107 265	4.07 3.98	1.02 1.05	.75	370	.454
Activity							
Provided awareness of different value systems	Female Male	109 266	3.91 4.03	.91 .73	-1.31	373	.189
Activity as a significant emotional event	Female Male	110 266	2.83 2.97	1.19 1.13	-1.25	374	.261
Activity is relevant to job as EO Advisor	Female Male	110 261	4.43 4.55	.71 .62	-1.64	369	.101
Activity met my personal expectation	Female Male	109 264	3.83 3.85	.86 .90	-.172	369	.863
Activity increased and updated my knowledge	Female Male	110 266	4.07 4.06	.82 .89	-.089	371	.929
Activity reinforced information from the lecture	Female Male	110 266	4.09 4.10	.85 .84	-.071	374	.943
The time allotted was appropriate	Female Male	110 264	3.61 3.65	1.09 1.04	-.354	372	.723
Activity promoted new values and beliefs	Female Male	111 266	3.52 3.62	.95 .92	-.967	371	.334
Lesson objectives were clearly stated and understood	Female Male	110 266	4.02 4.01	.70 .86	.075	374	.941
Activity provided an opportunity for self appraisal	Female Male	110 265	3.83 3.88	.86 .84	-.581	373	.562
Trainer							
Trainer promoted a good atmosphere	Female Male	110 265	4.11 4.26	.926 .789	-1.58	373	.116
Trainer facilitated class discussions effectively	Female Male	110 266	4.08 4.15	.814 .785	-.850	374	.398
Trainer linked concepts to interpersonal situations	Female Male	110 265	4.06 4.15	.600 .795	-.990	373	.325
Trainer listened carefully	Female Male	110 265	4.13 4.22	.760 .760	-1.03	373	.306
Barriers							
Group activity content	Female Male	110 251	2.49 2.69	1.71 1.78	-.970	354	.333
Instructional format	Female Male	104 257	2.41 2.71	1.65 1.81	-1.42	359	.154
Personal interest and participation	Female Male	106 257	2.50 2.79	1.81 1.91	-1.31	361	.188
Students in the group	Female Male	105 258	2.71 2.79	1.82 1.85	-.358	361	.720
Trainer	Female Male	104 256	2.53 2.88	1.81 2.07	-1.52	358	.129
Trainers ability to facilitate	Female Male	104 257	2.53 3.03	1.88 2.18	-2.01	359	.045

Table 10.3
Group Statistics by Race

	Gender	N	Mean	Standard Deviation	T	df	Sig.
Global Ratings Ratings of the small group	Black White	165 145	3.92 3.63	.988 1.05	2.47	308	.014*
Ratings of the trainer(s)	Black White	163 146	4.06 3.94	.928 1.17	.97	307	.120
Activity							
Provided awareness of different value systems	Black White	166 146	4.04 3.90	.776	.85	310	.397
Activity as a significant emotional event	Black White	166 147	3.1 2.6	1.03 1.26	3.53	311	.000*
Activity is relevant to job as EO Advisor	Black White	165 146	4.52 4.43	.659 .633	1.21	309	.227
Activity met my personal expectation	Black White	165 145	3.95 3.02	.814 .939	2.34	308	.020*
Activity increased and updated my knowledge	Black White	165 147	4.1 3.9	.821 .891	1.63	310	.103
Activity reinforced information from the lecture	Black White	166 147	4.10 4.00	.749 .951	1.69	311	.092
The time allotted was appropriate	Black White	166 145	3.67 3.51	1.05 1.08	1.30	309	.196
Activity promoted new values and beliefs	Black White	163 147	3.73 3.48	.861 .982	2.30	308	.022*
Lesson objectives were clearly stated and understood	Black White	166 147	4.12 3.87	.764 .853	2.57	311	.010*
Activity provided an opportunity for self appraisal	Black White	166 146	3.89 3.85	.786 .910	.37	310	.713
Trainer							
Trainer promoted a good atmosphere	Black White	165 147	4.21 4.22	.741 .935	-.07	310	.947
Trainer facilitated class discussions effectively	Black White	166 147	4.17 4.08	.660 .918	1.04	311	3.00
Trainer linked concepts to interpersonal situations	Black White	165 147	4.13 4.08	.662 .906	.57	310	.568
Trainer listened carefully	Black White	166 147	4.20 4.10	.655 .871	.44	310	.662
Barriers							
Group activity contest	Black White	162 134	3.09 2.16	1.78 1.67	4.61	294	.000*
Instructional format	Black White	161 138	3.09 2.19	1.84 1.60	4.47	297	.000*
Personal interest and participation	Black White	162 138	3.10 2.20	1.98 1.79	3.86	298	.000*
Students in the group	Black White	163 138	3.10 2.40	1.85 1.84	3.28	299	.001*
Trainer	Black White	162 136	3.20 2.44	2.10 2.02	3.24	296	.001*
Trainers ability to facilitate	Black White	161 138	3.40 2.46	2.14 2.04	3.88	297	.000*

trainer effectiveness were high, 3.95 for whites and 4.06 for African Americans.

In general, students perceived few barriers that impeded the effectiveness of the small group laboratory activities. The scale ranged from 1-5 with 1 and 2 indication a low-level, 3 a medium level, and 4 and 5 a high level. The group ratings averaged 2.7. However, there were significant differences by race on six of the items when students were asked specific perceptions of issues related to barriers during the group activity. African Americans reported higher mean scores, or greater perception of potential barriers than whites. Concerning trainer effectiveness, ratings were high, averaging 4.2.

Trainer Perception of Small Group Process

Despite students' positive perceptions of trainer effectiveness and the curriculum, per se, successful implementation of DEOMI's mission requires a more comprehensive method of assessing trainer effectiveness. Training is a key dimension of maintaining mission readiness and, currently, the U.S. Air Force Occupational Measurement Squadron is in the process of conducting an Occupational Task Analysis to assess skill needs in the military, including training. Faculty, staff, and graduates from DEOMI will participate in this project. The results from this study will assist trainers and curriculum specialist in implementing the Instructional Development Systems (IDS) approach that the Institute uses to plan, design, and implement the instructional program. This research is a preliminary assessment to begin the process of a formal systematic approach to diversity training that focuses on how the training program is designed. The systematic approach to training (i.e., IDS) would include (1) analysis, (2) design and development, and (3) implementation (Dick & Carey, 1996). The analysis includes needs assessment, job analysis, performance standards, and survey of existing courses.

Members of the training staff can provide useful data for evaluations of several essential elements of training: student reactions, knowledge, behavior change, and results of on job behavior change (Kirkpatrick, 1975). Trainers can be effective in helping to develop a need assessment with respect to course design and delivery because of their direct involvement in these areas. As group facilitators and group leaders they are in a position to identity further training needs of their participants. As training designers, they respond to needs-assessment findings and critique their own efforts and the work of their colleagues. Further, trainers can analyze and interpret training data in order to determine how the information will affect future training activities.

In addition, the roles that trainers are required to perform are an important aspect of the process of diversity training and should be understood and evaluated. In addition to the traditional teaching and facilitating roles, Ferdmann and Brody (1996) include modeling and consulting competencies as important aspects of the training process. Of course, teaching is a primary role of the DEOMI trainers and all learning blocks include platform lectures. However, given the group experiential learning mode of training used at DEOMI, the trainer's ability to facilitate and process group interactions is also critical. It is important for trainers to provide a learning environment that allows each participant to take risks in learning new behaviors and sharing knowledge and insights with other members of the group. Another unique and critical function that trainers serve is consultant to broad-based constituents that include senior military and civilian leaders and military senior executive staff. Finally, DEOMI trainers serve as models for new trainers who are part of the class and students in the small groups.

It is clear that these training roles are varied and complex and include stills that are geared to individual, interpersonal, and intergroup changes as well as skills required to provide interventions targeted toward organizational effectiveness and change. Three surveys were used to capture trainer's self-assessed perceptions of their roles and competencies.

Methodology

Subjects

Twenty-four DEOMI trainers, block coordinators, and training management staff completed a three-part questionnaire. The questionnaire was sent to the respondents, who were asked to return the completed survey in a sealed envelope. Table 10.4 presents the trainer profile by race, gender, service, rank, and experience. The majority of trainers are males (62 percent). Fifty-four percent of the trainers were white and 46 percent were African American. Forty-six percent of the trainers are officers and 50 percent are enlisted, and 4 percent were civilians.

More than 54 percent of the trainers had participated in a formal instructor-training course, while the remainder had not had this training. All have completed the EOAC. At the time of this study, most of the trainers were inexperienced and had less than six months of training at DEOMI. Twenty-one percent of the trainers had six months to twelve months of training. More than 17 percent had two to three

Table 10.4
Profile of DEOMI Trainers by Gender, Race, Education, Service and Experience

Gender	Male	62.5
	Female	37.5
Race	African American	45.8
	White	54.2
Rank	Officer	45.8
	Enlisted	50.0
Education	Some College	16.7
	Bachelor Degree	20.8
	Masters/Doctoral	29.2
	High School	33.3
Experience as DEOMI Trainer	Less than 6 months	16.7
	6-12 months	20.8
	1-2 years	25.0
	2-3 years	16.7
	3+ years	4.2
Service	Army	41.7
	Navy	20.8
	Air Force	20.8
	Marine Corps	8.3
	Coast Guard	8.3
EO Experience	None	45.0
	Army EO Specialist	20.0
	Navy EOPS	12.0
	Air Force Social Actions Officer	12.0
	Coast Guard Civil Rights Counselor	8.34

years of training and 4 percent of the sample had more than three years of training experience at DEOMI.

Measurement

The measurements consisted of three surveys. The first, developed by Malcolm Knowles, was a self-diagnostic rating scale of competencies for the role of adult educator/ trainer (Knowles, 1975). Gudykunst, Guzley and Hammer (1996) view self-assessments as an effective technique to help trainers determine their attitudes and perceptions of their training competence. Trainers were asked to indicate on a five-point scale their present, self-assessed, competence level or ability, on roles that included competencies in facilitating learning, designing and implementing learning experiences, and selecting methods, techniques, and materials for planning and implementing a systematic learning process. Five indicated high, 4 moderate high, 3 moderate, 2, low moderate and 1 low.

The second self-report questionnaire included general statements of thirty skills that trainers use in performing their roles. This training and development survey model was developed by the American Society for Training and Development. Trainers are asked to read statement of trainer skills and indicate their perception of need for more training in that skill. The scale ranged from 1-5, with 1 and 2 indicating a low need, 3 moderate need, and 4 and 5 high need.

The third questionnaire was the Trainer Type Inventory (TTI) developed by Mary Wheeler and Jeanie Marshall (1986). This survey measures the individual's training approach or way of presenting content, as well as the relationship that the trainer has with the trainees. This inventory is based on Kolb and Fry's (1981) work on learning style preference. This model includes four types of learning and four training types. Learning types include the following:

- *Concrete experiencers* are receptive learners who enjoy experience based learning, learning from group discussion, role-plays, and simulations.

- *Reflective learners* rely on careful observation and processing of information.

- *Abstract conceptualizers* have an analytical approach to learning and rely on logical thinking and rational evaluation.

- *Active experimenters* have a pragmatic approach and rely on information gained from projects and trying things out.

Table 10.5
Learning Style Preference with Most Effective Trainer Type/Style

Listener (L)

Concrete Experiencer

Creates an affective learning environment
Trains the Concrete Experiencer most effectively
Encourages learners to express personal needs freely
Assures that everyone is heard
Shows awareness of individual group members
Encourages learners to be self-directed
Prefers that trainees talk more than the trainers

Coach (C)

Active Experimenter

Creates a behavioral learning environment
Trains the Active Experimenter most effectively
Allows learners to evaluate their own progress
Involves trainees in activities and discussions
Encourages experimentation with practical application
Puts trainees in touch with one another
Draws on the strengths of the group
Uses trainees as resources
Helps trainees to verbalize what they already know

Director (D)

Reflective Observer

Creates a perceptual learning environment
Trains the Reflective Observer most effectively
Takes charge
Gives directions
Prepares notes and outlines
Appears self-confident
Is well organized and outlines what is to be learned

Interpreter (I)

Abstract Conceptualizer

Creates a symbolic learning environment
Trains the Abstract Conceptualizer most effectively
Encourages learner to memorize and master terms and rules
Makes a connection with the past and present
Integrates theories and events
Separates self from learners; observes
Shares ideas but not feelings
Acknowledges others; interpretations, as well as his/her own
Uses theory as a foundation
Encourages generalizations

Cited in J. William Pfeiffer & Leonard D. Goodstein (Eds.). *The 1986 Annual: Developing Human Resources.* San Diego, CA: University Associates.

Table 10.6
Trainer Type

Listener (L)
Creates an affective learning environment
Trains the Concrete Experiencer most effectively
Encourages learners to express personal needs freely
Assures that everyone is heard
Shows awareness of individual group members
Reads nonverbal behavior
Prefers that trainees talk more than the trainers

Coach (D)
Creates a behavioral learning environment
Trains the Active Experimenter most effectively
Allows learners to evaluate their own progress
Involves trainees in activities and discussions
Encourages experimentation with practical application
Puts trainees in touch with one another
Draws on the strengths of the groups
Uses trainees as resources
Helps trainees to verbalize what they already know

Director (D)
Creates a perceptual learning environment
Trains the reflective Observer most effectively
Takes charge
Gives directions
Prepares notes and outlines
Appears self-confident
Is well organized

Interpreter (I)
Creates a symbolic learning environment
Trains the Abstract Conceptualizer most effectively
Encourages learner to memorize and master terms and rules
Makes connections (ties the past to the present, is concerned wit the flow of the
    training designs
Integrates theories and events
Separates self from learners, observes
Shares ideas but not feelings
Acknowledges others; interpretations, as well as his/her own
Uses theory as a foundation
Encourages generalizations
Presents well constructed interpretations

The four trainer styles are, "listener," "coach," "director," and "interpreter." According to Kolb and Fry (1981), a particular training approach (i.e., method of presenting content) and the relationship between the trainer and trainees characterize each of the four training types. Table 10.5 shows the learning style preference and the training types that are the most effective match. Research suggests that students have very different learning styles, therefore, there is no best approach to training. And while trainers often use all four trainers' styles, it is appropriate for trainers to be aware of their preferred style when working with diverse groups. The "listener" style trains the concrete experiencer most effectively. The "director" is most effective in training the reflective learner. The abstract conceptualizer favors the "interpreter" style and "coaches" are most effective in training the active experimenter.

Given DEOMI's experiential laboratory approach to training, the current clarification method of training used in the small groups, and the current skill training given to trainers, it was hypothesized that the highest percentage of trainers would be coaches.

Results

Twenty-one of the twenty-four trainers completed the Trainer Style Inventory (TSI). Table 10.6 outlines the TSI and shows the matrix of possible forced choices. Sixty-seven percent of the of the trainers scored high as "Coaches." Twenty-four percent of the trainers scored high on "Listener" as a preferred training style. Four percent scored as an "Interpreter" and 4 percent scored as a "Director." As predicted, these trainers scored high as coaches and listeners, the style most compatible with the approach and methodology of the DEOMI training program.

Tables 10.7 and 10.8 include mean scores in descending order for trainer self-assessed competencies and training needs assessment. Results indicated that trainers have positive perceptions of their interpersonal skills and competence in-group process skills and in their ability to provide a positive learning community for students. However, they believed that they need more training in group process skills and consultant and counseling skills that are utilized in the small group laboratories and feedback session to students as well as in presentation skills. These findings are not surprising given the fact that only 21 percent of the current trainers had had more than two years training, and more than half had not taken a formal instructor training course. The findings indicated a clear need for more time for preparation and research for teaching new lessons, and opportunities for professional development and feedback.

Discussion

The results of the first phase of the research indicated a generally high level of student satisfaction with individual trainers and the small group experience. Training is perceived as relevant for EO job tasks. Also, students thought that the objectives were stated clearly. However, more African Americans than whites felt that the exercises provided a significant emotional event, which some researchers believe is important for students to confront their own biases and prejudices toward others and change attitudes and behaviors (Day, 1983). It may be that the block courses under investigation in this small group study, i.e., *women in the military, sexual harassment,* and *affirmative action,* had a personal impact on the African-American students, precipitating an emotional event for many members of this subpopulation. Various explanations could be advanced to explain the lower rating by white males. Data from the MEOCS indicated that white males rated the EO climate more positively than any other demographic group. This high rating reflects, in part, a lack of awareness about the problems experienced in the military by racial/ethnic minorities and women. When confronted with these issues in the small group setting, many white males may react defensively and experience a type of cognitive dissonance of a problem as it relates to women in the military or affirmative action. Such a response constitutes a significant barrier to achievement of DEOMI's objectives, particularly at a time when debates between African Americans and whites and between males and females about affirmative action and sexual harassment in the larger civilian society are intensifying.

Students observed that the most salient potential barrier to training was the expertise of the trainer. The *Cultural Factors and Unit Cohesion* block provides a considerable challenge to trainers to manage the group interaction in areas where the cultural group distinctions are heightened and are mirrored in the group. These cultural differences can be manifested in communication styles, leadership orientation, locus of control (the belief about the causes of events in life), and different value systems concerning individualism versus collectivism. Data suggested that in-depth exploration of racial

Table 10.7
Self-Diagnostic Rating Scale

Competencies for the Role of Adult Educator/Trainer
Trainer Self-Assessed Skills

Mean Ranking

4.08   Ability to establish warm, empathic relationships with learners.
3.87   Ability to foster climate of respect, trust, openness and safety.
3.83   Confront new situations with confidence and a high tolerance for ambiguity.
3.74   Ability to involve learners in planning and evaluating learning activities.
3.67   Use a wide variety of presentation methods effectively.
3.67   Use audience-participation methods effectively.
3.63   Ability to engage learners responsibly in self-diagnosis of needs for learning.
3.63   Ability to engage learners in formulating objectives that are meaningful to them.
3.59   Describe difference between a content and process plan.
3.58   Use a wide variety of experimental and simulation methods effectively.
3.58   Use group dynamics and small group techniques
3.54   Identify materials as resources for learning.
3.54   Ability to model the role of self-directed learner.
3.50   Explain role of teacher as facilitator for self directed learners.
3.42   Apply adult learning principles to training in cross-cultural contents.
3.42   Invent new techniques to fit new situations.
3.42   Describe concepts and research findings regarding adult learners.
3.38   Apply principles of learning to intercultural communication.
3.30   Select appropriate methods, techniques, and materials.
3.33   Ability to facilitate self-directed learning skill development.
3.30   Assess effects of forces affecting learners from the environment.
3.29   Select a method, techniques and materials for educational outcomes.
3.29   Describe techniques available for facilitating learning.
3.29   Ability to design learning experiences that takes into account individual
         differences among learners.
3.29   Understand adult learner and implications for learning.
3.26   Describe theories of learning relevance.
3.25   Evaluate learning outcomes and processes.
3.25   Describe methods for organizing learning.
3.09   Evaluate effectiveness of various methods in achieving educational outcomes.
3.04   Ability to assess application of self-directed learning in the context of cross-
         cultural work.
3.00   Ability to describe and implement the basic steps of planning process.
2.92   Construct and use tools and procedures for assessing competency-development needs.
2.92   Develop and manage procedures for models of competency.
2.83   Ability to explain the difference between didactic instruction and
         self-directed learning.
2.83   Ability to interpret contribution of self-directed learning to the learning contexts
         of other cultures.
2.79   Develop and use instruments and procedures for assessing the needs of individuals,
         organizations and subpopulations in the social system.
2.75   Involve representatives of the client system in the planning process.
2.74   Ability to design and conduct one hour, three hour one day learning experience
         to develop skills of self-directed learning.
2.65   Use systems analysis strategies in program planning.

Legend: 1. Low; 2. Low Moderate; 3.Moderate; 4. Moderate High; 5. High
Source: Malcolm S. Knowles (1988). *Self-directed learning: A guide for learners and teachers.* Boston: Cambridge Book Co.

Table 10.8
Training Needs

Question: Please provide feedback on whether you believe **additional training** is needed in each area

Mean Ranking	N=24
3.92	Group Process Skills
3.92	Feedback Skills
3.91	Presentation Skills
3.87	Counseling Skills
3.87	Competency Identification Skills
3.75	Computer Competence
3.71	Negotiation Skills
3.70	Relationship Versatility
3.67	Questioning Skills
3.65	Training and Development Techniques
3.63	Performance Observation Skills
3.57	Intellectual Versatility
3.55	Organization Behavior Understanding
3.50	Research Skills
3.50	Adult Learning Understanding
3.43	Writing Skills
3.38	Personnel and Human Resource Understanding
3.38	Training and Development Field Understanding
3.35	Data Reduction Skills
3.33	Cost Benefit Analysis Skill
3.33	Objective Preparation Skills
3.26	Organization Understanding
3.17	Career Development Knowledge
3.17	Model Building Skill
3.04	Industry Understanding
3.04	Library Skills
2.88	Audio-Visual Skills
2.82	Records Management Skill
2.77	Futuring Skills
2.75	Delegation Skills
2.58	Facilitation Skills

Legend: 1. Low Need; 2. Low Moderate Need; 3.Moderate Need; 4. Moderate High Need; 5. High Need and gender issues is important to gain an understanding of how to enhance personal relationships and team effectiveness.

Trainers' self-assessment of needs in the second phase of the study focused on skills relevant to performance in platform instruction and in the small group. One limitation of the methodology used in this phase of the investigation is that the trainer skills checklist and self-assessed competency scale were general evaluations, not specific to the major tasks of DEOMI trainers. A more systematic approach to training those responsible for disseminating information to students and guiding them through individual and group exploration is needed.

Recommendations

Assessment and Evaluation

While participant evaluations of perceptions of training are an essential first step in the evaluation process, it is not sufficient in itself. This initial step should be followed by further evaluation at later times, using a variety of the technologies described below:

1. Direct and indirect observation as a data collection technique is very powerful for gaining insight as to who, what, where, when, why, and how, participants approach and interact within a training environment. However, it is important that the findings are kept in context.

2. Training participants and others may be asked to explain what they have learned and how successfully the have used that knowledge. This can be done either orally or in writing.

3. Pretests and post-tests constitute a special type of direct observation. Often the same test is administered prior to the training course and again at the end to determine the extent to which instructional objectives have been achieved.

4. Focus groups can generate invaluable qualitative data on a variety of training issues.

A systematic approach to training would include a needs assessment and evaluation in conjunction with the design of the instructional program. When implementing a systematic approach, these important steps would be followed. First, the objectives of the training program should be precisely defined in behavioral terms so that the results are observable and measurable. Second, the purpose of evaluation must be clearly defined. Finally, feedback on the evaluation should be given to trainers, and supervisors and interested management directors. Several areas can be evaluated.

- *Trainee Progress*: Assess pre- and post training performance of trainers to determine differences in trainer job behavior.

- *Training Program*: Determine whether the training objectives are congruent with the organizational objectives, policy and structure.

- *Trainers, Methods, Techniques and Materials*: Measure whether the methods, techniques, and materials are effective.

Personnel

Staffing is the greatest challenge to the stability and success of the DEOMI training program. One factor contributing to this challenge is the variation in types of competencies that trainers must possess. Currently, instructors must be competent platform lecturers and curriculum specialists, as well as small group facilitators. This can be a difficult challenge for staff to be equally competent in all of these roles, given the short three-year time frame of most assignments. Another challenge is the inevitable turnover of experienced trainers and the inexperience of new trainers.

The changing mission of the DoD requires differential training to meet the needs of different target groups. These groups include all DoD and Coast Guard military and civilian personnel assigned to EO, EEO, and human relations programs. Groups also include senior civilian and military leaders, including all officers newly appointed to the grade of brigadier general and rear admiral (lower half), and all members of the Senior Executive Service. With limited resources, and the demands of scheduling and supporting all of these activities and groups can drain the resources of the training division. Recommendations to approach these challenges include:

- Identify training needs, choose the appropriate training approach to support the targeted outcomes, review schedule to insure adequate time for training, planning, and feedback to trainers.

- Specialize trainer roles as instructors or facilitators.

- Provide a core of training, but include differential training based on the level of experience and assigned participant group, and training activity.

- Infuse civilian faculty and administration positions into curriculum and training division to minimize the impact of military personnel turnover.

- Develop "train-the-trainer" workshops to maximize in-house expertise.

- Review manpower requirements based on changing mission and roles.

The selection of trainers is another critical challenge. The DoD Directive 1350.2 allows the ASD (FMP) to establish criteria for assigning officers and enlisted personnel to serve as faculty and staff a DEOMI. Minimum criteria include: (1) completion of the DEOMI EO Staff course; (2) an undergraduate degree if the trainer is an officer; (3) completion of the Service Instructor Training School; (4) one tour as an EOA; (5) possession of an associate degree or equivalent level of college credit or experience if the trainer is enlisted, and (6) individual and service action to ensure a minimum of three years service following assignment to DEOMI. Unfortunately, not all of these criteria are being met at DEOMI. To insure the quality of the training staffs these minimum criteria must be met or exceeded.

Conclusion

From an organizational perspective, quality training is important in establishing excellence in the organizational work culture. Far ahead of the corporate initiatives, the military diversity training programs have a rich history of including both education and training that focus on behavioral change and compliance with military EO policy and affirmative action plans.

As important, the methodological approach used in the military's diversity training program is an acknowledgement that equal opportunity and intergroup and intercultural understanding are critical links to military readiness. The more learners participate in experiential training, the greater will be learning effectiveness and the more likely that the learners will understand the concepts and use their skills on the job. Laboratory small group training approaches and group dynamics training allow students to gain skill in understanding others from different cultures and gain skills in intergroup processes.

While based on a small sample size, this chapter has also documented the need for more awareness of the competencies needed by trainers, the importance of personnel selection and training, and the potential challenges and barriers to effective training outcomes. These barriers can be the trainer style and ability, the content of the training, and the participant's perceptions. Gender and racial issues continue to be major diversity concerns in the military as they are in the larger civilian work force. This chapter has demonstrated differing perceptions of the training process by race on selected training units.

The military's increasingly diverse workforce and changing mission has forced diversity training at the DEOMI to evolve into an integrated strategy that includes awareness, knowledge, skills, and action plans to help services institute organizational change and to incorporate diverse methodologies that include an awareness of adult learning styles and intergroup processes. Given the importance of training as an intervention strategy, more research is needed on trainer competencies, training methodologies and curriculum content, and evaluation of training. DEOMI's Academic and Research directorates work together in facilitating and implementing training that is essential to the military's diversity management plan. This chapter has provided some useful information on critical elements of that training.

Diversity training is not a passing fad and will continue to be one of the principal tools used to improve interpersonal and intergroup dynamics and insure EO for all. DEOMI offers an integrated, behavioral, experiential approach that could serve as a model for other institutions and organizations.

References

Adelman, J., & Larkin, T. (1980). *Fundamental assessment of military equal opportunity staffs: Policy and personal analysis, Vol. II.* A final report to the Deputy Assistant Secretary of Defense. Equal Opportunity, Logistical Technical Services Corporation, Vienna, VA.

Arrendondo, P., Toporek, R., Brown, S., Jones, J., Locke, D., Sanchez, J., & Stadler, H. (1996). *Operationalization of the multicultural counseling competencies.* Alexandria, VA: Association for Multicultural Counseling and Development.

Bahad, E., Birnbaum, M., & Beene, K. D. (1978). The C-group approach to laboratory learning. *Group and Organization Studies, 3,* 168-184.

Bahad, E., Birnbaum, M., & Beene, K. D. (1983). *The social self: Group influence on personal identity.* Beverly Hills, CA: Sage.

Benne, K., Bradford, L., Gibb, J., & Lippit, R. (Eds.). (1975). *The laboratory method of changing and learning.* Palo Alto, CA: Science and Behavior Books.

Bernthal, P. R. (1995). Evaluation that goes the distance. *Training and Development, 49*(9), 41-45.

Bhagat, R. S., & Prien, K. O. (1996). Cross cultural training in organizational contexts. In D. Landis & R. S. Bhagat, (Eds.), *Handbook of intercultural training.* Thousand Oaks, CA: Sage.

Birnbaum, M. (1975). The clarification group. In K. Benne, L. Bradford, J. Gibb, and R. Lippit (Eds.), *The laboratory method of changing and learning.* Palo Alto, CA: Science and Behavior Books.

Black, J. S., & Mandenhall, M. (1990). Cross cultural training effectiveness: A review and theoretical framework. *Academy of Management Review*, *15*, 112-136.

Brussow, H. L. (1995). *Training know-how for cross-cultural and diversity trainers.* Duncanville, TX: Adult Learning Systems, Inc.

Cox, T., Jr. (1994). *Cultural diversity in organizations: Theory, research & practice.* San Francisco: Berret-Koehler Publishers.

Cox, T., Jr. (1994a). The effects of diversity and its management on organizational performance, *The Diversity Factor*, *2*(3), 16-22.

Dansby, M. R., & Landis, D. (1996). Intercultural training in the military. In D. Landis & R. S. Bhagat, (Eds.), *Handbook of intercultural training.* Thousand Oaks, CA: Sage.

Day, H. R. (1983). Race relations training in the U.S. Military. In D. Landis & R. W. Brislin (Eds.), *Handbook of Intercultural training (volume 2): Issues in training methodology,* 241-289. Elmsford, NY: Pergamon.

Dick, W., & L. Carey (1996). *The systematic design of instruction* (4th ed.). New York: Harper Collins.

Dinges, N. G. (1996). Intercultural competence: A research perspective. In D. Landis & R. S. Bhagat, (Eds.), *Handbook of intercultural training,* Thousand Oaks, CA: Sage.

Ferdmann, B. M., & Brody, S. E. (1996). Models of diversity training. In D. Landis & R. S. Bhagat, (Eds.), *Handbook of intercultural training.* Thousand Oaks, CA: Sage.

Gagne, R., & Medsker K. (1996). *The conditions of learning: Training applications.* Fort Worth, TX: Harcourt Brace.

Gallegos, R. C., & Phelan, J. G. (1975). Using behavioral objectives in industrial training. In D. Kirkpatrick. *Evaluation training programs.* Madison, WI: American Society of Training and Development.

Geber, B. (1995). Prove it! Does training make a difference? *Training*, *32*(2), 27-35.

Gudykunst, W. B., Guzley, R., & Hammer, M. R. (1996). Designing intercultural training. In D. Landis & R. S. Bhagat, (Eds.), *Handbook of intercultural training.* Thousand Oaks, CA: Sage.

Hope, R. O. (1979). *Racial strife in the U. S. military: Toward the elimination of discrimination.* New York: Praeger.

Johnson, J. L. (1995). *A preliminary investigation of DEOMI training effectiveness* (DEOMI Research Series Pamphlet 95-7). Patrick Air Force Base, FL: Defense Equal Opportunity Management Institute.

Johnson, J. L. (1996). *Local effects and global impact of DEOMI training.* (DEOMI Research Series Pamphlet 96-7). Patrick Air Force Base, FL: Defense Equal Opportunity Management Institute.

Knouse, S. B., Landis, D., Bach, S., & Dansby, M. (1996). *Recent diversity research at the Defense Equal Opportunity Management Institute (DEOMI): 1992-1996.* (DEOMI Research Series Pamphlet 96-14). Patrick Air Force Base, FL: Defense Equal Opportunity Management Institute.

Kolb, D., & Fry, R. (1981). *Experiential learning theory and learning experiences in liberal arts education: New directions for experiential learning.* San Francisco, CA: Jossey-Bass.

Kirkpatrick, D. L. (1975). *Evaluating training programs.* Madison, WI: American Society of Training and Development.

Kirkpatrick, D. L. (1994). *Evaluating training programs: The four levels.* San Francisco, CA: Berrett-Koehler.

Kirkpatrick, D. L. (1996, Jan). Great ideas revisited: Techniques for evaluating training programs. *Training & Development, 50*(1), 54-57.

Knowles, M. (1988). *Self-directed learning: A guide for learners and teachers.* Boston: Cambridge Book Co.

Landis, D., & Bhagat R. (1996). A model of intercultural behavior and training. In D. Landis & R. S. Bhagat, (Eds.), *Handbook of intercultural training*. Thousand Oaks, CA: Sage.

Pfeiffer, J. W., & Ballew, A. (1988). *Presentation and evaluation skills in human resource development.* San Diego, CA: University Associates, Inc.

Potts, J., & Brantley, C. (1994, summer). On measuring diversity: Race and gender dimensions. *The Diversity Factor*, 2(4), 20-26.

Thomas, J. A. (1988). *Race relations research in the US Army in the 1970s: A collection of selected readings.* Alexandria, VA: U.S. Army Research Institute of the Behavioral and Social Sciences.

Underwood, W. J. (1975). Evaluation of laboratory-method training. In D. Kirkpatrick (Ed.), *Evaluating training programs.* Madison, WI: American Society of Training and Development.

Wheeler, M., & Marshall, J. (1986). Trainer type inventory. In J. Pfeiffer & L. Goodstein (Eds.), *The 1986 annual developing human resources*, (pp. 93-97), San Diego, CA: University Associates, Inc.

Part 2

Diversifying Leadership:
Equity in Evaluation and Promotions

Introduction to Part 2

Representation of Minorities and Females

As a result of a variety of initiatives, the representation of minorities and females in the Armed Services has expanded dramatically during the last half century. The demographic transformation has been most evident in the enlisted ranks, where minority group members account for over one-third of total active duty enlisted personnel. While there has also been progress in diversifying the officer corps, the pace of change has been much slower. Concerns about this pattern led then Secretary of Defense William Perry to issue a memorandum March 3, 1994, requesting, in part, "a study of the officer pipeline," and, where necessary, recommendations "to improve the flow of minority and female officers from recruitment through general and flag officer ranks."

As of March 1999 minority group members constituted 16.9 percent of all active-duty officers and 36.4 percent of all active-duty enlisted personnel. The representation of females was essentially identical in the officer corps (13.8 percent) and in the enlisted ranks (14.0 percent). The representation of minorities and women varies significantly across the various groups and services, as indicated in the table below.

The Pipeline Model

The pipeline model (see Figure I.1 below) focuses on accession, training, assignment, evaluation, promotion, and retention as critical processes where disproportionate losses of minority and female officers may occur. Each service submits a report annually to the Deputy Assistant Secretary of Defense (Equal Opportunity) that includes data relevant to each of these areas. The analyses included in these reports contribute to an assessment of the equity of outcomes for demographic subgroups.

Table I.1
Demographic Composition of Active Duty Armed Services By Race, Gender,
Service Officers and Enlisted Personnel
March 1999
Percentage Representation

Race/Ethnicity	ARMY Officer	ARMY Enlisted	NAVY Officer	NAVY Enlisted	MARINE CORPS Officer	MARINE CORPS Enlisted	AIR FORCE Officer	AIR FORCE Enlisted	DoD Officer	DoD Enlisted
White	78.6	85.6	83.9	62.4	84.7	66.3	86.6	72.6	83.1	63.6
Black	11.8	29.5	6.5	20.1	7.3	16.5	6.1	17.9	8.2	21.9
Hispanic	3.9	7.9	4.0	9.2	4.8	12.6	2.2	5.2	3.5	8.2
Other	5.7	7.0	5.6	8.3	3.2	4.6	5.1	4.3	5.2	6.3
Total	100.0	100.0	100.0	100.0	100.0	100.0	100.0	100.0	100.0	100.0
Gender										
Male	86.8	84.9	85.8	87.1	95.2	94.6	83.3	81.3	86.2	86.0
Female	13.2	15.1	14.2	12.9	4.8	5.4	16.7	18.7	13.8	14.0
Total	100.0	100.0	100.0	100.0	100.0	100.0	100.0	100.0	100.0	100.0

Source: Defense Equal Opportunity Management Institute, *Semiannual Race/Ethnic/Gender Profile of the Department of Defense Forces (Active Duty and Reserve), The United States Coast Guard, and Department of Defense Civilians* (September 1999).

FIGURE I.1
The Officer Pipeline

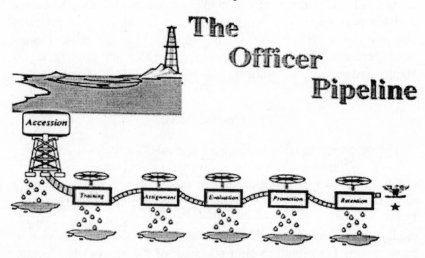

Source: Officer Pipeline Study (Draft)

In the case of the officer corps, the data that have received the most attention in recent years have been discrepancies in promotion rates to the ranks of O-4 and O-5. In fact, discrepancies in promotion rates to these ranks in the early 1990s contributed significantly

Table I.2
Demographic Composition of Active Duty Officer Corps By Paygrade, Service, Race, and Gender Percentage Representation

March 1999

Race/ Ethnicity	ARMY	NAVY CORPS	MARINE	AIR FORCE	DoD
White					
O-1 -O-3	57.5	56.8	62.4	55.6	57.1
O- 4 -O-6	41.9	42.8	37.1	44.0	42.5
O- 7- O-10	0.6	0.4	0.5	0.4	0.4
Black					
O-1-O-3	60.5	71.8	74.9	59.0	63.6
O-4-O-6	39.2	28.0	24.8	40.8	36.1
O-7-O-10	0.3	0.2	0.3	0.2	0.3
Hispanic					
O-1-O-3	68.7	73.2	81.2	54.5	68.7
O-4 -O-6	31.2	26.7	18.6	45.2	31.2
O-7-O-10	0.1	0.1	0.2	0.3	0.1
Other					
O-1 -O-3	68.8	72.8	78.3	76.7	73.2
O-4 -O-6	31.1	27.2	21.1	23.2	26.7
O-7-O-10	0.1	0.0	0.4	0.1	0.1
Gender					
Male					
O-1-O-3	57.6	58.7	63.9	54.9	57.3
O-4 -O-6	41.9	40.8	35.6	44.7	42.0
O-7-O-10	0.5	0.5	0.5	0.4	0.7
Female					
O-1 -O-3	66.9	62.5	78.7	66.8	66.3
O-4 -O-6	33.0	37.4	21.1	33.1	33.6
O-7-O-10	0.1	0.1	0.2	0.1	0.1

Source: Defense Equal Opportunity Management Institute, *Semiannual Race/Ethnic/Gender Profile of the Department of Defense Forces (Active Duty and Reserve), The United States Coast Guard, and Department of Defense Civilians* (September 1999).

to former Secretary Perry's decision to request for an officer pipeline study.

Over time, discrepancies in accession, promotion, and retention rates across demographic groups accumulate to create imbalances in the distributions of officers across paygrades. The distribution of officers by paygrade, service, race, and gender as of March 1999 is presented in Table I.2.

Accessions

The first segment of the officer pipeline is the accession (or recruiting) process. Although none of the services have specific accession goals for minority or female officers, each has implemented specific programs to diversify their officer corps. These initiatives support the goal of achieving a demographic profile that is similar to the representation of comparable minority and female personnel in the civilian sector.

College graduates provide the large majority of new entrants into the officer corps. Of course, talented college graduates are also highly sought by private sector organizations. The four service academies —Army, Navy, Air Force, and Coast Guard—provide some degree of insulation from this competition. However, these institutions account for less than 20 percent of the officers commissioned each year. The Reserve Officer Training Corps (ROTC) provides the majority of new officers for all services combined, through scholarship and non-scholarship programs offered at colleges and universities across the country. In the face of competition with private sector employers, some of the services have created more flexible ROTC scholarship programs that require less up-front time commitment.

A number of new officers are appointed directly to fill specialized needs such as medical doctors, dentists, lawyers, and chaplains. Such appointments are the largest source of new officers following ROTC programs. Obviously, some of the fields where such appointments are made are ones where significant competition exists with private sector organizations.

The officer corps is also extremely dependent upon the continual infusion of new officers recruited from the pool of talented personnel who entered the Armed Services in the enlisted ranks. Overall, the number of new officers commissioned through Officer Candidate Schools (OCS) and Officer Training Schools (OTS) is of the same general magnitude as the number commissioned through service academies. The vast majority of officers in the Marine Corps are, in fact, acquired through this source.

Training and Assignment

Training and assignment are the next segments of the officer pipeline. Movement into the higher paygrades, e.g., O-5 and O-6, generally requires that officers have experience in "career enhancing assignments" and also complete essential professional military education programs. Commanding officer and executive officer billets are especially important career enhancing assignments, and each service reports annually on the allocation of such billets across demographic subgroups, service postgraduate schools, and advanced degrees. Each service provides intermediate and senior level professional education curricula. Competition for these opportunities is intense and requires a well-planned career strategy as well as continual demonstration of a high degree of competence and commitment. The most successful senior officers have been effective in networking with key players in their specialty community. Officers also regularly pursue advanced degrees and specialized training on their own initiative as a means of career enhancement.

Performance Evaluation Practices

Performance evaluation practices are the next segment of the officer pipeline. Increasingly, use is made of team approaches to evaluation as opposed to evaluations conducted solely by an officer's commander. The objective is to develop more comprehensive evaluations than could be achieved by any single assessor. The rater, senior rater, and reporting senior must work together to ensure consistent, accurate interpretation and application of military standards. Where a division of effort is required, the rater collects input from the member being evaluated, primary and collateral duty supervisors, and other work center supervisors. The rater then reviews the member's performance, assigns trait ratings using the performance standards, propose career recommendations and writes justifying statements, if necessary. The senior rater will then review the rater's ratings, career recommendations and edit the comments, if necessary. The reporting senior will ensure that evaluation standards have been followed and will determine the final distribution of promotion recommendations within the member's summary group. The final report will then be prepared and signed by all members of the evaluation team.

As part of the evaluation process, counseling is regarded as a vital part of developing professional performance and competence. The objectives are to provide feedback to the member and to motivate and facilitate improvement. Performance counseling starts with a fair assessment of the member's performance and capabilities; it identifies the member's strengths and motivates their further improvement. Seniors are instructed to avoid discussing personality or personal attributes of the member and concentrate only on professional performance. Although performance counseling can take place at any time during the evaluation cycle, performance counseling, at a minimum, must be provided at the mid-point of the evaluation cycle and when the evaluation report is reviewed and signed by the member. These periodic evaluations support the promotion process, the next segment of the pipeline.

Promotion

Each service has a set of procedures to select and promote personnel that have consistently displayed superior professional performance across a number of categories. One important factor that distinguishes the military from the civilian sector is that promotions occur at relatively predictable intervals. In general, promotions are scheduled to occur after four years for captain/lieutenant (O-3), ten years for major/lieutenant commander (O-4), sixteen years for lieutenant colonel/commander (O-5), and twenty-two years for colonel/captain (O-6). However, depending upon the military's needs at the time, length of service can vary from the prescribed schedule. Small percentages of officers are promoted one or two years ahead (i.e., below zone [BZ] or "deep selected") or behind the scheduled promotion ladder (i.e., above zone [AZ]). The *Defense Officer Personnel Management Act* (DOPMA) limits the number of active-duty officers at O-4 through O-6. Retirements, previous promotions, separations, changes in work-force structure, and the drawdown therefore determine the overall number of officers that can be promoted. The Secretary of each service, in turn, determines the specific number of officers in each competitive category that can be promoted.

Promotion evaluations are made by a promotion board. Promotion boards consist of at least five active-duty officers who serve in the same military branch, community, or corps as the promotion candidates and hold a higher rank than the candidates. They include at least one officer from each competitive category of officers considered for promotion.

Each promotion board member is selected by the service several months prior to the board convening. The board members are selected on the basis of professional record with consideration given to military occupational specialty, duty assignment, gender, and minority representation. The duties of the board are guided by service instructions. Each member of the board is responsible to maintain the integrity and independence of the selection board process. An oath is administered to each member before the selection process.

The selection standard as contained in the precepts is as follows:

The board shall carefully consider without prejudice or partiality the record of every eligible officer. The officers selected will be those officers who a majority of the members of the board consider best qualified for promotion. In addition to the standard of best qualified, all officers recommended for promotion by the board must be fully qualified.

Once the oath is taken and the president of the board provides his/her guidance, the work of individual case preparation begins. Each member of the board receives a number of records of individuals who are above, in, and below the promotion zone. Records are assigned arbitrarily to each member and include the individual's photograph, microfiche file, and a chronological overview of evaluation reports up to their present assignment. To assist the board members, there is a case preparation and briefing guide provided. This is particularly helpful for those who may be serving on a selection board for the first time.

In light of each service's need for officers with particular skills, promotion boards recommend the promotion of officers who are the "best qualified" within each competitive category. In determining the best qualified, boards typically evaluate a candidate's job performance, job responsibilities, functional specialization, breadth of experience, academic and military training, leadership ability, and specific achievements. Each service also has height, weight, and physical fitness requirements for promotion. The board assesses the extent to which each candidate meets these requirements.

Normally, each officer's case requires one hour for a board member to prepare a brief for presentation during the executive sessions. It is during this deliberation period that the briefer would then provide the descriptive information gleaned from the record and then recommend to the board a numerical recommendation based on the individual's promotion standing among all the cases he or she is briefing. The briefer would then indicate the overall strengths and standing of the officer's career path and provide a recommendation to the board members as to whether or not the officer should be recommended for selection. After all cases are briefed, a period of time is allotted by the president of the board for each member to make their final preparations prior to the voting process. Once all members are ready, then voting begins on each individual case predicated upon the guidance contained in the precept and the strength of the individual's record of service as briefed to the board. Results are tabulated and the "best of the best" are selected for promotion.

Several of the services have established special procedures to minimize the possibility that bias influences the aggregate outcomes of promotion boards. As an example, in some of the services in cases where equal opportunity goals are not met, files of fully-qualified but not tentatively best-qualified officers are reviewed for evidence of past personal or institutional discrimination. Where such evidence is found, another vote is held for these files as appropriate, and the final standing is adjusted to reflect the new scores.

The military adopts an "up or out" philosophy with respect to promotions. For example, if an officer is not selected for promotion twice, then he or she is involuntarily separated from the service. However, the timing and conditions associated with such separations vary depending on the rank of the officer, the number of years of active-duty, and his or her occupational specialty.

Retention

Involuntary separations due to failure to be selected for promotion constitute only one of the sources of attrition from the officer corps. Attrition also results from voluntary separations due to family circumstances, change of career intentions, quality of life issues, perceived lack of a supportive climate, and dissatisfaction with compensation and benefits. Planned retirements also constitute a major source of attrition, particularly after twenty years of service have been completed. Involuntary separations under other-than-honorable conditions and involuntary selective early retirement separations to meet required downsizing targets also contribute to attrition. Each service is required to monitor involuntary separations to ensure that there are no disparate impacts on specific demographic groups.

All services are required to monitor and report the retention experience of each officer cohort five, ten, and fifteen years after original accession. The retention rates differ significantly across the services. As an example, at the end of fiscal year (FY) 1997 the retention rate for officers entering the Navy five years earlier was 62 percent compared to 75 percent for Air Force officers. The rate for Navy officers who accessed ten years prior to FY 1997 was 30 percent versus 46 percent for Air Force officers. Differences across services decline as the career life cycle progresses. To illustrate, the retention rate for Navy officers accessed fifteen years prior to FY 97 was 21 percent compared to 29 percent for Air Force officers. Retention rates are tracked separately by race/ethnic group and gender.

Research Overview

The analyses presented in this section illustrate various approaches to the examination of accession, promotion practices and outcomes, and retention. "Looking for a Few Good Men: Predicting Patterns of Retention, Promotion, and Accession of Minority and Women Officers" by James Stewart and Juanita Firestone generates estimates of year-to-year retention and promotion rates for individual race/gender/service cohorts that entered the armed forces from 1979 through 1987 and forecasts of likely patterns of retention and promotion for these cohorts over the next decade. In general, the results revealed few discrepancies, although some disparities in promotion rates to O-4 were identified. The more general problem was and remains the relatively small number of cohort candidates eligible for promotion consideration at the higher paygrades. "Trends in Gender and Racial Equity in Retention and Promotion of Officers" by Firestone and Stewart is an update of the previous study incorporating information about the subsequent promotion experience of the various cohorts as of 1992 and 1993. The results indicated slightly lower retention rates for women than for men and slightly slower promotion rates for blacks than for whites.

In recent years all services have instituted special procedures to ensure that biases do not influence the review of individual candidates for promotion. As described above, in some services in cases where promotion boards do not meet equal opportunity goals, some files are reviewed for evidence of past personal or institutional discrimination and, if such evidence is found, files are reevaluated. Such procedures underscore the importance of officer evaluation reports or officer fitness reports in promotion decisions. Biases in fitness reports have the potential to adversely affect promotion outcomes for both women and minority officers. Thomas, Perry, and David (1994) found that although gender-typed words were absent from narratives found in female officer reports, women were consistently rated lower than men with respect to leadership and were less likely to be recommended for promotion or for career enhancing command positions.

The last two papers in this section explore the extent to which biases in fitness reports contribute to promotion disparities among Navy officers. Everett Greene and Amy Culbertson provide useful insights in "Officer Fitness Report Ratings: Using Quantitative and Qualitative Methods to Examine Potential Bias." Although little evidence of bias in promotion rates was found in the analysis of quantitative data, examination of qualitative information revealed how the broad discretionary authority granted to senior officers can allow bias to be introduced into fitness reports.

Olenda Johnson's study entitled "'The Content of Our Character': Value Differences in the Narrative Comments of Navy Officer Fitness Reports" examines the descriptors used in promotion recommendations contained in Navy officer fitness reports to determine if subtle differences exist in descriptors applied to black and white officers. She found that descriptors often associated with early promotion were disproportionately applied to white officers. This finding is consistent with Firestones and Stewart's conclusion that various factors lead to black officer cohorts being promoted more slowly than white cohorts.

In combination these studies suggest the need for ongoing review of the processes used to assess the performance and promotability of officers. The studies also point to the complexity of determining the extent to which subtle biases significantly influence promotion outcomes.

References

SECNAV Instruction 1920.6A (1983, Nov #21). *Administrative separation of officers.* Washington, DC: Department of the Navy.

Thomas, P.J., Perry, Z.A., & David, K. (1994). *Fitness reports of naval warfare officers: A search for gender differences.* NPRDC TR 94-10. Navy Personnel Research and Development Center: San Diego, CA.

11

Looking for a Few Good Men: Predicting Patterns of Retention, Promotion, and Accession of Minority and Women Officers

James B. Stewart and Juanita M. Firestone

Introduction

This paper is concerned with social representativeness in the officer corps. We briefly review the literature on officer accession, retention, and promotion that documents the conventional wisdom that officers are predominantly white males. This may in turn, sustain a process in which white males are stereotyped as having the attributes of successful officers; hence more white males will be sought to fill force requirements. In view of this possibility, it is of special interest to see how well minorities and women fare in the officer accession process.

Review of Literature

The "democratization" of the U.S. military's officer corps envisioned by Janowitz in 1971 was reinforced by the genesis of the All-Volunteer Force (AVF) in 1973. By "democratization" Janowitz meant that the social background of military officers would broaden to include increasing proportions of (1) individuals with working class backgrounds; (2) self-recruits from enlisted/noncommissioned parentage; (3) individuals claiming religious affiliations such as Baptist, Methodist, and Roman Catholic as opposed to Presbyterian; and (4) minority group service academy graduates (Janowitz, 1971: xvii-xviii). The shift to a voluntary military reinforced these trends by emphasizing the monetary rewards of military service over the intrinsic rewards of duty and service to country (Moskos, 1977; Fitzgerald, 1981).

Whether characterized as a change from institutional to occupational utilities (Moskos, 1977), professional to occupational values (Janowitz, 1977), or divergence to convergence with civilian norms (e.g., civilianization; Huntington, 1957; Biderman & Sharp, 1968; Cotton, 1988), researchers agree that the change from conscription to a voluntary military system transformed both the cultural definition of military service and the organizational outcomes of that transformation. Put simply, the voluntary military must compete with civilian organizations for participants. Among the most important outcomes associated with this change are member recruitment, retention, and promotion.

Recruitment

Over the past fifteen years, the military response to recruitment focused on monetary rewards as well as educational programs and equal opportunity initiatives for minorities, to compete with civilian employers for members. As a result, recruitment of enlisted personnel has been sensitive to economic conditions of society in general as well as unemployment rates (Snyder, 1984; see Brown, 1985; Ash, Udis, & McNown, 1983 for alternative views). Recruitment of officers, on the other hand, appears less sensitive to prevalent economic trends. Because military officers must have at least a baccalaureate (BA) degree or equivalent, recruitment appears more closely associated with need for financial aid during college (Snyder, 1984). While many of the issues affiliated with civilian recruitment also apply to the military, there are important differences. Most importantly, personnel strengths as well as pay levels of the military are established by congressional decree and based on national security needs rather than market incentives (i.e., profitability). Thus, as the male cohort on which the AVF has typically relied for volunteers (ages 17-24) shrinks, the cost to procure recruits will increase. One way around this problem has been to increase the participation of minority group members and women, often through initiating and/ or emphasizing equal opportunity (EO) programs. The 1979-1989 cohort data analyzed for this report are particularly relevant, because significant cutbacks in personnel and monetary support for EO programs have occurred during this period.

Turning to officer recruitment, it is important to note that all services currently support specific affirmative action programs to increase minority and female representation among officers, in spite of resource constraints which necessitated scaling down equal opportunity programs in FY88 (Department of the Army, 1988; Department of the Navy, 1988). The Army and Navy programs illustrate such initiatives. New promotion guidance designed to emphasize equitable selection rates for all officers considered was provided for the Army promotion boards in 1989. In addition, procedures for branching of officers to achieve representative minority/female distribution across occupations are under review.

The Navy now seeks to commission annually at least 7 percent black and 4 percent Hispanic officers. The Navy also has a special program to provide upward mobility for disadvantaged students desiring a naval commission. Changes to increase the number of minorities/women in designated career fields, most notably aviation, and insure their representative selection for service schools and colleges for postgraduate education have been initiated.

Despite these efforts, officers remain less socially representative than enlisted personnel. Minority and women officers remain underrepresented in all services, especially among field grade officers and above (Quarterly Statistical Profile, 1989).

As in the civilian market, military recruiters typically have limited information on which to base their decision to accept individuals into the organization. "Objective" criteria (such as various test scores), as well as aggregate information about specific categories of individuals are often used to proxy information about individual competence or precise job requirements, because complete background information on individual applicants is too costly. The effect of this process can be to discriminate against individuals based on group characteristics and to perpetuate stereotypes. For example, the U.S. officer corps is still overrepresented by white men and this pattern increases with higher rank cohorts. Thus, the characteristics associated with success as an officer may be identified with those stereotyped as white, male characteristics (Heilman, 1983). This, in turn, can lead to less priority for the recruitment of minorities and women into officer accession programs (e.g., Reserve Officers Training Corps [ROTC], Officer Candidate School [OCS]/Officer Indoctrination School [OIS], Service Academies).

Until recent cutbacks, the combined effect of equal employment opportunity (EEO) legislation and affirmative action programs (such as Title ix) has been to counter stereotypes and create a more heterogeneous work force (e.g., Fernandez, 1981). Certainly, the military has been in the vanguard of the EO/AAP programs, especially with regard to the enlisted force. Information presented in this paper, suggest that the officer corps of all services is still predominantly white male and will remain so unless there is continued focus on recruitment of minority group members and women.

Retention

Unlike the original decision to join the military, the decision to remain a member after initial obligation has always been voluntary (Quester & Thomason, 1984). Attrition of first term enlistees as well as mid-career noncommissioned officers and officers has increased with the advent of the AVF (Moskos & Faris, 1982; Moskos, 1988; Faris, 1984). The "easy-out" system associated with voluntary service and market utilities reflects the fact that a sense of obligation to the service has been replaced with criteria emphasizing organizational "fit" with individual motivations and skills (Eitelberg & Binkin, 1982). In other words, individuals no longer presume an obligation to fulfill commitments unless they perceive economic/occupational benefits accruing from completing their tour of duty (Moskos, 1988).

Research on civilian manager retention supports the contention that minority and women managers are more likely than comparably situated white men to leave their jobs because they perceive a lack of challenging/interesting assignments or lack of career opportunities/ advancements (Fernandez, 1981). Similarly, Kim (1982) found that job satisfaction was the only significant variable associated with commitment to military service; with good pay, learning valuable skills, and pleasant physical surroundings (listed in order of importance) as the most important components of job satisfaction.

Apparently, pay has little direct effect on commitment, but operates indirectly through job satisfaction, and this effect is stronger for officers than enlisted members (Faris, 1984). Furthermore, because the military has offered equal pay for equal rank as well as nontraditional opportunities for minorities and women, black men and women have shown increasingly high levels of retention (i.e., Butler & Holmes, 1983; Shields, 1988). Thus, of critical importance to the retention of military officers within the market structure of voluntary benefits may be a value system stressing duty and obligation over and above the contractual relationships (Korb, 1981; Faris, 1984) as well as a concentrated effort to support and retain minority and women officers.

Promotion

The present "up or out" system of officer retention means that if an officer is passed over twice for promotion, regardless of the reason, s/he must exit the service. Thus, to some extent, promotion rates must be correlated with the structure of the military force. Also, because promotion to the next grade depends on subjective as well as objective criteria (for example, promotion boards still require a photograph of the candidate included in the applicant file), rates may vary on the basis of individual characteristics (i.e., race, ethnicity, sex) and membership in upper grades may reflect underlying stereotypes about which individuals make better officers.[1]

In the past, empirical analyses reflect lower promotion rates of black officers (Moskos, 1988) as well as women officers (Thomas, 1987) relative to white men. Recent EO/AAP programs in the military have attempted to rectify this situation with some success, most notably in the lower enlisted and company grade ranks. Gains are less apparent for high level non-commission officers (NCO) and field grade officers and higher (O4+). This situation is in part due to the structure of entry and promotion in the military; that is, everyone (with the exception of medical department officers) enters the military at the lowest rank and is promoted internally. Thus, if the number of women and minority officers in the company grade ranks was minimal, they can not be represented in field grade ranks now. This circumstance may further reflect the fewer numbers of black and women officers relative to white male officers as well as their over representation in enlisted ranks. For example, blacks comprise only 6.6 percent of all DoD officers; Hispanics, comprise only 1.9 percent of all DoD officers; and women comprise only 11.4 percent of all officers (*Quarterly Statistical Profile*, 1989). These numbers vary somewhat by branch of service and considerably by grade and occupation. For example, blacks are 7.7 percent of all those holding grade O1, 7.3 percent of those in grade O2, and 8.4 percent of those in grade O3 (*Quarterly Statistical Profile*, 1989). Women are 15.6 percent of grade O1; 15 percent of grade O2; 12.8 percent of grade

O3; 9.7 percent of grade O4, and 4.9 percent of grade O5 (*Quarterly Statistical Profile*, 1989).

Furthermore, black men officers are concentrated in the technical/operational occupational category (35.3 percent) and most women officers are concentrated in the medical/dental category (41.8 percent), with most of the latter found in the field of nursing (29 percent) (Firestone, 1989). Because real numbers of black and women officers are quite low, excluding those occupations with high representation, both groups may lack the critical mass to significantly increase their representation at higher levels of command without institutional intervention.

While sources other than military academies will continue to provide the bulk of officers, the relative under-representation of women and minorities at the academies has critical implications for promotion patterns and the demographic profile of the career officers corps. Snyder (1976) has suggested that: a significant gap exists in the degree of preparation for military service between the academies and ROTC programs. Snyder suggests that ROTC graduates are particularly deficient in familiarity with the overall range of service activities. Rose and Dougherty (1976) note that service academy graduates are likely to obtain more positive early Officer Effectiveness Reports which constitute the primary criteria for assignments selection and shape an individual's initial career pattern.

Increasingly, promotion to higher grades is tied to the attainment of post-baccalaureate degrees in addition to successful completion of professional military training. In examining the 1973 Officer Graduate Education Study, Rose and Dougherty (1976) found that 21 percent of all graduate degrees in the officer corps of all services were held by service academy graduates even though they constituted only 10 percent of all active duty officers. Moreover, they note that the present system of selecting attendees at the intermediate and Senior Service Schools discriminates against "late bloomers" and inadequately reflects the nonlinear growth and developmental patterns of individuals.

Objectives

In the context of the preceding perspectives the present study examines the extent to which differences exist across race, sex, and service group in rates of retention and promotion of officers. Models of retention and promotion are developed and estimated using cohort data for the period 1979-1988. The empirical results are used to develop predictions of the degree of representation and the distribution of individuals across ranks for the cohorts over the next decade.

Data, Variable Construction, and Selected Descriptive Statistics

The data analyzed in this study were taken from a special DoD tabulation containing original accessions and retentions of commissioned officers by service group, race, and sex for ten cohorts (1979-1988), as of September 1988. Cohort also provided the numbers of retainees by grade and the overall retention rate. The original tabulations were provided by the Defense Manpower Data Center (DMDC) to the Defense Equal Opportunity Management Institute (DEOMI), Patrick Air Force Base, Florida. Several adjustments to these original data were made to facilitate analysis.

Warrant officers and officers of unknown rank were subtracted from the number of original accessions and retainees. This algorithm permitted parallel treatment of each service group given the absence of the rank of warrant officer in the Air Force. The procedure introduced some imprecision because the numbers of original warrant officer accessions were not available.[2]

The racial-ethnic groups for which data were available are whites, blacks/African-Americans, Hispanics, Native Americans, Asian/Pacific Islanders, and Unknown. Individuals classified as "Unknown" were excluded from all phases of the investigation. This exclusion introduced no bias because accession and retention information is tabulated separately for each group. Although data for Native Americans were originally included in the detailed analyses described in the methods section, the small numbers necessitated exclusion of Native Americans in the final iterations.

Complete information was available for the Army, Navy, Marine Corps, and Air Force. However, significant differences in the typical timing of promotion from rank to rank between the Marine Corps and the other service groups necessitated the exclusion of Marine Corps cohorts from the statistical analyses.

Four independent measures were developed from the modified data for each race/ethnic-sex cohort: (1) the retention rate (RETRATE); (2) the proportion of retainees promoted to grade O3 or higher (PRO-O3+); (3) the proportion of retainees promoted to grade O4 or higher (PRO-O4+); and (4) the proportion of retainees promoted to grade O5 or higher (PRO-O5+). The computation of each measure was straightforward, defined simply as the number of individuals fitting each classification divided by the number of original accessions (adjusted). It will be noted that for a given cohort measure (4) is a subset of the data used to compute measure (3), and measures (3) and (4) are included in the computation of measure (2). Each is examined independently so that problems of colinearity do not arise.

The principal goals of the study are again to determine the extent to which systematic differences in each of the four measures of retention and promotion exist across race, sex, service group, and cohort, and to use the results to predict future retention and promotion profiles of cohorts.

Methods

The first phase of the study involved the development of estimates of the year-to-year retention and promotion rates for individual cohorts. In the second phase of the study the predicted retention and promotion rates are used to forecast likely patterns of retention and promotion of race/ethnic/gender cohorts over the next decade. The logic associated with the first phase of the study can be illustrated by referring to Table 11.1, which contains the actual retention rates for white males in the Army for each cohort. The retention rates can be described as "well-behaved," (i.e., they decline monotonically as length of time since accession for each cohort increases). The characterization "well-behaved" is meant to imply that the pattern is consistent with *a priori* expectations that normal patterns of voluntary and involuntary attrition should result in cohorts of more recent vintage having a higher proportion of original accessions surviving than older ones.

The period of time over which an observed pattern is "well-behaved" is especially critical. Because data were available for only ten cohorts, the extremely important phenomenon of attrition of career officers completing 20+ years of service could not be examined. This is because the pattern of retention differs dramatically in that time range. Longer-term analyses of retention patterns focusing on officer retention have, however, been undertaken. An example is provided by the Fifth Quadrennial Review of Military Compensation (DoD, 1984). Fiscal and force-strength impacts of alternative retirement compensation schemes were examined using, among other tools, the Annualized Cost of Leaving (ACOL) model. In the ACOL

Table 11.1
Actual Adjusted Retention Rates by Cohort
White Male Army Officers
as of 9/88

Accession Year	Retention Rate
1987	.983
1986	.939
1985	.821
1984	.663
1983	.606
1982	.563
1981	.509
1980	.483
1979	.474

Source: Computed from data provided by the Defense Manpower Data Center (DMDC)

model retention rates are assumed to be functionally related to the differences in compensation between the military and civilian alternatives. Seven-year average retention rates covering FY76-FY82 were used.

The level of detail necessary to undertake a comparable investigation in this study was unavailable, as noted previously. The retention rates examined here, however, cover a more recent and longer period of time. In the absence of the capability of undertaking civilian-military compensation comparisons, systematic errors would be introduced by attempting to develop out-of-sample predictions for cohorts approaching the twenty years of service plateau. The slope of the retention-years of service profile for officers changes in the 10-year range and shifts again in the 20-year range. As a consequence, predictions in this study are restricted to periods less than ten years. The basic approach is illustrated in the example below.

Referring again to Table 11.1, suppose it were desired to predict the retention rate for the 1988 cohort that would be observed in 1991 (three years in the future). Ideally, it would be desirable to have retention data available for each cohort for every year to facilitate predictions. Unfortunately, the only information available to undertake the present analysis is for a single year (i.e., 1988). As a consequence, it is necessary to use the experiences of individual cohorts measured in 1988 as a proxy for time series information about each cohort. The cautions necessary in using such an approach for both retention and promotion analyses are discussed in Stewart and Firestone (1989).

In the present study an especially critical problem is the small numbers of black, Hispanic, and Asian officers. This problem is exacerbated for women officers. The small numbers can produce dramatic fluctuations in the year-to-year retention and promotion rates. This phenomenon can be seen from Table 11.2, which contains actual retention rates for black women Army officers. The retention rate for the 1983 cohort in Table 11.2 is lower than that for the 1982 cohort. Similarly, the rate for the 1981 cohort is larger than for the 1982 cohort. Such patterns would not occur in time series cohort data.

For large cohorts it is reasonable to assume that the probabilities of retention (or promotion) for individuals in a given cohort are normally or log-normally distributed allowing clear inferences to be drawn about population characteristics from the analysis of a sample distribution of mean cohort retention (promotion) rates. Those assumptions are obviously problematic for cohorts of small size, introducing potential bias in statistical analyses.

To address the various estimation problems, three separate statistical models were developed to examine the retention and promotion experience of men and women in the ten cohorts. The models differ in the treatment of the possible effects of race/ethnicity on variation in retention and promotion rates. The models are termed "statistical" rather than "behavioral" because no information about the mean background characteristics of cohorts is available that could be used to test hypotheses about factors accounting for observed differences in retention and promotion rates.

The detailed specifications for each model are presented below. In general terms Model 1 treats differences in retention and promotion rates across race/ethnic collectives as being invariant across cohorts and service groups. Variation across service group and cohort is treated as being unrelated to race/ethnicity.

Model 2 allows for the possibility that the experience of each race/ethnic collective differs systematically for each service group. Race/ethnicity is not allowed to affect retention and promotion rates independently. Variation across cohorts is again assumed to be unrelated to race/ethnicity. In contrast to the other models, Model 3 allows race/ethnicity to directly influence the retention/promotion experience of each individual cohort. Variation across service groups is assumed to be unrelated to race/ethnicity.

Table 11.2
Actual Adjusted Retention Rates by Cohort
Black Female Army Officers
as of 9/88

Accession Year	Retention Rate
1987	.974
1986	.931
1985	.741
1984	.676
1983	.504
1982	.531
1981	.552
1980	.533
1979	.430

Source: Computed from data provided by the Defense Manpower Data Center (DMDC)

Ordinary least squares regression (OLS) was used to estimate each model and generate the predicted retention and promotion rates. Using the predicted rates generated through regression analysis can smooth out some of the distortion that would occur by using actual rates for individual cohorts to predict the subsequent experience of other cohorts.

Specification of Model 1

The specification of Model 1 took the form:

(1) $Y_i = a_0 + a_1 \text{NAVY} + a_2 \text{AIRFORCE} + a_3 \text{BLACK} + a_4 \text{HISP} + a_5 \text{ASIAN} + b_i \text{YR}_i + u$

In (1) Y_i denotes one of the dependent variables RETRATE, PRO-O3+, PRO-O4+, and PRO-O5+ defined previously with the subscript " referring to a given cohort. The error term is denoted by "u". NAVY and AIRFORCE are service group dummy variables assigned the value 11 if a cohort is associated with that service group and zero otherwise. No dummy variable is created for the Army because it is the reference service group. BLACK, HISP, and ASIAN are also dummy variables assigned the value 1 if measurement Y_i is for that particular racial/ethnic group and zero otherwise. No dummy variable is created for whites because this is the reference racial ethnic/group. Note that this specification requires the influence of race/ethnicity, per se, to be constant across both service groups and cohorts.

YR is a vector of nine dummy variables each indicating a particular cohort year from 1980 to 1988. Each dummy variable is assigned the value 1 if the measurement of Y_i is for that year and zero otherwise. No dummy variable is created for 1979 because this year serves as the reference cohort. Thus this formulation treats whites in the 1979 Army cohort as the reference group whose experience is reflected in the constant term.

Specification of Model 2

The specification of Model 2 parallels that of Model 1. Equation (2) differs from Equation (1) in the substitution of dummy variables that are constructed by interacting the race/ethnicity variable with the service group indicator. Thus, unlike the specification in Equation (1) the effect of race/ethnicity, per se, is not constrained to be constant: across service groups. To maintain the convention of using the constant term to capture the experience of white officers in the 1979 Army cohort it is necessary to create interaction dummy variables for white officers in the other service groups. In this formulation it is also necessary to create a dummy variable ARMY defined analogously to the other service group dummy variables to allow the creation of the race-Army interactions for racial groups other than whites.

(2) $Y_i = d_0 + d_1$ WHITE * NAVY + d_2 WHITE * AIRFORCE + d_3 BLACK * ARMY
+ d_4 BLACK * NAVY + d_5 BLACK * AIRFORCE
+ d_6 HISP * ARMY + d_7 HISP * NAVY + d_8 HISP * AIRFORCE
+ d_9 ASIAN * ARMY + d_{10} ASIAN * NAVY + d_{11} ASIAN * AIRFORCE + e_i YR$_i$
+ v

As in (1) a vector of dummy variables designating cohorts is included and "v" is an error term. This specification retains the convention of (1) where race/ethnicity per se is not allowed to have different effects for different cohorts.

Specification of Model 3

The specification of Model 3 in (3) treats service groups in a manner identical to the treatment in (1). Unlike the case in (1) and (2), the effect of race/ethnicity, per se, is allowed to vary across each individual cohort.

$$(3) \ Y_i = f_0 + f_1 \ NAVY + f_2 \ AIRFORCE + g_i \ WHITE*YR_I + h_i$$
$$BLACK*YR_i + m_i \ HISP*YR_i + n_i \ ASIAN*YR_i + w$$

Separate dummy interaction terms are introduced for each race/ethnic cohort with the exception of whites in 1979. This convention again uses the experiences of the 1979 cohort of white Army officers as the reference. It should be noted that the race-cohort interaction vectors for the groups other than whites have ten elements unlike in (1) and (2).

Each of the three models was estimated to obtain sets of predicted year-to-year retention and promotion rates. Information for all cohort years was not used in the estimation of equations (1), (2), and (3) for promotion rates (PRO-O3+, PRO-O4+, PRO-O5+). In the estimation of (1), (2), and (3) with. PRO-O3+ as the dependent variable only the data for relatively newer cohorts (i.e., those acceding in 1983 or earlier) was used. Conversely, in the estimations with PRO-O4+ and PRO-O5+ as the dependent variables only data for relatively older cohorts was examined (i.e., those cohorts acceding in 1986 or before). The cutoff points, selected arbitrarily, were designed to reflect the typical temporal pattern of promotions to the ranks in question. In addition, the convention serves to reduce distortions caused by the fact that some direct appointments to higher ranks are made for officers with particular specialties (e.g., physicians).

The second phase of the investigation entailed using the different sets of predicted retention and promotion rates to calculate ranges of future numbers of retainees and promotees in current cohorts. The procedure is straightforward, simply involving multiplication of the original cohort size by the appropriate retention or promotion rate. However, the more critical task involved assessing the reasonableness and comparative accuracy of the alternative predictions.

The large volume of intermediate results for retention and promotion rates and predictions of numbers of retainees and promotees generated cannot be presented in total. As a consequence, only selected results for phases (1) and (2) are presented in the next section.

Results

Patterns of Retention and Promotion

The predictions of year-to-year retention rates for white and black men for all three service groups generated by each estimation method are presented in Table 11.3 along with the actual rates. The rates are computed using the coefficients of appropriate variables that were significant at the 80 percent level of confidence or higher. Comparable information for Hispanic and Asian males is contained in Table 11.4.

Table 11.5 presents the predicted year-to-year retention rates for white and black women and Table 11.6 contains the results for Hispanic and Asian women. In Tables 11.3-11.6 rows (a)-(c) contain the predictions generated by estimating equations (1)-(3), respectively. Row (d) contains the actual adjusted retention rates.[3]

The overall fit of the models of retention rates is good as reflected by the R^2 values indicated in the tables. Several general observations can be made about the results. First, the models exhibit significantly greater explanatory power for men than for women. This reflects, in part, the problem of small cohort sizes noted previously. In addition, however, the underlying structural constraints affecting retention (and also promotion) probably differ. Evidence can be seen by comparing the actual retention profiles of white men and women in the Army shown in Table 11.7. As can be seen, in the early years the retention rate for women officers approximates that for men. However, after the initial service obligation has been met the retention rate of women falls significantly below that for men.

A second conclusion that can be drawn from the results is that race-specific effects are relatively limited. To illustrate, the experiences of black men more closely approximate those of white men than do those of Hispanics or Asians. At the same time, the race-specific effects for Asian and Hispanic men appear to be service specific (Army) and to some extent cohort specific.

A third general observation is that there are systematic differences in patterns of retention across service groups. Retention rates in the Air Force are consistently higher than in the Army or the Navy.

Drawing conclusions about the relative explanatory power of the models on bases other than the R^2 value, for example, by examining how well-behaved the rates are was not possible. All models produced well-behaved rates. Estimates generated from equation (3) generated fewer differences among older cohorts than the other equations.

Table 11.3
Retention Rate Predictions
White and Black Men

Years In		White Men Army	Navy	Air Force	Black Men Army	Navy	Air Force
1	(a)	.920	.966	1.000	.920	.966	1.000
	(b)	.933	.933	1.000	.933	.933	1.000
	(c)	.909	.955	1.000	.900	.946	1.000
	(d)	.983	.963	.955	.988	.912	.974
2	(a)	.894	.940	1.000	.894	.940	1.000
	(b)	.907	.907	1.000	.907	.907	.995
	(c)	.883	.929	1.000	.860	.906	.987
	(d)	.939	.946	.937	.926	.887	.939
3	(a)	.817	.863	.990	.817	.863	.990
	(b)	.830	.830	.933	.830	.830	.918
	(c)	.817	.863	.944	.760	.806	.887
	(d)	.821	.898	.906	.752	.811	.888
4	(a)	.692	.738	.865	.692	.738	.865
	(b)	.705	.705	.808	.705	.705	.793
	(c)	.698	.744	.825	.681	.727	.808
	(d)	.663	.774	.831	.658	.747	.811
5	(a)	.584	.630	.757	.584	.630	.757
	(b)	.596	.596	.699	.596	.596	.684
	(c)	.630	.676	.757	.604	.650	.731
	(d)	.606	.678	.779	.642	.603	.738
6	(a)	.569	.615	.742	.569	.615	.742
	(b)	.582	.852	.685	.582	.582	.670
	(c)	.478	.524	.605	.478	.524	.605
	(d)	.563	.598	.729	.588	.488	.668
7	(a)	.497	.543	.670	.497	.543	.470
	(b)	.510	.510	.613	.510	.510	.598
	(c)	.478	.524	.605	.478	.524	.605
	(d)	.509	.515	.661	.500	.470	.607
8	(a)	.497	.543	.670	.497	.543	.670
	(b)	.510	.510	.613	.510	.598	.598
	(c)	.478	.524	.605	.478	.524	.605
	(d)	.474	.484	.649	.518	.452	.658
9	(a)	.497	.543	.670	.497	.543	.670
	(b)	.510	.510	.613	.510	.510	.598
	(c)	.478	.524	.605	.478	.524	.605
	(d)	.474	.484	.649	.518	.452	.658

R^2 (a)= .882   N = 120
(b)= .893
(c)= .864

Table 11.4
Retention Rate Predictions
Hispanic and Asian Men

Years In		Hispanic Men			Asian Men		
		Army	Navy	Air Force	Army	Navy	Air Force
1	(a)	.920	.966	1.000	.881	.927	1.000
	(b)	.933	.933	1.000	.837	.933	1.000
	(c)	.863	.909	.990	.884	.930	1.000
	(d)	.991	.905	.914	.968	.934	.985
2	(a)	.894	.940	1.000	.855	.901	.982
	(b)	.907	.907	1.000	.811	.907	.985
	(c)	.863	.909	.990	.884	.930	1.000
	(d)	.905	.929	.929	.927	.959	.938
3	(a)	.817	.863	.990	.778	.824	.905
	(b)	.830	.830	.930	.734	.830	.908
	(c)	.805	.851	.932	.798	.844	.925
	(d)	.789	.878	.920	.741	.911	.916
4	(a)	.692	.738	.865	.653	.699	.780
	(b)	.808	.808	.908	.609	.609	.705
	(c)	.668	.714	.795	.631	.677	.758
	(d)	.628	.731	.813	.545	.773	.747
5	(a)	.584	.630	.757	.545	.591	.672
	(b)	.699	.699	.799	.500	.596	.674
	(c)	.478	.524	.605	.478	.524	.605
	(d)	.519	.559	.748	.514	.644	.690
6	(a)	.569	.615	.742	.530	.576	.657
	(b)	.582	.652	.682	.486	.582	.660
	(c)	.478	.524	.605	.478	.524	.605
	(d)	.500	.571	.727	.480	.619	.729
7	(a)	.497	.543	.670	.458	.504	.585
	(b)	.510	.510	.610	.414	.510	.588
	(c)	.500	.571	.727	.480	.619	.729
	(d)	.439	.460	.733	.414	.566	.714
8	(a)	.497	.543	.670	.458	.504	.585
	(b)	.510	.510	.610	.414	.510	.588
	(c)	.478	.524	.605	.478	.524	.605
	(d)	.308	.548	.647	.436	.443	.535
9	(a)	.497	.543	.670	.458	.504	.585
	(b)	.510	.510	.610	.414	.510	.588
	(c)	.478	.524	.605	.478	.524	.605
	(d)	.500	.514	.658	.349	.545	.590

R^2 (a)= .882   N = 120
(b)= .893
(c)= .864

None of the models generated particularly accurate predictions of promotion rates, although the R^2 values obtained in the analysis of promotion to grade O3 or higher were generally comparable to those obtained in the analysis of retention rates. The R^2 values for the estimations of equations (1), (2), and (3) for promotion rates of men to grade O3 or above were respectively, .864, .855, and .846. For women the comparable statistics were .825, .826, and .789. The overall explanatory power dropped dramatically, however, when promotion rates to grade O4 and above and grade O5 and above were analyzed. To illustrate, the highest R^2 obtained in the analysis of promotion rates to O4 or higher and O5 or higher, respectively, were .509 (equation 2), and .487 (equation 2). The comparable results for women were .202 (equation 2), and .256 (equation 3).

The relatively high degree of explanatory power of the models of retention and promotion to grade O3 or higher provides an opportunity to test the internal consistency of each estimation approach. The predictions associated with a particular approach are internally consistent to the extent that the predicted numbers of officers retained is greater than the predicted number of officers promoted to the grade of O3 or higher. Predictions generated using equation (1) for men produced five inconsistent cases (Army—all groups, and Asians in the Navy). Predictions generated using equation (2) yielded only one inconsistent case-Asian Army officers. Estimations of equation (3) produced six cases of inconsistent predictions (Army—all groups, and Hispanics in the Navy and Air Force). Comparisons for women for equations (1) and (3) indicated four and five inconsistent predictions, respectively.[4]

A second check of internal consistency is the stability of the predictions of the numbers of officers promoted to a given grade or higher by cohort. If the estimated year-to-year promotion rates are not well-behaved the result will be that both positive and negative fluctuations in the number of officers predicted to be promoted to a given grade or higher will occur. If, however, we could observe an individual cohort over time the proportion of individuals promoted to a given rank or higher would increase monotonically.

All of the models produce internally consistent estimates in the analysis of promotion to grade O3 or higher. However, none of the models produces internally consistent estimates for promotion rates to grades O4 or higher or O5 or higher for men or women. Given these patterns only the promotion rate estimates to grade O3 or higher

Table 11.5
Retention Rate Predictions
White and Black Women

Years In		White Women			Black Women		
		Army	Navy	Air Force	Army	Navy	Air Force
1	(a)	.910	1.000	.985	.910	1.000	.985
	(b)	.935	.935	.935	.880	.974	.955
	(c)	.917	1.000	.993	.918	1.000	.944
	(d)	.980	.970	.970	.931	.970	.908
2	(a)	.880	.974	.955	.880	.974	.955
	(b)	.905	.905	.905	.905	.985	.905
	(c)	.880	.975	.956	.879	.975	.955
	(d)	.935	.958	.917	.931	.970	.908
3	(a)	.719	.813	.794	.719	.813	.794
	(b)	.744	.744	.744	.744	.824	.824
	(c)	.711	.806	.787	.718	.814	.794
	(d)	.745	.778	.656	.718	.814	.794
4	(a)	.622	.716	.697	.622	.716	.697
	(b)	.647	.647	.647	.647	.727	.727
	(c)	.585	.681	.661	.645	.741	.797
	(d)	.595	.674	.656	.676	.740	.688
5	(a)	.534	.628	.609	.464	.558	.574
	(b)	.561	.561	.561	.561	.641	.561
	(c)	.513	.609	.589	.535	.631	.611
	(d)	.530	.594	.584	.504	.614	.656
6	(a)	.464	.558	.575	.464	.558	.575
	(b)	.489	.489	.489	.489	.569	.489
	(c)	.356	.452	.432	.549	.645	.625
	(d)	.798	.583	.526	.531	.727	.559
7	(a)	.434	.528	.509	.434	.528	.509
	(b)	.459	.459	.459	.459	.539	.459
	(c)	.356	.452	.432	.498	.594	.574
	(d)	.423	.521	.501	.552	.577	.534
8	(a)	.417	.511	.492	.417	.511	.492
	(b)	.442	.442	.442	.422	.502	.422
	(c)	.356	.452	.432	.356	.452	.432
	(d)	.409	.498	.470	.533	.487	.591
9	(a)	.286	.380	.561	.311	.391	.311
	(b)	.311	.311	.311	.311	.391	.311
	(c)	.356	.452	.432	.356	.452	.432
	(d)	.339	.462	.437	.430	.344	.496

R^2 (a)= .858   N = 119
(b)= .877
(c)= .850

Table 11.6
Retention Rate Predictions
Hispanic and Asian Women

Years In		Hispanic Women Army	Navy	Air Force	Asian Women Army	Navy	Air Force
1	(a)	.910	1.000	.985	.910	1.000	.985
	(b)	.935	.935	.935	.794	1.000	.935
	(c)	.939	.909	.926	1.000	1.000	.920
	(d)	.939	.909	.926	1.000	1.000	.920
2	(a)	.880	.974	.955	.880	.974	.955
	(b)	.905	.905	.905	.764	1.000	.905
	(c)	.855	.951	.931	.917	1.000	.993
	(d)	1.000	.858	.857	.929	.944	.964
3	(a)	.719	.813	.794	.719	.813	.794
	(b)	.744	.744	.744	.603	.805	.744
	(c)	.699	.795	.775	.740	.836	.816
	(d)	.500	.941	.800	.708	.775	.806
4	(a)	.622	.647	.647	.622	.716	.697
	(b)	.690	.786	.766	.506	.748	.647
	(c)	.690	.786	.766	.552	.648	.628
	(d)	.625	.857	.759	.444	.750	.632
5	(a)	.534	.452	.432	.534	.628	.609
	(b)	.561	.610	.561	.420	.622	.561
	(c)	.356	.452	.432	.549	.645	.625
	(d)	.600	.500	.659	.400	.810	.667
6	(a)	.464	.558	.509	.464	.558	.575
	(b)	.486	.489	.489	.348	.590	.489
	(c)	.356	.452	.432	.356	.452	.432
	(d)	.600	.533	.455	.167	.500	.520
7	(a)	.434	.528	.509	.434	.528	.509
	(b)	.459	.459	.459	.317	.560	.459
	(c)	.356	.452	.432	.356	.452	.432
	(d)	.429	.375	.524	.250	.600	.552
8	(a)	.417	.511	.492	.417	.511	.492
	(b)	.442	.442	.442	.301	.543	.442
	(c)	.356	.452	.432	.356	.452	.432
	(d)	.571	.333	.522	.143	.692	.375
9	(a)	.286	.380	.361	.286	.380	.361
	(b)	.311	.311	.311	.170	.412	.311
	(c)	.356	.452	.432	.163	.259	.239
	(d)	.143	.400	.348	.000	.286	.375

R^2 (a)= .858   N = 119
(b)= .877
(c)= .850

Table 11.7
Adjusted Actual Cohort Retention Rates
White Male and Female Army Officers

Accession Year	White Males	White Females
1987	.983	.980
1986	.939	.935
1985	.821	.745
1984	.663	.595
1983	.606	.530
1982	.536	.498
1981	.509	.423
1980	.483	.409
1979	.474	.339

Source: Computed from data provided by the Defense Manpower Data Center (DMDC)

generated by estimating equation (2) for men and women are reported in Tables 11.8 and 11.9, respectively. In both tables the predicted promotion rates are invariant across racial groups. While greater
inter-racial variation occurs in the other models, these results are useful
for simple comparisons of the rates for men and women. A crossover
effect can be observed whereby the predicted promotion rate for
women is initially lower than, then becomes larger than, and again
fall below that for men. The second crossover is likely due in part to
the higher attrition rate of women officers suggested in Table 11.7.

The inability of the models to generate internally consistent estimates of promotion rates to grades O4 or higher and O5 or higher
suggests that using cross-sectional cohort data as a substitute for
time-series cohort data has fundamental limitations for analyzing
promotions at these levels. There is, however, also the broader question of whether even time series cohort data are sufficiently rich to
answer some of the critical questions regarding the extent to which
differences exist in retention and promotion rates by race, gender,
and service group. Answering many of the more interesting questions, including the impact of civilian opportunities on retirement
decisions, is likely to require the analysis of individual level rather
than cohort data.

Predictions of Retention and Promotion

As indicated previously, in Phase II the predicted rates were used to generate forecasts of the numbers of officers expected to be retained and promoted from each cohort in future years. Only illustrative results are presented in Table 11.10 since the original number of accessions drives the numbers and questions of reliability of the estimates are unresolved. What is shown in Table 11.10 are simply the estimates of the number of black men Army officers retained from each cohort for selected years from 1989 to 1997. The blank cells reflect the decision not to attempt out-of-sample predictions. The presentation is simply designed to illustrate the potential usefulness of the framework for planning and monitoring purposes. Comparable predictions are presented for white women Army officers in Table 11.11.

Although the detailed results obtained from the prediction of numbers of officers that will be promoted to various grades are not presented, several illustrations underscore the criticality of expanded

Table 11.8
Predictions* of Promotion Rates to Grade O3 or Higher
Males in the Army, Navy and Air Force by Race/Ethnicity

	White Males			Black Males		
Years In	Army	Navy	Air Force	Army	Navy	Air Force
1	.090	.090	.090	.090	.090	.090
2	.091	.091	.091	.091	.091	.091
3	.147	.147	.147	.147	.147	.147
4	.593	.593	.593	.593	.593	.593
5	.593	.593	.593	.593	.593	.593

	Hispanic Males			Asian Males		
Years In	Army	Navy	Air Force	Army	Navy	Air Force
1	.090	.090	.090	.090	.090	.090
2	.091	.091	.091	.091	.091	.091
3	.147	.147	.147	.147	.147	.147
4	.593	.593	.593	.593	.593	.593
5	.593	.593	.593	.593	.593	.593

$R^2 = .855$
$N = 72$

*Computed from the results of OLS estimations of Equation (2), excludes Native Americans and Marines

Table 11.9
Predictions* of Promotion Rates to Grade O3 or Higher
Females in the Army, Navy, and Air Force by Race/Ethnicity

	White Females			Black Females		
Years In	Army	Navy	Air Force	Army	Navy	Air Force
1	.082	.082	.082	.082	.082	.082
2	.091	.091	.091	.091	.091	.091
3	.151	.151	.151	.151	.151	.151
4	.554	.554	.554	.554	.554	.554
5	.554	.554	.554	.554	.554	.554

	Hispanic Females			Asian Females		
Years In	Army	Navy	Air Force	Army	Navy	Air Force
1	.082	.082	.082	.082	.082	.082
2	.091	.091	.091	.091	.091	.091
3	.151	.151	.151	.151	.151	.151
4	.554	.554	.554	.554	.554	.554
5	.554	.554	.554	.554	.554	.554

$R^2 = .826$

$N = 71$

*Computed from the results of OLS estimations of Equation (2), excludes Native Americans and Marines

initiatives if long-term diversity is to be achieved. The maximum number of black men officers in any service group and any cohort predicted to attain grade O5 or higher by any of the three models was twenty-three (Army 1984 and 1985 cohorts). The comparable figures for Hispanic and Asian men were, respectively, seven and eight.[5]

Information about expected retention and promotions must be combined with information about expected accessions to determine whether force requirement shortfalls are likely to occur.

Conclusion

This analysis has demonstrated the potential and limitations of utilizing cross-sectional cohort data to examine differences in retention and promotion profiles by race and gender/sex. Given the importance of increasing diversity in the officer corps, a number of possibilities exist for building on this preliminary effort. As a starting point, the present analysis should be replicated annually combining data from each of several years. The first step would be obtaining comparable data as of September 1989 for the cohorts acceding from 1979 to 1989. Eventually, this process will produce a combined cross-sectional-time series data base that can generate more reliable predictions than either a cross-sectional or time series data base individually. Moreover, such a database will en-

Table 11.10
Predictions of Numbers of Black Male Army Officers
Retained 1989-1997

Cohort	Original Number	1989	1990	1991	1992	1993	1994	1995	1996	1997
1988	563	525	511	467	397	336	336	328	287	287
1987	580	526	481	409	346	338	296	296	296	
1986	634	526	447	378	369	323	323	323		
1985	742	523	442	432	378	378	378			
1984	728	434	424	371	371	371				
1983	408	237	208	208	208	208				
1982	437	223	223	223						
1981	426	217	217							
1980	461	235								
1979	465									

Table 11.11
Predictions of Numbers of White Female Army Officers
Retained 1989-1997

Cohort	Original Number	1989	1990	1991	1992	1993	1994	1995	1996	1997
1988	947	868	833	673	554	486	337	337	337	337
1987	1034	910	735	605	530	368	368	368	368	
1986	1078	766	631	553	384	384	384	384		
1985	1196	700	614	426	425	426	426			
1984	1187	609	423	423	423	423				
1983	702	250	250	250	250					
1982	818	291	291	291						
1981	1053	375	375							
1980	987	351								
1979	961									

able the examination of the aggregate impact of retirement decisions on the demographic profile of the officer corps. Simultaneously, an individual level data base should be developed that
includes the complete service histories of officers and former officers so that timing of promotions can be determined. Analysis of such
data using life event history analysis techniques can produce information of extensive value to planners as well as complement analyses using cohort data.

Finally, additional scrutiny should be undertaken to determine the
extent to which systematic barriers to the production of minority
and women officers exist in the various accession sources. Such a
combined research program will help insure that the search for officers is more than looking for a few good men.

Notes

1.   Some of this may take place prior to the board's convening through supervisor
     ratings.
2.   Subtraction of retained warrant officers (and officers of unknown rank) from the
     original accessions implies a *de facto* retention rate of 100 percent for this (these)
     category (ies) for all cohorts. The degree of imprecision introduced is limited
     by the relatively small number of warrant officers. The maximum effect occurs
     for older cohorts. In the 1982 cohort of white men army officers there were
     865 warrant officers remaining out of 5,848 original accessions. Remaining war-
     rant officers thus accounted for slightly fewer than 15 percent of original acces-
     sions.
3.   As noted previously the data were tabulated as of September 1988. This meant that
     the retention rate for 1988 was less than 100 percent. The 1988 retention rate was
     included in the database but in the calculation of predicted retainees and promotees
     the coefficient associated with the 1987 cohort is used as the one-year rate. This
     convention has the effect of assuming a September to September measurement for
     the various variables.
4.   For equation (1) all the inconsistent predictions were obtained for the Army. For
     equation (3) all groups except Asians had inconsistent predictions for the Army and
     Hispanics had inconsistent predictions for the Navy and Air Force.
5.   The highest predictions for Hispanics were generated for the 1988 Army cohort, the
     1988 Navy cohort, the 1986 Navy cohort, and the 1985 Air Force cohort. The
     highest predictions for Asians were for the 1988 and 1986 Army cohorts.

References

Ash, C., Udis, B., & McNown, R. (1983). Enlistments in the all volunteer force: A military
    personnel supply model and its forecasts. *American Economic Review, 73*, 145-55.
Biderman, A. D., & Sharp, L. M. (1968). The convergence of military and civilian occupa-
    tional structures; evidence from studies of military retired employment. *The American
    Journal of Sociology, 73*, 381-399.
Brown, C. (1985). Military enlistments: What can we learn from geographic variation? *The
    American Economic Review, 75*, 228-234.

Butler, J. S., & Holmes, M. D. (1983). Changing organizational structure and the future of race relations. In R. K. Fullinwider (Ed.), *Conscripts and volunteers*. Totowa, NJ: Rowman & Allanheld, 167-177.

Cotton, C.A. (1988). The institutional organization model and the military. In C. C. Moskos & F. R. Wood (Eds.), *The Military: More than Just a Job?* Washington, DC: Pergamon-Brassey's, 39-55.

Defense Equal Opportunity Management Institute. (1988). *The academies as a source of minority and female officers*. Patrick AFB, FL: Research Division.

Department of the Army. (1988). *Annual-equal opportunity assessment*. Washington, DC: Office of the Deputy Chief of Staff for Personnel, Human Resources Division, Equal Opportunity Branch. (DAPE-MPH-E).

Department of Defense. (1984). *Fifth quadrennial review of military compensation*. Washington, DC: Office of the Secretary of Defense.

Department of the Navy. (1988). *U.S. Navy annual assessment of military equal opportunity programs*. Washington, DC: Office of the Chief of Naval Operations.

Eitelberg, M. J., & Binkin, M. (1982). Military service in American society. In A. J. Goodpaster, L. H. Elliott, & J. A. Hovey, Jr. (Eds.), *Toward a consensus on military service*. New York: Pergamon Press, 235-259.

Faris, J. H. (1984). Economic and noneconomic factors of personnel recruitment and retention in the AVF. *Armed Forces and Society, 10*, 251-275.

Fernandez, J. P. (1981). *Racism and sexism in corporate life, changing values in American business*. Lexington, MA: D.C. Heath and Company.

Firestone, J. M. (1989). *Occupational segregation: Comparing the civilian and military workforce*. Summer Research Report prepared for Defense Equal Opportunity Management Institute (DEOMI), Patrick AFB, FL.

Fitzgerald, J. A. (1981). Changing patterns of officer recruitment at the U.S. naval academy. *Armed Forces and Society, 8*, 111-128.

Heilman, M.E. (1983). Sex bias in work settings: The lack of-fit model. In L. L. Cummings and B. M. Staw (Eds.), *Research in organizational behavior*, Vol. 5. Greenwich, CT: JAI.

Huntington S. P. (1957). *The soldier and the state*. Cambridge, MA: Harvard.

Janowitz, M. (1971). *The professional soldier: A social and political portrait*. New York: Free Press.

Kim, C. (1982). *The all-volunteer force: 1979 NLS studies of enlistment, intention to serve, and intentions to reenlist*. Columbus, OH: Center for Human Resource Research, The Ohio State University.

Korb, L. J. (1981). Future challenges. In J. H. Buck & L. J. Korb (Eds.), *Military leadership*. Beverly Hills, CA: Sage, (pp. 235-241).

Moskos, C. C. (1988). Institutional and occupational-trends in armed forces. In C. C. Moskos & F. R. Wood (Eds.), *The military: More than just a job?* Washington, DC: Pergamon-Brassey's, 15-26.

Moskos, C. C. (1977). From institution to occupation: Trends in the military organization. *Armed Forces and Society, 4*, 41-49.

Moskos, C. C., & Faris, J. H. (1982). Beyond the marketplace: National service and the AVF. In A. J. Goodpaster, L. H. Elliott, & J. A. Hovey, Jr. (Eds.), Toward a consensus on military service. New York: Pergamon Press, 131-151.

Quarterly statistical profile of minorities and women in the Department of Defense armed forces, reserve forces, and the United States coast guard. (1989). Patrick AFB, FL: Defense Equal Opportunity Management Institute.

Rose, M. R., & Dougherty, A. J. (1976). The system and the challenges: An overview. In L. J. Korb (Ed.), *The system for educating military officers in the U.S.* (Occasional Paper, No. 9). University Center for International Studies: University of Pittsburgh,

18-34.

Shields, P. M. (1988). Sex roles in the military. In C. C. Moskos & F. R. Wood (Eds.), *The military: More than just a job?* Washington, DC: Pergamon-Brassey's.

Snyder, W. P. (1984). Officer recruitment for the all-volunteer force: Trends and prospects. *Armed Forces and Society, 3*, 401-425.

Snyder, W. P. (1976). Leaders for the volunteer force: The problems and prospects of ROTC. In L. J. Korb (Ed.), *The system for educating military officers in the U.S.* (Occasional Paper, No 9). University Center for International Studies: University of Pittsburgh, 71-94.

Stewart, J. B., & Firestone, J. M. (1989). *Looking for a few good men?: Predicting patterns of retention, promotion, and accession of minority and women officers,* Summer Research Report prepared for Defense Equal Opportunity Management Institute, Patrick AFB, FL.

Thomas, P. J. (1987). Appraising the performance of women: Gender and the naval officer. In B. A. Gutek & L. Larwood (Eds.), *Women's career development.* Beverly Hills, CA: Sage, 86-109.

12

Trends in Gender and Racial Equity in Retention and Promotion of Officers

Juanita M. Firestone and James B. Stewart

Introduction

All branches of the military have implemented specific affirmative action (AA) programs to increase minority and female representation among officers, in spite of resource constraints experienced in recent years (Department of the Army, 1988; Department of the Navy, 1988; see Segal, 1989: Ch 5 for a history of attempts to eliminate ascriptive criteria as a basis for evaluating personnel). What yet remains unclear is the standard by which social representation should be decided—the population in general, only comparable age cohorts in the population, the military population, or the military subdivided into officer and enlisted groupings. Conceivably examination of the degree of social representation could be applied at even finer levels of disaggregation, for example, individual occupational classifications or individuals entering a service group in a particular year. With respect to the enlisted force, concern seems to focus on overrepresentation of blacks compared to the general population (e.g., Butler, 1988). For the officer corps, the standard seems to be the officers currently in the military.

AA programs implemented by the Army and Navy included procedures for branching of officers to achieve representative minority and female distribution across occupations and guidance to ensure representative selection for women and minorities for service schools and for postgraduate education.

Of course, organizational practices can either overtly or covertly counteract even the best AA programs. For example, systematic barriers to the production of minority and women officers may exist in the various accession sources. Additionally, for promotions at the officer level, a photograph is used as part of the assessment. If race/ethnic minorities, or women do not fit the expected image of high-ranking officers, this could bias chances of promotion.

For women, family constraints may impinge on women's choices, regardless of concerted attempts to prevent gender from negatively impacting women's military careers. Segal (1988) discusses the "greedy" nature of family/household responsibilities and the equally "greedy" nature of military career demands. When demands of both are incompatible, it may be that socialization of women to meet family demands over career pushes them out of the military. Since career demands increase as rank increases, this would mean women would be less likely than men to attain higher ranks.

Most recently the necessity of downsizing (see Kozlowski et al., 1993) may have placed what may be competing demands with equal opportunity (EO) and AA initiatives on the military organization. These competing requirements may show up in women's lower retention rates.

This study updates our earlier research (Stewart & Firestone, 1992) which examined the extent to which differences exist across race/ethnicity, sex and service group in rates of retention and promotion of military officers. The addition of two years of new data to the original data analyzed expands the cross-sectional database to three points in time, allowing for more reliable predictors. Each additional year permits more robust analyses, particularly with respect to the examination of the aggregate impact of retirement decisions on the demographic profile of the officer corps.

Our original research reported that in the early years, retention rate for women officers approximated that for men, however, after the initial service obligation was met, the retention rate of women fell significantly below that for men (Stewart & Firestone, 1992). Additionally, race-specific effects were relatively limited, service specific, and to some extent cohort specific. Finally, retention rates for the Air Force were consistently higher than in the Army or Navy.

Objectives

Building on our original research, this study examines the extent to which there is a pattern of increasing or decreasing gender and racial equity in retention and promotion rates as the number of years since accession for each cohort increases.

Data and Variable Construction

The data analyzed in this research were taken from a special Department of Defense tabulation of original accessions and retention of commissioned officers by service group, race, and sex for cohorts at three different points in time: September 1989 (original data), September 1992, and September 1993. Cohort data also provided the numbers of retainees by grade and the overall retention rate. The original tabulations were provided by the Defense Manpower Data Center (DMDC).

Warrant officers and officers of unknown rank were subtracted from the number of original accessions and retainees. This algorithm permitted parallel treatment of each service group given the absence of the rank of warrant officer in the Air Force. The procedure introduced some imprecision because the numbers of original warrant officer accessions were not available. Subtraction of retained warrant officers (and officers of unknown rank) from the original accessions implied a *de facto* retention rate of 100 percent for these categories of all cohorts. The degree of imprecision introduced is limited by the relatively small number of warrant officers. The small numbers of Native Americans necessitated their exclusion in the analysis, as were individuals classified as "unknown." These exclusions introduced no bias because accession and retention information are tabulated separately for each race/ethnic group. Significant differences in the typical timing of promotion from rank to rank between the Marine Corps and other service groups also required the exclusion of Marine Corps cohorts from the analysis.

Four independent measures were developed from the modified data for each race/ethnic-sex cohort: (1) the retention rate, (2) the proportion of retainees promoted to grade O3 or higher, (3) the proportion of retainees promoted to grade O4 or higher, and (4) the proportion of retainees promoted to grade O5 or higher. The computation of each measure was straight-forward, defined simply as the number of individuals fitting each classification divided by the number of original accessions (adjusted).

The adjusted retention rates by cohort and gender for all branches combined are presented in Table 12.1. Note that the divergence between retention rates for males and females generally increases for individual cohorts over time.

Methods

Estimates of the normalized year-to-year retention and promotion rates for individual cohorts are constructed using multiple regression techniques. This approach is used to determine whether observed differences in retention and promotion rates are statistically significant. The model used to generate the estimates is a modification of those employed in Stewart and Firestone (1992) that includes controls for race, branch and cohort. There are three principal differences between the methods used in the present investigation and those employed in the earlier analysis.

The first change is the weighting of observations based on the size of the original acceding cohort as opposed to the unweighted scheme used in the original study. This procedure controls for large percentages that result in cases where the cohort size is small.

The second modification is that direct comparisons between the retention and promotion rates of men and women are generated directly by estimating the model using data for both men and women. In the earlier study retention and promotion patterns for men and women were analyzed separately.

Table 12.1
Adjusted Retention Rates by Cohort and Gender As of 9/89, 9/92 and 9/93,
All Branches Combined

Cohort	Male	Female	Male	Female	Male	Female
1979	.533	.338	.357	.245		
1980	.513	.469	.384	.340		
1981	.550	.487	.393	.348		
1982	.605	.517	.425	.383		
1983	.618	.603	.450	.417	.375	.336
1984	.727	.673	.478	.467	.399	.426
1985	.853	.771	.548	.487	.451	.431
1986	.930	.933	.608	.496	.527	.450
1987	.956	.962	.682	.591	.603	.497
1988	.983	.988	.709	.651	.631	.576
1989			.826	.772	.635	.643
1990			.901	.916	.817	.795
1991			.966	.950	.917	.898
1992					.963	.955

The third modification reflects the availability of three data sets rather than the single source in the earlier study. The original analysis included dummy variables for each cohort-year. The coefficients of those dummy variables provided not only an estimate of differences in retention and promotion among cohorts, but also the year-to-year distribution of retention rates as time since accession increases. In the present investigation it is not possible to use this technique alone to infer information about year-to-year changes in retention rates because there are multiple observations for all cohorts at different periods of time. As a consequence, it was necessary to create a different type of set of dummy variables that equilibrated years since accession across the three samples. Using the cohort of officers acceding in 1988 as an example, the information reported in 1989 would reflect this cohort's experience one year after accession. This experience should be directly comparable to the experience of the cohort of officers acceding in 1992 reported in 1993 (sample 3). In 1993, the information reported for the cohort acceding in 1988 reflects the experience of this cohort five years after accession. This experience should be comparable to the information provided for the cohort acceding in 1984 as reported in 1989.

Results

Retention Rates. The analysis of the combined samples indicated that blacks have a slightly higher retention rate overall than other racial groups (+.010). This result reflects higher probabilities of retention of black women officers identified in separate analysis of samples 1 and 2. No other differences in retention rates among racial groups were uncovered.

Table 12.2 contains the results of the comparison of retention rates by gender. The differential between the retention rates of men and women increases to slightly over .17, seven years after accession and then declines to approximately .10 after 13 years. Female Navy officers have a retention rate approximately .10 higher than other women officers. Male Army officers are retained at a rate approximately .07 less than men in other branches. These gender specific differentials are layered on top of an existing pattern of structural retention differentials across branches. Retention rates for naval officers are .028 below that of Army officers. Retention rates for Air Force officers are .037 higher than Army officers.

Table 12.2
Mean Difference in Retention Rates between Men and Women

Years Since Accession	Male Retention Rate — Female Retention Rate
1	.002
2	.006
3	.016
4	.081
5	.113
6	.171
7	.116

Promotion Rates. No differences in promotion rates to rank O3 were found. Women have slightly higher promotion rates up to four years after accession. After the fourth year, men have higher promotion rates with the differential generally tracking with the differential in retention rates. Female naval officers have a promotion rate approximately .10 higher than women in other branches. Male Army officers have lower promotion rates than their counterparts in the Navy and Air Force.

The promotion rate for blacks to rank O4 is slightly less than for whites (-.013) while the rate for Asians is slightly higher (.003) than for whites. The differential between the promotion rates of men and women cluster around .01 irrespective of years since accession.

Similar patterns are observed when promotions to ranks of O5+ are analyzed. Again, blacks are promoted at slightly lower rates (-.003) and Asians are promoted at slightly higher rates (.006) than whites.

Conclusion

Our analyses suggest that the military's EO and AA initiatives are operating effectively with respect to race/ethnic minorities with the exception of promotions to the rank of major or its equivalent (O4). In the latter category blacks are significantly less likely to be promoted than other groups. Interestingly, when the three data points are analyzed separately, black women in the first two cohorts (1989 and 1992) have higher retention rates than other groups.

With respect to women, our findings indicate that perhaps downsizing may have dampened the effectiveness of EO and AA efforts. Peck (1994) found that military education and belonging to the World War II (WWII) commission cohort significantly enhanced the possibility of promotion, especially to field grade ranks (O5) in the Army. Women are far less likely to attend military academies, and, of course, are not able to be part of the WWII commission cohort. With two such important strikes against them, other organizational factors may "push" them out of the military.

For example, lack of adequate support for family responsibilities has been a major complaint of women (Segal, 1988) in the military. Family responsibilities are probably most strongly felt by women as they move from the rank of O3 to O4. The lack of institutional support for roles as wives and mothers, along with recognition that they do not have either the WWII commission or the "academy" advantage (Janowitz, 1960; Segal, 1967) may offset the attempts of EO and AA efforts to retain and promote women officers.

References

Butler, J. S. (1988). Race relations in the military. In C. C. Moskos & F. R. Wood (Eds.), *The Military: More Than Just a Job?* Washington, DC: Pergamon-Brassey, 115-127.

Department of the Army (1988). *Annual Equal Opportunity Assessment.* Washington, DC: Office of the Deputy Chief of Staff for Personnel, Human Resources Division, Equal Opportunity Branch (DAPE-MPH-E).

Department of the Navy (1988). *U.S. Navy Annual Assessment of Military Equal Opportunity Programs.* Washington, DC: Office of the Chief of Naval Operations.

Janowitz, M. (1960). *The professional soldier.* New York: Free Press.

Kozlowski, Chao, Smith, & Hedlund. (1993). Organizational downsizing strategies, interventions, and research implications. In C. L. Cooper and L. T. Robertson (Eds.), *International Review of Industrial and Organization Psychology* (Vol. 8). New York: Wiley.

Peck, M. (1994). Assessing the career mobility of U.S. army officers: 1950-1975. *Armed Forces & Society, 20*(2), 217-237.

Segal, D. (1967). Selective promotion in officer cohorts. *Sociological Quarterly, 8,* 199-206.

Segal, D. (1989). *Recruiting for Uncle Sam.* Lawrence, KS: University of Kansas Press.

Segal, M. (1988). The military and the family as greedy institutions. In C. C. Moskos & F. R. Wood (Eds.), *The Military: More Than Just a Job?* Washington, DC: Pergamon-Brassey's.

Stewart, J. B., & Firestone, J. M. (1992). Looking for a few good men: Predicting patterns of retention, promotion and accession of minority and women officers. *The American Journal of Economics and Sociology, 51*(4), 435-458.

Wong, L., & McNally, J. (1994). Downsizing the Army: Some policy implications affecting the survivors. *Armed Forces & Society, 20*(2), 199-216.

13

Officer Fitness Report Ratings: Using Quantitative and Qualitative Methods to Examine Potential Bias

Everett L. Greene and Amy L. Culbertson

Introduction

Potential bias in performance evaluations has been an area of continuing concern for those wishing to guarantee equal opportunity for women and minorities in the work place. This bias has been proposed as one explanation for the glass ceiling effect, which finds women and minorities unable to progress to top management levels in organizations (Department of Labor, 1991). Like civilian organizations, the military services have for a number of years noted the disparity in performance evaluation ratings between majority and minority service members. The underrepresentation of women and minorities in senior military grades is also attributed to potential bias in performance appraisals. However, understanding the causes of this disparity has not been straightforward. Although performance ratings are tracked at a service-wide level these global numbers offer little insight as to why the disparity exists.

Qualitative research methods are increasingly being used to enrich our understanding of complex social and organizational phenomena (Carey, 1993; Patton, 1990; Searight, 1989). The qualitative approach is particularly used to expand our understanding of female and minority experiences in military organizations. The qualitative approach encourages the development of new models that take into account variables that may not have been considered when studying the experiences of majority personnel (Bennett, Clansy, McGaha, & McWherter, 1994; Searight, 1989). Military sociologists have employed the qualitative approach for quite some time.

This paper uses both quantitative and qualitative research methods to examine the fitness report (FITREP) process. It highlights how this approach is useful in gaining a deeper understanding of parameters of the FITREP process, and highlights scenarios of how potential bias can occur. The data presented are from the Navy, but similar data and case studies concerning lower performance ratings for women and minorities may be found in all services (CNO, 1988).

Background

FITREPs document a naval officer's performance. The FITREP form is a single, two-sided page. The front page contains letter grades to describe specific aspects of performance (e.g., goal setting & achievement, equal opportunity (EO), tactical proficiency, and desirability for command). Letter grades range from "A" to "I," with "A" being the highest (always meets or exceeds highest standards) and "I" being the lowest (unsatisfactory with no evident capability for improvement). A "C" indicates meeting minimum standards, and a "D" denotes being below minimum standards. A "D" or lower grade is adverse by definition. The front also contains recommendations for promotion (recommended accelerated promotion [RAP], regular [REG], and none). The back contains narrative comments by the reporting senior, which generally highlight significant accomplishments and provides recommendations for promotion and future assignments.

As in industry, military performance appraisals suffer from inflation. The lack of variability in quantitative marks (i.e., top one percent, "all A," RAP syndrome) forces selection boards to rely on qualitative parameters in the narrative. Thomas et al. (1983) pointed out that "such material is vulnerable to the influence of personal biases or stereotypes..." (p. 2). Potential bias in the performance evaluation process has been acknowledged on a number of occasions over the past ten years. The impact on promotions of gender differences in the narrative portion of enlisted performance evaluations was the first formal study of potential bias in the FITREP process (Nieva, Mallamd, Eisner, Mills, & Thomas, 1981). Although no gender differences were found to exist in the number of positive statements made about performance, an interaction between sex and selection status was found. Thomas, Holmes, and Carroll (1983) found significant differences in the comments appearing in the FITREPs of male and female unrestricted line officers. Men's narratives were longer, contained more recommendations, and described traits valued by the Navy. The only areas in which women's evaluations exceeded men's were their support for equal opportunity and their appearance. Another FITREP study of majority and minority officers commissioned from the U.S.Naval Academy revealed higher average FITREPs for the majority officers over their minority counterparts (CNO, 1988).

The Navy's comprehensive review of equal opportunity in1988 included the study of potential bias in performance evaluations (CNO, 1988). The Study Group was tasked to explore why, after extensive efforts to create an equal opportunity organization, minority shortfalls continued to exist in particular areas, such as accessions and promotions. While studying the promotion process, the Study Group reviewed the fairness of the FITREP process. A review of 450 black and white officer FITREPs showed that black officers received fewer top ratings (see Figure 13.1). Based on the data examined, the Study Group concluded that "... bias whether intentional or unintentional - is believed to be a factor in lower fitness reports" (CNO, 1988, p. ES-25). The Study Group also, observed that lower minority fitness reports result in lower selection rates for minorities on promotion and screening boards.

As a result of the EO Study, the Bureau of Naval Personnel (BUPERS) conducted four FITREP analyses between 1989 and 1993. Findings from these examinations confirmed a statistically significant disparity along demographic lines (BUPERS, 1992). Thus, despite aggressive actions by the Navy to diminish the gap between ratings of minority/majority and male/female personnel little change was noted.

Separation questionnaire data provides another indicator of potential bias in the FITREP process. For the last three years, the top two reasons why black officers say they separate from the Navy has been the FITREP process. In contrast, FITREPs are no longer one of the top five reasons why white officers separate from the service (BUPERS, 1992). Although the sample size of the questionnaires is inadequate to generalize to the Navy overall, the data suggest different experiences and perceptions depending on one's race or gender.

Recently, Thomas, Perry, and David (1994) examined gender differences in the narratives of FITREPs to determine the impact of interventions to address potential bias. The positive findings indicated that now gender-typed words were not found in the narratives of female warfare officers. Instead, women were described to be dynamic, assertive, and energetic more often than men. But leadership remained an area where women were rated significantly lower than their male counterparts. In addition, men were found to be recommended more often for promotion or for command.

Although these studies shed light on disparities in the FITREP process, why these differences occur is unclear. The use of a multi-method approach that employs both quantitative and qualitative data provides insight into the phenomena behind these differences.

Method

A multi-method approach to data collection and analysis was used employing both quantitative and qualitative data to better understand the FITREP process and how potential bias could occur. Information regarding sampling, data collection instruments, and statistical analyses as they apply to each type of data is described below.

Figure 13.1
1988 Comparison of Black v. White FITREP Rates

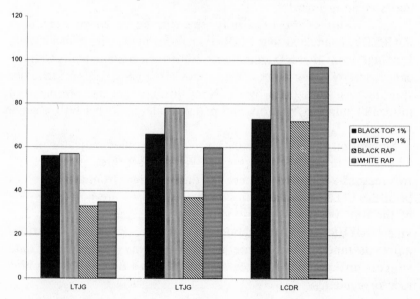

Promotion Data

Officer promotion data were gathered and analyzed for fiscal years 1990 to 1993 from annual military equal opportunity assessments (MEOA) (CNO, 1991; 1992; 1993; 1994). The MEOAs tabulate official in-zone promotion data (above and below zone selections are not factored into the overall or demographic rates) from service headquarters files. Promotion rates were calculated for whites, blacks, men, and women. Statistical tests were conducted using the z-test to determine if significant differences in promotion rates existed between black and white officer rates, and male and female officer rates.

Perceptual Data

Perceptual data concerning the FITREP process were gathered through the Navy Equal Opportunity/Sexual Harassment (NEOSH) Survey. The NEOSH is a biennial Navy-wide survey that is sent to stratified random sample of over 10,000 active-duty personnel. The survey has been administered in fiscal years 1989, 1991, and 1993 (Rosenfeld, Culbertson, Booth-Kewley, & Magnusson, 1992; Rosenfeld, Culbertson, & Newell, in press). The response rates for the NEOSH Survey have ranged from 40 to 60 percent. Statistical analyses compared the findings between years.

Case Studies

Active-duty service members can contest perceived unfair FITREPs through a variety of channels. These cases are generally routed to the headquarters office that reviews equal opportunity cases. It is the headquarters review process that often highlights trends that may have applicability service-wide. Based on the review of over 100 cases, patterns began to emerge which provided insight into gender and race disparities in FITREPs. Representative case studies were selected to describe various scenarios that indicated the potential for bias to be a factor in the FITREP process.

Results

Promotion Rates

Selection rates to O-4 through O-6 between 1990 to 1993 were examined to determine the potential impact of differences in black

Table 13.1
Comparison of Black v. White Promotion Rates

YEAR	O-4 BLACK	O-4 WHITE	O-5 BLACK	O-5 WHITE	O-6 BLACK	O-6 WHITE
93 LINE	0.69	0.70	0.61	0.62	0.64	0.47
STAFF	0.74	0.76	0.62	0.63	0.42	0.47
92 LINE	0.50*	0.75	0.61	0.68	0.50	0.51
STAFF	0.71	0.76	0.72	0.66	0.33	0.52
91 LINE	0.73	0.75	0.57	0.66	0.50	0.51
STAFF	0.86	0.77	0.77	0.66	0.50	0.53
90 LINE	0.75	0.74	0.46*	0.62	1.00	0.45*
STAFF	0.66	0.78	0.70	0.66	1.00	0.48*

*Statistical tests found a significant difference (p £ .05) when comparing the rates of black and white officers.

FITREPs on promotion board results (see Table 13.1). The examination revealed four instances when black promotion rates were statistically different from white rates: two lower (92 Line O-4, $z = 3.97$; 90 Line O-5, $z = 1.97$) and two higher (90 Line O-6, $z = 2.20$; 90 Staff O-6, $z = 3.07$). On 22 of 24 boards, the black rates were comparable to or exceeded their white counterparts.

Selection rates to O-4 through O-6 between 1990 to 1993 were examined to determine if differences in female FITREPs had impact on promotion rates (see Table 13.2). The results revealed two instances where female promotion rates were statistically different from male rates: lower (92 Line O-5, $z = 2.26$) and higher (92 Staff O-5, $z = 2.02$). On 23 of 24 boards, the female rates were comparable to or exceeded their male counterparts.

NEOSH Survey

Data from the biennial NEOSH Survey are summarized in Table 13.3 (Rosenfeld, Culbertson, Booth, Kewley, & Magnusson, 1992; Rosenfeld, Culbertson, & Newell in press; Rosenfeld & Thomas, 1994). On all three surveys, less than half of the black female officers responding to the survey felt they got the recognition they deserved on FITREPs. In general, within each demographic group, female responses were less positive than their male counterparts. Responses for black male officers ranged from 49 to 64 percent and were lower than white males on all three surveys. In general, black officers perceive that their performance is inadequately recognized.

Case Study #1

Description. The subject is a black male O-3. The supervisor a white male O-4. The reporting senior is a white male O-9. The FITREP is a top 1 percent, "all A" report except for one "B". The subject is ranked 1 of 1.

Analysis. This FITREP is a moderately competitive report. The narrative is very strong, including statements such as "his performance was singularly outstanding... this is a superior achievement and is indicative of his ability to set and subsequently achieve goals which many would not attempt...." But the rating component of the FITREP contained one flaw - the "B" in foreign shore.

Some of the performance criteria for the foreign shore dimension include the appreciation of foreign laws and customs; knowledge of or potential to learn foreign languages; and presenting a positive image of the Navy.

Table 13.2
Comparison of Female v. Male Promotion Rates

YEAR	O-4		O-5		O-6	
	FEMALE	MALE	FEMALE	MALE	FEMALE	MALE
93 LINE	.73	.69	.57	.63	.46	.47
STAFF	.75	.77	.65	.63	.45	.46
92 LINE	.76	.74	.60*	.69	.50	.51
STAFF	.75	.36	.73	.64*	.44	.52
91 LINE	.75	.75	.67	.66	.43	.51
STAFF	.73	.78	.68	.67	.45	.50
90 LINE	.71	.74	.57	.62	.45	.46
STAFF	.79	.78	.70	.66	.52	.49

* Statistical tests found a significant difference (p £ .05) when comparing the rates of female and male officers.

Table 13.3
NEOSH Survey Officer Responses: "I usually get the recognition I deserve."

	WM	WF	BM	BF
1989	68	59	49	47
1991	67	59	64	49
1993	75	66	59	49

Percent agreeing with survey question

The FITREP contains no weaknesses for the foreign shore trait. The subject had already served successfully overseas for three and a half years prior to this FITREP. In addition, the FITREP period only covered duty in the continental United States. This report is indicative of what may be referred to as the "token B" junior minority and women officers might receive. Although not technically adverse, a "B" has a negative impact in an inflated FITREP system.

Case Study #2

Description. The subject is a black male O-5. The reporting senior is a white female O-6. The FITREP is a top 10 percent report with grades of "C" in leadership and "Ds" in judgment and command. The recipient was not recommended for promotion or command. The subject was removed from command based on a "loss of confidence" in anticipation of a detachment for cause (DFC) and Special Courts-Martial (SPCM). But the subject was acquitted at the SPCM and the DFC was disapproved. An Uniform Code of Military Justice (UCMJ) Article 138 complaint was filed against the reporting senior to, *inter alia*, expunge the adverse FITREP from the complainant's record.

Analysis. The FITREP is adverse. The FITREP narrative misrepresents the truth concerning results of the investigations that led to the DFC and SPCM. The phrase "I have lost complete confidence in his judgment and ability to provide effective leadership and maintain morale..." attempts to hold the subject accountable despite disapproval of his DFC and SPCM acquittal in violation of service policy.

FITREPs may not be used as punishment or as an alternative to proper disciplinary procedures. Also, FITREPs can not reflect alleged misconduct, which was the subject of a courts-martial acquittal or finding of not guilty. The UCMJ Article 138 complaint ruling stated that the reporting senior's comments inappropriately addressed prohibited information and were being used as an alternative to the proper disposition of allegations of misconduct to circumvent the findings of not guilty at a special court-martial. The FITREP was expunged from the subject's record based on this ruling.

Case Study #3

Description. The subject is a white male O-6 who was in command. Several minority enlisted personnel complained about unfair treatment by this commanding officer. Despite this, the O-6 received a top one percent, "all A," RAP report at the end of his command tour, and was given command of an even larger unit.

Analysis. A formal investigation of the complaints was initiated, and the report detailed disparate treatment of minorities by the commanding officer. The report also recommended that the commanding officer's suitability for command be reevaluated. Despite this strong indication of loss of confidence in the subject's ability to command, no grades or comments in his detaching FITREP reflected this concern.

Case Study #4

Description. The subject is a white female O-4. The reporting senior is a white male O-6. The FITREP is a top one percent, "all A," RAP report. The subject is ranked 4 of 4. The reporting senior rationalizes the ranking by stating that "...should not be interpreted to indicate any weakness in her performance. The three officers ranked ahead of her are sure bet screeners for..." aviation commands.

Analysis. This FITREP is moderately competitive. Being ranked last detracts from the competitiveness of this FITREP. The subject felt that she was the victim of gender discrimination and petitioned to have the FITREP removed from her record. Her male peers were warfare qualified (aviators), and she was not. Additionally, her narrative contained the following statement which she viewed as evidence of gender bias: "A hard working talented young lady, who tirelessly applies herself to her career, in addition to running a household for her husband and three children." Similar statements were not found in the FITREPs of the male officers, who were husbands and fathers. Higher authority directed removal of this FITREP.

Discussion

Examining potential bias in officer FITREPs is not a simple and straightforward task. New methods of data collection and analysis are necessary, for global numbers on a service wide, level provide little insight as to the actual experiences of active-duty members. Based on the quantitative data concerning promotion rates, large disparities between the rates of minorities/majorities and women/men are not found. But the assumptions that equal promotion rates are a reflection of an unbiased system is not accurate. In fact, often the case has been made that women and minorities have to work harder to receive the same benefits in terms of performance appraisal and promotions compared to majority members. The NEOSH data indicates that women and minorities believe they have to work harder to get promoted/advanced (Rosenfeld et al., 1992; Rosenfeld et al., in press; Rosenfeld & Thomas, 1994). By using only quantitative data such as promotion rates when assessing this matter inaccurate conclusions about the fairness of the FITREP process may be made.

The subjective nature of the FITREP process makes it potentially susceptible to bias. This bias can manifest itself either as actions detrimental to minorities or as action protective of majorities. Most bias that is detrimental to minorities is probably the result of unconscious, or what has been referred to as aversive bias, by well-intentioned officers (Dovidio, 1993). However, conscious bias occurs when some supervisors deliberately abuse their discretionary authority by manipulating technicalities in the FITREP process to discriminate against minorities and women. Bias continues to be supported when discriminatory behavior is engaged in the FITREP process specifically to protect majority personnel.

The Navy is using several diagnostic tools to detect and analyze potential bias in the FITREP process. These tools include demographics, statistical analyses of ratings and promotion data, surveys of perceptions, and cases that are contested. These tools can serve as indicators of potential disparate treatment of minorities in the rating of performance. Senior officers routinely make subjective decisions in evaluating a person's performance. Research has shown that race can factor in on a subconscious level to subjective ratings of performance (Dovidio, 1993).

Conversely, the broad discretionary authority available to senior officers does not establish a process that prevents bias in the FITREP process. There is no diagnostic tool with which to detect protective bias of majority personnel. One way to begin to flag potential problems in this arena is by examining the FITREP ratings of supervisors who were involved in substantiated discrimination complaints. The connection between discrimination findings and ratings on the equal opportunity element of the FITREP for these supervisors could then be checked for consistency. Too often it seems that personnel are given a top rating ("A") in equal opportunity despite evidence of disparate treatment against women and/or minorities. In addition, identifying individuals with substantiated discrimination complaints allows closer scrutiny to the subsequent FITREP ratings given to both majority and minority personnel by the individual.

The Navy has taken action on a number of occasions over the past decade to address the issue of fairness in the FITREP system. The issue is one of concern not only for the Navy, but also for all the military services, whose data represent similar patterns of lower ratings for minority and women officers. In an environment of downsizing, the ability of the military services to attract high quality women and minority officers will hinge on perceptions of equal opportunity held by potential volunteers. To ensure that high quality candidates choose the military as a career, emphasis must be placed on guaranteeing equal opportunity in the performance appraisal rating and promotion procedures.

By using a multi-method approach that combines both quantitative and qualitative types of data, a much more comprehensive understanding of the FITREP process is possible. The qualitative data also provide examples that depict how potential bias can manifest itself. Without the case study data, an understanding of the intricacies of the FITREP process and the impact of potential bias is not possible. As others have showed the validity of this approach, more military researchers need to apply both quantitative and qualitative research methods to understand complex phenomena in military organizations.

Acknowledgment

The authors would like to thank Patricia J. Thomas and Paul Rosenfeld for their review and comments on this paper.

References

Bennet, S. E., Clansy, C. D., McGaha, S., & McWherter, P. L. (1994). *Critique of methodologies: Toward an integrated approach.* Presentation at the Annual meeting of the American Psychological Association, Los Angeles, CA.

Bureau of Personnel. (1987). *FY87 U.S. Navy Annual Assessment of Military Equal Opportunity Programs.* Washington, DC: Department of the Navy.

Bureau of Navy Personnel. (1992). *Navy Equal Opportunity Command Seminar Brief.* Washington, DC: Department of the Navy.

Carey, J. W. (1993). Linking qualitative and quantitative methods: Integrating cultural factors into public health. *Qualitative Health Research, 3*(3), 298-318.

Chief of Naval Operations. (1988). *CNO Study Group's Report on Equal Opportunity in the Navy.* Washington, DC: Department of the Navy.

Chief of Naval Operations. (1991). *U.S. Navy Fiscal Year 1990 Military Equal Opportunity Assessment.* Washington, DC: Department of the Navy.

Chief of Naval Operations. (1992). *U.S. Navy Fiscal Year 1991 Military Equal Opportunity Assessment*. Washington, DC: Department of the Navy.

Chief of Naval Operations. (1993). *U.S. Navy Fiscal Year 1992 Military Equal Opportunity Assessment*. Washington, DC: Department of the Navy.

Chief of Naval Operations. (1994). *U.S. Navy Fiscal Year 1993* Military *Equal Opportunity Assessment*. Washington, DC: Department of the Navy.

Department of Labor. (1991). *A Report on the Glass Ceiling Initiative*. Washington, DC: Author.

Dovidio, J. (1993, April). The subtlety of racism. *Training and Development*, pp. 51-57.

Nieva, V. F., Mallamd, S. M., Eisner, E. J., Mills, S. H., & Thomas, P. (1981). *Performance evaluation narratives of Navy women and men: An examination for bias in promotion* (NPRDC TR 81-14). San Diego, CA: Navy Personnel Research and Development Center.

Patton, M. Q. (1990). *Qualitative evaluation and research methods*. Newbury Park, CA: Sage Publications, Inc.

Rosenfeld, P., Culbertson, A. L., Booth-Kewley, S., & Magnusson, P. (1992). *Assessment of equal opportunity climate: Results of the 1989 Navy-wide Survey* (NPRDC TR 92-14). San Diego, CA: Navy Personnel Research and Development Center.

Rosenfeld, P., Culbertson, A. L., & Newell, C. (1995, Dec.). *Assessment of equal opportunity climate: Results of the 1991 Navy Survey*. San Diego, CA: Navy Personnel Research and Development Center.

Rosenfeld, P., & Thomas, K. J. (1994). *Results of the 1993 Navy Equal Opportunity Sexual Harassment Survey*. Presentation to the Chief of Naval Personnel, Washington, DC.

Searight, H. R. (1989). Psychology's neglected child. *Journal of Social Behavior and Personality, 4*(1), 1-16.

Thomas, P. J., Holmes, B. L., & Carroll, L. (1983). *Gender differences in the evaluations of narratives in officer performance ratings* (NPRDC TR 83-14). San Diego, CA: Navy Personnel Research and Development Center.

Thomas, P. J., Perry, Z. A., & David, K. M. (1994). *Fitness reports of naval warfare officers: A search for gender differences* (NPRDC TR 94-10). San Diego, CA: Navy Personnel Research and Development Center.

14

"The Content of Our Character": Value Differences in the Narrative Comments of Navy Officer Fitness Reports

Olenda E. Johnson

Introduction

Recently, Thomas, Edwards, Perry, and David (1998) conducted a detailed content analysis of fitness report (i.e., performance evaluation) narratives for a sample of male Navy officers. Consistent with findings from earlier studies on gender differences (e.g., Thomas, Holmes, & Carroll, 1983), Thomas et al. found statistically significant racial differences in some of the descriptors ascribed to black officers and those ascribed to white officers.[1] White Navy officers, for instance, were more likely to be described as "Thorough," whereas black officers were more likely to be described as "Dedicated." Arguably, both descriptors appear to be favorable assessments. In discussing the pattern of results, Thomas et al. noted that although clear evidence of racial bias was not demonstrated, the findings did indicate the performance and potential of black officers were viewed *differently* (emphasis added) from that of white officers. Operating under the assumption that certain traits probably had little effect on selection boards (the process used to determine promotions), Thomas et al. asked several Navy officers with selection board experience to evaluate the lists of traits used to describe black officers and white officers.[2] These officers concluded that both lists were "equally positive"—neither list appearing to be more favorable than the other.

While there may be general agreement on the overall favorability of the descriptors identified in the Thomas et al. study, differences

277

may exist in the relative value of the descriptors for promotion assessments. It may be that certain descriptors are more closely associated with conceptions of leadership—and, hence, promotabiltiy —than other descriptors (cf., Atwater & Yammarino, 1993; Lord, De Vader, & Alliger, 1986). This distinction is important because perceived leadership potential is a key factor in promotion decisions (Drewry, 1993; Gonzales, 1997; Thomas, Perry, & David, 1994; Wallace, 1991). Since terms used to describe an individual's character may imply more than just the word's surface meaning (see Ruscher, 1998 for complete discussion), the racial differences discovered in Thomas et al.'s study raise the possibility that subtle bias may occur through the language of the written comments.

To investigate this possibility, an expanded analysis of Thomas et al.'s data was conducted. Of particular interest was the possible relationship between the descriptors and the promotion recommendation included in the fitness reports. Specifically, were officers more likely to be recommended for early promotion (versus regular promotion) if they were described as "thorough," while less likely to be recommended if described as "dedicated"? If such a distinction exists, then it would follow that ascribing specific characteristics to certain racial groups may, in essence, create subtle bias—even if unintended.

Leadership Traits and Perceptions

People vary in their conceptions of leadership. According to social-cognitive leadership theories, the traits associated with leadership are dependent upon the perceiver's perspective (Lord, Foti, & Phillips, 1982). People, through their experiences, develop their own idea of the "prototypical leader," assigning certain traits to their ideal. Consequently, when making assessments of leadership potential and leader behavior they make trait *inferences* about the individual being evaluated (Lord et al., 1986). That is, they ascertain how the information they are provided matches the traits they ascribe to their prototype. Research shows that certain traits appear to be consistently associated with leadership perceptions (e.g., intelligence), while the correlation for other traits (e.g., warmth) may vary (Atwater & Yammarino, 1993; Lord et al., 1986).

Leadership perceptions and trait inferences are particularly relevant to the selection board process because, in most instances, members of the selection board have not had any personal interaction with those being evaluated. The selection board relies solely on the officer's record to determine promotions (Eisman, 1998; Wallace, 1991). Therefore, rather than basing assessments on personal observation, the selection board bases its promotion decisions on *perceived leadership potential* as portrayed in the individual's record (fitness reports, in particular) (Drewry, 1993; Gonzales, 1997; Wallace, 1991). This suggests trait inferences are likely to influence promotion decisions; increasing the value of certain descriptors while diminishing the value of others. Accordingly, the present analysis explored three questions:

1.   Is there a relationship between traits listed in the written comments and the promotion recommendation?

2.   Are the traits associated with the recommendation (if a relationship exists) ascribed more often to a particular racial group?

3.   If so, what are the implications?

Method

Using the fitness reports from a matched sample of 582 Navy officers (i.e., 291 officers of each race, matched by rank and designator), Thomas et al. (1998) identified eight categories of descriptors from the written comments: general performance, personality traits, relations with others, self-expression, leadership and management, unique Navy behaviors, impact on command, and recommendations. The number of items in each category ranged from 3 (self-expression) to 24 (personality traits). Although no differences were found in the total number of descriptors extracted from the fitness reports of black or white officers, the data revealed statistically significant racial differences among the individual items in each of the eight categories.

Table 14.1 summarizes the descriptors more often ascribed to black officers and those more often ascribed to white officers for the character-related categories personality traits and relations with others. The character-related categories reflect the perceived "inner" qualities of the officer—a subjective assessment of who the officer "is" (Drewry, 1993: 153). The other categories are, for the most part, performance-related assessments and are excluded from this analysis. As noted by Thomas et al., their content analysis could not account for the actual performance of the officer. Consequently, any findings using the performance-related descriptors might be confounded by the unknown performance factor (See Arvey, 1998; Dipboye, 1985).

Data Analyses

Regression analysis was used to explore the possible relationship between the narrative descriptors and the evaluation recommendations. Regression would indicate whether certain descriptors explained any of the variation in the promotion recommendation included in the fitness reports. The dependent variable, the recommendation for promotion, is marked as either "early," "regular," or "no" (coded 1-3, respectively). An early promotion recommendation is critical for advancement in the Navy's "up and out" hierarchical promotion system. A regular promotion recommendation, on the other hand, can inhibit advancement possibilities. This results in extreme and inherent ratings inflation in Navy officer fitness reports (Kozlowski & Morrison, 1990; Thomas et al., 1998). Indeed, the mean of the promotion recommendations for the sample was 1.51 (on a scale of 1 - 3), with a standard deviation of .37. For the present study, the range restriction may limit the possibility of finding any statistically significant relationships. At the same time, however, to the extent that statistical significance surfaces, an argument could be made for the meaningfulness of the effect given the limited variability.

Table 14.1
Descriptors More Often Ascribed to Black Officers and White Officers

	Black Officers	White Officers
Personality Traits	Motivated and dedicated	Energetic
	Displays initiative	Intelligent
	Organized and sets priorities	Flexible
	Aggressive	Thorough
	Positive and optimistic	Perceptive
		Honest
		Creative
Relations with Others	Team player	Instructive
	Attentive to needs of others	Motivating
	Gets along well with others	Demanding
	Displays good counseling skills	

The independent variables used in the regression were the twelve personality descriptors and the seven relations descriptors in which Thomas et al. found statistically significant racial differences. They were coded as binary variables (1 - mentioned, 0 - not mentioned). The frequency percentages (i.e., percent mentioned) for the personality traits ranged from 14.1 to 63.7, with 44.0 as the median. The

Table 14.2
Results of the Regression for the Personality Descriptors

Descriptor	b	t
Intelligent (W)	.00	.04
Honest (W)	-.01	-.45
Creative (W)	-.10	-2.73**
Energetic (W)	.00	.05
Aggressive (B)	-.02	-1.98*
Positive and optimistic (B)	.12	2.77**
Thorough (W)	-.01	-.59
Organized and sets priorities (B)	-.00	-1.48
Flexible (W)	.00	.36
Motivated and dedicated (B)	.00	.21
Displays initiative (B)	.00	-1.35
Perceptive (W)	.00	-1.71

B = black   W = white
  *p<.05
  **p<.01

Table 14.3
Results of the Regression for the Relations Descriptors

Descriptors	b	t
Team player (B)	-.00	-.64
Attentive to the needs of others (B)	.12	3.05**
Instructive (W)	-.01	-1.20*
Motivating (W)	-.11	-2.69**
Gets along well with others (B)	.13	2.37*
Displays good counseling skills (B)	-.00	-.29
Demanding (W)	-.01	-1.24

B = black   W = white
  *p<.05
  **p<.01

percentages for the relations descriptors ranged from 5.0 to 19.9, with 16.5 as the median.

Results

Personality traits. Table 14.2 shows the results of the regression analysis for the personality descriptors. The racial group ascribed each characteristic is indicated in the parentheses. As shown in the table, three traits—creative, aggressive, and positive/optimistic— were significantly related to the recommendation for promotion. Because of the binary coding, a negative *t*-value connotes a favorable relationship. That is, officers characterized as creative or aggressive—ascribed to white or black officers, respectively—were more likely to be recommended for early promotion. Conversely, officers characterized as positive/optimistic were less likely to be recommended for early promotion. As indicated, Thomas et al.'s findings showed the positive/optimistic descriptor was more often ascribed to black officers.

Relations with others. The analysis for the relations descriptors revealed four significant main effects (Table 14.3). Officers described as instructive or motivating were more likely to be recommended for early promotion, while officers described as "attentive to the needs of others" or "gets along well with others" were less likely to be recommended for early promotion. The former two descriptors were more often ascribed to white officers, whereas the latter two descriptors were more often ascribed to black officers.

Summary

Table 14.4 summarizes the statistically significant relationships between the narrative descriptors and the promotion recommendation. Of the nineteen descriptors, four were favorably related, three were less favorably related, and twelve were unrelated to the recommendation for promotion. Notably, none of the less favorable descriptors were more often ascribed to white officers, while only one of the favorable descriptors was more often ascribed to black officers.

Discussion and Implications

Thomas et al. (1998) found statistically significant racial differences in the written comments of Navy officer fitness reports. In spite of the significant differences, they cautiously noted that their

Table 14.4
Summary of the Descriptors Related to the Promotion Recommendation

Favorable	Less Favorable
Creative (W)	Positive and Optimistic (B)
Aggressive (B)	Attentive to the needs of others (B)
Instructive (W)	Gets along well with others (B)
Motivating (W)	

results could not be construed as clear evidence of racial bias (p. 141). The present study was undertaken to determine if evidence of bias could be demonstrated from the data collected by Thomas and her colleagues. The results suggest the possibility of bias. More specifically, the findings reveal potential racial biases, whether intended or not, in the descriptors as a function of leadership conceptions.

This extended analysis first examined whether there was a relationship between officers' described character and promotion recommendation. Since the basis of the recommendation was perceived leadership potential, the underlying assumption was that a favorable relationship between the descriptor and the recommendation indicated a match with the Navy's conception of leadership. A less favorable relationship indicated the descriptor did not fit the prototypical leader, while no relationship indicated the descriptor was unrelated to leadership perceptions. The study found creativity, aggressiveness, instructiveness, and the ability to motivate were likely to be associated with an early promotion recommendation and, thus, more highly valued in terms of leadership potential. Surprisingly, less valued were interpersonal skills and a positive outlook. Such characterizations were more likely to be associated with a "regular" or "no" promotion recommendation. Thus, irrespective of racial group, certain words used to describe officers were significantly related to the recommendation for promotion in their fitness reports — favorably or less favorably.

The next question, then, was whether the descriptors were more often ascribed to one group or another. The analysis showed that with the exception of aggressiveness, all of the favorable descriptors were more often ascribed to white officers, whereas all of the less favorable descriptors were more often ascribed to black officers. The inference from this finding is that subtle, if unintended, racial bias may appear in the written comments of Navy officer fitness reports.

The first implication from these findings is that despite the current focus on teambuilding and the development of other interpersonal skills, these qualities are not yet valued by Navy supervisors (i.e., those who write the evaluations) with regard to leadership potential. Indeed, the results seem to indicate that the evaluators perceive these characteristics as antithetical to the prototypical leader. This perception is perhaps a function of the traditional military leadership paradigm which values authoritative presence over "softer" ideals. As a consequence, descriptors relating to interpersonal behavior can be career-inhibiting rather than career-enhancing.

The second implication from this study is that military supervisors may unintentionally create institutional disadvantage for some officers, while creating institutional advantage for others, by consistently associating certain descriptors with a particular group of people. The findings from the study suggest that black officers are more likely to be disadvantaged by career-inhibiting descriptors, while white officers are more likely to be advantaged by career-enhancing descriptors. Although the differing descriptors may not reflect negative stereotypes, they may reflect cultural assumptions (Ruscher, 1998). In light of continuing differences in promotion rates for minority and nonminority Navy personnel (Baldwin, 1997), and the increasing importance of narratives for promotions boards due to ratings inflation, this suggests written comments in fitness reports may be one source of the disparities.

Racial and gender differences in performance evaluations have long been a concern for both military and civilian organizations (see Arvey & Murphy, 1998 for a review). Because evaluations play such a significant role in career advancement, any subgroup differences in performance ratings may negatively impact equal opportunity by inhibiting promotional opportunities for certain groups. The challenge, then, is to find ways to eliminate the potential biases revealed in this research. The author concurs with Thomas et al., who suggested that training supervisors to appropriately evaluate subordinates is of critical importance. In this particular instance, the training should impress upon the supervisors that the perceived content of an officer's character can influence his/her future career. Society as a whole attaches certain values to words in our vernacular—some are perceived in a more favorable light than others. Awareness of these subtleties is important for maintaining an equal opportunity environment for all members.

Notes

1.   This research uses the terms "black" and "white" (as opposed to African American and Caucasian) to remain consistent with Thomas et al.'s original analysis.
2.   The lists included descriptors such as aggressive, creative, honest, optimistic. See Thomas et al. for complete list.

References

Arvey, R. D. (1998). Performance evaluation in work settings. *Annual Review of Psychology*, *49*, 141-168.

Atwater, L. E., & Yammarino, F. J. (1993). Personal attributes as predictors of superiors' and subordinates' perceptions of military academy leadership. *Human Relations*, *46*, 645-667.

Baldwin, J. N. (1997). Equal promotion opportunity in the United States Navy. *Journal of Political and Military Sociology*, *25*, 187-209.

Dipboye, R. L. (1985). Some neglected variables in research on discrimination in appraisals. *Academy of Management Review*, *10*, 116-127.

Drewry, D. L. (1993). *Enlisted eval & officer fitrep writing guide*. Pensacola, FL: Professional Management Spectrum.

Eisman, D. (1998, May 18). Navy chaplain claims that religious discrimination stopped his rise to commander's rank. *Norfolk Virginian-Pilot*.

Fiedler, F. E., & House, R. J. (1994). Leadership theory and research: A report of progress. In C. L. Cooper & I. T. Robertson (Eds.), *Key reviews in managerial psychology* (pp. 97-116). New York: Whiley.

Gonzales, J. A. (1997, October). Chief offers advice on enlisted promotions. *Airman*, 21.

Kozlowski, S. J., & Morrison, R. F. (1990). *Officer career development: Mapping rater strategies in officer fitness ratings*. (Rep. No. NPRDC TR-91-2). San Diego, CA: Navy Personnel Research and Development Center.

Lord, R. G., De Vader, C. L., & Alliger, G. M. (1986). A meta-analysis of the relation between personality traits and leadership perceptions: An application of validity generalization procedures. *Journal of Applied Psychology*, *71*, 402-410.

Lord, R. G., Foti, R., & Phillips, J. (1982). A theory of leadership categorization. In J. G. Hunt, U. Sekaran, & C. Schriesheim (Eds.), *Leadership: Beyond establishment views* (pp. 104-121). Carbondale, IL: Southern Illinois University Press.

Ruscher, J. B. (1998). Prejudice and stereotyping in everyday communication. *Advances in Experimental Psychology*, *30*, 241-307.

Thomas, P. J., Edwards, J. E., Perry, Z. A., & David, K. M. (1998). Racial differences in male navy officer fitness reports. *Military Psychology*, *10*, 127-143.

Thomas, P. J., Holmes, B. L., & Carroll, L. L. (1994). *Gender differences in the evaluations of narratives in officer performance ratings*. (Rep. No. NPRDC TR-83-14). San Diego, CA: Navy Personnel Research and Development Center.

Thomas, P. J., Perry, Z. A., & David, K. M. (1994). *Fitness reports of naval warfare officers: A search for gender differences*. (Rep. No. NPRDC TR-94-10). San Diego, CA: Navy Personnel Research and Development Center.

Wallace, D. M. (1991, October). Don't end up in the gray area. *Space Trace*, pp. 4-5.

Part 3

Gender Intergration and Sexual Harassment

Introduction to Part 3

Gender Integration

Many women in the United States are living in a paradox. While changes in American culture have led to significant improvements in women's work and family lives, they still are frequently exposed to discriminatory polices and actions. This section examines the United States military context, an institution that embodies this paradox. While the military offer women certain opportunities, such as specialized training, college education, travel, and adventure, it is still steeped in male domination and gender discrimination.

Some might assume that the issue of women in the military is a relatively new one, coinciding with social movements and reforms. On the one hand, the 1960s to mid-1970s can be characterized as a period of significant social and legal reform, one during which women (and ethnic minorities) fought for equal rights and opportunities. In response, key legislation was passed that opened doors for these groups. Modeled after race discrimination laws, the majority of these laws were targeted at dismantling barriers in education and the workplace that had restricted women's freedom to make choices and advance. Predictably, this movement found its way into the military sector and demands critical reexaminations of the history, policy, and procedures relative to women. Members of Congress, feminists, special interest groups such as Defense Advisory Committee on Women in the Services (DACOWITS), Women in International Security (WIIS), and the Women's Research and Education Institute (WREI) provide the necessary leadership and applied research to challenge traditional policies effectively.

On the other hand, others know that debates over gender representation are much older than the modern civil rights movement, and they have arisen in both draft and voluntary years (post-1973) over the past two hundred years. The fact that women would actually be deployed to combat zones to perform side-by-side with men in combat support jobs should not come as news to anyone familiar with the United States military of the 1990s. Still, many people are surprised to learn that women could become involved in international hostilities, largely because politicians and military leaders had been arguing for years that women should be excluded from combat by law and service policies (Holm, 1992).

Advocates of women in combat like to compare their efforts to the integration of African Americans into the United States military. However, that comparison must be made with qualification. The integration of African Americans in the ranks of the U.S. military stands in stark contrast to the attempt to integrate women. A major cause of successful racial integration of the military is that the services eliminated double standards. In their book, *All That We Can Be*, Moskos and Butler (1997) argue that from the beginning of racial integration in the 1950s, the Army was adamant that professional merit would not be subordinated to quotas achieved by lowering standards, which would "stigmatize applicants by raising doubts about their true qualifications."

To place women's roles in the modern military in perspective, it is important to note that the concept of American women serving in the military is not a new phenomenon. Women have been granted formal military status for less than 100 years, yet throughout the history of the U.S. Armed Services, women have served bravely and with distinction in official and semi-official capacities, though their military status has often relegated them to peripheral assignments. Moreover, women have served honorably and competently during this country's wars and conflicts. Since women compose more than half the population of the United States, wartime mobilization has always included them out of necessity. Over the past two centuries, the wartime role that women have been permitted to take by society has slowly expanded to include a formal military role, even in peacetime.

From the Revolutionary War to World War II to the Persian Gulf War, women were generally restricted to combat support, nursing, and related medical jobs, but during these wars selected administrative and clerical jobs were opened to women due to severe manpower shortages. For example, there is a little known historical account that a select group of young women pilots served in the Army Air Corps during World War II. In September 1942, the Army Air Force (AAF) created the Women's Auxiliary Ferry Squadron (WAFS) which was renamed the Women's Air Service Pilots (WASP) (Holm & Bellafaire, 1998; McCaffrey, 1998), the first women in history trained to fly American military aircraft. Although thirty-eight WASP members gave their lives during WWII, the WASP was not granted full military status until many years later.

Another commonly overlooked fact is that women have served and died along side their male counterparts. Moreover, it is the extent of their participation and the degree to which they have been integrated into the military forces that sets the present so dramatically apart from the past. Another significant departure from earlier periods is the fact that military women are now bonafide, respected professional members of the Armed Services, rather than serving in some quasi-official capacity. Yet, there is still a paucity of public information about women's contributions in forging and protecting this nation.

It has been fifty years since President Truman signed the *Women's Armed Services Integration Act*, which formalized the role of women in the Armed Services. Paradoxically, this same act excluded women from combat roles and adopted a two-percent quota. In fact, for the next two decades job opportunities were severely restricted and only about one percent of the active-forces included women. The two-percent ceiling was lifted in 1967 during the Vietnam War.

Between 1948 and 1980, the role of women in the Armed Services expanded considerably as a result of political pressure, legislation, court rulings and DoD initiatives. Women were admitted to the military academies, the policy of involuntary discharge for pregnancy was ended, basic training was gender integrated, and women were allowed to go to sea. This trend slowed during the Reagan administration, and some policies were reversed (e.g., Army basic training was resegregated). Nevertheless, the role of women in the military has expanded greatly, with many women serving in the Persian Gulf during the 1991 war, where they often shared tents, latrines, and shower facilities with men (Schneider & Schneider, 1992).

The drafters of the 1948 law, which allowed each branch of the services to appoint one female senior officer, would be perplexed by the number of current female pilots, and ship and submarine drivers, as well as admirals and generals. For example, as of March 1999 there were a total of twenty-three female flag officers on active duty (DMDC, 1999). The steps toward full gender integration have been significant. Under *Public Law 94-106*, women were admitted to the three Service academies in 1976. Two years later, Congress passed legislation abolishing the Women's Army Corps (WAC) as a separate unit. In more recent years, active-duty women have deployed to combat zones—Grenada, Panama, the Persian Gulf, and Kosovo.

The debates on the viability of efforts to integrate women into our Armed Services have continued despite evidence of their significant contributions. The various perspectives from members of Congress, military departments, feminists, economists, historians, psychologists, special committees, active- and reserve-duty men and women, and the public in general, have been used in an attempt to influence military policy regarding the integration of women. To be sure, some rationales are more persuasive than others. Some are based on facts while others are emotional, culturally–based, and borrow heavily from traditional beliefs. This admixture of diverse opinions seems to rekindle an impassioned debate inside and outside the Pentagon about the decades-long efforts to integrate women into the military. Historically, these debates surrounding women in the military seem to have been recycled continuously from World War II to the mid-1970s, yet it was not a priority issue. It can be argued that much of these debates and negotiations had taken place in Congress (prior to C-SPAN) and the offices of the Pentagon until recently.

Currently, there appears to be a general acceptance of women in the ranks, but with qualification. To some extent, animosity toward female military members still exists in the Armed Services, despite training and policy implementation designed to facilitate acceptance. It can be argued that this paradox persists in large part because some male members continue to perpetuate a tradition of sexism. At times, it seems as if our modern military remains at war with itself over issues of sex. Recently, a top government official remarked that the Armed Services *"still have an environment...where women face intimidation and harassment..."* (*The Economist*, 1998). In contrast to the services' success with African Americans, a sordid series of scandals has cast serious questions over the military's employment and integration of women as well as the efficacy of efforts to control or prevent sexual harassment.

The most heated debate concerns the issue of combat restrictions (Roush, 1997; Armor, 1996; Segal, 1995). Maintaining the exclusion for special flight operations units and for ground troops, for example, continues to reinforce stereotypes and perpetuate inequality for women. Women in military and civilian sectors argue for a full acknowledgement that the issue of women in the military is a question of equal opportunity and that assumptions and arguments supporting the exclusion from the past to the present are deeply flawed.

Another burgeoning contention is gender-integrated training. The Army, Navy, and Air Force are still struggling with recommendations that the nation's Armed Services should separate men and women for much of basic and advanced training and house them in separate barracks. In contrast, women's rights advocates criticize the same recommendations by opposing the idea that the military return to segregating men and women. Women should be integrated into the military with the same opportunities as men. It can be successfully argued that, in fact, the military is now so dependent on women that without them, it would need to re-institute the draft.

The ongoing gender integration debate has obvious spillover effects on other seemingly benign matters. For example, should men in the Army be able to carry umbrellas and wear jewelry, just as female soldiers can? On the surface, the issue seems trivial and mundane, especially when compared with base closings and regionalization, restructuring and right sizing, and constrained military budgets. Something else is going on here, and it is related to the current gender integration arguments. After the sexual harassment scandals, the military is sensitive about the subject of women in the military and the umbrella debate provides an outlet for an honest discussion of this taboo subject. Thus, the debate is really about whether military traditions and standards are under siege; it's about whether women have *"feminized"* the military and whether women soldiers, sailors, airmen, and marines should receive special accommodations. This begs the question, *Is the military closer to figuring out how to persuade men and women to get along better?*

Sexual Harassment

Sexual harassment (and sexual discrimination) of military personnel is a real and serious problem at all levels of the chain of command, including enlisted and officer ranks. Sexual harassment can take two forms: *quid pro quo* and *hostile environment*. *Quid pro quo* is a Latin phrase that means "this for that." Sexual harassment in the form of *quid pro quo* occurs when unwelcome sexual advances are made and an employee is required to submit—either to obtain or keep employment, or because employment decisions or benefits could be adversely affected. The *quid pro quo* type of sexual harassment is easier to recognize than the hostile environment form. Specifically, hostile environment sexual harassment is a situation in which the employer (or a supervisor or co-worker) does or says things that make the victim feel uncomfortable because of his or her sex. It is the creation of an uncomfortable, offensive environment. The concept was first legitimized in the *Meritor Savings Bank v. Vinson* case decided by the U.S. Supreme Court in 1986. The principle established in this case is that an employer can be held liable in actions alleging sexual harassment even if sexual favors were not being exchanged for employment benefits. The Court ruled that a corporate environment could be pervasively hostile or abusive to women (or, conceivably, men). Thus sexual harassment can affect any member of an organization, regardless of sex, race, rank, or age. Sexual harassment can threaten a member's physical or emotional well-being, influence how well a member performs on and off duty, and may make it difficult for a member to achieve his or her career goals. Preventing sexual harassment in the military is essential for ensuring nondiscriminatory, safe environments for all members.

Until recently, sexual harassment and victimization in military work settings received little attention. However, the growing number of women in military service and the much-publicized sexual harassment scandals have drawn widespread attention to the problem of sexual harassment and assault of women in the United States armed forces. To date, relatively little empirical data have objectively documented the prevalence of these events. However, Martindale (1990) reported that five percent of female respondents described attempted or completed sexual assault during military service over an 18-month period. Rates of sexual harassment were considerably higher, with 15 percent reporting pressure for sexual favors and 38 percent describing unwanted physical contact (e.g., touching). This survey provided important information about sexual victimization during peacetime service but did not address the prevalence of these experiences during wartime deployment.

To measure the extent of this problem, a 1995 DoD-wide sexual harassment survey was sent to 90,000 active-duty service members —65,000 women and 25,000 men. The results showed that 55 percent of the women and 14 percent of the men reported they had experienced unwanted or uninvited sexual behavior within the past year. These figures represent a drop from the 1988 DoD survey, when 64 percent of the women and 17 percent of the men reported a harassment incident. Although the 1995 survey shows sexual harassment declining, it remains a major concern for the DoD.

Until the last decade, little was published about females in the military, but awareness of the issues has been dramatically increased by a variety of high profile public events surrounding the Navy's Tailhook and Great Lakes Training Center scandals; the Army's Aberdeen Proving Ground, Fort Leonard Wood, Fort Jackson, and Sergeant Major of the Army incidents; the Air Force's Lackland Air Force Base and Lieutenant Kelly Flinn and General Joseph Ralston cases; congressional hearings on sexual harassment in the military, and women finally being assigned to combatant units. These widely publicized incidents of sexual harassment and gender discrimination in the military raise broader questions about the services' treatment of women. How, after almost 25 years of experience with an all-volunteer military that offers expanded opportunities for women, can it be that women are still not treated fairly in the military?

Current military personnel policies regarding gender (and race) representation are in a rather curious state. Interestingly, three of four services maintain no recruiting objectives for women, even though laws and regulations have opened many formerly closed jobs to women. Moreover, the segregation of men and women into different occupations is one of the most important and enduring aspects of the military job structure. Occupational gender segregation has been at the heart of debates about gender inequality. High levels of occupational gender segregation and concentration have been considered to be significant factors in the military and civilian workforce. Clearly, both factors, occupational gender segregation and concentration, are concerned with the distribution of men and women in military occupations. It is easy to see why they have been grouped together; on the other hand it is clear that there are two distinct ideas here. According to the recent data, women are usually assigned to "traditional" service and support billets.

For example, significant differences in occupational categories across gender groups in the military population have received widespread attention (Anker, 1998; Blau, Simpson, & Anderson, 1998). In general, males are concentrated in technical occupations and women are concentrated in administrative and support positions. A similar pattern has existed within the military job classification system for decades. Data in DEOMI's *1998 Annual Occupational Pro-*

file of Minorities and Women in the Department of Defense indicated that a vast majority of women officers were assigned in categories that are designated service, support, or supply positions. As of September 1998, the enlisted women populations of DoD were disproportionately overrepresented in service, support, and supply categories across military service. Males were assigned across designators and overrepresented in combat arms. In contrast, women were disproportionately assigned to medical, maintenance, and service and supply job codes.

Mary McCloud Bethune, renowned American educator and civil rights activist, said, *"The best measure of a people is the treatment of their women...."* With women being funneled into a few narrow job categories, the future of a fully gender integrated military may be compromised. With equal opportunity and operational readiness being inextricably linked one would ponder the current readiness of the U.S. military. Without the full integration and equal opportunity of women, the question should be asked, *Can the U.S. military realize its full readiness potential?*

Research Overview

The contributors to this section examine several important dimensions of gender integration and sexual harassment. In the paper entitled, "Cultural Diversity and Gender Issues," Mickey Dansby shares a comprehensive and introductory work that encompasses contemporary issues of cultural diversity, gender integration, and sexual harassment in the military. His paper sets the stage for the subsequent papers in this section. It considers a host of issues that remain areas of future diversity research consideration for the Department of Defence and military sociologists and psychologists.

Gender segregation has been reduced since the civil rights legislation of the 1960s, but reductions in inequalities are uneven, temporary, and incomplete. To that end, Juanita Firestone's contribution, "Occupational Segregation: Comparing the Civilian and Military Workforce," compares the differential assignment of women and men across occupations in the civilian labor force to the distribution of women and men in military occupations. One of the conclusions is that delimiting or precluding women from primary-mission jobs compromises their full integration into the military.

Brenda Moore addresses the question, "How do active duty women perceive the Army's EO climate?" by examining the perceptions of active-duty Army members to determine their satisfaction with the climate for equal opportunity. Her findings indicate concomitant race and gender effects referred to in the literature under a variety of terms such as the *double-whammy effect, gendered racism, double jeopardy*, or *double bind*. Her major finding is that race is a more powerful predictor of the attitudes of Army personnel toward the equal opportunity climate than is gender. The data also suggest that African-American, Hispanic, and white members do not always share the same perceptions of the EO climate. Moreover, to some extent African-American women on active-duty experience unique stresses due to their race and gender unlike their males and white female counterparts.

The theoretical underpinnings of the next paper, "Towards an Integrative Model of Sexual Harassment: An Examination of Power, Attitudes, Gender/Role Match, and Some Interactions," are drawn from psychological, organizational and socio-cultural models. In this study, Gary Whaley argues that although sexual harassment is a serious and complex problem in organizations, it is treated in an oversimplified manner in the literature. He attempts to integrate three models into a single, more comprehensive model of sexual harassment. His recommendations, which are based on a multilevel strategy, call for a proactive approach for managing and eliminating sexual harassment.

Collectively, these papers highlight the complexities and barriers that must be overcome to achieve complete gender integration and eliminate the environmental factors that contribute to sexual harassment. In addition, according to the former Undersecretary of Defense of Personnel and Readiness, Dr. Edwin Dorn, "One person who experiences sexual harassment is too many. Sexual harassment affects people's performance, good order and discipline" (Kozaryn, 1996).

References

Armor, D. (1996). Race and gender in the U.S. military, *Armed Forces & Society, 23*(1), 7-27.

Anker, R. (1998). *Gender and jobs: Sex segregation of occupations in the world.* Washington, DC: Brookings Institute.

Blau, F.D., Simpson, P., and Anderson, D. (1998). Continuing progress? Trends in occupational segregation in the United States over the 1970s and 1980s, *Feminist Economics, 4*(3), 29-71.

Defense Management Data Center (DMDC) (1999). *3035EO Report.* Washington, DC.

DePauw, L.G. (1998). *Battle cries and lullabies: Women in war from prehistory to the present*. Norman, OK: University of Oklahoma Press.

"Eight Air Force trainers cited for harassment," *Washington Post*, November 15, 1996, p. A4.

Harrell, M.C., and Miller, L. (1997). *New opportunities for military women: Effects upon readiness, cohesion, and morale*. Santa Monica, CA: RAND.

Holm, J. (1992). *Unfinished business: Women in the armed forces*. Novato, CA: Presidio Press.

Holm, J., and Bellafaire, J. (Eds.). (1998). *In defense of a nation : Servicewomen in world war II*. New York: Vandamere Press.

Kozaryn, L. (1996, July). *Sexual harassment declining, remains major concern*. Press release. Washington, DC: Armed Forces Press Service.

Martindale, M. (1990). *Sexual harassment in the military*. Arlington, VA; Defense Manpower Data Center.

McCaffrey, M. (1998). Constructing gender through representation: The women airforce service pilots (WASP) of World War II, *Dissertation Abstracts International*, 60/01, p. 113, July 1999.

Moskos, C., and Butler, J.S. (1997). *All that we can be: Black leadership and racial integration the Army way*. New York: Basic Books.

O'Neil, W. (1998). Sex scandals in the gender-integrated military, *Gender Issues*, *16*(1/2), 64-85.

Research Directorate (1998). *Annual occupational profile of minorities and women in the Department of Defense*, Patrick AFB, FL: DEOMI.

Roush, P. (1997, Aug) A tangled web. *Proceedings*, 123(3), 42-45.

Schneider, D., & Schneider, C. (1992). *Sound off! American military women speak out* (2nd ed.). New York: Paragon House.

Segal, M. (1995). Women's military roles cross-nationally: Past, present, and future. *Gender & Society*, *9*(6), 757-775.

The Economist (1998, Jun 27). United States: Women of war, pp. 30-33.

Whiteley, S. (1996, Dec 15). Women in the United States military, 1901-1995. *The Booklist*, *98*(8), 750.

15

Cultural Diversity and Gender Issues

*Mickey R. Dansby**

Introduction

In their book, *All That We Can Be*, military sociologists Charles Moskos and John Sibley Butler (1996) compare the prevailing negative paradigms for racial integration in America to one institution where African-Americans have been uniquely successful:

> It is an organization unmatched in its level of racial integration. It is an institution unmatched in its broad record of black achievement. It is a world in which the Afro-American heritage is part and parcel of the institutional culture. It is the only place in American life where whites are routinely bossed around by blacks. The institution is the U.S. Army (p. 2).

Moskos and Butler discuss the remarkable success (with caveats) of racial integration in the Army and suggest it may be instructive for the rest of American society. Because of its historical precedent (MacGregor, 1981) and its contemporary significance, race must be a key issue in any discussion of diversity and military psychology.

But race is not the only major concern for psychologists interested in diversity within the military. Incidents like the Navy's Tailhook scandal and the sexual assaults at Aberdeen Proving Ground, Maryland, and Fort Leonard Wood, Missouri, remind us that gender issues are also of paramount importance. Therefore, in this chapter we concentrate on these two key diversity topics from a military psychology perspective. We close the chapter with some brief thoughts on the future of diversity issues in the military. But before

---

* The views expressed in this chapter are those of the author and do not necessarily reflect the views of the Department of Defense or any of its agencies.

we discuss the two major content areas, let us establish a context for understanding how the military deals with diversity and gender issues.

Background

President Truman's Executive Order 9981 (July 26, 1948), which established racial equality as a policy and called for desegregation of the military services, was a watershed event for diversity within the military. Born out of questions relating to military efficiency (MacGregor, 1981) and Mr. Truman's concern about treatment of black soldiers returning from World War II (Nalty, 1986), this unprecedented policy faced stiff opposition (MacGregor, 1981). Even so, it established a tradition that would result in the successes described by Moskos and Butler (1996) and led to a long line of commissions and studies on how to implement such a broad social change (MacGregor, 1981). Equality of treatment existed on paper and in policy, but effective integration did not come easily.

Despite the revolutionary and immediate impact of Executive Order 9981, it was not until some time later that the military came to grips with the important question of training service personnel (coming from all walks of American life and all regions of the nation) on how to deal with racial issues. As Hope (1979), points out, "Like most institutions, the Army did not 'get serious' about the problem of racism until there were riots and 'fraggings' (fire bombing of top-ranking officers and enlisted personnel)" (p. 1). In early 1971, the military services openly recognized the racial unrest and seriously considered what might be done to combat such divisiveness (Hope, 1979). Almost immediately, a broad strategy of education and training was implemented to meet the challenge.

Hope (1979), Day (1983), and Dansby and Landis (1996) chronicle the military's response to the racial unrest of the late 1960s and early 1970s. Perhaps the keystone in the services' strategy was the establishment of the Defense Race Relations Institute (DRRI), later redesignated the Defense Equal Opportunity Management Institute (DEOMI). Unique in American society, DRRI/DEOMI has served a distinctive purpose in preparing trainers and advisors to help the services deal with diversity issues. Dansby and Landis (1996) note five key elements in the military's approach to equal opportunity (EO) and diversity:

(a)   a focus on *behavioral change* and *compliance* with stated policy;

(b)   an emphasis on EO and intercultural understanding as *military readiness issues*;

(c)   an understanding that *equal opportunity is a commander's responsibility* and that the *DEOMI graduate's function is to advise and assist the commander* in carrying out this responsibility;

(d)   a belief that *education and training* can bring about the desired behavioral changes; and

(e)   reliance on *affirmative action plans* as a method for ensuring equity and diversity. (pp. 206-207)

Several of these elements lend themselves to psychological inquiry (e.g., behavioral change, compliance, training), and psychologists have frequently been called upon to explore diversity issues in the military. Hope (1979), Day (1983), and Thomas (1988) summarize much of the race relations research that was generated in the 1970s and 1980s—perhaps the "golden period" for research on these issues in the services. A useful reference to set the context for this period is Binkin and Eitelberg's (1982) excellent overview of black participation and the unprecedented rise in black representation in the military (especially the Army). Thomas' (1988) collection of readings and reports from this era is most helpful in demonstrating the scope and depth of research conducted at the U.S. Army Research Institute for the Behavioral and Social Sciences (ARI). Though many studies were conducted by "think tanks" (like RAND Corporation, the Brookings Institution, and the Human Resources Research Organization), the work at ARI appears to be the most cogent and best organized effort to apply a behavioral science perspective to race relations questions in the military. The ARI's race relations research diminished after this early work, perhaps due to a redirection toward other issues or to a belief that the major questions had been resolved.[1]

For many reasons, interest in gender issues developed after that for race. Participation of women in the military was restricted by law or policy for many years, and women are still prohibited by Congress from serving in a number of direct combat military specialties. The Women's Armed Services Act of 1948, while giving women a permanent place in the military, had placed many limitations on women's service: women could constitute no more than 2 percent of a branch's personnel; only 10 percent of the women in a service could be officers; women could not serve as general or flag officers; each service was limited to one woman at the rank of O-6 (colonel or Navy captain), and that woman's rank was temporary—she held it only so long as she was head of the women's corps for that service. In 1967, Congress passed a law repealing these restrictions (though women's participation in direct combat was still prohibited). (See Holm, 1992, and Dansby & Landis, 1996, for a discussion of these issues.) Representation of women in the services increased very rapidly after 1967, and by the end of 1996, women comprised over 13 percent of active duty service personnel (13.4 percent of officers and 13.2 percent of enlisted members; DEOMI, 1996). The military has been a particularly popular career choice for minority women (over 40 percent of the women in the services are from minority groups; DEOMI, 1996), perhaps due to the many benefits of military service (e.g., gender equity in pay, retirement, and other benefits).

Gender topics were added as a significant part of DEOMI's curriculum only in the late 1970s and early 1980s, and little psychological research had been conducted on gender issues in the military until about the same time. However, gender research rapidly overtook racial/ethnic questions as a topic of interest, and many key studies on gender issues have been conducted by several military research agencies, including the Defense Manpower Data Center (DMDC), Navy Personnel Research and Development Center (NPRDC), and DEOMI, or by individual researchers.

The initial sluggish pursuit of research on gender issues in the military may have been due to several factors, including: the smaller representation of women in the services, the early concentration of women in relatively few (usually gender-stereotyped) jobs (e.g., nursing), a belief by research sponsors that race was a more pressing concern, or the lack of "crisis" events (e.g., race riots) to focus attention on gender issues. However, questions related to integration of women into the service academies, expansion of opportunities for women in the services, and possible problems in gender relations (e.g., sexual harassment, the source of several later "crisis events") led to the rapid expansion of research on gender issues.

The military's public support for diversity concerns is codified in the Department of Defense (DoD) Human Goals. This document, signed by the Secretary of Defense, Deputy Secretary of Defense, service secretaries, and military chiefs of the services, lists a number of objectives. The basic premise of the Human Goals is, "Our nation was founded on the principle that the individual has infinite dignity and worth. The Department of Defense, which exists to keep the Nation secure and at peace, must always be guided by this principle." The DoD aspires, "To make military and civilian service in the Department of Defense a model of equal opportunity for all..." and "To create an environment that values diversity and fosters mutual respect and cooperation among all persons..." Military psychologists have contributed to these lofty ideals through their research on race and gender issues within the services and by helping develop the training programs used to combat racism/sexism and improve human relations.

Unfortunately, a large proportion of the research done by military psychologists is never published in professional journals or books. This is not a function of the quality of the work, for much has very high technical merit, but rather because it tends to address issues of immediate practical importance, based on the needs of a particular sponsor (i.e., a senior manager in the service who needs to make a policy decision, a training institution that needs a methodological question answered, etc.), and occurs under the purview of a military laboratory, school, or other agency (e.g., the ARI, NPRDC, DEOMI, Naval Postgraduate School, and DoD Accession Policy Office). A great deal of this "fugitive" literature is accessible (using computer assisted searches) through the Defense Technical Information Center and the National Technical Information Service. (The author of this chapter is pleased to note a movement toward increased publication in standard professional journals and books—a trend that should be encouraged in the interest of enhancing scientific community and cross-utilization of military psychologists' work.) Military psychologists also frequently make presentations at meetings of professional societies (such as the American Psychological Association [APA], Society for Industrial and Organizational Psychology, and American Management Association). Certainly, creation of Division 19 (Military Psychology) and its associated journal (*Military Psychology*) of the APA has contributed substantially to the opportunity to share results from military research. In addition, specialized forums, such as the Applied Behavioral Sciences Symposium, sponsored by the U.S. Air Force Academy, and the International Military Testing Association Annual Conference often feature presentations by military psychologists. Frequently, these professional activities include presentations or reports on diversity issues.

With a basic understanding of the context, let us now consider the first of the two major diversity issues in the military: the racial/ethnic concerns.

Racial/Ethnic Issues

A number of sociologists, psychologists, and other professionals have explored race and ethnic issues within the military. Many, spurred by concerns raised in the general society, have done so without formal sponsorship of the services. However, identification of major issues and initiation of most research are direct results of the efforts of behavioral scientists from military organizations. The research has covered many key areas, including racial/ethnic questions related to personnel (e.g., entrance testing, recruitment, assignment, performance, personnel evaluation, promotion, retention, and training), discipline, diversity training, and human relations (e.g., equal opportunity climate, fostering positive relations, group dynamics, and cohesion). A comprehensive review of all these topics is beyond the scope of this chapter. However, the author shall attempt to discuss representative studies and give the reader some sense of the scope of the work that has been done.

Personnel

Much of the research on race and ethnicity involves personnel issues and has been conducted under the auspices of major military personnel research centers (e.g., ARI, NPRDC, or the Air Force's Armstrong Laboratory Human Resources Directorate—formerly the Human Resources Laboratory [HRL]). In many instances, broader studies of personnel issues (e.g., entrance testing, occupational assignment) addressed racial/ethnic questions, though the main thrust was not diversity concerns. Many such studies were sponsored through the Office of the Secretary of Defense, frequently by the Accessions Policy Office. For example, Eitelberg, Laurence, and Waters (1984) and Eitelberg (1988) offer extensive summaries on screening, selecting, and classifying personnel for military service. These reports include analyses based on race, ethnicity, and gender, in addition to a number of other relevant dimensions. A great deal of the information relates to data from the Armed Services Vocational

Aptitude Battery (ASVAB), a test battery introduced in 1968 that has been used by all services since 1974 as a tool for screening enlistees and assigning them to occupations (Eitelberg, 1988).

Since the ASVAB (or its predecessors and composites, such as the Armed Forces Qualification Test, or AFQT) is used to make critical personnel decisions (i.e., entry qualification, occupational field, etc.), it has been the subject of much research on gender and race issues. Two notable incidents in the use of the ASVAB should be mentioned. The first is Project 100,000 (a result of the "Great Society" initiatives), in which 100,000 men who fell below current admission standards were allowed to enter the services annually. Many of the accessions were minority group members. The project was designed to provide employment for many of America's "subterranean poor" (Eitelberg, 1988). The second is the inadvertent misnorming of the AFQT between 1976 and 1980 (Sellman & Valentine, 1981). The misnorming resulted in the admission of nearly 360,000 men who actually fell below minimum standards (if the test had been normed properly). Clearly, both these incidents resulted in increased admission of minority group members, who traditionally had not done as well on standardized testing and may have lacked educational advantages.

For the interested reader, Eitelberg (1988) discusses both Project 100,000 and the misnorming in some detail. He reports that military commanders often complained of what they perceived as a diminished quality of the force during this period; however, statistical analysis indicates those scoring below the accepted standard did about as well as those in the lowest qualified group. Eitelberg's (1988) conclusion is noteworthy:

> It is probably safe to say that, from the standpoint of "military effectiveness" or "readiness," the jury is still out on both Project 100,000 and its unplanned replacement. Lower aptitude standards tend to be viewed more favorably when expedience demands it . . . [S]everal gross misconceptions about the two events have become a permanent part of the military's folklore. But Project 100,000 and the ASVAB misnorming did make at least one lasting contribution to defense manpower policy: they helped to raise some serious questions about the appropriateness of established selection standards and forced the military's policymakers to examine more closely the performance measures used to set those standards (pp. 182-183).

Eitelberg's (1988) analysis of the status of women and minorities indicates significant progress by these groups in securing assignment to higher skilled jobs between the late 1970s and late 1980s. However, he points out there are still significant differences in the job distribution of minorities and women compared to white men (though the distribution in the military may be more equitable than in U.S. society as a whole). These issues (representation and distribution by occupation) continue to be of interest to social scientists exploring diversity issues in the military. For example, Moskos and Butler (1996) outline the significant rise of African Americans into leadership positions within the Army. Between 1970 and 1990, the proportion of senior noncommissioned officers who were black grew from 14 percent to 31 percent; during the same period, black officers increased from 3 percent to 11 percent of commissioned officers; and by the mid-1980s, 7 percent of the Army's generals were black.

Another area of inquiry is the propensity of American youth to join the military. Major attitude studies by race, ethnicity, and gender are common. For example, Segal and Bachman (1994) report results from high school seniors surveyed as part of the *Monitoring the Future* project at the University of Michigan's Institute for Social Research. The DoD also sponsors the annual *Youth Attitude Tracking Study* (YATS; Ramsberger, 1993; Nieva, 1991), generating a number of analyses of attitudes toward the military. Such efforts provide many opportunities for psychologists to explore attitudinal data and behavioral propensities of minority group members and women who are potential recruits.

Many other personnel issues related to race have been researched in the military. A few examples: Thomas (1988) describes a number of reports dealing with institutional discrimination issues (assignment, promotion, selection for schooling, access to reenlistment, retention, etc.); Dansby (1989) and St. Pierre (1991) look at retention by race (and gender); Rosenfeld, Thomas, Edwards, Thomas, and Thomas (1991) provide a historical review of the Navy's research on race (and gender) issues, including personnel research such as studies of Hispanic representation and turnover in the Navy's civilian work force; Greene and Culbertson (1995) present an analysis of potential racial bias in promotion fitness reports within the Navy; Smither & Houston (1991) explore issues related to fairness and redress of grievances within the military. In short, personnel issues within the military have been, and continue to be, a rich source for racial/ethnic (and gender) research.

Discipline

Another major topic for racial/ethnic research within the services is military discipline and punishment (i.e., military justice). There are three broad categories of discipline within the military: adminis-trative discipline (e.g., separation from the service), nonjudicial pun-ishment (NJP; minor punishments and fines administered by a local commander), and formal legal proceedings conducted under the Uniform Code of Military Justice (UCMJ). Military psychologists have explored all three.

To a large degree, the research interest in race and military justice is the result of questions of equity raised by black civilian leaders. For example, in 1971 the National Association for the Advancement of Colored People (NAACP) and the Urban League challenged the racial fairness of military justice in the Army's European theater (Nalty, 1986). Members of these organizations, along with others, served on a task force commissioned by Secretary of Defense Melvin Laird to investigate the allegations. The majority of the task force concluded that racial discrimination existed in the administration of military jus-tice, and that it resulted from pervasive discrimination in American society (Nalty, 1986). Nalty summarizes the report as follows:

> Statistics indicated that blacks were more likely than whites to run afoul of regulations. Furthermore, black servicemen had the greater probability of undergoing trial by court-martial, being confined before the trial, being convicted, and receiving long sentences. Blacks were also more likely to receive . . . administrative discharge . . . and . . . nonjudicial punishment, administered on the authority of the commanding officer for comparatively minor offenses. The statistical disparity . . . existed despite what the task force agreed was a genuine effort on the part of the armed forces to ensure equal treatment (p. 329).

The report of the task force was administrative and lacked the rigor of a scientific study. Yet the basic disparity in rates of military discipline for white and black soldiers was not in dispute. A statisti-cal disparity persists, though the absolute numbers of disciplinary actions (especially for UCMJ offenses) has declined dramatically since the 1970s. (See, for example, Walker, 1992, who reports that while the total number of court-martial convictions across the DoD fell from 15,739 in fiscal year [FY] 1987 to 7,485 in FY1991, the proportionate overrepresentation of black servicemembers actually increased during the same period because of the faster decline in white convictions as compared to black convictions.) Landis and Dansby (1994) report that between 1988 and 1993, blacks were overrepresented in NJP (by 20-40 percent, depending on service) and UCMJ actions (by as much as 100 percent). While the overrepresentation of blacks in military prisons is less than half what it is in the penal system at large (Moskos & Butler, 1996), it is still an issue of some concern. Why does the disparity exist? This important question, raised by Secretary Laird's task force in the 1970s, remains to a large degree unanswered and continues to be the basis of many studies within the military.

Dansby (1992) outlines a structure for systematically addressing the issue. Using the analogy of a tree, three "roots" in the soil of society are discussed as potential exogenous (i.e., outside the military) sources leading to black overrepresentation in the military justice system: psychological, physiological, and sociological variables. Within the military several "branches" are discussed as endogenous factors: differential treatment by race, differential involvement in crimes by race, and statistical artifacts. Landis and Dansby (1994) continue to develop this model.

After a review of numerous empirical studies, Dansby (1992) concludes that a substantial portion of the disparity can be traced to exogenous sociological factors. In a study of incarcerated military members, Knouse (1993) presents empirical evidence of racial differences in exogenous variables such as socioeconomic, familial, and personality factors. Based on available results, it appears racial discrimination within the military justice system is not the major cause of the disparity. Consequently, Dansby (1992) and Landis and Dansby (1994) recommend an action research strategy addressing the sociological factors. Two possible techniques are special training programs: one for recruits and another for military supervisors. These programs are described as the *inoculation approach* and the *cultural assimilation model* (see also Knouse, 1994a, and Knouse & Dansby, 1994). Neither strategy has been fully developed or validated as of this writing.

Numerous studies relating to discipline have been conducted or sponsored by the NPRDC (see Rosenfeld et al., 1991, and Culbertson & Magnusson, 1992, for reviews), ARI and Department of the Army (e.g., Bauer, Stout, & Holz, 1976; Bell & Holz, 1975; Nordlie, Sevilla, Edmonds, & White, 1979; and Verdugo, 1994), Office of the Secretary of Defense (e.g., Flyer, 1990; Flyer, 1993; Flyer & Curran, 1993), and DEOMI (see Knouse, 1996a, for a review). Despite the large number of studies, much remains to be explored (Dansby, 1992).

Diversity Training

Hope (1979), Day (1983), Thomas (1988), and Dansby and Landis (1996) offer reviews of the structure, policies, and research for diversity training in the military. Many of the studies in this area are evaluation research relating to the impact of the training on servicemembers in general or the effectiveness of DEOMI's training programs in preparing equal opportunity advisors and instructors (also see Knouse, 1996a; Johnson, 1995; and Johnson, 1996).

Day (1983) offers an extensive review of the effectiveness of diversity training in the military, especially in the Army. In general, there are many problems associated with evaluation research, making it difficult to determine the effectiveness of the DEOMI training or the training offered by the services to their members in general. Evidence reviewed by Day (1983) indicates the training varies in effectiveness (based on numerous criteria such as whether it was implemented seriously or just as a "paper-and-pencil" exercise). The overall program appears to have improved the race relations climate in the services (Day, 1983). Hope (1979) summarizes a number of studies concerning the effectiveness of the DEOMI training as measured by several approaches, including attitude change; cognitive change; and the opinions of the faculty, graduates, and commanders the graduates served. All sources indicated positive impact of the training, both personally and organizationally. Johnson (1995; 1996) found similar positive results in her surveys of commanders and supervisors of DEOMI graduates.

In addition to analysis of the impact of diversity training, many studies have considered the adequacy of the content of the DEOMI training to prepare equal opportunity advisors for their jobs. Most of the studies were occupational analyses conducted by the services (e.g., the Air Force Occupational Measurement Squadron) or contractors (e.g., Kinton & Associates). The results have been used to refine the curriculum to make sure graduates are adequately prepared to meet the needs of the field commands. Such studies have led to evolutionary changes in DEOMI's curriculum (such as an increased emphasis on gender issues and the addition of a writing and speaking program).

Human Relations

Fostering positive human relations is a key concern in military organizations. Without mutual respect and recognition of each person's dignity and contributions to the organization, it is difficult to develop a cohesive, smoothly functioning team. The DoD Human Goals emphasize the "infinite dignity and worth" of each indi-

vidual in the service, and military commanders generally acknowledge the need for a positive human relations climate in order for
their units to function effectively. Much of the diversity research
conducted by military psychologists has focused on this issue.

The range of research in this area is quite extensive (see Thomas,
1988, for examples of research on cross-cultural communications,
racial separatism, unit race relations, cultural assimilation, and training for racial harmony). For the sake of brevity, we will focus on
general EO climate issues and confine our consideration to two major sources of EO climate research: DEOMI and NPRDC. The work
of each institution has been documented in numerous articles and
technical reports (for the DEOMI program, see Dansby & Landis,
1991; Landis, Dansby, & Faley, 1993; Landis, Dansby, & Tallarigo,
1996; Dansby, 1995; and the summary in Knouse, 1996a; for information on the NPRDC effort, see Rosenfeld et al., 1991; Culbertson
& Rosenfeld, 1993; Rosenfeld & Culbertson, 1993; Rosenfeld &
Edwards, 1994; and Newell, Rosenfeld, & Culbertson, 1995).

At DEOMI, most EO climate research involves the Military Equal
Opportunity Climate Survey (MEOCS) or its various derivatives (i.e.,
the small unit, equal employment opportunity, senior leader, and
short versions). The MEOCS is an organizational development survey and analysis service provided free to military commanders at all
levels to help them assess EO and organizational effectiveness (OE)
within their units and plan strategies to improve the organizational
climate. There are four EO climate sections in the MEOCS: perceptions of unit EO behaviors, OE perceptions, general EO perceptions
(i.e., in the total context and not just unit conditions), and a global
measure called *Overall EO Climate*. Issues addressed include race/
gender discrimination, racist/sexist behaviors, sexual harassment,
positive EO behaviors, the so-called "reverse" discrimination, desire for racial separatism, job satisfaction, commitment to the organization, and perceptions of work group effectiveness (Dansby,
1994a). Commanders voluntarily request MEOCS for their units, and
DEOMI keeps unit results confidential. After a commander receives
his or her report, identifying information is stripped from the unit's
data and the data are added to an overall database used for comparison and research purposes (i.e., to allow each command to compare
their results to their service's results and those from all services). In
addition, occasional probability samples are gathered across entire
services to compare results to the overall unit database results. Since

the program began in June of 1990, over 4,000 units have participated and a database of well over half a million respondents has
been accumulated.

Results from the MEOCS have demonstrated several consistent
patterns. Although most demographic subgroups rate the EO climate as "average" or better for their organizations, the perceptions
vary by group. In general, the most favorable climate ratings are
from majority men, and the least favorable are from minority women
(Dansby, 1994a; Moskos & Butler, 1996). More specifically, the most
favorable ratings are from majority officer men and the least favorable are from minority officer women (Dansby, 1994a). (In a recent
article, Dansby & Landis, in process, present evidence that one reason minority officer women rate the climate less favorably than minority enlisted women is because of their smaller representation in
units.) Results from the Senior Leader Equal Opportunity Climate
Survey (Dansby, 1996), a version of MEOCS developed for the gen-
eral/admiral/Senior Executive Service level, and from the normal
MEOCS indicate that high ranking white men have the most favorable ratings of all.

The MEOCS database has been the source of many empirical studies on diversity issues, including the relationship between EO climate and Total Quality Management (Knouse, 1994b, 1996b), group
cohesiveness and performance (Niebuhr, Knouse, Dansby, &
Niebuhr, 1996), career commitment (Landis, Dansby, & Faley, 1994),
demographic representation within the organization (Dansby &
Landis, in process), organizational characteristics (Tallarigo &
Landis, 1995), and acceptance of diversity (Niebuhr, 1994a). In addition, the MEOCS program has inspired numerous studies on EO
climate survey development and improvement (e.g., Dansby &
Landis, 1991; Landis et al., 1993; Dansby, 1994b; Niebuhr, 1994a;
Albright & McIntyre, 1995; McIntyre, 1995; McIntyre, Albright, &
Dansby, 1996; Dansby, 1996).

The NPRDC's extensive EO climate program includes both the
Navy and the Marine Corps. The Navy assessed EO climate as part
of its Human Resources Management organizational survey program
as far back as 1975 (Rosenfeld & Edwards, 1994). There were also
efforts to measure race relations in the Navy during the 1970s
(Rosenfeld et al., 1991) that were similar to the Army's efforts at
ARI (Thomas, 1988). The current NPRDC program involves measurement at two levels: the Command Assessment Team Survey Sys-

tem (CATSYS), at the individual unit level, and service-wide probability sample surveys (the Navy Equal Opportunity/Sexual Harassment Survey [NEOSH] and the Marine Corps Equal Opportunity Survey [MCEOS]) (Rosenfeld & Edwards, 1994; Newell et al., 1995; Thomas & Le, 1996).

The NEOSH (and MCEOS) is composed of nine modules, addressing a number of areas where discrimination might occur. The modules include: assignments, training, leadership, communications, interpersonal relations, grievances, discipline, performance evaluation, and Navy satisfaction (Rosenfeld, Culbertson, Booth-Kewley, & Magnusson, 1992). Results on each module are compared by demographic group, much as MEOCS results are compared by group for MEOCS scale scores.

For the most part, results of the NPRDC EO climate program are very similar to those for the MEOCS. Newell et al. (1995) summarize the EO results of the 1991 NEOSH as follows:

> 1) Navy personnel generally had positive EO climate perceptions; 2) men had more positive EO climate perceptions than women; 3) White male officers had the most positive EO climate perceptions, African-Americans, particularly African-American women had the least positive perceptions; and 4) Hispanics' EO perceptions typically fell between those of Whites and African-Americans and most often were closer to the perceptions of Whites (p. 160).

The close correspondence between NEOSH and MEOCS, which use different instruments and methodologies, supports the construct validity of the two surveys and increases confidence in the findings.

The NEOSH and MCEOS are divided into two major sections: EO climate issues and sexual harassment issues (Rosenfeld & Edwards, 1994; Thomas & Le, 1996). The fact that a single EO issue (sexual harassment) carries such weight in the NPRDC's assessment of EO climate indicates the importance of this issue in military research efforts. We now turn our attention to the this sensitive and often discussed topic, along with other gender issues in the military.

Gender Issues

In recent years, gender issues in the military have occupied a prominent place in the popular press as well as the scientific literature. Questions regarding the impact of women's increased accessions and entry into traditionally male military specialties, along with gender discrimination and sexual harassment concerns, have occupied newspaper and television reporters, movie makers, political pundits, feminists, special interest organizations, congressional oversight committees, senior leaders within the services and executive branch, and behavioral scientists alike. Perhaps the most often discussed issue is sexual harassment, so we address it first, followed by a brief synopsis of other gender issues of interest to military psychologists.

Sexual Harassment

The DoD definition of sexual harassment parallels that of the Equal Employment Opportunity Commission (EEOC). DoD Directive 1350.2 states:

> Sexual harassment is a form of sex discrimination that involves unwelcome sexual advances, requests for sexual favors, and other verbal or physical conduct of a sexual nature when:
> (1) submission to such conduct is made either explicitly or implicitly a term or condition of a person's job, pay, or career, or
> (2) submission to or rejection of such conduct by a person is used as a basis for career employment decisions affecting that person, or
> (3) such conduct has the purpose or effect of unreasonably interfering with an individual's work performance or creates an intimidating, hostile, or offensive working environment.

This definition encompasses two basic forms of sexual harassment: *quid pro quo* (i.e., "something for something"), a more severe form in which sexual favors are demanded in exchange for job benefits (e.g., continued employment, advancement), and *hostile environment*, a less severe form in which sexual behavior in the work place interferes with a person's performance or creates an intimidating environment. (See Eisaguirre, 1993, for a lay person's discussion of the general EEOC definition, the two basic categories, legal issues, and a summary of studies concerning sexual harassment. Pryor (1985) also provides an excellent summary of the issues.) Another key feature of the definition is that the sexual behavior is unwelcome (i.e., uninvited and unwanted; Farley, 1978; MacKinnon, 1979). Secretary of Defense William Perry (in a 1994 memorandum to the secretaries of the military services, joint chiefs of staff, and other defense agencies) further clarified the policy to indicate that hostile environment harassment "need not result in concrete psychological harm to the victim, but rather need only be so severe or pervasive that a reasonable person would perceive, and the victim does perceive, the work environment as hostile or abusive." Secretary Perry's memorandum also indicated that the definition applied both on or off duty for military members, and that anyone in DoD "who makes deliberate or repeated unwelcome verbal comments, gestures, or physical contact of a sexual nature in the workplace is also engaging in sexual harassment." Goldman (1995) offers an excellent summary of the issue as it is understood in the military; and Bastian, Lancaster, and Reyst (1996) give a succinct history of sexual harassment policy concerns and deliberations in the DoD.

Several major studies of sexual harassment in the military have been conducted in the last 20 years. Two, while not specifically focused at the military, included information concerning the sexual harassment of civilians working in every service. These studies were conducted by the U.S. Merit Systems Protection Board (MSPB) (1981, 1988) in 1980 and 1987. The MSPB defined several categories of sexual harassment, varying in severity. The *most severe* form was actual or attempted rape or assault; the *severe* forms were deliberate touching, pressure for sexual favors, and letters and calls; the *less severe* forms were sexual remarks, suggestive looks, and pressure for dates. The survey asked respondents to indicate whether they had experienced any of these forms of harassment during the 24 months prior to completion of the survey. Table 15.1 below shows the reported incidence rate, by gender and service, for the two surveys. As the table indicates, there was relatively little change in the incidence of sexual harassment of civilian employees of the military between 1980 and 1987.

Since the MSPB surveys did not address the rate of sexual harassment for military members, the DoD conducted its own studies, modeling its survey after the MSPB survey. The military surveys,

Table 15.1
Results of the MSPB Surveys of DoD Civilians:
Those Experiencing at Least One Incident in the Previous Two Years

Service	*1980 Survey*		*1987 Survey*	
	Men	*Women*	*Men*	*Women*
Air Force	12%	46%	16%	45%
Army	16%	41%	11%	44%
Navy/Marine Corps	14%	44%	14%	47%
Federal Government Average	15%	42%	14%	42%

Source: Adapted from U.S. Merit Systems Protection Board, 1981, 1988.

conducted by DMDC in 1988 and 1995, used probability samples representing military personnel from all services (Martindale, 1990; Bastian et al., 1996). The rates for military women were higher than those reported by civilians in the MSPB surveys, though the rates for military men were similar to those of the male civilian employees. A major finding of the 1995 survey was a significant decline in reported sexual harassment from the 1988 survey. While 64% of the women in the 1988 survey reported at least one incident during the preceding 12 months, 55% gave a similar report in 1995. Similarly, the rates for men dropped from 17% to 14%. This drop in reported incidents is consistent with perceptions reported in the MEOCS (see Figure 15.1 below) and other climate surveys, which indicate sexual harassment is on the decline in the services.

Though several notable incidents have brought sexual harassment in the military to the public's attention recently, the overall trend is toward an improved climate. However, DoD still has a long way to go before it reaches its goal of "zero tolerance" (Bastian et al., 1996).

In trying to understand the levels of sexual harassment, care must be taken in interpreting incidence rates. There are many different operational definitions used in measuring sexual harassment: per-

Figure 15.1
MEOCS Results
Sexual Harassment/Discrimination Scale*
(All Services - by calendar year a/o 12/96)

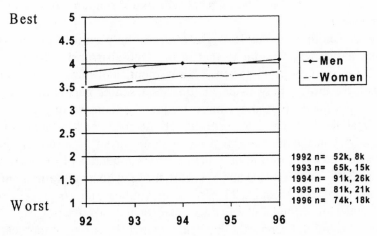

* Source: Defense Equal Oppurtunity Managment Institute, Patrick AFB, FL.

ceptions of what has happened to others, reports of personal experience, and reports of formal complaints, to name a few (Eisaguirre,
1993; Culbertson & Rosenfeld, 1994). Furthermore, studies may use
different time references (i.e., have you *ever* experienced, experienced in the *last year*, etc.), selection of participants may vary (i.e.,
self-selected or randomly selected), and the behaviors reported may
not be considered harassing by the respondent. (For example, the
1995 DoD survey included a Form B listing additional behaviors
not included in the original survey. Respondents were asked to report whether they considered the behaviors they experienced to be
harassing. Many did not think of some of the incidents as sexual
harassment.) A final consideration is differences in working conditions and exposure to sexual harassment. Although the military rates
are higher than those reported by civilian employees in the MSPB
surveys, the surveys do not consider the difference in working conditions for civilian and military employees (i.e., while civilians are
typically "on duty" for normal 8-hour work days, military members are on duty 24-hours a day and often live in military quar-
ters; this expands the opportunities for work-related harassment,
as clarified by DoD's expansive definition of sexual harassment;
also, the higher ratio of men to women—over six to one—in the
military increases opportunities for military women to experience sexual harassment). However, even with consideration for all
these caveats, sexual harassment remains an issue of major concern
to the services (Bastian et al., 1996), and developing strategies for
the prevention of sexual harassment will likely continue to be a high
interest item.

Other findings of the 1995 DoD survey help paint a picture of
sexual harassment similar to that in the civilian world: women are
much more likely to experience harassment than men; junior personnel are more likely to be victims than senior personnel; black
men experience harassment more frequently than white men; and
the most likely perpetrators are coworkers, followed by superiors,
then others in the service. Most incidents occurred on a military installation, at work, during duty hours. About a quarter of the victims
reported the incident(s), and most of those who complained said
action was taken (though 23 percent of women and 16 percent of
men said their complaint was discounted or not taken seriously). Of
those who did not report the incidents, over half said they took care
of it themselves or didn't consider it important. About a quarter of

the nonreporting women indicated they failed to report the incident(s) because they thought it would make work unpleasant, and 20 percent thought nothing would be done. A small but significant number of victims (20 percent of women and 9 percent of men) reported some degree (to a small, moderate, or large extent) of reprisal, but 80 percent of women and 85 percent of men said they felt free (to a small, moderate, or large extent) to report sexual harassment without the fear of something bad happening to them. About a third of those making complaints said they were dissatisfied with the resolution of the complaint (another third were neither satisfied nor dissatisfied, and the remaining third were satisfied). Eight in ten had received training about sexual harassment in the last year, and almost nine in ten knew how to report sexual harassment. (Bastian et al., 1996; cf., Eisaguirre, 1993)

Niebuhr (1997) summarizes recent research findings on sexual harassment in the military, though his work was published before the second DoD survey had been released. Table 15.2 lists some of the findings reported by Niebuhr (1997).

As this brief overview has indicated, there is a wide range of research on sexual harassment in the military. While this topic remains the most prominent gender issue in the military, others have been considered as well. The next section provides a sampling of some of the other research.

Other Gender Issues

Besides sexual harassment, researchers have addressed a wide variety of other gender issues in the military. An early interest was the impact on the military of increased accessions of women after Congress removed the limits on numbers of women in the services. Binkin and Bach (1977) consider several such issues, including the economic impact (both on the military and for the women themselves), institutional attitudes (both within and outside the military), and military effectiveness; Holm (1992) discusses the expanding access to military occupations (i.e., job specialties); Shields (1988) explores sex roles in the military. Another interest has been the impact of pregnancy and single parenthood (e.g., Thomas & Thomas, 1992). Related to the latter is the questions of gender differences in absences from work (e.g., Thomas, Thomas, & Robertson, 1993; Thomas & Thomas, 1993a, 1993b).

Table 15.2
Sexual Harassment in the Military

Finding	Researcher(s)	Date
1. Women in lower-status positions were more frequently harassed.	Fain & Anderton	1987
2. Women in male-dominated groups or who are gender pioneers in their jobs were more likely to be harassed.	Niebuhr & Oswald	1992a
3. Organizational climate concerning sexual harassment contributed to the degree of perceived harassment.	Niebuhr	1994b
4. More sexual harassment of women occurred in large units, where contact with larger numbers of men occurred.	Niebuhr & Oswald	1992b
5. Different survey designs may lead to substantially different estimates of sexual harassment incidence rates.	Culbertson & Rosenfeld	1994
6. Men and women may have different interpretations of what is sexual harassment.	Thomas	1995
7. There was a negative relationship between gender discrimination climate and both group cohesion and perceived group performance.	Niebuhr, Knouse, & Dansby	1994
8. The better the balance between the percentages of males and females in a work group, the greater their agreement in perceptions of how much sexual harassment occurs.	Niebuhr	1994b

Gender equity in promotions and retention has been an issue of some concern as well (e.g., Firestone & Stewart, 1995). The data indicate women generally fare well in military promotions, doing about as well as their male cohorts in most promotion decisions. One interesting theme in the research on promotions has been the effort to determine how narrative descriptions in evaluation reports differ by gender (Thomas, Holmes, & Carroll, 1983; Greene & Culbertson, 1995). These studies have found that women's narratives may be shorter and have fewer dynamic, action words. Such deficiencies can have a negative impact on individuals, despite the equitable overall promotion statistics.

Table 15.3 summarizes some other gender issues that are recent research interests for military psychologists:

Table 15.3
Gender Issues in the Military

Finding	Researcher(s)	Date
1. Female aviators in the Air Force had more masculine or androgynous scores on a sex role scale (the Bem Sex Role Inventory) compared to other military and civilian women.	Dunivin	1990
2. Younger, more highly educated respondents with better paying jobs were more likely to support women's participation in a variety of military roles.	Matthews & Weaver	1990
3. Female Air Force aviators who planned to separate from the service were more likely to cite family concerns than job, career, or other concerns.	Schissel	1990
4. The relationship between stress, general well being, and job absences is more complex for women than for men.	Hendrix & Gibson	1992
5. Male service academy cadets were less approving of women serving in combat roles than their counterparts in a private civilian college.	Matthews	1992
6. Women had higher naval aviation qualifying test scores, yet had lower scores and completion rates for pre-flight training.	Baisden	1992
7. Compared to their male counterparts, women USAF pilots had higher ex traversion, agreeableness, and conscientiousness personality scores.	King, McGlohn, & Retzlaff	1996
8. Scores on the Bem Sex Role Inventory were not predictive of ratings of military development for U.S. Military Academy cadets.	Stokan & Hah	1996
9. There was a negative correlation between sexism and both cohesion and group performance for an active duty military unit.	Niebuhr, Knouse, Dansby, & Niebuhr	1996

Gender issues will, no doubt, continue to be central to diversity concerns in the military for some time to come. Because the proportion of women recruits is on the rise, women will likely become a larger proportion of military personnel, even though the military has experienced a reduction in overall force levels. We can expect military psychologists will have more than a passing interest in this phenomenon and its related issues.

In our discussion of race and gender issues, we have covered the "big two" diversity concerns in the military. Yet, many see diversity as encompassing issues "beyond race and gender" (Thomas, 1991). In the next section we briefly address some of these issues.

Future Diversity Issues

What does the future hold for diversity issues within the military? We can safely project that race and gender will continue to be important; but what else will researchers address? We see several potential "hot topics" for the next few years, including the status of homosexuals in the military, racial identity issues (specifically, dealing with multiracial individuals), concerns about the "white male backlash" (i.e., reactions to affirmative action programs and perceptions of "reverse" discrimination), the conflict between individual rights and the need for cohesion in the military, and dealing with racial/ethnic/gender issues in foreign countries as the military takes on more humanitarian and peacekeeping missions.

Of all these issues, certainly the most prominent is the status of homosexuals in the military. Traditionally, military leaders have maintained that homosexuality is incompatible with military service because it is considered contrary to morale, good order and discipline, and cohesion within units. Congress and the courts have supported this position. Senate Bill 1337 (September 16, 1993) amends Chapter 37 of Title 10 (US Code) to clarify the policy (which has been characterized as "don't ask, don't tell, don't pursue") on issues of gender orientation. The law is clear that homosexual behavior is still forbidden within the military. However, homosexual orientation, per se, is not a reason for dismissal from the service, nor does it prevent entry into the service. So long as a person shows no *propensity to engage in homosexual acts*, does not openly state that he or she is homosexual or bisexual, and does not marry or attempt to marry a person of the same sex, the individual may serve in the military. The law reaffirms that military service is not a constitutional right. It also provides for continuation of a January 1993 policy that suspends questioning about homosexuality as a condition for entry into the military, but allows the Secretary of Defense to resume such questioning as necessary to implement the revised policy on homosexuality.

Very little research has been conducted on this issue. Since law and policy preclude homosexual behavior in the military, service laboratories are reluctant to sponsor research on the subject. At the request of the Congress, the United States General Accounting Office (1992) conducted an analysis summarizing previous research and incorporating findings of their own. The DoD contested the conclusions of the GAO's report, which indicated increasing support for permitting homosexuals in the services. The highly political and controversial nature of this issue will, no doubt, influence the course of research on the topic. Perhaps the most important question—the impact on military effectiveness—remains to be addressed from a scientific perspective.

As more and more interracial marriages occur, racial identity issues are becoming increasingly important in society at large, as well as in the military. The basic questions are how to identify racial categories in an increasingly multiracial society and what the impact of using multiracial (or nonracial) categories will be on various programs used to ensure racial equity in organizational decisions. Although more individuals are asking for a statistical category that reflects blended racial/ethnic background, the laws establish protected groups based on the traditional census categories. This is a very practical issue that should be addressed from a scientific perspective.

Another emerging trend is the "white male backlash" to affirmative action and other programs white males may perceive as discriminatory toward them. As the MEOCS data below indicate (Figure 15.2), servicemembers perceived more "reverse" discrimination as occurring between 1992 and 1995, with a possible reversal of the trend beginning in 1996. (Note that the scale has been abbreviated to better depict the difference in scores. Also note the overall high scores on the 5-point scale, indicating an overall favorable perception.)

While the issues of homosexuality, racial classification, and white male backlash may become more important in the future, other diversity issues are also likely to emerge. We toss two more onto the table: the conflict between individual rights and the need for group cohesion and preparation for dealing with the potential racial/gen-

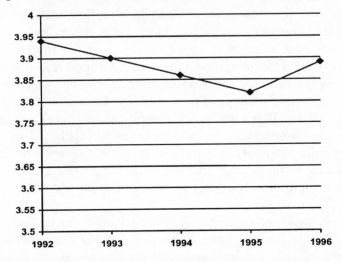

Figure 15.2
Average MEOCS "Reverse" Discrimination Scale Scores, 1992-1996*
(Higher score indicates perception of better climate; all services, a/o 12/96)

Source: Defense Equal Oppurtunity Managment Institute, Patrick AFB, FL.

der/ethnic conflicts in other parts of the world. As the services become more diverse, we can expect more conflicts between individual rights and organizational requirements. For example, as the military recruits more individuals from diverse religious backgrounds, we may see increasing demands for accommodation of particular religious views and practices (i.e., Sabbath observances, clothing requirements, etc.). Issues of religious discrimination may also become of more concern. Finally, as American troops take on more peacekeeping and humanitarian duties, they are likely to be stationed in countries where their primary duties require close contact with people of different racial/ethnic backgrounds and customs. Dealing with such diversity may be a problem for some military members. Therefore, we should research methods to prepare and train servicemembers to face such issues.

As this chapter has demonstrated, the military psychologist has a wide range of diversity issues to research in the military. The field has a rich heritage and challenging future. As long as our services consist of people from across America's diverse population, one has difficulty imagining a time when some issue related to diversity will not be "on the front burner."

Note

1.   Indeed, in the foreword to Dr. Thomas' book, the Technical Director of ARI may
     have presaged this view when he indicated, "Dr. Thomas provides a proven model
     for future research, *should it be needed.*" (emphasis mine)

Glossary

administrative discipline - use of administrative actions, rather than courts-martial or
nonjudicial punishment, to enforce discipline. For example, individuals who violate
rules may be discharged from the service, reassigned, or subjected to other administrative actions.

behavioral change - modification of individuals' behaviors to meet institutional standards, irrespective of whether the individuals' attitudes or values are modified. For
example, the military's main focus in deterring racism is to ensure that all members
behave in a non-racist manner, regardless of their personal *attitudes* toward other races.
Certainly, attitude change is desirable and may be a product of behavioral change, but
the goal is to have *behaviors* meet the standard.

cultural assimilation model - a training model designed tc increase intercultural sensitivity by using simulation, role play, computer-based training, or other techniques to allow
members of one group (e.g., the dominant group) to gain insight into the behavior,
motivations, cultural meanings, etc., of another group (e.g., the nondominant group).
For example, a white drill sergeant may respond to a scenario depicting interactions
involving black soldiers by selecting (from a list) a description of the most likely
meaning of the black soldiers' behavior. If the drill sergeant fails to select the culturally
sensitive alternative, an explanation is provided and the sergeant is allowed to choose
another alternative. This continues until the preferred alternative is selected. The preferred alternative is accompanied by an explanation as to why it is preferred.

cultural diversity - a term used to indicate differences among individuals in cultural
background, or sometimes to indicate the statistical level of such differences (as in
"cultural diversity is high in the Army"). Though the term may be used expansively to
include myriad differences (e.g., regional, educational), in the military it is generally
applied to differences based on race, national origin (or ethnicity), color, gender, religion, disability, and/or age.

discrimination - in general, the act of distinguishing differences; in diversity issues, this
term usually indicates actions or policies that have a differential adverse impact on one
group (or more) as compared to others.

disparity - statistical inequity between compared groups in the rate of some action (either
positive or negative) affecting both groups. Typically, when diversity issues are considered, disparity indicates the rate of occurrence for one group (e.g., percentage of black
soldiers who are incarcerated) is statistically different from the rate for another group (e.g.,
percentage of white soldiers who are incarcerated). Since disparity may occur for many
reasons, it does not necessarily indicate illegal discrimination has occurred, though the
presence of a disparity may lead to a determination of whether discrimination has occurred.

gender-stereotyped jobs - jobs that have historically been considered by society (or some
reference group) to be more appropriate for one gender or the other. For example, *nurse*
and *secretary* have traditionally been considered jobs that are more appropriate for
women, while *firefighter* (usually called fire*man*) and *infantry soldier* (i.e., infantry-
man) have been considered more appropriate for men.

inoculation approach - when applied to military discipline issues, a method of discourag-
ing individuals (usually recruits) from engaging in actions that may result in their being
disciplined by educating them in advance as to the rules of behavior and allowing them

to experience vicarious examples of discipline-generating interactions in a "safe" (e.g., training) environment. By experiencing the troublesome interactions in a mild form (such as a video presentation, role play, etc.), individuals might learn to avoid behaviors that would result in punishment.

institutional discrimination - a form of discrimination in which institutional rules, policies, or practices (whether legal or illegal) have a differential adverse impact (e.g., reduced opportunities for promotion, retention, access to benefits) for one demographic group (or more) as compared to others. For example, restrictions on women entering direct combat specialties may prevent women from obtaining experience that would help them gain promotion to the highest military grades. At this time, such restrictions are required by Congress and are legal, despite possible adverse impact for women.

misnorming - using incorrect information to establish the norms (standards) on standardized tests, such as the Armed Services Vocational Aptitude Battery (ASVAB). The ASVAB was inadvertently misnormed due to statistical errors between 1976-1980. During this time, nearly 360,000 individuals whose test scores would have been too low if the test had been normed properly entered military service.

nonjudicial punishment (NJP) - a form of military discipline that is administered by a commander or other designated authority to punish relatively minor offenses at the option of the offending party in lieu of a court-martial. NJP is intermediate in severity between minor corrective discipline (e.g., extra duty, short-term restriction) and court-martial. NJP does not involve incarceration, but may result in reduction in rank, fines, restriction to base, or extra duty.

organizational effectiveness - a general field of research and practice dealing with how to improve the management, communications, job, and human resources climates in organizations in order to make them more effective in accomplishing their goals; also used to indicate the degree to which such effectiveness has been obtained (e.g., "the 33rd Fighter Squadron demonstrates a high degree of organizational effectiveness).

racial separatism - a desire to have separate activities, facilities, etc., for different races. For example, where this desire is high one may see people separating themselves by racial groups in dining facilities, clubs, etc., on military installations. On college campuses, this may be reflected in the desire for separate dormitories and student centers for different racial groups.

sexual harassment - a form of gender discrimination in which the victim is subjected to unwelcome behaviors of a sexual nature. There are two basic types: quid pro quo, in which sexual favors are demanded in return for some job benefit (such as retention, promotion, etc.), and hostile environment, in which sexually related behaviors establish an environment that is hostile, intimidating, or offensive or interferes with a person's work.

References

Albright, R. R., & McIntyre, R. M. (1995). *Measuring equal opportunity climate in small units: Development of scales to evaluate the acceptance of diversity* (DEOMI RSP 95-10). Patrick Air Force Base, FL: Defense Equal Opportunity Management Institute.

Baisden, A. G. (1992). Gender and performance in naval aviation training. *Proceedings, Psychology in the Department of Defense 13th Symposium* (pp. 217-220). Colorado Springs, CO: USAF Academy.

Bastian, L. D., Lancaster, A. R., & Reyst, H. E. (1996). *Department of Defense 1995 sexual harassment survey.* Arlington, VA: Defense Manpower Data Center.

Bauer, R. G., Stout, R. L., & Holz, R. F. (1976). *Predicting military delinquency* (Research Problem Review 76-4). Alexandria, VA: U.S. Army Research Institute for the Behavioral and Social Sciences.

Bell, D. B., & Holz, R. F. (1975). *Summary of ARI research on military delinquency* (Research Report 1185). Alexandria, VA: U.S. Army Research Institute for the Behavioral and Social Sciences.

Binkin, M., & Bach, S. J. (1977). *Women and the military.* Washington, DC: The Brookings Institution.

Binkin, M., & Eitelberg, M. J. (1982). *Blacks and the military.* Washington, DC: The Brookings Institution.

Culbertson, A. L., & Magnusson, P. (1992). *An investigation into equity in Navy discipline* (TR-92-17). San Diego, CA: Navy Personnel Research and Development Center.

Culbertson, A. L., & Rosenfeld, P. (1993). Understanding sexual harassment through organizational surveys. In P. Rosenfeld, J. E. Edwards, and M. D. Thomas (Eds.), *Improving Organizational Surveys* (pp. 164-187). Newbury Park, CA: Sage.

Culbertson, A. L., & Rosenfeld, P. (1994). Assessment of sexual harassment in the active-duty Navy. *Military Psychology, 6,* 69-93.

Dansby, M. R. (1989). Military retention by gender, racial/ethnic group, and personnel category. *Proceedings, 31st Annual Conference of the Military Testing Association* (pp. 744-749). San Antonio, TX: Flamingo.

Dansby, M. R. (1992). *Racial disparities in military incarceration rates: An overview and research strategy* (DEOMI RSP 92-3). Patrick Air Force Base, FL: Defense Equal Opportunity Management Institute.

Dansby, M. R. (1994a, December). The Military Equal Opportunity Climate Survey (MEOCS). Presentation to the Equal Opportunity Research Symposium, Cocoa Beach, FL.

Dansby, M. R. (1994b). Revising the MEOCS: A methodology for updating the Military Equal Opportunity Climate Survey. *Proceedings, Applied Behavioral Sciences 14th Symposium* (pp. 59-64). Colorado Springs, CO: USAF Academy.

Dansby, M. R. (1995). *Using Military Equal Opportunity Climate Surveys for organizational development* (DEOMI RSP 95-11). Patrick Air Force Base, FL: Defense Equal Opportunity Management Institute.

Dansby, M. R. (1996). The Senior Leader Equal Opportunity Climate Survey: What do the bosses believe? *Proceedings, Applied Behavioral Sciences 15th Symposium* (pp. 310-316). Colorado Springs, CO: USAF Academy.

Dansby, M. R., & Landis, D. (1991). Measuring equal opportunity climate in the military environment. *International Journal of Intercultural Relations, 15,* 389-405.

Dansby, M. R., & Landis, D. (1996). Intercultural training in the military. In D. Landis & R. S. Bhagat (Eds.), *Handbook of Intercultural Training, Second Edition* (pp. 203-215). Thousand Oaks, CA: Sage.

Dansby, M. R., & Landis, D. (in process). Race, gender, and representation index as predictors of equal opportunity climate in military organizations. *Journal of Military Psychology.*

Day, H. R. (1983). Race relations training in the U.S. military. In Landis, D., & Brislin, R. W. (Eds.), *Handbook of intercultural training (volume II): Issues in training methodology* (pp. 241-289). New York: Pergamon Press.

DEOMI. (1996). *Semi-annual race/ethnic/gender profile of the Department of Defense forces (active and reserve), the United States Coast Guard, and Department of Defense civilians* (DEOMI SSP 96-4). Patrick Air Force Base, FL: Defense Equal Opportunity Management Institute.

Dunivin, K. O. (1990). Gender identity among Air Force female aviators. *Proceedings, Psychology in the Department of Defense 12th Symposium* (pp. 71-76). Colorado Springs, CO: USAF Academy.

Eisaguirre, L. (1993). *Sexual harassment: A reference handbook.* Denver, CO: ABC - CLIO.

Eitelberg, M. J. (1988). *Manpower for military occupations.* Alexandria, VA: Human Resources Research Organization.

Eitelberg, M. J., Laurence, J. H., & Waters, L. S. (1984*). Screening for service: Aptitude and education criteria for military entry.* Alexandria, VA: Human Resources Research Organization.

Fain, T. C., & Anderton, D. L. (1987). Sexual harassment: Organizational context and diffuse status. *Sex Roles, 5,* 291-311.

Farley, L. (1978). *Sexual shakedown.* New York: McGraw-Hill.

Firestone, J. M., & Stewart, J. B. (1995). Trends in gender and racial equity in retention and promotion of officers. *Proceedings: Equal Opportunity Research Symposium* (pp. 43-49). Patrick Air Force Base, FL: Defense Equal Opportunity Management Institute.

Flyer, E. (1990). *Characteristics and behavior of recruits entering military service with an offense history.* Arlington, VA: Defense Manpower Data Center.

Flyer, E. (1993, August). Inservice criminal behavior: Another measure of adjustment to military life. Paper presented at the 101st Annual Convention of the American Psychological Association, Toronto, Canada.

Flyer, E., & Curran, C. (1993, August). Relationships between preservice offense histories and unsuitability discharge. Paper presented at the 101st Annual Convention of the American Psychological Association, Toronto, Canada.

Goldman, J. L. (1995). *The issue is . . . sexual harassment* (DEOMI STSP 95-1). Patrick Air Force Base, FL: Defense Equal Opportunity Management Institute.

Greene, E. L., & Culbertson, A. L. (1995). Officer fitness report ratings: Using quantitative and qualitative methods to examine potential bias. *Proceedings: Equal Opportunity Research Symposium* (pp. 31-41). Patrick Air Force Base, FL: Defense Equal Opportunity Management Institute.

Hendricks, W. H., & Gibson, G. S. (1992). Gender differences: Stress effects on general well-being and absenteeism. *Proceedings, Psychology in the Department of Defense 13th Symposium* (pp. 202-206). Colorado Springs, CO: USAF Academy.

Holm, J. (1992). *Women in the military: An unfinished revolution.* Novato, CA: Presidio.

Hope, R. O. (1979). *Racial strife in the U.S. military: Toward the elimination of discrimination.* New York: Praeger.

Johnson, J. L. (1995). *A preliminary investigation into DEOMI training effectiveness* (DEOMI RSP 95-8). Patrick Air Force Base, FL: Defense Equal Opportunity Management Institute.

Johnson, J. L. (1996). *Local effects and global impact of DEOMI training* (DEOMI RSP 96-7). Patrick Air Force Base, FL: Defense Equal Opportunity Management Institute.

King, R. E., McGlohn, S. E., & Retzlaff, P. D. (1996). Assessment of psychological factors in female and male United States Air Force pilots. *Proceedings, Applied Behavioral Sciences 15th Symposium* (pp. 1-5). Colorado Springs, CO: USAF Academy.

Knouse, S. B. (1993). *Differences between black and white military offenders: A study of socioeconomic, familial, personality, and military characteristics of inmates at the United States Disciplinary Barracks at Fort Leavenworth* (DEOMI RSP 93-2). Patrick Air Force Base, FL: Defense Equal Opportunity Management Institute.

Knouse, S. B. (1994a). *Preliminary development of the military socialization inoculator: A means of reducing discipline problems by early socialization into appropriate military behaviors* (DEOMI RSP 94-9). Patrick Air Force Base, FL: Defense Equal Opportunity Management Institute.

Knouse, S. B. (1994b). *Equal opportunity climate and Total Quality Management: A preliminary study* (DEOMI RSP 94-3). Patrick Air Force Base, FL: Defense Equal Opportunity Management Institute.

Knouse, S. B. (1996a). *Recent diversity research at the Defense Equal Opportunity Management Institute (DEOMI): 1992-1996* (DEOMI RSP 96-14). Patrick Air Force Base, FL: Defense Equal Opportunity Management Institute.

Knouse, S. B. (1996b). *Diversity, organizational factors, group effectiveness, and total quality: An analysis of relationships in the MEOCS-EEO test version 3.1* (DEOMI RSP 96-6). Patrick Air Force Base, FL: Defense Equal Opportunity Management Institute.

Knouse, S. B., & Dansby, M. R. (1994). The organizational socialization inoculator. *Proceedings of the Southwest Decision Sciences Institute, 25*, 35-39.

Landis, D., & Dansby, M. R. (1994). *Race and the military justice system: Design for a program of action research* (DEOMI RSP 94-3). Patrick Air Force Base, FL: Defense Equal Opportunity Management Institute.

Landis, D., Dansby, M. R., & Faley, R. H. (1993). The Military Equal Opportunity Climate Survey: An example of surveying in organizations. In P. Rosenfeld, J. E. Edwards, and M. D. Thomas (Eds.), *Improving Organizational Surveys.* (pp. 210-239). Newbury Park, CA: Sage.

Landis, D., Dansby, M. R., & Faley, R. H. (1994). The relationship of equal opportunity climate to military career commitment: An analysis of individual differences using latent variables. *Proceedings, Applied Behavioral Sciences 14th Symposium* (pp. 65-70). Colorado Springs, CO: USAF Academy.

Landis, D., Dansby, M. R., & Tallarigo, R. S. (1996). The use of equal opportunity climate in intercultural training. In D. Landis & R. S. Bhagat (Eds.), *Handbook of Intercultural Training, Second Edition* (pp. 244-263). Thousand Oaks, CA: Sage.

MacGregor, M. J. (1981). *Integration of the Armed Forces, 1940-1965.* Washington, DC: Center of Military History, United States Army.

MacKinnon, C. (1979). *Sexual harassment of working women.* New Haven, CT: Yale University.

Martindale, M. (1990). *Sexual harassment in the military: 1988.* Arlington, VA: Defense Manpower Data Center.

Matthews, M. D. (1992). Women in the military: Comparison of attitudes and knowledge of service academy cadets versus private college students. *Proceedings, Psychology in the Department of Defense 13th Symposium* (pp. 212-216). Colorado Springs, CO: USAF Academy.

Matthews, M. D., & Weaver, C. N. (1990). Demographic and attitudinal correlates of women's role in the military. *Proceedings, Psychology in the Department of Defense 12th Symposium* (pp. 77-81). Colorado Springs, CO: USAF Academy.

McIntyre, R. M. (1995). *Examination of the psychometric properties of the Senior Leader Equal Opportunity Climate Survey: Equal opportunity perceptions* (DEOMI RSP 95-6). Patrick Air Force Base, FL: Defense Equal Opportunity Management Institute.

McIntyre, R. M., Albright, R. R., & Dansby, M. R. (1996). *The development and construct validation of the Small Unit Equal Opportunity Climate Survey* (DEOMI RSP 96-8). Patrick Air Force Base, FL: Defense Equal Opportunity Management Institute.

Moskos, C. C., & Butler, J. S. (1996*). All that we can be: Black leadership and racial integration in the Army.* New York: Basic Books.

Nalty, B. C. (1986). *Strength for the fight: A history of black Americans in the military.* New York: The Free Press.

Newell, C. E., Rosenfeld, P., & Culbertson, A. L. (1995). Sexual harassment experiences and equal opportunity perceptions of Navy women. *Sex Roles, 32*, 159-168.

Niebuhr, R. E. (1994a). *Measuring equal opportunity climate in organizations: Development of scales to evaluate the acceptance of diversity* (DEOMI RSP 94-5). Patrick Air Force Base, FL: Defense Equal Opportunity Management Institute.

Niebuhr, R. E. (1994b). *The relationship between organizational characteristics and sexual harassment.* Patrick Air Force Base, FL: Defense Equal Opportunity Management Institute.

Niebuhr, R. E. (1997). Sexual harassment in the military. In W. O'Donohue (Ed.), *Sexual harassment: Theory, research, and treatment*. Boston: Allyn & Bacon.

Niebuhr, R. E., & Oswald, S. L. (1992a). The impact of workgroup composition and other work unit/victim characteristics on perceptions of sexual harassment. *Applied H. R. M. Research, 3*, 30-47.

Niebuhr, R. E., & Oswald, S. L. (1992b, April). The influence of workgroup composition on sexual harassment among military personnel. Paper presented at the Psychology in the Department of Defense 13th Symposium, Colorado Springs, CO.

Niebuhr, R. E., Knouse, S. B., & Dansby, M. R. (1994). *Workgroup climates for acceptance of diversity: Relationship to group cohesiveness and performance* (DEOMI RSP 94-4). Patrick Air Force Base, FL: Defense Equal Opportunity Management Institute.

Niebuhr, R. E., Knouse, S. B., Dansby, M. R., & Niebuhr, K. E. (1996). The relationship between racism/sexism and group cohesiveness and performance. *Proceedings, Applied Behavioral Sciences 15th Symposium* (pp. 322-327). Colorado Springs, CO: USAF Academy.

Nieva, V. F. (1991). *Youth Attitude Tracking Study: Propensity report (final)*. Rockville, MD: Westat, Inc.

Nordlie, P. G., Sevilla, E. R., Edmonds, W. S., & White, S. J. (1979). *A study of racial factors in the Army's justice and discharge system*. McLean, VA: Human Sciences Research.

Pryor, J. B. (1985). The lay person's understanding of sexual harassment. *Sex Roles, 13*, 273-286.

Ramsberger, P. F. (1993). *Influences on the military enlistment decision-making process: Findings from the 1991 Youth Attitude Tracking Study* (DMDC 93-004). Arlington, VA: Defense Manpower Data Center.

Rosenfeld, P., & Culbertson, A. L. (1993, August). Assessing equal opportunity climate: Integrating Navy-wide and command-level approaches. Paper presented at the 101st Annual Convention of the American Psychological Association, Toronto, Canada.

Rosenfeld, P., & Edwards, J. E. (1994, September). Automated system assesses equal opportunity. *Personnel Journal*, 99-101.

Rosenfeld, P., Culbertson, A. L., Booth-Kewley, S., & Magnusson, P. (1992). *Assessment of equal opportunity climate: Results of the 1989 Navy-wide survey* (NPRDC TR-92-14). San Diego, CA: Navy Personnel Research and Development Center.

Rosenfeld, P., Thomas, M. D., Edwards, J. E., Thomas, P. J., & Thomas, E. D. (1991). Navy research into race, ethnicity, and gender issues: A historical review. *International Journal of Intercultural Relations, 15*, 407-426.

Schissel, B. L. (1990). Factors affecting career decisions of Air Force female aviators. *Proceedings, Psychology in the Department of Defense 12th Symposium* (pp. 162-166). Colorado Springs, CO: USAF Academy.

Segal, D. R., & Bachman, J. G. (1994). Change in the all-volunteer force: Reflections in youth attitudes. In Eitelberg, M. J., & Mehay, S. J. (Eds.), *Marching toward the 21st century: Military manpower and recruiting* (pp. 149-166). Westport, CT: Greenwood.

Sellman, W. S., & Valentine, L. D. (1981, August). Aptitude testing, enlistment standards, and recruit quality. Paper presented at the 89th Annual Convention of the American Psychological Association, Los Angeles, CA.

Shields, P. M. (1988). Sex roles in the military. In Moskos, C. C., & Wood, F. R., *The military: More than just a job?* (pp. 99-113). New York: Pergamon-Brassey's.

Smither, R. D., & Houston, M. R. (1991). Racial discrimination and forms of redress in the military. *International Journal of Intercultural Relations, 15*, 459-468.

St. Pierre, M. (1991). Accession and retention of minorities: Implications for the future. *International Journal of Intercultural Relations, 15*, 469-489.

Stokan, L. A., & Hah, S. (1996). Psychological androgyny and its relationship to leadership grades of cadets at the United States Military Academy. *Proceedings, Applied Behavioral Sciences 15ᵗʰ Symposium* (pp. 97-102). Colorado Springs, CO: USAF Academy.

Tallarigo, R. S., & Landis, D. (1995). *Organizational distance scaling: Exploring climates across organizations* (DEOMI RSP 95-13). Patrick Air Force Base, FL: Defense Equal Opportunity Management Institute.

Thomas, J. A. (1988). *Race relations research in the U.S. Army in the 1970s: A collection of selected readings.* Alexandria, VA: U.S. Army Research Institute for the Behavioral and Social Sciences.

Thomas, M. D. (1995). *Gender differences in conceptualizing sexual harassment* (NPRDC TR-95-5). San Diego, CA: Navy Personnel Research and Development Center.

Thomas, P. J., & Le, S. K. (1996). *Sexual harassment in the Marine Corps: Results of a 1994 survey* (NPRDC TN-96-44). San Diego, CA: Navy Personnel Research and Development Center.

Thomas, P. J., & Thomas, M. D. (1992). *Impact of pregnant women and single parents upon Navy personnel systems* (NPRDC TN-92-8). San Diego, CA: Navy Personnel Research and Development Center.

Thomas, P. J., & Thomas, M. D. (1993a). Mothers in uniform. In F. Kaslow (Ed.), *The military family in peace and war.* (pp. 25-47). New York: Springer.

Thomas, P. J., & Thomas, M. D. (1993b). Surveying pregnancy and single parenthood: The Navy experience. In P. Rosenfeld, J. E. Edwards, and M. D. Thomas (Eds.), *Improving Organizational Surveys.* (pp. 145-163). Newbury Park, CA: Sage.

Thomas, P. J., Holmes, B. L., & Carroll, L. (1983). *Gender differences in the evaluations of narratives in officer performance ratings* (NPRDC TR 83-14). San Diego, CA: Navy Personnel Research and Development Center.

Thomas, P. J., Thomas, M. D., & Robertson, P. (1993). *Absences of Navy enlisted personnel: A search for gender differences* (NPRDC TN-93-3). San Diego, CA: Navy Personnel Research and Development Center.

Thomas, R. R. (1991). *Beyond race and gender.* New York: AMACOM.

United States General Accounting Office. (1993). *DoD's policy on homosexuality: Report to Congressional requesters on defense force management* (GAO/NSIAD-92-98). Washington, DC: United States General Accounting Office.

U.S. Merit Systems Protection Board. (1981). *Sexual harassment in the federal workplace: Is it a problem?* Washington, DC: U.S. Government Printing Office.

U.S. Merit Systems Protection Board. (1988). *Sexual harassment in the federal government: An update.* Washington, DC: U.S. Government Printing Office.

Verdugo, N. (1994, December). Research on the Army's criminal justice system. Presentation to the Equal Opportunity Research Symposium, Cocoa Beach, FL.

Walker, M. R. (1992). *An analysis of discipline rates among racial/ethnic groups in the U.S. military: Fiscal years 1987-1991* (DEOMI RSP 92-4). Patrick Air Force Base, FL: Defense Equal Opportunity Management Institute.

16

Occupational Segregation: Comparing the Civilian and Military Work Force

Juanita M. Firestone

Introduction

If the labor force were completely integrated by sex, the percentage of men and women in each occupation would equal their representation in the labor force. As one sex increased or decreased in proportion in the labor force relative to the other, percentages of that sex in a given occupation would increase or decrease proportionately. Sex segregation exists when men and women are not representatively distributed across occupations.

This article compares the differential location of women and men across occupations in the civilian labor force to the distribution of women and men in military occupations. The data reported suggest that segregation of occupations by sex remains in both the civilian and military work force.

Occupational Segregation

In spite of dramatic increases of women into the labor market during this century, differences in the occupational distribution of men and women remain. Women are disproportionately overrepresented in clerical and service jobs, while men are much more likely to be in management, executive, and blue-collar (especially skilled production), positions (Openheimer, 1970; Blau and Ferber, 1986). Some recent works suggest that the extent of the segregation of men and women in different occupations is declining, although, overall, the occupational structure in the United States remains highly segregated (Beller, 1984). Beller describes a decline in occupational segregation during the 1970s, reporting that three out of five workers of one sex would have to change occupations to make the sex distribution of most jobs comparable. The decline noted appears concentrated in male professional and managerial jobs and among younger cohorts of women (Beller, 1984).

Occupational segregation is not confined to broad occupational classifications, but continues within each occupational category. For example, among professional and technical workers, women are more likely to be elementary school teachers and nurses, while men are more likely to be physicians and lawyers (Bibb & Form, 1977). Furthermore, vertical segregation exists within similar classifications. The distribution of full-time university faculties, where women comprise about 50 percent of non-tenure-track positions (lecturers and instructors), 36 percent of assistant professors, 21 percent of associate professors, and only about 10 percent of full professors, provides a good illustration (Blau & Ferber, 1986).

Considerable controversy exists concerning whether the causes of occupational segregation are voluntary choices of individuals or result from discrimination within the labor market. For example, neoclassical human capital theorists argue that women generally anticipate shorter and less continuous employment than do men, and therefore their best interest is served by "choosing" occupations that presumably require less human capital investments (education, on-the-job training, geographical mobility, etc.) and have lower wage penalties for discontinuous participation, part-time or more flexible work schedules (Becker, 1964; Polachek, 1981). Most research does not support this contention. Conclusions drawn from recent empirical tests of this hypothesis indicate that women's earnings do not show lower rates of depreciation or appreciation in female than in male occupations (England, 1982). Rather, females earned less in female jobs at all levels of experience, suggesting that women cannot maximize lifetime earnings by choosing female occupations (England, 1982).

Support for structural discrimination within the labor market also exists. Analyses report that as the percentage of female workers in an occupation increases, all else being equal, earnings decrease (England, 1982; Jusenius, 1977; Stevenson, 1975). Blau (1984) reports that 76 percent of the unexplained pay gap between men and women in the United States was due to sex differences in distribution among occupational categories within a firm. Women are also more likely than men to be concentrated in smaller, peripheral organizations and less stable industrial sectors (Hodson, 1983; Rosenfeld, 1983).

Women in the U.S. Military

In contrast to civilian jobs, where sex-based occupational segregation is the rule, women in the military perfom the same overall duties as men and compete for jobs and ranks within the military as soldiers rather than women. A key difference between the roles of women in civilian organizations and those in the military exists: military roles are decreed by federal statute and military policies. Thus, the same laws that increase the number of women in the military can also be used to define their roles within its structure. At present, the only jobs closed to women based on those constraints are direct combat roles, and a few direct combat-support roles. Furthermore, all service branches currently use the "risk rule'" based on likelihood of geographical jeopardy during war regardless of the mission (combat or not) of the job.

The establishment of the All-Volunteer Force (AVF) was an important factor in dramatically increasing the numbers of women in the U.S. military and expanding their roles in unprecedented ways. Women comprise approximately 11 percent of the active-duty Department of Defense forces and 12 percent of the reserve forces, for an 11 percent proportion of the total force (although this varies by service), and it seems unlikely that participation will return to earlier force levels (previous to AVF) of 2 percent or less. Women have, of course, served in the military in the past, although for the most part this was in response to the exigencies of war: women were needed to fill traditionally female-typed jobs (secretary, typist, clerk, etc.) and thus release men for battle. Women who join the AVF, on the other hand, are responding to decisions about employment. The types of jobs women perform have also expanded to include such traditionally male domains as combat-support positions. A few women even hold combat occupational specialty codes as instructors in combat skill areas.

Two other conditions impact the distribution of women in military occupational categories relative to their civilian counterparts. First, because pay in the military is based on rank and tenure rather than occupation or individual characteristic, (i.e., race, sex), women receive equal pay to that of men of comparable rank. Minor exceptions exist, but for the most part, a male master sergeant supply custodian and a female master sergeant computer specialist draw the same pay if they have equal years of service. Second, women are very nearly comparably represented across officer and enlisted categories, unlike their underrepresentation in management and executive categories in the civilian work force (Department of Defense, 1989).

In spite of these recent changes, evidence persists that the institutional role of soldier remains stereotyped as male, and that the utilization of women in the military remains largely based on the conventional definition of women's work in American society (Holm, 1982; Steihm, 1982; Shields, 1988).

Data Sources

The military data were compiled from all active-duty military member records collected and stored at the Defense Manpower Data Management Center (DMDC) on a quarterly basis. DMDC organized the data to reflect the occupational category of all active-duty personnel by sex and ethnicity and provided the results to the Defense Equal Opportunity Management Institute for analysis. Figures provided represent the entire active-duty enlisted and officer population of the Army, Navy, Marine Corps, and Air Force as of March 1989.

The civilian data are taken from a representative sample of individuals from the 1988 General Social Survey. Data from only the 1988 sample were used, although this limited the total civilian sample size (N = 249), because structural differences in the labor force of previous years could cause their inclusion to render the civilian sample incomparable with the cross-sectional military data. Each survey is an independently drawn sample of noninstitutionalized, English-speaking persons 18 years of age or over. For purposes of this analysis, only respondents employed full-time are included. Data used in the analysis were weighted to correct for oversampling of minorities

Methods

The differential location of women and men in the labor market can be typically referred to as occupational segregation, and is measured by an index developed by Duncan and Duncan (1955). The occupational segregation index indicates the percentage of women, or men, who would have to change jobs in order to duplicate the distribution of the other group. The index would be equal to zero if the proportion of men and women in an occupation were representative of their distribution in the labor force as a whole, and would equal 100 if the occupation were completely segregated.

The index is calculated by the following formula:

$$s = \tfrac{1}{2} \, S \, |m_i - f_i|$$

where m_i = the percentage of the male labor force employed in occupation and i and f_i = the percentage of the female labor force employed in occupation i. Occupational segregation indices are calculated across civilian and military occupations, and comparable groups are contrasted. Initial calculation of the occupational segregation index for the civilian sample uses the U.S. Census Bureau Industrial Classification Codes.

Occupations for the civilian sample were then reclassified using the U.S. Census Bureau three-digit number code. The *Occupational Conversion Manual – Enlisted/Officer/Civilian* (Department of Defense, 1987) was used to create comparable categories for the civilian sample and the military population. The military classification system was used as the base and civilian job classifications were recoded to match the military categories. Only officer DoD Occupation Codes I (General Officers and Executives) and 3 (Intelligence Officers) did not have comparable civilian census job codes. All categories were used to create the segregation index across occupations, because all military categories are considered full-time military employees. Specific comparisons were not affected as individuals in either of the above categories were not compared.

In addition, structural differences between enlisted and officer cohorts in the military render each analytically distinct, therefore each cohort must be analyzed separately. The primary basis for this distinction is level of education: enlisted personnel are not required to have completed a baccalaureate degree (B.A.) or equivalent, while officers generally must have at least a baccalaureate degree or equivalent. Therefore, the civilian sample was divided into two groups based on education level. The civilian subsample with less than a B.A. is compared to the enlisted cohort, and those with at least a B.A. are compared to the officer cohort.

Findings

Table 16.1 indicates that for the civilian sample with at least a B.A. or equivalent, 58 percent of either men or women workers would have to change occupations to achieve an equitable distribution of men and women across occupations, and 50 percent of those with less than a B.A. degree or the equivalent would have to change occupations. Furthermore, data reported in Table 16.1 suggest that 47 percent of the DoD officer corps and 35 percent of the DoD enlisted force would have to change occupations for the distribution of men and women to approach equality. Put simply, this means that 47 percent of male officers in the DoD would have to change occupations for the distribution of males across occupations to match that of females, or vice versa. This suggests that, while military occupational categories are still segregated based on sex, the distribution of men and women across categories is more equitable than that in the civilian work force.

When the results are compared across services, differences emerge among the various branches. Overall differences are not large; however, they present interesting patterns. The occupational segregation index for Army officers is 44.03 and for Army enlisted personnel, 39.8 (see Table 16.2); for Navy officers the index is 63.69 and for Navy enlisted, 28.45 (see Table 16.3); for Marine Corp officers the index is 49 and for Marine enlisted, 37.1 (see Table 16.4); for Air Force officers the index is 39.29 and for Air Force enlisted, 35.45 (see Table 16.5). This reflects both the fact that women are excluded from most combat occupational categories by a combination of federal law and service policies and that they are still concentrated in the medical categories for officers in all services. Because combat jobs are almost exclusively held by men, those services where combat assignments are a high priority should reflect more occupational segregation. The Army and Marine Corps have the highest levels of occupational segregation by sex among the enlisted force. This reflects the high proportion of combat-related jobs in these services, as well as the fact that the Marines have no individuals in medical/dental occupational categories, as Navy medical facilities and personnel are used by the Marine Corps. The latter is also reflective of the low proportion of women in the Marine Corps, especially among officers. Women comprise only 5 percent of Marine enlisted and 3.4 percent of Marine officers (Department of Defense, 1989) The Navy

Table 16.1
Occupational Distributions of Civilian and Military Labor Forces

Occupational Category	Civilian						Military					
	Degree			No Degree			Officer			Enlisted		
	% of Males	% of Females	Absolute Difference	% of Males	% of Females	Absolute Difference	% of Males	% of Females	Absolute Difference	% of Males	% of Females	Absolute Difference
0	--	--	--	--	--	--	--	--	--	18.6	3.9	14.7
1	24.2	20.0	4.2	7.4	3.6	3.8	0.6	0.1	0.5	10.5	5.8	4.7
2	45.5	6.7	38.8	14.8	3.6	11.2	46.0	8.0	38.0	9.4	10.9	1.5
3	12.1	6.7	5.4	--	--	--	4.0	6.0	2.0	4.7	13.4	8.7
4	6.1	40.0	33.9	0.0	14.3	14.3	14.0	11.0	3.0	2.4	2.3	0.1
5	3.0	6.7	3.7	7.4	10.7	3.3	5.0	4.0	1.0	13.1	35.6	22.5
6	0.0	20.0	20.0	3.7	32.1	28.4	11.0	42.0	31.0	21.9	8.4	13.5
7	6.1	0.0	6.1	29.6	7.1	22.5	6.0	19.0	13.0	4.3	1.9	2.4
0	--	--	--	3.7	0.0	3.7	10.0	8.0	2.0	9.0	9.6	0.6
9	--	--	--	--	--	--	5.0	1.0	4.0	6.1	8.1	2.0
10	--	--	--	3.7	0.0	3.7	--	--	--	--	--	--
11	--	--	--	22.2	25.2	3.0	--	--	--	--	--	--
12	3.0	0.0	3.0	7.4	3.6	3.8	--	--	--	--	--	--
Totals	100.0	100.1	115.1	99.9	100.2	97.7	101.6	99.1	94.5	100.0	99.9	70.7
S^a			115.1/2 = 57.5			97.7/2 = 48.85			94.5/2 = 47.25			70.7/2 = 35.35

Note: Dashes in cells indicate that the given occupational category is not an option for that group of individuals.

[a]S = Occupational Segregation Index

and the Air Force have the least occupational segregation with respect to the enlisted force. The Army and the Air Force have the highest proportion of women of all services. The proportion of Army enlisted who are women is 11.1 percent and of Army officers who are women is 11.1 percent, while the proportions for the Air Force are 13.4 percent and 12.5 percent respectively. These findings are consistent with the traditional military roles (especially combat roles) associated with the Army, and Marine Corps, and the more highly technical occupational structures of the Navy and the Air Force.

The Air Force is also unique in that most of its combat positions are held by officers rather than enlisted personnel. This is reflected in the relatively high occupational segregation index for Air Force officers compared to that for enlisted members. The relatively high segregation for Navy officers may reflect the importance of combat ship duty for career advancement.

The relatively equitable distribution of men and women across Army occupations, in spite of high proportions of combat jobs, may

Table 16.2
Occupational Distributions of Army Personnel

	Officer			Enlisted		
Occupational Category	% of Males	% of Females	Absolute Difference	% of Males	% of Females	Absolute Difference
0		-	-	30.80	2.60	28.20
1	0.04	0.00	0.04	4.60	2.90	1.70
2	48.00	7.00	41.00	12.40	12.30	0.10
3	6.00	7.00	1.00	5.40	15.90	10.50
4	13.00	12.00	1.00	2.70	2.30	0.40
5	5.00	2.00	3.00	12.50	38.00	25.50
6	14.00	44.00	30.00	15.30	6.90	8.40
7	6.00	13.00	7.00	2.00	0.80	1.20
8	9.00	14.00	5.00	12.20	12.80	0.60
9	0.02	0.00	0.02	2.30	5.30	3.00
Totals	101.06	99.00	88.06	100.20	99.80	79.60
S^a	88.06 / 2 = 44.03			79.60 / 2 = 39.80		

Note: Dashes in cells indicate that the given occupational category is not an option for that group of individuals.
[a]S = Occupational Segregation Index

Table 16.3
Occupational Distributions of Navy Personnel

	Officer			Enlisted		
Occu-pational Category	% of Males	% of Females	Absolute Difference	% of Males	% of Females	Absolute Difference
0	-	-	-	9.60	8.90	0.70
1	0.40	0.03	0.37	16.70	9.60	7.10
2	44.00	4.00	40.00	9.50	13.60	4.10
3	3.00	3.00	0.00	5.30	12.00	6.70
4	12.00	3.00	9.00	0.80	1.60	0.80
5	3.00	4.00	1.00	8.60	23.20	14.70
6	13.00	44.00	31.00	28.50	10.40	18.10
7	3.00	35.00	32.00	6.00	3.40	2.60
8	7.00	4.00	3.00	5.20	5.20	0.00
9	14.00	3.00	11.00	10.00	12.10	2.10
Totals	99.40	100.03	127.37	100.20	100.10	56.90
S^a	127.37 / 2 = 63.69			56.90 / 2 = 28.45		

Note: Dashes in cells indicate that the given occupational category is not an option for that group of individuals.
^aS = Occupational Segregation Index

Table 16.4
Occupational Distributions of Marine Corps Personnel

	Officer			Enlisted		
Occu-pational Category	% of Males	% of Females	Absolute Difference	% of Males	% of Females	Absolute Difference
0	—	—	—	27.30	0.00	27.30
1	4.00	2.00	2.00	6.20	4.50	1.70
2	51.00	4.00	47.00	7.20	10.10	2.90
3	3.00	6.00	3.00	—	—	—
4	10.00	10.00	0.00	2.10	2.70	0.60
5	3.00	5.00	2.00	13.80	42.40	28.60
6	—	—	—	17.00	9.50	7.50
7	7.00	39.00	32.00	2.60	2.00	0.60
8	12.00	21.00	9.00	13.90	15.70	1.80
9	10.00	13.00	3.00	9.90	13.10	3.20
Totals	100.00	100.00	98.00	100.00	100.00	74.20
S^a	98.00 / 2 = 49.00			74.20 / 2 = 37.10		

Note: Dashes in cells indicate that the given occupational category is not an option for that group of individuals.
^aS = Occupational Segregation Index

Table 16.5
Occupational Distributions of Air Force Personnel

	Officer			Enlisted		
Occu-pational Category	% of Males	% of Females	Absolute Difference	% of Males	% of Females	Absolute Difference
0	—	—	—	8.00	2.20	5.80
1	0.40	0.02	0.38	13.60	6.60	7.00
2	43.00	10.00	33.00	5.90	7.40	1.50
3	4.00	6.00	2.00	4.70	13.40	8.70
4	17.00	15.00	2.00	3.80	2.70	1.10
5	7.00	5.00	2.00	18.70	41.30	22.60
6	10.00	41.00	31.00	26.10	8.70	17.40
7	8.00	14.00	6.00	5.80	2.10	3.70
8	8.00	8.00	0.00	8.70	8.40	0.30
9	3.00	.80	2.20	4.60	7.40	2.80
Totals	100.40	99.82	78.58	99.90	100.20	70.90
S^a	78.58 / 2 = 39.29			70.90 / 2 = 35.45		

Note: Dashes in cells indicate that the given occupational category is not an option for that group of individuals.
$^a S$ = Occupational Segregation Index

manifest the high proportion of African-American women in the Army compared to the population in general. African-Ameican women comprise 42.5 percent of all active-duty Army women, while they are only about 11.9 percent of women in the United States (Department of Defense, 1989; U.S. Bureau of the Census, 1990). African-American women are more likely than white women to hold nontraditional jobs in the civilian labor force (Malveaux & Wallace, 1987). If this holds true for the military, occupational segregation should be lower for those services with higher proportions of African American women. Data from Table 16.6 seem to support this contention, as the distribution of African Americans in DoD by sex, across occupational categories, is more equitable than that of the total DoD population. As shown in Table 16.7, the distribution across occupations of African Americans in the Army is also more equitable than that of the total Army force.

The extent of sex segregation in the work place can be seen in greater detail by examining the employment of women and men in specific occupation categories. Table 16.8 shows the concentration of men and women in civilian occupational categories. Table 16.9

summarizes recent employment data available for selected military occupations. The occupations are classified in this table as male-intensive, female-intensive, or neutral according to a conservative 20-point spread around the female (or male) proportion of the work force (Rytina & Bianchi, 1984). This allows room for individual choice in entering occupations, while allowing a comparison of the proportion of men and women in a given occupation. In March 1989, approximately 56 percent of all women were in the civilian labor force (U.S. Bureau of the Census, 1990). Therefore, a male-intensive occupation is one in which 36 percent or less of the work force is female. Female-intensive occupations are defined as those in which 76 percent or more of the work force is female. Those occupations in which 37 percent to 75 percent of the workers are female are classified as sex neutral.

Because women are such a small percentage of the active-duty military force (10.7 percent), using the same 20-point spread would mean that all jobs were at least sex-neutral even if no women worked in them. Keeping in mind that the military as an occupational category is highly male intensive, the proportional representation of women is used as a conservative basis for differentiation between male-intensive and sex-neutral jobs. In other words, jobs with less than a proportional representation of women (10.7 percent) are classified as male-intensive, those with 30.7 percent or more women are female-intensive, and those with between 10.7 percent and 30.6 percent are sex-neutral. Both groups are classified based on the representation of women and men, thus results can be compared, although statistical significance of the differences cannot be assessed.

Results presented in Table 16.8 indicate that for the civilian subsample with less than a B.A. degree, over half (55 percent) of all women were working in female-intensive occupational categories, while only 2.9 percent worked in male-intensive classifications. Almost half (46.9 percent) of the female work force in this group worked in functional support occupations, and another 8.2 percent worked in medical/dental service or support jobs. Only 11.6 percent of men in this group were employed in functional support jobs, and only 1.2 percent in medical/dental service or support occupations. Over one third (36.6 percent) of the men in this group worked in precision production-, craft-, and repair-oriented categories, while only 11.9 percent of the women workers were employed in these job classifications.

Table 16.6
Occupational Distributions of Black DoD Personnel

Occu-pational Category	Officer % of Males	% of Females	Absolute Difference	Enlisted % of Males	% of Females	Absolute Difference
0	—	—	—	17.80	3.70	14.10
1	0.00	0.00	0.00	5.40	3.20	2.20
2	35.30	5.60	29.70	10.00	9.90	0.10
3	3.40	3.70	0.30	6.60	12.60	6.00
4	19.30	14.00	5.30	2.10	1.60	0.50
5	3.60	2.40	1.20	23.20	45.00	21.80
6	8.30	34.10	25.80	14.80	6.00	8.80
7	11.10	23.00	12.10	2.90	1.30	1.60
8	15.20	16.50	1.30	11.70	10.90	0.80
9	3.30	0.60	2.70	5.50	6.20	0.70
Totals	99.50	99.90	78.40	100.00	100.40	56.60
S^a		78.40 / 2 = 39.20			56.60 / 2 = 28.30	

Note: Dashes in cells indicate that the given occupational category is not an option for that group of individuals.
^aS = Occupational Segregation Index

Table 16.7
Occupational Distributions of Black Army Personnel

Occu-pational Category	Officer % of Males	% of Females	Absolute Difference	Enlisted % of Males	% of Females	Absolute Difference
0	—	—	—	27.70	2.30	25.40
1	0.30	0.10	0.20	4.00	2.20	1.80
2	40.00	5.80	34.20	11.90	8.90	3.00
3	4.00	4.30	0.30	6.00	13.60	7.70
4	19.00	15.30	3.70	2.50	1.80	0.70
5	2.30	1.20	1.10	19.00	47.60	28.60
6	9.30	31.60	22.30	12.80	5.90	6.90
7	9.00	18.00	9.00	2.00	0.90	1.10
8	16.10	22.70	6.60	12.30	12.90	0.60
9	0.00	0.00	0.00	2.30	3.60	1.30
Totals	100.00	99.00	77.40	100.50	99.70	77.10
S^a		77.40 / 2 = 38.70			77.10 / 2 = 38.50	

Note: Dashes in cells indicate that the given occupational category is not an option for that group of individuals.
^aS = Occupational Segregation Index

Table 16.8
Concentration of Men and Women In Civilian Occupational Categories

A. Less Than B.A. Degree

Occupation	% of Male Labor Force	% of Female Labor Force	% Female Workers	Type
Electrical/repair	5.0	0.0	0	M
Communications/intelligence	2.1	.5	16	M
Medical/dental	1.2	8. 1	85	F
Technical/allied	2.5	1.4	33	M
Functional support	11.6	46.9	77	F
Electrical/mechanical	7.5	.5	5	M
Crafts	7.1	1.9	19	M
Service/supply	14.1	7.6	32	

B. At Least a B.A. Degree

Occupation	% of Male Labor Force	% of Female Labor Force	% Female Workers	Type
Engineering/maintenance	18.8	1.3	5	M
Scientist/professional	13.9	15.4	46	
Medical/dental	6.9	10.3	53	
Administration	39.6	29.5	37	
Support/procurement	7.9	7.7	43	

Table 16.9
Concentration of Men and Women In Military Occupational Categories

A. Enlisted

Occupation	% of Male Labor Force	% of Female Labor Force	% Female Workers	Type
Electrical/repair	5.9	10.5	6.3	M
Communications/intelligence	10.9	9.4	12.2	
Medical/dental	13.4	4.6	25.6	
Technical/allied	2.3	2.4	10.3	M
Functional support	35.6	13.1	24.7	
Electrical/mechanical	8.4	21.9	4.4	M
Crafts	1.9	4.3	5.1	M
Service/supply	9.6	9.0	11.2	

B. Officers

Occupation	% of Male Labor Force	% of Female Labor Force	% Female Workers	Type
Engineering/maintenance	8.8	13.9	8.8	M
Scientist/professional	3.6	4.6	8.7	M
Medical/dental	11.1	41.8	31.5	F
Administration	19.0	6.2	27.0	
Support/procurement	9.7	8.2	12.6	

All occupations examined for the subsample with at least a B.A. degree were sex-neutral with the exception of engineering, which was male-intensive. Only 1.3 percent of the female workers in this group were classified as engineers, while 18.8 percent of male workers were included in this category. Administrative management, medical, and scientist/professional classifications are gender-neutral in composition. Of course, these broad categories do not give a complete picture. Women managers are employed to a far greater extent at the lower managerial levels than they are in top management positions (O'Neill, 1985). In other words, while the lower levels of management and administrative ranks have become sex-neutral, the upper levels often remain male-intensive (O'Neill, 1985).

Data from Table 16.9 indicate that 36.1 percent of the female active-duty enlisted personnel work in the four sex-neutral occupational categories (communications, medical, functional support and service/supply). The remaining 63.9 percent work in male-intensive categories. Over two-thirds of military men (69.5 percent) work in sex-neutral job categories, while 30.5 percent work in male-intensive categories.

Among the categories examined for the officer corps, one (medical) was classified as female-intensive in composition, while two (engineering and scientists) were classified as male-intensive. About 2 out of 5 female officers (41.8 percent) work in the female-intensive medical occupational category, while only about 1 out of 10 men (11.1 percent) are in this category. Looking at the two sex-neutral categories, we find that 28.7 percent of male officers and 14.4 percent of female officers work in these areas.

Comparing the data from Tables 16.8 and 16.9 demonstrates that the two female-intensive categories for the civilian subsample without B.A. degrees (medical/dental and functional support) are sex-neutral for the enlisted military members. Service/supply jobs were classified as sex-neutral for both the civilian and military groups. Overall, more individuals work in sex neutral occupational categories in the enlisted military force than in the comparable civilian labor force.

In contrast, the civilian group with at least a B.A. degree are more likely than military officers to work in sex-neutral occupational categories. None of the civilian job categories for this group was classified as female intensive, while the medical/dental job category was classified as female-intensive for military officers. Interestingly, although it is classified as male-intensive for both the military and civilian groups, women officers comprise a much higher proportion of individuals in the military's engineering/maintenance category than for the comparable civilian group.

The categories of engineering (officer/civilian with at least a B.A.) and technical/allied skills (enlisted/civilian with less than a B.A.) are particularly interesting because military affirmative action programs currently focus in these areas (see Tables 16.8 and 16.9). The military has instituted programs to increase access to these traditionally white male occupational areas for women and racial minorities for two important reasons. First, more complex military technology requires increasing numbers of engineers and other technical specialists. Second, the military has been unable to compete with civilian salaries for white men in these occupations. Thus, affirmative action and equal economic opportunity programs to increase representation of women (and minorities) in engineering and technical skills benefit both the military and the workers.

Once again, as in the civilian group, looking at broad classification categories can obfuscate existing occupational segregation b), sex. Tables 16.10a and 16.10b report data for specific occupations. For example, 10.3 percent of women officers and only 6.9 percent of male officers are classified in the medical/dental category. Closer inspection of data reported in Table 16.10b reveals, first, that 11.8 percent of women in this classification are physicians, while 38 percent of men in this classification are physicians and second, that 69.4 percent of women in this classification are registered nurses, while only 10.4 percent of men are registered nurses.

Thus 75 percent of military nurses are women, and 8.9 percent of the physicians are women. For the civilian sample, 83 percent of nurses are women, and 20 percent of physicians are women (see Table 16.10a).

The proportionate distribution of women among the military occupations examined is very similar to that in the civilian population. The one exception is air traffic controller, which is male-intensive for the civilian sample but sex-neutral for the military group. Because fewer women are in the military than the civilian work force, a higher proportion of jobs for the enlisted group are classified as sex-neutral. Overall, the occupational distribution of enlisted men and women is far more representative than that of the officer corps. The selection of civilian jobs compared to those of the officer corps shows a similar distribution of men and women also. For both groups, nurses are classified as female-intensive, while engineers, physicians, and pilots are male-intensive.

Table 16.10
Comparison of Sex-Typing of Specific Occupations

A. Civilian

Occupation	% of Male Labor Force	% of Female Labor Force	% Female Workers	Type
Computer specialist	15.4	8.3	29.0	
Engineers *	30.8	4.2	14.0	M
Physicians *	6.2	2.1	20.0	M
Nurses *	3.1	20.8	83.0	F
Health technician	4.6	8.3	58.0	
Health service	1.5	29.2	93.0	F
Engineering technician	15.4	4.2	17.0	M
Pilots *	1.5	-	0.0	M
Air traffic controller	1.5	-	0.0	M
Food service	15.4	20.8	50.0	
Pohce	4.6	11	25.0	M

* Compared to military officers

B. Military

Occupation	% of Male Labor Force	% of Female Labor Force	% Female Workers	Type_
Computer specialist	1.3	2.6	19.1	
Health technician	1.3	2.9	20.5	
Health service	3.8	7.4	18.7	
Engineering technician	22.9	8.4	4.2	M
Air traffic controller	0.6	0.8	14.1	
Food service	2.7	3.0	11.7	
Police	2.6	2.3	8.7	M
Engineer *	2.0	3.3	6.7	M
Physician *	38.0	11.8	8.9	M
Nurse *	10.4	69.4	75.0	F
Pilot	1.9	2.7	7.8	M

* Military officers

Conclusion

A comparison of the distribution of full-time workers across occupations in a representative sample of the 1988 civilian labor force to that of individuals on active duty in all branches of the Armed Services as of March 1989 reveals that although the military as a whole is extremely male-intensive, the proportionate distribution of women and men in the military, across occupational categories, is more representative than the distribution of women and men across civilian occupational categories. This holds true, across services, even for the Army and Marine Corps, which have a high proportion of combat jobs that are closed to women by a combination of U.S. statute and service policies. Of course, an important caveat should be introduced. Suggesting that the military has a more equitable distribution of men and women across occupational categories *compared to the civilian labor force* may be faint praise: the civilian labor force has shown remarkably stable occupational segregation through the past thirty years (Beller, 1984). Furthermore, overall, the military remains a male-intensive occupation.

In the case of the Marine Corps, the equitable distribution may result from the fact that no jobs in the medical/dental categories are available, as Marines use Navy medical/dental facilities. Overall, a high proportion of individuals classified in this category is female, especially among officers. For the Army, this may result from an overrepresentation of African-American women, who appear more likely to enter nontraditional occupations than white women, compared to the population in general.

The distribution of officers across occupations is less representative than that of enlisted personnel, but still more equitable than comparably situated civilian workers. Women officers are few, especially in the higher grades (O4 and above), and tend to be disproportionately located among military nurses (Department of Defense, 1989).

The higher representation of women among military engineers and technical specialists may be indicative of the emphasis on equal opportunity programs and an example of the changes in the work force necessitated by future occupational demands and clanging demographics. Technological change and international competitive pressures will create the need for an increasing number of technical specialists in the civilian work force in the twenty-first century.

Women will be called upon to provide much of this highly trained work force.

Of course, comparing numbers of individuals in various occupational groups is only part of the picture. As mentioned earlier, anecdotal accounts abound documenting that the qualitative experiences of women are distinct from those of men (Schneider & Schneider, 1988; Steihm, 1988). Women's small representation in the military as a whole reinforces these differences. As Steihm (1988, p. 45) notes:

> If promotion or uniform boards are selected without regard to sex, men can count on having a majority (and possibly a monopoly) on those bodies. Women cannot count on automatic representation. They must expect always to operate as a minority and sometimes to be wholly unrepresented.

Implications for Policy

Overall, this analysis suggests that if we use the proportion of men and women in the service as a base, the military is attempting to create a representative distribution of men and women across occupations. The data also suggest the necessity for increasing recruitment of women and for promoting women into high-level non-commissioned officer and officer ranks. If assignments continue to be based, in part, on the sex distribution of members, increasing numbers of women should create a more representative distribution of women and men across occupations. This effect is highlighted by the more equitable distribution of African-American women, who are overrepresented among military women, especially those in the Army, compared to military women in general.

Finally, the higher segregation of women in ranks and services with high proportions of combat-related jobs suggests the importance of combat exclusion policies and utilization of the "risk rule" when determining available positions for women. Excluding women from jobs related to the primary mission of the military seems to reinforce their segregation among the military male majority.

References

Becker, G.S. (1964). Human capital: A theoretical and empirical analysis, with special reference to education. New York: Columbia University Press.

Beller, A.H. (1984). "Trends in occupational segregation by sex and race, 1960-1981," in Sex segregation in the workplace: Trends, explanations, remedies, B.F. Redskin (ed.) Washington, D.C.: National Academy, 11-26.

Bibb, R. & W.H. Form,W.H. (1977). "The effects of industrial, occupational and sex stratification on wages in blue-collar markets," Social Forces 55, 975-96.

Blau, F.D. (1984). "Occupational segregation and labor market discrimination," in Sex Segregation in the Workplace: Trends, Explanations. Remedies, B.F. Redskin, ed. Washington, National Academy, 117-43.

Blau, F.D. & Ferber, M.A. (1986). The economics of women, men, and work. (Englewood Cliffs, NJ: Prentice-Hall, 1986).

Department of Defense (1987). The occupational conversion manual. Washington, D.C.: Department of Defense.

Department of Defense (1989). The quarterly statistical profile of minorities and women in the Department of Defense, armed forces, and the United States Coast Guard. Patrick AFB, FL.: Defense Equal Opportunity Management Institute.

Duncan, O.D. & B. Duncan, B. (1955). "Residential distribution and occupational satisfaction," American Journal of Sociology 60, 493-503.

England, P. (1982). "The failure of human capital theory to explain occupational sex segregation,"' Journal of Human Resources 17, 358-70.

Hodson, R.A. (1983). "Corporate structure and job satisfaction: A focus on employment characteristics," Sociology and Social Research 69, 22-49.

Holm, J. (1982). Women in the military: An unfinished revolution. Novato, CA: Presidio Press.

Jusenius, C.L. (1977). "The influence of work experience, skill requirement, and occupational segregation on women's earnings," Journal of Economics and Business 29, 107-15.

Malveaux, J. & P. Wallace, P. (1987). "Minority women in the workplace," in Working Women: Past, Present, Future, K.S. Koziara, M.H. Moskow, & L.D. Tanner, eds. Washington, D.C.: Bureau of National Affairs, 265-98.

O'Neill, J. (1985). "Role differentiation and the gender gap in wage rates," in Women and Work: An Annual Review, vol. 1, L. Larwood, A.H. Stromberg, & B.A. Guick, eds. Beverly Hills, CA: Sage.

Oppenheimer, V.K. (1970). The female labor force in the United States. Berkeley: University of California Press.

Polachek, S.W. (1981). "Occupational self-selection: A human capital approach to sex differences in occupational structure," Review of Economics and Statistics 63, 60-69.

Rosenfeld, R. (1983). "Sex segregation and sector," American Sociological Review 48, 637-55.

Rytina, N.F. & S.M. Bianchi, S.M. (1984). "Occupational reclassification and changes in distribution by gender," Monthly Labor Review 107, 11-17.

Schneider, D. & Schneider, C.J. (1988). Sound off! American military women speak out. New York: E.P. Dutton.

Shields, P.M. (1988). "Sex roles in the military," in The Military: More Than Just A Job?, C.C. Moskos & F.R. Wood, eds. Washington, D.C.: Pergamon-Brassey's, 99-113.

Steihm, J.H. (1982). "Women. men, and military policy: Is protection necessarily a racket? in Women, Power and Policy. E. Boneparth, ed. New York: Pergamon Press.

Steihm, J.H. (1988). Arms and the enlisted woman. Philadelphia. PA: Temple University Press.

350   **Managing Diversity in the Military**

Stevenson, M.H. (1975). "Relative wages and sex segregation by occupation," in Sex, Discrimination, and the Division of Labor, C.B. Lloyd, ed. New York: Columbia University Press, 175-200.

U.S. Bureau of the Census (1990). Current Population Reports, Series P-23, no. 159, Population Profile of the United States. Washington, D.C.: U.S. Government Printing Office, 1990).

17

Army Women Assigned to Combat Units: Perceptions of the Military Equal Opportunity Climate

Brenda L. Moore

Introduction

The U.S. Army has been assigning women to serve in "combat service support" units since World War II. These units provide service support (such as medical, finance, signal, transportation, etc.), or administrative services to the Army. For the most part, combat and combat support units in all of the services were formerly closed to women until the late 1990s.[1] Since 1993, some 259,199 additional military occupations have opened to women. This process began in April, with a Department of Defense (DoD) directive removing barriers that had prevented women from serving on aircraft that engage in combat. In November 1993, Congress repealed the naval exclusion law, which opened 136,000 new positions to Navy women. In 1994, DoD rescinded the "risk rule," thereby opening new career fields and jobs to women in all of the services.

Still, of the 259,199 new jobs that opened to women since 1993, women fill only 843 of them (Harrell & Miller, 1997). In FY 1997, most of the enlisted women in DoD were assigned to administration (33 percent), followed by medical (17 percent), and supply (11 percent). Similarly, female officers were assigned mostly to health care occupations (46 percent), followed by administration (13 percent), and engineering and maintenance (10 percent).[2] On the other hand, fewer than two percent of the enlisted women were assigned in the occupational area of "infantry, gun crew, and seamanship," and fewer than 9 percent of the women officers were assigned to "tactical operations." These low numbers are, attributable to the relatively low percentage of women in the military (14 percent), too few women trained for these positions (Harrell & Miller, 1997), and a lack of interest on the part of women to enter these fields (Collier 1985; Willis 1998).

Currently, women are eligible to be assigned to all military units with the exception of those involving direct physical fighting, (such as infantry, armor, and special forces), or units that work in proximity (collocate) with combat units. Because so many of the Army units involve direct ground combat, they still remain officially closed to women. Since the "risk rule" has been rescinded, only sixteen of the Army's twenty-six previously closed units have been opened to women (see Table 17.1). Still, women in the Army are assigned to combat units at the level of Brigade Headquarters or higher, i.e., Corps or Division,[3] and tend to perform "traditional" female occupational roles. Regardless of one's occupational assignment, the cultural environment of combat units differ from those of combat support and service support units; where women have historically been present. A central question is how well are women being integrated into these previously all-male units, and are they being given the same opportunities as are their male counterparts.

This paper explores the perceptions of Army women toward the equal opportunity climate of their units. Responses to the Military Equal Opportunity Climate Surveys (MEOCS) are examined to determine whether the attitudes of active-duty Army personnel, in general, and women, in particular, vary significantly by unit of assignment. This study is similar to a previous study which examined the effects of race, gender, and the intersection of race and gender on the responses of Army personnel to the MEOCs controlling for paygrade (Moore, 1997; Moore & Webb, 2000). The present analysis, by contrast, focuses primarily on women, and controls for unit mission type (combat, combat support, and combat service support).

Background

Studies on the Integration of Women in the Army

Much of the scholarly literature on the integration of women into the U.S. military suggest that the exclusion of women from combat

Table 17.1
Army Units Open to Women Since 1994 and Units Still Closed to Women

Units Open Since 1994

Maneuver brigade headquarters (in open MOSs/AOCs only)
Division Military Police companies
Chemical reconnaissance and smoke platoons
Mechanized smoke platoons
Engineer bridge companies
Military Intelligence collection and jamming companies
Forward maintenance support teams
Military Police Company-minus attached to 3d U.S. Infantry Regiment (Old Guard)
Regimental Aviation squadron of Armored Cavalry Regiments
Air Calvary troops of a Divisional Calvary Squadron
Combat Engineer Battalion Headquarters (in open MOSs/AOCs only)
Headquarters and headquarters company/160th Special Operations Aviation Regiment (open MOSs/AOCs only)
Air Defense Artillery Battalion Headquarters (open MOSs/AOCs only)
Aviation Unit maintenance troops of division Calvary squadrons.

Units Still Closed To Women

Infantry Battalions and Companies
Armor Battalions and Companies
Field Artillery Battalions and Batteries
Special Forces Battalion, Companies and Detachments
Forward Area Air Defense Artillery Batteries
Combat Engineer Companies
Aviation Special Operation
Mechanized Maintenance (organizational)
Ranger Regiments, Battalions and Companies
Military Intelligence Ground Surveillance Radar Platoons

Source: U.S. Army, Office of the Deputy Chief of Staff for Personnel; Published by G.E. Willis, "Are Women Making Gains," *Army Times,* June 1, 1998, p.13.

occupations hinders their military careers, creating a "glass ceiling." This issue is supported by the fact that many of the military occupations opened to women are not available to them, as they are in infantry, armor, and other units currently off-limits to women.

A further implication of these studies is that male soldiers refuse to accept military women as equals; viewing them instead as interlopers trespassing on male turf (Becraft, 1992; Burke, 1996; Devilbiss, 1985; Holm, [1982] 1992; Peach, 1996; Segal, 1982; Stiehm, 1998, 1989). These feminist scholars view women as possessing the same abilities as men, and advocate for changes in government policies that remove restrictions on the assignments of women in the military. Some of these studies challenge the combat restriction rule by underscoring the fact that American women have always risked dying in combat. Indeed, women who masqueraded as men and actually fought during the Revolutionary and Civil Wars never received official recognition for their sacrifices (DePauw, 1981). Consistently, while some women aviators were killed ferrying planes during World War II (Merryman, 1998), it was not until the death of Major Marie Rossie in 1991 that the service of women aviators received recognition (Francke, 1997).[4] Hence, contrary to popular belief, American women have always played a role in combat but have not been appropriately acknowledged for their services. Therefore, the common belief that men fight wars to protect women is merely a myth (Stiehm, 1989).

On the opposite side of the spectrum, critics argue that the military is no place for women, as women are physically and emotionally weaker than men. One of the leading critics against women in the military is former Army infantry officer and intelligence agent, Brian Mitchell (1989). Military women, so Mitchell argues, "are less aggressive, less daring, less likely to suppress minor personal hurts, less aware of world affairs, less interested in military history, less respectful of military tradition, and less inclined to make military a career (1989, p. 7)." For Mitchell, this has caused a "feminization," or weakening of the American armed services.

Moreover, the problem is further exacerbated by proponents of women in the military who, according to Mitchell, encourage women to think of themselves and their careers before thinking of the good of the organization and of national defense (Mithcell, 1989, p. 9). This biological determinist theme is echoed by former Defense Advisory Committee on Women in the Services (DACOWITS) member, Elaine Donnelly. In a PBS documentary, Donnelly argued ardently against the removal of the restriction on women in combat on the grounds that women are not physically and emotionally capable of performing in that role (PBS, 1999).

Other studies, while not emphasizing the male domination theme and asserting no apparent political agenda, also acknowledge a tension in gender relations in the U.S. military. According to a National Defense Research Institute (RAND) report, there are some military occupations in which women are perceived by their male counterparts as not contributing as much to the overall mission of their units as do men in those occupations. Responding to a congressional directive, RAND launched a study in 1997 to evaluate the progress of integrating women into occupations and units previously closed to them (Harrell & Miller 1997). These researchers found that gender issues were not cited as affecting morale as often as were leadership issues.[5] Still, when respondents raised gender as being an issue, they usually objected to a double standard in policies for men and women. Harrell and Miller reported:

> Men . . . tended to assert that women demanded equal rights and recognition within the company but they were not equal in their performance or contribution to the unit. . . . Men claimed that female standards were too easy and that women were not being forced to meet even the lower standards (Harrell & Miller, 1997, p. 80).

Another interesting finding of this study is that depending upon the circumstances, the effects of gender integration on unit cohesion varied. The researchers found gender to have a positive effect on unit cohesion when the presence of women was perceived as raising the standards of the workplace. On the other hand, when the organization emphasized gender differences, or when men and women socially polarized themselves, gender had a negative effect on unit cohesion. Lastly, gender integration appeared to be inconsequential to unit readiness (Harrell & Miller, 1997). These data seem to lend some support to both social constructionists and biological determinists explanations for gender relations in the military.

Some studies have found that military women are often uninterested in being assigned to non-traditional, "male-dominated" occupations (Collier, 1985; Miller, 1998; Willis, 1998). A Congressional Research Service (CRS) report indicated that in 1985, military women preferred assignments in administration and medical occupations rather than those in nontraditional career fields (Collier, 1985). Miller (1998) argues that there is a gap between the issues raised by feminists who act as advocates for military women and those raised by military women themselves. Feminist activists, so Miller asserts, choose agenda that fail to represent the interest of military women, for whom they claim to speak. Based on multiple waves of field research of active-duty Army soldiers, and large scale survey data, Miller concluded that enlisted women in general, and women of color in particular, are more likely to oppose the idea of women serving in combat roles than are white women officers. Similarly, in an *Army Times* article published in June 1998, Captain Cindy Doane, a graduate of Army flight school in 1995, stated that she declined three invitations to be among the first women to fly Apache attack helicopters because, "the attack role just didn't turn me on at the time"(Willis, 1998, p. 12).

Even though gender restrictions on direct combat roles remain, women have gained access to combat and combat support units in the Army. The integration of women into these previously all-male units raise interesting questions about how they perceive the military equal opportunity (EO) climate. To be sure, women entering these units are pioneers, facing new challenges that often accompany members of previously excluded groups who enter career fields, or penetrate organizations for the first time. Because their numerical representation is low, these women are likely to face the pressures of high visibility, and performance expectations based on group stereotypes (Kanter, 1977).

Some of these women are members of racial or ethnic minority groups and may face additional pressures by virtue of their double minority status (Moore, 1991; 1995; Moore & Webb, 1998). Previous studies have shown African-American women to be less well satisfied with the equal opportunity climate in the military than women of other racial/ethnic backgrounds and men (Moore & Webb, 2000, 1998; Rosenfeld, et al., 1992). During a series of focus group studies launched by the Navy Personnel and Development Center (NPRDC) in 1995, African-American women Navy officers raised several EO concerns. For example, these women officers perceived a lack of leadership support for EO programs, unequal distribution of punishment, and a break in the step to promotion (Moore & Webb, 1998). Laura Miller (1998) asserts that women of color, given their overrepresentation in the enlisted ranks, have less to gain and more to lose by a removal of the gender restriction on combat. There is enough evidence to suggest that race and ethnicity must be considered when examining attitudes of women in the military if findings are to be representative.

Hypotheses

1.   Women assigned to combat units have a lower perception of the military equal opportunity climate than those assigned to either combat support, or combat service support units.

2. The perceptions of women do not vary significantly by race/ethnicity in units where their overall numbers are low (i.e., combat); conversely, the perceptions of women vary significantly by race/ethnicity in units where their overall numbers are high (i.e., service).

3. Women in combat units perceive the military EO climate to be less favorable than do minority men assigned to those units.

Data

Data from the Military Equal Opportunity Climate Surveys (MEOCS) were used for the present analysis. This survey was developed by the Defense Equal Opportunity Management Institute (DEOMI), to assess perceptions of race and gender inequality in military organizations. It contains 124 items, classified into four general categories: demographic characteristics, members' perceptions of equal opportunity in their units, perceptions of organization effectiveness, and members' global perceptions of equal opportunity.

Methodology

Based on prior factor analyses, survey items that measure the same perceptual domain were combined into 12 five-point factor scales (Dansby & Landis, 1995, p. 5). Scales 1 to 5 and 12 measure perceptions of equal opportunity behaviors within the respondent's unit; scales 6 to 8 measure perceptions of organizational effectiveness; and scales 9 to 11 measure the respondent's perception of equal opportunity in the overall military environment (Dansby & Landis, 1992; Landis, Dansby, & Faley, 1993). Possible scores on each scale range from 1 to 5; the higher the respondents' score, the more favorably (s)he perceives the equal opportunity climate to be.

Sample Description

Between June 1990 and May 1999, some 830,000 military and civilian personnel were surveyed from U.S. military installations all over the world. Almost half of the individuals surveyed were Army personnel. A data file was created keeping only Hispanic, African-American, and white men and women who were on active-duty, and who were assigned to Army installations. This left a total sample of 166,551 respondents (See Table 17.2). The independent variables in this study include: gender (male, female), race/ethnicity (African

American [non-Hispanic], white [non-Hispanic], Hispanic), and unit type (combat, combat support, combat service support). The variable "unit type" is generic, referring to a Division, Brigade Headquarters, Battalion, or Company. If, for example, a Division Commander requested that the MEOCS be administered to his/her command, then all of the respondents to the survey are identified by the primary mission of that Division (combat, combat support, or combat service support). By the same token, if a Company Commander requests that his/her command be surveyed, then all of the respondents were identified by the primary mission of that company. All of the women in this study who are assigned to combat units are assigned at the Brigade Headquarters level or above. The depended variable, "COMBUNIT," which is explained in greater detail below, is the attitude of the respondent toward the EO climate of his/her unit.

Method

Due to the fact that enlisted and officer personnel are governed by two distinct sets of policies, and have different types of responsibilities, the data were stratified by rank level (officers and enlisted) and cross-tabulated for each of the twelve scales by gender while controlling for race. Some of these preliminary findings are discussed below in the result section. Although the discussion in this section includes findings before a test of significance was done, these statistical trends are still noteworthy.

To determine whether or not the differences detected in the preliminary statistics were significant, two multivariate analyses were performed (one for officers, the other for enlisted personnel) with race, gender, and the intersection of race and gender as independent variables, and the twelve scales as dependent variables. The F-test was used in these models to determine level of significance. The results of the multivariate analyses showed each of the scales measuring the EO climate in the respondent's unit to be significant. The scales measuring perceptions of the EO climate in the overall military environment were also significant. On the other hand, none of the scales measuring organizational effectiveness were significant. For the final analysis in this study, all of the scales measuring perceptions of the EO climate of respondents' units were added into one variable labeled "COMBUNIT."

Given that the independent variables were categorical, the race variable had three levels: white, African American, and Hispanic,

Table 17.2
Demographic Statistics

Enlisted

	Gender			
	Women		Men	
	N	%	N	%
Unit Type				
Combat	8603	34.5	77151	53.3
Combat Support	6656	26.7	27940	19.3
Combat Service Support	9709	38.9	39558	27.3
Total	24968	100	144649	100
Race/Ethnicity				
African American	10858	43.5	35712	24.7
Hispanic	2589	11.9	17234	11.9
White	11520	46.1	91703	63.4
Total	24968	100	144649	100

Officers

	Women		Men	
	N	%	N	%
Unit Type				
Combat	978	25.1	9517	43.5
Combat Support	987	25.3	3597	16.4
Combat Service Support	1929	49.5	8788	40.1
Total	3894	100	21902	100
Race/Ethnicity				
African American	891	22.9	2945	13.4
Hispanic	241	6.2	1229	5.6
White	2762	70.9	17728	80.9
Total	3894	100	21902	100

and I was also interested in measuring the interaction effects of race and gender, the General Linear Model (GLM) was used in the final analysis (SPSS, 1997). The L-matrix was used to determine interaction effects of gender within racial categories.[6] Since large sample sizes often show significance where there are small actual effects, the Eta-Squared statistic was used to determine the proportion of variance explained by the independent variables. To control for unit type, the data were stratified by type of unit (combat, combat support, and combat service support) and the GLM model was tested on each part separately. Finally, F-tests, level of significance, and Eta-Squared statistics were compared for variation across control groups. The findings of these tests are reported in the Results section under the subtitle, "General Linear Model."

Results

Preliminary Findings on Women Controlling For Race and Organizational Type

For the exploratory data analysis, active-duty men and women were stratified by rank level (officers vs. enlisted) and the MEOCS scores of men and women at each rank level were plotted by unit-type. Figure 17.1 shows that officer men perceive the EO climate in their units to be higher than do officer women in comparable units.

A similar pattern exists for enlisted men and women in Figure 17.2. Noteworthy, is the fact that both men and women assigned to combat units score the EO climate of those units lower than do men and women in the other types of units. Men and women in combat service support units appear to be most satisfied with the EO climate

Figure 17.1
Perceptions of Men and Women Officers Toward the EO Climate of their Units

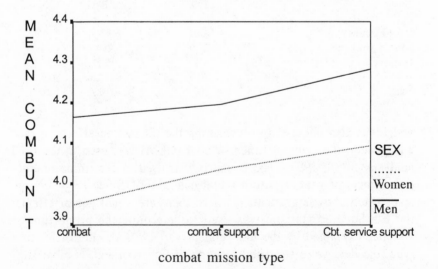

combat mission type

in their units when compared to men and women in combat and combat support units (See Figures 17.1 and 17.2).

Women were subsequently selected out, and their ratings of the EO climate of their units were plotted by rank level and unit type.

Figure 17.2
Perceptions of Enlisted Men and Women Toward the EO Climate of their Units

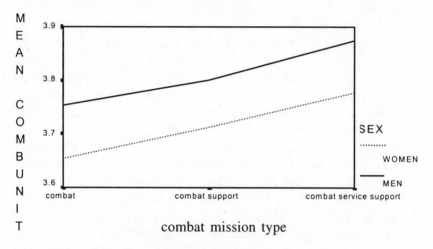

Figure 17.3
Perceptions of Active-Duty Army Women Toward the EO Climate of their Units

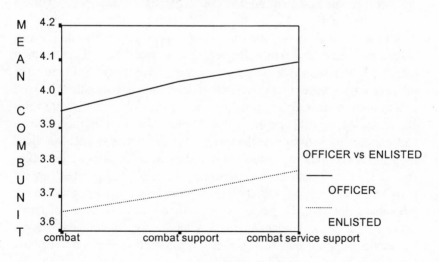

Results showed that women officers rated the equal opportunity climates of their units higher than did enlisted women, and the disparity between officers and enlisted was least for women assigned to combat units. In general, active-duty women assigned to combat units had a lower perception of the EO climate of their units than did women in other units (See Figure 17.3).

When plotting the data by race/ethnicity and unit mission type, I found that white women rated the EO climate of their units more favorably than did Hispanic women, who rated the EO climate more favorably than did African-American women. African-American women officers assigned to combat units had the lowest perception of the EO climate, and white women officers in service support units had the highest perception. The perceptions of Hispanic women officers more closely resembled those of African-American women officers (See Figure 17.4).

In general, women in combat units rated the equal opportunity climate of the overall military lower than did women in other units. Similarly, they perceived that there were more instances of overt sexual harassment and discrimination in their units. In addition, they perceived that there was more discrepancy in command behavior toward minorities and fewer instances of minority and majority members getting along well in their units. Finally, active-duty women in combat units were more likely to believe that minorities and women are discriminated against more in the larger society than were women in the other units.

Within combat units, Hispanic women generally rated the EO climate lower than did white women, and African-American women rated it lower than did Hispanic women. This trend held true for officers (see Figure 17.4) and enlisted women (see Figure 17.5).

Another interesting preliminary finding in these data, though not elaborated upon in this paper, is that African-American enlisted women had greater job satisfaction than Hispanic and white women, particularly those assigned to combat service support units. Among the officers, African-American women assigned to combat and combat support units had lower job satisfaction than white women officers, and greater job satisfaction than Hispanic women officers in those types of units. On the other hand, African-American women officers assigned to combat service support units had greater job satisfaction than white or Hispanic women in comparable units.

Figure 17.4
Perceptions of Women Officers Toward the EO Climate
of their Units by Race/Ethnicity

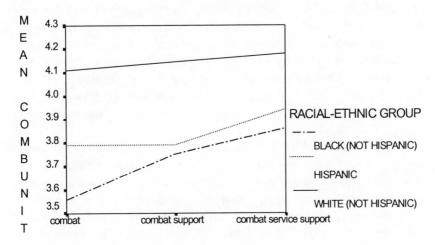

combat mission type

Figure 17.5
Perceptions of Enlisted Women Toward the EO Climate
of their Units by Race/Ethnicity

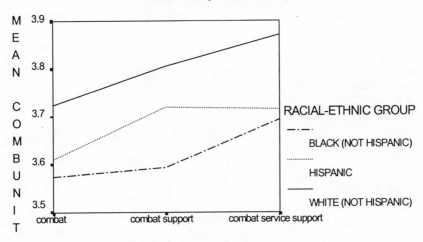

combat mission type

General Linear Model

In the final analysis, the data were stratified by rank level (officer and enlisted), and unit type (combat, combat support, and combat service support), and the GLM was tested on each part separately. The final results were subsequently compared across groups. Among the findings, the first hypothesis was partly supported by the data. Gender was significant in all of the models (see Tables 17.3 and 17.4). However, while the gender variable tested significant, it explained less than 1 percent of the variance in each of the models (see Tables 17.3 and 17.4).

The second and third hypotheses were not supported by the data. Perceptions of women varied significantly by race/ethnicity in the three unit types. Race was significant in each of the models testing for perceptions of the equal opportunity climate in the respondent's unit, and explained more of the variance than the other independent variables in the models (see Tables 17.3 and 17.4). The direction of the race effect was the same in all the models—white men and women scored the COMBUNIT scale higher than did Hispanics, and African-Americans scored the EO climate of their units least favorably.

Table 17.3

Officers	GLM by Unit Type (Dependent Variable COMUNIT)			
Source	**df**	**F**	**Sig**	**Eta Squared**
Combat				
Gender	1	47.213*	.000	.005
Race	2	288.578*	.000	.053
Race*Gender	2	2.419	.089	.000
Combat Support				
Gender	1	38.841*	.000	.008
Race	2	155.593*	.000	.064
Race*Gender	2	2.681	.069	.001
Combat Service Support				
Gender	1	37.542*	.000	.004
Race	2	218.998*	.000	.040
Race*Gender	2	.820	.441	.000

Significant at the <.05 level

Table 17.4

Enlisted	GLM by Unit Type (Dependent Variable COMUNIT)			
Source	df	F	Sig	Eta Squared
Combat				
Gender	1	47.443*	.000	.001
Race	2	353.576*	.000	.008
Race*Gender	2	9.357*	.000	.000
Combat Support				
Gender	1	13.579*	.000	.000
Race	2	310.958*	.000	.018
Race*Gender	2	4.218	.015	.000
Combat Service				
Gender	1	53.713*	.000	.001
Race	2	347.340*	.000	.014
Race*Gender	2	.654	.520	.000

Significant at the <.05 level

This held true for both officers and enlisted personnel (see Tables 17.5, 17.6, and 17.7). Moreover, white women assigned to combat units perceive the military EO climate more favorably than did minority men assigned to those units. This was true for officers, among whom the observed mean score for white women was 4.1110 compared to that of African-American and Hispanic men (3.7904 and 3.9484, respectively) (see Table 17.5). This was also true of enlisted members where the observed score for white women was 3.7337 compared to 3.6023 and 3.6631 for African-American and Hispanic men, respectively (see Table 17.5).

When examining the Eta-Squared statistic in Tables 17.3 and 17.4, race explained more of the variance in the perceptions of officers (.053, .064, and .040) than those of enlisted personnel (.008, .018, .014). Race was strongest in combat support units, and weakest in combat service support units for officers, and combat units for enlisted members.

Lastly, the interaction of race and gender did not explain variation in any of the models. With the exception of enlisted members assigned to combat units, there were no significant interaction ef-

Table 17.5
Observed Means for Combat Organizations

Officers

Gender	Race/Ethnicity	Mean	Std. Dev.	N
Women	African American	3.5595	.6978	239
	Hispanic	3.7905	.7011	81
	White	4.1110	.5533	651
	Total	3.9485	.6498	971
Men	African American	3.7904	.6491	1321
	Hispanic	3.9484	.6466	564
	White	4.2470	.4856	7527
	Total	4.1650	.5482	9412
Total	African American	3.7550	.6618	1560
	Hispanic	3.9286	.6552	645
	White	4.2362	.4926	8178
	Total	4.1448	.5620	10383

Enlisted

Gender	Race/Ethnicity	Mean	Std. Dev.	N
Women	African American	3.5742	.5980	3516
	Hispanic	3.6116	.6015	977
	White	3.7337	.6029	4056
	Total	3.6541	.6055	8549
Men	African American	3.6023	.5958	17573
	Hispanic	3.6631	.6079	9556
	White	3.8248	.5913	49216
	Total	3.7533	.6024	76345
Total	African American	3.5977	.5962	21089
	Hispanic	3.6583	.6074	10533
	White	3.8178	.5927	53272
	Total	3.7434	.6034	84894

Table 17.6
Observed Means for Combat Support Organizations

Officers

Gender	Race/Ethnicity	Mean	Std. Dev.	N
Women	African American	3.7526	.6176	211
	Hispanic	3.7931	.7426	62
	White	4.1433	.5358	706
	Total	4.0369	.5938	979
Men	African American	3.8606	.6299	679
	Hispanic	4.1034	.6426	230
	White	4.2897	.4864	2662
	Total	4.1961	.5538	3571
Total	African American	3.8350	.6283	890
	Hispanic	4.0375	.6758	292
	White	4.2590	.5007	3368
	Total	4.1619	.5664	4550

Enlisted

Gender	Race/Ethnicity	Mean	Std. Dev.	N
Women	African American	3.5930	.6019	2763
	Hispanic	3.7189	.6276	670
	White	3.8142	.5903	3178
	Total	3.7121	.6080	6611
Men	African American	3.6591	.6027	7061
	Hispanic	3.7049	.6292	3281
	White	3.8761	.5901	17417
	Total	3.8007	6062	27759
Total	African American	3.6405	.6032	9824
	Hispanic	3.7073	.6289	3951
	White	3.8666	.5905	20595
	Total	3.7836	.6075	34370

Table 17.7
Observed Means for Combat Service Support Organizations

Officers

Gender	Race/Ethnicity	Mean	Std. Dev.	N
Women	African American	3.8617	.6387	439
	Hispanic	3.9423	.6215	93
	White	4.1781	.5219	1383
	Total	4.0941	.5720	1915
Men	African American	3.9746	.6288	931
	Hispanic	4.0902	.7004	423
	White	4.3339	.4762	7349
	Total	4.2836	.5212	8703
Total	African American	3.9384	.6339	1370
	Hispanic	4.0636	.6886	516
	White	4.3092	.4870	8732
	Total	4.2495	.5357	10618

Enlisted

Gender	Race/Ethnicity	Mean	Std. Dev.	N
Women	African American	3.6946	.6044	4509
	Hispanic	3.7157	.6344	930
	White	3.8807	.6091	4199
	Total	3.7777	.6160	9638
Men	African American	3.7473	.6138	10817
	Hispanic	3.7951	.6321	4272
	White	3.9437	.6051	24156
	Total	3.8734	.6171	39245
Total	African American	3.7318	.6115	15326
	Hispanic	3.7809	.6332	5202
	White	3.9344	.6061	28355
	Total	3.8545	.6180	48883

fects in the models (see Tables 17.3 and 17.4). While the interaction effect among enlisted men and women assigned to combat units was significant according to the F statistic, it did not explain any of the variance in the model (Table 17.4).

Conclusion

The American armed services have made great progress in integrating women into the ranks. Still, the debate as to whether or not women should be fully integrated into the military and assigned to combat position according to their qualifications is far from being resolved.

The data presented in this study do not support arguments alleging that military women are victims of a sexist environment. At the very least, the Army women in this survey do not perceive themselves to be victims of oppression. On the contrary, white women rate the equal opportunity climates in their units relatively high. Surely there are gender issues that are yet to be resolved, but these data suggest that the Army is making progress in this area.

On the other hand, the effect of race on the attitude of men and women in the Army are is significant, and explain most of the variance in all of the models. Paradoxically, African-American women are least well satisfied with the EO climate, while being most satisfied with their job assignments. White women are more satisfied with the EO climate than are African-American and Hispanic men. The race effect in these data reflect race relations problems not only in the respondents' units, but also that which exists in the broader society as well. Military service has and continues to offer career opportunities for African Americans and Hispanics that do not exist in the civilian sector. Therefore, it is not surprising that African-American women would be satisfied with the job opportunity the Army has to offer, yet dissatisfied with the racial climate. In a previous study, an African-American woman officer is cited as saying that while the military has a less than desirable social climate, it is better than that which is found in the civilian sector (Moore & Webb, 1998). Nonetheless, these findings suggest that the armed services need to be ever vigilant in their attempt for racial equality.

The data reveal that both men and women assigned to combat units are less satisfied with the EO climates of their units than are men in women in combat support. As the structure of the U.S. Army changes to a "power projection force" for the twenty-first century, researchers should examine conditions affecting men and women assigned to combat units in greater detail. The Secretary of the Army, and the Army Chief of Staff established a vision for the Army to be a total and strategic force, trained and ready to fight, and capable of decisive victory as we approach the twenty-first century (U.S. DOA, 1994). The attainment of this goal depends heavily upon equipment, effective leaders, superior training, and most importantly, quality people. It is in the best interest of our services to develop ways of attracting talented men and women to serve in combat units. A good first step is to ascertain why so many men and women who are currently assigned to combat units perceive the EO climate to be less desirable than those assigned to combat service support units. Or conversely, why are men and women assigned to combat service support units more satisfied with the EO climate than those assigned to combat units?

Notes

1.   Combat arms are those branches whose soldiers are directly involved in the conduct of actual fighting such as Infantry, Corps of Engineers, Air Defense Artillery, Field Artillery, Armor, Special Forces, and Aviation. Combat support arms are those branches whose soldiers provide operational assistance to the combat arms, such as Civil Affairs, Corps of Engineers, Signal Corps, Military Police Corps, Chemical Corps, Military Intelligence, and Aviation. For a detailed explanation of each of the service branches see: U.S. *Army Regulation 600-3* June 1993, Chapter 3.

2.   U.S. Department of Defense. *Population Representation in the Military Services Fiscal Year 97*. Washington, D.C.: Government Printing Office, 1998, Tables B-29 and B-38.

3.   A corps is the primary command and control headquarters for the conduct of Airland Battle within a Theater of Operations. A brigade headquarters commands the tactical operations of two to five combat battalions. A battalion is composed of four to six companies. A company contains three to five platoons; a platoon consists of two to four squads; the squad is the smallest element in the Army organizational structure (consisting of 9-10 soldiers), and is the final step in the completion of the mission. For a detailed explanation about Army units and their missions, see U.S. Department of the Army Pamphlet 10-1. *Organization of the United States Army*. Washington, D.C.: Headquarters, Department of the Army.

4.   Major Marie Rossi's Chinook helicopter crashed in the Persian Gulf in 1991.

5.   Morale is defined in the study as the degree to which group members are enthusiastic about and committed to carrying out the duties of that group.

6.   I used the contrast coefficients matrix to study the between-subjects effects. This procedure is explained in *SPSS Advanced Statisitics 7.5*, pp. 348-364.

References

Becraft, C. H. (1992). "Women and the Military: Bureaucratic Policies and Politics." In E. A. Blacksmith (Ed.) *The Reference Shelf: Women in the Military*. New York: H. W.

Wilson Co., pp. 8-17.

Burke, C. (1996). "Pernicious Cohesion." In J.H. Stiehm (Ed.) *It's Our Military Too!: Women and the U.S. Military*. Philadelphia: Temple University Press, pp. 205-219.

Collier, E.C. (1985). *Issue Brief: Women in the Armed Forces*, Washington, D.C.: Congressional Research Service.

Dansby, M. R. (1994, December). *The Military Equal Opportunity Climate Survey (MEOCS)*. Paper presented at the World Wide Equal Opportunity Conference, Cocoa Beach, FL.

_____ (1995). "The Military Equal Opportunity Climate Survey: Overview Briefing to DACOWITS," 13 October, Phoenix, AZ.

_____ (1998). "Cultural Diversity and Gender Issues." In Chris Cronin (Ed.) *Military Psychology: An Introduction*. Newbury Park, CA: Sage Publications.

_____ & Landis, D. (1998). "Race, Gender, and Representation Index as Predictors of Equal Opportunity Climate in Military Organizations." *Military Psychology, 10*(2), 87-105.

_____ & Landis, D. (1991). "Measuring Equal Opportunity in the Military Environment," *International Journal of Intercultural Relations, 15*, 389-504.

Davis, J., Lauby, J. & Sheatsley, P.. (1983, April). *Americans View the Military: Public Opinion in 1982*, Report No. 131. Chicago: National Opinion Research Center.

DePauw, L. G. (1981). "Women in Combat: The Revolutionary War Experience." *Armed Forces and Society* (7)2, pp. 209-226.

Devilbiss, M.C. (1985). "Gender Integration and Unit Deployment: A Study of GI Jo," In *Armed Forces and Society* 11(4), pp. 523-552.

Defense Equal Opportunity Management Institute (1994). *Military Equal Opportunity Climate Survey: Commanders' Guide*. DEOMI, Directorate of Research, Patrick AFB, FL.

Defense Equal Opportunity Management Institute (1994). *A Report of the Army Database from the Military Equal Opportunity Climate Survey (MEOCS)*. DEOMI, Directorate of Research, Patrick AFB, FL.

Enloe, C. (1994). "The Politics of Constructing the American Woman Soldier." In E.Addis, V. Russo, & L. Sebesta (Eds.). *Women Soldiers: Images and Realities*. New York: St. Martin's Press, pp. 81-110.

Francke, L. B. (1997). *Ground Zero: The Gender Wars in the Military*. New York: Simon and Schuster.

Harrell, Margaret C. & Laura L. Miller (1997). *New Opportunities for Military Women: Effects Upon Readiness, Cohesion, and Morale*. Washington, D.C.: RAND.

Holm, J. [1982] (1992). *Women in the Military: An Unfinished Revolution*. Novato: Presidio Press.

Kanter, R. M. (1977a). *Men and Women in Corporations*. New York: Basic Books.

_____ (1977b). "Some Effects of Proportions on Group Life: Skewed Sex Ratios and Responses to Token Women." *American Journal of Sociology*, 82(5), 965-994.

Landis, D. & Dansby, M. (1996, May). "The Relationship of Equal Opportunity Climate to Military Career Commitment: An Analysis of the Impact of Race and Gender Using Latent Variables." Paper presented at the Joint Center for Political and Economic Studies Seminar, Washington, DC.

Landis, D., Dansby, M. & Faley, R. (1995). "The Military Equal Opportunity Climate Survey: An Example of Surveying in Organizations." In P. Rosenfeld, J. Edwards, & M. Thomas (Eds.) *Improving Organizational Surveys*. Newbury Park, CA: Sage Publications, pp. 210-239.

Landis, D., Fisher, G. & Dansby, M., (1988). "Construction and Preliminary Validation of an Equal Opportunity Climate Assessment Instrument." In F.E. McIntire (Ed.). *Proceedings of Psychology in the DoD Symposium* (Technical Report 88-1), pp. 487-491.

Colorado Springs, CO: U.S. Air Force Academy.

Merryman, M. (1998). *Clipped Wings: The Rise and Fall of the Women Air Force Service Pilots (Wasps) of World War II.* New York: New York University Press.

Miller, L.L. (1998). "Feminism and the Exclusion of Army Women from Combat." *Gender Issues* 16 *(3)*, 33-64.

Mitchell, B. (1989). Weak Link: The Feminization of the American Military. Washington, D.C.: Regnery Gateway.

Moore, B.L. (1997). *How Do Active Duty Women Perceive the Army's Equal Opportunity Climate?"* PAFB, FL: Defense Equal Opportunity Management Institute, DEOMI Research Series Pamphlet 97-14.

_____. (1996). "From Underrepresentation to Overrepresentation: African American Women," In J.H. Stiehm (Ed.) *It's Our Military, Too: Women and the U.S. Military.* Philadephia: Temple University Press, pp. 115-135.

_____(1991). "African American Women in the U.S. Military." *Armed Forces and Society* 17(3), pp. 363-384

_____ and S.C. Webb (1998). "Equal Opportunity in the U.S. Navy: Perceptions of Active-duty African American Women," In *Gender Issues* 16 *(3)*, pp. 99-119.

_____(2000). "Perceptions of Equal Opportunity Among Women and Minority Army Personnel," *Sociological Inquiry,* 70 *(2),* 215-239.

Moskos, C. (1990). "Army Women," *The Atlantic Monthly,* 266 *(2),* 71-77.

PBS. (1999). "Politics and Warriors," Video Documentary, Washington, D.C.: Public Broadcast System.

Peach, L. J. (1996). "Gender Ideology in the Ethics of Women in Combat," In J. H. Stiehm (Ed.) *It's Our Military Too: Women and the U.S. Military.* Philadelphia: Temple University Press.

Rosenfeld, P., Culbertson, A. Booth-Kewley, S., & Magnusson, P. (1992). "Assessment of Equal Opportunity Climate: Results of the 1989 Navy-Wide Survey." San Diego: Navy Personnel and Research Development Center.

Segal, M. W. (1982). "The Argument for Female Combatants." In *Female Soldiers: Combatants or Non-Combatants: Historical and Contemporary Perspective.* Westport: Greenwood Press, pp. 267-290.

SPSS, Inc. (1997). *SPSS Advance Statistics 7.5.* Chicago, IL: SPSS, Inc.

Stiehm, J. H. (1998). "Army Opinions about Women in the Army, In *Gender Issues* 16 *(3),* pp. 88-98.

_____. (1989). *Arms and the Enlisted Woman.* Philadelphia: Temple University Press.

_____. (1983). *Women and Men's Wars.* New York: Pergamon.

_____. (1981). *Bring Me Men and Women.* Berkeley:University of California Press.

U.S. Department of the Army. (1994). *Organization of the United States Army.* Washington, D.C.: Headquarters, Department of the Army, Pamphlet 10-1.

U.S. Department of Defense. (1998). *Population Representation in the Military Services.* Office of the Assistant Secretary of Defense (Force Management Policy) Washington, D.C.: Government Printing Office.

U.S. General Accounting Office. (1993). *Women in the Military: Deployment in the Persian Gulf War.* Washington, DC: GAO, July.

_____. (1988). *Women In The Military: More Military Jobs Can Be Opened Under Current Statutes.* Washington, DC: GAO.

U. S. Presidential Commission. (1992). *The Presidential Commission on the Assignment of Women in the Armed Forces.* Washington, D.C.: Government Printing Office.

Willis, G.E. (1998, June 12). "Are Women Making Gains in New Career Fields?" *Army Times,* pp. 12-14.

18

Toward an Integrative Model of Sexual Harassment: An Examination of Power, Attitudes, Gender/Role Match, and Some Interactions

Gary L. Whaley

Introduction

According to a 1995 report on sexual harassment by the National Council for Research on Women, at least 50 percent of working women will be sexually harassed during their careers. Research suggests that women in nontraditional jobs are especially likely to be sexually harassed. For example, surveys of female accounting professionals indicate that sexual harassment is widespread and pervasive in the traditional male accounting profession. A 1995 survey by Serepca of female internal auditors reported in *The Internal Auditor* revealed that 24 percent had been sexually harassed. As in the accounting profession, the Armed Forces is also a traditionally male dominated career environment which has experienced problems of sexual harassment. In 1990, approximately 10 percent of the active duty armed forces personnel were female, up from 2 percent in 1972 (Morris, 1994). The Defense Manpower Data Center conducted a worldwide sexual harassment survey of active-duty military personnel in 1988. Of the 20,000 respondents 64 percent of the females and 17 percent of the males reported that they had been sexually harassed (Webb, 1991).

The pervasiveness of sexual harassment of women in the traditionally male-dominated career fields leaves no doubt that sexual harassment is an issue whose time has come. Sexual harassment is an issue for victims and for the companies for which they work. There is much evidence to suggest that victims of sexual harassment suffer from more than the embarrassment and humiliation of the harassment itself. The experience is stressful and psychologically damaging with long-lasting effects. The cost of such occurrences can be dear to both the employer and the victim.

The corporate economic cost of this behavior is becoming more and more evident. In 1994, the *Wall Street Journal* reported the average sex discrimination/harassment verdict awarded in 1993 exceeded $255,000. Awards to some victims have run into the millions of dollars. For example, a freight clerk at Wal-Mart in Missouri was awarded $5 million after her supervisor made crude comments about her body and Wal-Mart management failed to take corrective action.

In addition to direct costs that include attorney's fees, settlements, and awards, there are indirect costs associated with sexual harassment. For example, a study conducted by *Working Woman* in 1988 concluded that sexual harassment costs the typical Fortune 500 firm $6.7 million per year in reduced productivity, increased absenteeism and employee turnover. Faley (1991) estimated that the dollar cost of sexual harassment in the military due to lost productivity and sick leave/absence was nearly $43,000,000!

The costs of sexual harassment to its victims are also monumental. The most common psychological effects of sexual harassment cited by women include fear, anger, anxiety, depression, self-questioning, and self-blaming. The physical manifestations of sexual harassment include such health problems as headaches, sleep disturbance, disordered eating, gastrointestinal disorders, and nausea. Many of these effects also result in additional costs to companies reflected in higher insurance claims, more sick leave taken, and failure to achieve maximum potential returns from their human resource investment.

The leaders and policy makers of private business and government institutions have realized the tremendous cost of sexual harassment in terms of human suffering as well as in dollars. The literature on sexual harassment contains strategies for organizational leaders to abate these costs. These strategies tend to be reactive in nature and primarily aimed at reducing the economic costs associated with sexual harassment once the problem has been made evident.

The reactive strategies outline a number of steps that firms can take to reduce the risk of litigation and financial loss resulting from job related incidents of sexual harassment. The firm's culpability against sexual harassment can be significantly reduced by:

1. Developing a definitive policy addressing sexual harassment that is clearly and regularly communicated to employees and effectively implemented;

2. Insuring that all management and nonmanagement members are provided a copy of the policy, are instructed as to its importance, and understand the sanctions for harassment;

3. Providing a grievance procedure for employees to report sexual harassment to one other than the alleged harasser;

4. Conducting prompt, thorough, and documented investigations of all complaints;

5. Taking swift remedial action to protect the victim from further harassment; and

6. Enforcing sexual harassment policies quickly, consistently, and aggressively.

But, beyond the suggestions for developing harassment policies, making those policies known to the organizational members, and providing organizational members with programs designed to raise their general awareness of behaviors which may be harassing, very little emphasis has been placed on proactive strategies for managing the risks associated with harassing behaviors.

A proactive strategy for managing the problem of sexual harassment is one which identifies areas within an organization where the potential for a sexual harassment problem is the highest and where intervention strategies would abate the risk prior to any incident. This proactive strategy has two very important advantages over a reactive strategy. First, whereas the reactive strategy seeks to reduce the suffering or compensate the victim for suffering as a result of harassment, the proactive strategy seeks to identify areas of greatest risk and take steps to reduce the risk of sexual harassment in the first place. Second, the proactive strategy suggested here allows an organization to utilize its scarce resources devoted to prevention of sexual harassment in a manner that will potentially benefit the organization and its members the most.

In this paper some organizational characteristics and individual attributes which contribute most prominately to the propensity for sexual harassment to occur will be identified. The primary purpose is to examine the interaction of these variables. Whereas the literature predominately examines the main effects of these variables on sexual harassment, it is argued here that the ability to truly understand sexual harassment lies in understanding how these terms interact with one another to produce different types of sexual harassment and the likelihood of the problem to exist. By identifying those organizational factors and personal attributes, and understanding how it is that they interact with one another, more effective strategies can be developed to prevent problems.

Environmental, Organizational, and Individual Attributes as Predictors of Sexual Harassment

There are numerous theories and models of sexual harassment in the literature of the 1980s and 1990s. Tangri and Hayes (1997) have provided an excellent summary/overview of the different approaches to understanding sexual harassment. They have identified natural/ biological models, organizational models, sociocultural models, and individual differences models. The model to be presented here reflects something from each of these approaches. Absent, however, will be coverage of the natural/biological models because they are beyond the scope of the present endeavor.

The magnitude of the impact that sexual harassment has upon an organization necessitates the development of more complex models so that a better understanding of the problem can be achieved and remedies can be developed. A general criticism of the existing models is their simplicity. They tend to focus on main effects of the factors relating to sexual harassment. That is, they fail to look at how new effects can arise as a result of unique combinations of contributing factors. The present model represents only a beginning effort to move towards more complex models. This model incorporates three factors: power, attitudes towards women, and gender/job match, drawn from existing models. The paragraphs that follow discuss the relationship that each of these three factors have with sexual harassment and some possible interactions among the factors.

Main Effect of Power on Sexual Harassment

The misuse and abuse of power is a common theme in promiscuous sexual behaviors, in sexual harassment and in sex crimes. Evidence of the misuse of power for selfish, sexual gratification has been demonstrated time and time again in the popular media. Some of the more sensational examples of this might include the following. Wilt Chamberlin used his "star power" as a sports personality and basketball superstar to sleep with a self-reported 20,000 women in his career. Michael Douglas, as his character in the popular Hollywood movie, "Disclosure" in speaking of his harassment by the character played by Demi Moore, stated accurately "...it's not a sex thing it's a power thing!" Senator Bob Packwood was investigated by the Senate Ethics Committee for the sexual harassment of this female subordinates and finally had to resign from his Senate seat. Finally, and most recently, the incidents which led to the court martial and conviction of several drill sergeants at the Army's Aberdeen Proving Ground were founded on the use of power over female recruits to obtain sexual favors.

Power is a factor central to sexual harassment. Power will be examined here as a dimension or characteristic of an organization's culture. The operationalization of power to be examined here is that of Hofstede's power distance. Hofstede (1991) defined power distance as "...the extent to which the less powerful members of institutions and organizations within a country expect and accept the fact that power is distributed unequally." Whereas Hofstede assessed power distance as a cultural characteristic of a country, the concept has been employed at the organizational level (see Bochner & Hesketh, 1994).

According to Hofstede, power distance is a measure of the power inequity between the more and the less powerful members of an institution. Power distance refers to how much inequity people are willing to accept and regard as proper in the organization's distribution of authority, prestige, status, wealth, etc. Bochner and Hesketh (1994) summarized the differences between high and low power distance organizational cultures in the following ways. In organizations with high power distance individuals behave submissively to superiors in terms of the organizational hierarchy. They are not willing to openly disagree with the higher authority. In fact, they prefer an autocratic or paternalistic supervisor, tend to be more task oriented, and are more likely to subscribe to McGregor's Theory X than Theory Y. Low power distance organizations, on the other hand, prefer a more participative or consultative leadership style in their supervisors, are not afraid to openly disagree with the boss, tend to be more people oriented, and tend to believe in the Theory Y perspective of the working person.

Based on the explanation of the power distance concept, the proposition that as power distance increases the likelihood of abuse of that power increases, it may be arguably assumed that members of a military institution measure high on the power distance index (i.e., that its members do expect and accept the fact that those with rank have the right to control and influence those with less rank). This would be especially true in the relationship between basic recruits and their instructors. Recruits are "drilled" to obey those of higher rank and are expected to be compliant to orders without debate or question.

The *quid pro quo* form of sexual harassment is most likely to occur in a high power distance organizational culture. *Quid pro quo* sexual harassment is the offer, by one in power, to enter into an exchange of organizational rewards for sexual favors from a subordinate. This type of harassment is likely because the supervisor has all the power and the subordinate is submissive and not likely to report the abuse of that power to anyone of higher authority. The motive for the act would be simple personal gratification. The perpetrator of the harassment is likely to view the behavior as within his power and right and the victim is likely to view the situation as just her own personal misfortune. Hofstede (1991) argued, "Being a victim of power abuse by one's boss is just bad luck; there is no assumption that there should be a means of redress against such a situation. If it gets too bad, people may join forces for a violent revolt." This seems to describe the basic events at the Aberdeen Proving Ground Training Center. The drill sergeants abused their power for their own personal sexual gratification. The abuse went unreported by the victims for several years until one victim spoke out, then many others joined in the revolt against the misuse of the power by the drill sergeants.

Main Effect of Attitudes Towards Women
on Sexual Harassment

Studies abound which find that women and men differ in their perceptions of the extent to which behaviors are sexually harassing (e.g., Fitzgerald & Ormerod, 1991; Reilly et al., 1986; Powell, 1986; Collins & Blodgett, 1981; Gutek et al., 1980). These studies and others have demonstrated that women tend to be more likely to recognize that sexual harassment is a problem and that men have a higher threshold for judging a particular harassing behavior as sexual harassment. Malovich and Stake (1990), in studying attitudes towards harassment, and Tucker and Whaley (1996), while examining perceptions of harassing behaviors, have suggested that the main effect of gender as a predictor of perceptions of sexual harassment is lost when attitude towards women is controlled. Gender, it is suggested, is just a surrogate measure of gender-based attitudes.

The focus here will be on attitudes towards women as a personal attribute influencing one's perceptions of sexually harassing behaviors. Attitude towards women represents one's perceptions of the appropriateness of traditional men's and women's behaviors and roles in our society. Traditional attitudes towards women may be characterized, for example, by the belief that women are better at certain jobs and tasks and that men are better at others, or that certain behaviors considered acceptable when displayed by men are less acceptable when displayed by women. A less traditional attitude towards women is characterized by an equality of men and women in their acceptable behaviors and jobs.

Main Effect of Gender/Job Match and Sexual Harassment

Research has demonstrated that women in traditionally male-dominated careers or blue-collar jobs experience more sexual harassment than women in other work settings (Gutek, 1992; Gutek et al. 1990, Izraeli, 1983; Hagman, 1988; Hogbacka et al., 1987 in O'Donohue, 1997). The sex-role spillover model (Gutek & Morasch, 1982) offers one explanation of this phenomenon. The spillover theory suggests that men hold role perceptions of women based on their traditional role in our culture. These traditional role expectations include the nurturing role (as mother), the sex-object role, and helper role (as wife). What have been traditionally viewed as women's careers is consistent with these role expectations. For example, as teachers and nurses, women are nurturing; as cocktail waitresses and cheerleaders they may be seen as sex objects; and as secretaries and dental assistants they are helpers. When women take jobs outside of these traditional areas to work with and for men there is the potential for the men to perceive the women in their gender role over and above their work role. It's argued that men in traditionally male-dominated careers and with little experience in working with women in these roles, may rely on these inappropriate gender-based role expectations in guiding their interactions with women. The result of the inappropriate expected role is male behavior which is likely to be inappropriate and perceived to be sexually harassing.

A different argument seeking to explain this behavior was put forth by Carothers and Crull (1984). They suggest that women in traditionally female occupations are more likely to experience *quid pro quo* harassment. This form of harassment arises from the harasser's internalization of the sex role for women in our culture, i.e., a sex object. Women in nontraditional careers are more likely to experience the hostile environment form of harassment. Here, women are perceived as a threat to the men's economic and social status. The harassment is the men's aggressive response to that threat (Carothers & Crull, 1984).

In general, the model suggested here would predict that women in traditionally female careers/jobs (e.g., teacher, nurse, or secretary) with male immediate supervisors are not likely to experience the more severe forms of hostile environment sexual harassment. Women in this situation are likely, however, to experience less severe forms of sexual harassment such as a mild form of hostile environment sexual harassment, *quid pro quo* sexual harassment, or sexism, the form of sexual behavior that does not reach the threshold of sexual harassment.

Interactions of Predictor Variables

A criticism of the models of sexual harassment mentioned above is their oversimplicity and in large part these models have not considered how different factors may interact with one another to result in different types of sexual harassment and differing levels of severity. Presented below is a three factor model of sexual harassment which considers how power distance, attitudes towards women, and gender/job match might interact (See Figures 18.1a and 18.1b).

The model suggests that power distance may interact with attitudes towards women and gender/job match to produce differing types of sexual harassment and differing levels of severity. The low power distance situation is represented in quadrants II and III of Figure 18.1a, where women are in traditionally female-dominated careers or jobs. In the low power distance situation in general we can expect fewer potential problems with sexual harassment. But, if we consider the attitudes towards women of the male supervisor and/or other males in the work environment, there may be observed

Figure 18.1a
A Model of Sexual Harassment Behaviors
for Women in Traditional Women's Work Roles
(i.e., secretaries, teachers, nurses, etc.) with Male Supervisors

		Attitudes towards Women	
		Traditional	Nontraditional
Power Distance	**High**	I *Quid pro quo* sexual harassment	IV Unconscious use of power resulting in hostile environment sexual harassment
	Low	II Simple sexism	III Least favorable environment for sexual harassment

Figure 18.1b
A Model of Sexual Harassment Behaviors for Women
in Nontraditional Women's Work Roles
(i.e., business executives, construction trades, etc.) with Male Supervisors

		Attitudes towards Women	
		Traditional	Nontraditional
Power Distance	**High**	I *Quid pro quo* and conscious use of power resulting in hostile environment sexual harassment	IV Unconscious use of power resulting in hostile environment sexual harassment
	Low	II Conscious use of illegitimate sources of power resulting in hostile environment sexual harassment	III Least favorable environment for sexual harassment

subtle differences in the behavior of the men towards the women. Where traditional attitudes towards women prevail (quadrant I), the type of behavior experienced by women on the part of their male supervisor and/or other males in the work environment would most likely be a form of sexism not generally classified as harassment. In the low power distance situation, supervisors and subordinates consider themselves as essentially equal (Hofstede, 1991). Only their roles within the organization are different, that difference being an artifact of the division of labor necessitated by the need for efficiency within the organization. In this situation the abuse of power cannot exist because there are no perceived power differences. A male supervisor and other males in that environment are likely to treat the women differently than the men. For example, they may compliment a women on her new dress or hair style (in a nonsexual way), but not men. The supervisor may ask a women to fix coffee and a male subordinate to help move a small table. Or, the males may express opinions which suggest that women are inherently better at certain tasks than men and *vise versa*. These attitudes may result in discrimination based on gender but will not likely cross the threshold of sexual harassment.

In quadrant III of Figure 18.1a, where contemporary attitudes exist these sexist behaviors are not as likely to occur, thus creating the most egalitarian work environment free from any forms of sexism or sexual harassment. As the attitudes of the males in the work environment towards women change from traditional to nontraditional the probabilities of women having to cope with sexism or suffering the pain of sexual harassment are the lowest. The lack of perceived power differences and a liberated attitude towards women and their role in the work environment alleviate some of the cultural and personal pressures resulting in sexual harassment. The sources of sexual harassment which may exist are not systemic. They are more likely to be attributable to a male person's uncontrollable, idiosyncratic attraction to a female subordinate or coworker.

The *quid pro quo* form of sexual harassment is most likely to occur in a high power distance organizational culture, when the immediate supervisor and/or male coworkers possess a traditional attitude towards women and the woman is in a traditionally female career or job (quadrant I in Figure 18.1a above). This type of harassment is likely because the supervisor has all the power and the subordinate is submissive to superiors and not likely to report the abuse of that power to anyone of higher authority. The motive for the act, as stated earlier, is simple sexual gratification. The perpetrator of the *quid pro quo* harassment is likely to view the behavior as within his power and his right. The victim is likely to view the situation as simply her own personal misfortune, a circumstance she will have to endure.

Moving from quadrant I to quadrant IV of Figure 18.1a, where only attitude towards women has changed from traditional to non-traditional, the type of harassment may be expected to change. In this situation the victim may expect to experience a hostile environment form of sexual harassment of which the perpetrator is not even aware. Bargh and Raymond (1995) explain how unintended sexual harassment is the result of an automatic mental link between the harasser's concepts of power and sex. In some men the idea of power is habitually associated with the idea of sex. For these men, the sex act itself is the woman's submission to the man's control and power. When an attractive women, in deference to a male supervisor's organizational power, behaves submissively, compliantly to his wishes, or politely laughs at his jokes, her behaviors trigger an unconscious sexual schema in the man's attribution of her behaviors. Thus, he perceives her behaviors as being sexually receptive to him and he responds accordingly. The outcome of this phenomenon is that she views herself as a victim of harassment and he sees himself as "led on" by the women. The harasser acknowledges his behavior but does not ascribe the same motive to that behavior as the victim; he perceives his actions as complimentary—she as threatening.

If the gender/job match dimension of the situation changes (occupational role held by women changes from "women in traditional women's work role" to "women in nontraditional women's work role"), the model suggests a change in the environment for sexual harassment in both quadrants I and II (See Figure 18.1b.). For quadrant I, the model suggests a change in the type of sexual harassment from just *quid pro quo* harassment to one with *quid pro quo* and hostile environment harassment. The *quid pro quo* sexual harassment is a function of the high power distance condition as describe above. The development of the additional hostile environment sexual harassment is explained by Pryor and Whalen (1997).

Pryor and Whalen (1997) argue that when women are the minority of a work group their gender becomes an outstanding identifying characteristic. This magnifies the use of gender-based categorizations and can lead to exaggerated and often stereotypical evaluations of the female in a predominately male environment. According to the social identity theory (Tajfel & Turner, 1986), the recognition of the interpersonal differences can also result in the development of an ingroup-outgroup perspective of the work environment which can result in the devaluation of the outgroup (Dovidio & Gaertner, 1993). Where the outgroup women are perceived as a threat, either an economic threat in the sense of competition for jobs or promotions for example, or as a threat to the ingroup's self esteem, such as a woman succeeding in a traditionally masculine job such as a policeman, fireman, coal miner, etc., thus taking away from the masculine image of the male ingroup. Either type of threat may result in a gender-based hostility directed towards the female outgroup. In other words, the males are likely to respond with a hostile environment form of sexual harassment which is meant to intimidate the victim and drive her away, thus eliminating the perceived threat.

In quadrant II with low power distance the likelihood of *quid pro quo* sexual harassment is diminished because of the absence of the organizational power base from which to negotiate for sexual favors. However, the hostile environment sexual harassment situation would remain unchanged. The male ingroup would still seek to retaliate against the perceived threat from the female outgroup.

Towards More Effective Strategies

The most effective way to manage the risk of sexual harassment is to develop a strategy which targets the underlying, causal factors of sexual harassment. The goal is to change or otherwise prevent those factors from initiating the offensive behaviors. The model presented above posits that sexual harassment is the result of an interaction of multiple factors. The interactions of these factors can produce different types of sexual harassment and differing levels of severity of the offensive behavior. The realization that harassing behaviors can have different sources strongly suggests that correcting these behaviors will require multiple strategies.

The strategy presented as the standard policy and punishment approach to remedy the harassment problem may be the most effective strategy for one type of harassment—*quid pro quo* sexual harassment. *Quid pro quo* sexual harassment is the result of a rational, calculated, cognitive process. The harasser attempts to enter into an exchange of services with the victim. Here policies can clearly define these types of behaviors as unacceptable and explain the punishment which would result from violation. These policies work in a fashion similar to speed limits on our highways. The maximum legal speed is posted and the penalty for violating the speed limit is publicized. When violators are caught they are punished in systematic fashion. All drivers on the highways, for the most part, make informed decisions factoring the risks involved and the potential benefits from speeding. Most, not all, choose to stay reasonably within the limits of the law.

Further, this strategy helps victims of sexual harassment understand their rights and outlines grievance procedures for reporting offenses. This approach may go a long way to remove the sense of helplessness for the victim by outlining a proper course of action for all involved. Clear sanctions create an expected remedy to the situation. The policy and punishment strategy, however, falls far short of reducing significantly the hostile environment form of sexual harassment.

Based on the logic presented in the integrative model presented above, the policy and punishment strategy would seem not to be very effective in preventing hostile environments. The hostile environment form of sexual harassment is not the result of the same type of thinking that produces *quid pro quo* sexual harassment. Hostile environment sexual harassment is the result of errant cognitive processes involving inappropriate stereotypes, misattributions of behaviors, and/or attitudes inconsistent with the organizational culture. An effective strategy for reducing the risk of hostile environment sexual harassment must be more involved than the relatively simple policy and punishment approach. An effective strategy to reduce the risk of hostile environment sexual harassment must focus on education concerning the complex issues of gender-based stereotypes, attribution theory, attitudes, and organizational culture. Educational remedies require a deeper intervention into the organization.

Such a strategy must be designed with several levels of intervention. The first level should focus on education about sexual harassment policy, grievance procedures and consequences, appropriate sexual and social relationships, gender-based stereotypes, and role expectations. It should also incorporate the topics of gender-based discrimination and equal rights in the workplace without gender bias. The first level is similar to the policy and punishment strategy. All members of an organization should receive this training beginning first with the highest level leadership and proceeding down the organizational hierarchy.

The second level of the intervention strategy should involve all persons with subordinates, again starting from the top down. At this level, the instructional content should focus on developing an understanding of the psychological processes discussed above in reference to *quid pro quo* sexual harassment (Figure 18.1a, quadrant I) and hostile environment sexual harassment (Figure 18.1a, quadrant IV and Figure 18.1b, quadrants I and IV). At this level the discussions of *quid pro quo* and hostile environment sexual harassment should be designed to reinforce the experience participants had with the level one intervention and to go beyond the basic level of understanding the sexual harassment. Discussions of the ways in which traditional values with respect to women's roles in society, gender-based stereotypes, role expectations, and "spillover theory" work to create the environment in which sexual harassment can become a serious problem. Only through an awareness of these issues can one be protected from the problems associated with them.

The third level of intervention would be used on an *ad hoc* basis for those work groups or units about to experience a change in the dominant gender composition of their work group. This would be a change from a "single gender" or "predominant gender" work unit to a "mixed gender" work unit. The intervention here should precede the anticipated change and should be designed to eliminate any perceived threat, economic or otherwise, which might cause the situation described in Figure 18.1b, quadrant II. It is here that harassers utilize hostile environment sexual harassment to drive out the source of that threat.

The fourth level of intervention is designed for persons found, after due process, to be harassers. The typical range of outcomes for a harasser can vary from a written reprimand attached to their personnel file and a "Don't do that again," to financial penalty and termination. For many, the event is an absolute barrier to any further career growth. In the military a harasser may face imprisonment. The recent $26.6 million judgment found against Miller Brewing Company for firing Jerold MacKenzie for sexual harassment (Jones, 1997) suggests that organizations should examine avenues other than termination of harassers as a cure for sexual harassment.

Rather than looking to punishment, the organization might explore treatment for the harasser. Because some forms of sexual harassment are the result of errant cognitive processes, treatment to correct those processes is possible. As a company invests in programs to treat employees who abuse alcohol or other drugs, organizations might invest in similar programs to change the cognitive processes and behaviors which result in sexually harassing environments. These programs would be conducted by professional therapists and involve cognitive and behavior therapy. Policies should govern participation in these programs in a fashion similar to the drug treatment programs currently in existence in many large organizations today.

Conclusion

Sexual harassment is a serious problem in organizations today. Attempts to effectively cope with the problem have not achieved the success level desired. It is argued here that to reduce the risks of sexual harassment it is essential to first understand the nature of the problem and its causes. Without the understanding of the problem, one is faced with a trial-and-error approach to finding a solution. The model presented here is only representative of the type of model needed to comprehensively understand sexual harassment and to work towards its elimination. As the whole sexual harassment process becomes more fully understood, strategies for attacking the problem will become more effective. It will allow those in leadership positions to identify groups with the greatest likelihood for problems and implement preventive action rather than corrective action for that specific area.

The multilevel strategy suggested in this paper should serve only as a guide or general model for more fully articulated efforts. The development of the content of such a strategy is beyond the scope of this paper and represents an area of research yet to be explored in the literature. I believe this type of information will be key to implementing a proactive strategy for managing the risk of sexual harassment.

References

Bargh, J. A., & Raymond, P. (1995). The naive misuse of power: nonconscious sources of sexual harassment. *Journal of Social Issues, 51*(1), 85-96.

Bochner, S., & Hesketh, B. (1994). Power distance, individualism/collectivism, and job-related attitudes in a culturally diverse work group. *Journal of Cross-Cultural Psychology, 25*(2), 233-257.

Carothers, S. C., & Crull, P. (1984). Contrasting sexual harassment in female and male-dominated occupations. In K. B. Sacks & D. Remy (Eds.), *My troubles are going to have trouble with me: Everyday trials and triumphs of women workers.* New Brunswick, NJ: Rutgers University Press, 219-227.

Collins, E. G. C., & Blodgett, T. B. (1981). Sexual harassment...some see it...some won't. *Harvard Business Review*, March-April, 76-95.

Dovidio, J. F., & Gaertner, S. L. (1993). Stereotypes and evaluative intergroup bias. In D. M. Mackie & D. L. Hamilton (Eds.), *Affect, cognition and stereotyping: Interactive processes in group perception*. San Diego, CA: Academic Press, 167-193.

Faley, Robert H. (1991). Preliminary partial estimates of the annual dollar-value of overall lost productivity due to sexual harassment in the active-duty military. Unpublished Technical Report. Patrick AFB, FL: Defense Equal Opportunity Management Institute.

Fitzgerald, L. F., & Ormerod, A. J. (1991). Perceptions of sexual harassment. *Psychology of Women Quarterly, 15*, 281-294.

Guteck, B. A. (1992). Understanding sexual harassment at work. *Notre Dame Journal of Law, Ethics and Public Policy*, 6(2), 335-392.

Gutek, B. A., Cohen A. G., & Knorad, A. M. (1990). Predicting social-sexual behavior at work: A contact hypothesis. *Academy of Management Journal, 33*, 560-577.

Gutek, B. A., Nakamura, C. Y., Gahad, M., Handschumacker, I., & Russell, D. (1980). Sexuality in the workplace. *Basic and Applied Social Psychology, 1*(3), 255-265.

Hofstede, G. (1991). *Cultures and organizations: Software for the mind*. New York: McGraw Hill

Izraeli, D. (1983). Sex effects or structural effects? An empirical test of Kanter's theory of proportions. *Social Forces, 62*, 153-165.

Jones, D. (1997, July 17). 'Seinfeld' case fallout: Award creates Catch-22 for companies. *USA Today*.

Malovich, N. J., & Stake, J. (1990). Sexual harassment on campus: Individual differences in attitudes and beliefs. *Psychology of Women Quarterly, 14*, 63-82.

Murrell, A. J., & Dietz-Uhler, B. L. (1993). Gender identity and adversarial sexual beliefs as predictors of attitudes toward sexual harassment. *Psychology of Women Quarterly, 17*, 169-176.

Morris, Celia (1994). Bearing witness: Sexual harassment and beyond—everywoman's story. New York: Little, Brown and Company.

Powell, G. N. (1986). Effects of sex role identity and sex on definitions of sexual harassment. *Sex Roles, 14*(1/2), 9-19.

Pryor, J. B., & Whalen, N. J. (1997). A typology of sexual harassment: Characteristics of harassers and the social circumstances under which sexual harassment occurs, in *Sexual Harassment: Theory, Research, and Treatment*, William O'Donohue, (Ed.) Needham Heights, MA: Allyn and Bacon, 129-151.

O'Donohue, W., (Ed.) (1997). *Sexual harassment: theory, research, and treatment*. Needham Heights, MA: Allyn and Bacon.

Reilly, M. E., Lott, B., & Gallogly, S. (1986). Sexual harassment of university students. *Sex Roles, 15*(7/8), 333-358.

Tangri, S. S., & Hayes, S. M. (1997). Theories of sexual harassment. In *Sexual Harassment: Theory, Research and Treatment*, William O'Donohue (Ed.). Needham Heights, MA: Allyn and Bacon, 112-127.

Terpstra, D. D., & Baker, D. D. (1986). A framework for the study of sexual harassment. *Basic and Applied Social Psychology, 7*, 17-34.

Tajfel, H., & Turner, J. C. (1986). The social identity theory of intergroup conflict in W. G. Austin and S. Worchel (Eds.), *The social psychology of intergroup relations*. Monterey, CA: Brooks and Cole, 47.

Tucker, S. H., & Whaley, G. L. (1995, March). Perceptions of sexual harassment of women: Effects of demographics and attitudes towards women in *Academy of Business Administration Proceedings*, Reno, Nevada, 154-165.

Webb, Susan L. (1991). *Step forward: Sexual harassment in the workplace: What you need to know*. Redlands, CA: Mastermedia.

Part 4

Military Discipline and Race

Introduction to Part 4

Justice and Race in the United States

For three decades sociologists, criminologists, political scientists, and anthropologists have debated why people of color, and specifically African Americans, are over-represented in the justice system in this country. Public debate over the nature and causes of the significant racial disparities in prison incarceration rates in the United States has taken on renewed intensity. Social science researchers and judicial system pundits, as well as the American public have been increasingly attentive to the implications of findings that race affects judicial proceedings and incarceration rates. The large number of African-American male "clients" in the justice system is a major concern as suggested by the following findings:

- 25 percent of young African-American men have had an encounter with the judicial system, are in prison, on parole, or on probation (Chideya, 1995)

- In 1990, of every 100,000 whites, 289 were in prison; of every 100,000 African Americans, 1,860 were in prison (Lemann, 1998)

- In 1995, one in three African-American men between the ages of 20 and 29 was under some type of supervision by elements of the criminal justice system (Mauer & Huling, 1995)

The data clearly document that African Americans are arrested at rates disproportionate to their population representation. Although only 12 percent of the American population is African American, almost half (48 percent) of the federal prison population is African American (Jackson, 1994). Too often "black" is a sufficient physical description of suspects (e.g., racial profiling), and African Americans fare even worse relative to conviction and sentencing (Chideya, 1995).

Recent literature reviews on race and incarceration rates reveal that approximately two thirds of the studies identify race as an important factor, while on the contrary, one third argues that race has no effect (Conley, 1994; Pope & Feyerhern, 1992). Unfortunately, decades of research have not offered any definitive solutions or increased our understanding of why the problems exist. Basically, the majority of researchers have demonstrated empirically that in juvenile justice, "race makes a difference." People of color, specifically African Americans and Hispanics, are more likely to be arrested, detained, tried and found guilty, and sentenced for longer periods of time than whites (Petersilia, 1983). Explanations for why this happens typically highlight family problems, poverty, educational disparities, and even differential situational opportunities to commit crime. For some, the reason is simple and very direct, "the system is rife with racism" (Cole, 1999; Miller, 1996; Smith, 1995; Tonry, 1996).

However, the issue of whether African Americans are punished more severely than are white Americans by the criminal justice system and whether the system is racist has been fiercely debated in the literature for decades (Cole, 1999; Tonry, 1996). On one hand, some criminal justice professionals have called the charge of a racist criminal justice system a myth or have stated that the evidence is mixed. However, other professionals assert that the U.S. criminal justice system indeed is racist, and this racism traces itself back to the dehumanization of African Americans during the era of slavery and the following period during which systematic segregation was practiced. (Nunn, 1997). Many researchers regrettably conclude that *de facto* racial discrimination in capital sentencing on the basis of the race of the victim is legal in the U.S. Moreover, they suggest that regardless of the elegance of statistical manipulation and causal inference, such racial discrimination will no doubt remain legal, given the public and the courts' interest in stiffer penalties, including the death penalty.

In addition, President Clinton's Advisory Board on Race reviewed statistics that suggest law enforcement is struggling with the goal of being colorblind. African Americans are charged with less that half of violent crimes but constitute 60 percent of prison admissions. There is also growing evidence that law enforcement authorities regularly subject African Americans to racial profiling. One researcher reported that minorities were *"more likely to receive prison sentences, more likely to get longer sentences and more likely to serve longer in prison that whites,"* even when controlling for offense, prior record and prison record. Without understanding the distinctive set of remedial challenges posed in the context of criminal adjudication (i.e., legal procedures applied to individuals who have committed a crime or have been convicted of a crime), it is simply impossible to confront, let alone solve, the persistent problems of racial disparity in the administration of criminal justice. Unfortunately, these same problems and dilemmas present themselves in the military context.

The Military Justice System

"The military justice system not only must be impartial, but also must be perceived as being fair and impartial. Without a positive public opinion of the military justice system, the armed forces in general will not enjoy a positive public opinion; without a positive opinion of the armed forces, the national will suffers; and without a strong national will, the United States cannot expect to succeed in a protracted war."

— Lamb (1992)

The above quote summarizes the interdependence of the military justice system with public perceptions of fairness and impartiality, national will, and the mission of our military. Thus, to affect one of the components is to affect all of the components. To the extent that fairness and impartiality are associated with operational readiness and equal opportunity, observers are concerned with the seemingly unbalanced nature of the military justice procedures. Several researchers have opined that there is a legitimate cause for concern about the fairness rendered in military court decisions given recent racial demographic statistics.

According to recent statistics, African Americans comprise a disproportionate segment of the inmates in the military prisons or brigs, comparable to the proportion in the federal, state and county prison system. Data from a study of 2,747 cases[1] examined in *Correctional Populations in the United States* (1996) indicated that 52.2 percent of prisoners under military jurisdiction were white, 35.5 percent African-American, 8.0 percent Hispanic, and 4.3 percent were members of other racial/ethnic groups.

As of September 1998, the enlisted population of the combined Armed Services was 66.8 percent white, 20.0 percent African-American, 7.2 percent Hispanic, and 6.0 percent other or unknown. African-American offenders were found to have committed or were alleged to have committed a disproportionate number of major military and civilian offenses and confrontation or status offenses (e.g., offenses against other individuals in violation of the law). In contrast, white offenders were disproportionately involved in drug related offenses.

Over the last few decades a large number of studies have been conducted to ascertain the sources of disparities in the military justice system. Several of these studies are discussed in the following section.

The Uniform Code of Military Justice

The military environment has a unique organizational structure with features not found in the civilian sector. The military organization has often been identified as a strict, formalistic, conservative organization characterized by rigid hierarchical modes of operation, the pervasive authoritarian expectation for close adherence to rules and instruction, tight restraints on individual expression, rank status, and rigidly-defined social expectations for conduct. In addition, it is an organization that has evolved into a complex institution with advanced technology, and sophisticated systems, as well as being responsible for the welfare and quality of life of those personnel within the organization. To maintain prescribed military behavior (i.e., military bearing), a body of law called the *Uniform Code of Military Justice* (UCMJ),[2] is the guideline that is used across services to ensure *good order and discipline*. Moreover, military justice pundits emphasize the "separate society" of military service and the importance of enforcing discipline among service members, particularly during war (Hillman, 1999).

Specifically, the UCMJ is comprised of a list of prescribed military offenses (i.e., Articles) and an established system of military courts to litigate a broad range of criminal charges. It is applicable to members of the regular component of the Armed Services, cadets, aviation cadets, and midshipman, members of a reserve component while on inactive-duty training, members of the National Oceanic and Atmospheric Administration (NOAA), Public Health Service (PHS), and other organizations aligned with the Armed Services. Consequences for infractions under the UCMJ range from punishment by company commanders or commanding officers imposed for minor violations under *Article 15*, to separations under four types of unfavorable discharges: General, Other than Honorable, Bad Conduct, and Dishonorable—with the later two being the most punitive and awarded only as a result of court-martial.

Ironically, a racially motivated event precipitated a string of events that led to the drafting of the UCMJ. World War I had just begun, when on August 23, 1917, 63 enlisted members of the all-Black 24th Infantry at Fort Sam Houston in San Antonio "rioted" in protest of police brutality and *Jim Crow* ordinances. The tragic confrontation resulted in eighteen fatalities, including eleven civilians. Within a matter of days, the soldiers were tried and thirteen African-American soldiers were condemned to death, forty-one were sentenced to life with hard labor, four received shorter sentences, and five were acquitted. To date, this punishment of the African-American soldiers remains one of the largest mass executions without the benefit of a trial in U.S. military history.

In the wake of the incident, the Army issued two general orders directing that no death sentence could be carried out in the United States until after a Judge Advocate General (JAG) review and also established boards of review in the JAG office that would review death sentences, dismissals of officers, and dishonorable discharges of enlisted soldiers. The latter provision was forced upon the War Department by public opinion and the threat of congressional action. The ensuing debate and revisions/amendments to the *Articles of War* continued until the Korean War.

Intense public criticism of the military justice system arose during and after World War II. As a result, the Department of War established a War Department Advisory Committee on Military Justice, known as the Vanderbilt Committee. The committee's report led to the *Elston Act*, which was introduced to Congress in 1947 to amend the *Articles of War*. The year following the passage of the *Elston Act*, Congress began work on a bill to unify the disparate military justice systems of the Army, Navy, and Coast Guard, a goal characterized as a "high priority" in the national military establishment by Defense Secretary James Forestall. As part of its overhaul of military law, Congress revisited its then recent *Elston Act* amendments to the *Articles of War* to propose reforms applicable to all the armed forces under the newly proposed Uniform Code of Military Justice (UCMJ). Subsequently, former Supreme Commander of Allied Forces in the European Theater during World War II, President Dwight Eisenhower, signed Executive Order No. 10214, thereby establishing the *Uniform Code of Military Justice* on May 5, 1950. *The Manual for Courts-Martial* was established by Executive Order 10214 on February 8, 1951. The UCMJ superceded the Army's *Articles of War*, the *Articles for the Government of the Navy*, and the *Disciplinary Laws of the Coast Guard.*

In summary, the military justice system has evolved from a procedure designed to support the ultimate will of local commanders into an independent adversarial system with many uniquely paternalistic aspects ensured by Congress, the military appellate courts, and the President. In all probability, the UCMJ will continue to evolve as the institutions responsible for its maintenance change.

DEOMI/UCMJ Research Conference

In 1992, DEOMI sponsored a conference focusing on the UCMJ. A seven component model of factors was proposed as a framework to guide research examining the UCMJ. Those components were: antecedents to behavior including psychological, sociological and physiological; offense behaviors; punishment recipient decision process; moderators of the decision process; punishment rates and differential rates. This model has provided a foundation for a number of studies on racial disparities in the military criminal justice system. In this section five studies are presented that offer a broad array of perspectives. The results are complex and leave many research questions unanswered. Collectively our contributors set the stage for further research and inquiry into race and the military justice system.

"Racial Disparities in Military Incarceration Rates: An Overview and Research Strategy" by Mickey Dansby presents a conceptual model and guide to determine causes for the overrepresentation of African-American males in the military justice system. Dansby concludes that a substantial portion of the disparity can be traced to exogenous sociological factors. In addition, he proposes a strategy using a bilateral approach: (1) design and implement an "inoculation" training for African-American males during the entry stages into military cultural and protocol; and (2) conduct cultural awareness training for the implementers (i.e., Judge Advocate General Corps, commanders, and military police) at all levels of the military justice system.

Martin Walker's study, "An Analysis of Discipline Rates Among Racial/Ethnic Groups in the U.S. Military," examined annual discipline data sent by the services to the Secretary of Defense for a four year period, 1987-1991. Overall, discipline rates were declining, although African-American rates were remaining steady. African Americans were over-represented in courts martial and to a lesser extent in non-judicial punishment (NJP), such as *Article 15s*. There were, however, large variations in rates over service and time. Walker concluded that the underlying factor was the nature of the offense. African Americans were found to be involved in more serious crimes, while whites were more prone to be involved with crimes against property and violating military rules.

In a similar study, Dan Landis and Richard Tallarigo, investigated 3300 *Article 15* incidents for three Army posts in 1994. They found that African Americans were over-represented in the number of *Article 15s*, but underrepresented in severity of punishment. In addition, African Americans were older and of higher rank than whites when receiving *Article 15s*. There was a notable difference between African Americans and whites in the type of offense they committed. They also discuss the possibility of a double standard relative to NJPs.

In the last study, Stephen Knouse examined equal samples of African-American and white inmates at the Fort Leavenworth, Kansas military prison. Similar to the studies listed above, African Americans and whites were found to commit different types of offenses. Knouse discusses a number of compelling factors that may explain the results. One conclusion is that researchers should focus on comparing African Americans with high-risk backgrounds who have discipline problems with those who do not. Such research would facilitate and understanding of the extent to which social background contributes to military discipline problems.

As noted above, these selected studies do not answer all of the burning questions, but they do point the way for further research. Even though the problems in this area are unusually complex and the acquisition of the data is extremely difficult, there are numerous important issues that should be considered for future research programs. The main question that remains to be answered is why significant differences in separations and punishment under *Article 15* continue to occur. We hope that the readership will extend this critical research and attempt to resolve some of those burning questions that may lead to corrective policy and procedures.

Notes

1.   Excludes prisoners held in Air Force confinement facilities.
2.   Like most codifications of Western jurisprudence, the Uniform Code of Military Justice (UCMJ) can trace its lineage back through English common law and to the

Ten Commandments. The readership is reminded that the Seventh Commandment says: *"Thou shalt not commit adultery."* Not surprisingly, this and other tenets of the Judeo-Christian ethic are incorporated in the UCMJ.

References

Chideya, F. (1995). *Don't believe the hype: Fighting cultural misinformation about African Americans.* New York: Plume.

Cole, D. (1999). *No Equal Justice: Race and Class in the American criminal justice system.* New York: New Press.

Conley, D. (1994). Adding color to a black and white picture: Using qualitative data to explain racial disproportionality in the juvenile justice system. *Journal of Research in Crime and Delinquency, 31*(2), 135-148.

DEOMI (1998). *A review of data on black Americans,* Patrick AFB, FL, Defense Equal Opportunity Management Institute.

Elliott, C. (1998). *Crime and punishment in America.* New York: Metropolitan Books.

Higgenbotham, Jr., L. (1996). *Shades of freedom: Racial politics and presumptions of American legal process.* New York: Oxford University Press.

Hillman, E.L. (1999). The "good soldier" defense character evidence and military rank at courts-martial, *The Yale Law Journal, 108*(4), 879-911.

Jackson, J. (1994, Mar 28). Crime bill in discriminatory, sentencing fall most on minorities says Jesse Jackson. *USA Today,* p. 13.

Lemann, N. (1998). Justice for blacks? *The New York Review of Books,* 45(4), 25-28.

Mauer, M. (1999). *Race to incarcerate.* New York: New Press.

Mauer, M., Huling, T., & Sentencing Project. (1995). *Young black Americans and the criminal justice system: Five years later.*

Miller, J. (1996). *Search and destroy: African American males in the criminal justice system.* New York: Cambridge University Press.

Nunn, K, (1997). Law as a eurocentric enterprise. *Law and Inequality: A Journal of Theory and Practice, 15*(2), 323-271.

Petersilia, J. (1983). *Racial disparities in the criminal justice system.* Santa Monica, CA: Rand Corporate.

Pope, C., & W. Feyerhern (1992). *Minorities in the juvenile justice system.* Rockville, MD: U.S. Department of Justice, Office of Juvenile Justice and Delinquency Prevention, Juvenile Justice Clearing House.

Smith, R. (1995). *Racism in the post-civil rights era: Now you see it, now you don't.* Albany, NY: State University of New York Press.

Tonry, M. (1996). *Malign neglect: Race, crime, and punishment in America.* New York: Oxford University Press.

Tonry, M. (1994). Racial disproportion in U.S. prisons, *British Journal of Criminology, 34.* Special issue.

19

Racial Disparities in Military Incarceration Rates: An Overview and Research Strategy

Mickey R. Dansby

Introduction

For some time now, Department of Defense (DoD) officials, civil rights activists, and researchers have been concerned about the discrepancy in discipline and incarceration rates between black and white men in the military services. Despite recent declines in overall discipline rates for all races, black service member continue to receive punishments at about twice the rate of their white counterparts (Tong & Jaggers, 1992). Tong and Jaggers (1992) present a chronology that traces some key events and research between 1969 and the present. Though formal research efforts within the services have not been as intensive during the last several years, recent media reports (e.g., Timms & McGonigle, 1991) and an April 1992 conference (1992 UCMJ Conference) at the Defense Equal Opportunity Management Institute (DEOMI), Patrick Air Force Base, Florida, mark renewed interest in the area and portend expanded research efforts.

The work of Tong and Jaggers (1992) provides a good summary of the issues and findings thus far. In addition, the results of the conference (summarized in Figure 19.1) help bring additional focus to specific research concerns. The purpose of the present paper is to extend these previous efforts by accomplishing the following:

1. Develop an overall model (the "Tree") that summarizes significant research issues and helps bring further focus to potential research.

2. Propose an initial research effort to address one of the more promising hypotheses, with a goal of encouraging the services to take steps that will reduce the disparity in discipline between black and white men.

Overall Model—"The Tree"

To establish a framework for organizing hypotheses that might explain the disparity between black and white disciplinary rates, the author has chosen to use the tree as an analogy. This choice was inspired by a discussion with Colonel Ronald M. Joe, USA, former Commandant of DEOMI, who likened the proliferation of research hypotheses to the development of a tree. The analog is designed to present a simple model that summarizes the current research and points the way for future research. The author makes no claim that the model is exhaustive; other factors may be involved that are not considered here. Furthermore, the reader should consider the possibility that the disparities are not simply explained; in all likelihood, multiple factors, operating in concert, are involved. Some introductory explanation of the tree model may be helpful. The reader may wish to refer to Figure 19.2 for clarification.

In identifying possible causes of the disparity, several researchers distinguish between factors that are external and those that are internal to the military system (e.g., Butler & Holmes, 1981; Nordlie et al., 1979). As distinguished by Butler and Holmes (1981), these factors will be referred to as exogenous and endogenous. In the analogy, exogenous factors are those that occur below the surface (i.e., in the root structure, unseen to those who examine the tree); endogenous factors are those that are part of the military system (i.e., the trunk, branches, etc., which are observable within the military).

At the interface between the exogenous and endogenous variables (ground level) is the interaction between the two types. For example, biases in selection based on characteristics of individuals who seek entry (exogenous) and the rules for selection established by the services (endogenous) may interact to differentially select blacks who are more likely to have disciplinary problems and whites who are less likely to have problems.

Above ground level are the trunk and branches. These represent endogenous factors that may explain the disparity in punishments. Though these factors are seen within the military, they may nonetheless be direct results of exogenous variables. For example, a propensity to commit certain types of crimes may be due to socializa-

Figure 19.1
1992 UCMJ Conference Output
Factors to be considered for UCMJ Research

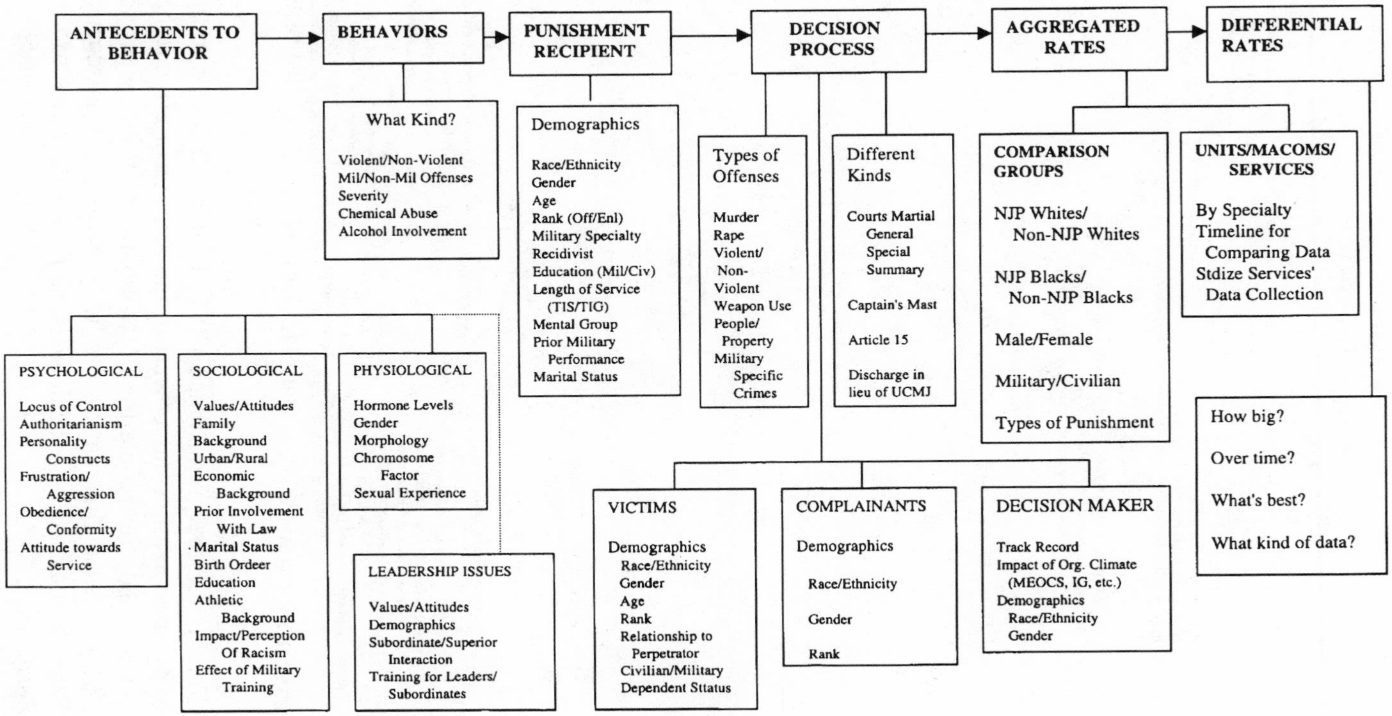

ANTECEDENTS TO BEHAVIOR → BEHAVIORS → PUNISHMENT RECIPIENT → DECISION PROCESS → AGGREGATED RATES → DIFFERENTIAL RATES

DIFFERENTIAL RATES

UNITS/MACOMS/SERVICES
By Specialty
Timeline for Comparing Data
Stdize Services' Data Collection

How big?
Over time?
What's best?
What kind of data?

AGGREGATED RATES

COMPARISON GROUPS
NJP Whites/ Non-NJP Whites
NJP Blacks/ Non-NJP Blacks
Male/Female
Military/Civilian
Types of Punishment

DECISION MAKER
Track Record
Impact of Org. Climate (MEOCS, IG, etc.)
Demographics
Race/Ethnicity
Gender

DECISION PROCESS

Different Kinds
Courts Martial
General
Special
Summary
Captain's Mast
Article 15
Discharge in lieu of UCMJ

Types of Offenses
Murder
Rape
Violent/ Non-Violent
Weapon Use
People/ Property
Military Specific Crimes

COMPLAINANTS
Demographics
Race/Ethnicity
Gender
Rank

VICTIMS
Demographics
Race/Ethnicity
Gender
Age
Rank
Relationship to Perpetrator
Civilian/Military
Dependent Status

PUNISHMENT RECIPIENT

Demographics
Race/Ethnicity
Gender
Age
Rank (Off/Enl)
Military Specialty
Recidivist
Education (Mil/Civ)
Length of Service (TIS/TIG)
Mental Group
Prior Military Performance
Marital Status

BEHAVIORS

What Kind?
Violent/Non-Violent
Mil/Non-Mil Offenses
Severity
Chemical Abuse
Alcohol Involvement

ANTECEDENTS TO BEHAVIOR

PHYSIOLOGICAL
Hormone Levels
Gender
Morphology
Chromosome Factor
Sexual Experience

LEADERSHIP ISSUES
Values/Attitudes
Demographics
Subordinate/Superior Interaction
Training for Leaders/ Subordinates

SOCIOLOGICAL
Values/Attitudes
Family Background
Urban/Rural
Economic Background
Prior Involvement With Law
Marital Status
Birth Order
Education
Athletic Background
Impact/Perception Of Racism
Effect of Military Training

PSYCHOLOGICAL
Locus of Control
Authoritarianism
Personality Constructs
Frustration/ Aggression
Obedience/ Conformity
Attitude towards Service

Figure 19.2
The Research Tree

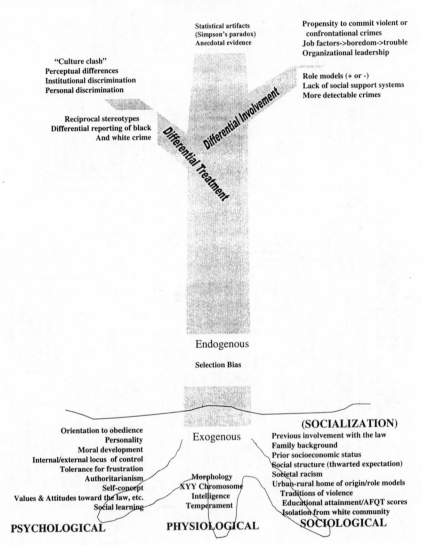

Statistical artifacts
(Simpson's paradox)
Anecdotal evidence

Propensity to commit violent or
confrontational crimes
Job factors->boredom->trouble
Organizational leadership

"Culture clash"
Perceptual differences
Institutional discrimination
Personal discrimination

Role models (+ or -)
Lack of social support systems
More detectable crimes

Reciprocal stereotypes
Differential reporting of black
And white crime

Differential Treatment

Differential Involvement

Endogenous

Selection Bias

Orientation to obedience
Personality
Moral development
Internal/external locus of control
Tolerance for frustration
Authoritarianism
Self-concept
Values & Attitudes toward the law, etc.
Social learning

Exogenous

Morphology
XYY Chromosome
Intelligence
Temperament

(SOCIALIZATION)
Previous involvement with the law
Family background
Prior socioeconomic status
Social structure (thwarted expectation)
Societal racism
Urban-rural home of origin/role models
Traditions of violence
Educational attainment/AFQT scores
Isolation from white community

PSYCHOLOGICAL   **PHYSIOLOGICAL**   **SOCIOLOGICAL**

tion outside the military and not to characteristics of military life; early socialization has powerful and long-term effects that would not be easily overcome by a few months of military service, especially if resocialization to a military culture did not occur rapidly. With the basics of the analogy in mind, we elaborate to include the specifics.

Exogenous Factors: The Roots and Soil

As the roots of a tree draw support for the trunk and branches from the soil, the soil of society, differential prior experiences, and individual differences may support the disparity between black and white punishment levels within the military services. The exogenous factors might be considered as having their influence through three main roots: psychological, physiological, and sociological. The psychological root includes such things as personality and attitudinal structure; the physiological includes genetic and physical differences; and the sociological includes factors such as social structure and socioeconomic status. These three major categories were identified at the 1992 UCMJ Conference. Hypothesized exogenous influences that could lead to the disparity in punishment within the services are considered for each root.

The Psychological Root

Some authors have suggested psychological differences between black and white men that may lead to differential involvement of black men in the military justice system. In many cases these differences are merely conjectures; research has not confirmed either that the differences exist or that they lead to disparate criminal activity. However, exploring such variables to determine whether differences exist and how the variables affect criminal behavior may lead to insights concerning differences between black and white men in involvement with the military justice system.

Nordlie et al. (1979) interviewed and surveyed a wide range of military personnel involved with military justice in the Army. The sources included implementers of the military justice system (i.e., first sergeant, commanders, military police, judges, etc.), prisoners, and ordinary soldiers. Among suggested causes was a difference in orientation to obedience and authority. Though there were some differences among black/white prisoners and nonprisoners on this variable, there was not strong support for the hypothesis that racial differences in attitude toward authority lead to differential involvement with the military justice system.

Laufer and Day (1983) compiled a series of papers suggesting several psychological factors that may lead to criminal activity. Among these factors are personality (e.g., personality factors that differ between criminal and noncriminal, such as interpersonal maturity, criminality, character structure, etc.) and moral development.

Another specific psychological factor hypothesized at the 1992 UCMJ Conference is tolerance for frustration. This factor would impact criminal behavior through the frustration-aggression relationship. Self-esteem and self-concept (Nordlie et al., 1979; Hogan & Jones, 1983; Berkowitz, 1980) have been proposed as influencing criminality. Also suggested as a key factor is values and attitudes toward the law, society, the military, etc. (Nordlie et al., 1979; Huba & Bentler, 1983).

Finally, researchers and theorists posit social learning as a psychological variable related to criminal behavior (e.g., Monahan & Splane, 1980; Hogan & Jones, 1983). Social learning emphasizes behaviors that are established by observation, imitation, and direct reinforcement from others. Consequently, the social learning view is highly related to the sociological perspective to be discussed later.

The Physiological Root

A number of biological (e.g., Mednick & Christiansen, 1977) and sociobiological (e.g., Mednick, 1980; Mednick et al., 1977) explanations of criminal behavior have been proposed. These explanations include reference to genetic variables such as temperament, the XYY chromosome factor, and intelligence. Some have tried to correlate various body forms (morphology) and crime (see Haskell & Yablonsky, 1983, for a summary of this generally unfruitful line of research). The most promising of the physiological studies are the sociobiological approaches, which consider the interaction between genetic influences (e.g., temperament) and societal influences (e.g., socialization).

A favored methodology in the physiological studies is to compare behaviors of dizygotic (fraternal) twins, who share similar environments but different genetic makeup, and monozygotic (identical) twins, who share essentially the same genetic makeup, to look for greater similarity in criminal activity among monozygotic twins. Such studies have some methodological problems, but in general lend some support to the proposal there is a physiological (genetic) basis for a tendency toward criminal activity (Christiansen, 1977).

The XYY chromosome studies generated a great deal of excitement (and controversy) when first introduced. They raised the prospect that males who had an extra chromosome (the second Y) were genetically more aggressive and more likely to be found in prisons. However, subsequent analyses tend to discount the XYY syndrome as a cause of aggressiveness (Witkin et al., 1976).

The Sociological Root

The sociological root includes those variables that are a function of society and the socialization process. These variables are quite powerful in determining behavior and are generally considered to have great impact on criminal behavior (Blumstein, 1982). Although the general process of socialization is pervasive, certain specific aspects have been suggested as relating to increased representation of black males in the military justice system. Some of these factors are summarized below.

Previous involvement (i.e., before entering the service) with the legal system has been suggested as a predictor of subsequent disciplinary difficulty in the military services (Nordlie et al., 1979; Flyer, 1990). Some researchers point to family background, especially non-traditional, unstructured homes where discipline was lacking or single-parent homes (e.g., Nordlie et al., 1979; Horne, 1988; Wilson & Herrnstein, 1985; McCord, 1980). Another suggested cause is prior socioeconomic status (e.g., Nordlie et al., 1979; Wilson & Herrnstein, 1985; Morris, 1988; Curtis, 1980), where deprivation leads to antisocial behavior and criminality. Related factors are social structure variables (Merton, 1938; Nordlie et al., 1979; Silberman, 1978), for example thwarted expectations of an improving place in society, and societal racism (Curtis, 1980; McNeely & Pope, 1981).

Another possible contributor is urban versus rural home of origin and the concomitant role models associated with these two different environments (Nordlie et al., 1979). The supposition is that the rural home does not engender the same "street-wise" behaviors that may lead to confrontations with military discipline. Some researchers propose a tradition of violence as a cause of subsequent criminality (Nordlie et al., 1979; Haskell & Yablonsky, 1983; Curtis, 1980; Gastil, 1971; Wolfgang, 1959). Some suggest educational attainment and Armed Forces Qualification Test scores as indicators (Flyer, 1990; Nordlie et al., 1979; Polan & Thomas, 1985). Morris (1988) believes some criminal behavior may be due to the growing black underclass and increasing isolation of black individuals from the white community.

The sociological root is replete with possible explanations for differences in black/white involvement with the justice system. If, indeed, some of these variables differentially affect black and white crime rates, there is a distinct possibility of the interaction of exogenous and endogenous factors to select black men for military service who are more likely than selected white men to have trouble with the military justice system. Such selection bias may be an inadvertent result of (for example) less complete screening of black men with regard to prior criminal activity. In the tree model, selection bias occurs at the juncture between the exogenous and endogenous factors (i.e., ground level). We now turn our attention to the trunk and branches of the tree: those variables that are internal to the services and that may explain the disparity in black and white discipline rates.

Endogenous Factors: The Trunk, Forks, and Branches

Endogenous variables operate within the military system itself. Though they are internal to the services, they may interact with any of the exogenous factors previously discussed. Our present focus is primarily limited to research that has been conducted within the services. The endogenous factors may be conveniently divided into those related to differential treatment (i.e., discrimination, etc.) and differential involvement (i.e., black males actually commit more acts that legitimately result in punishment). In addition to these major forks in the trunk, a third fork might be considered for artifactual effects (e.g., the rates of punishment for blacks and whites are to some degree due to anomalies in the reporting of data gathering process). First, we consider the possibility of differential treatment.

The Differential Treatment Fork

A frequent explanation for the higher representation of black men in the military justice system is discrimination. This explanation presumes prejudice on the part of various individuals throughout the disciplinary chain. Since most of the decision-makers in the disciplinary system are white males, it is a logical hypothesis that historical societal prejudices work to the disadvantage of black men. Several specific versions of how differential treatment might occur have been proposed.

The output from the 1992 UCMJ Conference summarizes a number of points at which discrimination might occur within the military justice system. Concern over possible racism in the military justice system have been raised over a span of at least 20 years by the NAACP (Wilkins, 1971), the Civil Rights Commission (McGonigle & Timms, 1991), and the Congressional Black Caucus (McGonigle, 1991). These concerns have been raised based on statistical disparities between black and white punishments and reports of discrimination from various individuals and groups within the services.

Researchers have also considered racism as a possible explanation, either in reality or as perceived by service members (e.g., Butler & Holmes, 1981; Moskos, 1991, quoted by Matthews in the *Army Times*; Morris, 1988, in civilian cases; Nordlie et al., 1979; Horne, 1988). Discrimination based ort race may have several sources, for example, discrimination may be due to *"culture clash"* (Nordlie et al., 1979). Culture clash may occur when the military culture (primarily based on white traditions) conflicts with a black subculture. The predominant and more powerful culture would be expected to exercise controls to resolve conflicts on its own terms.

Another source may be perceptual difference (Nordlie et al., 1979; Butler & Holmes, 1981; Horne, 1988), where black and white members have different perceptions of what behaviors are serious or punishable offenses. Institutional discrimination, where rules and policies of the military institution have unintentional discriminatory effects, is also a possibility (1992 UCMJ Conference).

Another powerful source is personal discrimination (Nordlie et al., 1979; Horne, 1988; Butler & Holmes, 1981). Personal discrimination could occur when individual prejudices of the implementers of the military justice system (i.e., first sergeants, commanders, military police, judges, etc.) influence their decisions. Finally, reciprocal stereotyping (Nordlie et al., 1979), where white implementers "expect" criminal behavior from black service members, and black members "expect" prejudicial treatment from white implementers, can exacerbate confrontations and lead to charges where an incident might otherwise be handled at a lower level and dismissed.

The Differential Involvement Fork

An alternative explanation for the disparity in discipline rates is the hypothesis of differential involvement. This explanation posits that black males, for whatever reasons (e.g., perhaps due to the exogenous factors discussed previously), commit more crimes and should therefore be overrepresented in the military justice system. From this perspective, the system operates fairly; discrimination within the services is not the primary cause of the disparity.

Several factors internal to the services could contribute to differential involvement of black men in various types of offenses. For example, there is some evidence that black members have a greater propensity to commit violent or confrontational crimes (Nordlie et al., 1979; Polan & Thomas, 1985). Such crimes are personal and more detectable and, therefore, more likely to be reported with a positive identification of the offender. Consider, for example, the difference between a property crime, such as stealing tools from the government, and a personal crime, such as assaulting another military member in the barracks. The property crime may not even be noticed for quite some time, making it more difficult to apprehend the offender; the personal crime involves at least one eyewitness (the victim) and immediate detection.

An interesting proposal by Nordlie et al. (1979) is that some differential involvement may be due to job factors. Black men, on average, have lower entrance test scores than white men. They consequently are more likely to have military jobs that are less interesting and lack intrinsic motivation (i.e., are unenriched). Such jobs can lead to low satisfaction, boredom, and, perhaps, dysfunctional behaviors resulting in disciplinary problems. A related explanation is a lack of effective organizational leadership (1992 UCMJ Conference). This hypothesis receives some support from the finding by Horne (1988) that within at least one service there is a wide difference in the disparity between black and white punishments based on the individual units observed. A corollary of this hypothesis is that the role models for black military members could influence behavior either in a positive or negative way (Horne, 1988). If appropriate role models are not available, greater disciplinary infractions may accrue. Also, lack of appropriate social support systems within the command (Horne, 1988) may contribute to greater involvement by black males in behaviors that result in disciplinary action.

The Artifactual Effects Fork

A third endogenous explanation is that some of the disparity is due to statistical and reporting artifacts. The reasoning is that with proper handling of statistical reports, especially the approach used to aggregate statistics from level to level, some of the disparity would be revealed as nonexistent (Horne, 1988). One such artifact is Simpson's Paradox. Horne (1988) provides an example of this phenomenon, and he reports evidence that it may be operative (at least within one service). The example is illustrated in Table 19.1.

As may be seen in this example, the rates of punishment within the two subunits of Command X indicate no disparity when considered separately (in fact, in each unit the rate for whites is slightly more than the rate for blacks). However, when the statistics are aggregated at the overall command level, there is an apparent 50 percent overrepresentation of black members in punishment rates. The paradox occurs when there are large differences in the proportions of black and white members in various subunits of an organization. The extent to which this occurs is not known, but Horne (1988) presented evidence that it does occur. Others have raised concerns about statistical procedures as well (e.g., Davison, 1972). Horne (1988) has recommended, along with others (e.g., 1992 UCMJ Conference; Polan & Thomas, 1985), that statistical procedures be scrutinized and standardized across services.

Table 19.1
NJP Statistics for Command X

Unit X1

Group	Punished	Not Punished	Punishment Rate
Black	1	59	1.7%
White	9	431	2.0%

Unit X2

Group	Punished	Not Punished	Punishment Rate
Black	38	162	19.0%
White	65	235	21.7%

Command X Overall

Group	Punished	Not Punished	Punishment Rate
Black	39	221	15.0%
White	74	666	10.0%

Others have suggested that especially black service members, based on anecdotal reports of incidents have also overestimated the degree of disparity. Both Horne (1988) and Hart (1978) present evidence that disparities may be perceived when there is no statistical difference between black and white punishment rates within a unit.

It is the author's speculation that such artifactual problems are relatively minor and not sufficient to account for a large portion of the overall disparity. These problems should be investigated and cleared up, however.

Having examined the tree from its roots to its branches, the logical question is where do we go from here? The answer to that question, in large measure, depends on how one frames the problem. The present author offers a starting place that is based on the tradition of action research.

Discussion and Research Proposal

Considerable research has been devoted to this issue, both in the civilian and military communities. A major question yet to be answered is how much of the disparity in discipline rates between black and white military members is due to exogenous factors and how much is due to endogenous factors? Furthermore, it is not clear how much is due to differences in treatment (i.e., discrimination) versus differences in involvement for black and white members. Certainly these issues are legitimate research concerns and should be addressed. Even when we find the answers, however, we will not solve the problem. Some form of intervention will be required to correct the disparity. As a next step, the present author advocates an action research program (based on the tree model) that makes some assumptions, based on current evidence and tests these assumptions by implementing interventions that might reasonably be expected to reduce the disparity.

Given the current evidence, where should an intervention program attack the problem? From the present analysis, it appears the most fruitful intervention program should be aimed at overcoming effects of the sociological root. This conclusion is based on several considerations. First, the effects of the sociological factors are well supported by research and theory (see review above). Second, there is evidence that at least a substantial portion of the disparity may be accounted for by differential criminal involvement of black and white males. This difference in involvement appears to be rooted in socialization differences between black and white males and persists even when possible discrimination is factored out (see, for example, Hindelang, 1978; Blumstein, 1982; Petersilia, 1983; Morris, 1988). This is not to deny differential treatment as another source of the disparity. As in most behavioral phenomena, causes may be multiple. However, discrimination, per se, does not appear to be the strongest contributor to the disparity (Blumstein, 1982; Morris, 1988). Third, there is only weak support for the hypothesis that the bulk of the disparity is due to discrimination within the military justice system (1992 UCMJ Conference; Horne, 1988; Tong & Jaggers, 1992; Nordlie et al., 1979; Polan & Thomas, 1985). Fourth, assuming a strong influence by the sociological root implies an intervention approach that is feasible. If a large part of the problem is due to socialization, then the military can use educational approaches to help resocialize incoming members and sensitize those who administer the military justice system to possible effects of exogenous factors on individual behavior.

With these factors in mind, the author proposes that the next research step should be to design an experiment to test the effects of early intervention to resocalize black males to the military system. This intervention should be designed to make incoming black males aware of the differential effects their behaviors may have in the military society (as opposed to the civilian society from which they came). For example, where confrontation may be an effective strategy in the inner city, it may be interpreted as disrespect and insubordination in the military service. If those most at risk to misread the military system (i.e., more often black males, due to typical differences in social factors between black and white recruits) receive effective orientation to military society, they may modify their behavior and avoid trouble with the military justice system.

The author is aware that some may consider this action research to be "victim focused." In a sense, it is, but only because it aims the intervention primarily at those who are victims of a socialization process over which they have no control. We must be clear in our thinking regarding this issue. The current proposal in no way assumes the victims (i.e., black males) are to blame. In the author's opinion, the major concern with a victim focus is the phenomenon of blaming the victim for the crime perpetrated against him or her. (The typical example is to blame a woman who is raped for "asking for it," etc.) However, to help a victim overcome his or her victimization is not discriminatory; it is in fact, the proper and moral course of action.

Perhaps, an example would help clarify the point. Assume a man is walking down the street and is mugged. The attacker severely injures the man and starts to flee. Just at that moment, a passerby sees what is happening and rushes to the scene. What should the passerby do? The mugger is to blame for what has happened and should be brought to justice. Doing so may prevent future muggings and help change society. So, it would seem the passerby should chase down the mugger, perhaps seeking help along the way, and detain the mugger for the authorities. But what about the victim? If the passerby leaves the victim with his injuries, he might die. Clearly, the first course of action for the passerby, no matter how much anger and disgust the criminal evokes, should be to try to help the victim survive and overcome his injuries.

The author applies the analogy to the present proposal as follows. Many black males entering the service may have been injured by sociological factors that have reduced their chances for success in the military. Though it is clear these factors are beyond their control, it is also clear that the passerby (the military system) cannot control them either. The military system should try to do what it can to help heal the victim's "injuries"; otherwise the victim's survival as an effective military member is in peril.

Having considered these background issues, let us reflect on how an experiment might be designed to implement this general line of research. The general approach is not original with the author (see Nordlie et al., 1979, for example). However, it appears not to have been implemented previously. Specifically, the following is proposed:

1. Design a training package that focuses on presenting behaviors that are appropriate and contrasts them with behaviors that are not appropriate in the military. A good design might be to have DEOMI (or another appropriate agent) created videotapes with vignettes depicting such scenes and showing the consequences of inappropriate behaviors (i.e., charges, punishment, incarceration, etc.). This strategy will be called the *inoculation* approach. A second package might be designed around the cultural *assimilation* model proposed by Landis et al. (1976). This model will be known as the assimilation approach. Both approaches could be used in the experiment, and the effectiveness of each compared to the other and to nontreatment control groups. Figure 19.3 shows the basic experimental design.

2. Implement the training packages either in the pre-entry stage or at the earliest possible point in a recruit's assimilation. Six randomly assigned, demographically matched groups should be used: black and white male control groups

(receiving no special training); black and white male inoculation training groups; and black and white male cultural assimilator training groups. Training should be implemented as a normal part of the assimilation process, insofar as possible.

3. Track the performance of the six groups over a period of at least two years to determine whether there are differences in contact with the military justice system.

From an action research perspective, a parallel effort that might enhance the effectiveness of early intervention with the black male population entering the military could be to provide sensitization training to those who implement the military justice system (including first sergeants, commanders, military police, etc.). They should be made aware of the effects of sociological factors exogenous to the military and the impact these factors may have on behaviors. Perhaps such increased awareness would temper implementers' decisions with greater wisdom at various levels within the system and help them make decisions that are culturally equitable. The effectiveness of such sensitization training should be determined through additional research.

Another possible line of research might help answer the question of differential involvement versus differential treatment for black males in the military justice system. A clever research strategy in the civilian sector tries to answer this question by examining victim reports (Wilson & Herrnstein, 1985; Hindelang, 1978). The basic approach is to consider only crimes which have a victim, contact the victims for identification of the race and gender of the perpetrator, and compare the rates reported, by race and gender, with arrest, conviction, sentencing, etc., statistics. The studies conducted thus far show a close correspondence between victims' reports of the race of the perpetrators and overall statistics, by race, for the type of crime considered. Although not all types of crime may be considered, at

Figure 19.3
Experimental Design

Condition*

Racial Group	Inoculation	Assimilation	Control
Black	X	X	O
White	X	X	O

*X =Treatment and observation; O =Observation only.

least for personal crimes we may be able to determine whether black males are arrested at a discriminatory rate.

Summary

The present paper presents a conceptual summary and guide for research to help determine causes for the overrepresentation of black males (compared to white males) in the military justice system. A number of factors external to the military (exogenous factors: psychological, physiological, and sociological) are considered, as well as several factors internal to the military system (endogenous factors: selection bias, differential treatment, differential involvement). Based on the author's analysis of the most influential causes of the disparity, an action research proposal is presented. The research proposal focuses on overcoming the effects of exogenous sociological factors through a program of training designed to facilitate black males' socialization into the military society. Two strategies are suggested: "Inoculation" training, using videotapes, to prevent adverse interactions with those in authority within the military; and cultural assimilation and transition training to aid black males in moving from a civilian to a military culture. A parallel recommendation is to provide cultural awareness training for the implementers (at all levels) of the military justice system. It is hoped that such programs will prove effective in reducing the overrepresentation of black males in military justice actions.

References

Berkowitz, L. (1980). Is criminal violence normative behavior? Hostile and instrumental aggression in violent incidents. In E. Bittner & S. L. Messinger (Eds.), *Criminology Review Yearbook.* Beverly Hills, CA: Sage.

Blumstein, A. (1982). On the racial disporportionality of United States' prison populations. *Journal of Criminal Law & Criminology, 73,* 1259-1281.

Butler, J. S., & Holmes, M. D. (1981). Perceived discrimination and the military experience. *Journal of Political and Military Sociology, 9,* 17-30.

Christiansen, K. O. (1977). A review of studies of criminality among twins. In S. A. Mednick & K. O. Christiansen (Eds.), *Biosocial bases of criminal behavior.* New York: Gardner.

Curtis, L. A. (1980). Violence, personality, deterrence, and culture. In E. Bittner & S. L. Messinger (Eds.), *Criminology Review Yearbook.* Beverly Hills, CA: Sage.

Davison, F. E. (1972, May). Coping with people problems. *Soldiers,* pp. 10-13.

Flyer, E. S. (1990). *Characteristics and behavior of recruits entering military service with an offense history.* Office of the Assistant Secretary of Defense (Force Management and Personnel). Arlington, VA: Defense Manpower Data Center.

Gastil, R. D. (1971). Homicide and a regional culture of violence. *American Sociological Review, 36.*

Haskell, M. R., & Yablonsky, L. (1983). *Criminology: Crime and criminality.* Boston, MA: Houghton Mifflin.

Hindelang, M. (1979). Race and involvement in common law personal crimes. *American Sociological Review, 43.*

Hogan, R., & Jones, W. H. (1983). A role-theoretical model of criminal conduct. In W. S. Laufer & J. M. Day (Eds.), *Personality theory, moral development and criminal behavior.* Lexington, MA: Lexington Books.

Horne, G. E. (1988). *Equity in disciplinary rates* (Research Memorandum 88-26). Alexandria, VA: Center for Naval Analyses.

Huba, G. J., & Bentler, P. M. (1983). Causal models of the development of law abidance and its relationship to psychological factors and drug use. In W. S. Laufer & J. M. Day (Eds.), *Personality theory, moral development and criminal behavior.* Lexington, MA: Lexington Books.

Landis, D., Day, H. R., McGrew, P. L., Thomas, J. A., & Miller, A. B. (1976). Can a black "culture assimilator" increase racial understanding? *Journal of Social Issues, 31,* 169-183.

Laufer, W. S., & Day, J. M. (1983). *Personality theory, moral development and criminal behavior.* Lexington, MA: Lexington Books.

McCord, J. (1980). Some child-rearing antecedents of criminal behavior in adult men. In E. Bittner & S. L. Messinger (Eds.), *Criminology Review Yearbook.* Beverly Hills, CA: Sage.

McGonigle, S. (1991, December 13). Black caucus chief joins call for military justice inquiry. *The Dallas Morning News.*

McGonigle, S., & Timms, E. (1991, November 5). Critics allege racial bias in military justice system. *The Dallas Morning News.*

McNeely, R. L., & Pope, C. E. (1981). *Race, crime, and criminal justice.* Beverly Hills, CA: Sage.

Mednick, S. A. (1980). A biosocial theory of the learning of law-biding behavior. In E. Bittner & S. L. Messinger (Eds.), *Criminology Review Yearbook.* Beverly Hills, CA: Sage.

Mednick, S. A., & Christiansen, K. O. (1977). Biosocial *bases of criminal behavior.* New York: Gardner.

Mednick, S. A., Kirkegaard-Sorensen, L., Hutchings, B., Knop, J., Rosenberg, R., & Schulsinger, F. (1977). An example of biosocial interaction research: The interplay of socioenvironmental and individual factors in the etiology of criminal behavior. In S. A. Mednick & K. O. Christiansen (Eds.), *Biosocial bases of criminal behavior.* New York: Gardner.

Merton, R. K. (1938). Social structure and anomie. *American Sociological Review, 3.*

Morris, N. (1988). Race and crime: What evidence is there that race influences results in the criminal justice system? *Judicature, 92*(2), 111-113.

Nordlie, P. G., Sevilla, E. R., Jr., Edmonds, W. S., & White, S. J. (1979). A study of racial factors in the Army's justice and discharge systems, (Rep. No. HSR-RR-79/18-Hr, in 4 vols.). Washington, DC: DAPE-HRR, The Pentagon.

Petersilia, J. (1983). *Racial disparities in the criminal justice system.* Santa Monica, CA: RAND.

Polan, S. L., & Thomas, P. J. (1985). *Military offense rates: Racial, ethnic, and gender differences,* (Rpt. No. MPL TN 86-2). San Diego: Navy Personnel Research and Development Center.

Silberman, C. E. (1978). *Criminal violence, criminal justice.* New York: Random House.

Timms, E., & McGonigle, S. (1991, November 24). Military's law system has abuses. *The Dallas Morning News,* pp. 1-5.

Tong, C. K., & Jaggars, C. A. (1992). *Phase I report: An investigation into the disparity of judicial and non-judicial punishment rates for black males in the armed services.* Patrick Air Force Base, FL: Defense Equal Opportunity Management Institute.

Wilkins, R. (1971). *The search for military justice.* New York: NAACP Special Contribution Fund.

Wilson, J. Q., & Herrnstein, R. J. (1985). *Crime and human nature.* New York: Simon & Schuster.

Witkin, H. A., Mednick, S. A., Schulsinger, F. Bakkestrom, E., Christiansen, K. O., Goodenough, D. R., Hirschhorn, K., Lundsteen, C., Owen, D. R., Philip, J., Rubin, D. B., & Stocking, M. (1976). XYY and XXY men: Criminality and aggression. *Science, 193,* 547-555.

Wolfgang, M. E. (1959). *Patterns in criminal homicide.* Philadelphia, PA: University of Pennsylvania Press.

20

An Analysis of Discipline Rates Among Racial/Ethnic Groups in the Military Fiscal Years 1987-1991

Martin R. Walker

Introduction

The Uniform Code of Military Justice (UCMJ) is a set of statutes governing military justice to which all service members are subject. The UCMJ contains articles that govern the administration of courts-martial, direct the commander in his/her implementation of Non-Judicial Punishments (NJP) procedures, and sets forth rules and regulations to which all personnel under UCMJ jurisdiction must adhere. NJP (sometimes known as *Article 15* after the section in the UCMJ where it is found) is part of the UCMJ and allows commanders to impose disciplinary punishments for minor offenses without convening a court martial. NJP is commonly used to correct the discipline of military personnel who have committed minor violations and/or infractions of the UCMJ. As shown in Figure 20.1, NJPs fall midway in terms of severity of punishment that a commander can impose against a service member.

More serious offenses against the UCMJ may be referred by the commander to a court martial. The *Manual for Court Martial* (MCM, 1984) describes three types: the summary, for minor non-capital offenses; the special, for more serious non-capital offenses; and the general, usually reserved for major offenses. The Summary Court Martial (SCM) is seldom used; commanders usually prefer to dispose of minor UCMJ infractions at NJP rather than convene a SCM.

Figure 20.1
Discipline Flow Diagram

Infraction

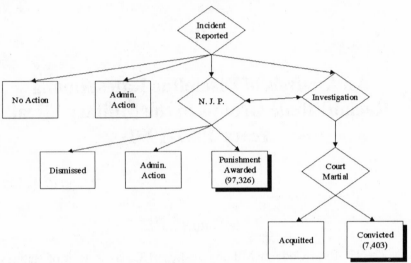

The Special Court Martial (SPCM) is used more frequently, and a SPCM conviction is considered a felony conviction. A General Court Martial (GCM) may adjudge harsher penalties than either the SCM or SPCM, including the death penalty. A GCM conviction is also a felony conviction.

The fundamental difference between a court martial and NJP is that a court martial requires a special investigation, legal representation, and a trial. *Article 15* proceedings, while providing for more punishment options than a commander can impose administratively, are not considered trials. Within NJP guidelines, a commander has the discretion to take no action, administrative action, or to impose NJP.

Problem. A recent review by the U.S. Commission on Civil Rights has placed the administration of the UCMJ under increased scrutiny. This review focused on allegations that minority service members receive a disproportionate amount, and more severe administration of disciplinary actions within the military services. Also, it alleged that within the military justice system, minority members were treated differently based on their race.[1]

Objective. This analysis analyzes data from Military Equal Opportunity Assessments (MEOA) reports quantifying punishments under the UCMJ. The objective is to determine changes over time in the representation of racial/ethnic groups among personnel receiving punishments.

Methodology. The study methodology involved the collection and analysis of data on the receipt of punishments (Courts Martials and NJPs) by racial/ethnic group. The data for FY87 through FY90 was collected from the MEOA reports that the services provide annually to the Office of the Secretary of Defense (OSD). The individual services were contacted in order to collect data for FY91. The data for FY91 were extracted from draft copies of the FY91 MEOA reports.

Analytical Techniques. Various descriptive statistics including measures of central tendency (means), frequency distributions, and percentages are examined. In addition, a Representation Index (RI) is used to determine the extent to which demographic subgroups are over or underrepresented among punishment recipients. Presentation of the statistical data is supplemented by graphical representations.

The following formula was used to compute the RI:

$$\text{Representation Index} = \frac{\text{Actual Number}}{\text{Expected Number}} \times 100 - 100$$

Where:

Actual Number   =   The discipline data reported in the MEOA by each military service.

Expected Number   =   Expected percentage times the base population (i.e., the number of court martial convictions or NJPs). The expected percentage is the population percentage of a particular group in question.

By dividing the actual number by the expected number, a ratio is created which indicates the extent to which the actual number is greater or lesser than the expected number. Multiplying by 100 converts the ratio to a more readily understood percentage. By subtracting 100 from the product, an indicator is created that is zero when actual and expected numbers are the same. If the index is zero or close to zero, this means that there is no difference between the actual and the expected dimension being considered. For the group and parameter in question, the formula yields the percentage over or underrepresented. If the RI is -20, this would mean that the subpopulation was 20 percent underrepresented relative to what would be expected given its population size.

Research Questions

The following questions provided the focus of this inquiry:

1.   What are the overall trends in discipline actions (courts martial convictions and NJPs) in the military justice system?

2.   Do discipline actions vary for the different armed services?

3.   How representative are minority groups with regards to discipline actions?

Limitations

As shown in Figure 20.1, the data analyzed in this report are limited to the outputs of the UCMJ system, i.e., courts martial convictions and NJPs assessed. Data on service members entering the system, how they were handled, and infractions committed were not available. Therefore, this study alone does not answer the question of whether the UCMJ system is racially unbiased.

Courts Martial Convictions

1. Trends in Courts Martial Convictions

a. Number of Courts Martial Convictions.

1. Figure 20.2 shows the total number of military courts martial convictions in the Department of Defense (DoD). Total courts martial convictions decreased more than 52 percent between FY87 and FY91 (from 15,739 in FY87 to 7,485 in FY91). The number of courts

martial convictions for each of the military services steadily decreased. In FY87, the Navy had nearly twice as many courts martial convictions as any other service. However, the number of Navy courts martial convictions decreased dramatically (71 percent) from 7,088 in FY87 to 2,025 in FY91. The other services experienced more modest decreases in the number courts martial convictions: 40 percent for the Army, 36 percent for the Marine Corps, and 31 percent for the Air Force.

2. One theory advanced by both DEOMI personnel and participants at the UCW conference sponsored by the Defense Equal Opportunity Management Institute Directorate of Research, held on April 6, 1992 at Patrick Air Force Base, Florida was that the improvements in the overall quality of service members have translated into the need for fewer courts martial. These improvements included tougher recruiting standards in terms of higher Armed Forces Qualification Test scores, a higher percentage of high school graduates, and fewer criminal and moral waivers. The exploration of the extent to which a relationship exists between service member quality and service behavior was beyond the scope of this report.

Figure 20.2
Courts Martial Convictions by Military Service

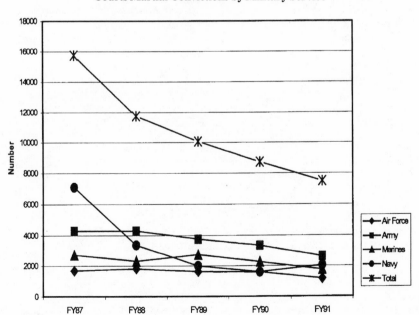

b. Percentage of Courts Martial Convictions.

1. The percentage of members from each service who have been court martialed is presented in Figure 20.3. The Marine Corps had nearly as many courts martial convictions as other services, but had fewer service members. Therefore, the Marine Corps had the highest rate of courts martial convictions among the services, between 1.0 and 1.5 percent of its population. Two possible explanations have been suggested as to why the courts martial convictions rate in the Marine Corps is higher than the other services - a greater emphasis on discipline, and the gender composition of the Corps. The percentage of females in the Marine Corps is much smaller than in the other services.

2. The percentage of courts martial convictions for each of the military services decreased between 1987 and 1991. The most significant decline was found within the Navy, with a change from 1.34 percent in FY87 to .41 percent in FY91, followed by the Marine Corps, where the percentage declined from 1.5 percent to 1 percent. For the Army, the percentage declined from .55 percent to .35 percent, and for the Air Force, the percentage declined from .3 percent to .2 percent.

Figure 20.3
Percentage of Courts Marterials by Service (FY87-91)

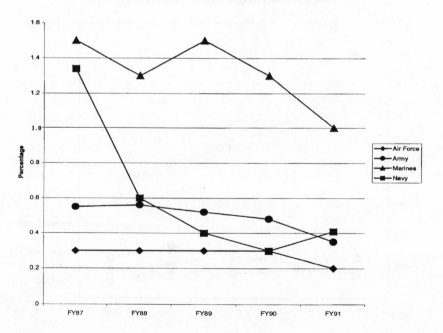

3. The most meaningful statistic identified in Figure 20.3 is the relative infrequency of courts martial convictions for all services. In FY91, the average rate of courts martial convictions for all service members was equal to four-tenths of one percent (.4 percent or .004) of the total military population. Additionally, the number of courts martial convictions and the percent of courts martial convictions declined over the five fiscal years.

2. Minority Courts Martial Convictions

a.   Number of Minority Courts Martial Convictions.

While the total number of courts martial convictions has decreased dramatically, the decrease in the numbers of courts martial convictions has varied considerably across racial/ethnic groups. Figure 20.4 exhibits the number of courts martial convictions by racial/ethnic groups. The number of courts martial convictions has decreased most significantly among white service members. The number of courts martial convictions decreased more than 60 percent for white service members compared to 35 percent for African-American service

Figure 20.4
Number of Courts Martial by Racial/Ethnic Group (FY87-FY91)

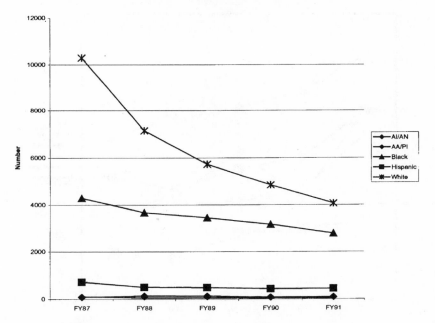

members, and 38 percent for Hispanic service members. Also, the number of courts martial convictions decreased more than 63 percent for American Indian (AI)/Native Alaskan (NA) service members, the number of courts martial convictions decreased 1 percent for Asian-American (AA)/Pacific Islander (PI) service members. Note, however, that the number of AI/NA and AA/PI courts martial convictions was relatively insignificant (less than .15 percent) when compared with the total number of courts martial convictions throughout DoD.

b.   Percentage of Courts Martial Convictions.

The percentage of members from each racial/ethnic group convicted of courts martial offenses is presented in Figure 20.5. The percentage of courts rnartial convictions for white service members decreased faster than for minority service members, with the exception of the AI/AN subgroup. The percentage of white service members court martialed decreased from .69 percent of their population in FY87 to only .31 percent in FY91, a decrease of more than 55

Figure 20.5
Percentage of Courts Martials by Racial/Ethnic Group (FY87-FY91)

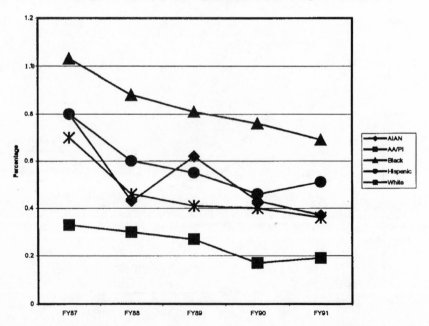

percent. The percentage of Hispanic and AA/PI service members courts martialed decreased more than 42 percent. The percentage of African-American service members court martialed decreased only 33 percent, the lowest rate of decline for all racial/ethnic groups.

3. Minority Representation Among Courts Martial Convictions

a. Percentage of Courts Martial Convictions by Race.

1. Since the number of white courts martial convictions decreased faster than the number of African-American courts martial convictions, the racial/ethnic mix of courts martialed service members changed considerably. Figure 20.6 shows the percentage of courts martial convictions assessed to African Americans and whites. In FY87, 65 percent of the service members who received courts martial were white, and 27 percent were African American. By FY91, white service members represented 54 percent, and African-Ameri-

Figure 20.6
Percentage of Courts Martial Convictions for Blacks and Whites (FY87-FY91)

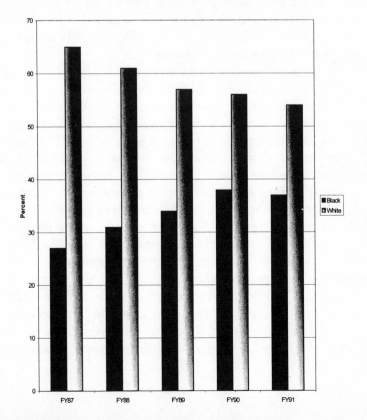

can service members represented 37 percent of those being courts martialed. The percentage of courts martial received by African Americans and whites for each individual service is presented in the Appendix.

b. Minority Over/Underrepresentation Among Courts Martial Convictions.

1. The RI, as previously discussed, was computed using total military courts martial convictions data for FY87 through FY91. The results are shown in Figure 20.7. The RI for African-American service members indicated that they were 36 percent overrepresented in courts martial convictions in FY87. The overrepresentation of African-American service members increased steadily during the five fiscal years, reaching more than 74 percent in FY91. Conversely, white service members were underrepresented with respect to courts martial convictions. The underrepresentation of white service members increased from 9 percent in FY87 to more than 22 percent in FY91. Additionally, AA/PIs were nearly always underrepresented, usually significantly underrepresented. The RI for all other minority groups varied considerably from period to period with no discernible patterns or trends in group representation. The RIs for individual services are presented in the Appendix.

2. The increased overrepresentation of African Americans was not caused by an increase in their number of courts martial convictions. Rather, it resulted from the more rapid decline in the number of courts martial convictions among other racial/ethnic groups, particularly white service members than among African Americans.

3. The degree of minority overrepresentation in courts martial convictions varied considerably among the different services. For all services, African-American service members were consistently overrepresented among courts martial convictions. Figure 20.8 shows the overrepresentation of African-American service members in courts martial convictions for the different services. In the Air Force, African-American service members are the only minority that was consistently overrepresented with regards to courts martial convictions. For the five years, nearly twice as many African-American service members were court martialed as would be expected given their population size. African-American and Hispanic service members were overrepresented in courts martial convictions within the

Figure 20.7
Representation of Racial/Ethnic Groups in Courts Martial Convictions

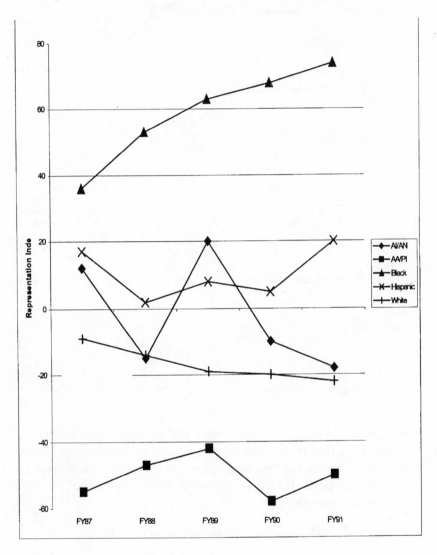

Figure 20.8
**Overrepresentation of Black Service Members in Courts Martial Convictions by
Military Service (FY87-FY91)**

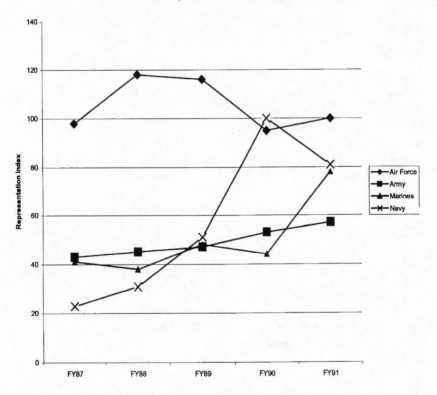

Navy and Marine Corps. For these two services, the
overrepresentation of African-American service members increased
significantly during the five fiscal years. In the Army, the percent of
overrepresentation of African-American service members showed
more modest growth.

Non-Judicial Punishments: Article 15

1. Trends in Non-Judicial Punishments

    a.   Number of Non-Judicial Punishments.

Figure 20.9 shows the total number of military NJPs between FY87
and FY91. The total number of NJPs decreased more than 47 per-

Figure 20.9
Number of Non-Judicial Punishment by Military Service (FY87-FY91)

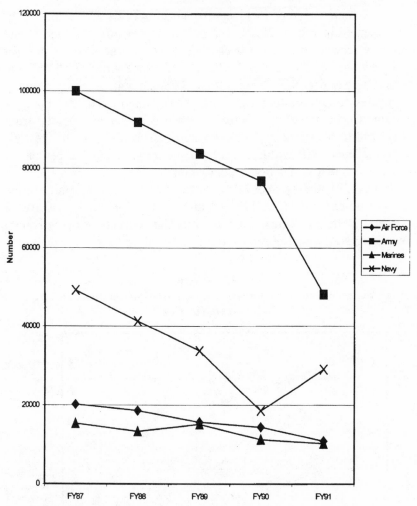

cent—from 184,601 in FY87 to 98,173 in FY91. The number of NJPs for each of the military services steadily decreased. In FY87, the Army had nearly twice as many NJPs as any other service. However, the number of Army NJPs decreased considerably (52 percent) over the five years, from 100,088 in FY87 to 48,025 in FY91. The other services had similar decreases in the number of NJPs. The Air Force had a decrease of 46 percent since FY87, the Navy decreased by 41 percent, and the Marine Corps by 33 percent.

b. Percentage of Non-Judicial Punishments.

1. The percentage of members from each service who were a NJP is presented in Figure 20.10. The percentage of NJP for each of the military services decreased over the five years. The most significant decrease in the NJP rate of NJP occurred in the Army. In FY87, the Army assessed a NJP to more than 12.9 percent of Army soldiers compared to only 6.6 percent in FY91. The rate of NJPs for both the Marine Corps and Navy decreased about 3 percentage points, from 9 percent to 6 percent of their populations. The Air Force has historically awarded NJP within a very narrow range, from 2.1 percent to 3.4 percent of the Air Force population.

2. In FY91, the average NJP rate for the Army, Navy, and Marine Corps combined was 6.3 percent, and for the Air Force just over 2 percent. Both the number of NJPs and the percentage of personnel receiving NJPs, declined over the five fiscal years.

Figure 20.10
Percentage of Population Receiving Non-Judicial Punishments by Military Services (FY87-FY91)

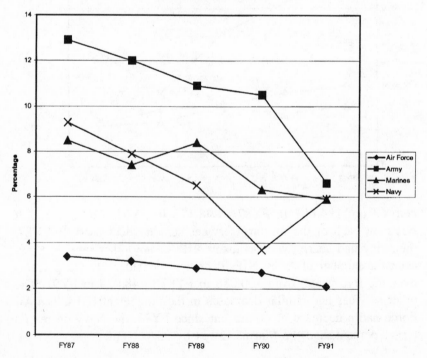

2. Minority Non-Judicial Punishments

a. Number of Minority Non-Judicial Punishments.

Figure 20.11 presents the number of NJPs by racial/ethnic group. While the total number of NJPs decreased considerably, the decrease in the number of NJPs varied significantly among racial/ethnic groups. The number of NJPs decreased most significantly among white service members. The number of NJPs decreased more than 46 percent for white service members compared to a 36 percent decrease for African-American service members, a 23 percent decrease for Hispanic service members, and a 13 percent decrease for AI/AN service members. The number of NJPs increased more than 26 percent for AA/PI service members. Note, however, that the percent of AA/PI NJPs was relatively insignificant (less than .61 percent) compared to the total NJPs throughout the military.

b.   Percentage of Minority Non-Judicial Punishments.

The percentage of members from each racial/ethnic group who received NJPs is presented in Figure 20.12. The percentage of NJPs

Figure 20.11
Number of Non-Judicial Punishments by Racial/Ethnic Group (FY87-FY91)

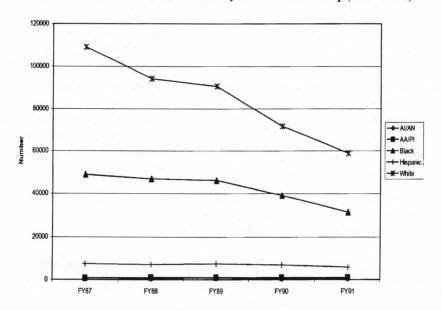

Figure 20.12
Percent of Population Receiving Non-Judicial Punishments
by Racial/Ethnic Group

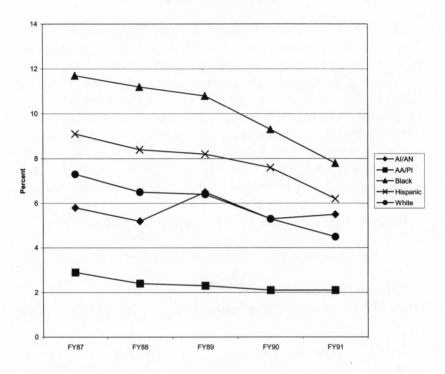

by racial/ethnic group decreased most significantly among white service members - a change from 7.3 percent in FY87 to 4.5 percent in FY91, or a decrease of more than 38 percent. This compared to decreases of 33 percent for African-American service members, 32 percent for Hispanic service members, 28 percent for AA/PI service members, and 5 percent for AI/AN service members. The number of NJP infractions committed by AA/PI service members increased, while the percentage of the population decreased as a result of significant increases in the population of AA/PI service members.

3. Minority Representation Among Non-Judicial Punishments

a. Percentage of NJPs by Race.

Figure 20.13 shows the percentage of NJPs assessed to African Americans and whites. In FY87, 64 percent of the service members

Figure 20.13
Percentage of Non-Judicial Punishments Received by
Blacks and Whites (FY87-FY91)

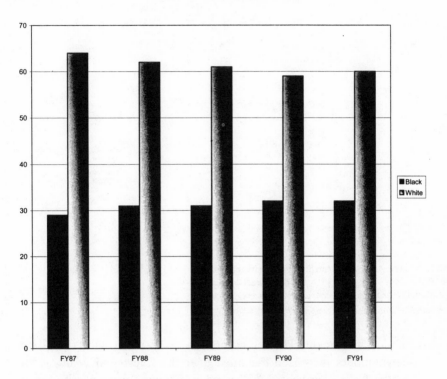

assessed NJP were white and 29 percent were African American. By FY91, white service members represented only 60 percent and African-American service members represented 32 percent of those receiving NJPs. The percentages among different racial/ethnic groups remained fairly constant after FY88. The percentage of NJPs assessed to African Americans and whites by service is presented in the Appendix.

b. Minority Over/Underrepresentation Among NJPs.

1. The RIs for each racial/ethnic group are shown is Figure 20.14. The data indicate that African-American service members were overrepresented by 44 percent among NJPs relative to what would have been expected based FY87 population. After FY88, the representation of African-American service members stayed relative constant

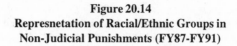

Figure 20.14
Represnetation of Racial/Ethnic Groups in
Non-Judicial Punishments (FY87-FY91)

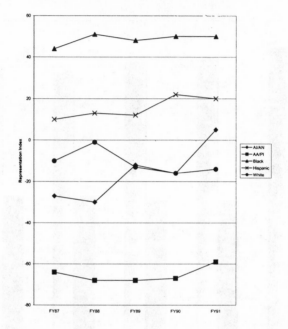

at about 50 percent. The representation of Hispanic and AI/AN service members increased the most over the five fiscal years. Additionally, for all services AA/PI service members were nearly always
underrepresented, usually significantly. The RIs for individual services are presented in the Appendix.

2. The degree of minority overrepresentation in NJPs varied considerably across the different services. For all services, African-
American service members were consistently overrepresented. Figure 20.15 shows the overrepresentation of African-American service members in NJPs for each service. The Air Force and Navy had
similar degrees of overrepresentation for African-American service
members. The Army and Marine Corps had the same degree of
overrepresentation of African-American service members receiving
NJPs and similar trends over time. The Army and Marine Corps had
the highest percentage of African-American service members, 29
and 20 percent respectively.

3. In the Air Force, African-American service members were the
only minority that was consistently overrepresented with regard to

Figure 20.15
Overrepresentation of Black Service Members in Non-Judicial Punishments by
Military Service (FY87-FY91)

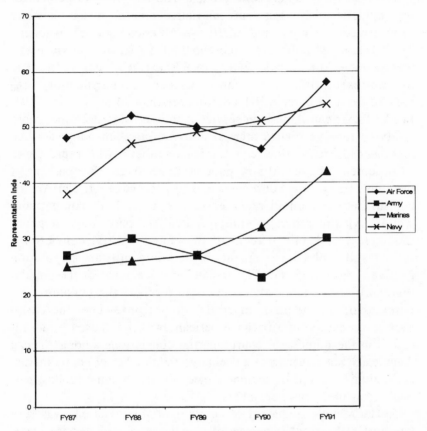

NJPs. In the Army, the overrepresentation of African-American and Hispanic service members ranged between 20 and 30 percent. In the Marine Corps, African-American service members were the only minority that was consistently overrepresented in NJPs. All minorities in the Navy, with the exception of AA/PI service members, were overrepresentated. The percentage of overrepresentation increased for African American and AI/AN service members.

Conclusions

1. The total number of courts martial convictions decreased significantly, by 48 percent, over the five fiscal years (FY87-FY91).

The percentage of courts martial convictions for all services and racial/ethnic groups also decreased; however, the decline varied considerably across racial/ethnic groups. The number and percent of the population receiving court martials decreased faster for white service members compared to African-American service members. This explains why the overrepresentation of African-American service members increased steadily over the five fiscal years. The overrepresentation of African-American service members increased from 33 percent in FY87 to more than 74 percent in FY91. In FY91, African-American service members were 2.2 times more likely to receive courts martial convictions than white service members. African-American service members, who represented 21.6 percent of the military population received 37.6 percent of the convictions. As a consequence, 0.69 percent of African-American military personnel received courts martial. In comparison, white service members, who represented 70.3 percent of the population, received 54.9 percent of the courts martial convictions. As a result, only 0.31 percent of the white military population received courts martial. The remaining 8.1 percent of the population consisted of other minorities, who received the remaining 7.5 percent of the courts martial convictions. The increased overrepresentation of African-Americans was not caused by an increase in the number of courts martial convictions among African Americans, but rather from a decline in the number of courts martial convictions received by members of other racial/ethnic groups, particularly white service members.

2. The relative frequency of courts martial convictions was very low. In FY91, the average rate of convictions for all service members was equal to .4 percent of the total military population.

3. As with courts martial, the total number of NJPs decreased significantly, by 47 percent, over the five fiscal years (FY87-FY91). The percentage of NJPs for all services and racial/ethnic groups decreased. The decrease in NJPs varied across racial/ethnic groups. The overrepresentation of African-American service members stayed relatively constant, at about 50 percent, for the last four fiscal years. However, in FY91, African-American service members were still 1.7 times more likely to receive NJPs than white service members. African-American service members made up 21.6 percent of the military population yet received 32.2 percent of the NJPs, resulting in a 7.81 percent NJP rate. White ser-

vice members made up 70.3 percent of the population and received 60.2 percent of the NJPs, translating to a 4.5 percent NJP rate. The remaining 8.1 percent of the population were other minorities, who received the remaining 7.6 percent of the NJPs. The representation of Hispanic and AI/AN service members increased the most over the five fiscal years.

4. The fact that the overrepresentation of African-American service members among recipients of courts martial convictions was greater than their overrepresentation among NJPs, suggests that African-Americans were involved in more serious offenses. This conclusion is supported by Nordlie et al. (1979), who found that African American service members were overrepresented in the commission of violent and confrontation crimes, while white service members committed the majority of crimes against property, and military specific offenses.

5. Commanders have greater discretion over handling NJPs compared to court martial convictions. If the UCMJ system is racially biased, then one may expect that overrepresentation among African Americans would be greater for NJP infractions as compared to courts martial. However, the data suggest just the opposite, the degree of overrepresentation among African Americans was less for NJPs, and African-American overrepresentation grew at a slower rate for NJPs than for court martial convictions. Also, the percent of African-American service members receiving NJPs decreased faster than other racial/ethnic groups. While this finding does not definitively answer the question of whether the NJP system is racially unbiased, it tends to contradict claims that the NJP system is unfair.

6. The rate of courts martial convictions and NJPs varies considerably from service to service. Undoubtedly, this is a function of many different factors such as the way the different services administer discipline, tolerance to offenses, population characteristics of service members, etc. Further research into issues of discipline and disparities among service members should be undertaken as a coordinated effort to ensure that the conclusions and recommendations of studies of one service are applicable to the others.

Note

1.   Editor's Footnote: This research uses the terms 'Black' and 'White' as racial descriptors. The terms 'Black' and 'African American' are used interchangeably.

References

Nordlie, P., Sevilla, E., Edmonds, W., & White, S. (1979). *A study of racial factors in the Army's justice and discharge systems.* (Report Number. HSR-RR-79/18-HR, in 4 volumes). Washington, DC: DAPE-HRR, The Pentagon.

United States Air Forces 1990 Military Equal Opportunity Assessment. San Antonio, TX: Air Force Military Personnel Center.

United States Air Forces 1991 Military Equal Opportunity Assessment, draft. San Antonio, TX: Air Force Military Personnel Center.

United States Army 1990 Military Equal Opportunity Assessment. Department of Army, DAPE-HR-L, The Pentagon. Washington, DC: Office of the Deputy Chief of Staff for Personnel.

United States Army 1991 Military Equal Opportunity Assessment, draft. Department of Army, DAPE-HR-L, The Pentagon. Washington, DC: Office of the Deputy Chief of Staff for Personnel.

United States Marine Corps 1990 Military Equal Opportunity Assessment. Washington, DC: Office of Naval Operations.

United States Marine Corps 1991 Military Equal Opportunity Assessment, draft. Washington, DC: Office of Naval Operations.

United States Navy 1990 Military Equal Opportunity Assessment. Washington, DC: Office of Naval Operations.

United States Navy 1991 Military Equal Opportunity Assessment, draft. Washington, DC: Office of Naval Operations.

Appendix

Table 20.A1
Percentage of Courts Martial Convictions of Blacks
and Whites for Individual Services
(FY87-FY91)

	FY87	FY87	FY88	FY88	FY89	FY89	FY90	FY90	FY91	FY91
Service	Black	White	Black	White	Black	White	Black	White	Black	White
Air Force	29	62	33	58	33	59	30	60	30	64
Army	39	55	40	53	41	49	44	50	45	47
Marine Corps	29	62	30	62	31	59	31	60	36	54
Navy	18	75	20	72	26	65	35	58	32	58

Table 20.A2
Percentage of Non-Judicial Punishments Received
by Blacks and Whites for Individual Services
(FY87-FY91)

	FY87	FY87	FY88	FY88	FY89	FY89	FY90	FY90	FY91	FY91
Service	Black	White	Black	White	Black	White	Black	White	Black	White
Air Force	22	69	23	68	23	69	22	69	24	71
Army	34	59	36	58	36	57	36	56	37	55
Marine Corps	26	65	26	65	26	65	28	62	29	61
Navy	20	73	23	69	25	66	27	63	27	62

Table 20.A3
Representation Indices for Racial/Ethnic Groups
Courts Martial and Non-Judicial Punishments - Air Force
(FY87-FY91)

	FY87	FY88	FY89	FY90	FY91
COURTS MARTIAL					
AI/AN	36	-20	-5	10	4
AA/PI	-34	-30	-37	-10	-56
Black	91	119	117	97	100
Hispanic	2	-16	-20	-15	4
White	-20	-23	-22	-21	-20
NJPs					
AI/AN	-16	-22	-18	-19	-10
AA/PI	-45	-40	-46	-45	-51
Black	47	52	50	45	57
Hispanic	-4	-10	-8	4	-10
White	-10	-10	-10	-9	-8

Table 20.A4
Representation Indices for Racial/Ethnic Groups
Courts Martial and Non-Judicial Punishments - Army
(FY87-FY91)

	FY87	FY88	FY89	FY90	FY91
COURTS MARTIAL					
AI/AN	5	-20	-4	-25	-55
AA/PI	-60	-30	192	-40	-4
Black	43	45	46	50	56
Hispanic	-17	-20	-15	-20	-19
White	-17	-19	-20	-19	-21
NJPs					
AI/AN	-33	-40	-25	-27	-24
AA/PI	-70	-66	-67	-67	-65
Black	26	30	27	24	30
Hispanic	19	18	19	32	22
White	-7	-8	-7	-7	-9

Table 20.A5
Representation Indices for Racial/Ethnic Groups
Courts Martial and Non-Judicial Punishments – Marine Corps
(FY87-FY91)

	FY87	FY88	FY89	FY90	FY91
COURTS MARTIAL					
AI/AN	-63	-22	10	-20	-26
AA/PI	-46	-40	10	-50	-23
Black	42	38	49	48	79
Hispanic	10	40	5	7	8
White	-10	-11	-15	-12	-20
NJPs					
AI/AN	-35	-58	20	-8	10
AA/PI	-50	-48	-44	-42	-41
Black	24	25	27	35	43
Hispanic	26	21	-5	-3	1
White	-6	-5	-5	-7	-10

Table 20.A6
Representation Indices for Racial/Ethnic Groups
Courts Martial and Non-Judicial Punishments - Navy
(FY87-FY91)

	FY87	FY88	FY89	FY90	FY91
COURTS MARTIAL					
AI/AN	35	14	70	-30	2
AA/PI	-60	-57	-70	-83	-78
Black	23	31	53	98	80
Hispanic	-3	-1	14	5	30
White	0	-1	-8	-18	-20
NJPs					
AI/AN	13	20	42	86	70
AA/PI	-42	-75	-70	-60	-62
Black	36	46	49	52	54
Hispanic	10	18	10	22	17
White	-3	-7	-8	-11	-11

21

Race and the Administration of Non-Judicial Punishments in the U.S. Army[1]

Dan Landis and Rick S. Tallarigo

Introduction

Military discipline is a term that covers many administrative actions. At its most informal and unstructured level, the term can refer to such actions as extra duty, extra instruction, short-term confinement, counseling, and similar responses. At the other extreme, military members can be sent to prison for terms up to life for serious felonies such as murder and even receive the death penalty. Somewhere in the middle of this dimension lies the domain of the non-judicial punishment, a series of actions in response to less than felony offenses, but more than simple errors of omission or commission.

In many ways the military system parallels the civilian environment, albeit in a more structured and confined fashion. So, one could argue that the informal system of military education/correction corresponds to the discipline meted out by superiors in the work, school, and home environments. In place of memory or sporadic record keeping, a more formal system is introduced, exemplified in the Army by the Soldier Miscellaneous Information File (SMIF). The non-judicial punishments are incrementally more formal and correspond, to some degree, to misdemeanors with the corresponding more permanent keeping of records (though, of course, the level of "permanency" is a matter of service discretion). Finally, there is the court-martial system, which is very similar, with significant differences, to the criminal court structure in the civilian world.

Racial disparity in the administration of criminal justice has been of interest to criminologists for some time (see Landis & Dansby, 1994 for a review of some of these studies). These studies have drawn their impetus from the universal findings that blacks are over-represented in the criminal justice system when compared to their proportion in the population (e.g., in 1992, 50.3 percent of prison inmates were black [Snell, 1995]). The amount of overrepresentation has varied, though, and, depending on the offense can range as high as 500 percent. Indeed, in some localities, close to 50 percent of young black men are involved in some way with the criminal justice system, accused, on trial, on probation, or on parole (Miller, 1993). Within the military, the overrepresentation ranges up to approximately 250 percent, again depending on the offense (Landis & Dansby, 1994).

Much of the research cited above has focused on the court-martial system. The reasons for this are obvious. First, the potential penalties that can be levied on a convicted offender can be quite serious. Second, as a formal legal proceeding, there is a requirement for complete and permanent record keeping. Hence, the data are more available than with the more informal parts of the military justice system.

Minor offenses may be disposed of under the Uniform Code of Military Justice (UCMJ), but not involve a full military adjudication. That is, determination and penalties may be levied by local commanders with incarceration[2] not being an option (though, of course, restriction to prescribed areas is an option). The so-called non-judicial punishment is handled somewhat differently by each service. In the Army, offenses falling under Article 15 of the UCMJ (i.e., non-judicial punishments) are seen as a way to provide correction to some behavior. Hence, they are comparatively common and do not become (except in the cases of senior enlisted personnel) part of the military member's permanent personnel file. Assuming good conduct, non-judicial punishments (NJPs) are routinely discarded after two years or when the member goes to a new assignment. In the Air Force, by contrast, NJPs are viewed as representing serious offenses and are used sparingly and as a last resort. Receiving one or two NJPs can mean automatic expulsion from the service.

A court-martial can be viewed as the tail end of a complex process that begins before the service member exits military life. It could be argued that once a person has been charged with an offense serious enough to warrant a court-martial, that person is lost to the service. Even if charges are not preferred or the person is acquitted, a question has been raised about the value of the individual to the service. So, in the sense of rehabilitating the person for a successful military career (however "successful" is defined), the court-martial is the wrong place to intervene.

Earlier in the process is expectations set up by receipt of either NJPs or other forms of military correction. Since these are processes in which there is greater command discretion, they are much more subject to discretionary treatment based on race or other irrelevant characteristics. As Bell and Holz (1975) noted some years ago, the single best predictor of military delinquency is the belief by commanders that the military person will do wrong. The receipt of a NJP may function as either a confirmation or initiation of that belief. For this reason it is important to examine the NJP system for possible racial disparities.

There is little literature dealing specifically with the administration of the Article 15 system. An early paper by Crawford and Thomas (1977) found that the human relations climate aboard ship was related to level of Captain's Masts (the Navy's version of NJP) being awarded. The literature is silent with regard to any racial differences in offense profiles or in patterns of punishment. This project is a first attempt to lift this veil.

We hypothesize the following:

1. Minorities will receive Articles 15 in our sample in greater numbers than their representation in post populations. This hypothesis is based on the three observations: (a) across the Army, minorities are overrepresented in NJPs (Landis & Dansby, 1994); (b) minorities are overrepresented in courts-martial (Landis & Dansby, 1994); and (c) minorities (particularly blacks) are overrepresented in the civilian criminal justice system (Miller, 1993; Snell, 1995). The first consideration speaks to the representativeness of our sample. While we might expect that the overall incidence for minorities in the military will be lower (due to the enlistment selection process), it will still be greater than the group's fraction of the total armed forces.

2. There will exist location and mission differences in the level of racial disparities in the awarding of Articles 15. The first part of this hypothesis recognizes the role of the commander in setting the parameters of permissible behavior. The second part derives from the consistent finding that equal opportunity climate varies as a function of mission type. That is, combat units tend to have the poorest climate, while service support units have the highest (Landis, Dansby, & Tallarigo, 1996).

3. There will exist offense profile differences between white and black service people. Tonry (1995) and others have noted that blacks are disproportionately more likely to be charged with drug and related offenses, while whites are more likely to be found in so-called white-collar offenses. In analyzing several years of Army courts-martial, Landis, Hoyle, and Dansby (1996) found that blacks were overrepresented in assaults, sex-related crimes, and some forms of drug offenses. This same group was slightly underrepresented in three marijuana-related offenses. We suggest that similar differences in offense profiles will exist at the NJP level.

4. There will exist racial disparities in the level of punishment levied from Articles 15. We state this hypothesis, recognizing that there is considerable disagreement over racial disparities in punishment in the civilian and military systems (e.g., Tonry, 1995; Wilbanks, 1987; Connelly, 1993; Landis, Hoyle, & Dansby, 1996). The present data will add to this debate by providing an analysis of an important part of the discipline system.

5. There will be racial disparities in the age, tenure, and rank of service people receiving Articles 15. This hypothesis derives from the finding that blacks who receive courts-martial are older, have been in the Army longer, and are of higher rank than whites similarly situated (Landis, Hoyle, & Dansby, 1996). It is reasonable to suppose that the same relationship will hold at the NJP level. Given that NJPs for senior enlisted personnel carry serious consequences (e.g., the termination of a career), evidence supporting this hypothesis would lead to an underlying phenomenon of "derailment" for minorities as a possible explanation.

Method

Sample

Three Army division-level infantry posts were selected. The posts were geographically dispersed within the continental United States. Infantry posts were selected in order to minimize any variance due to mission. Division-level sites were needed to assure a sufficiently large sample of Article 15. Table 21.1 gives the racial and gender breakdown of the sample.

For each post, all Articles 15 awarded during calendar year 1994 were captured. Defense Department (DD) Form 2627 is used to record

Table 21.1
Composition of sample by race and sex

Race	Male	Female	Unknown	Total
African-American	1026	114	1	1141
Asian-American	17	3	0	20
Hispanic	166	10	0	176
Native-American	17	1	0	18
White	1769	68	1	1838
Other	137	4	0	141
Totals	3132	200	2	3334

Note: Based on number of incidents.

details of the action. Capturing was accomplished by physically entering the data from each DD Form 2627 and subsidiaries into a database. Database construction was facilitated by use of a computer program (NJP.EXE)[3] written expressly for this project. The program was developed in dBase 5.0, compiled and installed on laptop computers that the research team carried to each site. The total number of Articles 15 thus captured numbered approximately 3300. Once the sample was gathered, the social security numbers were submitted to Defense Manpower Data Center (DMDC) and additional data were obtained. The two databases (our NJP and the DMDC) were then merged.

Data

From the DD Form 2627 (and subsidiaries), the following data were obtained for each Article 15: type (formal, summarized), social security number (SSN), birth date, gender, ethnic group, offense, subsidiary offenses (if any), article under which offense(s) was charged, level of offense (company vs. field grade), date of offense, date of filing appeal, date of appeal decision, request for court-martial, request for closed hearing, decision of original hearing, penalties levied (restriction, rank reduction, fines, extra duty), suspensions of penalties and their respective outcomes. From the DMDC matches, we obtained the individual's primary occupation code, educational level, Armed Forces Qualification Test (AFQT) percentile, birth date, marital status, dependents, ethnic group, gender, basic active service date, interservice separation code, character of service, and date of separation.

Procedure

After permission had been obtained from the post Commander, arrangements were made to visit each site. An in-briefing was conducted after which the data were extracted from the hard copy DD 2627s and other relevant forms. The computer program (NJP.EXE) mirrored the data on the form so that virtually all of the information was automatically entered into the database. Each post provided approximately 1000 Article 15s. Before leaving each post, an out-brief was conducted with the designee of the post commander (either the Staff Judge Advocate General [JAG] or the Chief-of-Staff for the Division).

Analyses of Data

For analyses of incidence rates (both-overall and by offense), data were cast into sets of contingency tables by race. Included in those tables were the expected frequencies obtained from post equal opportunity (EO) reports. These tables were analyzed using appropriate chi-square (Chi²) statistics.

In order to analyze punishments, three approaches were taken. In the first, each punishment (e.g., extra duty) was analyzed as an ordinal variable (0=absent, 1=present) and contingency tables prepared. These were analyzed as described above. In the second analysis, those punishments which were continuous (e.g., fines) were examined by analysis of variance with race as the independent variable. The third analysis developed a metric for scaling the total effect of the punishment, since in the majority of cases, an offender received some amount of all possible categories of punishment, defined as:

$$SI=(k_1(PG)*5)+k_2(FINE/10)+k_3(RD)+k_4(XD)$$

Where: SI=Severity Index

k_1	=	16 if punishment not suspended, 8 if suspended
k_2	=	8 if punishment not suspended, 4 if suspended
k_3	=	4 if punishment not suspended, 2 if suspended
k_4	=	2 if punishment not suspended, 1 if suspended

and	PG	=	Pay grade (Enlisted only)
	FINE	=	Amount of Fine in dollars
	RD	=	Days restricted
	XD	=	Days extra duty

Note: Each component is standardized by paygrade

It will be noted that the metric assumes that immediate punishment is more severe than a penalty which is suspended.[4] These values were calculated automatically as the relevant data were captured.

Results

Table 21.2 presents the incidence of Articles 15 by race over all three sites:

Table 21.2
Observed Versus Expected Representation in Articles 15 (all sites combined)

Race	Observed Percent	Observed Frequency	Expected Percent	Expected Frequency
White	58	1714	64	1895
African-American	36	1061	31	936
Hispanic	5	168	3	112
Total	100	2943	100	2943

Note 1. Expected frequencies based on official strength statistics.
Note 2. Chi^2=61.96, df=2, p<.001

Both the Hispanic and black groups are overrepresented. A breakdown by site indicates that this pattern (for blacks) holds true, however, for only 2 of the 3 locations (Figure 21.1).

In terms of primary[5] offense profile, significant differences appear with blacks being overrepresented in crimes against persons and property and confrontation with authority. Whites are overrepresented in drug offenses and failure to appear, while Hispanics and whites are charged more often with alcohol offenses (Figure 21.2 – Chi^2 (df=20) = 77.3, p<.0001; N = 2943).

Figure 21.3 indicates that whites tend to be overrepresented with respect to expected frequencies at the lower grades and underrepresented at high ranks, while the opposite is true for blacks.

Distribution of Penalties

There are four classes of penalties that can result from an Article 15 conviction:[6] reduction in rank, fine, restriction to base, and extra duty. Each of these penalties can be suspended for a specific amount of time. The pattern across all penalties is that minorities (particularly blacks) are underrepresented in receiving the penalty, and over-

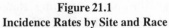

Figure 21.1
Incidence Rates by Site and Race

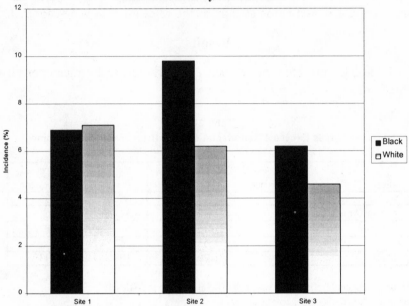

Figure 21.2
Relative Representation in Primary Offense for Blacks, Hispanics, and Whites

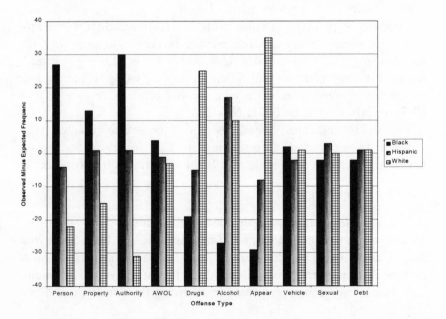

Figure 21.3
Percentage Receiving Article 15 by Race and Paygrade

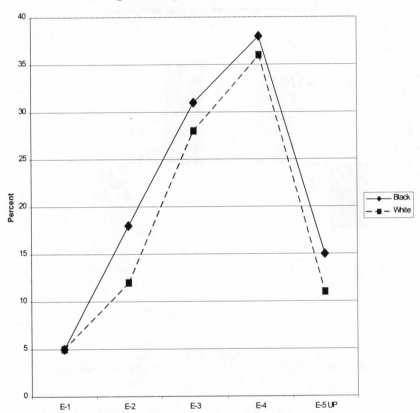

represented in having the result suspended. Figure 21.4 illustrates this pattern for rank reductions (reduction imposed Chi² (df=2) = 8.41, p<.05; n=2943; reduction suspended Chi² (df=2) = 7.04, p<.05; n=2943). While the same pattern is found for restrictions and extra duty, the imposition of fines presents a somewhat different schema: both the imposition and suspension of fines show underrepresentation of minorities (Figure 21.5 – fines imposed Chi² (df=2) = 7.02, p<.05; fines suspended Chi² (df=2) = 3.77 n.s.).

When fines are scaled as a percentage of salary, an interesting pattern appears: blacks at the E-1 and E-2 paygrades have a slightly higher percentage of their pay taken than whites (3.8 percent vs. 3.5 percent, respectively). The reverse is true at paygrades E-6 and higher (Figure 21.6).

Figure 21.4
Observed Minus Expected Frequencies of Reductions in
Rank and Suspensions of Reductions by Race

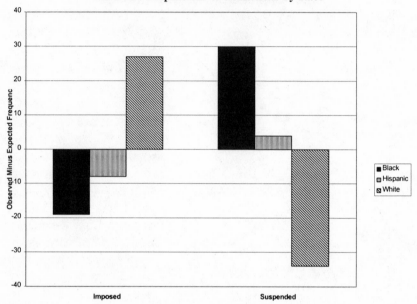

Figure 21.5
Observed Minus Expected Frequencies of Forteitures by Race and Suspensions

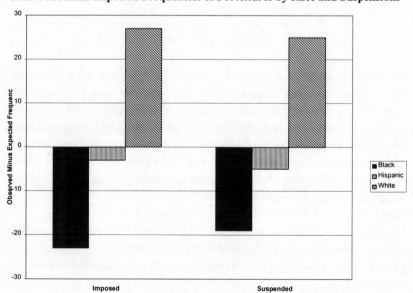

Figure 21.6
Fines as a Percentage of Annual Salary by Race and Rank

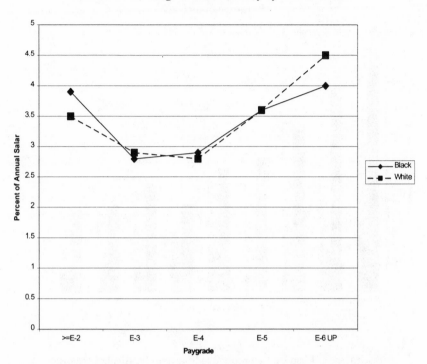

Severity of Punishments

There were no significant differences ($p>.05$) between sites in the amount of punishment levied with paygrade controlled. There were also no differences when the data were collapsed across sites and offenses as a function of race. However, when offense type and race were considered jointly, a significant interaction appeared ($p<.001$). Figure 21.7 indicates that this interaction was due to blacks receiving significantly more severe punishments for alcohol-related offenses and no other significant differences being apparent. Figure 21.8 indicates that this effect is due to blacks charged with alcohol offenses being given field grade NJPs at a higher rate than whites similarly charged. The punishments imposed for field as opposed to company level NJPs are much more severe ($Chi^2 = 7.15$, $df=2$, $p<.05$).

Although the interaction between race and offense is significant, the major component of that effect is type of offense. That effect is shown in Figure 21.9.

Figure 21.7
Punishment Severity as a Function of Offense Category and Race
(Paygrade Controlled)

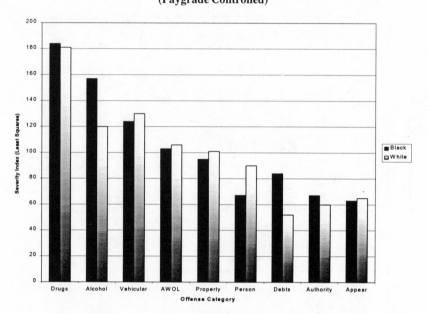

Figure 21.8
Percentage of Field vs. Company Grade Actions for Alcohol Offenses

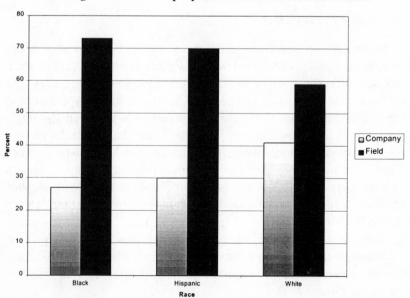

Figure 21.9
Punishment Severity as a Function of Offense Category (Paygrade Controlled)

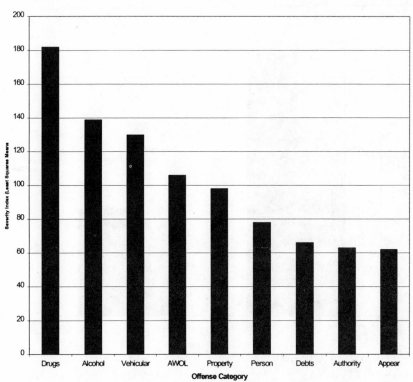

Figure 21.9 indicates that, in terms of punishment severity, there are four clusters of offenses: (a) drugs, (b) alcohol and vehicular, (c) offenses against property and AWOL, and (d) offenses against person, failure to pay debts, confrontation with authority, and failure to appear. These groupings probably reflect the likelihood of a particular offense being seen as requiring a field rather a company grade Article 15. It interesting to note that offenses against persons (e.g., fighting, hitting a spouse) receive less severe penalties than offenses against property. One can speculate that aggressive behavior may be perceived as a necessary, if unfortunate, by-product of military training or a "domestic issue" when involving a spouse and therefore more "private." Offenses against property and going AWOL are more serious—the former because property has intrinsic value and the latter because of its effects on good order and discipline.

Figure 21.10
Severity Adjusted for Paygrade by Race and Mission

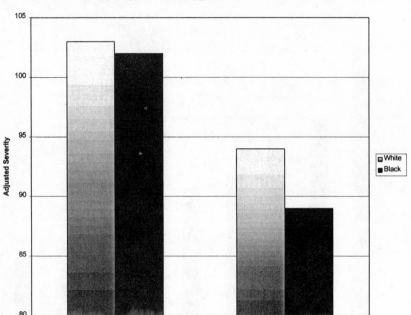

Effect of Unit Mission

Units were categorized in terms of their basic mission: combat or support. When severity was analyzed in terms of race and mission, the interaction was significant (p<.05). (Figure 21.10). While both groups received higher levels of punishment in combat units, the interaction was produced by blacks receiving more severe punishments than whites in support units as compared to combat units.

Effect of Time in Service

Overall, blacks who receive NJPs have been in the service a little over eight months longer than whites similarly situated (M=47.68, 39.31, respectively, p<.0001). When these data are disaggregated by offense type (Figure 21.11), blacks have had significantly (p<.01) longer tenure when receiving NJPs for drugs, alcohol, vehicular, and failure to pay debts. There is no offense for which whites have had longer tenure. At the time of discharge, blacks have served significantly longer than whites (M=1522.53 days, 1227.42 days,

Figure 21.11
Relationship Among Time in Service, Race, and Offense Type

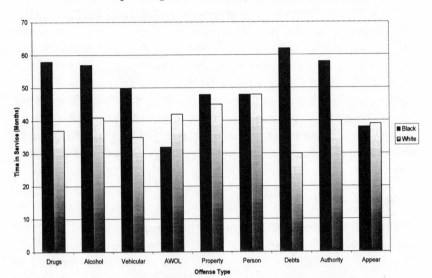

p<.0001, respectively. However, the time between Article 15 hearing and discharge is not significantly different for blacks and whites (M=83.86 days, 76.08 days, p=<.116, respectively).

Effect of Race and Offense Type on Time Between Offense and Charge Being Filed

Both whites and blacks waited approximately thirty-six days for a hearing on the charges (36.93, 35.81, respectively, n.s.). The interaction between race and offense type on time to file charges was also non-significant.

Rank at Time of Discharge

Blacks who were charged with Article 15 offenses were of significantly higher rank on discharge than similarly charged whites (M= 2.71, 2.45, t=3.15, df=1053, p<.002, respectively).

Race, NJP, and Discharge

This question was examined by comparing the relative proportions by race of those members of the sample who were no longer in the service (as of 31 December 1994) and who had received a less than favorable condition of service. Discharge might well be a way to remove disproportionate numbers of a minority from the service thus making the Article 15 into less of a corrective mechanism for that group. For whites, the NJP would retain its warning characteristic. Of the sample, 36.85 percent had been discharged (38.99 percent black). Using 36.1 percent as the expected black discharge rate (from Table 21.2), blacks were overrepresented in the following categories: (Early release—other [40.43 percent], discreditable incidents [41.27 percent], For the good of service in lieu of court-martial [66.27 percent], and unsatisfactory performance [39.16 percent]); blacks were underrepresented in "Failure to meet qualifications"(19.64 percent).

Discharge and Offense Type

Thirty-five percent of the sample had been discharged as of the end of 1994. A cross-tabulation for this subsample by race and offense type revealed the following: Blacks were overrepresented in the offenses of crimes against persons (51.28 percent), crimes against property (46.94 percent), confrontations with authority (54.13 percent), AWOL (40.21 percent), and vehicular offenses (46.51 percent). It would seem that there is a tendency to see these offenses when committed by blacks as being more serious and therefore more worthy of discharge.

Discussion

The results of this study may be summarized as follows: Blacks are overrepresented in the awarding of Articles 15 (Hypothesis 1), although that phenomenon seems to be site and offense specific (Hypothesis 2). In two of the sites overrepresentation of blacks was found, in the third, it was not. Such site totals tell only part of the story. More interesting are the different offense patterns. Blacks were overrepresented in crimes against persons, property, alcohol, and confrontations with authority. They were underrepresented in drug-related offenses (Hypothesis 3). This is different from the civilian situation where the "war against drugs" has resulted in very high percentages of blacks being incarcerated for such offenses. The difference is, however, easily explained.

As Tonry (1995) notes, the war against drugs has targeted those substances, which are most prevalent in minority communities.

Hence, the arrests and conviction rates fall disproportionately among these groups. Simultaneously, Miller (1993) has reported very high percentages of young blacks are involved with the criminal justice system. Since such involvement has traditionally been a bar to military recruitment the group of young blacks being accessed contained proportionately fewer individuals interested in drug involvement.

The age and tenure differences are most intriguing and offer support for a "derailment" (i.e., Hypothesis 5). Here we found that blacks are older, have been in the Army longer, are of higher rank when they offend, and are of higher rank when they are discharged. Disproportionately, they also received some categories of general discharges. And, for five out of the nine offense categories, blacks were more likely to be discharged than were whites. Given that derailment occurs, what are the possible explanations?

The most obvious interpretation is that higher ranking blacks (a level at which the NJP is most damaging to a career) are targeted as recipients of disciplinary actions. An individual racism form of this explanation requires that the judging and charging authorities be mainly white. Given the high proportion of blacks in the senior NCO ranks (where the NJPs originate), this explanation is not very satisfactory. However, a systemic version in which the process is administered by both blacks and whites that have accepted its basic premises may have some validity. Such an explanation is similar to the rational bias theory of Larwood and her colleagues (e.g., Larwood, Gutek, & Gattiker, 1984; Larwood & Gattiker, 1985). Finally, our data are in contrast to the findings and speculations of other researchers (Edwards & Newell, 1994; Knouse, 1993) who suggest that blacks that get into trouble in the military are junior in tenure and age.

A better explanation is that as blacks progress through the rank, the range of allowable behavior becomes disproportionately smaller as compared with whites. The limits of such behavior are enforced equally by whites and blacks in authority; whites because, possibly, a dislike of high ranking blacks, and blacks because of their desire to see only good role models achieve high status. A self-restriction of the range of acceptable behavior is a common pattern among groups that have historically been the victims of discrimination.[7,8]

The explanation suggested above has its roots in social identity theory (Taijel & Turner, 1986) and social categorization theory (Turner, Hogg, Oakes, Reicher, & Wetherell, 1987). As outlined by Brewer (1996), this theory rests on two basic propositions, which can be used to understand the behavior of black NCOs toward their race mates. First, the process of categorization of social experience minimizes in-group differences and enhances outgroup differences. Second, the distinctiveness of the in-group -- outgroup is one with affective and emotional properties because of its relevance to the self. Further, according to Brewer (1996), three principles guide the formation of intergroup schemas: First, members of the in-group are perceived be similar to the self and hence, more similar than those from the outgroup (the intergroup accentuation principle). Second, positive affect is given to in-group and only rarely, if at all, to the outgroup (the in-group favoritism principle). Third, negative affect is associated with intergroup competition (social competition principle). The first schema principle suggests a need to maintain in-group similarity (or homogeneity) and that this need will be stronger as a direct function of the perceived hostility of the outgroup (the third principle). We would suggest that as the perceived threat is increased, the need for homogeneity of the in-group also increases. Members of the in-group who disturb the perceived homogeneity threaten the security of the group hence must be dealt with.

Under threat, social categories become rigid; the boundaries between the in-group and the outgroup are less permeable and the range of acceptable behavior by members of the in-group narrowed. This increases the homogeneity of the in-group and its ability to act in concert against the perceived threat. Hence, behaviors that in less threatening times are acceptable become less so. Members of the in-group treat violations of the rules of acceptable behavior more severely.

Applying the theory outlined above to the situation of the black non-commissioned officer (NCO) dealing with the behavior of his/her race/rank mate is quite direct. The black NCO is expected to behave in a way that supports the self-interest of the larger group of black NCOs. Such behavior is that which is seen as similar to that emitted by other members of the group. As the level of perceived threat from the white majority increases, the level of acceptable deviance from the standard narrows. Hence, the punishment levied for deviation becomes greater.

The set of hypotheses outlined above may explain why blacks are proportionately more likely to receive Articles 15 and why that is particularly true for senior level minorities. However, it would also seem to predict that these individuals should receive more severe punishments, which appears not to be the case. However, we should remember that for a NCO to receive a NJP, suspended or not, is often tantamount to a career termination since a notation is placed in the permanent microfiche available to future promotion boards.

We emphasize that the theory outlined above depends on a significant number of Articles 15 on blacks being recommended by blacks. Unfortunately, the race of the recommender is not routinely gathered in the Army. The Air Force, on the other hand, has begun to code the race of the imposing officer, an improvement certainly that the Army should consider. However, the Air Force approach does not recognize the critical role that the NCO plays in the process.

These data provide a mixed picture when seeking support for a finding that blacks who are seen as troublesome are discharged early. On the one hand, blacks that have been charged with Article 15 are slightly more likely to be discharged (when compared with their representation in the units) than whites. However, when the cases involve those personnel who have received disciplinary actions, the difference is non-significant. When the discharge data are disaggregated by interservice discharge code, blacks are overrepresented in three, possibly four, categories and underrepresented in one. Further, the offense by race frequencies for those discharged lends some credence to the charge that discharges for offenders are racially disparate. For blacks, Article 15 may be administered in a fashion more typical of the Air Force than of the Army. While the present data do illuminate the issue, a definitive answer will have to wait on further study.

On the positive side, blacks, once they are charged with an Article 15 offense, are procedurally treated the same as whites. That is, they progress through the system at the same rate as whites and, for the most part, receive the same or more lenient sentence (thus failing to find support for Hypothesis 4).[9] The fly in the ointment is the suggestion, outlined above, that blacks (particularly those who are relatively senior) may be diverted into discharge actions at a higher rate am white soldiers.

The present data can be compared to that obtained from court-martial records (Landis, Hoyle, & Dansby, 1996). In that study, it was found that blacks do not spend the same amount of time in the system as whites. For non-sex-related crimes, blacks spend more time, are older, and have more tenure. For sex-related crimes, the reverse pattern was found. The present data look very much like the results from non-sex-related court-martial records. This is not surprising since there are few sex-related crimes in the present data set.

Certainly, the data reported here should alert military justice officials to examine all parts of the discipline system for possible race-based disparities. Prejudice can come in many forms and operate in many different venues. Focusing on just the Article 15 system itself may blind the organization to the reality of how the discipline system operates and its tertiary effects. For example, discharges may be only occasionally *officially* linked to disciplinary actions, yet they may follow such actions. Discharges or resignations may reflect the career stifling influences of Article 15 action for senior ranks, yet may be categorized as "honorable," the military equivalent of "Resignation to pursue other opportunities."

The present results (which indicated that blacks not only receive Articles 15 at a higher rate than whites but that once having received a NJP they are discharged at somewhat higher rates) have to be distressing to policy makers. Unfortunately, our data do not permit tracing a direct path from the NJP to discharge. The results are suspicious but by no means conclusive. Further research will be needed to determine just the existence and magnitude of the hypothesized link.

An important avenue of future investigation is the relative conduct leeway allowed for minorities as they move up the promotion ladder. It as we suggest above, blacks are held to higher standards of conduct, compared to whites, as they are promoted, then some sort of training for senior NCOs and officers would seem to be in order. If, as we further suggest, this standard is held equally by whites and blacks (though for completely different reasons), then the training may be as important for minorities as for whites in those positions. For until all groups involved with any part of the military discipline system are treated equally, the process can hardly be said to be fair.

Notes

1.   This research (the third in a series of studies dealing with race and the Uniform Code of Military Justice) was completed during the first author's sabbatical leave from the University of Mississippi. The second author was a Major in the U.S. Air Force assigned to the Defense Equal Opportunity Management Institute (DEOMI). The first two studies are Landis & Dansby (1994) and Landis, Hoyle, & Dansby (1996). We wish to acknowledge the invaluable aid of MSG Ashley Davis of DEOMI and Andrea J. Dettner of Defense Manpower Data Center in the prosecution of this research. Comments on this paper can be addressed to the first author at: Center for

Applied Research and Evaluation, University of Mississippi, University, MS 38677 (e-mail: ijir@vm.cc.olemiss.edu). The opinions in this paper are solely those of the authors and do not represent official policy of the U.S. Government, the Department of Defense, or their agencies.

2. Actually, commanders may impose "correctional custody," though this is rarely used in practice. In the Navy, custody on "bread and water" is on the books, but again is almost never used.

3. This program is available from the first author.

4. The weights were derived based on the research team's experience with the Article 15 system. Thus, reduction in paygrade was assumed to be a more severe penalty because it involves future earnings, prestige, and career possibilities. Extra duty, by contrast, is more of an annoyance and carries little permanent damage. Of course, these weights could be made more precise by a scaling study—a study that we fully expect to complete in the near future.

5. The program captured both primary (i.e., main offense charged) and secondary (e.g., subordinate or additional charges) Article 15.

6. Purists will argue that individuals are not "convicted" of offenses under Article 15. Indeed, the Army's Form 2627 ("Record of Proceedings under Article 15, UCMJ") speaks only of "imposing punishment" not of guilt or innocence. However, from the viewpoint of the person being accused, punishment means being guilty of something (i.e., being convicted). Hence, it is a difference that, in our opinion, makes no difference except to those who, like the medieval scholastics, enjoy dancing on the heads of pins. The only advantage is that the accused can say, with perfect honesty, that they have never been "convicted" of a crime. There is, however, some advantage to the individual in this distinction. Should the occurrence of a NJP be used as evidence in an administrative separation hearing, the servicemember can contest the facts. Had he/she been convicted in a court-martial, the hearing board would consider the issue closed.

7. For example, many Jews of middle age or older can recall being told by their parents that they must be twice as good (in every way) as non-Jews in order to succeed.

8. Another interesting possibility (suggested by COL Ronald Joe, USA) is that the early application of NJPs to whites serves as a corrective device which insulates them from difficulties later in their careers. Blacks are deprived of that corrective device, thus depriving them of information useful in avoiding later problems. Unfortunately, our data do not allow a test of this hypothesis (which is a variation of the "derailment" suggestion), but it is certainly worthy of further research.

9. The failure to find punishment severity differences may be a real (lack of) effect or it may reflect the insensitivity of a non-empirically derived measure. Before the finding can be accepted as definitive, the scaling study mentioned earlier should be completed and the analyses rerun.

References

Bell, D., & Holz, R. (1975, June). *Summary of ARI Research on military delinquency.* (Research Report 1185). Arlington, VA: U.S. Research Institute for the Behavioral and Social Sciences.

Brewer, M. B. (1996). When contact is not enough: Social identity and intergroup cooperation. *International Journal of Intercultural Relations, 20,* 291-303.

Connelly, J. (1993). *Equitability of treatment in the Army Judicial Proceedings (ETAJUP).* (Report SR-93-14). Bethesda, MD: U.S. Army Concepts Analysis Agency.

Crawford, K., & Thomas, E. (1977). Organizational climate and disciplinary rates on Navy ships. *Armed Forces and Society, 3,* 165-182.

Edwards, J., & Newell, C. (1994). Navy pattern-of-misconduct discharges: A study of potential racial effects. San Diego, CA: Navy Personnel Research and Development Center.

Knouse, S. E. (1993). *Differences between black and white military offenders: A study of socioeconomic, familial, personality, and military characteristics of inmates at the United States Disciplinary Barracks at Fort Leavenworth.* Patrick AFB, FL: Defense Equal Opportunity Management Institute.

Landis, D., & Dansby, M. (1994). *Race and the military justice system: Design for a program of action research.* (DEOMI Research Series Pamphlet 94-3). Patrick AFB, FL: Defense Equal Opportunity Management Institute.

Landis, D., Dansby, M., & Tallarigo, R. (1996). The use of equal opportunity climate in intercultural training. In D. Landis & R. Bhagat (Eds.). *Handbook of intercultural training, 2nd Ed.* (pp. 244-263). Thousand Oaks, CA: Sage.

Landis, D., Hoyle, M., & Dansby, M. (1996). *Race and procedural justice: The case of the Uniform Code of Military Justice.* (DEOMI Research Series Pamphlet 96-3). Patrick AFB, FL: Defense Equal Opportunity Management Institute.

Larwood, L., & Gattiker, U. (1985). Rational bias and interorganizational power in the employment of management consultants. *Group and Organization Studies, 10,* 3-17.

Larwood, L., Gutek, B., & Gattiker, U. (1984). Perspectives on institutional discrimination and resistance to change. *Group and Organization Studies, 9,* 333-353.

Miller, J. (1993). *Hobbling a generation: Young African-American males in the Washington, DC criminal justice system.* Alexandria, VA: National Center for Corrections Alternatives.

Snell, T. (1995, January). *Correctional populations in the United States 1992.* (Report NCJ-146413). Washington, DC: U.S. Department of Justice.

Tajfel, R., & Tumer, J.C. (1986). The social identity theory of intergroup behavior. In S. Worchel and W. Austin (Eds.). *Psychology of intergroup relations* (pp. 7-24). Chicago: Nelson-Hall.

Turner, J., Hogg, M., Oakes, P., Reicher, S. & Wetherell, M. (1987). *Rediscovering the social group: A self-categorization theory.* Oxford: Basil Blackwell.

Tonry, M. (1995). *Malign neglect.* New York: Oxford University Press.

Wilbanks, W. (1987). *The myth of a racist criminal justice system.* Monterey, CA: Brooks/Cole.

22

Differences Between Black and White Military Offenders: A Study of Socioeconomic, Familial, Personality, and Military Characteristics of Inmates at the U.S. Disciplinary Barracks at Fort Leavenworth

Stephen B. Knouse

Introduction

Minority involvement in the military justice system is a significant issue. Military authorities, civil rights activists, and researchers have been concerned for some time about the high level of black discipline rates in the military (Dansby, 1992). A number of studies have substantiated higher discipline rates for blacks (e.g., Polan & Thomas, 1985; Walker, 1992). These types of studies have examined aggregates of data (percentages of blacks and whites in various discipline areas) from large databases. While providing valuable descriptive information, this type of study cannot show any linkages with antecedent variables that may provide explanations. In other words, it is difficult to answer why blacks have higher discipline rates.

An alternative approach is to examine data derived from individual discipline cases. For example, Edwards and Knouse (1990) found blacks had higher discipline rates among first-term Navy enlistees, but found that a number of variables, such as grade and time in service, were related to these rates. They called for discipline databases tracking a number of these types of background variables.

The present study is a first effort in this direction. Background characteristics of a sample of black and white inmates at the United States Disciplinary Barracks at Fort Leavenworth, Kansas were examined as possible influences on disparate offense rates between blacks and whites. Fort Leavenworth was chosen because it contains in one place serious offenders, found guilty in a general court martial, from all the military services.

Literature Review

There is a growing literature identifying a number of background variables in both the civilian and military justice systems that may influence offense rates between blacks and whites. The basic profile, if you will, of the black offender is a young single male from a disadvantaged socioeconomic, educational, and familial background.

Age

Civilian Justice System. The highest incidence of violent crimes (i.e., rape, robbery, and assault) according to the National Crime Survey is among black males in the 18 to 20 year old group (Hindelag, 1981). In addition, Christianson (1982) reported that blacks in prison were younger than white prisoners for all crimes except drug-related offenses. In a longitudinal study of crime in Columbus, Ohio, Schuster (1981) found young black males were more apt to be arrested for multiple violent crimes.

Military Justice System. In a study of Marine Corps offenders, Perry (1981) found a higher rate of violent offenses among young black males than young white males. Hayles and Perry (1981) also found higher incarceration rates among young black sailors than among young whites in the Navy.

Socioeconomic Status

In a review of thirty-five studies, Tittle, Villemez, and Smith (1978) found a slightly negative association between social class and crime. Interestingly, they found that the association appears to be becoming weaker over time. On the other hand, Bridges and Crutchfield (1988) reported in a national study that blacks with lower social standing in the community were more apt to be imprisoned than whites.

On the economic side, Sampson (1987) in a study of 171 large American cities found consistently higher rates of violent crime (robbery and homicide) among blacks who were unemployed and at the bottom of the economic ladder. In addition, in his longitudinal study, Schuster (1981) found that the strongest association between race and crime was accounted for by socioeconomic status. Lower socioeconomic status blacks were more apt to commit violent crimes. Moreover, Joe (1987) argues that the reason that black youth are more apt to be in the criminal justice system is that they perceive poor prospects for economic success in the traditional employment route.

One of the best indicators of socioeconomic status is one's own and one's parents' employment status and occupation, which reflects economic power and social status (Gordon, 1978). Blacks who come from a background of welfare, unemployment, and low status jobs may perceive that the traditional work route does not yield results and turn to alternative routes, including crime (Pepinsky, 1986).

Education

Civilian Justice System. Perkins and Reeves (1975) found that Virginia inmates who committed crimes against persons had completed fewer grades in school regardless of race.

Military Justice System. In parallel fashion, Hayles and Perry (1981) found that incarceration rates in the Navy decreased as education level increased for all races. In another Navy study, Conway (1983) found that high school graduates had fewer courts-martial than nongraduates.

It would appear logical that blacks from disadvantaged educational backgrounds would have lower academic abilities and hence score lower on ability tests, such as the Armed Forces Qualifying Test (AFQT) (Dansby, 1992). Polan and Thomas (1985) found that black Navy offenders had lower AFQT scores than did white offenders. Similar findings occurred for Army and other military recruits (Flyer, 1990; Nordlie, Sevilla, Edmonds, & White, 1979).

Family

The Disrupted Family. Disruption in some black families can be a factor in crime. Family instability and marital conflict influence juvenile delinquency among blacks (Ensminger, Kellam, & Rubin, 1983; Loeber & Stouthamer-Loeber, 1986). In a study of violent crime (robbery and homicide) in U.S. cities, Sampson (1987) found that rates of black violent juvenile offenses were most strongly influenced by family disruption.

Troubled families can produce a number of problems eventually leading to crime. Disrupted families have lower participation in the community (e.g., neighborhood watches) and in the educational process (Bloom, 1966; Kellam, Adams, Born, & Ensminger, 1982). Disrupted families and single parent families may be less able to control negative peer influences (e.g., hanging out and vandalism) that may lead to more serious crime (Sampson, 1987). Moreover, the family is a primary conduit of society values. In a study of incarcerated and nonincarcerated black men, Parson and Midawa (1988) reported that incarcerated blacks were less apt to have had come from a family environment of strong family values (e.g., working hard to support their families) and active participation in black churches. And in a recent study examining children's behavioral problems and quality of parent-child relations at home, Parcel and Menaghan (1993) found that for both black and white families lower parental self-esteem can lead to less effective parenting styles, while less frequent, lower quality parental interaction with children may lead to less internalization of parental values, such as self control, in their children.

Birth Order. An interesting tangent is birth order (Dansby, 1992). There is some research that shows that first-born children have higher expectations from their parents and are more apt to internalize their problems, which produces perhaps more internal physical problems but less societal problems. Younger children, on the other hand, particularly from larger families, who simultaneously get less interest from their older (and more weary) parents and who have to deal with pressures from older siblings, may be less well adjusted and more apt to externalize their problems in socially unacceptable ways (Green, 1978). In the disrupted larger family where the parents are separated or divorced or there is only a single parent, the lack of structure and hence control may produce even more problematic behavior in the younger black child.

Military Justice System. While there are relatively few military studies examining family influence, Horne (1988) reported black Marines who had higher disciplinary rates were less apt to be from traditional family backgrounds.

Personality

It has been suggested that personality may be a factor explaining some of the difference between black and white offenders (Laufer & Day, 1983; Nettler, 1982). If personality is a function of socioeconomic, education, and family factors, then for some blacks, a disadvantaged background may influence certain personality variables. It has been suggested that black offenders may have different orientations to authority (Nordlie et al. 1979), moral values (Laufer & Day, 1983; Dansby, 1992), tolerance for frustration, and self-esteem (Dansby, 1992; Nordlie et al. 1979) than do whites. In addition, some studies show that blacks are more apt to show external locus of control (feel others control their lives) during adolescence and early adulthood (Tashakkori & Thompson, 1991), which is the primary age for offenses to occur.

Prior Offenses

Civilian Justice System. It has already been pointed out that prior offenses, particularly juvenile delinquency, are related to subsequent offenses of a more serious nature (Sampson, 1987; Schuster, 1971). Welch, Fruhl, and Spoohn (1984) reported that prior records of arrest and convictions are more strongly related to subsequent convictions for blacks than for whites. Moreover, Farrell and Swigert (1978) argue that there may be a self-fulfilling prophecy operating here. Blacks tend to receive more severe sentences because they are more apt to have prior records, but they are more apt to have prior records because they are more apt to be arrested and convicted differentially in the criminal justice system.

Military Justice System. In the military justice system, an indicator of initial tendency toward serious offenses may be the nonjudicial punishment system (NJP). NJPs, such as Articles 15 and letters of reprimand, may be given out for less serious offenses, such as drunkenness, missing a formation, or leaving one's duty station for a short period of time. Studies show that blacks in the Navy received more NJPs than had whites (Culbertson & Magnusson, 1992; Polan & Thomas, 1985). Further, Edwards and Knouse (1990) found that the blacks who were more apt to be separated from the Navy with other than honorable discharges had a higher frequency of NJPs than whites separated with misconduct discharges. Moreover, Horne (1988) reported that black Marines received more NJPs than did white Marines, regardless of the race of the local commander. There is evidence, then, that black NJPs are a function of factors other than bias. For example, blacks have received more NJPs for confrontational offenses, such as insubordination, than whites (Conway, 1983; Culbertson & Magnusson, 1992).

Quality of Employment and Occupation

Civilian Sector. Based on the Uniform Crime Reports, Allan and Steffensmeier (1989) found that low quality of employment (low pay and poor working hours) was associated with higher rates of property crime among both blacks and whites.

Military Sector. Two studies of Marines reported that black Marines in the lower grades (E1-E3) who were older than their colleagues were more apt to commit violent crimes (Hayles & Perry, 1981; Perry, 1980). The authors speculate that these older blacks in the lower grades had lower levels of education, which hindered their advancement. Carrying this idea further, it could be argued that some blacks who enlist from educationally deprived environments (lower levels of education completed from financially and academically poorer schools) receive lower scores on initial ability tests and hence are routed into the lowest status military occupations. The high degree of boredom, lack of advancement opportunities, and accompanying frustration may be factors precipitating the tendency toward criminal offenses.

Type of Offense

Blacks and Violent Crime. There is substantial evidence that blacks tend to be associated with a different type of offense than whites. Blacks tend to be arrested and incarcerated more often for violent crimes against persons (murder, rape, robbery, and assault), while whites are more apt to be associated with less violent property crimes (theft, auto theft, and drug use) (Christianson, 1982).

Of course, there are many possible reasons for this disparity. Because of psychological and sociological factors, blacks may actually commit more of this type of crime (e.g., Dansby, 1992). Or there may be bias. Individuals and institutions may believe that some blacks, because of economic, educational, and familial disadvantage, have a greater tendency toward violent offenses and may even live in a "subculture of violence" (Hindelag, 1978). Such bias may occur at any or all points along the criminal justice process from eyewitness testimony (witnesses more apt to perceive black involvement), to police discretion (police more apt to arrest blacks), to discretion in prosecution (prosecutors less apt to plea bargain, more apt to go to trial with blacks), to discretion of judges in sentencing (longer sentences for blacks) (Christianson, 1982; Hindelag, 1981). In fact, such bias may result in an "accumulated disadvantaged status" where initial differential treatment may become magnified as the individual moves through the criminal justice process (Pope & McNeely, 1981). Moreover, attempts to reduce bias, such as mandatory sentencing, which removes discretion (and hence potential bias) from the judge, may actually increase discrimination in the system by concentrating discretion (and hence possible bias) earlier in the process (i.e., with initial police and prosecutor decisions) (Christianson, 1982).

Military Justice System. In a Navy study, Polan and Thomas (1985) found that blacks were more apt to commit major Uniform Code of Military Justice (UCMJ) offenses (e.g., murder, manslaughter, rape, larceny, robbery) than whites.

Method

Data Site

Data were collected from the United States Disciplinary Barracks (USDB) at Fort Leavenworth, Kansas. The mission of the USDB is to incarcerate those persons sentenced to confinement under the Uniform Code of Military Justice (UCMJ) and to provide treatment, care, and training to return inmates to civilian life (United States Disciplinary Barracks, 1993). The USDB was chosen for this study because it houses offenders of major crimes (sentenced under a general court martial) for all the military services.

Data Collection

Data were collected 25-27 May 1993 by the author from the Mental Health Files of the Mental Health Directorate. A listing of the black and white inmates was generated on 25 May. From that list a random sample of fifty-one blacks and fifty-one whites was determined by selecting those inmates with a "0" in the first place of their registration number.

The Mental Health Files yielded data on inmate background (age, education, family, and prior civilian problems), inmate military experience (military branch, entry date, time in service, grade, and military specialty), and offense information (type of offense, general court martial adjudication date, sentence, and incarceration date).

The files also contained ability test information. For Army inmates, the General Technical Test (GT) scale of the Armed Services Vocational Aptitude Battery (ASVAB) was available, which is used for occupational placement and whose score is given as an intelligence quotient (IQ) equivalency. In addition, the USDB had academic equivalency test data for all inmates in reading, mathematics, and English, which are scored in academic grade level equivalents.

For some recent inmates psychological test data were included. A few inmates in the sample had taken the Anger Inventory to determine level of anger relative to the average USDB inmate and the Buss-Durkee Hostility Inventory, a 75-item true-false scale used to predict assaultive behavior (Brodsky & Smitherman, 1983). Thirty-eight of the inmate sample had completed the Minnesota Multiphasic Personality Inventory - 2 (MMPI-2), a 566-item true-false personality test that is the most widely used test in criminal justice (Brodsky & Smitherman, 1983). Among the MMPI scales that were available in the files were Amorality, Authority Problems, Hostility, Impulsivity, Inhibition, Overcontrol, Masculinity, Projecting Blame, Self Alienation, Self Esteem, Self Indulgence, Social Alienation, and Viewing Others as Dishonest.

Data Coding

Socioeconomic Status. One of the most direct indicators of socioeconomic status is occupation (e.g., Gordon, 1978; Office of the Assistant Secretary of Defense, 1992). Therefore, the occupation of the inmates' parents was used to determine socioeconomic status of the family environment in which the inmate grew up. If the parents were listed as on welfare or unemployed, socioeconomic status was coded as lower class. If the parents' occupations were blue or white collar for which a lower level of formal education was sufficient (e.g., manufacturing assembler, mechanic, carpenter, beautician, teacher's aide, nurse's aide, seamstress, truck driver, clerk), socioeconomic status was coded as working class. If the parent's occupations were white collar for which advanced education was required (e.g., teacher, social worker, nurse, engineer, accountant, manager), socioeconomic status was coded as middle class. If there was a discrepancy between mother's and father's occupational level, the focus was placed on the father's occupation for determining socioeconomic status, considering that the father's occupation was probably more influential on the family's life style. If father's occupation was listed as retired, deceased, or not given, socioeconomic status was coded as "Other."

Results

Comparison of Population to Sample Characteristics

Table 22.1 shows inmate characteristics for the entire population of the Disciplinary Barracks as compared to the inmates in the sample drawn for the present study. It can be seen that there were no appreciable differences between the sample and the population characteristics. Therefore, it can be concluded that the sample was fairly representative of the inmate population.

Table 22.1
Comparison of Characteristics of Disciplinary Barracks
Inmate Population to Study Sample

Characteristic	Disciplinary Barracks	
	Population	Study Sample
Number of Inmates	1379	102
Black Inmates	44%	50%
White Inmates	48%	50%
Percentage of Males	96%	99%
Average Inmate Age	30.5 years	31.2 years
Average Inmate Education	High school	High school
Average General Technical	105	106.9
Test Score		
Average Time in Service	6.3 years	7.6 years
Average Grade	E5	E4/E5
Marital Status	46% Married	46% Married*
Offense Profile		
Crimes against Persons	75%	80%
Sex related Crimes	50%	32%
(pedophilia, rape#)		
Violent Crimes	25%	48%
(assault, murder, robbery)		
Drug related Crimes	13%	7%
Crimes against Property	11%	13%
Military related Crimes	1%	0%
Average Sentence Length	13.8 years	12.9 years
Inmates with Life Sentences	6%	9%

Source: *Fort Leavenworth United States Disciplinary Barracks*
*Separated inmates were included in the married category as they are technically still married.

#The Disciplinary Barracks in their categorization scheme includes rape among sex-related crimes. The present study, however, used the category of sex-related crimes only for sex crimes against minors (pedophilia) and included rape in the category of violent crimes against others.

Age

Table 22.2 shows a summary of analyses of variance for the inmate continuous (nonfrequency) data. For the variable age, black inmates (M age = 30.02 years) were somewhat younger than white inmates (M age = 32.33 years), although this difference was nonsignificant, $F(1,100) = 2.51$. These ages are at the time of the present study, however. There may be differences due to the time served between the commission of the offense and the present time. When inmate age at the date of the court martial adjudication is examined, which is perhaps the closest indicator of offender age at the time of the offense, black offenders (M age = 26.57 years) are shown to have committed their offenses at a younger age than white offenders (M age = 29.14 years), although the significance is marginal, $F(1,100) = 3.56$, $p < .10$.

Table 22.2
Summary of Analyses of Variance on Inmate Continuous-Type Data

Variable	Black Mean	White Mean	F	df	p	eta
Inmate Age at Present	30.02 years (6.88)	32.33 years (7.84)	2.51	1,100	ns	
Inmate Age at Date of Adjudication	26.57 years (6.07)	29.14 years (7.60)	3.56	1,100	.10	.03
GT Score (IQ equivalent)	103.49 (10.36)	111.12 (14.70)	6.63	1,70	.05	.09
Reading Test Score (grade level)	11.81 (1.40)	12.38 (1.06)	5.24	1,99	.05	.05
Math Test Score (grade level)	9.56 (2.21)	11.26 (2.07)	15.78	1,99	.001	.16
English Test Score (grade level)	9.21 (2.65)	10.57 (2.52)	7.07	1,99	.01	.07
Time in Service at Offense	5.76 years (4.64)	9.53 years (6.54)	11.30	1,100	.001	.10
Sentence	13.47 years (12.25)	12.36 years (12.17)	0.16	1,91	ns	

Note: Numbers in parentheses under the means are the standard deviation for that racial group; eta gives the variance accounted for by the effect. It is comparable to R^2 in regression.

Socioeconomic Status

Very few whites or blacks had parents who were unemployed or on welfare. The largest category for both blacks and whites was working class background. Somewhat more whites compared to blacks came from a middle class background. These differences were not significant, however, chi-square (3) = 4.93.

Educational Background

Educational Level. An equal number of black and white inmates had dropped out of high school, entered the service, and then completed their General Education Diploma (GED). About the same number of blacks as whites were high school graduates. Few blacks and whites had gone to college or beyond. These slight differences were nonsignificant, chi-square (3) = 4.74.

Ability Level. Table 22.2 also shows ability test scores. Overall ability level as measured by the General Test score showed blacks (M = 103.49) to be significantly lower than whites (M = 111.12), $F(1,70) = 6.63$, $p < .05$. The smaller sample size here (n = 72) is due to the fact that test data were only available for Army inmates.

The Disciplinary Barracks administers an academic equivalency test during in processing which gives scores on inmate reading, mathematical, and English ability, in terms of academic grade levels. Blacks were significantly lower than whites in all three areas: black M = 11.81, white M = 12.38 for reading, $F(1,99) = 5.24$, $p < .05$; black M = 9.56, white M = 11.26 for math, $F(1,99) = 15.78$, $p < .001$; black M = 9.21, white M = 10.57 for English, $F(1,99) = 7.07$, $p < .01$.

Home Background

Marital Status of Parents. A majority of both black and white inmates came from homes where the biological parents were no longer married. More blacks came from homes where the parents were separated or divorced or had been single parents. More whites came from homes with stepparents, chi-square (5) = 11.96, $p < .05$.

Family Size. The majority of blacks (n = 28) grew up in larger families of five or more children. The majority of whites (n = 33) grew up in smaller families of four or fewer children, chi-square (1) = 3.96, $p < .05$.

Inmate Birth Order. The pattern of birth for blacks and whites is surprisingly similar; there were no significant differences, chi-square (8) = 4.14. The modal birthplace was first for both whites and blacks. The majority of both whites and blacks were either first or second born.

Personality Data

There were very few high inmate scores on the Anger Inventory (black n = 3, white n = 3) and the Buss-Durkee Hostility Inventory (black n = 3, white n = 0).

Of the thirty-eight inmates who completed the MMPI-2, eighteen were black and twenty were white. More blacks fit the external profile (problems with others and with societal norms), while more whites fit the internal profile, chi-square (2) = 10.29, p < .01.

Prior Legal Problems

Prior Civilian Problems. Prior civilian problems included school suspension, skipping school, and problems with the legal system, such as DUI, charges, arrests, and convictions. The pattern for blacks and whites is fairly similar. There were about equal numbers of inmates who experienced prior problems (black n = 29, white n = 30). When the different types of problems are examined, there were no differences found in school problems. Interestingly, more whites (n = 20) than blacks received traffic tickets (n = 11), although this difference was not significant, chi-square (1) = 2.62.

When prior civilian legal problems (DUI, charges, arrests, and convictions) are examined, there again are similar patterns. About the same number of blacks (n = 14) as whites (n = 15) experienced some type of legal difficulty. The types of problems were also very similar. In particular, violent interpersonal acts (charges of rape, arrests for assault or assault and battery, arrests for carrying a concealed weapon) were relatively infrequent and equally distributed among blacks (n = 5) and whites (n = 5).

Prior Military Discipline. Prior military disciplinary procedures included Article 15, letters of reprimand or counseling or prior courts martial. Although a larger number of black inmates (n = 36) than white inmates (n = 24) received prior military discipline, the numbers of inmates were not significantly different, chi-square (1) = 2.40. On the other hand, as a group blacks received almost twice as many

Articles 15 (n of Articles 15 = 55) as did whites (n of Articles 15 = 30), chi-square (1) = 7.35, p < .01.

When the number of inmates receiving prior discipline for military confrontation offenses (disrespect to an officer or NCO, disobeying an order, according to the classification by Nellum and Associates, 1973) is examined, there were a larger number of black inmates (n = 8) than white inmates (n = 2), although these small numbers are not significant, chi-square (1) = 2.40. When the total number of military-related offenses (confrontation offenses and other military offenses including AWOL, missing or late for duty, unattended or lost government property, drunk or sleeping or faking sickness on duty, female in room, fraternization, poor attitude, dereliction of duty) is examined, however, there were a significantly greater number of black offenders (n = 24) than white offenders (n = 12), chi-square (1) = 4.00, p < .05.

There was no difference between black inmates (n = 20) and white inmates (n = 15) who encountered both prior civilian and prior military discipline, chi-square (1) = 0.71.

Military Service

Branch of Service. Most black and white inmates were from the Army. There were, however, a larger number of whites (n = 14) compared to few blacks (n = 5) from the Air Force. There were few numbers of either Marine Corps or Navy inmates. The number of whites versus blacks in the Air Force subsample was not enough to make a significant difference in the larger sample, chi-square (3) = 6.91.

This white Air Force subsample should still be briefly examined, however. It tended to be older (average age = 36.9 years) and had more time in service (average time = 12.9 years) than the larger sample. Most of the inmates were sentenced for sodomy for an average sentence of thirteen years. This was a sizeable number of the total number of inmates sentenced for sodomy.

Grade. Although the average grade for black inmates was E4 and for white inmates was E5, there were no significant differences in the overall distribution of grades by race, chi-square (9) = 7.81.

Time in Service. Table 22.2 shows that blacks had significantly less time in service at the time of the offense (M = 5.76 years) than did whites (M = 9.53 years), F(1,100) = 11.30, p < .001.

Military Occupational Specialty. More blacks tended to be in lower ability jobs, while more whites were in higher ability jobs, although these differences were not significant, chi-square (3) = 3.66. It should be noted that the author created this ability classification. To the author's knowledge, there is no consistent ability classification for occupations across the services.

Incarceration Offense

Type of Offense. Table 22.3 shows the distribution of type of crime by race. The majority of the whites were sentenced for sex crimes against minors (sodomy or indecent acts), while almost twice as many blacks as whites were sentenced for violent crimes against others (assault, attempted murder, murder, rape, robbery), chi-square (3) = 24.89, p < .001.

Sentences. Table 22.2 shows that blacks (M = 13.47 years) had slightly longer sentences than whites, although the difference was nonsignificant (M = 12.36 years), F(1,91) = 0.16. The number of life sentences was equivalent for blacks (n = 5) and whites (n = 4).

Discussion

Education and Ability Level

There were no real differences in education level. On the other hand, blacks had significantly lower ability test scores than whites. It should be noted, however, that if the General Technical Test score is an indicator of overall intelligence and thus reflects overall IQ,

Table 22.3
Type of Incarcerated Offense for Black and White Inmates

Type	Number of Blacks	Number of Whites
Sex Crime with Minor (sodomy, indecent acts with a minor)	5	28
Violent Crimes against Persons (assault, attempted murder, robbery, rape)	32	17
Property Crimes (larceny, forgery)	8	5
Drug related Crimes (use, distribution of drugs)	6	1

both blacks and whites fell more or less within the average IQ range (90 - 110). At the same time the academic skills of blacks (reading, math, and English) were significantly lower than whites indicating that many of the blacks came from educationally disadvantaged environments.

Home Environment

Parents' Marital Status. A majority of both blacks and whites came from homes where the parents were no longer married. One difference, however, is that more blacks came from homes where a parent was missing, while in some white homes the missing biological parent had been replaced with a stepparent. Moreover, several black inmates claimed that a grandparent, which perhaps meant that they did not even have access to one parent, had actually raised them. On the other hand, having a stepparent was not necessarily always beneficial as several white inmates claimed that their stepparents had abused them as children.

Family Size. Blacks tended to come from larger families than whites. And many tended to be the younger children in these larger families. While the data do not give definitive answers, several possible linkages between family size and tendency toward problems can be suggested. One speculation is that larger families create more tensions among siblings as they compete for parental attention and scarce family resources. Indeed, several inmates in their in processing interviews claimed that siblings had physically abused them as they were growing up. This might be an indicator of family tension.

A larger family may also mean that a child may spend more time away from the crowded family environment. This time may be spent on the street in the company of peers and thus there may be more opportunity to learn peer-influenced problematic behaviors.

For black offenders, in many cases the absence of one parent coupled with the fact that they tended to come from larger families may have resulted in less individual attention and perhaps less control overall when they were growing up, a pattern identified in other studies (Sampson, 1987). In other words, the lack of attention and concomitant lack of guidance and at the same time the greater freedom earlier in life may have led to more opportunities to learn maladaptive behaviors and eventually to get into trouble.

Personality

The MMPI-2 data show a trend for white inmates toward personality traits associated with internal problems of control and self and for black inmates traits associated with external problems with others and society. Two cautions should be pointed out at this time. First, this is a small subsample of inmates (only thirty-eight). Second, the internal-external dichotomy may reflect factors associated with race, but it may also reflect type of offense. The majority of blacks committed violent crimes against persons, while the majority of whites committed sex crimes with minors. These personality profiles, then, may be representing the type of individual who commits a certain type of crime; i.e., a person with interpersonal problems may be more apt to commit violent crimes against others, while a person with internal psychological problems may be more apt to be involved in incest or pedophilia.

The important point is that these preliminary personality data show a need for more research in this area. More extensive personality data should be collected from larger offender samples.

Prior Problems

Prior Civilian Problems. There were no differences found between blacks and whites on problems at school and prior legal difficulties. About 30 percent of both black and white offenders had a record of prior DUIs, charges, arrests, or convictions. There was no difference, however, between blacks and whites on confrontational interpersonal violent acts (i.e., rape, assault, battery, or carrying a concealed weapon). Therefore, based on these data, there does not appear to be a greater propensity toward prior civilian legal problems among black offenders. And there does not appear to be a greater propensity among these black offenders toward a history of violence.

Prior Military Discipline. A large majority of black inmates (71 percent) had a history of prior military discipline in the form of Articles 15, letters of reprimand or counseling, or prior courts martial, although almost half of the whites (47 percent) also had prior experience with military discipline. On the other hand, blacks received almost twice as many Articles 15 as did whites, which reflects the findings of a number of military studies (Culbertson & Magnusson, 1992; Edwards & Knouse, 1990; Polan & Thomas, 1985). This could indicate that this particular group of blacks was more apt to get into trouble. The data on prior civilian problems, however, show no greater propensity for prior legal difficulties for blacks than for whites. Moreover, only 34 percent of blacks that had prior civilian problems went on to have military discipline problems prior to their incarceration offense. In other words, these data do not show a pattern of blacks that have a long history of getting into trouble.

A second explanation is that there is some type of problem in the system, perhaps institutional bias, whereby blacks as a group were more apt to get an Article 15 for a problem, while whites were apt to get some other type of perhaps less visible punishment, such as an informal reprimand.

A third explanation espoused by some in the military is that the large number of black military disciplinary problems may be a function of the difficulty of some blacks in dealing with the predominantly white authority structure of the military; these blacks may react with an "in your face" confrontational attitude toward military authority. While more blacks than whites received discipline for confrontation offenses to military authority (disrespect to an officer or NCO or disobeying an order), the small numbers were not significant. When the total number of military-related offenses was examined (confrontation offenses and other offenses such as AWOL, missing duty, dereliction of duty), however, significantly more blacks than whites experienced disciplinary problems. Therefore, there may be a problem of adjustment for some blacks to the military, which is exhibited in some type of clash with the military environment, which in turn results in disciplinary actions, such as Articles 15. The present data reflect small numbers of these problematic instances, however. Future research should examine larger data sets to verify this speculation.

Military Service

Branch of Service. Although a majority of both black and white inmates were from the Army, a number of white inmates were from the Air Force. This subsample tended to be older, more senior, and to have been convicted almost exclusively of sodomy. This may possibly indicate a tendency for the Air Force to look particularly closely and harshly at this offense.

Time in Service. Blacks tended to commit the major offense for which they were incarcerated earlier in their military career. For many it was during their first enlistment. It must be noted, however, that the difference between blacks and whites is partly due to the fact that many whites were incarcerated for a sex crime against a minor that occurred much later in their military careers. In other words, these white offenders may be skewing the time in service data.

Military Occupational Specialty. There was a slight tendency for blacks to have had a lower status occupational specialty than did whites. This is no doubt due partially to their lower test scores which would direct them into lower ability and hence lower status specialties.

Offense

Type of Offense. These data show a trend identified in a number of civilian and military studies (e.g., Christianson, 1982; Polan & Thomas, 1985); i.e., blacks are more likely to be sentenced for violent crimes against others (i.e., assault, murder, rape, robbery). On the other hand, the majority of whites were sentenced for sex crimes against minors, which may reflect the unique tendency of all the military services, not simply the Air Force, to look more harshly on this offense than does the civilian justice system.

Sentence. Blacks were given slightly longer sentences than whites, which may possibly be attributed to the nature of their offense. More blacks had been convicted of violent crimes, which would result in a longer sentence. Moreover, the intercorrelational data did not show any significant correlates with sentence length for the black subsample. From this data, then, there does not appear to be bias in sentencing.

Future Research

Examination of Personality Test Data. In addition to the demographic data in its files, the Mental Health Directorate at the Disciplinary Barracks at Fort Leavenworth maintains extensive inmate data on a number of personality and behavioral tests. It would be fruitful to study the relationship of this test data to various background factors. For example, the present study showed indications of interpersonal problems in some black inmates based upon the limited test data available in the basic mental health file. Further research could examine linkages between potentially significant problematic family variables, such as one or both parents not at home and family size, and problematic educational variables, such as truancy, suspensions, and low academic achievement, and the subsequent influence upon personality and behavioral variables and ultimately the influence upon initial problems in the military, such as nonjudicial punishments.

Larger Sample Sizes. There are patterns of differences found here between blacks and whites, which must be deemed tentative, however, because of the small sample sizes. To reiterate what has already been stated several times, future research should examine larger databases to confirm these findings.

Comparison of Black Offenders and Nonoffenders. It should be pointed out that the basic comparisons examined here were between black inmates and white inmates. A number of these differences might be alternatively explained as not due to factors associated with race, but rather with various social and psychological background factors that may predispose individuals to problems with the criminal justice system. And these individuals also happen to be black. In other words, there may be certain factors in the life experiences of individuals regardless of race, such as a disadvantaged upbringing and disadvantaged education, that cause them to get into legal troubles. In order to test this alternative explanation, it is necessary to focus not so much on differences between black and white offenders, but rather differences within subgroups of blacks. Specifically, it is important to compare the differences between black offenders who come from disadvantaged environments with a matched group of blacks who come from the same type of environment but have not had trouble with the law. Recent studies have shown, for example, that incarcerated black males had more childhood problematic behavior, less involvement with black churches, less family influence on values, and associated more with peers who got into trouble than nonincarcerated black males who came from similar environments (Parson & Mikawa, 1988).

It would be fruitful, although perhaps not easy, to create a database of black offenders in the military matched to a group of black nonoffenders in the military with similar demographic characteristics and then examine unique differences in their backgrounds, such as differences in upbringing, educational experiences, and peer relationships, which may contribute to their problems with the military justice system.

Recommendations

Overall the data show indications that the tendency to commit an offense in the military relates to two antecedent areas: family and educational background and early experience in the military. Recommendations are presented for these two areas.

Family and Educational Background

1. *Provide early help to enlistees.* The data show that some black inmates came from larger families particularly where one parent was absent. The data also show from ability test scores that a number of blacks came from educationally disadvantaged backgrounds. Therefore, some blacks may not have learned the requisite interpersonal skills for effectively dealing with others in various types of social environments.

The military certainly cannot prevent individuals from enlisting because they come from a "broken" home. After all divorce is almost becoming the norm. But the military can be aware of certain factors that *may* predispose some individuals to trouble in their first tour of duty and provide early help, such as counseling, to circumvent these potential problems (Horne, 1988).

Such early help may be particularly important when blacks from troubled backgrounds are sent overseas in their first tour of duty. Among the black inmates in the present study, their intake interviews showed that a number committed their offense overseas, particularly in Europe during their first tour. The sudden cultural change coupled with perhaps inappropriate social skills for dealing with the resultant stress may have precipitated the frequently violent response that led to their court martial.

2. *Be more selective on ability levels of recruits.* The data show that blacks had lower ability scores across the board than whites, which perhaps reflects the larger societal problem of educational disadvantage for many blacks. At least for the military, however, this problem may be partially resolving itself. The data show that more recent inmates tended to have somewhat higher scores on some ability measures, which may mean that the military has been recruiting higher ability blacks than in the past. In addition, with the recent force reductions, the emphasis in future recruiting will most likely be in highly technical areas, which demand higher ability recruits. In other words, after the military has stabilized from its present

downsizing, it may have higher ability blacks (and whites) than in the past. To the extent that disciplinary problems are due to lower educational levels of individuals (i.e., lower education places them in boring dead end jobs, and lower education may provide them fewer psychosocial mechanisms for dealing with frustration and stress), disciplinary problems among both whites and blacks may decline in the future in the military.

Early Experience in the Military

1. *Provide socialization inoculation.* These data and that of other studies (e.g., Culbertson & Magnusson, 1992; Edwards & Knouse, 1990; Polan & Thomas, 1985) show that blacks, who were largely first term, had more NJPs than whites, even when they had fewer prior civilian problems. This points to something in their early military experience that triggers disciplinary problems.

Some type of device that inoculates them to military rigor and stress early in their process of being socialized into the military is important. The Defense Equal Opportunity Management Institute (DEOMI) has proposed such a device (Dansby; 1992, 1993). The socialization inoculator is a series of videotapes and vignettes that present appropriate and inappropriate interpersonal responses in military situations, such as dealing with a NCO or officer. The emphasis is upon avoiding aggressive confrontational approaches that may be effective in an urban inner city environment but may be considered disrespectful and even insubordinate in the military environment.

2. *Provide foreign culture inoculation.* A combination of socialization inoculation and cultural sensitivity training might reduce the sense of frustration and stress caused when first-term blacks from the urban environment of large cities encounter very different foreign cultures when they are posted overseas.

3. *Provide early mentors.* Mentors provide help both for psychosocial problems and for career problems (Kram, 1988; Zey, 1984). Mentors can serve as guides, coaches, teachers, resource experts, and supportive persons for new persons in organizations. In addition, minorities can receive special understanding and special help from minority mentors (Knouse; 1991, 1992).

The military might consider using older more experienced black NCOs as mentors to newly trained black enlistees. Research shows that mandating formal mentoring programs where mentors are assigned to mentees many times does not work (Kram, 1988). The crucial chemistry between mentor and mentee does not develop. At the same time, organizations have been successful in providing situations, such as formal and informal get-togethers, where potential mentors and mentees can meet, get to know one another, and let the mentoring process take its course. In like fashion, the military could provide formal and informal functions where first-term black enlistees could meet experienced black NCOs, who could serve as their guides through the military bureaucracy, their coaches on appropriate interpersonal behaviors, and their support persons for dealing with stress and frustration.

References

Allan, E. A., & Steffensmeier, D. J. (1989). Youth, underemployment, and property crime: Differential effects of job availability and job quality on juvenile and young adult arrest rates. *American Sociological Review*, *54*, 107-123.

Bloom, B. (1966). A census tract analysis of socially deviant behaviors. *Multivariate Behavioral Research*, *1*, 307-320.

Bridges, G. S., & Crutchfield, R. D. (1988). Law, social standing and racial disparities in imprisonment. *Social Forces*, *66*, 699-723.

Brodsky, S. L., & Smitherman, H. O. (1983). *Handbook of scales for research in crime and delinquency*. New York: Plenum.

Christianson, S. (March 1982). *Disproportionate imprisonment of blacks in the U.S.* Prepared for the National Association of Blacks in Criminal Justice. Center on Minorities and Criminal Justice, State University of New York at Albany.

Conway, S. W. (1983). *Effects of race and gender on court-martial rates and punishments*. NPRDC-SR-83-20. San Diego, CA: Navy Personnel Research and Development Center.

Culbertson, A. L., & Magnusson, P. (1992). *An investigation into equity in Navy discipline*. NPRDC TR-92-17. San Diego, CA: Navy Personnel Research and Development Center.

Dansby, M. R. (1992). *Racial disparities in military incarceration rates: An overview and research strategy*. DEOMI 92-3. Patrick AFB, FL: Defense Equal Opportunity Management Institute.

Dansby, M. R. (1993). *Socialization as an inoculation to reduce black males' involvement with the military justice system*. DEOMI Research Proposal Number 10. Patrick AFB, FL: Defense Equal Opportunity Management Institute.

Edwards, J. E., & Knouse, S. B. (1990). *Racial- and ethnic-group differences in character-of-separation and disciplinary rates among first-term enlistees who are ineligible to reenlist*. NPRDC TN-91-1. San Diego, CA: Navy Personnel Research and Development Center.

Ensminger, M. E., Kellam, S. G., & Rubin, B. (1983). School and family origins of delinquency. In K. T. Van Dusen & S. A. Mednick (Eds.), *Antecedents of aggression and antisocial behavior*. Boston: Kluwer.

Farrell, R. A., & Swigert, V. L. (1978). Prior offense record as a self-fulfilling prophesy. *Law and Society Review*, *12*, 437-453.

Flyer, E. S. (1990). *Characteristics and behavior of recruits entering military service with an offense history*. Office of the Assistant Secretary of Defense for Force Management and Personnel. Arlington, VA: Defense Manpower Data Center.

Gordon, M. M. (1978). *Human nature, class, and ethnicity.* New York: Oxford University Press.

Green, E. J. (1978). *Birth order, parental interests, and academic achievement.* San Francisco: R & E Research Associates.

Hayles, R., & Perry, R. W. (1981). Racial equality in the American naval justice system: An analysis of incarceration differentials. *Ethnic and Racial Studies, 4,* 44-55.

Hindelag, M. J. (1978). Variations in sex-race-age-specific incidence rates of offending. *American Sociological Review, 46,* 461-474.

Horne, G. E. (1988). *Equity in disciplinary rates.* CNA CRM 88-26. Alexandria, VA: Center for Naval Analyses.

Joe, T. (1987). Economic inequality: The picture in black and white. *Crime and Delinquency, 33,* 287-299.

Kellam, S., Adams, R., Brown, C., & Ensminger, H. (1982). The long-term evolution of the family structure of teenage and older mothers. *Journal of Marriage and the Family, 44,* 539-554.

Knouse, S. B. (1991). Social support for Hispanics in the military. *International Journal of Intercultural Relations, 15,* 427-444.

Knouse, S. B. (1992). The mentoring process for Hispanics. In S. B. Knouse, R. Rosenfeld, & A. Culbertson (Eds.), *Hispanics in the workplace* (pp. 137-150). Newbury Park, CA: Sage.

Kram, K. E. (1988). *Mentoring at work.* New York: University Press of America.

Laufer, W. S., & Day, J. M. (1983). *Personality theory, moral development and criminal behavior.* Lexington, MA: Lexington.

Loeber, R., & Stouthamer-Loeber, M. (1986). Family factors as correlates and predictors of juvenile conduct problems and delinquency. In M. Tonry & N. Morris (Eds.), *Crime and justice* (Vol. 7, pp. 29-149). Chicago: University of Chicago Press.

Nellum, A. L., & Associates. (1973). *Analysis of the military and civilian criminal justice system.* Report ALNA-79 to the Office of Naval Research.

Nettler, G. (1982). *Explaining criminals.* Cincinnati: Anderson Publishing Company.

Nordlie, P. G., Sevilla, E. R., Edmonds, W. S., & White, S. J. (1979). *A study of racial factors in the Army's justice and discharge systems.* Report No. HSR-RR-79/18. Washington, DC: DAPE-HRR, The Pentagon.

Parcel, T. L., & Menaghan, E. G. (1993). Family social capital and children's behavior problems. *Social Psychology Quarterly, 56,* 120-135.

Parson, N. M., & Mikawa, J. K. (1988). Incarceration and nonincarceration of African-American men raised in black Christian churches. *Journal of Psychology, 125,* 163-173.

Pepinsky, H. E. (1986). A sociology of justice. *Annual Review of Psychology, 12,* 93-108.

Perkins, M. L., & Reeves, J. E. (1975). The Cattell 16 PF as a measure of inmate offense types. *Journal of Clinical Psychology, 31,* 35-50.

Perry, R. W. (1981). The American dilemma at sea: Race and incarceration in the naval justice system. *Phylon, 41,* 50-58.

Polan, S. L., & Thomas, P. J. (1985). *Military offense rates: Racial, ethnic, and gender differences.* MPL TN 86-2. San Diego, CA: Manpower and Personnel Laboratory, Navy Personnel Research and Development Center.

Pope, C. E., & McNeely, R. L. (1981). Race, crime, and criminal justice: An overview. In R. L. McNeely & C. E. Pope (Eds.), *Race, crime, and criminal justice.* Beverly Hills, CA: Sage.

Sampson, R. J. (1987). Urban black violence: The effect of male joblessness and family disruption. *American Journal of Sociology, 93,* 348-382.

Schuster, R. L. (1981). Black and white violent delinquents: A longitudinal cohort study. In R. L. McNeely & C. E. Pope (Eds.), *Race, crime, and criminal justice.* Beverly Hills, CA: Sage.

Tashakkori, A., & Thompson, V. D. (1991). Race differences in self-perception and locus of control during adolescence and early adulthood. *Genetic, Social, and General Psychology Monographs, 117*, 133-152.

Tittle, C. R., Villemez, W. J., & Smith, D. A. (1978). The myth of social class and criminality. *American Sociological Review, 43*, 643-656.

United States Disciplinary Barracks (1993). Fort Leavenworth, KS.

Walker, M. R. (1992). *An analysis of discipline rates among racial/ethnic groups in the U.S. military.* DEOMI 92-4. Patrick AFB, FL: Defense Equal Opportunity Management Institute.

Welch, S., Gruhl, J., & Spohn, C. (1984). Sentencing: The influence of alternative measures of prior record. *Criminology, 22*, 215-227.

Zey, M. G. (1984). *The mentor connection.* Homewood, IL: Irwin.

Part 5

Where Do We Go from Here?

Introduction to Part 5

Importance of Continuing Research

Additional research will be increasingly needed to generate the detailed information necessary for creating a workable equal opportunity (EO) climate and to enable the Armed Services to perform their ever-expanding missions effectively. The issues facing future diversity management and equal opportunity programs may be demonstratively different both in content and in complexity from those of the past, if for no other reason than that the country's demographic profile is projected to undergo considerable change. African-American, Hispanic, and Asian sub-populations are increasing at a faster rate than that of whites. Consequently, it is projected that non-white sub-populations will be entering the military at rates exceeding current levels. It has been predicted that the Hispanic representation will be greater than that of African Americans by the first decade of the twenty-first century. Asian Americans will also increase their numbers in the ranks significantly. Changes in the Armed Services will be accompanied by changes in values and perceptions. It will be absolutely critical that the instruments used to assess the EO climate are designed and subsequently redesigned to accommodate differences across individual groups rather than aggregating groups into a "minority" classification. Indeed, DEOMI is currently engaged in designing a new Military Equal Opportunity Climate Survey (MEOCS), MEOCS 2000, with that goal in mind.

The need for new approaches to diversity management will undoubtedly increase as the anticipated population shifts occur. As an example, extensive research and planning will be required to enable the Armed Services to meet their recruitment goals. Such research should focus, in part, on developing subculture-specific recruitment strategies. An example of recent developments consistent with such a thrust is the recent decision by the Navy to contract with filmmaker Shelton "Spike" Lee for development of new recruitment advertisements. Beyond recruitment issues there is also a need for new approaches to long-term force planning incorporating not only projections of population growth trends for individual demographic groups, but also group-specific retention targets.

As the military environment becomes increasingly more diverse, the focus of diversity management will require adjustment. As an example, the anticipated demographic shifts are likely to engender hostile responses on the part of some constituencies who feel displaced by the growing presence of previously underrepresented groups. One manifestation of such resistance may be the growing presence of extremist groups in the U.S. and in other parts of the world. The military may hold a special attraction for some of these groups as a result of warfare training opportunities and access to weapons. The Department of Defense has a longstanding policy of intolerance for organizations, practices, or activities that are discriminatory. Nevertheless, several instances where military personnel have been found to belong to extremist groups and engage in hate violence have received significant media attention and prompted official inquiries. There is a need for much more detailed research examining this phenomenon. Is it possible to identify individuals whose prior socialization makes them more predisposed to be receptive to extremist ideas? Can targeted training programs be developed to counter such tendencies in addition to the standard training provided to all personnel?

New challenges in the international arena will also serve as a catalyst for future research. The U.S. military has been called on increasingly in recent years to play a peacekeeping role in various parts of the world. In several cases, for example Somalia, cross-cultural conflicts have contributed to U.S. fatalities in the line of duty. While total avoidance of such catastrophes may be impossible, it is absolutely critical that U.S. military personnel have adequate international cross cultural communication skills to interact constructively with the indigenous residents of the areas where they are assigned. Are there lessons that can be learned from the recent experiences of U.S. military personnel who served in Haiti, Somalia, and Kosovo? Research designed to identify problem areas and develop strategies to minimize potential conflicts could be invaluable as the U.S. military's international peacekeeping role expands. In the same sense that DEOMI has spearheaded the training of military personnel to manage internal domestic diversity, it may well be called upon in the future to play a vanguard role in training personnel to perform externally focused international diversity management missions. Such a training curriculum would have the goal of providing an optimal and working understanding of military, political, social, cultural, psychological, and economic factors that influence the success of deployments outside the U.S. The development of long-term research strategies can position DEOMI and other research facilities to assist the Armed Services in meeting future challenges more effectively. Possible approaches to developing such strategies are discussed in this section.

Research Overview

The studies presented in the preceding sections highlight research conducted primarily by visiting faculty participating in the Summer Faculty Research Program at DEOMI. This type of partnership can play a pivotal role in the future in supporting the types of research projects necessary to facilitate effective diversity management in the Armed Services.

In this section there is also an effort to highlight research conducted at other installations. "Women and Minorities in the Military: Charting a Course for Research," by Mark Eitelberg describes several recent research studies conducted by students and faculty in the Manpower Systems Analysis Curriculum at the Naval Postgraduate School. The studies focus on areas such as the officer pipeline, international comparisons of military sexual harassment policies, and attrition among females in the Navy.

"The Future of Intercultural Research: Application to the Military Setting," by Dan Landis identifies fifteen areas where additional research can be fruitful. Landis emphasizes the need for more complex models of intercultural behavior. One of the most crucial issues highlighted by Landis and other researchers is the need for more systematic evaluation of EO training and management programs.

The research agenda proposed by Landis could be effectively pursued through collaborative efforts of the type represented by the work of academic researchers under the auspices of DEOMI as well as through cooperation between DEOMI and other DoD research facilities. In addition to the research agenda proposed by Landis, the studies presented in the preceding sections have identified some specific research topics that warrant additional attention. Several of these are highlighted below.

Specific Research Issues

As discussed previously, the primary concern in managing diversity in the Armed Services is the maintenance of unit operational readiness. Consequently, research examining the linkage between unit demographic composition and readiness should be a high priority. In particular, is there a methodology (or are there methodologies) that can accurately predict unit readiness based on its racial and gender composition? If so, how accurate are such predictions across units with differing missions and demographic profiles? Further, how do military teams with diverse membership become cohesive units?

Demographic characteristics are, of course, simply crude indicators of potential intercultural communication and human relations problems. The broader research questions that require additional scrutiny are how unit readiness is influenced by the degree of multicultural harmony, the actions of command leadership, and specific interventions designed to improve the EO climate.

Historical and empirical evidence has shown that any organizational problem can not be fully resolved without the "buy-in", i.e., commitment and support, from the chain of command including the commanding officer. In order to assure that "buy-in," it is necessary to demonstrate to commanders that multicultural understanding and respect are essential to operational effectiveness or readiness. Even though DEOMI training includes this element in its curriculum, there have been only a few studies using real world criteria as measures of effectiveness.

The principal mission of DEOMI is to train equal opportunity advisors (EOAs) to assist commanders in managing diversity in their units. There is an ongoing need to ascertain if EOAs are effective in their efforts to foster a favorable EO climate. What are the best practices of EOAs? What are the optimal characteristics of EOAs? Is there a best mix of personal and professional factors (i.e., personality factors, biodata traits, etc.) that would predict EOA success? These are among the questions that need to be answered as part of an expanded research agenda.

In a related vein, the MEOCS database provides an opportunity to identify exceptional commands that have significantly reduced or eliminated gender and racial conflict and enhanced overall command EO. Intensive studies should be conducted to highlight best practices and the diversity management efforts of these commands and share this information with other units as a follow-up to a pilot DEOMI initiative.

The time is ripe to undertake this type of expanded research program. Now that the drawdown is nearing completion, it is important to determine if it has impacted command EO climate and, if so, to what extent? More generally, the most crucial question is whether the Pentagon leadership will continue to prioritize EO in the face of more opposition to EO and affirmative action matters from some civilian groups. The answer to this question will depend strongly upon the level of funding provided in the future to EO research and management programs.

Unforeseen circumstances will undoubtedly create new challenges in diversity management that can be met effectively only if the DoD has research capabilities that take full advantage of the nation's intellectual capital. The unique partnership between the military and the civilian sector in place at DEOMI reflected in the research presented in this volume constitutes a valuable asset that must be nurtured and expanded into the twenty-first century.

23

Women and Minorities in the Military: Charting a Course for Research

Mark J. Eitelberg

Introduction

This paper reviews a number of studies conducted in 1996 and 1997 by students and faculty in the Manpower Systems Analysis Curriculum at the Naval Postgraduate School (NPS).[1] These studies share a common focus on women and minorities (singularly or together) in the military. They include the following: a statistical assessment of the accession, assignment, retention, and career advancement of women in the military; a study of women and racial/ethnic minorities in the military's "officer pipeline"; a study of attrition among women in the Navy; a study of attrition among twenty categories of racial/ethnic groups in the Navy; an evaluation of diversity management in the Navy; a study of sexual harassment policies and programs in the militaries of five nations; and three studies relating to the U.S. military's "Don't Ask, Don't Tell" policy on homosexuals.

Additionally, this paper looks at three studies currently in progress at NPS: a study of possible linkages between a recruit's socioeconomic status and his or her performance in the military; an assessment of the boot camp (i.e., basic military training) experience (as part of "progressive integration") for women in the Marine Corps; and an exploratory study of civilian "following spouses" of female officers in the Navy. The paper then summarizes the basic premise of a forthcoming article on understanding organizational "culture change" and its relationship to women and minorities in the military.

A common thread runs through all of the studies addressed here. That thread is one of both progress and hope for the future. Each

497

study, in its own way, reveals a positive step in behalf of equal opportunity. At the same time, each study tends to point in the direction of continuing research for positive change in the years ahead.

Statistical Assessment of Women in the Military

A joint-service workshop was held at NPS in August 1996. It was convened by the Defense Advisory Committee on Women in the Services (DACOWITS), Subcommittee on Forces Utilization and Development. The workshop helped to design the basic content of a statistical report that was subsequently produced by the Defense Manpower Data Center (DMDC) and NPS.[2]

The statistical information in the report reveals several noteworthy trends regarding women in the military. As of 1996, proportionately more women were in the military than ever before—13 percent of active-duty personnel and 14 percent of reservists. As relatively more women enter the enlisted and officer "pipelines," correspondingly increased numbers are rising to senior positions of authority. An index of equality in promotions suggests remarkable fairness between men and women; and the greatest disparities, where found, tend to "favor" women.[3]

Proportionately more women have been enlisting in the Armed Forces as a whole—even though the "military propensity" of young women is considerably below that of their male counterparts.[4] In 1996, for example, women accounted for 26 percent of active-duty recruits in the Air Force and 21 percent of recruits in the Army—up from 19 percent and 14 percent, respectively, nine years earlier. On the other hand, female representation among newly commissioned officers has apparently changed little over the period examined here.

The continuation rates of men and women in the active-duty force are generally similar by Service and officer or enlisted status.[5] Certain variations can be seen in different measures of continuation—but, on average, there are more similarities than differences between men and women up to typical retirement (i.e., twenty years). Continuation by women can also be evaluated by their use of voluntary separation incentives during the force drawdown. As it turns out, women took advantage of these incentives at about the same level as their representation in the force as a whole. Further, female personnel who remain in the military appear to advance educationally to a greater extent than do their male counterparts.

Male-female differences were found in average years of service at time of promotion. These particular differences tended to "favor" women in the officer corps (active duty) and "favor" men in the middle grades of the enlisted force. Promotion rates by gender further confuse the issue—showing higher rates for men within all grades of the officer corps except O-4 and higher rates for men in most enlisted grades.

Other indicators suggest that a number of "gender gaps" exist in the duration, condition, or nature of military service. Most notably, women are still concentrated in traditionally female occupations— specifically, in health care and support/administration. Women are gaining entrance to a wider variety of jobs, but the proportions of female personnel in traditional fields have apparently changed very little over the years examined in the report. Occupational differences within the officer corps may help to explain why men and women are so unevenly distributed by sources of commission. At the same time, proportionately fewer women than men in the military are married or have dependents—suggesting, perhaps, gender-related differences in the personal life choices of military personnel. The first-term attrition rates of women in the enlisted force are considerably higher than of those men—largely due to the early separation of women who become pregnant. Female officers (grades O-4 and above) are less likely than their male counterparts to receive a joint-duty assignment, which is a critical step in advancement to the rank of general or admiral—but these disparities may be tied to long-standing differences between the occupational tracks of women and men. Finally, women appear less likely than men (by entry cohort) to stay in the active-duty military for ten, fifteen, or twenty years.

No attempt has been made to explore the causes or implications of the various trends revealed in this report. A vast amount of data is presented in the tables—compiled from Service sources by DMDC, and based on a plan developed at the DACOWITS-led workshop. The report marked a first, "quick-response" effort to create a new body of information on women in the military—information that could serve as a reference and guide for those who may wish to further study the subject.

The "Officer Pipeline" Study

The "Officer Pipeline" study was initiated at the request of Secretary of Defense William J. Perry in the fall of 1994. The primary objective of the effort was to study the flow of women and minorities into the officer corps and through its ranks—from recruitment and commissioning through the organization's highest positions—and to recommend areas for improvement, if necessary. Specific areas of concern included the relatively low representation of women and minorities in the senior ranks of the officer corps, the relatively low representation of women in certain career tracks (e.g., aviation), and differing perceptions of the equal opportunity climate and fairness in promotions, evaluations, and assignments.

The draft report looks at the following: demographic composition of the officer corps; officer recruitment, assignment, and career progression; officer performance evaluation and recognition; and equal opportunity perceptions and interventions. Generally, the report finds that racial/ethnic minorities and women have made substantial progress over the period of study, but "there remains room for improvement," and "more remains to be done."[6]

Female Attrition in the Navy

Numerous studies of enlisted attrition have been conducted since the draft ended in 1973. Many more studies will likely be undertaken in the coming years as well, since over one-third of all new recruits fail to complete their first term of service. This level of attrition has remained fairly constant for the past two or more decades, despite dramatic increases in the quality of new recruits and accumulated knowledge from many years of research devoted to the problem.

Several recent studies of gender differences in attrition reveal the following: women tend to have higher rates of first-term attrition than do men, but the differences in rates are primarily due to pregnancy-related factors; women are more likely than men to experience certain medical problems that lead to early discharge from the military; and women tend to experience lower rates of attrition than do men in certain occupational areas, such as support or shore-duty jobs in the Navy (see Sealey, 1997).

Sealey (1997) focused on recruits who enlisted in the Navy from 1986 through 1990. These recruits were tracked over their first term of enlisted service with the aid of DMDC's cohort accession data file. The study was especially interested in exploring gender differences that were related to job categories or the mix of men and women in Navy occupations.

The results of the study indicated that the official reasons for attrition (as recorded in Defense Department records) tend to be similar for men and women across Navy occupations, with two exceptions: pregnancy, as previously noted, and "alcohol/drugs," which is typically more prevalent for men. The data also show that the major reasons for attrition by women are similar in occupations that have relatively high rates of female attrition and those that have relatively low rates. Further, the primary reasons for female attrition in occupations with a high proportion of women (the so-called "traditional" jobs) are similar to the reasons for female attrition in occupations with a relatively low proportion of women.

Racial/Ethnic Groups and Attrition in the Navy

There is no shortage of research on the causes and correlates of personnel attrition from the military. Indeed, this area of research can trace its modern-day origins to the 1950s, when education and aptitude test scores were first linked in determining an applicant's qualifications for enlistment (see for example, Eitelberg, Laurence, & Waters, 1997). Personnel attrition is still one of the most studied—yet perplexing—aspects of the All-Volunteer Force.

Studies of first-term attrition traditionally compare personnel discharge rates across the usual demographic categories—such as gender, age, educational level, aptitude test scores, marital status, and race or ethnicity. Studies that include race or ethnicity, in turn, are usually limited to just a few major categories: white, black, Hispanic, and a catch-all "other," which combines small populations of Asians, Native Americans, and persons of various other backgrounds.

Espiritu (1997) compensates for the relatively small numbers of "other" racial and ethnic groups in annual cohorts of recruits by aggregating recruit populations from a ten-year period. Specifically, data for the study consisted of longitudinal information (from DMDC's cohort accession file) on recruits who entered the Navy from 1983 through 1992. The study population—a total of more than 500,000 male enlisted personnel—was tracked over a 48-month period (e.g., recruits who entered the Navy in 1992 as of 1996). The attrition experiences of this population were then examined for three racial groups (white, black, and other), six racial/ethnic groups (white, black, Hispanic, North American Indian/Alaskan Native, Asian, and unknown), and the following ethnic groups: Mexican, Puerto Rican, Cuban, Latin American, other Hispanic descent, Aleutian, Eskimo,

North American Indian, Chinese, Japanese, Korean, Indian, Filipino, Vietnamese, other Asian descent, Melanesian, Micronesian, Polynesian, other Pacific Islander descent, and other/unknown.

The results by ethnic group reveal that Asians had the lowest attrition rate—about 17 percent—which was almost half the rate for the Navy's male recruits as a whole. Filipinos (who number 6,248 in the database) had the lowest attrition rate (13 percent) among Asian groups and all other ethnic groups (with the exception of Melanesians, who numbered just fifty-one). Among the racial/ethnic groups, North-American Indians/Alaskan Natives had the highest attrition rate at 37 percent.

As previous research shows, Hispanic subgroups tend to differ somewhat with respect to their attrition experiences. Among Hispanics in the study population, Cubans had the highest attrition rate (35 percent), and Mexicans had the lowest rate (26 percent).

Overall, 21 percent of recruits in the study population were discharged from the Navy for failure to meet minimum behavior or performance criteria (which accounts for about 70 percent of all reasons for attrition). This compares with rates of 24 percent for blacks, 28 percent for North American Indians/Alaskan Natives, and 19 percent for Mexicans. Filipinos had the lowest attrition rate for reasons connected to behavior or performance—just about 8 percent.

The attrition experiences of racial and ethnic groups were also examined by several variables, including education and enlistment test scores. It is interesting to note here that controlling for "high quality" (a combination of education and aptitude test scores) sometimes led to different results for ethnic groups. Generally, "high quality" recruits had a lower rate of attrition than did their counterparts when examined by race or race/ethnicity. But, several ethnic groups—including Filipinos—did not follow this pattern.

The study by Espiritu (1997) underscores the importance of breaking down larger categories of racial or ethnic minorities into their component subgroups. As seen here, combining certain groups of minorities into large categories, such as "Asian" and "Hispanic," can mask meaningful differences between the groups that compose these categories. Future research should thus seek to examine subgroups separately whenever possible. And, taken further, such research should seek to discover why certain ethnic groups—such as Filipinos—tend to have attrition rates that are so much lower than the average for their fellow recruits.

Diversity Management in the Navy

Manning (1997) examines private and public efforts at managing diversity, using published research and case studies to identify the most effective strategies and techniques. Managing diversity is defined generally as "a comprehensive managerial process for developing an environment that works for all employees"—an environment that allows an organization to "tap the potential of all employees" and expands the notion of valuing diversity at all levels of the organization (Thomas, 1996).

The study assesses various approaches to diversity management, including multicultural organizational development (used by New Perspectives, Inc.), "high-performing inclusive organizations" (developed by Kaleel Jamison Consulting Group, Inc.), and the managing diversity model (used by the American Institute for Managing Diversity). Additionally, the study looks at approaches employed by Avon, Procter and Gamble, Xerox, Environmental Protection Agency, National Aeronautics and Space Administration, and the U.S. Navy and Marine Corps.

Manning (1997) recommends using a "total systems change" approach—a long-term process for organizational change—to manage diversity. This approach focuses on the organization in its entirety, the individual, and interpersonal relationships, as well as the organization's systems, policies, and practices. Thus, an organization must first design a plan for total systems change, if it lacks one. Then, it can proceed to develop an improved diversity management strategy, meaningful training programs, and feedback procedures to evaluate the effectiveness of its training and longer-term outcomes.

Sexual Harassment Policies and Programs in TTCP Countries

Bennett (1997) evaluates sexual harassment policies and programs in the militaries of nations in The Technical Cooperation Program (TTCP). TTCP is a consortium of defense scientists from the United States, Canada, United Kingdom, Australia, and New Zealand. The study of sexual harassment was conducted as a cooperative effort of the TTCP panel on "Military Human Resources Issues" (officially designated as Technical Panel HUM-TP3).

More specifically, Bennett (1997) looks at the following topics: the background surrounding sexual harassment in each of the countries, including initial recognition of problems or issues, associated watershed events, and the role of women in the nation's military; each country's national and military sexual harassment policies; sexual harassment training and associated programs, assessment groups, measurement instruments, and the scope of sexual harassment; common themes across the countries; and highlights of the most effective programs. On the last topic, the study identifies several exemplar approaches—including the so-called "umbrella approach" employed by both the New Zealand and Canadian militaries. This approach treats sexual harassment as one of many forms of harassment. It is of key importance, since sexual harassment is actually a subset of gender harassment, which demands a more comprehensive treatment in policies, programs, and training. Another area of note is the Support Harassment and Racism Prevention (SHARP) program introduced by the Canadian Forces. SHARP is recognized in the study for it unique mission, approach, and method of implementation. Canadian Forces are also recognized for their positive efforts at changing the military culture. Additionally, the study singles out the U.S. Navy's Command Managed Equal Opportunity (CMEO) program for its "unique preemptive approach to managing sexual harassment and other equal opportunity issues" (Bennett, 1997; pp. 193-194). Finally, the study emphasizes the importance of a well-conducted investigation, as evidenced in Australia, Canada, and New Zealand; and it discusses the need for further efforts at ensuring accountability, using mentoring and support groups, and improving the informal complaint process.

Bennett (1997) identifies several areas that are considered "critical" in eliminating sexual harassment. These areas are drawn from the "lessons learned" in TTCP countries as well as from the positive results of exemplar approaches. Thus, the author recommends that greater efforts be taken as follows: first and foremost, evoke culture change; expand the focus of sexual harassment to include all types of harassment; further strive to improve training; use prevention measures and conduct regular assessments of the command climate; ensure that program guidelines are clearly communicated, service members are held accountable for their actions, and that the accountability process is periodically inspected; improve questionnaires and other data-gathering procedures; centralize data collection and track informal and formal complaints; and use top-level study groups to underscore the importance of programs and to pinpoint necessary courses of action.

Gays in the U.S. Military: Three Studies

A minority group can be defined as a number of "persons who share the experiences of being objects of discrimination, exclusion, and persecution by members of non-minority groups who hold ethnocentric beliefs and stereotypes" (Sarbin, 1996; p. 180). As Sarbin (1996) observes, sexual orientation has been identified as a feature of a minority group in areas of our society, most notably through legislation that guarantees to homosexuals equal access to housing and jobs in certain jurisdictions. The recent debate over the U.S. military's ban on gays—along with the resulting policy of "Don't Ask, Don't Tell" and trends in the militaries of other nations—suggests that homosexuals may one day achieve the protected status of a minority within the military. Sarbin sees "minority" as the latest social construction of homosexuality—preceded by homosexuality as a sin, a crime, and a sickness, each of which endures to some extent in society and among those who guide military policy.

Three studies of note were undertaken at NPS on the subject of homosexuals in the military:

1. A survey of the attitudes of naval officers toward homosexuals and officers' levels of understanding regarding the "Don't Ask, Don't Tell" policy (Friery, 1997).

2. A study of the possible effects of the "Don't Ask, Don't Tell" policy on unit cohesion (Rea, 1997).

3. A study of the possible influence of a service member's religious values and understanding of church teachings on his or her acceptance of gays in the military (Peterson, 1997).

Friery (1997) replicated a survey that was administered in 1994 at NPS, so that any shifts in attitudes or understanding could be compared over time. It involved two phases: a 50-question, structured survey distributed to all naval officers attending NPS; and focus group interviews to explore issues raised in the surveys. The results suggested that officers were even more uncertain in 1996 than in 1994 (when the previous survey was administered) about basic elements of the policy; and officers tended to evaluate the policy in pragmatic terms, balancing mission requirements against individual needs. Further, most officers in the two samples held negative attitudes about serving with homosexuals—but the intensity of their feelings appeared "softer" in the later survey.

Rea (1997) similarly examined the attitudes and opinions of naval officers toward the "Don't Ask, Don't Tell" policy—but attempted to focus more specifically on aspects of unit cohesion, rather than on general feelings. A series of seven focus group interviews revealed that naval officers (in early or mid-career) may be far more tolerant toward differing sexual preferences than is currently assumed. There is still a strong sentiment that homosexuals may disrupt the cohesion of military units; but there is a clear lack of agreement on what constitutes the root causes of the disruption—and virtually no experiential data in recent times supporting the claim, since military policy excludes "known" homosexuals. Indeed, some officers felt that the military's present method of dealing with homosexuals is detrimental to unit cohesion. The policy is intended to protect unit cohesion, but it actually supports the stereotypes (e.g., regarding intolerant heterosexuals and predatory gays) that make cohesion so difficult to achieve. Military personnel are essentially *instructed* by the policy that heterosexuals and known homosexuals cannot work side-by-side. Rea (1997) drew three general conclusions from the interviews: (a) there was little evidence to support the contention that homosexuals weaken unit cohesion; (b) a homosexual's identity is often defined solely by his or her sexual orientation, and heterosexuals tend to believe that they do not share the same values, goals, and experiences with homosexuals; and (c) a lack of privacy on naval vessels leads to feelings of discomfort among heterosexuals, which tends to outweigh concerns about unit cohesion. As the author concludes: "In the end, then, 'Don't Ask, Don't Tell' is only an artificial protection. Real protection of unit cohesion will be achieved if the stereotypes supporting the ban are broken. And these stereotypes will only be broken if the military allows an opportunity for the 'contact theory' to work." (It is important to note here that this study, as well as the surveys conducted in 1994 and 1996, evidenced support for the "contact theory" or "contact hypothesis." The "contact hypothesis" states that intergroup prejudice or hostility can be reduced by personal contact between groups that share or pursue a common goal (Allport, 1957; Herek, 1996).[7]

Peterson (1997) broke important, new ground—not only with respect to the U.S. military's policy on gays, but regarding any policy that a service member may perceive as involving a "moral" issue. The author looked specifically at whether personal religious beliefs may influence a service member's response to such policies. The study began with a review of the religious heritage of the U.S., the First Amendment to the Constitution, and the history of military policies toward gays. The author then described the religious demographics of the active-duty military and assessed the doctrines on homosexuality of the largest denominations represented in the U.S. military. Finally, he evaluated the expressed moral beliefs of active-duty service members regarding homosexuality (using extant data from three surveys).

The primary conclusion of the study was that opposition by service members to the integration of homosexuals in the U.S. military is likely influenced by teachings of the dominant Christian faiths. This conclusion, as the author observes, suggests that the nation's decision makers should weigh the importance of religion and associated personal beliefs on organizational effectiveness when considering a policy that may involve a "moral" issue.

Research in Progress

Four studies, currently underway at NPS, may be of interest to the community of scholars and practitioners in equal opportunity/equal employment opportunity. The largest research effort is a study of the relationships between a new recruit's socioeconomic status (SES) and his or her performance in the military over time. Questions concerning the SES origins of recruits have been raised for decades— dating at least as far back as the Vietnam-era draft. When an end to the draft was first proposed in the late 1960s, a great deal of debate centered on the very same issue. For example, people asked: would an all-volunteer military become an "army of the poor"; would a draft-free system tend to attract the hard-core unemployed, the labor-market rejects of society; would the military become an "employer of last resort"; and, would the burdens of defense be placed unfairly on the shoulders of America's poor—as the Civil War slogan said, with "rich men's money and poor men's blood"?

The Department of Defense (DoD) is required by Congress to assess population representation in the military, and it prepares a lengthy report each year that looks at a variety of demographic variables. The Defense Department also conducts an annual survey (the "Survey of Recruit Socioeconomic Backgrounds") of new recruits regarding their SES origins. This survey was first administered in March 1989, and the results of the survey have since become a fixed part of the annual report on population representation. The results of the survey continue to show that recruits come from all levels of SES; however, they tend to be concentrated in the lower three-quarters of the SES distribution. In fact, today's recruits are often characterized as being over-representative of "middle America," drawn heavily from "average" SES brackets.

The study of SES linkages with performance involves merging the SES survey results with DMDC's enlisted cohort files (which tracks recruits longitudinally). This allows researchers to examine the service careers and military performance of the SES survey population over time. There are approximately 14,000 respondents (active-duty recruits) for each annual survey—providing a total sample size of over 100,000 with some respondents having as many as eight years of service since the time they were surveyed. Measures of performance include items currently available in the DMDC database (e.g., first-term attrition, time-to-promotion, reenlistment eligibility, etc.), as well as service-specific measures, such as fitness report scores, skill qualification scores, disciplinary cases, and other variables.

The results of the study are likely to be of general interest, well beyond the community of military researchers. It should also be noted that the study focuses more on recruiting and enlistment policies of "selecting in" as opposed to "selecting out." That is, it seeks to identify "at risk" individuals with the intent of devising innovative strategies that would help these young men and women succeed in military service. The study is scheduled for completion in March 1998.

Another, more modest research effort seeks to assess the effects on women of gender segregation in Marine Corps boot camp. Segregation of men and women at this point of Marine Corps training is part of a master plan called "progressive integration." This study involves interviews with women Marines prior to boot camp, during boot camp, and one year after boot camp. Research only covers the period since the Marine Corps first initiated the "crucible" as part of initial training. The study will be finished by March 1998.

The military family of today has become increasingly removed from the classic, traditional arrangement of yesteryear. For example, in dual-parent households, more and more men are taking on the role of the "following spouse," sometimes assuming the position of "Mr. Mom," or primary caregiver for young children. A newly-initiated study at NPS seeks to describe this trend and identify related issues such as spousal satisfaction with military life and the possible effects of "role reversal" on the retention of women in the military. The study uses extant data, including information from Defense Department surveys, as well as interviews with both men and women in this type of military family. The results of the study will be published in March 1998.

A fourth study, which is still in a very preliminary stage, seeks to understand the long-term consequences of "diversity" policies on organizations. In particular, the study explores possible problems that develop when the promises and expectations for immediate change go unfulfilled—and when attempts at rapid change confront the barriers of an organization's prevailing and conflicting culture. A recent shift in "reinventing government" strategies serves as a focal point of the research. The study also highlights the importance of maintaining a strong sense of history.

Summary Comment

This paper reviews a number of studies, some of which are still in progress. All of the completed studies provide some direction for further research. All point to continuing issues of concern for equal opportunity and equal employment opportunity. All studies demonstrate that there have been positive changes in behalf of equal opportunity and a military that values the diversity of its membership. And all provide some hope for a future that will be better than the past.

The studies that are summarized here also emphasize the importance of taking the long view, of seeking to gain historical perspective. Surely, one cannot fully appreciate the present—for its gains as well as lingering problems—until it has been properly weighed against the past. History can be the "Great Teacher," as we separate the myth from reality, value the efforts of those that preceded us, and recognize that progress toward equal opportunity has indeed occurred within the military in our time. But it is likewise important that progress not be used as an excuse for inaction—because progress requires even more diligence, so that two steps forward, one step back does not become one step forward, two steps back. History, too, is replete with examples of apathy and neglect among leaders who believe that they have somehow triumphed over a problem and that progress, once achieved, is a force of its own. This is where *research* can help, as it sheds light on unsettled areas, points the way to possible solutions, and raises awareness of the need for positive change.[8]

Notes

1. This paper was prepared for the Defense Equal Opportunity Management Institute (DEOMI) Equal Opportunity/Equal Employment Opportunity Research Symposium, Cocoa Beach, Florida, December 1997. The author participated—as either an advisor or researcher—in the studies discussed here. For further information, contact the author at the Department of Systems Management, Code SM/EB, Naval Postgraduate School, Monterey, CA 93943. The e-mail address is as follows: meitelberg@nps.navy.mil.
2. Department of Defense, *Utilization of Women Indicator Report*, Draft Report (Monterey, CA: Defense Manpower Data Center and Naval Postgraduate School, September 1996). See also, Department of Defense, *Response to Request for Information, Standard Reporting Format* (Monterey, CA: Defense Manpower Data Center, December 1996).
3. The *index of equality* has been used previously in studies of this nature. It examines average rank equality, comparing the average rank of men with that of women, controlling for occupation, education, length of service, racial/ethnic group, and marital status. The resulting ratio (weighted to reflect the number of women) is then a representation of men and women working in the same occupation, with equal education, length of service, and so on. A separate analysis focused on officers and enlisted personnel in higher grades. This was undertaken to test for possible "smoothing" of gender differences—because of virtually automatic promotions in lower grades, where personnel are more heavily concentrated. The results again showed little or no difference in average rank equality between women and men.
4. The "propensity" of women to join the military—that is, those claiming (on a nationwide survey) to have a "definite" or "probable" chance of enlisting—has been stable at about 11 or 12 percent between 1986 and 1995. The "propensity" of young men has ranged from 24 to 30 percent over the same time period. There is a relatively greater discrepancy between young women and men on unaided mentions of interest in the military—2 percent for women, compared with 7 percent for men.
5. The "continuation rate" is the number of persons on active duty at the end of a year divided by the number at the start of the year, computed by matching social security numbers in personnel files at both points. Continuation was also examined by years of service.
6. Department of Defense, *Minorities and Women in the Officer Pipeline*, Draft Report (Washington, DC: Office of the Under Secretary of Defense for Personnel and Readiness, November 1996), p. 94. The final report is now available, see Department of Defense, 1999.
7. Herek (1996) notes that most research in this area has looked at interethnic and interracial prejudice; but, it is reasonable to assume that the "contact hypothesis" can be applied to attitudes and groups based on sexual orientation.
8. Readers who are interested in the details of these studies and related research at the Naval Postgraduate School should contact Professor Mark Eitelberg in the Department of Systems Management. Readers are also encouraged to convey their comments and ideas for future research, especially projects that may be suitable for a Master's thesis.

References

Allport, G. (1954). *The nature of prejudice*. New York: Addison-Wesley.
Bennett, D. R. (1997, June). *Sexual harassment policies and programs in the militaries of TTCP countries*. Master's Thesis. Monterey, CA: Naval Postgraduate School.

Department of Defense (1996, September). *Utilization of women indicator report*. Draft Report. Monterey, CA: Defense Manpower Data Center and Naval Postgraduate School.

Department of Defense (1996, December). *Response to request for information, standard reporting format*. Monterey, CA: Defense Manpower Data Center.

Department of Defense (1996, November). *Minorities and women in the officer pipeline*. Draft Report. Washington, DC: Office of the Under Secretary of Defense for Personnel and Readiness.

Department of Defense (1999, August). *Career progression of minority and women officers*. Washington, DC: Office of the Under Secretary of Defense, Personnel and Readiness.

Espiritu, E. M. (1997, March). *Study of first-term attrition among racial/ethnic minorities in the Navy*. Master's Thesis. Monterey, CA: Naval Postgraduate School.

Eitelberg, M. J., Laurence, J. H., & Waters, B. K. (1984, September). *Screening for service*. Washington, DC: Office of the Assistant Secretary of Defense [Manpower, Installations, and Logistics].

Friery, M. R. (1997, March). *Trends in Navy officer attitudes toward the "Don't Ask, Don't Tell" policy*. Master's Thesis. Monterey, CA: Naval Postgraduate School.

Herek, G. M. (1996). Why tell if you're not asked? Self-disclosure, intergroup contact, and heterosexuals' attitudes toward lesbians and gay men. In G. M. Herek, J.B. Jobe, & R. M. Carney (Eds.), *Out in force: Sexual orientation and the military*. Chicago: University of Chicago Press.

Manning, C. D. (1997, March). *Managing diversity in the United States Navy*. Master's Thesis. Monterey, CA: Naval Postgraduate School.

Peterson, M. A. (1997, March). *Homosexuality, morality, and military policy*. Master's Thesis. Monterey, CA: Naval Postgraduate School.

Rea, T. M. (1997, March). *Unit cohesion and the military's "Don't Ask, Don't Tell" policy*. Master's Thesis. Monterey, CA: Naval Postgraduate School.

Sarbin, T. R. (1996). The deconstruction of stereotypes: Homosexuals and military policy. In G. M. Herek, J. B. Jobe, & R. M. Carney, (Eds.) *Out in Force: Sexual orientation and the military*. Chicago: University of Chicago Press.

Sealey, V.D. (1997, March). *Study of attrition among enlisted women in the Navy*. Master's Thesis. Monterey, CA: Naval Postgraduate School.

Thomas, R. (1996). *Redefining diversity*. Atlanta: American Management Association.

24

The Future of Intercultural Research: Application to the Military Setting[1]

Dan Landis[2]

Introduction

In 1983 and again in 1996, I was involved in publishing the two editions of the *Handbook of Intercultural Training* (Landis & Brislin, 1983; Landis & Bhagat, 1996). I became involved in these projects despite the fact that most of my research had involved intracultural studies (studies of race relations in various American institutions, e.g., Landis, Day, McGrew, Thomas, & Miller, 1976; Landis, Brislin, & Hulgus, 1985). However, I was convinced that intra- and intercultural studies have a common basis and therefore each edition included both types of contributions. At the same time, beginning in the early 1970s, we conducted a number of studies of racial issues in the military. These studies continued sporadically until the late 1980s when, at the invitation of DEOMI and Mickey Dansby, we embarked on the conceptualization and operationalization of the military equal opportunity climate construct resulting in the Military Equal Opportunity Climate Survey (MEOCS). Parallel with this work, I continued an interest in the intercultural aspect of the domain through the editorship of the *International Journal of Intercultural Relations*, involvement with the Society for Intercultural Education, Training, and Research (SIETAR), and active participation in the formation of the International Academy for Intercultural Studies.[3]

The above recitation of a personal history is not presented for narcissistic reasons, but rather to show how superficially disparate strains can coexist. It is those strains that I will attempt to integrate in this paper. My purpose is to summarize what I believe to be the major challenges for intercultural relations research in the near future and how those tasks have implications for the prosecution of military studies on fields like prejudice, discrimination, and equal opportunity training.

Structure of the Paper

The *leitmotif* of this paper is a sampling of papers that have appeared in the *International Journal of Intercultural Relations* over the past two or three years. This sample gives, I propose, a fairly good picture of where the field is and where it needs to be going. While few of these papers deal directly with military topics, almost all have implications for the military. It is those implications that I will attempt to draw. I make no pretense that the field has been completely covered or that all the implications have been drawn. Others may disagree on my ability to discern patterns and I have no problem with such disagreement. This is, most assuredly, a personal look into the nexus of a field. I invite others to make similar journeys.

My sojourn suggests some fifteen issues. There are, of course, many more; but, these are ones that speak particularly clearly to the military situation. For convenience, these are grouped into those involving theory and methodology and those involving specific contexts. Again, while this distinction is arbitrary, it does make some sense when we reflect on how the field is organized into scholars and researchers on the one hand and trainers on the others.

Issues Involving Theory and Methodology

Issue 1: The contact hypothesis is increasingly under attack

It is arguably true that most of what we do in intercultural and equal opportunity training has its intellectual roots in a single work: Allport's *The Nature of Prejudice* (1954). In this seminal work, Allport outlined what has come to be called the "contact hypothesis." Allport noted that prejudice:

> ...may be reduced by equal status contact between majority and minority groups in the pursuit of common goals. The effect is greatly enhanced if this contact is sanctioned by institutional supports (i.e., by law, custom or local atmosphere), and if it is of a sort that leads to the perception of common interests and common humanity between members of the two groups. (Allport, 1954, p. 267).

In the years since the Allport book was published, many variants of the contact hypothesis have appeared. Such versions have included the Common Ingroup Identity Model (e.g., Gaertner, Dovidio, & Bachman, 1996) and Brewer's Theory of Optimal Distinctiveness (e.g., Brewer, 1991; Brewer, 1996). Both models deal with an implication from the contact hypothesis: that prejudice decreases when the boundary between the in- and out-group becomes thin or nonexistent. Each model has produced mainly laboratory data to support their propositions. However, when real groups which have experienced considerable intergroup tension are used with conditions arranged to favor "decategorization," it is not clear that using crosscutting (an operationalization of the Optimal Distinctiveness Model) produces the desired positive changes. For example, when Rich, Kedem, and Schlesinger (1995) used groups of religious and secular Israeli preteen children, they found that the model worked for "natural" categories like gender and failed when a value category like religion was used. That is, greater social acceptance after treatment occurred for religious outgroup persons only when they were of the same gender as the person in the ingroup. Since the setting for the study was a fairly natural one and the religious distinction one that engenders considerable hostility in the Israeli situation, the results suggest that decategorization would appear to be quite resistant to change. It may be that categorization on the basis of gender is a more primitive form of stereotyping (e.g., Smith & Branscombe, 1984) than is religious affiliation. Hence, the latter is easier to change than the former.

Despite the negative findings of the Rich et al. study, other researches continue to suggest that some aspects of the contact hypothesis may be valid. For example, Wood and Sonleitner (1996) using survey data from Oklahoma City, found that childhood interracial contact in schools was a significant predictor of adult stereotype disconfirmation and decreased prejudice. When childhood interracial contact occurred, the level of adult negative stereotypes decreased and the opposite was also true. The effect remained robust even when control variables (e.g., gender, age, education, and family income) were added to the predictor equation. Findings supporting the contact hypothesis were also reported by Horenczyk and Bekerman (1997). These authors measured ingroup and outgroup stereotyping from a group of American Jewish teenagers visiting Israel and participating in a structured contact situation. Positive changes were reported as a result of the contact irrespective of participation in the structured experience. More important, in my opinion, is the observation that the boundaries between ingroup and outgroup could hardly be said to contain as much affect as for example between Arab and Jew in Israel, black and white in America, or Protestant and Catholic in Northern Ireland. Again, the contact model, and its descendants seem most applicable in situations where the borders between groups have not been encrusted with years of mistrust, anger, and hate.

The best research design calls not for testing a theory against the absence of an effect (the "null" hypothesis), but for testing contrasting models against one another. This is rarely done in any area of social science research, much less in intercultural studies. One study that did attempt such a contrast was reported by Tzeng and Jackson (1994).

The Tzeng and Jackson study involved testing the effects of levels derived from three models (contact, social identity, and realistic group conflict [e.g., Sherif, 1979]). Scales were developed to measure each model as well as three types of hostile reactions (behavioral intentions, affective, and cognitive evaluations). Results indicated that all three models predicted level of hostile reactions for the white subjects only, but for blacks only the contact theory seems to hold up. An implication from this finding would be that whites (or majority groups) can find many reasons for negative reactions to minority groups, but for blacks such decisions are based on the nature of past (real) interactions.

The upshot of many years of research since the Allport book is that the effects of contact are far more complex that we might have thought at one time. More intriguing is the possibility that all theories might be true for some groups and that there, consequently, may not exist reciprocity between in and out-groups. The implication is that in any intercultural training situation we need to take account that the treatments might have differential effects on the groups involved. Hence, totally different experiences might be necessary for members of in- and out-groups.

Implications for the military. The military has generally taken the position that it is irrelevant to its mission as to whether or not contact does in fact decrease prejudice, reduce ingroup/outgroup distinctions, or change stereotypes. These are *attitudes* and what is important is how military members behave while on the job. At the same time, the military has, in its actual behaviors, acted as if the contact hypothesis (at least as propounded by Allport) were, in fact, true. So, the various policies surrounding equal opportunity provide the "institutional supports;" the stress placed on unit *esprit de corps* provides a common task, and separation by ranks, across groups, in work and social environments deals with the third leg of the hypothesis. However, there is little evidence of changed attitudes or beliefs about other groups as a result of these policies and activities. A study by Lawrence and Kane (1996) found no change in racial attitudes as a function of military service. It is most probable that race is like gender in that it is a default social categorization, most likely because it is marked by clearly discernible physical characteristics. In more recent years, the emphasis has been on the first part of the hypothesis. Here I refer to the decision by then Secretary of Defense Perry to require all flag rank officers, serving and designate, to undergo equal opportunity training. The underlying rationale for this training is, clearly, to enhance the perception of a strong institutional support for a policy of equal opportunity. This is certainly important, but one has to wonder if it is enough given the possibility that stereotyping by race and gender may be quite basic ways of categorizing people in the social world. If so, then more vigorous actions may be necessary and it may, indeed, be necessary to focus once again on the changing of attitudes to provide a support for changed behaviors. There has been recent evidence that the use of normative pressure may change private beliefs in a direction favorable to antiracist sentiments (e.g., Blanchard, Lilly, & Vaughn, 1991). Such procedures should be investigated to move the military to a racially free attitude as well as behaviorally neutral institution.

A rather neglected area of investigation is the behavior of military members when assigned to foreign bases. It is here that intercultural relations theory and practice may make important contributions. The intercultural behavior of service people has generally been ignored, the assumption being that military members will generally socially interact with others of their own kind and have relatively little to do with the host populations. That this assumption has been false can be confirmed by simply counting the number of intercultural marriages on any military base or post. In the past few years there have been a number of particularly egregious events (for example in Okinawa and actions by Canadian Airborne forces in Somalia [Winslow, 1997]) which call into question the policy of ignoring the need to provide effective intercultural training.

Issue 2: The need to develop more complex and rich models

In 1983, and again in 1996, my colleagues and I proposed a model of intercultural behavior (Brislin, Landis, & Brandt, 1983; Landis & Bhagat, 1996). Those models are individualistic in focus and path analytic in format. Those models attempted to place the major antecedents of intercultural behavior into some sort of a logical scheme from which predictions could be made. It was hoped when we formulated the original version in 1983 that researchers would begin the process of putting quantitative indexes on the links in the models. Sadly, that was not the case. Perhaps, it was because the models were too complex, containing too many variables. Nevertheless, it should be apparent that intercultural behavior is a complex phenomenon that demands many variables for its explication.

Others in the past few years have echoed the need for going beyond the two- or three- variable model. And, still others (e.g., Anderson, 1994) have reminded us that intercultural behavior is not unique in human experience. In Anderson's view the process of cross-cultural adaptation can best be thought of as a special case of sociopsychological adjustment. She suggests that since all adaptation is cyclical, we should not be surprised if the same holds true of adjusting to a new culture. The import of her theorizing is that intercultural behavior becomes linked to well researched theories in other domains of social science, in this case psychology. Based on her model (Anderson, 1994; pp.310-311), she defines six major categories of reactors to another culture: returnees (those who withdraw at an early stage); time servers (those who appear to be doing their jobs, but are really simply serving out their time, otherwise known as "brown-outs"); escapers (those who remain, but are always motivated by the urge to leave it all behind); beavers (counterparts of the escapers—they escape their work by burying themselves in the minutiae of their tasks); adjusters (people who are activity coping, still trying to fit in and working at it—they are conscious of the lack of fit and are constantly worried by it); and participators (people who are effective, demonstrate a willingness to learn and to expand their own subjective cultures to include the host). While her model is even more complex than the one that we have described in the *Handbook*, it has value in alerting us to the many variables to go into determining how a person reacts to an unfamiliar culture.

Complex model building requires the use of rather sophisticated statistical tools. We are beginning to see the application of such tools in understanding the development and maintenance of culture (e.g., Gaertner et al., 1996; Ruggiero, Taylor, & Lambert, 1996). In both the Gaertner and Ruggiero papers, structural equation modeling (SEM) has been used to develop causal nets describing relevant phenomena. The research by Ruggiero and colleagues probed a previously unstudied variable (ethnic discrimination) in maintaining an ethnic heritage. In a very carefully designed study, these authors demonstrated a robust relationship between host discrimination and culture maintenance. Though such a relationship had often been speculated about by observers of the rise of the black consciousness movement in American, this is the first time that I can recall that it is has been quantitatively determined. However, contrary to expectation and in line with common sense, it was found that the occurrence of personal discrimination (e.g., by police) produced lower ethnic heritage maintenance. The multiple R^2 was .90, quite good for these types of data. As more and more multivariable data sets become available, the use of powerful statistical methods to tease out causal paths will become more common.

Implications for the military. The military has generally ignored the possibility that working with the culturally/ethnically different may be a disturbing and transitional experience for some people. Thus, in the process of living and working in an integrated environment, the unprepared military member may go through a process not unlike the person entering a new culture for the first time. The process of decategorization may not be a pleasant one and may hold the possibility of a person's recoiling into an even more extreme level of prejudice.

A second implication deals with the requirements for validating complex social theories. One of the procedures that the military is very good at is the construction of very large and well-designed databases. The MEOCS is one, of course. But others exist that are more pertinent to the topic of this paper (e.g., the sexual harassment database produced by the Department of Defense Management Data Center). Such databases provide the Ns necessary for the testing of multivariate models using more powerful analytic techniques than those available in ordinary regression techniques. The studies of causal antecedents of commitment to a service career by Landis, Dansby and Tallarigo (1996) and Bartle, McIntyre, Landis and

Dansby (1997) are examples of this approach. Both of these studies used structured equation modeling (SEM) and although they came to somewhat different conclusions, one thing they did agree on was that equal opportunity climate is a significant precursor of several important indicators of organizational functioning.

Issue 3: Development of psychometrically adequate scales for measuring cross-cultural adaptation and other dimensions

Many studies fail to find significant results (or they present weak findings) because the measures are psychometrically flawed. These measures will have low reliability and, consequently, low validity. At least four recent papers have included rigorously developed measuring instruments (Pruegger & Rogers, 1994; Dawson, Crano, & Burgoon, 1996; Dunbar, 1997; Landis, Dansby, & Tallarigo, 1996). Two of these researches present new quantitative measures and the third refines an already existing scale. Pruegger and Rogers (1994) developed a new measure, the Cross-cultural Sensitivity Scale (CCSS). The CCSS has quite good reliability (a=.93) and has two parallel forms, thus permitting use in repeated measures designs. Since the measure was developed in Canada, it is no surprise that the items have a strong Canadian emphasis. However, other investigators in other countries could easily follow the same procedure to develop equally good versions of the CCSS.

Dunbar (1997) presents a three-factor measure of multigroup identity. Developed using a large multiethnic sample, reported reliability is quite good for each of the three factors: perceived social support, empowerment, and ascribed identity. The importance of this measure is that it can be used to evaluate the progress of groups who are subjected to racial or ethnic awareness programs. Having a well developed and multidimensional scale would relieve the program designer of the responsibility to construct and validate their own psychometrically sound measures.

Dawson et al. (1996) take an already existing measure, The Acculturation Rating Scale for Mexican-Americans (ARSMA) and statistically examine its internal structure. Though the ARSMA had been reported to have a multifactor structure, Dawson et al. extracted a shorter, but factor-pure version that had an equally high reliability as the full measure. And, they demonstrated that the short (10 item) version measures the same construct as the full (21 item) version. Having a ten-item scale to use to assess program effectiveness is certainly more conserving of participant time than longer testing procedures.

To summarize, the development of psychometrically sound measures has two advantages. One, it conserves the energy of the program developer. Two, it provides an assessment of program effectiveness which allows the separation of treatment from random effects. To the extent that the measure has high reliability it will be sensitive to small but significant changes due to the treatment. All of these are highly desirable, since treatments that are effective will be retained and those that are not can be discarded.

Implications for the military. The import for the military is the same as for all social sciences. It is arguably true that the military has generally paid more attention to the psychometric properties of its measuring instruments than have others engaged in intercultural research. Such attention is probably due to the long history of measurement research in the various military personnel research centers such as the Army Research Institute and the former Navy Personnel Research Development Center. (Currently known as Navy Personnel, Research, Science and Technology). The challenge will be to use these well-developed instruments to assess the effectiveness of the various programs now in place and those to be developed to reduce intercultural friction. This means that pressure to use "quick and dirty" measures of program success must be resisted and that will, I suspect, be difficult in the military and political setting.

Moving away from the internal situation in the United States and recognizing that the military is an international organization whose members interact with host nationals, the development of intercultural training programs will become increasingly important. As such the evaluation of such programs will require data being gathered from host nationals. Of particular interest will be measures tapping how the military members and host nationals see one another. These will require measures that are functionally equivalent—that is, have been back translated (Brislin, 1980).

The reason for the failure to develop such measures in the military is twofold. The first issue is the failure to find meaningful differences in predictability using aptitude measures in the civilian and military sector. That is, the regression lines for ethnic minorities and Caucasian military members generally parallel one another. This would suggest that the measures function equally well in both populations. On the other hand, this consistent finding may mean that the ethnic minorities have learned to be bicultural and act "white" when such behavior is demanded by the situation. This is particularly likely with individuals and groups who are striving to become either assimilated or integrated, to use John Berry's analysis of group reactions to migration (Berry, 1997).

Complementary to the technical and psychometric reason outlined above is the political aspect. Acceptance of the idea of conceptually equivalent measures implies acceptance of the concept of multiculturalism. Politically, the concept of multiculturalism slides easily over into the construct of quotas, even though the two ideas are quite unrelated. In the military, as in today's society, programs directed only at minority servicepeople are unacceptable to many interest groups because they are special efforts not available to others or likely to stigmatize the receiving group. The development and use of different measuring instruments are likely to be seen in a similar fashion and seen as unacceptable to both majority and minority groups.

While it is politically dangerous to develop equivalent measures to be used to assess aptitudes, attitudes, and behaviors between groups in the military, it is certainly less problematic to conceive of such instruments in the international context. I suggest that as the military becomes involved in more nonmilitary tasks outside the boundaries of the United States the development of such measures will come to be seen as necessary.

Issue 4: Investigators will continue to question the generality of theories of intergroup conflict

The Rich et al. (1995) and Tzeng and Jackson (1994) studies described earlier suggest, beyond questioning the truth of certain theories, that those theories might not be adequate descriptions for all culture groups engaged in intercultural conflict. Hence, in order to make those theories work, additional variables or constants might have to be added—in other words, the theories have to become more complex.

Perhaps a theory that has the distinction of being one of the most researched derives from the work of Hofstede (1980; Kim, Triandis, Kagitcibasi, Choi, & Yoon, 1994). In that well-known work, Hofstede put forth the construct that cultures can be organized along four dimensions: individualistic-collectivistic, power distance, uncertainty avoidance, and masculinity. Many studies have used the four-part structure in explaining cultural differences—especially the individualistic factor. However, Fons Trompenaars ignited a small controversy with his book, *Riding the Waves of Culture: Understanding Cultural Diversity in Business* (Trompenaars, 1993; Hofstede, 1994; 1997; Hampden-Turner & Trompenaars, 1997). The argument is rather arcane, but revolves around whether the seven Tropenaars dimensions (universalism, individualism, emotionalism, specific versus diffuse, achievement versus ascription, time orientation, and attitudes toward the environment) are really derivations of the individualistic[4] factor of Hofstede. Even more bothersome is the possibility that both approaches are faulty because they base their generalizations on the use of etic approaches to study emic phenomena as well as committing the ecological fallacy. More to the point of this section, however, is Trompenaars' belief that the dimensions organize themselves in different ways in different cultures, thus calling into question the linear combinations implied by the Hofstede approach. I am not going to even attempt to resolve this debate here. But, to the extent that the debate centers around the issue of the applicability of the Hofstede dimensions (which were derived from a questionnaire based on a number of well-known American scales, e.g., the California Psychological Inventory) across cultures, the implications for research are pervasive. Perhaps the reduction to four dimensions in the Hofstede structure fails to capture the real differences in ways people in different cultures view their social world. These are issues that will continue to excite us in the years ahead.

Implications for the military. Considerable evidence (e.g., Albert, 1996; Buriel, 1975) has indicated that, for example, Hispanic groups tend to be more collectivistic in outlook than Caucasian groups and may have had different socialization patterns. Members entering from other ethnic backgrounds may have developed similar cultural "syndromes" (Triandis, 1994). The prevailing military doctrine varies between individualistic and collectivism in how individuals should perform. On the one hand, a team performance doctrine implies a collectivistic set of behaviors. On the other hand, the member is encouraged to assume leadership and exhibit initiative when called for by the situation—an individualistic approach. But, it may be easier for Caucasian members to adapt to this variance since they have had experience with institutions (e.g., schools) which often demand similar switching. Minority members may not have had as much experience. The experience from their homes may have emphasized the collectivistic syndrome. In the military they may, thus, function much more effectively in collectivistic roles. However, advancement in the military goes much more commonly to those who can effectively switch from one syndrome to the other (i.e., can act individualistically when dealing with those who are lower in their chain of command and collectivistically with those are superordinate). The training of individuals who can effectively switch syndromes may be the key to the military becoming truly integrated.

Issue 5: Development of a bridge between culture specific and culture-general assimilators

Some may wonder why I place a clearly "technique" discussion under "Theory and Methodology." I do it because the culture assimilators (Cushner & Landis, 1996) are one of the few techniques derived directly from theory—the theory of attributions and Triandis' statement of isomorphic attributions. In the past few years, assimilator development has diverged into two paths: the culture specific and culture general. These are analogues of the distinction between emic and etic, which has also framed much of the discussion in cross-cultural research. To put a fine point on the discussion: are there certain commonalties in the subjective culture of societies such that a person who grasps those similarities will be able to function quite well no matter on what shore they wash up upon? This concept forms the logic behind the culture-general assimilator (Brislin, Cushner, Cherrie, & Yong, 1986; Cushner & Brislin, 1996). At the same time, the development of culture-specific assimilators proceeds apace (e.g., Tolbert & McLean, 1995). What is needed is an overarching theory to guide development of both the general and specific assimilators (Bhawuk, 1997). Furthermore, there is, to my knowledge, no study comparing the effects of each against the other to determine which is most efficient. Put another way, the challenge is to determine what attributions are common to all human experience and which are unique to particular groups of humans. This is a challenge that has yet to be met.

Perhaps the challenge can be addressed by suggesting the following: "Arrival" behaviors (those that are necessary upon arrival or first contact with another culture) are more likely to be universal. Hence, these are efficiently addressed by the culture general approach. Behaviors which deal with the roles and values of the host culture are more likely to be unique; hence, best trained using culture specific assimilators. An implication from this formulation is that for brief sojourns (less than a month or so), the culture general assimilator will suffice. For more extensive sojourns (particularly those that include spouses and other members of the family) the culture specific assimilator will be most useful. A further implication is that for the long sojourns, the two types of assimilators should be used in tandem with the culture general being applied predeparture and the culture specific used once the person has begun to be settled in the host country.

Implications for the military. There are two implications that can be discussed under this rubric. First, the military constantly faces the issue of how best to socialize minority group members into the culture of the military. Attempts have been made (e.g., Landis, Day, McGrew, Thomas, & Miller, 1976) to develop assimilators for Army leaders in dealing with minority enlisted personnel. It is certainly politically more acceptable to provide training programs for majority persons in positions of authority. However, if we consider the military to represent a culture which reflects primarily majority norms and if those norms are unlikely to change significantly, then techniques are needed to aid minorities to assimilate those norms. By "assimilate" I do not mean destroy or forget indigenous norms of behavior, thought, and attitudes. Rather, we would point to the extensive literature suggesting that as a result of assimilator training an expansion of the trainee's subjective culture (Triandis et al., 1972) occurs.

The second implication comes from the need to train servicepeople to interact positively with non-American nationals that they meet in the prosecution of their assigned duties. Present intercultural training in the military is minimal at best. One can speculate that military doctrine is that servicepeople serving overseas need have only fleeting contact with host nationals. Such contact is justified on the basis that assignments overseas are generally short and focus on technical aspects largely achievable without extensive involvement of non-military personnel. This is unlikely to be the case for many overseas deployments as we move more and more into limited actions around the world. We have evidence that the failure to provide effective cross-cultural training can have disastrous results.

Issue 6: The need for reality-based assessments of cross-cultural training effectiveness

Kealey and Protheroe (1996) reviewed the state of assessing cross-cultural training and came to the conclusion that it is "...seriously deficient" (p. 159). They suggested that a "reliable" study of the impacts of expatriate training would need to include, at a minimum, the following five criteria:

1.   A comparison between trained and untrained groups which have been matched on most important criteria.

2.   Pre- and post-knowledge measures of change in both cognitive and behavioral competencies.

3.   Random assignment of subjects to trained and untrained groups.

4.   longitudinal measures of subsequent performance on the job lasting fairly long periods of time.

5.   Impact measures which are more objective that self-reports of the trainees, including peer, supervisor, and host national assessments.

To these, I would add:

6.   The sequential and interactive effects of multiple training techniques should be assessed.

The optimum evaluation design is one that compares training approaches against one another. This has rarely been done because of the difficulty of selecting comparable treatments and groups. Three studies, however, have attempted such a design (Pruegger et al., 1994; Landis et al., 1985; Harrison, 1992). Of the three studies, only the Landis et al. (1985) used a design in which the sequential effects of two training approaches could be assessed. In this study, groups were formed which engaged in culture assimilator and/or role play training in a black-white situation. The culture assimilator was either presented alone, before the role playing or after the role playing. The role playing was similarly presented with regard to the assimilator. A control group which received no training was also used. This modified Solomon four-group design was used to study the interactive effects of the two types of training. Results gave support to the notion that a culture awareness approach (the assimilator) worked best when it preceded an experiential technique since it appeared to reduce what W. Stephan and C. Stephan (1985) have called "intergroup anxiety."

The Pruegger et al. (1994) study compared the simulation game, Bafa Bafa, with a lecture-based cognitive presentation. The treatments were not compared within but rather between groups, in contrast to the Landis et al. (1985) study. Results indicated that the two treatments did not differ when they were compared on a quantitative measure—the Cross-cultural Sensitivity Scale (CCSS), which was administered some two months later. A personal three-page document was also prepared by each subject and submitted after the posttest CCSS was administered. This document was subjected to content analysis, with the experiential group showing significant attitude change appearing on both the experiential and lecture groups. This study is interesting because of its use of rigorous evaluation methods, a relatively long follow-up data gathering, and the finding that when objective measures are used neither technique produced changes, but that the participants reported significant subjective changes. In other words, the self-perception of the participants had changed, but their actual attitudes had not. This apparently paradoxical result begs further investigation since it does bear on the how we measure the effectiveness of our training activities.

After reviewing much of the literature on cross-cultural training effectiveness, the authors concluded that few, if any, studies meet all of the criteria. The two studies that came closest to meeting the criteria (Sorcher & Spence, 1982; Landis, Brislin & Hulgus, 1985) were focused on domestic intergroup relations and may, therefore, be of doubtful application to the expatriate setting. Kealey and Protheroe (1996) went on to describe an "ideal" study which, at the time of writing, appeared likely to be implemented by the Canadian government. Unfortunately, such implementation has turned out not to be the case. Two reasons for this reluctance to carry out, or even approximate, the study design may be given. First, there exists considerable cynicism among the foreign service establishment about the value of cross-cultural training and, second, paradoxically, there exists considerable fear among training professionals that proper evaluation might show that the foreign service professionals have been correct all along. These two reasons result in decisions by government officials not to invest the necessary funds and human capital in evaluations and a willingness of training professionals to accede to those decisions. Despite this gloomy assessment, the need for good evaluations will continue to be what my mentor, Charlie Solley called a "Socratic gadfly" (Solley & Murphy, 1960) ever buzzing around our ears and demanding that we assess what it is that we do.

Implications for the military. The evaluation of military equal opportunity training virtually ceased by the late 1970s as a serious scientific enterprise (Thomas, 1988). The result has been little change in the doctrine governing such training. In response to this need, Johnson (1995, 1996) developed a plan for evaluating the training at DEOMI; comparable plans could and should be developed for the training in Europe and elsewhere. The criteria outlined above for the evaluation of intercultural training programs can be equally applied equal opportunity/race-relations training.

Issue 7: Is re-entry different or the same as entry?

In general, trainers and their organizations tend to lose interest in expatriates once they leave their home country. Rarely are they followed when they return. Over the past few years, there have been a spate of researches focused on reentry problems (Martin & Harrell, 1996; Gama & Pedersen, 1977; Gullahorn & Gullahorn, 1963). Generally, these studies report that: (1) younger returnees face more readaptation than older sojourners; (2) females have more difficulty readapting than males, particularly those who have sojourned in countries with more liberal gender attitudes than their home settings; (3) religion appears to affect readaptation though few studies have looked at this variable; and (4) previous intercultural experience is thought to be a predictor (Adler, 1981), but there have been no reported empirical studies to verify this claim. There are also many other variables that require empirical investigation: social class, personality characteristics, ethnicity, and socioeconomic status.

Implications for the military. The military has certainly done a better job of aiding reentry than it has entry. This is accomplished mainly through the buddy or mentor system. In this system, a person inbound to a new post or base is assigned a local contact whose job it is to help the new assignee navigate all of the problems attendant upon settling in a new locale. In effect, the system provides a ready-made support system. I suspect the system works best when the family of the serviceperson comes from an American background.

When the family is of mixed background (e.g., when the spouse is Asian), the system may work less efficiently. In this case, the spouse may be entering a new culture for the first time, while the serviceperson is returning to his or her home culture. The needs of the spouse may be different from those of the servicemember. So, while the spouse may need cross-cultural training, the serviceperson may need only to reacquaint him/herself with the ways in which everyday tasks are accomplished. The cross-cultural needs of the returning family are often placed in the hands of some sort of family services agency or the Chaplain. Some more structured training may be necessary and desirable.

Issue 8: Shift to more of an interdisciplinary focus in the development of models of intercultural relations

Intercultural research traditionally has been dominated by two disciplines: psychology and communications. An individualistic point-of-view has dominated versions of these disciplines that we have found most congenial. Some (e.g., Anderson, 1994) have found the basis of cross-cultural adaptation in well known and researched psychological mechanisms. Others (e.g., Gudykunst, 1985) have introduced terms (e.g., uncertainty reduction) which are clearly psychological in nature. Still others (e.g., Landis & Bhagat, 1996) have used models which give rather brief attention to macro-level variables in determining a person's adaptation to a new culture. While these models and theories have the comfort of familiarity, it is uncertain that they ultimately provide solutions to such questions as the authenticity of intercultural communication or how to resolve the apparently intractable intergroup problems when conflict is based on long standing religious or cultural differences. Sociological and political theorists are clamoring to be heard (e.g., Lustick, 1996) and they may have approaches that we can incorporate into our models.

Implications for the military. Within the military the domination of cross-cultural and equal opportunity training has been by variations of pedagogy, while most of the serious work in cross-cultural training has occurred in psychology and communication. This state of affairs is a puzzle and I suspect it deprives the military of the best thinking in the field. The rich skein of programs and theories derived out of the contact hypothesis could be brought to bear on the intercultural issues which are of interest in the military.

Issues Involving Content and Technique

Issue 9: Expansion of definition of "culture group"

Traditionally, culture has been correlated with either national boundaries or visible characteristics (e.g., gender or skin color). Indeed, our field started when scholars began to traverse national boundaries in the search for knowledge or cultural artifacts. It has only been since certain political acts have occurred that intra-national subgroups have been considered to be distinct cultures. Now, few would dispute that not only do such groups as Pacific Islanders represent different cultures from those located in North America but that groups such as African Americans, Asian Americans, Hispanic Americans, etc., also form separate cultures. Whether women also form a separate culture is still a matter of considerable debate (despite the pseudo-scientific assertions of writers such as John Gray). However, there is a constant pressure to enlarge the definition of "culture" so as to include previously excluded groups. Recently, the deaf and gay groups have been suggested to form distinct cultures from the mainstream American society (Siple, 1994; Ross, Fernandez-Esquer, & Seibt, 1996). I suspect that other writers will attempt to apply some criteria (e.g., Porter & Somovar's [1988] model of culture and communication) to bring other groups into the "culture fold." I suspect also that as these attempts are made, the definitions of culture will change. The fear is that they may change beyond all recognition and then cease to have any explanatory power at all.

A second issue concerns the identification of culture with national boundary. Paradoxically, this has been exacerbated by the success of the Hofstede individualism-collectivism contribution. Triandis (1994b), among others, has warned us about committing the "ecological fallacy;" that is, using culture-level concepts to interpret individual behavior. Triandis has used the terms *idiocentric* and *allocentric* to describe individual differences within a cultural trait. As these considerations become more prevalent among researchers, we will see more care in defining the characteristics of research samples.

Implications for the military. The military has largely confined its identification of ethnic groups to those officially named in various civil rights laws and in the applicable Department of Defense directives. So, most samples are described as Asian-Americans, Hispanics, blacks, whites, Native Americans, and others. With recent changes in the designations used by the Census Bureau and the fact that many servicepeople are members of mixed race families, the old designations would seem to be ripe for a change. Furthermore as the trend toward privatization of military functions proceeds, the military may come more and more under other portions of the civil rights laws: those affecting people with disabilities and those of differing sexual orientations. While some of these groups may never perform some uniquely military functions (e.g., being in front-line combat), they will perform, and are already performing, functions once the exclusive purview of the armed forces and in some cases in dangerous locations (e.g., in Bosnia).

Issue 10: Issues of sexuality in cross-cultural communication are coming under scrutiny

Some of the earliest recorded cross-cultural interactions involved sexual contact. Alexander the Great mandated that his soldiers should marry women from the conquered countries, thus cementing control from Greece. While the Greek wives left behind were not terribly thrilled by this policy, it is one that has been followed by conquerors throughout the ages. As people travel across national boundaries contact beyond the merely verbal is bound to occur. Some of these result in marriage, many more do not.

Cross-cultural training and research tends to avoid sexuality issues. Why that is so is understandable. These are issues that many of us feel uncomfortable discussing or which we feel belong within that sphere of privacy that we want to accord others. Some of us may even feel that to discuss such issues borders on the unethical. However, foreign students report that these issues are among the most bothersome and which their advisors are reluctant to discuss.

Beyond the training research issues are the problems of doing research on sexual issues in countries where the standards of such work are quite different from those in Western countries. Goldman (1994) has illustrated these difficulties in a cross-national study of children's sexual cognitions. This author notes that as a result of her study, three lessons can be drawn:

1.   "...paradigms assumed to be common to countries roughly comparable in social characteristics may not be suitable due to many other intervening variables, particularly cultural factors, especially relating to sexuality."

2.   "...all cultures restrict in different ways access to information about its population's sexuality..."

3.   "...politicians, especially those responsible for education, local school boards, superintendents, and teachers play a strong role in this cultural restriction."

(Goldman, 1994, p.22-23)

In training we often avoid discussions of "sensitive" topics that may make some members of the group uncomfortable and there are certainly ethical reasons to be cautious here (Paige & Martin, 1996). Nevertheless, when the discussion may save avoid embarrassing situations in-country, it may be worthwhile to take the risk. In any case, research on how to introduce and manage topics involving sexuality would seem to be a necessary addition to our corpus of knowledge.

Implications for the military. Perhaps no other issue has galvanized public awareness more than the issue of sexual conduct in the military setting. While there is a certain amount of prurient interest in the public following of the sexual exploits of people in uniform, the issue cannot be dismissed so lightly. The spectacle of training personnel taking sexual advantage of trainees shocks and disgusts most of us. Yet at the same time, that emotional reaction should not prevent a rational analysis of the situation. That analysis should start with a recognition that there are really two situations here: the case of superior/subordinate sexual interaction and the case of peer sexual interaction. Cutting across these two categories is the issue of consensuality. The waters are further muddied by the criminalization in the Uniform Code of Military Justice of sexual behavior by married servicepeople with non-spousal individuals. In the public consciousness all of those types of sexual behavior have become merged and fall under the category of "prohibited behaviors." Moskos, at this symposium, suggests that all sexual contact in the military be prohibited. Short of draconian measures, this is a bit like forbidding the tide to roll in; the last person who was successful at that task was Moses and even he had to have some help. Furthermore, blanket prohibitions ignore the dynamic that may occur when people are placed in situations where propinquity, presumed attitude similarity, acceptance of a common goal, and power all intersect. As many years of social psychological studies have taught us, such situations (be they in a university research laboratory or in Advanced Individual Training) are the petri dish in which attraction, on the part of both parties, grows and flourishes. Since sexual contact between military people is unlikely to cease, any policy must recognize the reality of human (and therefore sexual) beings operating in work situations. I suspect that this issue will be one that will occupy more and more policy makers in the years ahead as the military becomes more and more gender integrated.

Issue 11: What is the impact on the spouse of the international assignment?

In a recent paper, de Verthelyi (1995) lamented the lack of research on the adaptation of the spouses of international students. These are the "invisible" people in sojourner research. When spouses do appear, it is in terms of their impact on the international student or expatriate manager (Black & Gregersen, 1991). Indeed, the de Verthelyi study is the only one, to my knowledge, which deals with the spouse as a sojourner in his or her own right. Although the sample in de Verthelyi study was quite small, restricting her to a qualitative methodology, it is clear that the spouse suffers more from adaptation problems than does the sojourner in most cases. The level of adaptation seems to the related to the following events: (1) simultaneous or separate arrival in the country; (2) relocating from another campus or location; (3) lack of purposeful activity; (4) loss of professional identity; (5) difficulty with language barrier; (6) living on a tight budget; (7) missing family and friends; and (8) lack of use of what programs and services are available. Research on programs directed at spouses to ameliorate these problems is sorely needed. Unfortunately, such research is probably not high on the priorities of funding agencies.

Implications for the military. The military family is given great deference in public pronouncements. There seems to be general recognition that the success of the married serviceperson is partly dependent on the role of the spouse. Why else would the spouse be given a prominent role at retirement ceremonies? But, if the training of the serviceperson to function in an intercultural environment is minimal, the support given the spouse is even less. Given what we know about the role of the spouse in such settings, it is to be expected that difficulties will occur in the assignment. One can wonder if the difficulty being experienced in retention of field level officers has to do with the satisfaction of spouses or their servicemember's satisfaction in the job. Perhaps also the increasing importance of family satisfaction has to do with the change of military career from a calling (institutional model) to a job (occupational model) as Moskos has described.

Issue 12: The ethics of intercultural training and practice remains an unresolved issue

In both editions of the *Handbook of intercultural training* (Landis & Brislin, 1983; Landis & Bhagat, 1996), Michael Paige and Judith Martin wrote chapters on the need for considering ethical issues in training. They based their exposition on the proposition "...that intercultural training is an inherently transformative form of education, for learners and trainers alike." (Paige & Martin, 1996, p.35). They defined three questions that served as the structure for their discussions: (1) "What are the ethical dilemmas facing intercultural trainers?" (2) "What does ethical conduct mean for interculturalists?" and (3) "What is the role of professional organizations in promoting ethical conduct?" They make many recommendations for the behavior of ethical trainers. For researchers, the question is what is the harm or benefit to occur from being ethical or unethical? A related question comes from the conflict that occurs between the ethical norms of the trainer's home country and the country for which he/she is training sojourners. How do trainers handle such conflict, and what are the effects on the trainers and trainees from the various attempts to deal with the conflicts? The research is lacking on these issues and is necessary if the discussion of ethics is to move beyond philosophical imperatives to a resolution based on solid and verifiable foundations.

Implications for the military. Equal opportunity training is no less a transformative experience than cross-cultural training. As such it can have profound impact on the emotional and educational state of the trainee. Even though the serviceperson who is to be an equal opportunity advisor accepts that role more or less willingly, more attention needs to be given to determine if the candidate has the psychological wherewithal to profit from the training. At the present time, the training institutes are left with accepting whomever the services decide to send. While rejection can occur, it is rare. Goals are set by doctrine with little consideration given to whether or not the goals are attainable for a particular individual.

And, if the ethical issues are given short shrift at the training of the trainer level, they are awarded even less attention at the field level. Trainers are given little instruction on the ethics of the activities that they are expected to perform at the local level. Hence, since raising ethical questions is likely to produce discomfort and may even have career implications, such issues are not addressed.

Issue 13: Previously under researched areas of the world need to come under study

Probably a good 75 percent of the studies published over the past two decades have dealt with three areas of the world: the United States, Israel, and Japan. This phenomenon reflects the geographical distribution of researchers and the interests of funding agencies. While those locales remain important, other nationalities are likely to become important as the result of geopolitical events. We are beginning to see research dealing with Europe (particularly the former Soviet bloc), Africa (particularly South Africa, now that apartheid is a thing of the past), South and Central America (as a result of the North American Free Trade Association) and mainland China (the largest market in the world). Initially, I would expect that many of the studies focusing on these countries will fall prey to the "ecological fallacy." But, as researchers working in those locales become more common, more sophisticated analyses will be forthcoming.

Issue 14: Do almost all overseas managers really fail?

It has become rather traditional to start off a paper, or workshop, on expatriate manager success (or lack thereof) to assert that most such assignments are failures. While this undoubtedly gets the attention of editors and potential sponsors, it is apparently a figure built on a rather nebulous base. Harzing (1995)[5] has traced almost all such assertions back to a single article by Rosalie Tung (1981) which has been wildly misquoted as giving failure rates of around 40 percent for American firms (actually, her report suggests that only 7 percent of American firms had recall rates between 20 and 40 percent). It is apparent that most writers have been content to cite either Tung or one of the many other writers who cite her. In any case, some really serious research needs to be done to deal empirically with this interesting issue.

Implications for the military. One of the problems with the Tung research is that failure is very hard to define. As Anderson (1994) noted there are many ways that supervisors can perform at less than optimum levels. This is no less true in the military. The military has spent many years and untold dollars on trying to predict and identify sub-optimal performance in leaders without a lot of success. The well known inflation in the various versions of fitness reports only compound the problem. When it comes to providing leadership in equal opportunity issues, the problem becomes even more murky. The best that the military has been able to come up with is adding a check mark to the fitness reports with the inevitable result: nobody scores below a perfect mark unless they clearly fail. Further, when considering success in an overseas environment, one that requires considerable cross-cultural skills, there are no "tick" marks on the evaluation forms. This is one domain where civilian organizations seem to be more aware of the pertinent issues than is the military. Many civilian corporations spend significant funds identifying and then training managers to take up overseas posts. Technical competence is only part of the criteria for selection. Openness to cultural differences and ways of doing business are even more important. Contrast this with the military process: technical competence is the only criterion. And yet, a career may be built on success in the overseas assignment—failure may mean the premature end of that career. We can certainly do better in selecting and training leaders to function overseas.

Issue 15: Do diversity and intercultural training have the same outcomes?

The aim of much diversity training is to reduce or remove the boundaries between the in- and outgroups (i.e., to "decategorize"). Hence, the outgroup becomes part of the ingroup. Intercultural training, on the other hand, is often directed to decategorizing within the training situation (i.e., perceiving the "others" in the situation as individuals) leaving members of the outgroup who do not have the same characteristics as those in the training situation still outside the boundaries. Those outgroup persons will still be seen as homogeneous. In this case there would be a reintroduction of the stereotype with the only change that some people formerly included in the category would now be outside of it. Indeed, some theories would predict an increase in the impermeability of the in-group/out-group boundaries. This is not a finding that would hold much comfort for intercultural trainers, and there certainly needs to be research directed at explicating the conditions under which such negative results could occur.

Concluding Remarks

The fifteen issues described above are neither exhaustive nor exclusive. They are a selection of what this writer considers to be the foci of much research in the future. There are certainly others and I do not mean to stifle any researcher's work. This is truly an enterprise in which we should see "a thousand flowers bloom." Having made a plea for diversity, I now make a overture for more care, focus, and theoretical foundation in intercultural research. In general the era of pushing here and probing there just to see the reaction is wasteful of time and resources. The time in which we use convenience samples, available because the researcher happens to be located in a particular country, should be at an end. Rather, samples should be selected because they enable testing of some theoretical proposition. Failing such carefully drawn research, this field will never attain respectability. Without respectability, we can provide no direction to the design and implementation of intercultural training. The past twenty years has been prologue; the next twenty should bring real and solid achievements based on the prologue. The making of those achievements will belie the cynicism that abounds in government circles as to the efficacy of intercultural training. This will truly be an exciting time.

Notes

1.   The views expressed are those of the author and do not necessarily reflect the views of the DoD or any of its agencies.
2.   This paper is a revised version of a paper given upon completion of the author's term as the Col. Shirley J. Bach Visiting Professor at the Defense Equal Opportunity Management Institute.
3.   Information on the Academy can be had at its home page: http://www.watervalley.net/users/academy/academy.htm
4.   Tropennaars does not deal with the possibility that the first Hofstede factor is not bipolar, but really two unipolar dimensions (Wink, 1997).
5.   I am indebted to Geert Hofstede for calling my attention to this interesting and important paper.

References

Adler, N. (1981). Reentry: Managing cross-cultural transitions. *Group and organization studies, 6*(3), 341-356.
Albert, R. (1996). A framework and model for understanding Latin American and Latino/ Hispanic cultural patterns. In D. Landis & R. Bhagat (Eds.) *Handbook of intercultural*

training. Thousand Oaks: Sage. (327-349).

Allport, G. (1954). *The nature of prejudice*. Garden City, NY: Doubleday Anchor Books.

Anderson, L. (1994). A new look at an old construct: Cross-cultural adaptation. *International Journal of Intercultural Relations, 18*, 293-328.

Bartle, S., McIntyre, R., Landis, D., & Dansby, M. (1997). *The effects of equal opportunity climate on job satisfaction, organizational commitment, and work group effectiveness.* Unpublished manuscript.

Berry, J. (1997). Immigration, acculturation, and adaptation. *Applied Psychology: An international review, 46*, 5-34.

Bhawuk, D. P. S. (1997). *Evolution of culture assimilators: Toward theory-based assimilators.* Unpublished manuscript, Honolulu, HI: College of Business, University of Hawaii.

Black, J., & Gregersen, H. (1991). The other half of the picture: Antecedents of spouse cross-cultural adjustment. *Journal of International Business Studies, 3*, 461-477.

Blanchard, F., Lilly, T., & Vaughn, L. (1991). Reducing the expression of racial prejudice. *Psychological Science, 2*, 101-105.

Brewer, M. (1991). The social self: On being the same and different at the same time. *Personality and Social Psychology Bulletin, 17*, 475-482.

Brewer, M. (1996). When contact is not enough: Social identity and intergroup cooperation. *International Journal of Intercultural Relations, 20*, 291-303.

Brislin, R. (1980). Translation and content analysis of oral and written materials. In H. Triandis & J. Berry (Eds.), *Handbook of cross-cultural psychology: Vol. 2—Methodology*. Boston: Allyn & Bacon, Inc. (389-444).

Brislin, R., Cushner, K., Cherrie, & Yong, M. (1986). *Intercultural interactions: A practical guide*. Beverly Hills, CA: Sage.

Brislin, R., Landis, D., & Brandt, M. (1983). Conceptualizations of intercultural behavior and training. In D. Landis & R. Brislin (Eds.), *Handbook of intercultural training. Vol. I*. Elmsford, NY: Pergamon. (p. 1-35).

Buriel, R. (1975). Cognitive styles among three generations of Mexican-American children. *Journal of Cross-cultural Psychology, 6*, 417-429.

Cushner, K., & Brislin, R. (1996). *Intercultural interactions: A practical guide (2nd. ed.).* Thousand Oaks, CA: Sage.

Cushner, K., & Landis, D. (1996). The intercultural sensitizer. In D. Landis & R. Bhagat (Eds.), *Handbook of intercultural training (2nd. ed.)*. Thousand Oaks, CA: Sage.

Dawson, E., Crano, W., & Burgoon, M. (1996). Refining the meaning and measurement of acculturation: Revisiting a novel methodological approach. *International Journal of Intercultural Relations, 20*, 97-114.

de Verthelyi, R. (1995). International students' spouses: Invisible sojourners in the culture shock literature. *International Journal of Intercultural Relations, 19*, 387-412.

Dunbar, E. (1997). The personal dimensions of difference scale: Measuring multi-group identity with four ethnic groups. *International Journal of Intercultural Relations, 21*, 1-28.

Gaertner, S., Dovidio, J., & Bachman, B. (1996). Revisiting the contact hypothesis: The induction of a common ingroup identity. *International Journal of Intercultural Relations, 20*, 271-290.

Gama, E., & Pedersen, P. (1977). Readjustment problems of Brazilian returnees from graduate studies in the United States. *International Journal of Intercultural Relations, 1*, 46-58.

Goldman, D. (1994). Some methodological problems in planning, executing and validating cross-national study of children's sexual cognition. *International Journal of Intercultural Relations, 18*, 1-28.

Gudykunst, W. (1985). A model of uncertainty reduction in intercultural encounters. *Language and Social Psychology, 2*, 79-98.

Gullahorn, J. T., & Gullahorn, J. E. (1963). An extension of the U-curve hypothesis. *Journal of Social Issues, 14*, 33-47.

Hampden-Turner, C., & Trompenaars, F. (1997). Response to Geert Hofstede. *International Journal of Intercultural Relations, 21*, 149-159.

Harrison, J. K. (1992). Individual and combined effects of behavior modeling and the cultural assimilator in cross-cultural management training. *Journal of Applied Psychology, 77*, 952-962.

Harzing, A. (1995). The persistent myth of high expatriate failure rates. *International Journal of Human Resource Management, 6*, 457-474.

Hofstede, G. (1980). *Culture's consequences: International differences in work-related values*. Beverly Hills, CA: Sage.

Hofstede, G. (1996). Riding the waves of commerce: A test of Trompenaars' "model" of national culture differences. *International Journal of Intercultural Relations, 20*, 189-198.

Hofstede, G. (1997). Riding the waves: A rejoinder. *International Journal of Intercultural Relations, 21*, 287-290.

Horenczyk, G., & Bekerman, Z. (1997). The effects of intercultural acquaintance and structured intergroup interactions on ingroup, outgroup, and reflected ingroup stereotypes. *International Journal of Intercultural Relations, 21*, 71-83.

Johnson, J. L. (1995). *A preliminary investigation into DEOMI training effectiveness* (DEOMI Report #RSP 95-8). Patrick AFB, FL: Defense Equal Opportunity Management Institute.

Johnson, J. L. (1996). *Local and global effects of DEOMI training* (DEOMI Report #RSP 96-7). Patrick AFB, FL: Defense Equal Opportunity Management Institute.

Kealey, D. J., & Prothroe, D.R. (1996). The effectiveness of cross-cultural training, for expatriates: An assessment of the literature on the issue. *International Journal of Intercultural Relations, 20*(2), 141-165.

Kim, U., Triandis, H., Kagitcibasi, C., Choi, S., & Yoon, G. (1994). *Individualism and collectivism: Theory, method and applications*. Thousand Oaks, CA: Sage.

Landis, D., & Bhagat, R. (1996). A model of intercultural behavior and training. In D. Landis & R, Bhagat (Eds.), *Handbook of intercultural training (2nd. ed.)*. Thousand Oaks, CA: Sage. (p.1-16).

Landis, D., & Bhagat, R. (Eds.). (1996). *Handbook of intercultural training (2nd. ed.)*. Thousand Oaks, CA: Sage.

Landis, D., & Brislin, R. (Eds.). (1983). *Handbook of intercultural training (3 vols.)*. Elmsford, NY: Pergamon.

Landis, D., Brislin, R., & Huglus, J. (1985). Attributional training versus contact in acculturative learning: A laboratory study. *Journal of Applied Social Psychology, 15*, 466-482.

Landis, D., Dansby, M., & Tallarigo, R. (1996). The use of equal opportunity climate in intercultural training. In D. Landis & R. Bhagat (Eds.), *Handbook of intercultural training (2nd. ed.)*. Thousand Oaks, CA: Sage.

Landis, D., Day, H., McGrew, P., Thomas, J., & Miller, A. (1976). Can a black "culture assimilator" increase racial understanding? *Journal of Social Issues, 31*, 169-183.

Lawrence, G. & Kane, T. (1996). Military service and racial attitudes of white veterans. *Armed Forces and Society, 22*, 235-256.

Lustick, I. (1996). Hegemonic beliefs and territorial rights. *International Journal of Intercultural Relations, 20*, 479-492.

Martin, J., & Harrell, T. (1996). Reentry training for intercultural sojourners. In D. Landis & R. Bhagat (Eds.). *Handbook of intercultural training (2nd. ed.)*. Thousand Oaks, CA: Sage.

Paige, R., & Martin, J. (1996). Ethics in intercultural training. In D. Landis & R. Bhagat (Eds.) *Handbook of intercultural training (2nd. ed.)*. Thousand Oaks, CA: Sage.

Porter, R., & Somovar, L. (1988). Approaching intercultural communication. In L. Somovar & R. Porter (Eds.). *Intercultural communication: A reader.* Belmont, CA: Wadsworth.

Pruegger, V., & Rogers, T. (1994). Cross-cultural sensitivity training: Methods and assessment. *International Journal of Intercultural Relations, 18*, 369-387.

Rich, Y., Kedem, P., & Schlesinger, A. (1995). Enhancing intergroup relations among children: A field test of the Miller-Brewer Model. *International Journal of Intercultural Relations, 19*, 539-554.

Ross, M., Fernandez-Esquer, M., & Seibt, A. (1996). Understanding across the sexual orientation gap: Sexuality as Culture. In D. Landis & R. Bhagat (Eds.), *Handbook of intercultural training (2nd. ed.).* Thousand Oaks, CA: Sage.

Ruggiero, K., Taylor, D., & Lambert, W. (1996). A model of heritage culture maintenance: The role of discrimination. *International Journal of Intercultural Relations, 20*, 47-67.

Schwarzwald, J., & Yinor, Y. (1977). Symmetrical and asymmetrical interethnic perception in Israel. *International Journal of Intercultural Relations, 1*(1), 40-47.

Sherif, M. (1979). Superordinate goals in the reduction of intergroup conflict: An experimental evaluation. In W. G. Austin & S. Worchel (Eds.), *The social psychology of intergroup relations.* Monterey, CA: Brooks/Cole.

Shuter, R. (1977). Cross-cultural small group research: A review, an analysis, and a theory. *International Journal of Intercultural Relations, 1*(1), 90-104.

Siple, L. (1994). Cultural patterns of deaf people. *International Journal of Intercultural Relations, 18*, 345-367.

Smith, E. R., & Branscombe, N. R. (1984). *Stereotype traits can be processed automatically.* (Technical Report TR-ONR-3). Department of Psychological Sciences, Purdue University: West Lafayette, IN.

Solley, C., & Murphy, G. (1960). *Development of the perceptual world.* New York: Basic Books.

Sorcher, M., & Spence, R. (1982). The interface project: Behavior modeling as social technology in South Africa. *Personnel Psychology, 35*, 557-581.

Stephan, W., & Stephan, C. (1985). Intergroup anxiety. *Journal of Social Issues, 41*, 157-176.

Tolbert, A., & McLean, G. (1995). Venezuelan culture assimilator for training United States professionals conducting business in Venezuela. *International Journal of Intercultural Relations, 19*, 111-125.

Thomas, J. (1988). *Race relations research in the U.S. Army in the 1970s: A collection of selected readings.* Arlington, VA: United States Army Research Institute for the Behavioral and Social Sciences.

Triandis, H. (1994a). Theoretical and methodological approaches to the study of collectivism and individualism. In U. Kim, H. Triandis, C. Kagitcibasi, S. Choi, & G. Yoon (Eds.), *Individualism and collectivism: Theory, method and applications.* Thousand Oaks, CA: Sage.

Triandis, H. (1994b). *Culture and social behavior.* New York: McGraw-Hill.

Triandis, H., Vassiliou, V., Vassiliou, G., & Tanaka, Y. (1972). *The analysis of subjective culture.* New York: Wiley-Interscience.

Trompenaars, F. (1993). *Riding the waves of culture: Understanding cultural diversity in business.* London: The Economist Books.

Tung, R. (1981). Selection and training of personnel for overseas assignments. *Columbia Journal of World Business, 15*, 68-78.

Tzeng, O., & Jackson, J. (1994). Effects of contact, conflict, and social identity on interethnic group hostilities. *International Journal of Intercultural Relations, 18*, 259-276.

Wink, P. (1997). Beyond ethnic differences: Contextualizing the influence of ethnicity on individualism and collectivism. *Journal of Social Issues, 53,* 329-350.

Winslow, D. (1997). *The Canadian Airborne Regiment in Somalia: A socio-cultural inquiry.* Ottawa, Canada: Minister of Public Works and Government Services.

Wood, P., & Sonleitner, N. (1996). The effect of childhood interracial contact on adult antiblack prejudice. *International Journal of Intercultural Relations, 20*, 1-17.

Contributors

Jose Bolton, Sr., Ph.D., Colonel, U.S. Air Force, Commandant, Defense Equal Opportunity Management Institute, Patrick Air Force Base, Florida

Amy L. Culbertson, M.A., Personnel Research Psychologist, Navy Personnel Research and Development Center, San Diego, California

Mickey R. Dansby, Ph.D., Director, Directorate of Research, Defense Equal Opportunity Management Institute, Patrick Air Force Base, Florida

Jack E. Edwards, Ph.D., Chief, Personnel Survey Branch, Defense Manpower Data Center, Washington, DC

Mark J. Eitelberg, Ph.D., Professor, Department of Systems Management, Navy Postgraduate School, Monterey, California

Carlos C. Huerta, M.A., Captain, U.S. Army Reserve, Chaplain Corps, Jewish Welfare Board, New York, New York

Juanita M. Firestone, Associate Professor, Department of Sociology, University of Texas at San Antonio, San Antonio, Texas

Everett L. Greene, M.S., Captain, U.S. Navy, Special Warfare Advisor to Joint Chiefs of Staff, Pentagon, Washington, DC

Ruth L. Greene, Ed.D., Professor, Department of Psychology, Johnson C. Smith University, Charlotte, North Carolina

Judith L. Johnson, Ph.D., Professor, Department of Behavior Sciences and Psychology, Louisiana Tech University, Ruston, Louisiana

Olenda E. Johnson, Ph.D., Assistant Professor, School of Business and Economics, Department of Business Administration, North Carolina A&T State University, Greensboro, North Carolina

Stephen B. Knouse, Ph.D., Alvin and Patricia Smith Professor and Head, Department of Management, University of Southwestern Louisiana, Lafayette, Louisiana

Dan Landis, Ph.D., Professor, Department of Psychology, University of Mississippi, University, Mississippi

Robert M. McIntyre, Ph.D., Professor, Department of Psychology, Old Dominion University, Norfolk, Virginia

Brenda L. Moore, Ph.D., Associate Professor, Department of Sociology, The State University of New York at Buffalo, Buffalo, New York

Rupert W. Nacoste, Ph.D., Associate Professor, Department of Psychology, North Carolina State University, Raleigh, North Carolina

James B. Stewart, Ph.D., Professor of Labor Studies and Industrial Relations and African and African American Studies, The Pennsylvania State University, University Park, Pennsylvania

Rick S. Tallarigo, Ph.D., Major, U.S. Air Force, former Deputy Director, Directorate of Research, Defense Equal Opportunity Management Institute, Patrick Air Force Base, Florida

Martin R. Walker, M.S., U.S. Army, TRADOC Analysis Command, Fort Benjamin Harrison, Lawrence, Indiana

Schuyler C. Webb, Ph.D., Commander, U.S. Navy, former Deputy Director, Directorate of Research, Defense Equal Opportunity Management Institute. Currently, Director, Navy Life Assessment Group and Special Assistant to the Commander, Navy Personnel Command, Millington, Tennessee

Gary L. Whaley, Ph.D., Associate Professor, Department of Management and Decision Sciences, Norfolk State University, Norfolk Virginia

Index